THE OFFICIAL
ILLUSTRATED HISTORY of
MANCHESTER UNITED

THE OFFICIAL
ILLUSTRATED HISTORY OF
MANCHESTER UNITED

THE FULL STORY
AND COMPLETE RECORD 1878-2012
Foreword by Sir Bobby Charlton

Written by Alex Murphy
Statistics by Andrew Endlar

**SIMON &
SCHUSTER**

London · New York · Sydney · Toronto · New Delhi

A CBS COMPANY

This edition first published in Great Britain by Simon & Schuster UK Ltd, 2012

A CBS Company

Copyright © Manchester United Football Club Limited 2006, 2007, 2008, 2010, 2012

First published in 2006 by Orion Books

The authors would like to thank the following for their help in writing this book:

Arthur Albiston, Steve Bruce, Phil Chisnall, Tommy Docherty, Professor Steven Fielding, David Gill, Brian McClair, Roger Mellor, Johnny Morris, Ivan Ponting, Jo Riches, David Sadler, Karen Shodbolt, Alex Stepney and Philip Townsend.

1 3 5 7 9 10 8 6 4 2

Simon & Schuster UK Ltd
1st Floor
222 Gray's Inn Road
London
WC1X 8HB
www.simonandschuster.co.uk

Simon & Schuster Australia
Sydney

Simon & Schuster India
New Delhi

A CIP catalogue for this book is available from the British Library.

ISBN: 978-1-4711-0262-2

Edited by Julian Flanders
Designed by Craig Stevens
Index by Indexing Specialists (UK) Ltd
Printed and bound in China by LEO Paper Products Ltd

CONTENTS

FOREWORD   BY SIR BOBBY CHARLTON   7
INTRODUCTION   9

CHAPTER ONE   1878–1915   FROM NEWTON HEATH TO OLD TRAFFORD   10

CHAPTER TWO   1915–45   THE WILDERNESS YEARS   30

CHAPTER THREE   1945–51   BUSBY STARTS WORK   48

CHAPTER FOUR   1951–59   THE BUSBY BABES   66

CHAPTER FIVE   1959–67   BACK TO THE TOP   86

CHAPTER SIX   1967–69   CHAMPIONS OF EUROPE   110

CHAPTER SEVEN   1969–77   DECLINE AND FALL   130

CHAPTER EIGHT   1977–86   IN QUEST OF MORE GLORY   154

CHAPTER NINE   1986–93   THE WAITING ENDS   178

CHAPTER TEN   1993–99   THE DECADE OF DOUBLES AND TREBLES   202

CHAPTER ELEVEN   1999–2006   21ST CENTURY BOYS   230

CHAPTER TWELVE   2006–12   UNITED FOR THE FUTURE   252

CLUB STATISTICS   296
INDEX AND PICTURE CREDITS   366

FOREWORD

BY SIR BOBBY CHARLTON

It is with enormous pleasure that I write this foreword to *The Official Illustrated History of Manchester United.*

As I pen these words it seems like yesterday that I first arrived at Old Trafford as a nervous boy of 15, to start work on the groundstaff. Yet when I look at the records, I see it was 59 summers ago. I never imagined when I spent those first, few homesick months away from my home village of Ashington that United was to become such a big part in my life, and win such a special place in my heart.

It goes without saying that I am immensely proud of the small part I have played in the club's history, and to be our record goalscorer. I am also very fortunate to have won more than my share of medals and honours with United. But what I prize above everything else are the memories of the wonderful footballers I played alongside, and the hundreds of great friends I have made through my association with United. And there is sadness, too, to think that many of those people whose friendship I cherished are no longer with us to enjoy the success of the current generation of players who have stepped into our boots.

I am thrilled that this history tells the story of United with such warmth, and captures so beautifully the unique spirit that makes it such a special club. It is a history that lives and breathes. It brings the legends of the past vividly to life, in the words of many of the people who helped make the club what it is today.

Of course, the history of United is very much a work in progress. New heroes emerge to write fresh chapters in the club's engrossing story, and new generations of United supporters grow up to follow the club's exploits. This book gives young United fans the chance to learn more about what, to me, is the greatest football club in the world. And older supporters, like me, will revel in reliving so many happy moments from our past.

SIR BOBBY CHARLTON

INTRODUCTION

If you recounted the history of Manchester United solely in terms of trophies won, it would be a stirring volume. After all, there is plenty of scope for pride in the club's honours list. But it is the personal stories behind the statistics which really bring the tale to life. That's why the story is told here in the voices of the individuals who shaped the club and made all the glory possible.

It was a privilege to talk to some of the all-time legends of United, stretching all the way back to the great Johnny Morris, the Radcliffe lad who shone as an inside-forward in the first days of Matt Busby's time at Old Trafford immediately after the Second World War. His memories of those difficult early days, and then of United's illustrious 1948 Cup-winning campaign were razor sharp. Even then, aged 86, he recalled every twist and turn of that buccaneering run – including the final itself, in which United staged a dramatic comeback to beat Blackpool. Sadly, Morris passed away in April 2011, aged 87.

Morris was a stellar name in his day, but this is the story, too, of the journeymen who played their part in the unfolding drama. Stretford lad Phil Chisnall signed for the club he worshipped in the Easter after the tragedy at Munich, and witnessed the birth of the team that went on to win the European Cup. He provided a fascinating and honest account of how Matt Busby strived to rebuild the club following the awful catastrophe of February 1958.

Alex Stepney, United's admirable, long-serving keeper, talked us through the joy of 1968 from a player's perspective, and spoke candidly about the difficult era that followed. Tommy Docherty, in typically waspish fashion, told the tale behind the club's relegation in 1974, and how the club began the long, slow haul back to the top of the English game. The contrasting reigns of Dave Sexton and Ron Atkinson are described by one of United's most loyal players, the Scottish full-back, Arthur Albiston.

Then, finally, two United giants from the modern era, Steve Bruce and Brian McClair, explained how United blossomed under Sir Alex Ferguson, conquered Europe once again, and laid the platform for another century of triumphs – a century that is certain to provide many more gripping chapters in the rich human chronicle that is the history of Manchester United.

ALEX MURPHY

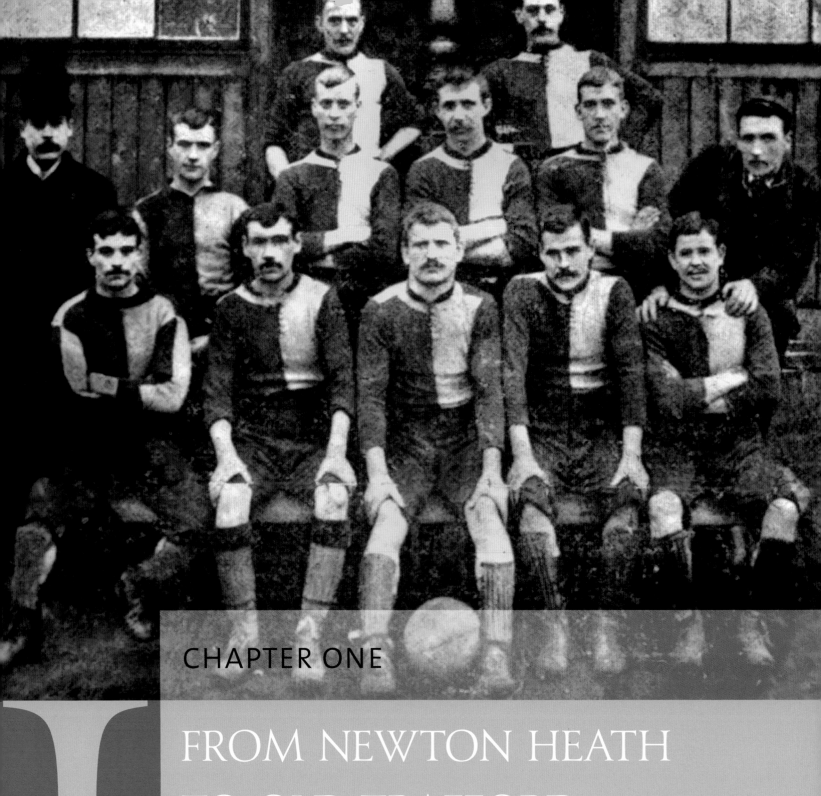

CHAPTER ONE

FROM NEWTON HEATH
TO OLD TRAFFORD

1878–1915

1878 WAS A GREAT YEAR FOR FOOTBALL – MANCHESTER UNITED WAS BORN

The name on the birth certificate might look oddly unfamiliar, but the world's best-supported football club began life in that year as Newton Heath L&YR (Lancashire and Yorkshire Railway) FC, launched by a band of railway workers looking for something to do on their Saturday afternoons off.

Those pioneers of United began by subscribing sixpences from their wages to buy a ball and meet other expenses, and quite quickly the men from the LYR's carriage and wagon works proved they were the best association football team in Manchester. They played all around the city in their familiar red and white quartered jerseys and blue shorts (red shirts and white shorts came later) taking on and beating all potential rivals, and they were formidable on their own patch of ground at North Road, close to the modern site of Piccadilly Station.

But who were these first United heroes, the men who laid the foundations of a sporting institution that would in time come to be revered in every corner of the globe? Glancing at the earliest formal team photographs of Newton Heath, the faces peering out from more than a century ago belong to tough men. Their gazes are steady and solemn, their burly frames testament to the hard, physical labour they carried out on the railway. Some of them wear the severe, straight moustaches men sported in that Victorian era

One of the earliest photographs ever taken of Newton Heath LYR FC, the pioneers of the modern Manchester United, dating from the 1890s.

and the overwhelming impression you gain of this football team is that you wouldn't want to mess with them. It is easy to understand how the 'Coachbuilders', as they were nicknamed, came to dominate football in Manchester and east Lancashire in the last quarter of the 19th century.

In those early days when football was finding its way as an organised sport, hundreds of football clubs were springing up all over the country, especially in the industrial cities of the north and the Midlands. Most of them have long-since been forgotten, and have left little or no impression on history. Others were the forerunners of the great clubs that still inhabit the higher reaches of our professional game. How was it that Newton Heath survived and prospered, to develop into what is arguably the mightiest club in the country? As is so often the case, the answer lies in economics, and the mysterious workings of pounds, shillings and pence.

Newton Heath held an advantage over their Mancunian rivals, because in those amateur days they had ways of luring the best players in the region to join Newton Heath. The railway works were enjoying something of a boom, and while new recruits might not be offered lavish wages to play football, they could be offered well-paid jobs at the depot. The recruitment of players was left in the capable hands of the works Dining Room Committee, and historians of the LYR suggest that they were not above finding employment for men who could strengthen their football team.

As early as the mid-1880s Newton Heath were flirting with professionalism. Records from the time reveal that one Jack Powell was offered a job as a fitter with the LYR – on condition that he turned out for the football team. It was a significant signing, as Powell went on to become a prominent captain of the club in its rise to Football League status.

The early Newton Heath players were working class, but they had enough leisure time to play games on Saturday afternoons, and were prosperous to the extent that they did not have to spend every waking hour earning money to live. Professor Steven Fielding, a United fan and history lecturer from the University of Salford, whose office is just a goalkick away from Old Trafford, said, 'The men who formed Newton Heath would have mostly been from a comparatively affluent section of the working class as, unlike many others, they were skilled and had regular work.

'It was a time when working class people were starting to enjoy what we would understand to be "leisure time". At the time the weekend began at Saturday dinnertime, so Saturday afternoon was the only time they had the opportunity to follow pursuits that they enjoyed. Sunday was meant for church and little else. This is why you find football clubs and other sporting bodies sprouting up all over the country at this time. Quite simply, working people in the towns and cities were starting to have the time and money to play and watch sport.

'Clubs like Newton Heath were founded and supported by the elite of the working class, because they had the resources to indulge in organised sport. If you look at very early photographs of football matches, you will see that most of the spectators are wearing hats or caps. This is a clear marker of status as the poor working class tended not to wear them. A hat was a symbol that showed you were better off than the poor unskilled labourer.'

At first Newton Heath played and beat other railway works teams, and they progressed to games against the football clubs that were mushrooming around Manchester in that era. In the early 1880s they were playing and beating sides such as Manchester Arcadians and West Gorton St Marks; Middleton and Haydock Temperance; Haughton Dale and Pendleton Olympic. In 1884/85 the club, by now more commonly known as the Heathens, played

A Newton Heath season ticket for 1882/83, when the club still played at the football and cricket ground near the railway yard in North Road.

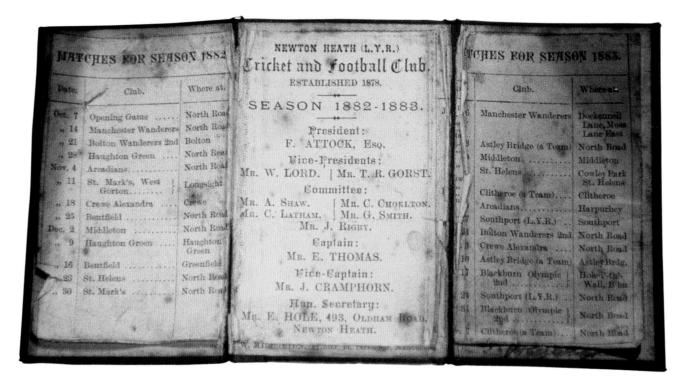

in the inaugural Manchester Cup and reached the final, which they lost 3-2 to Hurst at Whalley Range on 25 April 1885. But they were back in the final the season after, when they beat Manchester FC 2-1 on 3 April 1886. The magnificent, two-handled silver trophy was the fledgling United's first-ever trophy of consequence, and they went on to dominate the competition, appearing in the final eight years out of nine. Newton Heath were top dogs in the city and it was not long before they sought new worlds to conquer.

The national Football League had been launched in 1882, but Newton Heath did not feel ready to mix it with such giants of association football as Preston North End, who won the first-ever Championship without losing a game. But by the end of the 1880s Newton Heath were ready to take their club up a level and they applied to join the League. Sadly the founding members did not share their optimism and the Heathens' application attracted just

one vote of support. Undaunted, Newton Heath joined the Football Alliance instead, a national competition reserved for clubs who were not quite ready to join the big boys.

For three seasons Newton Heath battled away in the Alliance and every summer they re-applied to join the League. The breakthrough came in the 1891/92 season, when they finished second in the Alliance after a string of fine results. They hammered Lincoln City 10-1 at home and 6-1 away; Sheffield Wednesday were dispatched 4-2 in Yorkshire; and they won their first competitive match against Ardwick (soon to be re-named Manchester City), 3-1 at home. Their record was good enough to win them election to the First Division of the newly expanded Football League, along with Nottingham Forest and Sheffield Wednesday.

Newton Heath's first-ever season in the Football League proved something of a trial. Their debut game was a tough assignment at Blackburn Rovers, who were one of the top teams in English football. Contemporary reports note that Newton Heath's first foray in league football, on 3 September 1892, took place amid a rain storm in front of a crowd of 8,000, and the home team galloped into a 3-0 lead. Newton Heath showed plenty of fight to reduce the deficit and by the end could take credit from a 4-3 defeat. The honour of scoring the club's first-ever league goal went to Bob Donaldson, their Scottish centre-forward who had joined from the famous Airdrieonians club.

Despite the promising start it took the Heathens seven matches to chalk up a win, but it was worth waiting for, as they hammered Wolverhampton Wanderers 10-1 at home on 15 October. By a statistical quirk, their first-ever victory was also destined to be the biggest in the history of the club for the next 114 years and counting. Newton Heath also managed to demolish Derby County 7-1 at home, but on the whole their first league season was a chastening experience and they ended the campaign bottom of the table.

There was no automatic promotion and relegation at the time, and Newton Heath faced a so-called Test match against the Second Division Champions, Small Heath, for the right to play in Division One the following season. The Midlands side (soon to be re-named

The Manchester Cup, which Newton Heath came to dominate in the 1880s and 1890s.

Birmingham City) were a rising force in the game and widely tipped to see off the Mancunians without much difficulty. The play-off at Stoke City's ground finished 1-1 and the teams had to replay in Sheffield the following week. The Heathens saved their top-flight status with a 5-2 win.

Newton Heath marked their second season as a league side by moving grounds. Their first home had been the subject of numerous complaints from visiting league teams. Nobody had been impressed by the playing surface, which was a bog at one end and rocky as a quarry at the other, or the changing rooms, a 10-minute walk away in a room behind the Three Crowns pub in Oldham Road. Later on they switched their headquarters to another pub in Oldham Road, the Shears Hotel, but the change did little to win visitors' hearts and minds.

The Heathens found a new pitch at Bank Street in Clayton, but this was hardly a home fit for heroes either. Even by the unexacting standards of the day, the playing surface was shockingly bad – an uninviting morass of mud and wet sand, with just the odd, sorry tuft of scrubby grass. A factory adjoining the ground blasted thick clouds of foul-smelling smoke over spectators and players. Simon Inglis in his *Football Grounds of Great Britain* quotes a report from the *Guardian* on a visit by Portsmouth, 'All the time the struggle was waging the 30 Clayton chimneys smoked and gave forth their pungent odours, and the boilers behind the goal poured mists of steam over the ground.'

Some visiting teams could not believe their eyes when they saw the place. Walsall Town Swifts turned up at Bank Street for the first time and refused to play. They were finally persuaded to set foot on what they regarded as a toxic waste dump, but only after the groundsmen had dumped another layer of sand on top of the brown slime that passed for a pitch. Walsall proceeded to lose 14-0 and lodged a strong protest. The result was expunged from the record books. Swifts returned to Bank Street for the rescheduled game and left uncharmed by the environs of Clayton – this time they lost 9-0.

The move to Bank Street continued a gradual loosening of the club's railway ties. After they entered the Football League the club had become an independent company, appointed a full-time secretary and dropped the L&YR from their title to become simply Newton Heath FC. The gentlemen of the Dining Room Committee had played their historic role in helping to deliver the club to the world, but Newton Heath were destined to leave their humble origins behind forever, to embrace the future as Manchester United.

The Heathens did not appear to enjoy playing at Bank Street any more than their visitors and they finished their second season bottom of the table again. This time they failed to survive a Test match, against Liverpool, and were relegated to Division Two. They were to remain there for the next 12 years.

Results improved at the lower level and in 1897 they narrowly failed to win promotion via the Test matches. But while the Heathens' fortunes were better on the pitch, the club was heading for the first off-field crisis in its short history. In 1899 the club's directors clamped down on what they perceived to be a climate of indiscipline among the players. Three forwards were in the firing line – Harry Boyd and John Cunningham were placed on the transfer list, and Matthew Gillespie was suspended. The club did their best to wash their dirty linen in private, but the demon drink was known to be involved. Just to show there is nothing new under the sun, the sporting press railed about overpaid footballers running out of control and wasting their talent. The *Athletic News* thundered, 'If men who are paid good wages don't think it worth their while to keep themselves in condition they are better off out of the team.'

Meanwhile the Heathens had begun to struggle in the Second Division, crowds at their ramshackle ground were dwindling and the club was a financial basket case. They had been in existence for less than a quarter of a century, and they had been a league club for fewer than 10 years, but already they were facing extinction. Newton Heath lurched a step nearer oblivion in 1902 when their own president, William Healey, went to court to apply for a winding-up order – he was owed £242 17s 10d and the club's total debts amounted to over £2,500. Newton Heath were duly declared bankrupt and the official receiver padlocked the gates at Bank Street. The club needed a saviour – and in their hour of need, they found not one but two.

Harry Stafford was Newton Heath's captain and, more than any other individual, he saved Manchester United for the world.

On Saturday afternoons Stafford was a resolute full-back, but during the week he was a boilermaker by trade, a throwback to the club's artisan roots. He held the club close to his heart and but for his efforts it might have joined the other league clubs from those early years that never made it out of infancy – clubs such as Burton Swifts, Loughborough and New Brighton Tower. Beset by debt and short of public support, Newton Heath could easily have gone under. And if history had turned out only slightly differently, Manchester today could easily be a city like Newcastle, with just one professional football club. But Stafford protected the dying

embers of the nascent Manchester United. He begged and borrowed just enough money to cover the club's travelling costs for their next game (a 4-0 defeat at Bristol City) and even found a temporary ground at Harpurhey where they fulfilled the next home fixture (a 1-0 defeat against Blackpool). But to put the club back on an even footing, Stafford needed to find a major injection of funds.

1878–1915

Just in time, a trio of Manchester businessmen each chipped in £500 to give the club some semblance of stability – but the key contributor was a prosperous gent named John Henry Davies. Davies was the managing director of Manchester Breweries, a pillar of the city's mercantile aristocracy, and it was his wealth allied to Stafford's endeavour that saved Newton Heath. But Davies was more than just a benefactor. He rolled up his sleeves and took an important role in the running of the club, and in 1902 he was named club president. It was a lucky day for Newton Heath when Davies walked into the club – and they owed their good fortune to a dog, if the legends are to be believed.

The story has passed into folklore how it was not Stafford who found Davies, but the full-back's dog. The fable has taken many forms down the years. One has Stafford showing his prize St Bernard at a Newton Heath fund-raising event. Davies, a dog-lover, is much taken by the animal and asks to buy it. Davies declines the offer, but persuades Davies to make a donation to the club instead. In another version, Stafford's dog runs away and is found by Davies. He has been searching for a birthday present for his 12-year-old daughter, Elsie, and reasoning that the dog is a stray gives it to her. But Stafford tracks his lost dog down and calls to claim it back. The pair strike up an acquaintance, which ends with Davies throwing his lot in with the Newton Heath cause. It is debatable how much truth there is in these stories, but all that matters is that Davies and the club found each other, and Manchester United was the result.

John Henry Davies, the great benefactor who saved Newton Heath from financial ruin and set the penurious Manchester club on the way to becoming one of the most powerful in England.

Newton Heath certainly needed a boost. Until now they had been mired in the Second Division, generally finishing in the top four but never quite proving good enough to win promotion back to Division One. Worryingly, in their last season as Newton Heath, 1901/02, they finished fourth from bottom. But their fortunes were about to change with a new name – and a new manager.

Newton Heath had come a long way from its days as a railway works team and had also moved away from the area of Manchester where it was founded. To reflect the club's fresh start and new circumstances, it was decided to choose a new name. Various options were considered, including Manchester Celtic and Manchester Central. Finally the directors agreed on a new name that had a distinguished ring to it. At a board meeting one of the directors, an Italian immmigrant, Louis Rocca, said, 'Gentlemen, why don't we call ourselves Manchester United?' The other directors liked the name and, on 26 April 1902, Manchester United came into existence. As part of the club's new image, they also switched to a smart new strip: red shirts and white shorts.

The new name wasn't Rocca's last service to United. He worked ceaselessly for the club over the next decades and, a long way into the future, he became chief scout under Matt Busby. Rocca would be instrumental in overhauling the club's youth set-up and he unearthed many of the great players who formed the backbone of the club's success after the Second World War. But for millions of people all over the world his main legacy are the two words that mean so much to so many: Manchester United.

The first match ever played by the new Manchester United was an away fixture at Gainsborough Trinity, in Lincolnshire, on 7 September 1902, and it was an auspicious start as they won 1-0. It was also the month they welcomed a new manager.

At the start of the 1902/03 season, Newton Heath were managed by James West, but he resigned his position on 28 September after just a handful of games. The new manager was Ernest Mangnall, who would make his name as the first of the great Manchester United bosses.

But Mangnall's first season in charge ended in frustration once again, as United could finish no higher than fifth in Division Two. Mangnall spent that first campaign trying out new players and 28 men were given a run-out. But it was clear to the manager he needed new blood to reinvigorate the playing strength. In the 1903/04 season a new-look United surged to third in the Second Division. New stars such as goalkeeper Harry Moger, half-backs Charlie Roberts, Alex Bell and Dick Duckworth, and forwards Charlie Sagar and John Picken gave the team a new lease of life. United were beaten to the second promotion place by Woolwich Arsenal, one point ahead of them, while the Division Two Champions, Preston, were only two points clear. United had run them close and it was clear that the club was heading in the right direction under Mangnall's vigorous leadership.

Roberts, especially, proved to be a crucial signing for the success of Mangnall's regime. It cost United £400 to lure the centre-half away from Grimsby Town, which was a tidy sum then, but United received full value for their shillings. In an age when formations were far more static than they are today, and players seldom strayed from their allotted station on the field, Roberts roamed at will. He was a fine athlete, quick, and possessed enormous stamina. His all-action style made him a player ahead of his time and he was clearly one of the best footballers in England. United supporters grumbled that Roberts should have played far more often for England (he won just three caps), but there were reasons for that.

As well as being a wonderful footballer, Roberts was also a maverick and no respecter of authority. The Victorian age of deference was dead and Roberts had no difficulty in speaking his mind on any subject which might come up. When the launch of a players' union was mooted, Roberts was one of the movement's chief agitators. He also cut something of a sartorial dash on the pitch. In an era when footballers' shorts reached down to their shins, Roberts's barely covered his thighs. The gentlemen of the Football Association did not always look upon Roberts's antics with a benign eye and that perhaps explain why he earned so few national call-ups.

How good was Roberts? In the opinion of the great Italian coach, Vittorio Pozzo, he was the best footballer in the world.

Charlie Roberts, one of the first legends of Manchester United and a great character who exerted a huge influence on the club's emergence as a footballing power.

Pozzo led Italy to two World Cup triumphs in the 1930s and his tactical approach to the game was inspired by watching Roberts play. The Italian visited England on a scouting expedition, and was astonished when he visited Clayton and saw Roberts playing a brand of daring football he had not witnessed before. He remembered Roberts's style when he coached Italy, converted his centre-half into an attacking weapon and turned his team into world-beaters.

United fell agonisingly short of promotion once more in 1903/04, finishing third again, just behind Liverpool and Bolton Wanderers. But the breakthrough season was 1905/06, when United made enormous strides towards the summit of English football. In the past, United hadn't had much luck in the FA Cup, but now they set off on a swashbuckling run which took them all the way to the quarter-finals. In the first round they had little trouble in brushing aside Staple Hill 7-2 at Clayton. Next came non-league Norwich City, who were dismissed 3-0 at home. United's run was fully expected to end in the third round, when they were drawn to play Aston Villa at Clayton. Villa were, after all, one of the best teams in the First Division and the FA Cup holders. But United hammered their illustrious visitors 5-1 in front of a vast crowd estimated to be over 35,000. It was a stirring achievement. By now United fans were dreaming of the final with genuine optimism, with a day out at Crystal Palace just two wins away. But their opponents in the next round were Woolwich Arsenal, a mid-table Division One team, and the Londoners prevailed 3-2.

Any disappointment about that defeat was banished as United closed in on promotion at last. They had been in close touch with the Second Division leaders all season and made sure of their return to the First Division with a closing sprint of nine wins in 10 games. The burst did not close the gap on the Second Division Champions, Bristol City, but it was good enough to leave Chelsea trailing by nine points in third place. After so long suffering in the doldrums of the Second Division, and missing out by tiny margins on numerous occasions, Mangnall finally delivered promotion, which was confirmed by a 3-1 win at Leeds on 21 April 1906 and topped by a 6-0 thrashing of Burton United on the last day of the season.

Davies and Mangnall knew they would have to recruit some better players if they were to pose a threat in the First Division, and they were busy men in the summer of 1906. To the horror of their Division One rivals across town, they spent much of their time plundering Manchester City's playing squad. City had won the FA Cup in 1904, but the FA launched an inquiry into the club's financial dealings, with payments of illicit wages and secret bonuses coming in for special scrutiny. Clubs were only allowed to pay players a maximum of £4 a week and the investigation found that City were paying £6 or £7 a week. City were fined £250 and

Action from United's 1-1 draw with Chelsea at Stamford Bridge on 13 April 1906 in front of a vast crowd of 67,000.

their Hyde Road ground was shut for a month. In the fall-out from the scandal five City directors were booted out of the club and 18 players were barred from playing for the club ever again. Ever the pragmatist, Mangnall cherry-picked the best available talent, and signed up Billy Meredith, Herbert Burgess, Jimmy Bannister and Sandy Turnbull. The deals had to be done in secret, as the players were still suspended from the game. But Mangnall had laid the basis for a future soon at hand, when his United would emerge as the greatest team in England. And it was largely achieved thanks to half a team of City cast-offs.

By New Year's Day 1907 the City outlaws were eligible to play again and Mangnall unveiled his new-look team in a home game against Villa. United won 1-0 and, although it was too late for Mangnall's men to make an impact on the Division One table that season, everything was in place for a serious challenge for the Championship the following year.

Sure enough, United were unstoppable. Wherever they went in the country crowds gasped as the Mancunians served up a brand of skilful football never yet seen in England. Meredith was a wonder on the wing, and goals flew in from all positions. Turnbull top-scored with 25, George Wall contributed 19 and Meredith chipped in with 10. Crowds at Clayton averaged 22,315 during the campaign, higher than they had ever been before – at the turn of the century they were failing to attract an average of 5,000 for home games.

United set a murderous pace from the start, and on 21 September 1907 they beat Sheffield United 2-1 at home, the first of 10 consecutive victories. Among the season's many highlights

1878–1915

United lost 2-1 to Portsmouth in an FA Cup first round replay at their Bank Street ground in January 1907. The ground's distinctive atmosphere was created by the chimneys of the adjacent chemical works.

were a 6-1 win at Newcastle followed by a 5-1 victory at Bolton the following Saturday. The only black spot in their progress was a 2-1 FA Cup quarter-final defeat at Fulham – but that trophy could wait a little while longer.

United stuttered at the end of the campaign as teams who set a cracking tempo often do, but they still managed to wrap up the Championship by nine points from Villa. Along with Roberts, the captain and the mainstay of the defence, Meredith was the key personality in the make-up of the team. He played with a toothpick resting casually on his bottom lip and moved with a languid insouciance that belied his tigerish will to win. In Roberts he also found an ally in another off-field project close to both their hearts – the formation of a players' union.

Professional footballers had attempted to form a union a decade before and now the idea was resurrected, and it was United players who made the running. On 2 December 1907, in the middle of United's title-winning season, Meredith chaired a meeting at Manchester's Imperial Hotel. The gathering attracted 500 footballers, mainly from clubs in the north and the Midlands, and they were there to discuss the establishment of a union. Their grievances centred on the maximum wage, the attempted circumvention of which had landed City in the soup. The £4-a-week ceiling had been imposed in 1900, largely at the behest of smaller clubs who feared they would lose their best players to the richer teams if there was a wages free-for-all. The bigger clubs, including United, were in favour of relaxing the maximum wage and welcomed the chance of hiring the cream of the country's playing talent. But the artificial constraint placed on wages was irksome to the players, who had seen crowds increasing season by season while their pay stagnated. In 1900 when the pay limit was set crowds over 10,000 were infrequent. Now a team like Chelsea, for instance, were pulling in average crowds of 32,000 and many clubs had seen gates triple. The players wanted a greater share of the cash their labour was producing. In January 1908 the players' union was ratified at a meeting in Sheffield.

At this stage United's union members had the full backing of their employers. Davies, now United chairman, agreed to be president of the new union and leading officials from other big clubs were vice-presidents. Davies and like-minded men from other First Division clubs talked about launching a new breakaway league, which would allow them to pay their players whatever they liked, but the idea came to nothing. The Football League countered with a demand that the clubs introduce new contracts for their employees, which retained the maximum wage and gave the players less freedom of movement. They also insisted the clubs disown the union. The clubs caved in and the battle to free footballers from indentured slavery would continue until 1961.

The United players were rewarded for their title-winning efforts with a summer trip to Austria and Hungary, which combined sightseeing with some semi-serious matches against local opposition. United were half a century away from their first season in the European Cup, but Mangnall's men had an early taste of playing in a hostile environment in front of unfriendly fans, deep in the heart of the old Hapsburg Empire.

The tour began happily enough in Austria, where United beat a combined Vienna side 4-0. But events turned sour in Budapest. United played a double-header against Ferencvaros and won the first game 6-2. They also raced into a substantial, if undiplomatic, lead in the second game and the crowd grew restless. Stones flew. The referee responded by sending off three United players, but that did not stem the ugly scenes in the stands. The game ended 7-0 to the visitors and there was an equally clear-cut win for the police cavalry, as they quelled the unruly crowd by drawing their sabres and charging. United made the tactical error of riding back to their hotel on an open-topped bus, providing more sport for Budapest's stone-throwers. Hungarian officials apologised for the disorder, but Mangnall told them not to worry and insisted United would be back the following summer for another visit. Mangnall's first words when United's boat docked in England were that the team would never go near Hungary again.

The new Champions were also handed the distinction of playing in the first-ever Charity Shield. They took on Queens Park Rangers at Stamford Bridge and drew 1-1. United won the replay 4-0. But United failed to defend their title successfully and the league

---

Billy Meredith, the charismatic Welsh winger who helped bring early success to United and forged for himself a reputation as one of the greatest players in the history of the club.

campaign of 1908/09 was an anti-climax after the stirring deeds of the season before. United made up for it by winning the FA Cup for the first time. The journey began with home matches against non-league Brighton and Everton, which United won 1-0. The next visitors to Clayton for the third round, Blackburn Rovers, were riding high near the top of Division One while United were struggling in mid-table, but Mangnall's team swept them aside 6-1. In the quarter-finals United travelled to Burnley, who were bumping along near the bottom of the Second Division – but the favourites' Cup hopes were almost buried on a snowy day at Turf Moor. With 20 minutes of the game remaining Burnley were leading 1-0 and looking good value for a place in the semi-finals. But United were saved by the weather and by the referee. Snow had begun to fall during the first-half and as the match neared completion the flurry of flakes turned into a blizzard. The referee, a gentleman named Herbert Bamlett who was destined to manage United 18 years later, judged that the conditions were unplayable and called the match off. United made the most of their reprieve and won the re-match 3-2.

United were now just one step away from the final, but the semi-final opposition could not have been tougher. They had to face Champions-elect and Cup kings Newcastle, but United rose to the challenge and went through 1-0. Another 1-0 victory against Bristol City gave United their first-ever FA Cup.

Top United beat Queens Park Rangers 4-0 at Stamford Bridge in a replay of the first-ever Charity Shield in 1908. The first game ended 1-1.
***Above** George Robey, the famous music hall comic who provided the entertainment after United's glorious FA Cup final triumph in 1909.*
***Overleaf** The conquering heroes arrive back in Manchester with the English Cup, met by thousands of ecstatic well-wishers.*

1909 **FA CUP FINAL**

BRISTOL CITY 0 MANCHESTER UNITED 1 Sandy Turnbull

24 APRIL 1909 at Crystal Palace • Referee: J. Mason • Attendance: 71,401

The man who scored the goal which won United's first-ever FA Cup was lucky to be on the field at all. Alexander 'Sandy' Turnbull looked certain to miss the match with a painful knee injury, but on the morning he persuaded Mangnall that he could and should play. The captain, Charlie Roberts, was also desperate for the influential inside-left to turn out. 'Let him play,' Roberts implored the manager. 'He might get a goal and if he does we can afford to carry him.' Mangnall gave Turnbull the go-ahead and Roberts's words proved prophetic.

Midway through the first half Harold Halse fired a shot from a dozen yards out which smacked the bar. Despite his infirmity, Turnbull was first to the rebound and he poked it past Clay in the City goal. The thousands of Mancunians who had poured into London to watch the final on a freezing April day were ecstatic, even though the sporting press rated it a poor match.

There were no such happy endings in the short life of Sandy Turnbull. His football career was cut short when he was implicated in a match-fixing conspiracy and he was killed at the Battle of Arras on 3 May 1917.

BRISTOL CITY

Clay
Annan
Cottle
Hanlin
Wedlock
Spear
Staniforth
Hardy
Gilligan
Burton
Hilton

MANCHESTER UNITED

Moger
Stacey
Hayes
Duckworth
Roberts
Bell
Meredith
Halse
J. Turnbull
A. Turnbull
Wall

Sandy Turnbull (out of shot) scores the only goal of the game.

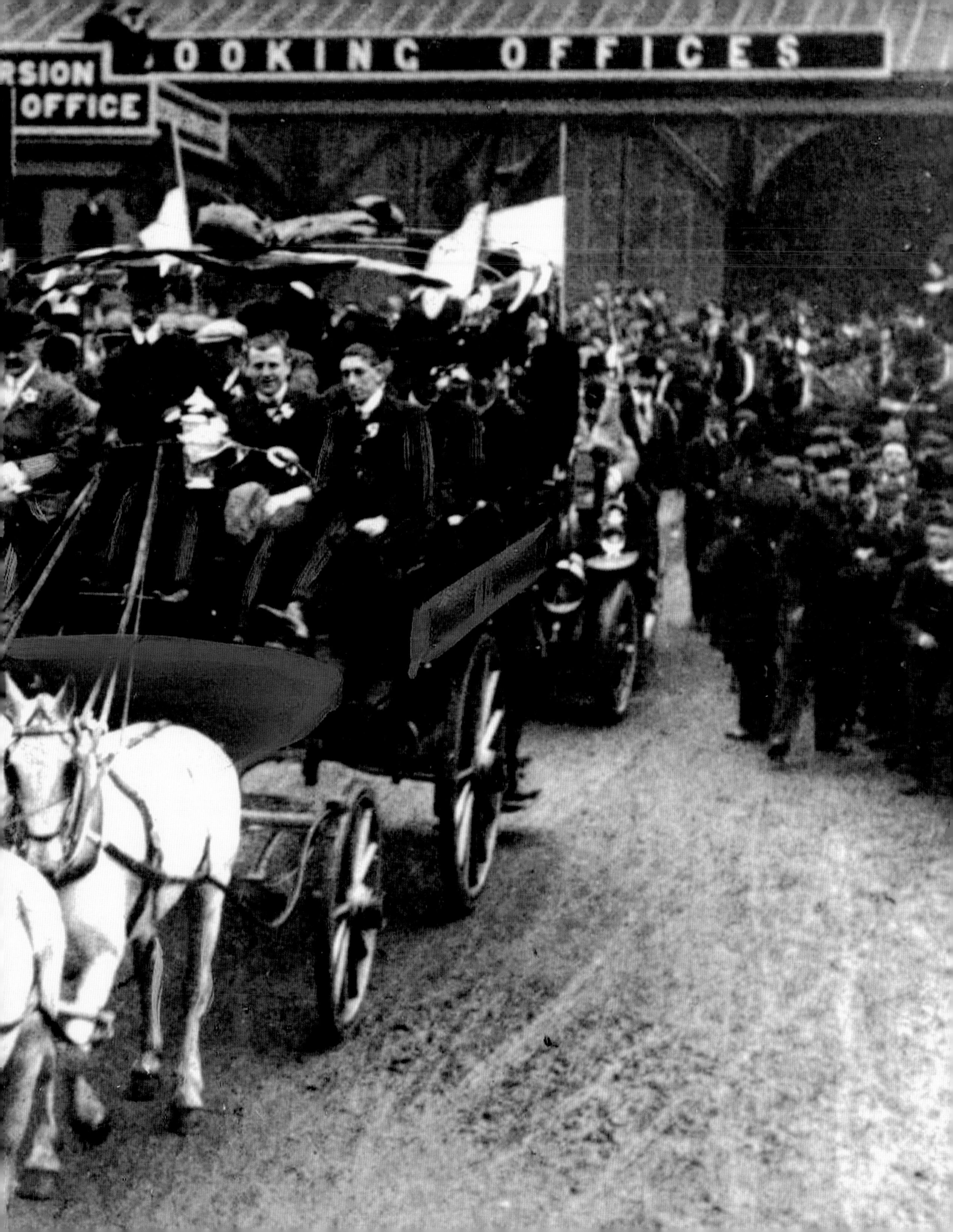
OOKING OFFICES
RSION
OFFICE

1878–1915

United's jubilant players celebrated with a night out at the music hall. They saw the country's most famous comic, George Robey, at the Alhambra Theatre – but it was no laughing matter the next morning when United could not find the trophy. After a frantic search it finally turned up wrapped in Sandy Turnbull's carelessly discarded coat. United almost became the first club to win the Cup and lose it again in the space of 24 hours.

The victorious team arrived back in Manchester the next afternoon and were astonished to find a vast crowd besieging the train station. A throng exceeding 250,000 had gathered to pay tribute to the Cup winners and a brass band belted out Handel's 'See, The Conquering Hero Come' on the platform. As a motor coach paraded the team and the trophy through the streets, a crowd dozens deep jammed the pavements, and people waving makeshift red and white flags hung out of every window. Even the roofs were packed with cheering well-wishers. The procession took in Albert Square and ended at the ground in Clayton, where more than 30,000 supporters had waited all day to see the team. You only win the Cup for the first time once in your history. United's supporters were determined to enjoy the moment and the whole city joined in with the festivities.

Despite those jubilant scenes, it was not all roses in the football garden. The festering row between the Football League and the players' union erupted once more in the summer of 1909 and United's steadfast players were in the thick of the trouble. The League had threatened to ban any player *sine die* if he continued to support the union. Players began to back down and it appeared as if the union would be strangled at birth. United's players were the last to remain solid for the union and they carried out their pre-season

The 1909 FA Cup-winning team pose with the trophy.

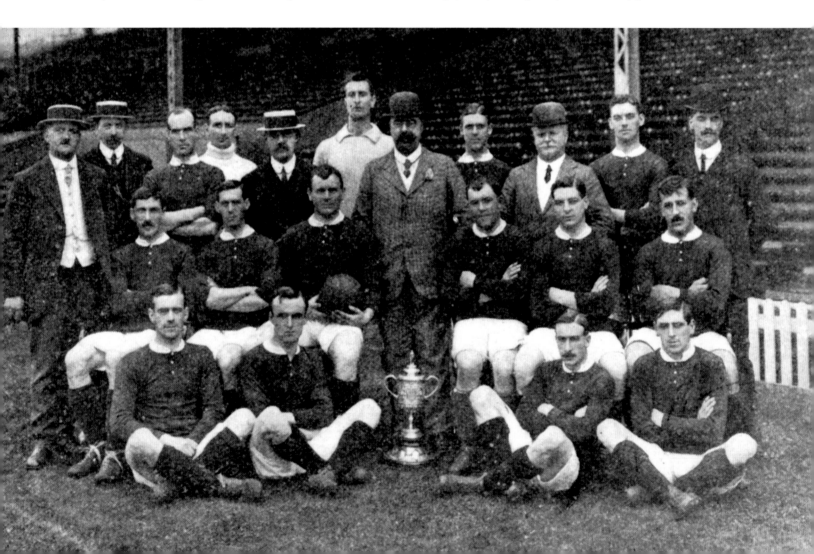

training under the name Outcasts FC. Alone, they were doomed to defeat, and there was a real prospect that none of the 1909 FA Cup winners would play professional football again. But the players of Middlesbrough, Newcastle, Sunderland, Liverpool and Everton threw their support back behind the union and the League were forced into a compromise, hours before the start of the season, which allowed the union to survive. Without the staunch United players, it would have died in the summer of 1909.

By now United had outgrown their old Bank Street home. Six weeks before the Cup final triumph, Davies had announced he was donating £60,000 to the club to buy a plot of land at Trafford Park, close to the Lancashire cricket ground, between the Bridgewater Canal, the railway line and Warwick Road. Davies envisaged a vast stadium that would house 100,000 supporters, 12,000 of them seated, and lavish facilities including a billiard room, gymnasium, laundry, massage room and tea room. He recruited a young Scottish architect named Archibald Leitch, who would become the doyen of football stadium designers, to plan the new ground, with a construction budget of a cool £30,000. Rising costs meant the blueprint had to be altered in due course, with the capacity reduced to 77,000, but United became the proud inhabitants of a stadium fit for the 20th century. The priciest seats would cost five shillings and it would cost sixpence to stand on the terraces.

The construction work was carried out astonishingly quickly by Messrs Brameld and Smith of Manchester, and the grand opening was set for 19 February 1910, when Liverpool were the visitors. The gala occasion, attended by 50,000 spectators, was marred slightly by a 4-3 away win, but the move did not come a day too soon. United had played Spurs in the last-ever game at Clayton on 22 January and won 5-0. A few days later one of the stands crashed to the ground during a storm.

The new ground – named Old Trafford – was hailed the finest in England, and before long it was home to the finest team in the country as United regained their First Division title the following season. United set the pace early and when they beat Newcastle 2-0 at Old Trafford, on 15 October 1910, it was their seventh victory in the first eight games of the season. From then on United were always pressing hard for the title, but Villa looked Championship favourites for most of the season.

The Birmingham team seized what seemed to be a decisive advantage when they beat United 4-2 at Villa Park in the run-in. But Villa failed to win either of their last two games, drawing at Blackburn and losing at Liverpool. To recapture the title United needed to win their last game of the season at home to Sunderland – and their 5-1 win was good enough. They owed much to the 19 goals of their leading scorer, Enoch 'Knocker' West, an all-action forward who had been a prolific goalscorer for Nottingham Forest. The ever-dependable Sandy Turnbull also contributed 18, and Billy Meredith and Charlie Roberts remained the creative geniuses that made the team tick.

United added another trophy to their expanding collection at the beginning of the 1911/12 season, when they beat Southern League Champions, Swindon Town, 8-4 in the Charity Shield at Stamford Bridge. But their form in the big competitions faded. They finished 13th in the First Division and lost 4-2 to Blackburn Rovers in an FA Cup quarter-final replay. But a far greater blow followed in August 1912 when Mangnall, the towering figure who had plotted United's rise to eminence, quit the club to join Manchester City.

Mangnall was replaced briefly by T.J. Wallworth and J.J. Bentley, who were both more comfortable with the secretarial side of the job rather than the football management. The next couple of seasons in the post-Mangnall era were featureless for United, mired in the middle of the First Division and exiting the FA Cup in the early rounds. But in the last season before football was suspended for war, United were embroiled in a scandal so serious they were lucky to escape with their First Division status intact.

Good Friday 1915 turned out to be Black Friday for the reputation of Manchester United. On that day they played Liverpool at Old Trafford, desperately needing points to avoid relegation. Liverpool were comfortably placed in mid-table, apparently with little to play for, so it was no great surprise when the home team won 2-0. But within days stories began to circulate that the game might not have been all it seemed. Rumours abounded that the match was, in fact, crooked. Manchester bookmakers took a disproportionate amount of cash on a 2-0 United victory and they plainly suspected skulduggery. These days they would be talking about irregular betting patterns. The angry bookies refused to pay out on the 2-0 win and they went further. They joined together to

produce a leaflet that was circulated around Manchester alleging that the Liverpool game had been bent. They offered a £50 reward for information that would unmask the conspirators.

The *Sporting Chronicle* newspaper took the story up and accused players from both sides of concocting a 2-0 scoreline. The paper also claimed that the players themselves weighed in with large wagers on a 2-0 United win, at odds of 7-1. The Football League launched an inquiry and it revealed its findings in December 1915. It concluded that 'a considerable amount of money changed hands by betting on the match and... some of the players profited thereby'. Four players from both teams were banned from the game for life.

The mastermind behind the scam was named as Liverpool's Jackie Sheldon, who had also played for United. The League stated that he met a United contingent in a Manchester pub and hatched the plot with them. The disgraced United quartet were the loyal club servant Sandy Turnbull; the top-scoring hero of the second Championship season, 'Knocker' West; Laurence Cook; and Arthur Whalley.

At the end of the war the bans on Cook, Whalley and Turnbull were rescinded in view of their service to King and Country. West, the only one of the four to have taken part in the tainted match, never played again. He protested his innocence ever afterwards. The reprieve for Turnbull was posthumous. He had been killed in action while serving with the Footballers' Battalion in France.

United's great title and Cup-winning team began to break up in the years before the First World War. The running costs of the huge new stadium were horrendous and United were saddled with a vast debt from building Old Trafford. When other clubs offered big money for their best players they were in no position to turn it down.

So it was that Roberts, for so long the inspiration of the team, was sold to Oldham Athletic for a club-record £1,500 in August 1913. He had been a great captain, leading them to their first two titles and the FA Cup, and in 10 years at the club he made 271 League appearances and scored 22 goals. His playing career continued at Oldham after the war, he chaired the players' union and he became manager of the Latics in 1921. But despite his sterling work at Oldham, it is as a United legend that he is best remembered and he never forgot the club he helped to make great. Roberts ended his working life as a tobacconist in Manchester and invented a cigarette named the Ducrobel, in honour of the great pre-war United half-back line he graced: Duckworth, Roberts, Bell. He died in Manchester on 7 August 1939.

Roberts's departure, following on from Mangnall's exit, marked the closing of a stirring chapter in the story of Manchester United. There were lean years ahead before the club could sample again the kind of glories they enjoyed in the first years of the 20th century.

Action from United's 3-1 win against Spurs at Old Trafford on 4 October 1913.

ERNEST MANGNALL

MANAGER (1903–12)

Ernest Mangnall, who took over as secretary-manager of Manchester United after James West resigned in September 1902, was an immediately recognisable figure around Manchester in the early years of the 20th century. He was a dapper fellow in his ever-present collar and tie, and had arresting features not easily forgotten, with a strong jaw jutting out from a round face, neat toothbrush moustache and penetrating gaze which gave a hint of the steely customer within. He had character to match and was a peerless motivator of players long before the phrase 'man-management' had even been dreamed of.

In truth, Mangnall was not a dyed-in-the-wool football man. He had played as a goalkeeper for Lancashire representative sides, but he also excelled at rugby and athletics. However, his first love was cycling and one of his proudest sporting achievements was riding from Land's End to John O'Groats.

But despite his prowess on two wheels, his claim on history rests with his record at United. Almost as soon as he arrived from his previous job as secretary at Burnley, Mangnall proved an inspired appointment. After two third-place finishes, he earned United a much-awaited promotion in his third season, and once in the First Division he built a team good enough to win the club's first two Championships in 1907/08 and 1910/11, and the FA Cup in 1909. Mangnall also oversaw the club's move from Bank Street in Clayton to its new stadium at Old Trafford in 1910.

Mangnall's training methods might fairly be described as old school. The players were denied use of a football during the week: Mangnall reasoned they would be all the hungrier for it on match day. Instead, their training sessions featured running, running and more running. Mangnall cared deeply about fitness.

He quit United to manage Manchester City in 1912, where he stayed throughout the First World War. He later became a director of Bolton Wanderers and he died in 1932.

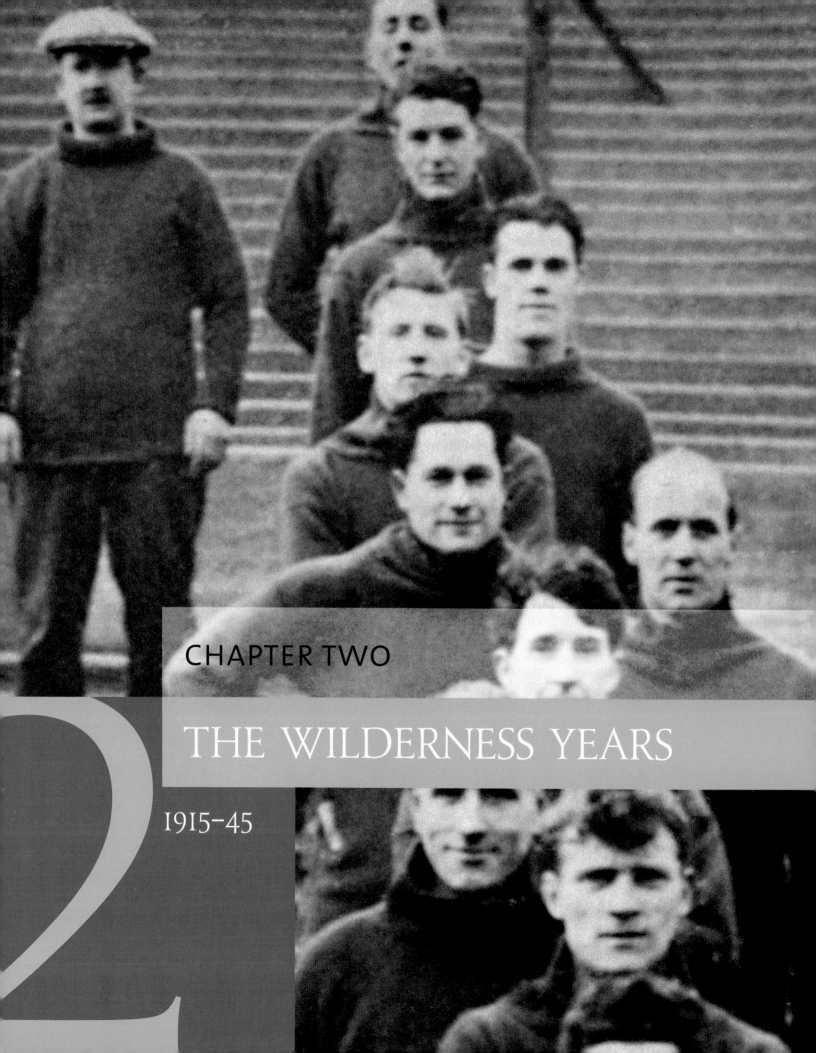

CHAPTER TWO

THE WILDERNESS YEARS

1915–45

THE PERIOD BOOKENDED BY TWO WORLD WARS WAS THE LEAST SUCCESSFUL IN MANCHESTER UNITED'S HISTORY

The days before the First World War when United had been the best team in England were an ever-fading memory as the club spent long stretches in the Second Division and failed to make much progress in the FA Cup either. During the grim days of the First World War there was already a sense that the club had lost its way.

The great team built by Mangnall had broken up and, although there was some semi-competitive regional football played, Old Trafford was like a mausoleum. The ornate edifice built in more confident times was now an albatross around the club's neck as running costs remained enormous in the long years when there were no spectators to fill the plush, tip-up seats in the grandstands.

At the end of the war United were in poor shape financially and weak in playing strength. The players from the pre-war team who hadn't been banned for match fixing, or sold, or killed in the conflict, were ageing. Billy Meredith stayed with the club until 1921 when, aged 47, a final row over money saw him go back to City as player-coach. United needed a visionary in the Mangnall mould to rebuild all over again. Alas, Mangnall was still at City.

United's manager in the first post-war seasons was John Robson, from County Durham, a man of wide experience who had already

United players take a break from training to pose on the Old Trafford terraces, May 1924.

managed Middlesbrough, Crystal Palace and Brighton with success. He had a reputation as a strict disciplinarian, but his methods failed to bring much prosperity to United, who spent the first couple of seasons after the war scuffling around the middle of the First Division.

United were, at least, able to start refilling their coffers when competitive football resumed after the armistice. Grounds all over the country were packed as a sport-hungry public lapped up all the entertainment they could. The war-weary populace were ready to be distracted by athletic heroes. In 1920/21, the first full season after the war, United's average gate was 35,525 – way in excess of anything they had experienced before. On 27 December 1920, a vast holiday crowd numbering 70,504 threatened Old Trafford's capacity for the first time, as United took on Villa and lost 3-1. At last, John Henry Davies's far-sighted decision to build Old Trafford on such a monumental scale began to pay off.

In 1921 Robson, who was 67 and in poor health, stood down from the manager's job to work as assistant to John Chapman, a Scot who had been recruited from Airdrieonians. But the club lurched into crisis. Of Chapman's first 15 games in charge, United won just one. From Boxing Day 1921 to 21 January 1922 they played six and lost six, and never recovered. They finished 22nd and last in the First Division, and were relegated along with Bradford City, a full eight points behind Everton and safety.

However, the Manchester sporting public continued to back the club. Average crowds at Old Trafford, though down on the previous season, still topped 28,500. That was 4,000 more than City were drawing in at Hyde Road. United remained the sixth-best supported club in the country. Chelsea were attracting 37,545 into Stamford Bridge; Liverpool, Cardiff and Villa also topped 30,000; and Arsenal were pulling in over 29,000.

United spent three unhappy years in the Second Division, but finally won promotion back to Division One in 1924/25 after pushing Leicester City all the way for the Division Two title. They roared away to a terrific start, reeling off seven straight wins from September 1924 and enjoying an unbeaten run that lasted 16 games right through the autumn. But it remained a close, three-way fight for promotion right through the campaign and going into the last weeks of the season it was any two from Leicester, United and Derby to go up. Luckily for United, Derby imploded on the run-in. From their last six matches the Rams could scrape only four points and the Reds took the second promotion spot behind Leicester. United ensured their return to the big league on 25 April 1925, beating Port Vale 4-0 in their last home game.

There were two major factors in that promotion team's success: Derby's demise which left the door ajar and the excellence of their own defence. United conceded just 23 goals in their 42 Second Division matches, which was an all-time low for the league. Much of United's attacking threat came from Geordie Joe Spence, a winger who loved to cut inside and score goals. In a fallow period for United, Spence was the man who lit up Old Trafford week after week and, from his debut in 1919 until his departure to Bradford City in 1933, he was the club's key player. Other men who stood out for United in the promotion season were the goalkeeper, Alf Steward, who kept 25 clean sheets, the colourful half-back Frank Barson and the indomitable full-back pairing of Charlie Moore and Jack Silcock.

United's first season back in the First Division was steady rather than spectacular, but they produced fireworks in the FA Cup for the first time since winning the trophy in 1909. They began their 1925/26 Cup run with a third-round tie at Port Vale, a middling Second Division team, and United won an exciting match 3-2. They travelled to Tottenham, like United a mid-table First Division team, in the fourth round. A 2-2 draw set up a replay at Old Trafford four days later, which United won 2-0. The odds were stacked against United going any further when they were pitted against title-chasing

Sunderland in the fifth round, but the dogged Mancunians fought out a 3-3 draw at Roker Park, and pulled off a 2-1 win in the replay.

By now United fans were beginning to anticipate their first-ever journey to the newly-opened Wembley Stadium, and they were handed a kind quarter-final draw. It was another away tie, but

Above Joe Spence, a free-scoring forward who shone for United during a difficult period. 'Give it to Joe!' was the common call around Old Trafford when United won possession.

Opposite Alf Steward, United's regular, reliable goalkeeper in the 1920s.

1915–45 the opponents were Fulham, who were struggling near the bottom of the Second Division. United won 2-1 to set up what was arguably the biggest match in Manchester's football history, a semi-final against arch-rivals Manchester City at Bramall Lane, a short hop over the Pennines, on 27 March 1926. Although City were having a poor season in Division One and ended up suffering relegation, the formbook made grave reading for United. Just two months earlier United had suffered their biggest-ever derby defeat, a 6-1 thrashing at Old Trafford.

It was not a good match, riddled with nerves and strewn with errors, and United were never on their game. One newspaper described the internecine battle as 'grim' entertainment for the 46,000 crowd and the result for United was even grimmer. City went ahead after quarter of an hour, when Tommy Browell headed the ball goalwards. United's players complained vehemently that the goal should not stand on two counts: they claimed Browell fouled his marker and that the ball didn't even cross the line. But the goal stood and Browell's second goal 15 minutes from time snuffed out any chance of a United revival. Frank Roberts applied the coup de grâce in City's 3-0 win.

No less an authority than United's pre-war stalwart, Charlie Roberts, said City deserved to win. Roberts, by this time a newspaper journalist, wrote, 'United were outplayed by a side who were all enterprise and dash, and never gave their rivals a moment to consider the next move.' It was little consolation to United fans that City went on to complete a relegation-Cup final defeat double, when their neighbours lost 1-0 to Bolton Wanderers at Wembley.

The next few unstable years saw managers come and go at Old Trafford, and United endured a precarious existence in the First Division. Chapman was suspended by the FA and left the club in 1926 following an investigation into crimes unknown. The FA released an opaque statement announcing Chapman's sentence without shedding any light on the charge. The document released on 8 October 1926 declared, 'For improper conduct in his position as secretary-manager of the Manchester United Football Club, the Football Association have suspended Mr J.A. Chapman from

Frank Roberts (third from left) scores for Manchester City in United's 3-0 FA Cup semi-final defeat at Bramall Lane, Sheffield, in March 1926.

BILLY MEREDITH

FORWARD (1906–21) • 335 APPEARANCES • 36 GOALS

In an age long before the cult of the celebrity had been invented, Billy Meredith was a superstar. Along with Edward VII, George V and his countryman, Prime Minister David Lloyd George, Meredith was one of the most famous people in Britain in the first two decades of the 20th century, an instantly recognisable icon whose image dominated the public prints. Even people who knew little of football and cared less knew all about Meredith: he was widely admired for his raffishness and rebellion, as much as for his prowess on the park.

If the cricketer W.G. Grace bestrode the sporting world in the Victorian age, the Edwardian era and those last years of peace before the carnage of Flanders belonged to Meredith. His roots in the tiny, strictly God-fearing village of Chirk, in Wales, could not have been humbler. Aged 12, Meredith went to work in the local mine. However, football turned out to be his saviour. He had shown some talent as a player in local football and Meredith wanted to try his luck in England. His family were reluctant to let him go, but in the end he joined Northwich Victoria as an amateur in 1892.

He was soon spotted and signed by Manchester City, and became an instant sensation, dazzling spectators up and down the country with his breathtaking wing play. He won his first Wales cap in 1895, the Second Division Championship in 1903 and the FA Cup in 1904 with City.

Meredith was already showing signs of the anti-authority streak that was such a feature of his career. In 1905 he was implicated in a financial scandal and accused of bribing an Aston Villa player to throw a match. He always denied the allegation, but was one of a number of players to be banned from playing for the club again. City's loss was United's gain, as Ernest Mangnall snapped up Meredith and a number of his team-mates for United. It was the start of one of the great United careers.

You wouldn't have picked Meredith out as an exceptional athlete if you had seen him in the street. He was pale as a ghost and had bandy legs which wouldn't

'stop a pig in a passage' as the saying has it. Yet get him on a football field and he was transformed. Meredith's skill with a ball, devastating acceleration and precise crosses, allied with an ability to inspire team-mates, all played a huge part in United's rise to the top of English football. Meredith was the team's best player as they won two Championships and the FA Cup in the years before the First World War.

Meredith's links with United ended acrimoniously after the war and money was the root of the problem. No player chafed against the restrictions of the maximum wage more than Meredith. He remained bitter throughout his career that players were not allowed to earn wages commensurate with their skills. Football was generating fortunes in gate money and Meredith was keenly aware that he pulled in more spectators than anybody else.

He left United in July 1921 to rejoin City as player-coach, but nothing in the rest of his career matched his achievements with United. He also played 48 times for Wales and scored 11 times.

Meredith died on 19 April 1958.

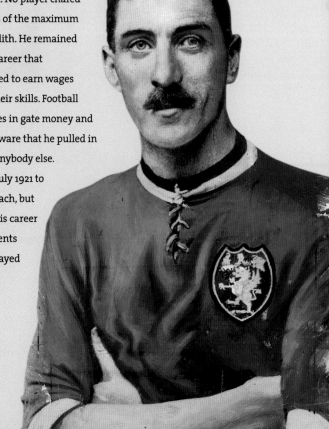

1915–45 taking part in football or management during the present season.' Amid dark mutterings about financial chicanery, he was summarily replaced by Clarrie Hilditch. A fine half-back for United, Hilditch carried on playing while managing the club in the 1926/27 season. But United's first and as yet only player-manager found it difficult to juggle the two jobs, and he was relieved to concentrate on playing and leave the management to somebody else in April 1927.

The new man was Herbert Bamlett, the former referee who had saved United from defeat with a timely postponement at Burnley in their Cup-winning season nearly two decades earlier. Bamlett had a patrician air, carried himself with an upright bearing, and wore rimless, round spectacles, which all contributed to his rather stern appearance. And after his years of refereeing he was quite capable of finding words to put footballers in their rightful places. Though he had all the right credentials for the job,

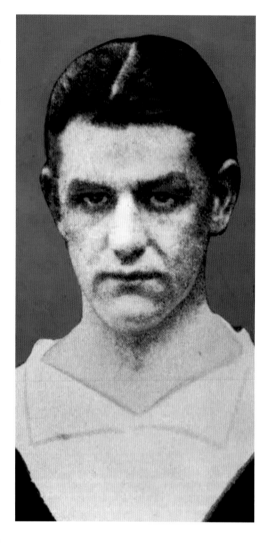

even in the 1920s it was highly unorthodox for a football club to appoint an ex-referee as manager. But Bamlett had plenty of experience in the role. The Geordie had already managed Oldham, Wigan Borough and Middlesbrough, and done well with those clubs. It was under Bamlett that Oldham recorded their highest-ever league finish – Division One runners-up in 1915. He had also turned around the failing Wigan club and set Middlesbrough on the road to promotion.

United's directors had done their homework well. Bamlett's speciality of reviving clubs on their uppers was precisely what they required at Old Trafford. But Bamlett could not repeat the trick in Manchester. In his first season, 1927/28, United finished just one

point ahead of relegated Tottenham in one of the most extraordinary battles against the drop the Football League has ever witnessed.

With three matches left to play United were planted in the bottom two, well adrift of a bunch of teams above them. They looked doomed, but won the first of the games 2-1 at home to Sunderland. United gave themselves an outside chance of staying up by winning the next one as well, 1-0 at Highbury. But they still needed to beat Liverpool by several goals at Old Trafford, then hope other results were kind.

Spence gave United an early lead against Liverpool, then his fellow forward Joe Rawlings scored twice, and Spence added his second to make the score 4-1 at half-time. The 30,000-strong United crowd were breathless with excitement in the second half, as Spence played as if his life was at stake. He completed his hat-trick, then scored a fourth, to make the final score 6-1. There followed a cruelly protracted wait while results came in from around the country. But when they arrived, United knew they were safe, and Tottenham and Middlesbrough were down instead. United's sixth goal saved them. Incredibly, they were one of seven teams to finish on 39 points. Spurs went down with 38.

Later that year the man who had saved United from extinction at the turn of the century and built Old Trafford did not live to see the dramatic finale. John Henry Davies, the club's wise benefactor, died in October 1927.

Clarrie Hilditch served United as player and manager in the troubled post-First World War era.

FRANK BARSON

HALF-BACK (1922–28) • 152 APPEARANCES • 4 GOALS

Frank Barson was not among the most skilful players in Manchester United's history, but few more colourful characters have passed through Old Trafford, and no footballer of his generation spawned so many stories.

He began his working life as a blacksmith in Grimethorpe, south Yorkshire, an occupation which helped sculpt the granite physique which made him such a commanding presence on the league pitches of England. And once he left hammer and anvil behind, he continued to make sparks fly in the world of football.

Barson began as a player with his local team, Barnsley, then moved on to Aston Villa before signing for United in July 1922 for the colossal sum of £5,000. The club had just been relegated, but they knew exactly what they wanted to revive their fortunes: a tough man to put some steel back into the side and inspire the men around him to win promotion. Barson was the right man. Just the fearsome sight of him was enough to demotivate some opponents: at 6 feet tall Barson loomed over most opponents and he had the sharp features and narrow, menacing eyes of an Aztec warrior.

The directors offered Barson an unusual bonus: if the club were back in the First Division within three years, they would give him a pub. United did it right on schedule and, good as their word, they handed Barson the keys to a hostelry in Ardwick.

Barson gave United exactly what they wanted on the pitch. He was considered a hard player even in an era when referees were far more lenient with physical contact. But he stepped across the line of fair play often enough to become a one-man disciplinary crime wave. That was partly due to his honesty. If an opponent fouled him or one of his team-mates, Barson would swear retribution. He also told the referee exactly what he was going to do,

just so there would be no mistake about his intentions. Unsurprisingly, opposition fans hated him and on several occasions team-mates or police officers persuaded him to leave grounds in secret to prevent a riot.

But Barson was not just a hatchet man. He could play and was especially fearsome in the air. The Yorkshireman was widely acknowledged to be the finest header of a football in the country and on one celebrated occasion he scored with his head against Sheffield United – from 30 yards.

Barson could be blunt and his plain-speaking often bordered on rudeness. But he was willing to help any footballer with advice, especially young players making their way in the game. But that cordial manner disappeared once he crossed the white line. Billy Walker, who knew Barson at Villa, said, 'Frank did more than any other player to help me when I started – but he had no friends on the field.' The words recalled a ruthless operator of a later generation, Denis Law, who booted Scotland team-mate Billy Bremner in the air during a United-Leeds game. The Lawman growled to Bremner, who thought Law was a pal, 'No friends on the park, son.'

Barson played 152 games for United before signing for Watford in May 1928. His career wound down at Hartlepool, Wigan Borough and Rhyl Athletic before he began a string of coaching jobs at Stourbridge, Villa, Swansea Town and Lye Town. His only international appearance was against Wales on 15 March 1920, at Highbury, when England lost 2-1. Perhaps he was blamed for the country's first defeat against Wales for 38 years.

He died on 13 September 1968.

United spent most of the following season, 1928/29, in danger of the drop again and only another remarkable end-of-season rally saved them. They finished with five straight wins then a draw, ending up in 12th place. The hero of that rearguard fight against relegation was a Scottish striker, Tom Reid, who had signed for United from Liverpool in February 1928. In the last 17 games of the campaign he scored 14 goals and became almost as much a favourite at Old Trafford as Spence.

But United plunged back into peril again the following season and only ended up two points clear of relegated Burnley. United's supporters were growing weary of their team dancing on the trapdoor, waiting for it to open, but the inevitable drop still came as a shock. By the late 1920s a pall of gloom had settled over Old Trafford, as even the ever-loyal, long-suffering supporters began to lose heart over the team's fortunes. The average crowd fell below 19,000. United hadn't seen such tiny crowds in peacetime since their Bank Street days and the writing was on the wall for Bamlett. His last chance to turn the club around was the 1930/31 season and it turned out to be the worst for results in the club's history.

United's form was catastrophic right from the start. The first game of the season was a 4-3 home defeat against Villa on 30 August, and United had begun as they meant to go on. That was only the first in a depressing run of 12 straight defeats, including back-to-back losses at Old Trafford when United were buried in an avalanche of goals. Huddersfield won 6-0 and three days later Newcastle put United to the sword 7-4.

There was serious unrest among the fans. A disgruntled group from the Manchester United Supporters' Club printed flyers and handed them out around Old Trafford, demanding a new manager, a better scouting system, new players, new directors and a share issue to raise funds for the club. United's beleaguered directors turned a deaf ear to the pleas, rejecting the pressure group as unrepresentative of the club's supporters.

But the Supporters' Club would not stay silent. After a limp 4-1 defeat away to City, followed by a 5-1 defeat at West Ham, a public meeting was held at Hulme Town Hall. The packed auditorium heard demands for a boycott of the home game against Arsenal on 18 October 1930. Despite an impassioned plea from Charlie Roberts for the fans to get behind the team, a motion to support the boycott was carried. The crowd at the game the following day was fewer

Police control a huge crowd for the FA Cup semi-final between Huddersfield Town and Sheffield Wednesday at Old Trafford in 1930. United's ground was one of the biggest and best appointed in the country, and a natural choice to stage important games.

than 24,000, when 40,000 might have been expected. United lost 2-1 to the Gunners, and gates continued to tail off for the rest of the season as disenchantment spread.

Amid the turmoil United finished bottom of the table nine points adrift of Leeds and 10 points short of Blackpool, who stayed up. The average crowd for the season was less than 12,000 – the lowest since 1902/03 – and the last game of the season, a 4-4 draw with Middlesbrough at Old Trafford, was seen by fewer than 4,000 spectators. Bamlett had already left the club by then. He was sacked on 5 April 1931, bizarrely, the day after United's first and only away win of the season, a 2-1 triumph at Sunderland.

Managing Manchester United looked like an impossible job in the early 1930s. The malaise at the club was so deep-rooted that the task of reviving United looked beyond any individual's powers. The directors seemed to be thinking along those lines because they did not appoint a full-time manager to replace Bamlett. Walter Crickmer was given temporary charge of the team for the first season back in Division Two in 1931/32, but he was never officially handed the title of manager. Whatever they called him, Crickmer held the fort manfully for that fraught season and steadied the ship well enough to steer United to a safe mid-table position. Even the crowd figures moved northwards, though only slightly.

The next man charged with the thorny task of improving United's fortunes was Scott Duncan, a Scotsman who had made his name as a player with Newcastle United. He later managed Hamilton and Cowdenbeath before answering the call from Old Trafford. Duncan, who came from Dumbarton, had one advantage not afforded to his immediate predecessors: money. At the start of the 1930s United had been staring at the prospect of bankruptcy as gate receipts continued to plummet. But an investment of £2,000 from a Manchester businessman named James Gibson came just in time, because United were sliding into a financial abyss and any one of a number of outstanding debts could have sunk the club.

United owed a substantial sum to the local council for the maintenance of the roads around Old Trafford, but the two sides agreed an instalment plan. The Inland Revenue was owed an even larger sum, but looked indulgently on United's plea for extra time to pay. But when United's bankers turned off the club's credit the crisis looked terminal. With no money to pay bills, including the players'

wages, the club looked doomed. But just as Davies appeared in 1901 to save United, so 30 years later Gibson emerged as a saviour. His money wiped out the debt, gave United stability and also allowed Duncan some clout in the transfer market.

Duncan set about rebuilding the team and looked to Scotland for new players. Although results weren't startling, United did manage to finish sixth in the Second Division at the end of 1932/33, Duncan's first season in charge. United were convinced they would make a serious push for promotion the following season. The cover of the programme (price tuppence) for the visit by Southampton on 11 November 1933 featured a cartoon encapsulating United's determined mood. The drawing showed a United player climbing a ladder leaning against the fortress walls of the Second Division. The ladder rests on the prone bodies of Fulham and Hull, and inside the battlements Port Vale, Grimsby and Bolton cower before the United onslaught. A United director, complete with shiny top hat, spats and a fat cigar dangling from his mouth, looks on gleefully while the caption boldly proclaims, 'Won't be long now lads!' United did win that match against the Saints 1-0, but it was a rare occurrence in a dreadful season.

They had to travel to Millwall's Den for the last game of the season on 5 May 1934, in a virtual play-off for survival. United won 2-0 and but for that victory would have dropped down to the Third Division (North) to share the company of teams like Barrow, New Brighton, Gateshead and Southport. The win at Millwall capped another amazing feat of escapology by United. With five matches to play they had looked finished, but somehow managed to draw three and win the other two to save themselves. But United had still fallen to their lowest-ever league position, finishing just one point and one place above Millwall and relegation. United's supporters were relieved to stay up and a crowd met them at the station on their return from London to hail their efforts. But the days when their team were winning Championships and FA Cups were growing ever murkier in the memory.

Duncan managed to turn the team around to the extent that they finished a respectable fifth the season after and the club took a huge step forwards in 1935/36 when they captured the Second

Overleaf *Scott Duncan (right) gets his point across to the United players.*

Division Championship. The team that won promotion was a hard-working United side rather than a star-studded outfit. They lacked idols of the calibre of Meredith or Spence, but Duncan had turned a collection of good players into an effective team. Among the crowd's favourites was Tom Manley, an outside-left who joined United from his hometown club, Northwich Victoria. He scored 41 goals in 195 games for United in the 1930s. In the Second Division Championship season he chipped in with 14 goals, including four in one game against Port Vale. The centre-forward was Welshman, Tommy Bamford, who set Wrexham scoring records before signing for United in 1934. In an Old Trafford career beset by injury he managed to score 57 goals in 109 games. Scottish left-half Billy McKay had come to Old Trafford from Bolton and he was a hugely influential player in the title-winning campaign, missing just a handful of games. In 182 matches for United he scored 15 times. The rock of the defence was George Vose, a Lancastrian who was a permanent fixture at the back for United in a turbulent era.

United won the title the hard way, starting the season in sluggish style before launching an all-out assault on the top of the table at the turn of the year. Towards the end of March they were still only fourth, but by April they were up into second place. Once again, United's season hung on the last match, when they travelled to Hull City needing a point to take the title. In the first 10 minutes Bamford chased a long through-ball, out-sprinted the Hull defence and lifted a shot over the goalkeeper. Hull scored just before half-time, and the United goal endured some close shaves in the second half, but they survived. The match finished 1-1 and United were Second Division Champions. Now they could look ahead to a fresh start in Division One.

Above *The United team that won the Second Division title in 1935/36.*

Opposite *George Mutch (centre) wins the ball in the air during United's 2-1 win over West Ham United at Upton Park on 7 March 1936.*

But it was a false dawn. United's first season back in Division One for six years was a miserable experience, and they went 11 matches without a win through to December and finished just one place from the bottom. They were back in the Second Division. Duncan had had enough and resigned his post in September 1937.

United's directors turned to a familiar face to get the club out of trouble. Walter Crickmer, who had handled the club's affairs competently for a season earlier in the decade, was installed as the new secretary-manager. In an era when league managers' jobs tended to be more secure than they are in the 21st century, it was United's fifth change at the top in 10 years. The club was crying out for stability and Crickmer offered just that.

United's yo-yo existence went on under Crickmer as he steered the team to their second promotion in three seasons at the end of another thrilling campaign. Villa had looked Second Division Champions in waiting for much of the 1937/38 season, but when the final day rolled around the second spot was still up for grabs, with United and Sheffield United in contention. Crickmer's team faced mid-table Bury at Old Trafford knowing a win should be good enough, and they closed the deal with a 2-0 victory. United were back in the First Division and this time they stayed there for 36 years.

In the last completed season before the Second World War Crickmer continued to refashion the team, and one newcomer in particular was destined to have a massive impact on the club. United's long-serving chief scout, Louis Rocca (the man who had coined the name 'Manchester United' all those years before), had spotted a young Dubliner he liked the look of. The club backed Rocca's instinct and signed Johnny Carey from a local Dublin team for £250. Carey made his debut on 25 September 1937, against

Southampton, and it was one of the first steps on the road to United's re-emergence as a great club in the aftermath of the Second World War.

Not that there were many signs of that rebirth on the pitch in 1938/39, when United were relieved to finish 14th – but at least the mid-table placing put an end to the damaging cycle of promotion and relegation. Off the pitch, however, there were definite signs of improvement, none more so than in the formation of the Manchester United Junior Athletic Club in 1938. One of the chief grumbles of supporters during the terrace unrest of the previous decade had been the club's poor record of finding and nurturing young talent. One of the Supporters' Club's five demands had been an overhaul of the scouting system. The situation had improved since the desperate days of the 1920s – witness Rocca's mission to Ireland and his inspired swoop for Carey. Now, though, United acted decisively to create the most advanced programme for youth development the game had ever seen. The architects of the plan were James Gibson, who helped bankroll the scheme, along with Crickmer and Rocca. The idea required patience and perseverance, but the pay-off was the emergence of a golden generation of talent after the Second World War.

The club's regeneration, though, was rudely interrupted by Adolf Hitler. United had lost their third game of a new season 2-0 at Charlton on 2 September 1939, when the Football League was

Above Johnny Carey in 1937, the year the Dubliner made his
United debut.

Right Bomb damage at Old Trafford during the Second World War put
the ground out of action for several years.

suspended until further notice. Britain was at war with Germany and nobody was more disappointed than Blackpool who were top of the table at the time.

Old Trafford was a sorry place in wartime. Its location right by the Trafford Park industrial estate, the canal and the railway line in Manchester's industrial heartland meant it took a fearful pounding from Luftwaffe bombs in the Blitz of 1941. On one night in March that year the German bombers were especially destructive. Old Trafford took two direct hits, one of them all but destroying the main stand, the other blowing up a large section of terracing and wrecking the pitch.

It would have taken a lengthy and costly programme of works to put Old Trafford back into commission as a football stadium, but there were more pressing uses for the nation's scarce resources in those perilous days. Of course, United's predicament was not unique. Other grounds suffered similar fates, especially those located in dock areas where Luftwaffe fire had been concentrated most heavily: Plymouth's Home Park, Millwall's Den and Bristol City's Ashton Gate also took a hammering. The football grounds would have to wait for happier and less hazardous days before they were restored.

United were now homeless and old enmities were set aside as City helped their neighbours when help was needed most. They allowed United to share Maine Road until their own ground was fit to use again.

Unlike in the First World War, competitive football was officially sanctioned through the 1939/45 hostilities. During the Great War the game had been tolerated at best and in some quarters footballers were excoriated for playing sport while other young men were dying for their country. There had been reports of footballers receiving white feathers. But Churchill's government perceived the game as vital for morale and the Prime Minister himself actively promoted it. Even in 1941, when the Allies' eventual victory was far from assured, Churchill made a point of attending wartime football internationals. He watched one England v Scotland game in the company of seven of his Cabinet ministers.

At first clubs were reorganised into ten regional leagues, but after one season that structure was scrapped and replaced with a northern and a southern league. There was also a cup competition played on a north-south basis, with a two-legged final. Games were generally

played in front of sparse crowds – it was difficult for people to travel to watch football, even if they weren't hard at work in factories or on active service. The games were also little reported or advertised, because paper shortages had slashed the size of newspapers and there was only limited space available for football coverage.

United always struggled to raise good quality teams during the war and their matches were usually watched by crowds which were tiny, even for the time. For the record they won one competition, the Lancashire Cup in 1941, and it would be an exaggeration to say that it provided any consolation for their ground being blown up.

But the players enjoyed wartime football. With a loosening of contractual ties they could play for fun, as a means of relaxation, and as a way of earning a little extra money to supplement their service pay. Players on leave from the services were allowed to guest for clubs near their bases and many were in such demand they played more football in wartime than they ever had done in peacetime. Players' pay was regulated, and set at 30 shillings per match, rising to £2 later in the war, although a little extra would often find its way into a jacket pocket left in the dressing room.

But the war was not, of course, all fun and games. Nearly a hundred professional footballers died while serving their country and many bright careers were snuffed out by injury.

EARLY YEARS' STALWARTS

**Along with Billy Meredith, the following
players were United's most loyal servants
during the years before the Second World War.**

JOE SPENCE **1919–33**
FORWARD • 481 Apps • 158 Gls

Geordie Joe Spence could play right across
the forward line, but he was most commonly
found at outside-right. He was stocky for a
winger, but his physical strength combined
with his trickery on the ball gave defenders
problems. His up-and-at-'em style made him
a huge favourite on the Old Trafford terraces
and, when United gained possession, the
crowd would chant 'Give it to Joe!'

Never was Spence more effective than
in the promotion season of 1924/25, when he
played in all 42 of United's league matches.
In 510 games in all competitions for United
Spence scored 168 goals, before moving to
Chesterfield where he enjoyed an Indian
summer. Spence only won two England caps
– a scandalous reflection of his status in the
English game. His international debut came
against Belgium on 24 May 1926, when England
won 5-3 in Antwerp. His second game was
against Ireland at Anfield and Spence scored
England's second in a 3-3 draw. The selectors
lost interest in him after that match.

He held the United appearances record
for 40 years until it was beaten by Bill Foulkes,
but he still lies third on the club's all-time
league appearances list.

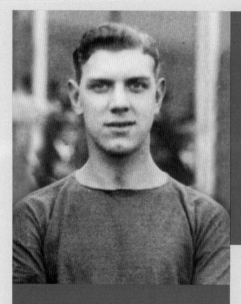

JOHN (JACK) SILCOCK **1919–34**
LEFT-BACK • 423 Apps • 2 Gls

Jack Silcock, from New Springs near Wigan,
was a left-back with a difference. At a time
when players in his position were not
expected to be ball players, Silcock was
one of the best passers around. When he
received the ball he did not resort to a hefty
boot up the field. He tried to link up with
his half-backs and pass to the forwards.

He joined United as a teenager on
amateur forms during the First World
War and made his professional debut
against Derby County in the first game
of the first season after the war. He
remained a permanent member of the
side for over a decade, and for several years
formed a seemingly eternal triangle with
goalkeeper, Jack Mew, and United's other
stalwart full-back, Charlie Moore.

Silcock was granted three England caps,
which would surely have been many more if
he had played for a successful team. His first
international was a 0-0 draw with Wales at
Ninian Park in May 1921, but after playing his
part in a 3-1 win over Sweden in Stockholm
in May 1932 he never played for the national
side again. He left Old Trafford for Oldham
Athletic in 1934, and after a brief spell at
Droylesden he retired.

CHARLIE MOORE **1919–30**
RIGHT-BACK • 309 Apps • 0 Gls

Charlie Moore's United career was written
off before it had even begun when he suffered
severe ankle damage, aged just 23. The club
thanked the right-back for his brief service and
wished him well in his life after football. But
Moore, a Black Country boy and tough as they
come, would not be beaten. He fought his way
back to fitness and was re-signed by the club
a year later. He went on to forge a long career
and for eight years was an automatic choice
on the opposite flank to Silcock.

ALF STEWARD **1920–32**
GOALKEEPER • 309 Apps

There is no doubt that Steward, a Mancunian,
paid his dues as a footballer, playing Army
football and for amateur sides around
Manchester for years before United signed
him up. He was not an overnight sensation at
Old Trafford and served in the reserves before
becoming an automatic choice in the first team.

He made his first-team debut in 1920, but it wasn't until 1923/24 that he became a regular.

His best season was the promotion campaign of 1924/45 when he played behind the formidable United defence which kept 25 clean sheets.

Steward also played county cricket for Lancashire. After leaving United he managed Altrincham and Torquay United.

CLARRIE HILDITCH 1919–32
HALF-BACK • 301 Apps • 7 Gls
Clarrie, or Lal as he was often known, Hilditch was a cultured half-back renowned for his fair play throughout football. In an era when football could be rough and ready, Hilditch stood out for his unwillingness to foul opponents.

He began his football career as a centre-forward for Witton Albion, in his home county of Cheshire, but dropped back to play a half-back role once he signed for United during the First World War. He made his professional league debut in 1919 and stayed in the team for the next 13 years.

He was very much a thinking footballer and a leader on the pitch, and when the club were in a jam and needed a temporary manager in 1926 Hilditch was given the job. He remains the only player-manager in the club's history.

GEORGE WALL 1905–15
OUTSIDE-LEFT • 287 Apps • 89 Gls
George Wall was a flying left-winger whose direct style and goalscoring incursions from the flank helped fire United to two Championships and the FA Cup. He was from mining stock in the north-east of England and signed for Barnsley as a professional footballer,

before switching to United in time to help spark the club's rise to pre-eminence in English football. In his first full season, 1906/07, he was the club's leading scorer with 11 league goals and he added an incredible 19 in the first title-winning campaign of 1907/08. After leaving United he turned out for Oldham, Hamilton Academicals and Rochdale.

ALEX BELL 1902–13
LEFT-HALF • 278 Apps • 10 Gls
An unflashy performer at left-half whose industry allowed the more flamboyant talents in the team to shine. The South African-born Bell was admired for his consistency and reliability as an accurate passer, and was also assiduous in his defensive responsibilities. These days Bell would probably be called a holding midfield player and he was a vital, if unglamorous, member of the side that carried all before it in the years before the First World War.

FRED ERENTZ 1892–1902
FULL-BACK • 280 Apps • 9 Gls
Fred Erentz, a Dundonian, was a Newton Heath pioneer who played in the team that first saw league action. He was famed for his composure and possessed an explosive shot, which helped make him a lethal penalty taker. His younger brother, Harry, also played at full-back for the Heathens.

CHARLIE ROBERTS 1903–13
CENTRE-HALF • 271 Apps • 22 Gls
Along with Billy Meredith, Roberts was the most important player in the early years of Manchester United. As an attacking centre-half he played a style of football that was revolutionary. As well as being a brilliant footballer, he was also a charismatic captain and an important personality in the side that won two titles and the FA Cup.

RAY BENNION 1921–32
HALF-BACK • 286 Apps • 2 Gls
The Welsh right-half suffered a traumatic start to his professional career. On his debut, the first match of the 1921/22 season, United lost 5-0 at Goodison Park, and the club finished the campaign bottom of the First Division. But Bennion survived the experience to become a regular first-team member over the next decade. He made his debut for Wales in a 3-0 defeat against Scotland at Ninian Park in October 1935 and went on to win 10 caps. In 1932 he left United for Burnley where he coached for 30 years.

CHAPTER THREE

BUSBY STARTS WORK

1945–51

ONE OF THE MOST SIGNIFICANT MEETINGS IN THE HISTORY OF MANCHESTER UNITED TOOK PLACE ON 15 FEBRUARY 1945

It was the day that a young Army PT instructor named Matt Busby travelled to Manchester with an appointment to see United director, James Gibson – the subject under discussion: the manager's job. For a 34-year-old who had never held a senior position in football, Busby went into the talks with a surprisingly hard line.

Yes, he would accept the task of rebuilding the shattered club, but he would go about it in his own way and brook no interference in playing matters. He would choose his own staff, decide which players to buy and sell, pick his own team, select the side's tactics and direct training. To the modern eye they do not look like unreasonable demands for a football manager to make, but at the time they were revolutionary. In the 1940s managers operated at the beck and call of powerful directors, and their independence was strictly limited.

Busby, though, was firm. He would do the job his way or not at all. He had already turned one job down over the same principle and Liverpool Football Club had to wait another 15 years before they found their own single-minded Scot to turn their club around. Gibson was in no position to argue. United were in a

Opposite *Matt Busby on the training field with his players in the early days of his United career.*

Right *Matt Busby, the man of destiny who made United the top club in Europe.*

1945–51 mess and they needed a young man with the vision, strength of character, energy and determination to do the work. He only had to see the steely glint in the young Scot's eye to know that this was the fellow for the job.

United were thrilled they had landed their man. Crickmer, by now club secretary, told the *Manchester Evening News*, 'Busby has had a number of offers, but he approached us himself as he particularly wanted to come back to Manchester. He will build up the team and put it where it belongs – at the top.' They were big words, but there was still so much work to do before the bold vision could be realised.

Busby was unable to start his employment at United until October 1945, by which time he had been demobilised from the Army – he ended the war as Company Sergeant Major Busby at the Sandhurst Military Academy. Busby also had to cut his ties with Liverpool, where he was under contract as a player-coach.

In the autumn of 1945 he took over a club with no ground, a patched up team and no income. Old Trafford remained a bomb site, with trees growing up through the bomb-blasted terracing, craters in the pitch and charred remains where a stand used to be. Many of the club's players from pre-war were scattered around Europe in the forces and six years had passed since United had pulled in any decent gate receipts on a regular basis. They were also £15,000 in debt.

One of his first decisions also turned out to be one of his best: he hired Jimmy Murphy for his coaching staff and the pair of them had until August 1946 to put together a team good enough to compete in the first post-war Division One season. They swung into action at once.

Busby had to stand his ground firmly when it came to interference in his domain. Old habits died hard among directors who were used to having their opinions heard and acted upon. Busby recalled an incident in his early days as United manager, 'I sat in the directors' box and a director sat behind me. During the game he leaned forward and said in a voice that people around him could hear, "Why didn't you do so-and-so?" Shall I turn round and give him a blast, I asked myself? But my judgement said, no, wait. I waited for the first convenient moment. Convenient? It was in the gents. I said to him, "Never dare to say anything like that to me when other people can hear you." And I put it on the agenda for the next board meeting, "interference by directors".'

If there had been any doubt until now, it had been removed. Busby was in charge. Several former players were eased out of the club and Busby acted decisively to recruit fresh talent. His eye for a player was unerring and in those frantic first few months he laid the basis of what would be his first great United team. The first new player to arrive was one of the most significant, Jimmy Delaney, a goalscoring winger who came from Celtic for £4,000. Busby also shuffled his pack by making a number of positional changes and, by the time the 1946/47 season kicked off, United were ready for the fray.

Busby's team began the new era against Grimsby Town at Maine Road on 31 August 1946. United supporters in the 41,025

Jimmy Delaney, the Celtic forward, was Busby's first significant signing for United and an important figure in the immediate post-war era.

crowd that day had some new players to watch, as well as a sprinkling of more familiar faces. In goal was Jack Crompton who had signed from Oldham as an amateur during the war. Carey was at right-back and Billy McGlen, spotted by Busby playing forces football in Italy, was at left-back. Allen Chilton, who had played in United's last league game in 1939, was at centre-half. The half-backs were Jack Warner, another 1930s survivor, and Henry Cockburn, a wartime signing from local football. The forward line featured Delaney and a quartet of locally-reared lads who had been with the club since before the war: Stan Pearson, Jimmy Hanlon, Jack Rowley and Charlie Mitten.

The team was good enough to win 2-1, and the first United goals of peacetime were scored by Rowley and Mitten. Busby's men played like a team from the start and strung together an impressive sequence of results. They won their first five matches and, but for a poor spell in October and November when they went five games without a victory, would surely have taken the title. As it was United lost out by one point to the Champions Liverpool, who they had beaten 5-0 at Maine Road. It was an exciting battle through a bitter winter for the title, with Stoke City and Wolves also pressing United and Liverpool for the top spot. But the Merseysiders lasted the course best in a season which stretched to 14 June after a flurry of postponements – but they needed a large helping hand. Stoke could have taken the title if they had won their final match against Sheffield United, but the Blades were victorious 2-1, gifting the Championship to Liverpool and the runners-up spot to Busby's side – United's highest league position since they won the title in 1911.

Some observers suggested that Liverpool won because they were the best fed team in England. Rationing was still in force in Britain and several commodities were in short supply. But Liverpool had been in the USA pre-season and spent several weeks gorging themselves on steak, limitless eggs and the kinds of foodstuffs which a pinched British populace could only dream of. It was a noticeably heavier Liverpool squad that arrived back in these hungry islands than the one which had left them.

Johnny Morris, who had signed for United as a 15-year-old before the war, was demobbed too late to take part in the first league game, but by the end of October 1946 he was in the side. Morris turned out at inside-right against Sunderland on 26 October 1945.

Morris recalled, 'I had been with United before the war, but I never got to play for the first team, and they had loaned me out to Bolton for 12 months. So that first game after the war was also my league debut for United.

'It was a good team to play in. A lot of the players already knew each other, because they had played together in the war, so they weren't like strangers. It felt good to be back home and playing football again. I had just come home from spending two-and-a-half years in India with the Tank Corps, so I was ready to come back. We played plenty of football over there. The Hearts player, Tommy Walker, and Denis Compton from Arsenal each had a team and we toured around India playing each other. It was enjoyable, but nothing like being at home.

'By the time I got back Matt was already in charge and he was doing a good job. But he couldn't have done anything without the players.'

Morris said that there was fierce determination among the players to get the club back on track, even in the months before Busby officially took over. 'In the season before the league started up again, the team never won any of their first half-dozen games,' Morris said. 'It was a crisis and there was a team meeting where it was all sorted out. Johnny Carey was the captain, but he was too nice a man to be captain really, and it was Allen Chilton who got hold of it and sorted it out. That's the way it was. The players knew what needed doing and it was done.'

Despite the disappointment of finishing second behind Liverpool, the first full season of league football was hugely encouraging for United. They played with an attacking vim which thrilled their supporters. Gates at Maine Road were frequently topping 50,000, with some crowds over 60,000. They amassed 95 league goals in the season, with Rowley bagging 26 and Pearson 19, and the bleak memories of pre-war mediocrity were blown away by Busby's fresh approach. United were on their way back.

The improvement continued in the 1947/48 season. United finished second in the First Division again, this time some distance behind the runaway winners Arsenal, but the team continued to enthral vast crowds with their attacking verve. One of the few occasions when the goals didn't flow was the first Manchester derby in over 10 years. On 20 September 1947, United and City drew 0-0

in a game fraught with the saved-up nerves of a decade, in front of more than 70,000 knuckle-biting supporters.

Crowds at Maine Road were huge all season, as United fans lapped up the expansive attacking football Busby's teams were serving up. On 17 January 1948 United attracted the biggest-ever crowd in their history when 81,962 crammed into Maine Road for the visit of Champions-elect Arsenal. The record-breaking attendance saw the sides draw 1-1. But it was the FA Cup that really set pulses racing. United began their campaign with a third round tie away to Villa, who were challenging at the top of the table along with United. In one of the most extraordinary Cup ties they have ever been involved in, United won 6-4, despite conceding a goal after only 13 seconds – George Edwards scored before United had even touched the ball. But Villa had made the tactical mistake of arousing their opponents' ire and United stormed back to score five before half-time. The match lurched back in Villa's direction after the break and they brought the score to 5-4 with 10 minutes left. Villa hammered away at Jack Crompton's goal, allowing United to break away and add their sixth goal. Morris and Pearson both scored twice and Delaney and Rowley also netted for United.

Morris said, 'It was such an exciting game, one of the best I ever played in. It was a shock to lose a goal so early, but it never bothered us. We just kept playing our football and we believed we would win. We were a good team and in the first half we played some of our very best football. It was marvellous. All the chances seemed to go in and to score five before half-time was wonderful.

'Then they hit us after half-time with three goals and it wasn't a case of us letting up at all. Villa were a good side themselves and they had their own crowd shouting for them, and it was one of those real Cup ties where there's plenty going on, and chances all the time at both ends. They put theirs away. But we never panicked. That team never did.'

In the fourth round United were drawn at home to Liverpool, but because Manchester City were entertaining Chelsea that day, United had to find another venue. The game was switched to Goodison Park, where a crowd exceeding 74,000 watched United rise to the big occasion again to beat the reigning League Champions 3-0.

There was a similar story in the fifth round, when United were scheduled to play struggling Charlton at 'home'. Once again

City were using Maine Road for their match against Preston, and itinerant United were forced to look elsewhere. This time they borrowed Huddersfield Town's Leeds Road. The match stood out in the memory for two reasons: it was played on one of the worst surfaces any of the players had experienced, with ankle-deep mud making United's free-flowing style impractical; and for an astonishing goalkeeping display by Charlton's Sam Bartram. The long-serving Addicks No.1 rated it as the best game he ever played for the club. United besieged the goal without luck for an hour asBartram flung himself over the cloying Yorkshire mud time and again to save his side. It took a freakish own goal from Charlton full-back Roy Bicknell to put United ahead, but still they strived frantically to put the game safe. Bartram said later, 'No Aunt Sally at a fairground ever underwent so prolonged and furious a peppering.' At last, five minutes from time, Charlie Mitten scored with a header to make the result 2-0 and United were just two matches away from their first Wembley cup final.

United played mid-table Preston North End in the quarter-finals and in another pulsating Cup tie won 4-2 in front of 74,213 at Maine Road. That set up a semi-final against Derby County, who were pressing for a top-four finish in the league. But the match belonged to Pearson, and his hat-trick led United to a 3-1 victory and bagged them their trip to London.

United's 4-2 win over Blackpool has been rated the best FA Cup final of all-time. Not as famous, perhaps, as the Matthews Final of 1953, when Blackpool were back to beat Bolton 4-3. But in terms of the purity of the football on display, it stands out in the annals as one of the great matches.

Morris said, 'It was every player's ambition to play at Wembley. It was the ultimate, really. I remember getting to the ground and the pitch looking so beautiful and green. You have to remember that for months we had been playing on wet pitches, just mud really. The pitches weren't as good in those days. But this was the first game Wembley had staged all season and it was so green. You just wanted to get out there and play football on that green grass.

Sam Bartram of Charlton put in a magnificent display between the sticks in the FA Cup fifth round tie at Leeds Road in 1948.

1948 **FA CUP FINAL**

MANCHESTER UNITED 4 Rowley 2, Pearson, Anderson **BLACKPOOL 2** Shimwell (pen), Mortensen
24 APRIL 1948 at Wembley • Referee: C.J. Barrick • Attendance: 99,000

MANCHESTER UNITED

Crompton
Carey
Aston
Anderson
Chilton
Cockburn
Delaney
Morris
Rowley
Pearson
Mitten

BLACKPOOL

Robinson
Shimwell
Crosland
Johnston
Hayward
Kelly
Matthews
Munro
Mortensen
Dick
Rickett

For many neutrals, this was the best FA Cup final Wembley had ever staged. For United fans, it was an emotional day as the club won its first trophy in 37 years – but for most of the afternoon it looked like the trophy might be heading for Blackpool. The Seasiders dominated possession for the first 70 minutes of the game. Stanley Matthews on the right wing threatened danger every time he had the ball and only an ever-alert display by United's left-back, Johnny Aston, stopped him wreaking havoc.

Blackpool went ahead on 12 minutes when the fleet-footed centre-forward Stan Mortensen ran clear of the United cover and bore down on Jack Crompton's goal. Allen Chilton made a last-ditch challenge, which brought the Blackpool marauder down. The trip looked like it was outside the area, but the referee awarded a penalty, which Shimwell put away.

United levelled when Blackpool prevaricated in clearing a loose ball, and Jack Rowley nipped in to lift the loose ball over the goalkeeper's head before rolling

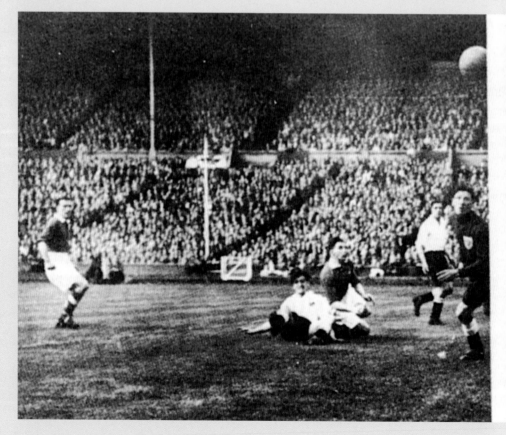

it over the line. But Mortensen grabbed a typical poacher's goal from close range to put Blackpool ahead at half-time, earning him the distinction of having scored in every round, and for most of the second-half they looked to be in comfortable possession of a winning lead.

Then Rowley crashed a spectacular diving header past Robinson from Morris's free-kick to equalise. Then with 10 minutes left Crompton pulled off an agile save to stop Mortensen scoring his 11th FA Cup goal of the season and United hit Blackpool on the break. Anderson passed to Pearson lurking outside the area and he smashed an unerring shot into the net via the inside of a post. United had turned the game in a few inspired moments and, as waves of passion rolled over the Wembley turf from the ecstatic Mancunians in the crowd, Anderson completed the scoring with a long-range, swirling shot which went in with a slight touch off a defender on the way.

The victory was a testament to Busby's team-building skills. Even with the odds stacked against them, United kept playing patient, constructive football and waited for their reward. Captain Carey, who had been switched to right-back by Busby, exuded composure and belief throughout the team. Morris, who had taken Carey's inside-right position, was tireless in probing for ways through the Tangerine defence. Pearson, who had slotted into Aston's place at inside-left, was a fount of attacking ideas. And Aston, who had been moved to left-back, looked like he had been there all his life. The United line-up was a Busby masterclass in making the most of the resources to hand. The young manager extracted every ounce of ability out of the men at his disposal and harnessed it for the good of all.

Other teams might have folded in those final 20 minutes: United never appeared to think defeat was possible. Morris said, 'We were never worried. We never did worry if we went a goal or two goals behind. We always had confidence in our ability and in our team-mates, and the final was no different. Even when the match was going into the last 20 minutes and we were a goal down, we kept playing our football and felt we would win.'

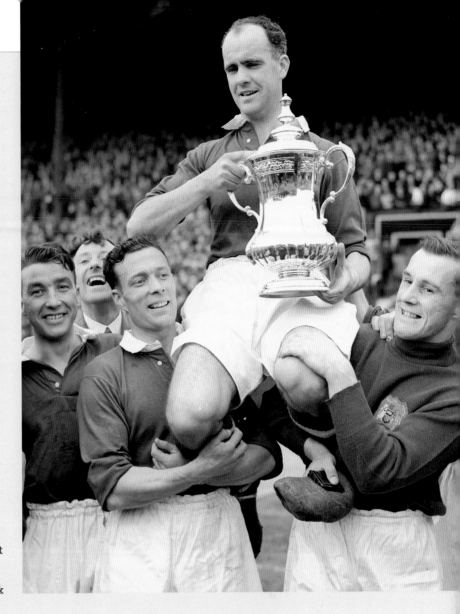

The next day's *News of the World* was in no doubt. It headlined its match report, 'This Was Wembley's Finest Final', and Harry J. Ditton's copy lavished praise on the event. 'What a magnificent Cup final,' he wrote. 'It had everything – tense drama, including six thrilling goals, and some of the most delightful ball play Wembley has ever seen... it was contested in a great sporting spirit in spite of the fact that fouls preceded both of Blackpool's goals... Yes, this was a game that will leave an imperishable memory with all who saw it – a classic exhibition which reflected nothing but credit on every one of the 22 players.'

Opposite Jack Rowley (centre) heads United's second goal to tie the scores at 2-2.
Above Johnny Carey, held aloft by his delighted team-mates, clutches the FA Cup – United's first major trophy for nearly four decades.

'We played well that day. We had a good team and we played to the best of our abilities. One man who sticks in my mind for having an especially good game was Johnny Aston at full-back. He was marking Matthews, who was their main man in attack, and Johnny did a very good job on him.'

The day was a terrific culmination to a Cup campaign that could not have been much tougher. United had faced opponents from the First Division in every round. If anybody has ever earned the FA Cup, United did that season.

The triumphant team were met by the traditional civic reception, with the city's streets thronged with celebrating supporters. All the players, and the Cup, squeezed through the sunroof of a single-decker coach for a tour of Manchester, ending in a tumultuous welcome at Albert Square.

'It was so exciting,' said Morris. 'I think I was the youngest in the team, I was about 22, and it was all new to me. Just to look around you and see all these happy people smiling, and the FA Cup there on show for the whole city. It was a wonderful occasion.'

Buoyed by the Cup win, United set off in pursuit of their first Championship in 37 years – but they were destined to fall just short once again. They finished runners-up to Portsmouth in 1948/49 and also missed out in the FA Cup after a promising run.

United thrashed Bournemouth from Division Three (South) 6-0 in the third round, but needed two replays to see off Second Division Bradford Park Avenue in round four. They enjoyed an eight-goal romp against the amateurs of Yeovil Town next, with Rowley scoring five times. Another Third Division team faced United in the quarter-finals and United squeaked a 1-0 win over Hull City at Boothferry Park. In complete contrast to their Cup-winning feats of the season before, United did not meet a First Division team until the semi-finals, when they came up against Wolves. They fought out a 1-1 draw at Hillsborough, but lost the replay 1-0 at Goodison Park a week later.

But any woes which lingered from United's near-miss 1948/49 season were banished on 24 August 1949, when the team returned in triumph to Old Trafford. It had been two days short of 10 years since they had last played a league game on their own ground and it felt good to be home. It certainly made sound financial sense for United to move back to Old Trafford: it was costing them

£5,000 a year to rent Maine Road, plus a slice of their gate receipts. And familiarity was beginning to breed contempt between the clubs: City were happy to see United leave. Bolton Wanderers were the visitors for the big day and United made it extra special by winning 3-0.

The ground had been passed fit for use, but work was far from finished. The main stand was roofless and remained so for another couple of years. Most of the terracing was still open to the elements and was not covered until building materials became more readily available. The battle-scarred stadium lacked the majesty of John Henry Davies's grand vision, but at least it was alive once again, full of all the noise, atmosphere and emotion that only a raucous, partisan football crowd can create. After long years when the only inhabitants had been builders, football and United were back.

That first post-war season at Old Trafford saw United challenging for the title yet again. Pompey successfully defended their title, but in a tight contest United finished fourth, just three points behind. Busby's team also enjoyed another stirring FA Cup run, which ended in a 2-0 quarter-final defeat at Chelsea.

That summer United's attacking left-back, Johnny Aston, became the first-ever player from the club to feature in a World Cup when he travelled to Brazil with England. As recently as 1946, when he had made his United debut, the lad from Prestwich had been operating as an inside-forward, but since Busby switched him to the back he had emerged as one of the country's best defenders.

He helped England win their first-ever World Cup game, when they beat Chile 2-0 in the Maracana Stadium in Rio on 25 June 1950, with goals from Stan Mortensen of Blackpool and Middlesbrough's Wilf Mannion. But Aston was made one of the scapegoats for England's cataclysmic 1-0 defeat at the hands of the USA in Belo Horizonte four days later. No matter that Aston was not at fault for

Opposite Johnny Morris, the inside-forward who packed a powerful shot and played an influential role in the 1948 FA Cup triumph.

Overleaf Charlie Mitten finds the back of the net to equalise against Wolverhampton Wanderers in the FA Cup semi-final at Hillsborough in March 1949. United lost 1-0 in the replay and Mitten walked out on the club that summer following a dispute over money.

the goal, or that England's all-star forward line failed to convert any of the numerous chances that fell their way, Aston was axed for the third and final group game. England lost 2-0 to Spain and were on their way home.

United continued to produce football of the highest quality throughout the 1949/50 season, but Busby knew it was time to think about the future. There was also some unrest in the dressing room to contend with.

The Cup run of 1948 brought the issue of pay to the fore again and some United players were unhappy. In the early 1950s the maximum wage was just £14. There was also a maximum win bonus of £2, which hadn't changed since it was introduced in 1920. These seemed like paltry rewards for successful First Division footballers, considering the cash generated by the vast crowds they were entertaining. Just like Meredith and his United team-mates four decades earlier, the players felt they were being short-changed. Other clubs got around the maximum wage by paying illegal bonuses. But Busby would not countenance dishonesty.

There was also a sense that an era was coming to an end at United. Many of the first-team players were in the twilight of their careers and the club's youth policy had begun to produce young players who deserved a chance. Morris had lost his place in the team and had been sold to Derby County for a club-record £24,500. And Charlie Mitten had flown in the face of football's restrictive contractual system by walking out on United.

Mitten fled to Colombia in the summer of 1950 to earn more money and broke his contract to do so. That meant he could not play for any other team from a country affiliated to FIFA – once a footballer signed for a club, that club owned his registration forever, even when the contract had expired. The club was entitled to dispose of its asset when and how it saw fit. But those legal niceties did not bother Mitten at the time: Colombia was not a member of FIFA and Colombian clubs could sign anybody they fancied. There could be no sanction against Mitten for breaking the punitively one-sided conditions of service he endured as an English professional footballer.

A handful of English players, including Mitten, were convinced Colombia was a footballing El Dorado. After joining Santa Fé FC in Bogotá, Mitten said, 'I have signed up for more money than I've earned in 14 years as a footballer.' The English contingent were reported to be earning anything from £3,500 a year to perhaps as much as £5,000 – at least five times what they would be picking up at home – plus a £1,000 signing on fee.

But a year later the gold rush came to an end. Colombia joined FIFA and the rebel players were forced to return to their old clubs and fulfill their old contracts or seek new jobs outside football. Busby, quite capable of being ruthless, suspended Mitten for six months, fined him £250 – an eye-popping amount for an English footballer of the times – and then sold him to Fulham for £25,000.

The flight of Mitten wasn't the only change as the great Cup-winning team gradually broke up. As the 1950/51 season kicked off Crompton was replaced as first-choice goalkeeper by Reg Allen, a Londoner who had joined from QPR. And they began the season with a new right-half – Eddie McIlvenny, a Scot, who had crossed the Atlantic from Philadelphia Nationals to join United. Aston knew all about him – McIlvenny was captain of the USA team which had beaten England in Belo Horizonte.

United finished the 1950/51 season in second place for the fourth time in five post-war campaigns, and this time it was Arthur Rowe's famous push and run Tottenham team who beat them to the top spot. It was a familiar story in the FA Cup as well, with another quarter-final exit. After comfortable Old Trafford victories against Oldham, Leeds and Arsenal, United lost 1-0 at Birmingham.

United's football was still earning them praise all across the country, but they had become perennial bridesmaids as Busby strived to find the missing ingredient for a title-winning team. In five years they had been pipped by Liverpool, Arsenal, Portsmouth twice and Spurs. The frustration around Old Trafford was palpable.

Looking back with the benefit of hindsight it is easy to imagine that United were destined for success under Busby, that they were racing to glory along golden rails. But at the time that was far from the case. In the summer of 1951 people began to wonder whether Busby was fated never to win the Championship he craved.

John Aston of United and England began his career as an inside-forward, but blossomed as a full-back after Matt Busby moved him into the defence.

MATT BUSBY

MANAGER (1945–69, 1970–71)

Lanarkshire, in the west of Scotland, was well known for producing two vital commodities in the early years of the 20th century: coal and football managers. Matt Busby began his working life excavating the former and ended it as one of the world's greatest examples of the latter.

Busby was born in Orbiston, near Belshill, Lanarkshire, on 26 May 1909, and was marked out for greatness from his first moments when the doctor who delivered him made an extraordinarily prescient prediction. The medic took one look at the Busby babe's sturdy legs thrashing about him and declared, 'A footballer has come into this house this day.' Perhaps he said that to all the mothers, but in any case the fledgling footballer had some obstacles to overcome before the doctor's wise words could be vindicated.

Like all the other boys from his background in that time and in that place, Busby's future was mapped out for him – and a dark and dangerous future it was at that. His schooling was over before it had barely begun and Busby was down the pit. Even as a teenager, Busby had to be a breadwinner for his family: has father had been killed in the First World War and his mother struggled alone to raise her children. At one point Busby's mother resolved that there was no future for her family in Scotland and, weary of their straitened economic circumstances, she decided they should emigrate to the USA. Busby was on the point of leaving the country when Manchester City came knocking at his door with a professional contract.

Busby had come to the notice of English scouts while playing for local junior sides, including Alpine Villa and Denny Hibernian. The boy was faced with three choices: he could venture over the ocean to a new, uncertain life in a foreign land; he could stay in the streets he had known all his life and work down the pit; or he could head for England and be a professional footballer. It was no choice

for the football-daft youngster and he was soon on his way to Maine Road in February 1928.

But his harsh early years in Lanarkshire and the long, punishing hours he spent hacking at the coalface miles underground were not wasted. Busby clung to his memories ever afterwards, reminding himself where he had come from even while he was plucking the greatest prizes in football. Busby did not need anybody to tell him about Kipling's twin impostors, triumph and disaster. He told himself every day of his life, 'So many good things in life have come my way since I became a professional footballer,' he said. 'It does me good to think back on the day when living was not so easy. It helps me keep my feet on the ground.'

Busby made a name for himself as an intelligent half-back with a fine eye for a pass and he won the FA Cup with City in 1934. Two years later he joined Liverpool for £8,000. Even while he was a player in his 20s Busby became interested in coaching and Liverpool viewed him as a potential manager in the making. At the end of the war he had a chance to manage at Anfield, but the deal wasn't right for Busby. He had formed firm opinions about how he wanted to manage and Liverpool did not share them. If he was going to manage anywhere, he would have to have complete freedom in playing matters, with no interference from directors or anybody else. United offered him the chance to do exactly that and Busby accepted their offer. It was the best decision either of the parties had ever made.

A select few managers have built great teams. Busby did more. He built a great club, which was necessary because when he became United manager there was hardly anything left to be manager of. He said later, 'It was not an easy assignment. The ground had been blitzed, they had an overdraft at the bank, and what is more I had no experience as a manager, and I felt they were taking a great risk in appointing me. All I had, apart from playing experience, was ideas about what a manager should do, faith in those ideas and faith in the future of the club.'

As well as trophies, Busby more than any other individual left United with a philosophy of how the game should be played. Football was not war by other means, it was a sport to be played for pleasure. His teams were sent out to win, but not for the sake of it. Thanks to Busby, Manchester United became synonymous with a brand of football full of skill, swagger and style.

He summed up his approach to football in a few well-chosen words, 'What matters above all things is that the game should be played in the right spirit, with the utmost resource of skill and courage, with fair play and no favour, with every man playing as a member of his team and the result accepted without bitterness and conceit.'

Matt Busby in conference with his right-hand man, Jimmy Murphy.

THE CLASS OF '48

Statistics are for appearances and goals in all competitions while playing for United.

Carey was a lead-by-example type of captain, rather than a fist-shaking, blood-and-thunder merchant, but his approach worked and helped set United on their way to post-war success. Never was that better displayed than in the 1948 FA Cup final. While United were losing 2-1 late in the game, Carey scotched any defeatism in the United ranks. 'Don't panic,' he exhorted his men. 'Keep playing football the way we have all season, the way the boss wants us to play.' United stayed calm and pulled away to win the match.

❸ JOHN ASTON (Snr) 1938–54
RIGHT-BACK • 284 Apps • 30 Gls

LEFT-BACK • 284 Apps • 30 Gls

Just as he had done with Carey, Busby moved Aston from inside-forward to full-back, ensuring that his defenders had just as much ability on the ball as his forwards. It was a bold move at a time when tactics were far less fluid and players less mobile than they were to become in later years.

A product of the youth system United launched in the 1930s, Aston enjoyed his finest hour for United during the 1948 FA Cup final. Few defenders ever did such a good marking job on Stanley Matthews as Aston did that day.

After retiring from playing he joined United's coaching staff and his son John Junior was also a fine player for the club.

❹ JOHN ANDERSON 1938–49
RIGHT-HALF • 40 Apps • 2 Gls

Anderson, from Salford, signed for United as an amateur before the war aged 17, but didn't make his debut until December 1947.

❶ JACK CROMPTON 1944–56
GOALKEEPER • 212 Apps

Appropriately enough for a man who served United so well, Crompton was born in Newton Heath, the Mancunian cradle of the club. He was a mainstay of the side immediately after the Second World War and his ebullient personality was almost as valuable to the side in those days as his reliable goalkeeping.

At the time of Munich Crompton was coaching at Luton, but he answered an emergency call to help out his old club. He remained an important member of the United staff for some time after Busby returned to

work and also served as reserve coach in Tommy Docherty's era.

❷ JOHNNY CAREY 1937–53
RIGHT-BACK • 344 Apps • 17 Gls

Carey was United's first great post-war captain and Busby's key lieutenant on the park. The Dubliner began his career as an inside-forward, but Busby switched him to full-back instead. It was the making of Carey and it was his skill at playing the ball from defence that helped make United such a progressive team. Carey brought the creative ability and passing vision of a fine inside-left to the full-back position.

He transferred to Nottingham Forest in October 1949 and later coached Peterborough.

⑤ ALLENBY CHILTON 1938–55
CENTRE-HALF • 391 Apps • 3 Gls

In the first league season after the war Busby was keen to find a solid centre-half who could anchor his defence. The manager's improvisational skills were displayed once again, as his eye fell on wing-half Chilton.

The Wearsider had been a boxer before taking up professional football and he gave United a daunting physical presence at the heart of their defence. And he was brave too. After his wartime experiences with the Durham Light Infantry, nothing he came up against in football was going to worry him. Chilton had been injured while storming the Normandy beaches on D-Day, so marking Stan Mortensen, however dangerous a centre-forward, was not going to upset him.

The muscular and athletic six-footer proved himself a commanding centre-half and he made the position his own. So much so that he set a United record for consecutive league appearances (166) which stood until Steve Coppell surpassed it in 1981.

⑥ HENRY COCKBURN 1943–54
LEFT-HALF • 275 Apps • 4 Gls

Cockburn was yet another inside-forward who was handed a key role in another position. Busby pitched the Mancunian into the unfamiliar left-half position while he was struggling to field a team in his first days in charge of the club. Cockburn's thoughtful passing game made him a great asset in the centre of the field and he filled the position capably until one of the great legends of United came along to replace him – Cockburn gave way to Duncan Edwards in 1953.

⑦ JIMMY DELANEY 1946–51
OUTSIDE-RIGHT • 184 Apps • 28 Gls

Busby's first signing gave United pace and trickery down the right, and was a useful source of goals as well. During the victorious FA Cup run of 1947/48 he scored a key goal that helped give United the edge in the 6-4 third-round thriller at Villa.

The Scot quit the club in November 1950 to join Aberdeen and he played in Ireland at the end of his career.

⑧ JOHNNY MORRIS 1939–49
INSIDE-RIGHT • 93 Apps • 35 Gls

Morris, from Radcliffe in Lancashire, enjoyed his best season for United in 1947/48, when he scored 21 times. In the victorious FA Cup run that year he scored twice in the third round at Villa and another in the 3-0 win over Liverpool in the fourth round.

But Morris found himself out in the cold the following season, when Busby rejigged the side, and left to play for Derby County.

⑨ JACK ROWLEY 1937–55
CENTRE-FORWARD • 424 Apps • 211 Gls

Rowley's prolific scoring record played a huge part in United's re-emergence as one of England's top teams after the war. He was not tall for a centre-forward, but his powerful, stocky physique gave defenders plenty of trouble. He packed a ferocious shot, especially with his left foot, and he was brave to the point of recklessness. Like Chilton he was a veteran of the D-Day landings, so going in for a 50:50 ball was not going to worry him unduly.

Rowley scored five goals in the FA Cup run of 1947/48 and contributed 30 goals in the title-winning season of 1951/52, which was a club record at the time. He left United in 1955 to manage Plymouth Argyle.

⑩ STAN PEARSON 1937–54
INSIDE-LEFT • 343 Apps • 148 Gls

Pearson began his career on the United groundstaff and spent months on his hands and knees weeding the Old Trafford pitch. But after the war he blossomed into one of the finest natural goal-scorers the club ever had.

His goals were crucial to United's 1947/48 FA Cup triumph. He scored twice in the third round at Villa, another two against Preston in the quarter-final, a hat-trick in the semi-final against Derby and another in the final itself against Blackpool.

The Salford boy moved to Bury in 1954, when his place was taken by Jackie Blanchflower.

⑪ CHARLIE MITTEN 1936–50
OUTSIDE-LEFT • 162 Apps • 61 Gls

Having been at the club almost ten years before he made his first-team debut, Mitten became a valuable player in United's forward line, keeping up a relentless supply of crosses for centre-forward Rowley. He could score goals himself and possessed a hard shot that he used to good effect in the 1947/48 FA Cup run, scoring in the fourth, fifth and sixth rounds.

Mitten's United career was overshadowed by his flight to Colombia in 1950 when he left the club to pursue South American gold. He returned to England and played for Fulham, and later managed Mansfield, Newcastle United and Altrincham.

CHAPTER FOUR

THE BUSBY BABES

1951–59

DURING THE EARLY 1950s MATT BUSBY'S VISION OF
AN ATTRACTIVE, ATTACKING TEAM BASED ON YOUTH
SLOWLY BEGAN TO TAKE SHAPE

Despite the years of near-misses Busby largely kept faith with the men who had served United so well since the war, and in some cases since before the war. There were bright young players straining to get their chance in the first team, but most of them would have to remain patient a while longer.

One man who did break through at the start of the 1951/52 season was Johnny Berry, but the winger was hardly a kid. When Busby signed him from Birmingham City, Berry was already 25 and a seasoned professional. He slotted in seamlessly at outside-right. Another newcomer, Roger Byrne, came into the side straight from United's prolific talent academy, a vindication of the far-sighted policy to nurture youth that had been set in train years before. The left-back from Gorton seized the number 3 shirt in November 1951 and made it his own.

By the New Year of 1952 United were level on points with Arsenal and Portsmouth at the top of the First Division table. United went clear in February, but the club's faithful fans must have feared another disappointment. They had been here before. In March and April the team suffered a stutter in their form when they lost consecutive games at Huddersfield and Portsmouth, and followed

Opposite Matt Busby shows his players how it's done.

Right Johnny Berry arrived at Old Trafford from Birmingham City and bolstered United's young team with his experience and ability on the wing.

1951–59   those up with a draw at Burnley. All the time Tottenham, Arsenal, Bolton and Pompey were threatening to overtake them at the top. But Busby kept cool and freshened up his team with a couple of astute positional changes: Aston was moved up front, but the real stroke of intuitive genius involved Byrne.

The boy who had only broken into the side as a full-back a few months earlier was switched to the left wing for the last six games of the season. He responded by scoring seven goals in United's decisive dash for the finishing line.

With two matches remaining United were within touching distance of the old silver trophy they had last won in 1911. Their opponents for the penultimate game of the season were Chelsea, and United held their nerve to win 3-0, with the old stalwarts Johnny Carey and Stan Pearson scoring the goals (there was also an own goal). The last match of the season brought their nearest challengers, Arsenal, to Old Trafford – but the only way the Gunners could deprive United of the title was by pulling off a seven-goal win. Arsenal's task was made even more difficult when they were reduced to ten men by injury midway through the first half, and they were down to nine by the full-time whistle. United swaggered to a 6-1 victory, with another of the old guard, Jack Rowley, bagging a hat-trick, and a delirious crowd of 53,651 saw Busby's team take the title in a carnival atmosphere.

It was the perfect culmination to a glorious season for Rowley, who had made a speciality of scoring hat-tricks in the title-winning campaign. He scored two in the first two matches of the season, against West Brom and Middlesbrough, and netted four in all. Rowley ended the season as the Champions' top scorer with 30

and Pearson contributed 22. The only ever-present in the side was the evergreen, ever-reliable Chilton, but a few significant names of the future made a handful of appearances. In a 0-0 draw at Anfield Jackie Blanchflower made his debut at right-half and Byrne also played his first game that day. It was the first occasion Tom Jackson of the *Manchester Evening News* wrote about the 'Babes' in the United line-up – a phrase which went on to have some resonance. Another new boy, Mark Jones, played three games at centre-half. The great Busby Babes side was waiting to be born.

United celebrated their Championship triumph with a short tour of north America. The football was hardly the most competitive United had been involved with all year and they lost two matches against Tottenham by wide margins. On 14 June 1952 they lost 5-0 to the Londoners at the University of Toronto, then travelled overnight to play them again at New York's Yankee Stadium the following day. In a bizarre ceremony Johnny Carey and Tottenham's captain, Ron Burgess, were obliged to lay a wreath on the memorial to America's baseball deity, Babe Ruth, and then stand to attention while a lone bugler sounded a lament. The funeral spirit extended to the match, as United were buried 7-1 after Rowley had given them the lead.

Despite the results, United's pioneering jaunt to the States was considered a success. More than 25,000 saw them play at Yankee Stadium, and the game attracted plenty of interest in the local press. The match report in one paper was headlined, 'The Mangling of the Mancs'.

The 1952/53 campaign was an anti-climax after the heroics which had gone before. As late summer gave way to autumn, Busby could already see that his ageing team was past its best. By October United were in one of the relegation places and in the

fourth round of the FA Cup they were embarrassingly held 1-1 at home by amateur side Walthamstow Avenue. They won the replay, but lost to Everton in the fifth round.

Busby made up his mind to let loose the gifted youngsters who were pushing for selection. As the season progressed a flood of talent burst into the first team: 17-year-old outside-left David Pegg was handed his chance; defender Bill Foulkes made his first mark on the team aged 20; 19-year-old centre-forward Dennis Viollet broke through; another extravagantly-gifted forward, Tommy Taylor, an old timer at 21, joined the club from Barnsley; and a 16-year-old wing-half named Duncan Edwards played his first game.

To be precise, Edwards was aged 16 years and 185 days when he took the field for United at Old Trafford to play Cardiff City on 4 April 1953. The Bluebirds took the shine off the tale somewhat by winning 4-1, but nevertheless it was the beginning of one of the great United careers. Many shrewd observers judge that he remains the club's greatest player ever.

Edwards first captured the attention of league scouts when he was a teenage star for Dudley Boys. Jimmy Murphy, especially,

Opposite Eddie Lewis scores in United's 5-2 FA Cup fourth round replay win against Walthamstow Avenue at Highbury on 5 February 1953.
Right Bill Foulkes (left) and Dennis Viollet broke through into the United first team as the great Busby Babes side emerged.

was desperate to sign the boy. Busby's assistant watched him on numerous occasions, and marvelled at the youth's maturity and technical ability. Finally, the manager himself travelled to the West Midlands to offer a deal to the player and his parents: but the Edwards family needed little persuading. Edwards had already decided he wanted to play for Busby, 'I think Manchester United are the greatest team in the world. I'd give anything to play for you,' he told Busby.

He signed for the club in June 1952, aged 15, but he already had the physique of a well-built man. Edwards combined physical strength with a fine eye for a pass, a thunderish tackle, natural athleticism and an equable temperament. He was also versatile; although nominally a left-half, Edwards was a good enough all-round footballer to fill any jersey from 2 to 11.

Busby's plan to play the youngsters was especially bold for the time, when players generally developed later. Edwards himself was struck by how youthful United's dressing room was. He said, 'The first time I entered the dressing room to meet the other players I wondered if I was in the right place. There were so many other youngsters that it seemed like being back at school.'

The changes worked and United recovered to end the season in eighth place. The country was already growing impressed with the ability of the boys emerging together at Manchester United. By the end of the 1952/53 season, the phrase 'Busby Babes' was already common currency and the world was about to witness the explosion of a sporting phenomenon – one of the finest club sides ever to grace a football field was about to burst into the world.

There was the sense of an old era coming to an end when Gentleman Johnny Carey played his last match for United and quit the club to manage Blackburn Rovers in the summer of 1953. His Old Trafford career had spanned the grim pre-war years, exile at Maine Road, the Cup glory of 1948 and the club's first Championship for over four decades. It was a sign of the club's new accent on youth that his replacement as captain should be the 25-year-old Roger Byrne.

The 1953/54 season saw the Busby Babes begin to grow and develop into the cohesive force which would come to dominate English football in the 1950s. The runaway Champions were Stan Cullis's utilitarian Wolverhampton Wanderers, a fearsomely

athletic and direct team, the polar opposite of Busby's team of young cavaliers. United ended the season in fourth place behind West Brom and Huddersfield in second and third, and they left the FA Cup in the third round, beaten 5-3 away at Burnley. But the campaign represented a significant forward step for Busby's radical young side.

The Babes were learning all the time and some of their lessons were painful. The following season, 1954/55, they finished in fifth place, just five points behind Champions Chelsea (the 'Drake's Ducklings' sobriquet for Ted Drake's young team never quite caught on). But United were not yet ready to strike out for the title themselves. A measure of how far they had to travel came on 12 February 1955, when they suffered a shocking 5-0 home defeat against City. Their local rivals had also beaten United 2-0 in the

FA Cup fourth round at Maine Road, and it was little comfort for United supporters that they ended the season a point and two places above City.

Before the start of the 1955/56 season, some football sages suggested that Busby's strategy was all wrong. As if to prove that there is nothing new in the game of football, many critics stated that the manager was putting too many youngsters in his team. The phrase might have been unfamiliar in the 1950s, but the gist was that you don't win anything with kids.

How wrong they were. The campaign turned out to be a glorious vindication of everything Busby stood for, as his fresh-faced, homegrown team – average age just 22 – stormed to the Championship. The extent of Busby's brilliant rebuilding job was revealed in the number of survivors from the title-winning side of four years earlier: there were just two, Byrne and Berry.

Opposite Duncan Edwards arrived at Old Trafford in 1953 with all the attributes needed for a top-flight footballing career.
Below Tommy Taylor scores in a 3-0 win against Chelsea at Old Trafford on 19 November 1955. United finished the season as Champions again.

The new players were almost all Mancunians or Lancastrians who had emerged from the youth programme; aided by a handful of key, relatively low-cost signings. The keeper, Ray Wood, had cost just £5,000 from Darlington; Berry had cost £15,000 from Birmingham; and the most expensive was Taylor, who cost £29,999 from Barnsley (Busby held back a pound from his transfer fee to save the player the burden of breaking the psychological £30,000 barrier!).

The Championship was won largely on the back of the huge volume of goals harvested by Taylor, the centre-forward, and Viollet at inside-left: Taylor scored 25 in 33 games, Viollet 20 in 34. United were also helped mightily by an impregnable home record – they went through the entire season without losing at Old Trafford, winning 18 games and drawing three.

United surged to the title on an especially hot streak of form, which lasted from the first week of February 1956 right through to the end of the season. A Championship-clinching 14-match unbeaten run began with a 2-0 home win against Burnley, and the run-in featured 10 victories and four draws. They made sure the Championship was coming back to Old Trafford on 7 April 1956, when Blackpool were the visitors. A match watched by a rapt audience of 62,277 ended 2-1 to United, with the goals coming from Berry and Taylor.

By the season's end United had opened up the biggest title-winning margin of the century – 11 points ahead of their nearest rivals, Blackpool. All the hard work begun by men like Davies, Crickmer and Norris before the war, then taken up by Busby and Murphy, saw its fruition in this season of seasons. It shows how far United's clear-minded planning had paid off that the Club also won the Central League easily and the Youth Cup for the fourth successive year. The fact that the Babes had grown up together and learnt their trades alongside one another at Old Trafford proved a huge benefit. The club was shot through with an unshakeable team ethic and a fierce will to win for the sake of the club. The players were gifted footballers as individuals, but everyone's ability was harnessed for the good of the team: that was the Busby philosophy and his players imbibed it from the first minute they walked through the gates of Old Trafford when they were boys starting out with the club. The captain, for one, was certain it contributed to their success. 'One of the secrets of Manchester United's success is that nearly all of us grew up together as boy footballers,' Byrne said. 'The Manchester United way is the only way we know.'

It was also a season when United remembered how to beat City. After a lean spell in derby encounters the Busby Babes beat City 2-1 at Old Trafford on New Year's Eve 1955 in front of a vast throng of 60,956, with 20,000 outside the gates unable to squeeze in. City went ahead in the first half, but Taylor and Viollet scored to give United their first derby victory since September 1951, and their first at Old Trafford since September 1949.

The Babes scored 83 league goals on the way to the title, but perhaps the most memorable goal by any United player that season was scored by the incomparable Edwards in the white of England. The date was 26 May 1956, the occasion a friendly with West Germany at the Olympic Stadium, Berlin. The Germans were a powerful side, the reigning World Champions, but England had pretensions to their crown, with a team full of great players, including the Wolves centre-half Billy Wright and the influential Fulham inside-forward, Johnny Haynes. England also fielded a strong United contingent, with Byrne at left-back and Taylor at centre-forward. But the best of the lot was Edwards, winning his ninth cap, and still only 19.

The score was 0-0 after 25 minutes when Edwards took control of the game in the way only great players can, with a few seconds of instictive genius. He won possession close to his own penalty area and began a progress up the field, which German after German tried and failed to interrupt. As the brawny left-half slalomed down the pitch, some of the best footballers in the world were made to look like novices as Edwards, superbly balanced and with faultless control, breezed by them. Finally, 25 yards from goal, he was ready to shoot and his effort flew past the goalkeeper. England won the game 3-1 and with Edwards in this kind of form, they looked likely contenders for the Jules Rimet trophy, to be contested in Sweden in the summer of 1958. Edwards, certainly the greatest teenage player in the world, and perhaps the greatest of any age at this time, had the world at his feet.

The 1956/57 season was the longest and perhaps the most satisfying season so far in the story of Manchester United. The 56-match campaign began with a 2-2 draw at home to Birmingham City on 18 August, the start of a second successive victorious Championship campaign. United retained their title with football that delighted neutral supporters almost as much as United diehards. Their play had been scintillating on the way to the title the season before – now they took it to another plane.

Busby's team didn't lose a match until 20 October, when Everton won 5-2 at Old Trafford, but by then United already had a handy cushion at the top after winning 10 and drawing two of their first dozen matches. It was during this run that a young forward from the north-east, who had been on the club's books since January 1953, made his first-team debut. Robert Charlton deputised for Taylor and took the number 9 jersey for the home game against Charlton Athletic on 6 October 1956. The 18-year-old scored twice in United's 4-2 win and, although he didn't manage to command a starting position in his debut season, Charlton still managed to score 10 goals in 14 games.

Goals were scored from every position for United that season. The inside-right, Liam Whelan, top-scored with 26 league goals, Taylor scored 22 and Viollet popped up with 16 from inside-left. Among the season's highlights was a resounding 4-2 win over City at Maine Road on 2 February, with Whelan, Taylor, Viollet and Edwards getting the goals.

The Championship was wrapped up at Old Trafford on 20 April, when Sunderland were routed 4-0. A crowd of 58,725 saw goals from Edwards and Taylor and two from Whelan win the title, and there were still three matches of the league season left. United finished the campaign with 103 goals – the first Champions to break a century since City did it in 1937.

The 1956/57 season was not just a record-breaking title-winning season – it also marked United's first experience in European competition. The European Cup had been launched the season before – without English representatives, because Chelsea had cravenly accepted a Football League order not to take part. The domestic game was still dominated by narrow-minded Little Englanders, who looked upon foreign club competitions as a threat to the League's own prestige, and the game's bosses wanted their Champions to ignore the new contest. They tried to exert pressure on United to boycott the European Cup, just as they had done with Chelsea. A League statement sniffed, 'Manchester United's participation is not in the best interests of the Football League.'

Busby and Manchester United, though, embraced the concept of pan-European competition. Busby retorted, 'Prestige alone demands that the continental challenge should be met, not avoided.' After United won the title in 1956 the board had voted unanimously to accept the invitation to take part in the 1956/57 edition of the European Cup.

United's first-ever European match was a preliminary round first leg tie played on 12 September 1956, away to the Belgian Champions, Anderlecht. Goals from Taylor and Viollet gave United a 2-0 win in the Parc Astrid, Brussels. The return was played at Maine Road, because Old Trafford was still without floodlights, and United raced to what remains their biggest-ever win in Europe.

Below Duncan Edwards (left) clearing the danger for England v Scotland at Wembley in April 1957. Edwards also scored in England's 2-1 win.
Overleaf Liam Whelan (right) slots the ball home in United's 2-0 win over Manchester City at Old Trafford on 22 September 1956.

1951–59

They smashed the pride of Belgium 10-0, with Viollet scoring four and Taylor adding a hat-trick.

United were handed a tough task in the first round proper – they had to face the Champions of West Germany, Borussia Dortmund. But United carved out a 3-2 lead in the first leg at Maine Road and shut out the Germans 0-0 in the second leg to reach the quarter-finals.

Athletic Bilbao were their next opponents in an extraordinary two-legged encounter, which began with a hair-raising adventure to the Basque country. In a chilling presentiment of the events of February 1958, the plane carrying the United party flew into difficulty on the descent to Bilbao. The pilot battled through a blizzard all the way and at journey's end he found that the airport runway was out of action. He was obliged to put the plane down in a nearby field. The nerve-shredding experience was no preparation

for a big European tie and United slid to a 5-3 defeat in a topsy-turvy encounter at Bilbao's Estadio San Mames. Before they were able to fly home, United's players had to grab shovels and help shift snow from the runway, another episode that takes on a macabre aspect with the knowledge of what was to take place at Munich.

Despite the trip and the poor first-leg result, United did enough in the home leg to reach the semi-finals. In one of the great United comebacks, the Babes pulled the match back at Maine Road, winning 3-0 to squeeze through on aggregate. Now they faced the biggest challenge of the lot – Real Madrid – rightly crowned the best team in Europe.

Tommy Taylor (left) scores the second in the 3-0 second-leg win over Athletic Bilbao to earn United a place in the semi-final against Real Madrid.

United travelled to the Bernabeu for the ultimate test in club football and did their best not to be dazzled by the frantic crowd of 135,000, or an opposition line-up featuring such stellar names as Kopa, Di Stefano and Gento. For an hour United kept out the swarms of white shirts that danced toward their goal, but finally Madrid found a way through and finished the game the victors by 3-1. But while Real were blessed with sumptuous talent, the British press were shocked by the Spaniards' physical approach to the game. Among the lurid headlines that dominated the next day's papers was one in the *Daily Herald*, 'Murder In Madrid', with the sub-heading, 'Manchester United hacked and slashed'.

The first, and still one of the greatest, European nights at Old Trafford unfolded on 25 April 1957, when United faced Real Madrid in the second leg under the ground's new lights. In one of the greatest exhibitions of football the old ground has ever seen, the teams fought out a scintillating 2-2 draw. Real Madrid raced into a 2-0 lead, which seemed to put the result beyond doubt.

But the Busby Babes remained undaunted and hit back through Taylor and Charlton to level the scores on the night. The comeback wasn't good enough to send them through, but it was magnificent nevertheless. Frank McGhee wrote in the next day's *Daily Mirror*, 'Brave failure. Fighting failure. Glorious failure. But that doesn't make it taste any better to those who cherished a proud illusion that in United England had the greatest football team in the world. They are not.

'Real Madrid are the real McCoy. They gave Matt Busby's League Champions a lesson in the basic arts and crafts of the game. They had the edge in skill and stamina. And above all they had a man called Alfredo Di Stefano.'

The second leg of the semi-final against Real Madrid was a thrilling match. Despite going 2-0 down United fought back, scored twice and had several other chances like this one.

United's first continental odyssey was over, but the memories of an enthralling night's sport would linger long in the memory. Busby was wise enough to realise that his young team had exceeded expectations and there was no shame in losing to a team as talented and as seasoned as Real Madrid. 'A great experienced side will always beat a great inexperienced side,' he observed.

The exit from Europe was a disappointment, but United were still in the hunt for the Double. All season long they had looked like Champions in waiting, while making significant strides towards another FA Cup final appearance. In the third round they had suffered a scare away to Hartlepool United of the Third Division (North) and only just made it into the next round with a jittery 4-3 win. There was more opposition from the same lowly division in the fourth round, but United made shorter work of the assignment this time, winning 5-0 at Wrexham. That set up a fifth round clash with Everton at Old Trafford and once again United had to sweat to make progress, with Edwards scoring the only goal of the game.

United came up against another Third Division side in the quarter-finals and played Bournemouth, who had reached the last eight after beating top sides like Wolves and Tottenham. United

survived yet another tight encounter at Dean Court and edged through 2-1 with two goals from Johnny Berry. Birmingham City were the last obstacle between United and Wembley and the Babes were guaranteed a difficult match. City were a mid-table First Division side, but they had reached the FA Cup final the season before and saved their best football for the competition. But in front of 65,000 at Hillsborough goals from Berry and Charlton were enough to send United through.

Their opponents at Wembley were Aston Villa and United were warm favourites to win back the Cup they had last held in 1948. After all, they had just won the Championship by a street and Villa were a largely anonymous, middling Division One team. But the odds lurched Villa's way after just six minutes when United lost their keeper, Ray Wood. Villa's outside-left, Peter McParland, recklessly challenged Wood for the ball and in the collision the keeper's cheekbone was smashed. Even for those times when keepers were afforded less protection than they are today, McParland's was a shocking foul. Wood had caught the ball and was standing in his six-yard area when the Irish international followed through and sent Wood crashing to the ground.

In those pre-substitute days United were down to ten men and centre-half Blanchflower volunteered to go in goal. Wood, concussed, bravely staggered back late in the first half, but the dazed keeper was able to do no more than stand ineffectually out on the wing. Blanchflower performed manfully between the sticks and made several impressive saves to keep his team in the game, but in the end the odds proved insuperable. United held out courageously for an hour before McParland scored twice in five minutes midway though the second half.

But the Babes were not quite beaten. Taylor pulled one back late in the game, heading home a corner taken by the makeshift centre-half, Edwards, to set up a late onslaught. United pinned Villa back into their own half for the rest of the game. Byrne even gambled outrageously by putting Wood, suffering from blurred vision, back in goal to give United ten fit outfield players. But the

The stricken United goalkeeper, Ray Wood, receives treatment during the 1957 FA Cup final against Aston Villa.

ploy was in vain. There would be no Double for United this season as Villa hung on for a 2-1 win.

If you could borrow a time machine and travel back to re-live any football season in history, a few campaigns would spring to mind. An obvious one would be 1998/99 and the Treble, but as that *annus mirabilis* lies fresh in the memory anyway it might be a wasted choice. Of course you could plump for 1967/68 and that magical night at Wembley when Benfica were defeated, but you would also have to put up with City winning the league again. Overall, it would be hard to beat 1956/57, the season when United retained the title, reached the FA Cup final, and enjoyed a first bravura foray into the European Cup, crossing swords with the might of Real Madrid in the semi-finals. This was the high-water mark of the Busby Babes – was football of a higher order ever played on these shores? For two seasons the Babes played football like young gods... and then they were destroyed.

The events of that black day in Munich have been rehearsed many, many times, and the stark cruelty of the event never fades. Even now, the scale of the tragedy barely seems credible, the enormity of it no easier to absorb. It breaks the heart to wind back time to 3 p.m. on that fateful, fatal Thursday, 6 February 1958. The BEA Elizabethan airliner had tried twice and failed twice to take off on the main runway at Munich airport, only for the pilot to abort both times because of the weather. It is easy to imagine the joshing banter and the nervous jokes shared by the young men inside the aircraft, as the plane revved its engines for a third take-off attempt. Then at 3.04 p.m., the crash, the explosion, the flames and the finest

The United party prepare to board their flight to Spain for the 1957 European Cup semi-final first leg against Real Madrid.

The twisted remains of the aircraft in the snow at Munich airport.

generation of footballers Britain had ever seen lay dead or dying in the burning carcass of the aircraft.

As always in large-scale catastrophes, it is the little details and ironies which grab the heart, because the full picture is too horrid to comprehend. The imagination seizes on tiny snapshots, which, all together, produce a nightmarish collage of grief. Like the image of Edwards's broken body in the German hospital bed and the young colossus valiantly clinging to life for two weeks, until his giant heart gave way at last. At the airport he had taken the trouble to telegraph the landlady of his digs in Manchester to say what time he would be in for his tea. The thought of that telegram lying on the mat while its sender was proceeding to his doom is almost too much to contemplate. Edwards stirred into consciousness briefly in hospital, and spied Jimmy Murphy on the ward. Edwards called out, 'Is the kick-off three o'clock Jimmy?' Doctors could not understand how Edwards stayed alive for so long with such grievous injuries: his kidneys were chronically damaged, a lung had collapsed, his ribs were smashed and his pelvis and leg were crushed. His fierce grip on life was finally loosened at 2.16 a.m. on 21 February 1958.

There was poor Liam Whelan, the sunny 23-year-old from Dublin, whose last recorded words were, 'If the worst happens, I am ready for death.' And the courage of Busby, who was not given a hope of life by the doctors and received the last rites. In extremis he whispered to Murphy, 'Keep the flag flying Jimmy. Keep things going until I get back.'

The final death toll stretched to 23 names: of the players, Roger Byrne, Geoff Bent, David Pegg, Duncan Edwards, Tommy Taylor, Eddie Colman, Mark Jones and Liam Whelan all perished; and from the club's staff, Walter Crickmer, Bert Whalley and Tom Curry also died. Eight journalists were among the dead: Alf Clarke, Don Davies, George Follows, Tom Jackson, Archie Ledbrooke, Henry Rose, Eric Thompson and Frank Swift.

At first it looked likely that Busby would join the roll call of the dead. But even though he fought back from the brink of death it would be a long time before the manager was fit enough to contemplate a return to work, and Busby wondered if he could ever face it. The feeling of guilt, that he had brought these extraordinary young men together only to see them die together while he survived, was crushing. He said, 'I was lost and sorrowing, and for a short period utterly defeated. A man's help at such a time is not his experience, but his faith and the love and encouragement of his friends.'

Busby had a great and trusted friend in Murphy, who stepped in as caretaker manager following the tragedy. Murphy would have been sitting next to the manager on the plane at Munich, except by one of those strange quirks of fate that had taken him to Israel for a World Cup qualifying match with the Wales team he managed.

Murphy was the quiet hero in the black weeks and months following the disaster, as he faced up to the task of rebuilding the shattered club with a sober determination.

He confessed he did not feel ready for the job. 'At first I felt I was going out of my mind, not knowing where to start,' he said. But Murphy found some solace in hard work and he pulled together a new coaching staff to help the recovery. Jack Crompton, who had been United's keeper in the first years of peace, was coaching at Luton Town, but he answered the call and turned up to help Murphy. And, somehow, United were able to put a team on the field for the first match after Munich, an FA Cup fifth round tie against Sheffield Wednesday on 19 February 1958.

Two survivors from the disaster were in the side; the new captain, Bill Foulkes, and the goalkeeper, Harry Gregg. The rest of the team were players promoted from the reserves or emergency signings. Stan Crowther joined from Villa and Ernie Taylor came

Below left Jimmy Murphy was on World Cup duty with Wales and missed the trip to Belgrade. He bravely kept United going in his role as caretaker manager following the horror at Munich.
Below Survivors of the crash grimly survey the scene of the disaster.

THE IMMORTALS

Eight Manchester United players were killed in the Munich air crash.

(Statistics are for appearances and goals in all competitions while playing for United)

❶ DAVID PEGG Age 22

OUTSIDE-LEFT • 150 Apps • 28 Gls

Pegg, from south Yorkshire, was an unorthodox left-winger for his time. He was far more than a touchline-hugging, by-line-hitting purveyor of crosses. Pegg loved to come inside off his wing to link up with his inside-forward and centre-forward, and he possessed a formidably hard left-foot shot.

He had lost his place in the starting line-up to Albert Scanlon at the time of Munich, but he was still highly regarded and certain of a bright future at the club. It wasn't just in the environs of Old Trafford that he was admired: Real Madrid were said to covet his services.

Pegg died with one England cap to his name: he played in a 1-1 draw with Ireland in May 1957.

❷ EDDIE COLMAN Age 21

RIGHT-HALF • 108 Apps • 2 Gls

The man the supporters called 'Snakehips', for his uncanny ability to swerve away from a challenge, was the perfect foil to Edwards in United's half-back line. Where Edwards was all physical presence and power, Colman's quicksilver talent was all to do with subtle passing and elusive runs.

He was an infrequent goalscorer, but he more than made up for that with the influence he had on United's attacking efforts.

Colman was proud of his Salford roots, and Salford was, and still is, proud of its illustrious citizen.

❸ DUNCAN EDWARDS Age 21

LEFT-HALF • 177 Apps • 21 Gls

Younger supporters will just have to accept the word of older witnesses that Edwards was the most complete footballer England has ever produced. Or you could believe Bobby Charlton, who said, 'He was the best player I've ever seen, the best footballer I've ever played with for United or England, the only player who ever made me feel inferior.'

Even as a teenager he was master of every footballing skill. He had wondrous passing ability with both feet, was strong in the air, could tackle cleanly and clinically, and to cap it off he was blessed with a calm temperament. At the time he was snatched away there seemed no limit to what he could achieve with United and England.

④ MARK JONES Age 24
CENTRE-HALF • 121 Apps • 1 Gl

Jones was another son of south Yorkshire who crossed the Pennines to serve United with distinction. He brought an uncomplicated method to his defensive duties and he was a highly effective centre-half. The 1950s was something of a golden age for the traditional English centre-forward, with the likes of Nat Lofthouse and Stan Mortensen rampaging in the First Division, yet Jones was equal to them all. He was unyielding in the tackle, unrivalled in the air and a good passer of the ball.

He spent much of his United career waging a good-natured duel with Jackie Blanchflower for the United number 5 shirt: Jones was in possession at the time of his death.

⑤ ROGER BYRNE Age 28
LEFT-BACK • 280 Apps • 20 Gls

Byrne, from Gorton, was not the most naturally gifted United player of all time, but he stands in the first rank of great leaders. He took over as captain following the departure of Johnny Carey and played a key role in helping the Busby Babes reach a new level of footballing brilliance.

Although only in his early 20s himself, the younger generation of Babes looked up to Byrne and he was an altogether tougher character than the genial Carey. He was quite prepared to have his say on team matters, and was one of the few people with the knowledge and the nerve to deal with Busby as an equal. Busby, in turn, recognised Byrne's special qualities and cherished his contribution to the team.

Byrne was also an outstanding player for England, with 33 caps to his name, and he would surely have been an important player in England's 1958 World Cup campaign, along with United's other lost England internationals, Duncan Edwards and Tommy Taylor.

⑥ GEOFF BENT Age 25
LEFT-BACK • 12 Apps • 0 Gls

Bent was Roger Byrne's understudy at left-back and, such was the captain's reliability, the Salford lad rarely had a chance of a game. When he did play, he displayed plenty of pace and a speed in the tackle that suggested he would have walked into any other First Division side.

⑦ LIAM WHELAN Age 22
INSIDE-RIGHT • 98 Apps • 52 Gls

The unassuming Dubliner was a star of United's all-conquering youth side and was on the verge of greatness with the senior team when his life was cut short at Munich.

Whelan did not have blistering pace, but he had an elusive quality with the ball at his feet that unsettled even the best defenders. For a player whose main responsibility and strength lay in setting up opportunities for others, he had an astonishingly prolific scoring record. In his last full season, 1956/57, he was the club's leading scorer with 26 goals from 39 games.

Whelan had recently broken into the Ireland national side and had won four caps for his country.

⑧ TOMMY TAYLOR Age 26
CENTRE-FORWARD • 191 Apps • 131 Gls

Taylor, another member of the Babes' south Yorkshire contingent, was born to score goals. His strike rate for club and country was mighty, running at two goals every three games for United and almost one a game for England.

He was adept at all the centre-forward's arts, but heading was his speciality. Taylor was the most powerful header of a ball in the English game, including Nat Lofthouse. Busby knew exactly what he was doing when he paid a record £29,999 to buy him from his home-town club, Barnsley, and other clubs soon became aware that Busby had picked up a bargain.

He made his England debut in a 0-0 draw with Argentina in May 1953 and scored 16 goals in 19 internationals. Taylor was especially deadly in the qualifying games for the 1958 World Cup, hitting eight goals to help his country reach a tournament he was destined never to grace.

Also pictured:

Ⓐ BILL FOULKES Survivor

Ⓑ RAY WOOD Survivor

Ⓒ DENNIS VIOLLET Survivor

Ⓓ JOHNNY BERRY Survivor

Injuries sustained in crash ended his career.

from Blackpool. It was only 13 days since the carnage at Munich and, on an extraordinary afternoon of raw emotion United won 3-0, with Shay Brennan, a reserve team full-back playing on the left wing, scoring twice.

With United now in the quarter-finals of the competition, the entire nation was willing them to go on and win it. Murphy's hastily assembled team was more than just a collection of 11 footballers: it became a vehicle for catharsis, as millions of people, whether they supported United or not, yearned to see something good, something joyful, emerge from the wreckage of Munich. It was as if United themselves held the antidote to the numbing grief that had gripped so many.

Murphy's makeshift team went to the Hawthorns next and drew 2-2 with West Bromwich Albion, winning the replay 1-0 at Old Trafford. They then faced Second Division Fulham in the semi-finals and, after a 2-2 draw at Villa Park, they reached the final with a thrilling 5-3 victory at Hillsborough in which Aberdonian centre-forward, Alex Dawson, scored a hat-trick.

The world watched and willed United to beat Bolton Wanderers in the 1958 FA Cup final, but it turned out to be a fairytale written by the Brothers Grimm, rather than Hans Andersen. There was to be no happy ending. Nat Lofthouse put Bolton 1-0 up after just three minutes and United were sunk by a second goal 10 minutes into the second half. It was the most unpopular goal Lofthouse scored in his long and illustrious career as a centre-forward, as he barged into United keeper, Harry Gregg, forcing him to drop the ball over the line. United were never able to find a way back into the game.

There was one pleasing aspect of the day for United. The match was attended by Busby, who had left hospital a fortnight earlier. He was well enough to watch from the touchline, although he was still unsteady on his feet and walking with the aid of sticks. The boss was still convalescing slowly after his dreadful ordeal – but he was alive and taking an interest in football, and United, once again. Busby was on his way back to resuming control of the club he loved.

The FA Cup final of 1958 was important, too, because it held out hope for the future of Manchester United. The Busby Babes were gone and nothing could replace that lost generation. But Murphy

and his assistants were building a new United and the club endured. The crushing sense of loss was still there, but life, football – and Manchester United – would go on.

It says much about Murphy's resolve and skills as a team builder that his hastily assembled United side finished second in Division One in the first post-Munich season. Wolves finished the 1958/59 season as Champions by six points, but United showed plenty of fight to stay in the hunt almost to the end. Busby returned to the helm during the campaign and a new group of United heroes emerged on the field. Gregg became the first-choice keeper and missed just one game; Charlton came through as the team's most dangerous striker and topped the club's scoring lists with 29 goals from inside-left; Viollet, who was back to fitness and filling the number 9 jersey brilliantly, contributed 21 goals; Albert Scanlon, too, had overcome injuries received at Munich and was an ever-present at outside-left. Ronnie Cope at centre-half, Foulkes at right-back, Wilf McGuinness at left-half, Ian Greaves at full-back on either side, Fred Goodwin at right-half and Albert Quixall at inside-right (a rare big-money Busby signing – he cost £45,000 from Shefield Wednesday, a record transfer between two British clubs) were all valuable members of the reborn United. The personnel might have changed, but the team's approach to playing the game had not. United continued to attack and they scored 103 league goals in their courageous pursuit of Wolves.

As United prepared for the 1959/60 season, they could look back on an era that brought the club its greatest glory and its deepest grief. The 1950s had been the best and the worst decade in the club's history. The conflicting experiences had left Busby with a burning desire to conquer one final mountain: he wanted to build one last, great team capable of winning the European Cup. He had lost one team in pursuit of the dream. Now it became an ambition bordering on an obsession to claim the prize that would surely in time have gone to his peerless Babes. The quest for the greatest prize in club football would define the 1960s and the rest of Busby's time in charge of United.

Bobby Charlton escaped from the carnage at Munich and was fit enough to play in the 1958 FA Cup final against Bolton Wanderers at Wembley.

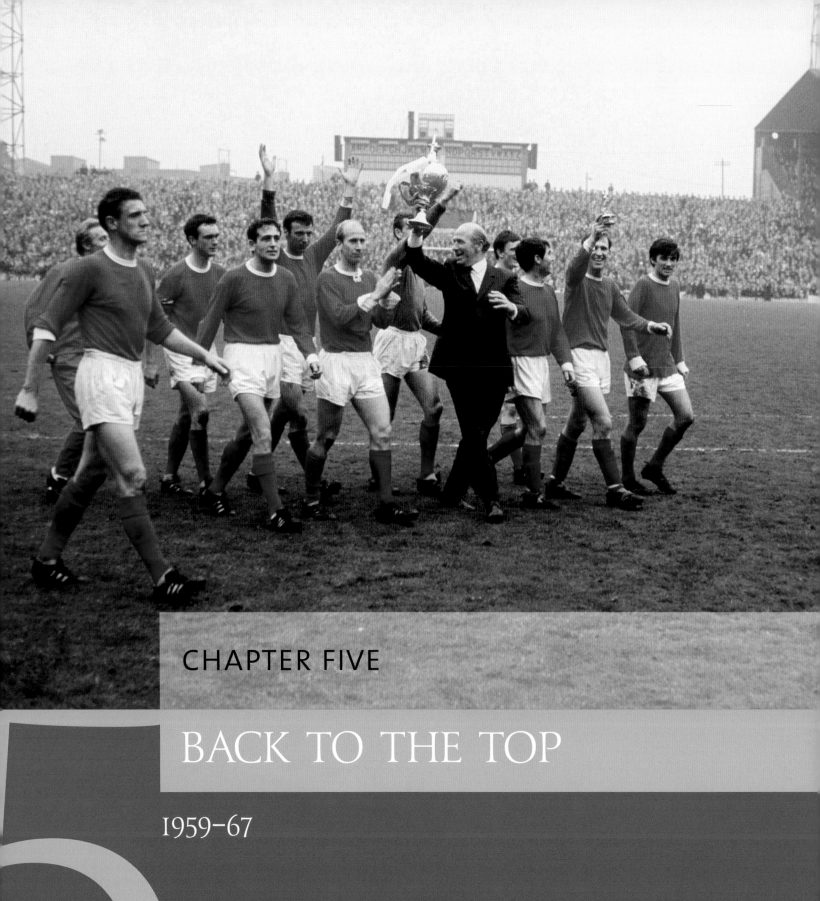

CHAPTER FIVE

BACK TO THE TOP

1959–67

PUTTING THE HORRORS OF MUNICH BEHIND HIM,
MATT BUSBY BEGAN REBUILDING HIS TEAM WITH ONE AIM –
GETTING BACK TO THE TOP

I n the 1959/60 season everything came up smelling of violets for one Manchester United forward. Dennis Viollet broke Jack Rowley's record for league goals scored in a season by hitting a remarkable 32 in 36 games, more than anyone else in the First Division. The goalscoring feat crowned an extraordinarily brave comeback by Viollet, who had escaped from Munich with his life, but sustained severe head injuries that threatened his career. But he battled back in time to captain United at the 1958 FA Cup final against Bolton, even though he was a long way short of full fitness.

The long road back to recovery found its glorious conclusion with his record-breaking exploits of 1959/60, and, even if nothing else that followed in his career equalled his performances then, it hardly mattered. He had won a personal fight to play again at the highest level and served United several seasons longer than anybody would have thought possible as he lay critically injured in 1958.

Despite Viollet's efforts United suffered a disappointing season in the league, finishing seventh, well adrift of Champions Burnley. The FA Cup campaign came unstuck with a 1-0 home defeat in the fifth round against Sheffield Wednesday. It was, though, a landmark

season for long-suffering Stretford Enders who had stood at the mercy of Manchester's moist climate for half a century. At last the popular terracing was roofed over, a big part of the rebuilding works which transformed Old Trafford during the 1960s.

On the face of it United appeared to tread water the next season, as they finished seventh in the league again and lost at home to Wednesday in the FA Cup fifth round just as they had 12 months earlier (except this time they were thrashed 7-2). The team was in a state of flux as Busby sought a settled line-up with enough quality to compete at the top of the table. There was some hope for the future as a handful of talented newcomers came into the team, including a Mancunian half-back named Norbert Stiles and a pair of reliable Irish full-backs – Noel Cantwell signed from West Ham for £29,500 and Tony Dunne arrived from Shelbourne for £5,000.

United were still scoring goals and Bobby Charlton led the way with 21 in 39 games mainly from outside-left but in truth

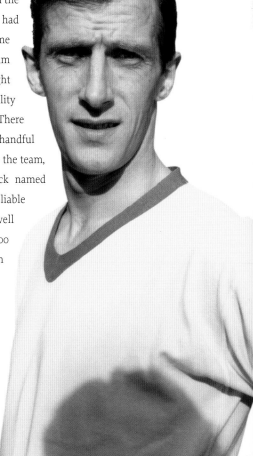

the team lacked consistency. They were potent enough to beat Chelsea 6-0 at Old Trafford, then poor enough to lose their next away game by the same score at Leicester. Bill Nicholson's 1960/61 Double-winning Spurs side had set a new standard and Busby, perhaps the greatest team-builder in the history of English football, was struggling to find a winning formula.

Performances were little better in 1961/62 when United stuttered to 15th place in the First Division. The club endured one of its worst runs since before the war, when a 2-0 home defeat against Wolves on 30 September 1961 triggered a 10-match spell without a victory. But even while they were stuck in the bottom half of the table United were still capable of showing flashes of the old brilliance, especially at Old Trafford, where they beat Blackburn 6-1, Forest 6-3, West Brom 4-1 and Ipswich 5-0.

Busby was still striving to mould together a stable side capable of challenging for honours once again. Just as he had done a decade earlier he gave youngsters their chance in the side, knowing that some would thrive and others would just fall short of the quality he needed. One member of the new generation given an opportunity to sink or swim was a young Stretford lad named Phil Chisnall. He was a promising forward who had signed for the club as a 15-year-old, in the first influx of schoolboys to join United after Munich, in Easter 1958.

'A load of us joined and over the next years we had our chances to play,' Chisnall recalled. 'For the next few years after 1958 the team was really makeshift, while Matt Busby and Jimmy Murphy did their rebuilding. Some players' progress into the first team was accelerated and Busby began to buy players, which he had never really had to do before. He had an assembly line of talent and it took a while for the next group of players to come through. Even into the mid-1960s Munich was a factor. The crash affected everything. It took years to recover, to find another team to take the club forward.'

Opposite Denis Law is measured up for his first United shirt by Matt Busby after moving to Old Trafford from Torino in August 1962.
Overleaf David Herd crashes the ball home for United in their 3-1 win at Arsenal on 25 August 1962.

United did at least enjoy their best FA Cup run since 1958, beating Bolton, Arsenal, Wednesday and Preston, before losing 3-1 to Spurs in the semi-final at Hillsborough.

That rousing Cup campaign was a portent of United's giddy run to the final in 1963 – and they were glad to have the excitement of the FA Cup to take their minds off their worst season in the league since they were relegated to the Second Division in 1937.

Busby had spent big money in 1962 to inject some vitality into his flagging squad, but for a long time it seemed as though his investment would not pay off. He bought Denis Law from Italian club Torino for the vast sum of £110,000 in August 1962. And in February 1963 another Scot arrived to freshen up the team as Pat Crerand, a midfield playmaker with a martial spirit signed from Celtic for £56,000. But even though Law top-scored for United with 23 league goals in 1962/63, the team still struggled to find any kind of consistent form.

Chisnall said, 'It was not surprising, really. It takes time to build a team and the whole club was still pulling itself back together after Munich. There were a lot of youngsters coming into the team and they weren't going to be great players overnight.'

With four matches left to play, United were in real danger of the drop. Leyton Orient had already been consigned to the Second Division and at that time, when two sides went down, United faced a battle with Birmingham and Manchester City to avoid dropping with the Os. United's outlook appeared bleak when they went to Birmingham and lost 2-1. As chance would have it, Busby's men faced another nerve-jangling relegation tussle in the next game too – at Maine Road on 15 May 1963. The derby match had virtually become a play-off to avoid relegation.

United's supporters' hearts were in their boots when Alex Harley gave City an early lead, and the game wore on with no sign of an equaliser. The match ticked into its last five minutes and all hope seemed lost. But United were gifted a goal by a defensive error, when Law stole a clumsy backpass and bore down on goal. Law was felled by City's keeper, Harry Dowd – penalty! Albert Quixall held his nerve from the spot to clinch a point that did United more favours than City. All United had to do to stay up was beat Orient in the penultimate game of the season and they managed that, 3-1 at Old Trafford. United survived by just three points, two places higher than City who joined Orient in Division Two.

BOBBY CHARLTON

FORWARD (1956–73) • 756 (2) APPEARANCES • 249 GOALS

It's impossible to name for sure the greatest Manchester United player of all time. How can you compare footballers from different eras and different positions, and come up with a definitive answer? But a few key individuals are bound to crop up on any shortlist: Edwards, Best, Charlton and Cantona would surely be there. But when it comes to the most influential player in the club's history, then you are picking from a list of one: it can only be Bobby Charlton.

A glance at the statistics alone establishes his status: he held the club's appearances record (605 League games, including two as a substitute) until Ryan Giggs beat it, and remains United's all-time top-scorer with 199 league goals. And for sheer longevity he stands out from the rest. Charlton made his first-team debut in 1956 and won two Championship medals with the great Busby Babes team.

He overcame the horror of Munich to become a mainstay of the side in the 1960s: throughout the transitional years while Busby re-built the team and on into the title-winning campaigns and the glory of the European Cup in 1968. Even into the 1970s Charlton was an effective midfield operator, until he made an emotional farewell to his time as a United player.

But the figures and dates tell less than half the story. Most importantly, he was a beautiful footballer to watch. There have been few more thrilling sights in United's history than that of Charlton running from deep with the ball at his feet, the perfect marriage of grace and power. Defenders trailed in his wake as he swept onwards, before unpacking his hammer of a shot to send the ball soaring into the net.

Charlton had a football intelligence that made him master in a series of different roles. In his early days he was a deadly penalty box operator, playing a striking role which suited him so well that he scored 29 League goals in 38 games in the first full season after Munich. In the early 1960s he was more commonly found on the left wing, where his direct running and ability to deliver an accurate ball made him one of the best wide players in the country. But his best role was probably the deeper, midfield position he made his own while United were climbing back to the summit of English football in the mid-1960s. It was also the place he played his best football for his country, and his surging runs and thoughtful passing made him a prime architect of England's triumph in the 1966 World Cup. It was that tournament that cemented Charlton's reputation as one of the world's greatest players. Out of all England's heroes that year Charlton was singled out for the European Player of the Year award.

By the time he played his last competitive game for United, a 1-0 defeat at Chelsea on 28 April 1973, Charlton had amassed a list of honours rivalled by few players: three Championships, an FA Cup, a European Cup and a World Cup. He played 106 games for England and remains top of his country's all-time goalscoring list with 49. Most importantly, he had earned the respect and admiration of his peers, and the game's most discerning judges. Busby said, 'There has never been a more popular footballer. He was as near perfection as man and player as it is possible to be.'

The perfect marriage of grace and power: Bobby Charlton scores in a 2-2 draw at Tottenham in the First Division on 20 January 1962.

JIMMY MURPHY

ASSISTANT MANAGER (1958–71)

Busby knew the truth. He knew that without Jimmy Murphy by his side he would never have reaped half the honours that came his way at Old Trafford. The Welshman was there right from the beginning for Busby. When the boss walked through the decrepit portals of Old Trafford for the first time as manager in 1945, one of his first actions was to appoint Murphy as his assistant. It was his first decision and his best – the start of a fruitful working relationship, which would last until Busby quit the boss's job.

Murphy had been an industrious wing-half for West Brom and Wales, until the Second World War halted his career, and it was while he was serving with the forces in Italy that Busby met him and decided he was a man he could work well with. Busby hired him as United's coach and in 1955 Murphy was named assistant manager, to formalise the job he was already filling.

Murphy was a key influence in the development of the Busby Babes in the 1950s, in tandem with Bert Whalley, and his work in bringing on players was spotted way beyond Old Trafford. He was approached with job offers from as far afield as Brazil and even Juventus wanted him to manage them. But Murphy was happy to avoid the limelight and stay with Busby at United.

In 1958 he had the United manager's job thrust upon him when Busby was horribly injured at Munich, but Murphy coped with calm assurance. He hardly had time to grieve for his slaughtered protégés before the task of rebuilding the team began. The world marvelled at Murphy's feat in steering United to the FA Cup final just three months after the disaster. But they should not have

been surprised by Murphy's ability to shape footballers into a team. As well as assisting Busby, Murphy was part-time manager of Wales and worked wonders to help them qualify for the 1958 World Cup in Sweden. Murphy's coaching ability helped a woefully-underprepared Wales side reach the last eight of the tournament and only Brazil, and a single goal from Pele, prevented the principality from reaching the last four.

After Busby's return to work Murphy was glad to retreat to his assistant's role once more and he continued to provide a perfect foil for the boss. Busby kept some distance between the players and himself, allowing Murphy a free rein to work with the team on the training ground. Busby was the general sorting out the strategy, Murphy was more the gruff but kindly sergeant major. He could tear into players when he felt they weren't giving of their best, but he was also capable of lending a sympathetic ear to players who did not want to share their troubles with the manager.

Murphy resigned as assistant manager in August 1971, but in retirement continued to scout for the club he loved. He died on 14 November 1989, aged 81.

Jimmy Murphy (centre) with Matt Busby and Jack Crompton in discussion during pre-season training on 7 August 1961.

It might have been United's worst season in the league for a quarter of a century, but it was an entirely different story in the Cup. United did not begin their FA Cup campaign until 4 March as the ice and snow of Britain's worst winter for decades played havoc with the fixture list. Busby's team kicked-off with a 5-0 home win against Second Division Huddersfield and Law scored a hat-trick against the club that had launched his career. Their fourth round opponents were Villa at Old Trafford and Quixall scored the only goal of the game to send United into the last 16.

United faced Chelsea, who were on their way to promotion from the Second Division, in the fifth round at Old Trafford. The Londoners made United work hard for their passage into the quarter-finals, but goals from Law and Quixall were just enough to earn a 2-1 win. Now United played their first away game of the Cup run when they travelled to take on Coventry City from the Third Division. By this stage of the season United were staring at the real prospect of relegation, while Coventry were chasing promotion to Division Two, and the match had all the ingredients of a Cup upset. But Quixall kept up his record of scoring in every round and Charlton added another two goals in United's 3-1 win.

The semi-final draw could not have been kinder to United. Leicester City and Liverpool were still in the competition and both those teams enjoyed far loftier positions in the First Division than United but Busby's side were paired with Southampton,

a mid-table Second Division team. The Saints, though, gave United a scare in their clash at Villa Park and only a single goal from Law separated the sides.

It had been a thrilling run to Wembley for United's success-starved followers, but they were widely expected to lose the final. Leicester, who had emerged from the other semi-final, were a strong First Division side while United had only just escaped relegation the Saturday before the final. But Busby's men defied the odds to win their first trophy since the Babes captured the title in 1957.

There was more cause than ever before for the city of Manchester to go berserk when their heroes returned with the Cup. Despite the difficulties encountered in the league, the Wembley triumph did much to dispel the gloom that had threatened to envelop the club. It was time for United to cast off the austere years and usher in the hedonistic 1960s.

As if galvanised by the Cup glory of May 1963, United roared back to form the following season. They threw off the uncertainty

---

Above David Herd scores United's second against Leicester City in the 1963 FA Cup final triumph.

Opposite Denis Law nets one of his three goals against Willem II of Holland during the 1963/64 Cup-Winners' Cup first round match.

which had dogged them throughout the previous relegation-haunted campaign and a bright new United team began to emerge. They finished second in the league table behind Liverpool and reached another FA Cup semi-final. Sadly, their hopes of retaining the trophy were wrecked by Second Division West Ham in a 3-1 defeat at a sodden Hillsborough.

'We should never have played,' Chisnall said. 'The pitch was already nothing but mud, then it rained hard on the day of the game and it was unplayable really. You'd kick the ball and it wouldn't travel two yards through the mud. It wasn't a football match. There were 22 players rolling around and sliding through the surface, but it wasn't a football match.'

The 1963/64 season also marked a return to European action for United as they competed in the Cup-Winners' Cup for the first time. 'We felt we belonged in Europe,' Chisnall said. 'United and Busby had been pioneers in continental football and when we got back into European competition we felt we were back in our

rightful place. Busby loved the challenge of playing against foreign sides and he was really motivated by European competition. He wanted United to test themselves against the best of the foreign sides. The European Cup was the ultimate challenge, but we were happy to be in the Cup-Winners' Cup.'

United's first test was against Willem II of Holland and, after a 1-1 draw at the Feyenoord Stadium in Rotterdam, the Reds swept their visitors aside at Old Trafford, with Law netting a hat-trick in a 6-1 win. United then faced the Cup-Winners' Cup holders, Tottenham, and after a 2-0 defeat at White Hart Lane it looked like Busby's men were on their way out. But a barnstorming comeback in the second leg at Old Trafford saw United win 4-1 to set up a quarter-final against Sporting Lisbon. Another hat-trick from Law gave United an easy 4-1 win in the first leg at Old Trafford, but now it was their turn to get on the wrong end of an unlikely turnaround. In the return leg Sporting won 5-0 to dump United, exhausted by an inhuman late-season workload, out of the competition.

1963 **FA CUP FINAL**

MANCHESTER UNITED 3 Law, Herd 2 **LEICESTER CITY 1** Keyworth

25 MAY 1963 at Wembley • Referee: K. Aston • Attendance: 100,000

Sometimes a single goal can change the direction of football history. That was the case in the 1963 final, when United turned back a rising tide of Leicester pressure with an opportunistic goal, which seemed to change the club's fortunes. Until they turned over the favourites to capture the Cup, United had been a shadow of the club that had dominated English football in the 1950s. It was difficult to see how they were going to recreate the swagger and verve of that era.

After half an hour of a tense match, Leicester were beginning to look likely winners. As half-time loomed a City goal looked on the cards as they began to monopolise possession. But United's striking genius, Law, stepped up to seize his moment and send the game United's way. He created space in the penalty area where none had seemed to exist and slammed a ball delivered by Crerand past Gordon Banks to give United the lead. The goal put fresh heart into United and from that moment on they were a transformed side. Gone was the hesitancy that had dogged their League performances: it was as if Law had given them a glimpse of what they could achieve if they played with the arrogance and audacity of old.

Law continued to stamp his class all over the match, although it was David Herd's two second-half goals which confirmed United as Cup winners. Herd's first came on the hour when Banks pushed out a shot from Charlton and United's centre-forward reacted quickest to boot the ball into the net. With 10 minutes left City's Ken Keyworth reignited the contest by scoring with an athletic header, but United simply moved up a gear and scored again to make the match safe. Banks failed to gather a shot from Quixall and Herd was on the spot once again to score.

Moments later United's captain, Noel Cantwell, was hoisting the FA Cup aloft for all the world to see. A new era of success had been launched and it could all be traced back to Law's deadly strike.

MANCHESTER UNITED

Gaskell
Dunne
Cantwell
Crerand
Foulkes
Setters
Giles
Quixall
Herd
Law
Charlton

LEICESTER CITY

Banks
Sjoberg
Norman
McLintock
King
Appleton
Riley
Cross
Keyworth
Gibson
Stringfellow

Skipper Noel Cantwell (centre) flings the FA Cup skywards after United's victory against Leicester City, with Maurice Setters (left) and Pat Crerand ready to catch the lid.

DENIS LAW

FORWARD (1962–73) • 398 (6) APPEARANCES • 237 GOALS

'The Lawman', as he was known, would be many people's pick of the greatest natural goalscorer ever to have appeared for United. During his magnificent spell at Old Trafford in the 1960s he formed an immortal attacking triumvirate with Best and Charlton, the memory of which will endure for all time.

He was at his greatest in the 1963/64 season when he rounded off a remarkable collection of scintillating individual performances by being voted European Player of the Year. He scored 30 League goals for United that season, as well as 10 in the FA Cup and 6 in Europe. It would have been even more but for a 28-day ban handed out by the FA in December 1963 for a string of on-field misdemeanours.

For Scotland, too, Law's golden season was stuffed with goals. It started with a hat-trick against Norway in Oslo as Scotland contrived to lose a game they dominated 4-3. Then they went to Spain and, inspired by Law, won 6-2. He scored four more in the return with Norway, which Scotland won 6-1 at Hampden. It was one of nine occasions that season when he scored three or more in a game.

But beyond the prosaic inventory of goals scored and games won, Law's style marked him out from the rest. His Scotland team-mate, Ian St John, said, 'Denis was two people. Away from the game he was a lamb, but put him on the pitch and he became a tiger. When he got the ball near the goal, he was electric, so quick.'

Law needed reservoirs of determination to become a footballer at all. He grew up with a chronic squint and it wasn't until he was an established pro that he had an operation to cure the condition. The young Law was also incredibly skinny. He turned up for a trial at Huddersfield Town and the team's assistant manager recommended he be sent home on the next available train. Bill Shankly later revised his hasty opinion, prescribed the boy a steady diet of steak and milk, made him into a professional footballer

and later bracketed him with Tom Finney as one of his two favourite footballers of all time.

Perhaps Law's finest hour and a half in that year of years came in October 1963, when he lined up for the Rest of the World XI which played England at Wembley in a game to celebrate the FA's centenary. The global all-star team lost 2-1, but Law stood out in a cast of talent featuring legends such as Di Stefano, Puskas, Eusebio and Gento.

Law's emergence as the best player in Europe overshadowed the arrival in the first team of yet another extravagantly talented youngster. George Best had signed as an apprentice for United in August 1961 and, although Busby and his staff knew they had a rare player on their hands, it was a month over two years before he made his first-team debut. The young Belfast boy was a weedy specimen and the wise heads at United did not want their prodigy to be kicked out of the game before he had a chance to make his mark. But the explosion of Best's talent was well worth waiting for. He played his first game on 14 September 1963, in United's 1-0 win over West Brom, and went on to make 17 league appearances in the season. His first goal came in a 5-1 win against Burnley at Old Trafford at Christmas time that year. By the following May it was already clear that United had unearthed a once-in-a-lifetime footballer.

Old Trafford continued its metamorphosis into the country's most magnificent football stadium in the mid-1960s. As early as 1962 the ground had been earmarked as a 1966 World Cup venue and United were handed a grant of £40,000 for major improvements. The roof over the old United Road section of the ground was demolished and replaced with the architecturally distinctive cantilever stand, which became such a well-known landmark. The new structure was ground-breaking in a number of ways and among its innovations was the provision of glass-fronted corporate boxes. The completed United Road stand had room for 10,000 supporters, seated and standing, and it cost £350,000 to build. The face-lift completely changed the old ground, lending it a stylish profile that was instantly recognisable.

By now United had a team to grace the plush new surroundings and the 1964/65 season marked a massive leap forward in the team's performances. After a hesitant start to the campaign United set off on a 15-match unbeaten run, which lasted from early September to December. After beating Sunderland 1-0 at Old Trafford on 10 October 1964 Busby's team embarked on a run of eight wins in eight games, which put them right in contention for the title. But they faced stern opposition from Don Revie's teak-tough Leeds team, who had won promotion to the First Division with an uncompromising approach to the game. Revie's mentality was to win at all costs and his combative attitude made Leeds deeply unpopular. By contrast, Busby had moulded another side brimming with skill and a new generation of supporters grew to love the verve of a United side filled with footballers like Law, Charlton and Best.

Above Denis Law, centre, with Scotland team-mates (left to right) Willie Henderson, Bobby Collins, Davie Wilson and Ian St John.
Right George Best in 1964, the brilliant focus of United's young and fast-emerging Championship-winning side.

GEORGE BEST

FORWARD (1963–74) • 470 APPEARANCES • 179 GOALS

George Best's career burned brilliantly for a few blessed seasons in the 1960s and he could, perhaps should, have played longer. But by the time his playing days had petered out messily, the Irishman had already proved himself the most naturally gifted footballer United had ever seen. You could go further and say he was the most talented player Britain has ever known and not hear much dissent.

It is one of the received wisdoms about Best that he frittered away his talent, but that seems a harsh verdict. It is true that he did not hang around until his mid-30s, plodding along to pick up the pay-cheques and the plaudits reserved for long-serving old pros. But Best packed enough achievement into his time at United to last several careers.

He was pretty much a spent force at the top level long before his 30th birthday – but he could look back on a career that featured 470 appearances and 179 goals for United; a European Cup winner's medal, two Championships, 37 international caps and a European Player of the Year award. He was United's top scorer of the season four times and in 1967/68 was the joint-leading scorer in the First Division with 28. It all adds together to make a decent haul of honours for a man whose top-flight career ended so prematurely.

You cannot measure Best's worth just in terms of medals. He was an artist who happened to use a ball and a rectangle of grass rather than brush and canvas, and it was a tragedy that his genius also bore the seeds of his own destruction. It was Best's fate that the only opponent he could never elude was drink, but his place in the pantheon is reserved for all time in spite of his unfortunate demise. Pele, many people's choice as the best ever, said simply, 'George Best was the greatest footballer in the world.'

It will do as an epitaph.

George Best and friends display some of the wares from his boutique business at Manchester's Tiffany's nightclub in September 1966.

Lest anyone imagine that United were all flash and no substance, they also had plenty of players who could stand up to anything the likes of Leeds could throw at them – men like Bill Foulkes and Nobby Stiles could play, but they were robust with it. Busby was weaving together a perfect combination of silk and steel.

It was a desperately close-run thing as Leeds and United fought for the title all the way through to May. But United edged ahead in the last furlong and with two matches to play they entertained Arsenal on 26 April 1965, knowing that a win would give them their first Championship since 1957. Two goals from Law and one

from Best wrapped up a 3-1 win and the trophy which had once been won by the Busby Babes was now in possession of another fine United side.

Above David Herd hammers home during United's 4-0 win against Chelsea at Old Trafford on 13 March 1965.
Opposite United's management brains trust toast Championship success at Old Trafford after the 3-1 win over Arsenal, which wrapped up the title in April 1965.

United won the Championship because they had the best players, but they also showed a tactical sophistication which was miles ahead of other First Division teams: Busby's side had a fluidity and a flexibility which their more rigid rivals completely lacked. Wingers were falling out of fashion in the English game, but Busby persevered with attackers down the flanks. George Best was a constant threat out wide and John Connelly would be probing down the right. Denis Law and David Herd were the attacking spearheads down the middle, while Pat Crerand and Bobby Charlton supplied the creativity in midfield. Nobby Stiles dropped back to play as an auxiliary centre-half alongside Bill Foulkes, and Tony Dunne and Shay Brennan were the dependable, no-frills full-backs. That was the basic structure, but the beauty of United's approach was that the attacking players would switch their positions right across the front line. Best would make runs down the middle or Law would drop deep to create mischief. United's attacking devilry caused consternation in opposing defences and was practically impossible to contain. The United attack was an ever-shifting kaleidoscope of skill and movement.

Some teams tried marking man for man, but United were ready for that tactic. The strikers would fall back to the halfway line with their markers in attendance, leaving vast acres in the opposition half for a Crerand or a Charlton to exploit. In addition, United's strikers were capable of scoring so many different types of goals. Best was brilliant in the air, he could shoot from long-range and he was also capable of dribbling the ball into the back of the net. Law was the best six-yard box poacher in the world, and was also fearless and lethal with his head. Herd and Charlton were among the hardest strikers of a ball in the country and could let fly from yards outside the penalty area. The array of attacking talent was usually enough to blow any opposition away. And Busby did not over-complicate matters. He simply gathered together the best footballers he could, then gave them licence to go out and perform. He knew it was pointless and self-defeating to put a natural genius like Best into a tactical straitjacket.

The Championship was plenty of consolation for two cup disappointments in 1964/65. In a long, hard season United also reached the FA Cup semi-final, only to lose a bruising replay against Leeds 1-0 at Forest's City Ground. And United faced an even tougher progress to the last four of the Fairs Cup. To get that far

United had already churned their way through four gruelling two-legged ties, against Djurgardens of Sweden, Borussia Dortmund, Everton and Strasbourg. Now in the last four they came up against the formidable Hungarian side, Ferencvaros. United won the first leg at home 3-2, but then lost 1-0 away and a replay was required – the away goals rule did not apply. After losing a toss United were obliged to head back to the Nep Stadion in Budapest on 16 June to end an unfeasibly long season with a 2-1 defeat.

That was all forgotten come the start of the new season, when Busby could set his sights on his heart's desire – the European Cup. The 1965/66 edition of Europe's top club prize featured many mighty sides. The list was headed by the holders, Internazionale, but there were plenty of other dangers lurking in the field, including Real Madrid, of course, Benfica, Werder Bremen, Ferencvaros, who had ditched United from the Fairs Cup, and the powerful Yugoslavian Champions Partizan Belgrade.

United were happy to have a gentle start in the preliminary round against the Finnish part-timers, HJK Helsinki. Despite one or two defensive alarms United won the away tie in the imposing Olympic Stadium 3-2. The home leg was a stroll for United and a hat-trick from outside-right John Connelly helped them to a 6-0 win.

United set off on a daunting trip behind the iron curtain to play East Germany's title-holders, Vorwaerts, in the first round proper. It was the kind of trek that was far more exhausting and nerve-wracking then than it would be now. United spent most of a day travelling to West Berlin via scheduled flights, then had to negotiate their passage into East Berlin. The United party was kept waiting for an interminable period of time at Checkpoint Charlie while suspicious East German policemen checked their credentials. Once they arrived on the other side of the Berlin Wall the players were holed up in a grim hotel with hardly anything to eat. The temperature never rose above freezing, but goals from Law and Connelly settled the tie 2-0. United were glad to fly out of the place and reflect on the glamour of being professional footballers playing in the European Cup. A Herd hat-trick in the home leg rounded off a comfortable 5-1 aggregate win.

In those pre-Champions League days the European Cup was more of a sprint than a marathon. The straight knockout format meant that the margin for error was tiny, but it also made for a more dynamic and exciting competition. The drama was not diluted by

endless qualifying rounds and neverending group stages. Now, after two sedate victories, United were in the quarter-finals where they came up against one of the giants of European football – Benfica – who had reached the final four times in the previous five years.

The first leg at Old Trafford was exciting enough, as United won 3-2 with goals from Law, Herd and a rarity from Foulkes. But the second leg produced one of the greatest United performances of all time and a show by Best which ranks as one of the finest individual displays in the club's history. United won the game 5-1, but it was the style of the victory rather than the margin that really stood out.

Best found the net first with a header from Tony Dunne's free-kick in the opening minutes, and moments later he scored his second. A mesmerising run saw him drift past a clutch of defenders, and he finished with élan. The way in which Best tore into the attack right from the kick-off astonished Benfica and put the tie beyond doubt: but it also flew in the face of Busby's tactical masterplan.

The manager had sent his team out with firm instructions to sit back for the first quarter of the game, to keep the crowd quiet, soak up the pressure and then to look for a goal on the break. Best kept the home support silent not by boring them to death, but by smashing their adored team to pieces. 'He must have had cotton wool in his ears during the team talk,' Busby ruefully observed. John Connelly notched the third and Benfica pulled a goal back, but United were irresistible. Crerand scored the fourth, then at the end Charlton showed that Best was not the only player in the team who could dribble, as he burst past a slew of defenders before scoring United's fifth. It was the first time in seven years of European competition that Benfica had been vanquished in the Stadium of Light.

But that glorious match proved to be the highwater mark of United's first season back in the European Cup. Fate decreed that United must return to Belgrade for a final reckoning in their European Cup comeback. In February 1958 they had been on their way home from an away leg against Red Star of Belgrade when they stopped to refuel at Munich. Now, as they closed in on the European Cup glory that had been denied the tragic Babes, they had to play Red Star's city rivals, Partizan.

Playing as if they carried the freight of history on their shoulders, a palsied United suffered a 2-0 defeat in the first leg in Yugoslavia. Law and Best had played despite being unfit, and Busby's team were

never in the game. They battled back bravely to win the home leg 1-0 with a goal from Stiles halfway through the second half, but Busby's quest for the European Cup was over one cruel step short of the final. Busby was inconsolable, imagining that his last chance of winning the one prize he craved had gone. 'We'll never win the European Cup now,' he sighed in the aftermath of the Partizan defeat. For a while the manager even contemplated retirement. But finally he resolved to make one last effort for the great trophy: he would strive to win another League Championship, then set off in pursuit of the European Cup one final time.

Opposite Denis Law in typically animated pose inside the penalty area during the home game against Finnish part-timers HJK Helsinki.
Above George Best – 'El Beatle' – looks the part after his demolition of Benfica in Lisbon, with John Fitzpatrick (left) and David Herd.

United's European adventures overshadowed their progress on the home front as they finished fourth in the league, 10 points behind the Champions Liverpool. In the FA Cup Busby's team reached the semi-finals for the fifth consecutive year, and for the fourth time they fell one match short of Wembley, beaten 1-0 by Everton at Burnden Park.

Old Trafford saw plenty of World Cup action in the summer of 1966, as United were handed the honour of hosting three Group Three games. In the first of them, on 13 July, a crowd of 29,886 saw two of the most talented teams in the competition in action. A gifted Portugal side featuring Eusebio beat Hungary, starring another great centre-forward Florian Albert, 3-1. Three days later Portugal were back at Old Trafford to play an ordinary Bulgaria team, and 25,436 spectators were delighted by a goal for Eusebio in Portugal's 3-0 victory. Then Hungary made sure that Brazil would be eliminated from the competition when they beat the hapless Bulgarians 3-1 at Old Trafford. United's involvement in the World Cup continued right through to the final, of course, as Bobby Charlton and Nobby Stiles played important roles in the 4-2 win over West Germany, which brought the Jules Rimet trophy to England for the very first time.

With no European campaign to distract them in 1966/67, United set off in single-minded pursuit of the title. Busby tweaked the line-up to deal with the loss of Connelly, who joined Blackburn early in the season, but disruption was minimal. John Aston was switched to the left wing and Best moved to the other flank, keeping the team's nominal 4-2-4 formation intact. Their results up to Christmas were nothing

special, but in the New Year United reeled off victory after victory and they hit the top of the table in the middle of March. They did not lose a match after Boxing Day and by time they faced West Ham at Upton Park on 6 May 1967 in the penultimate game of the season, United knew a victory would give them the title.

They made sure in fine style. Charlton, Crerand and Foulkes scored in the first 10 minutes and Best put away the fourth midway through the first half. Law added two more to make the final score 6-1, and Busy announced that the title triumph was his 'finest hour'. The *Sunday Times* reflected that United's victory was good for English football, at a time when sterile tactics threatened to stifle the game. 'This was a triumph for that ever-diminishing school of managers who believe soccer is primarily an entertainment,' the paper reported. 'Manchester United believe their customers should

Good news for Nobby Stiles on England duty at Lilleshall – a picture in the paper of Mrs Stiles with their new baby.

not only be granted the satisfaction of another victory, but should be delighted by the performance that earns it.'

Law finished as United's top scorer in the season with 23 goals, but all through the team players turned in terrific performances to bring the First Division trophy back to Old Trafford. Tony Dunne played impeccably at right-back and missed just two matches all season; Charlton and Best were both ever-presents; David Sadler emerged as a dependable centre-forward to replace Herd, who had broken his leg; Nobby Stiles and Pat Crerand anchored the team from midfield; and Alex Stepney, a youngster signed from Chelsea,

came through as United's first-choice keeper to replace the long-serving Harry Gregg, who was troubled by a shoulder injury.

Busby had set himself the task of winning one more Championship, which would give him one last shot at the European Cup. The first leg of the Double had been achieved: now it was time to reach out for the honour he coveted above all others.

Pat Crerand heads United's second in the 6-1 win at West Ham in May 1967 which clinched the Championship for United.

CHAPTER SIX

CHAMPIONS OF EUROPE

1967-69

IN 1968 BUSBY FINALLY ACHIEVED THE SUCCESS HE CRAVED
AS MANCHESTER UNITED WERE AT LAST CROWNED
CHAMPIONS OF EUROPE

B usby went into the 1967/68 season convinced that his squad was strong enough to make a serious challenge for the European Cup. The close-season came and went without any big signings, although he did make a couple of minor alterations to his line-up. Early in the season the young Scottish defender, Francis Burns, was given his chance at left-back, and an 18-year-old Mancunian, Brian Kidd, made his first-team debut up front.

It was quite a vote of confidence in the team considering the quality of the sides United could come up against. The field featured some impressive names from European football's aristocracy: Real Madrid were there as always, along with the Cup holders, Jock Stein's buccaneering

Celtic who had beaten the favourites Inter Milan in the final the previous May. The Dutch Champions, Ajax, were an emerging European power and the Soviet Union's title holders, Dynamo Kiev, were always dangerous. Italy's representatives were the mighty Juventus and the perennial European Cup challengers, Benfica, also lay in wait.

It came as a relief to United that their opponents in the first round would not come from that elite grouping – they were paired with the humble Hibernians of Malta instead. The first leg was at Old Trafford on 20 September 1967 and United kicked off their European campaign with an easy 4-0 win on a balmy late summer's evening. Sadler and Kidd both scored twice in an undemanding match, but the idyll would not last long. These were the first gentle steps on what was to prove a fraught progress to the final. The away leg in Malta finished 0-0 and United were safely through, which is more than could be said for Celtic. The reigning Champions were one of the real threats to United, but they were drawn to play Dynamo Kiev

Opposite Pat Crerand, Matt Busby
and George Best show off the European
Cup in front of massive crowds in
Manchester in May 1968.
Right Brian Kidd, the
Manchester boy who
emerged to play
a vital role in United's
victory over Benfica .

1967–69   in the first round. Stein's team fell by the wayside after losing the second leg at Parkhead. Already, United's progress to the final looked marginally less hazardous.

United drew Yugoslavian opposition once more in the second round, bringing back uncomfortable memories of the defeat to Partizan Belgrade two years earlier. This time United played Sarajevo, with the first leg away from home. Busby built his teams with attack in mind and they were hardly geared up to grinding out 0-0 draws. But they were no dilettantes either and were well capable of playing with a steely discipline when events dictated a tighter approach. It was not their natural game though. The match in Sarajevo was just the kind of testing tie that could have tripped United up, but they kept their concentration to come home with a valuable goalless draw. United's goalkeeper, Alex Stepney, said of their opponents, 'Let's put it this way, they were hard to beat and they weren't afraid to put their foot in.

'Busby was so angry about the way they played. The only time I ever saw him blow his top was at the final whistle in that game. He was normally a quiet, placid character, who did not let his emotions show, but he was furious that night.

'The goalless draw meant a lot to the players, because we realised now if we hadn't before that we were as good as any team playing any kind of game. We knew we could play football and we had some of the best players in Europe, and perhaps the world, in our team. But in Sarajevo we proved to ourselves that we could hold

our own against a dirty team like that. We felt we were equipped to beat anybody, anywhere, any way.

'It was typical of the determination that ran through that team. It was the first thing I noticed about the club, coming in as a Londoner, as soon as I joined from Chelsea the season before. There was a seriousness and a hardness about northern teams, especially United, I hadn't found in southern teams. United had great players, but they had that steely edge of determination with it.'

Opposite Alex Stepney, the Cockney who arrived from Chelsea to become one of the best goalkeepers ever to grace Old Trafford.
Above John Aston slides the ball into the net against Sarajevo to seal United's 2-1 win at Old Trafford, which sent them into the quarter-finals of the European Cup.

United closed the deal in the home leg against Sarajevo, but the result was far from straightforward. Late goals from Best and John Aston Jnr gave them a 2-1 win, but there were moments of worry for the 62,801 crowd, while the result remained in the balance and the Yugoslavs threatened on the break.

By now United were in the quarter-finals and another difficult visit to eastern Europe loomed. They were drawn to play Poland's top team, Gornik Zabrze, who had defeated Dynamo Kiev in the previous round, with the first leg at Old Trafford. By now United's supporters were revelling in the European Cup and anticipating a long-awaited appearance in the final. They were helped on their way with a 2-0 win in the first leg, with a goal from Kidd and an own goal. But the tie was not out of the Poles' reach as United still faced the away leg.

The return match was an ordeal for United in more ways than one. Firstly, the pitch at Gornik's Stadion Slaski was buried in snow, but the referee consulted the two managers and deemed the surface playable. Secondly, the Poles were roared on by a vast, noisy crowd numbering 105,000, who set up one of the most hostile environments United's players had ever experienced.

Stepney said, 'There was a lot of doubt about the game being played. The snow was six inches deep and the temperature was about 20 degrees below zero, and I understand the referee asked both managers if they wanted to play. Busby said he wanted to play, because travel was a lot more difficult in those days and he did not fancy going home then travelling all the way back again. He reasoned that it was the same for both teams, and, as we were leading 2-0, we had the advantage. So they packed the snow down, so it was roughly flat, and we played a game of football.'

Gornik were a strong side, and United needed all their reserves of character to come through the experience and survive to the semi-finals – a 1-0 defeat was sufficient to see them through. 'They were a dangerous team all right,' said Stepney. 'They had Lubanski, who was a terrific player and a real handful, and we had to play really well to hold them. They got their goal late and the last five minutes were fairly hectic, but for almost all of the game we had that two-goal cushion and we never panicked. But in the circumstances it was one of our best displays.'

The semi-final line-up could not have been stronger – as well as United, Real Madrid, Benfica and Juventus had all battled through to the last four. United drew Madrid. Stepney said, 'United had never beaten Real Madrid, but Busby turned that to our advantage. He said, "That has got to change, and it might as well be now."'

The first leg at Old Trafford was a nerve-ridden affair, very different to the open, flowing encounter when the sides had met in Manchester in 1957. That game 11 years earlier had ended in a 2-2 draw and spelt United's exit from the European Cup. This time United sneaked a 1-0 win thanks to Best's fabulous left-volley, but the lead looked too slight to defend at the Bernabeu. Madrid were odds-on favourites to make the final.

For the second leg there was never any prospect of United sitting back in massed defence to try to protect their lead. Busby judged it would have been fatal to invite Madrid to attack them, with 125,000 Spanish voices urging them on. He reasoned that attack was the best form of defence and the positive approach

provided the right conditions for one of the most exciting European matches of all time.

At half-time it seemed that Busby's bold approach had backfired. Madrid had torn into United from the kick-off and Busby's men could do no more than hang on. They held out for half an hour until Pirri levelled the aggregate score and a flurry of goals just before half-time went a long way to sinking United: the inimitable Gento gave Madrid the lead before Zoco carelessly conceded an own goal to give United new hope. But Amancio pounced just before the half-time whistle to give the Spaniards the advantage 3-2 over both games. Stepney said, 'To be honest we hadn't played well and they were worth their lead, but Matt's half-time team-talk was fantastic. He was a superb man-manager, and he told us, "You are great players, but you haven't played tonight. Go out now and play, and you will win."'

There was a whiff of complacency about Madrid as they came out for the second half a shadow of the team that had

---

Above *George Best scores the only goal of the game as United beat Real Madrid in the first leg of the European Cup semi-final at Old Trafford.*
Opposite *David Sadler levels the scores on aggregate in the second leg in a hostile Bernabeu stadium in Madrid.*

taken United apart in the first 45 minutes. For the first time all night United began to win possession and the Spaniards were content to let United have the ball. It was a big mistake and United were soon level on aggregate. Pat Crerand took a throw-in to Best and his early cross was met by the unmarked David Sadler, who put the ball into the net. United now had the momentum and Madrid found it impossible to reassert their grip on the game. For long periods they failed to get out of their own half as United pressed for the winner. It finally arrived as Best embarked on a tantalising run down the right wing before pulling the ball back into the area. Bill Foulkes, who had made a lung-bursting run from the back, met the ball and sent it crashing into the back of the net. The 3-3 draw in the Bernabeu sent United into the final.

'For Bill Foulkes to score that goal was fate,' said Stepney. 'He was a survivor of Munich, and for him to turn up at that moment to

score the goal, which took the club into the European Cup final at long last, seemed like it was meant to be.'

Benfica had beaten Juventus in the other semi-final, and they were the opponents United wanted. United had, after all, thrashed them two years earlier and now backed themselves to do it again. The choice of venues for the final also favoured United: as luck would have it they were to play the biggest game in the club's history at Wembley. It cut their travelling to a minimum and also ensured they had most of the support behind them. But those were all peripheral matters: what really counted was United's ability to match a team as good as Benfica. The Portuguese Champions were full of world-class performers and seasoned internationals: Eusebio, of course, was still one of the best strikers in the world and they had other fine, experienced players like Jose Augusto and Coluna. In contrast United suffered injury problems and were missing some

key names going in to the game. Most importantly, Denis Law did not play. The Scot needed an operation on his knee and the unlucky man had to watch the European Cup final from a hospital bed in Moss Side. United did, though, have one or two useful performers fit and well. It was the perfect stage for Best to display his outrageous talent and Bobby Charlton was at the top of his game as well. United also had the benefit of fearless youth: Brian Kidd won a place in the starting line-up on his 19th birthday.

When the day of the final dawned, United's players could have been forgiven for letting their minds dwell on the enormity of the challenge that lay in front of them. The memory of Munich might have been a crippling burden for the players, but they did a good job of distracting themselves in the hours leading up to kick-off: they used the odd combination of religion and racing to get through the day. In the morning Busby and his players – Catholic and non-Catholic alike – attended Mass together. Then in the afternoon a group were guests at the home of the racehorse owner, Robert Sangster, where they watched the derby on television. Plenty of the players liked a bet and several of them had backed Lester Piggott's mount, Sir Ivor, at fancy ante-post odds. Once the race was underway Piggott ratcheted up the tension by waiting until the last possible moment to hit the front – and the roars that went up from the delighted United players as Sir Ivor flashed across the line in first place were almost as loud as the ones that would echo around Wembley a few hours later. Even without the tidy sums the players picked up for backing the winner, the outcome of the race was valuable for United. The adrenalin of watching the race had obliterated all thoughts of the match, brought the players together and allowed them to relax. By the time they had travelled back to their hotel in high spirits and had a light tea it was time to go to the stadium: there was no time left for nerves to take their toll.

The players were lifted hugely by the enormous United support they saw in the streets around Wembley. It was a hot early evening, and there was a holiday mood among the shirt-sleeved crowd. They were in buoyant spirits, anticipating a United victory. Sometimes the fear of defeat can paralyse a team, but their supporters' optimism was infectious. Any hint that history would close in to stifle the heirs to the Busby Babes' legacy was banished in the carnival atmosphere. There would be no oppression of United's spirits as they won 4-1 after extra-time.

Football does not always provide the right ending, but on this night Busby had found his happy ever after. Ken Jones reported in the next day's *Daily Mirror*, 'When time has come to dim the

Eusebio relaxes during the build-up to the 1968 European Cup final, browsing in a record shop in Harlow.

emotion of this match, strong men will still remember it with tears in their eyes. Manchester United have the European Cup. Their illustrious manager Matt Busby has finally conquered his Everest... We shall remember it for what it meant to a great club, a great manager and to British football.'

It was a great party night too, as United celebrated becoming the first English side to win the European Cup in style. A banquet was laid on for them and their families at the Russell Hotel in London, and the Joe Loss Orchestra played in their honour. Touchingly, the club had invited the parents of the players who had died at Munich to join in with the festivities. The pioneers who lost their lives in the service of United were not forgotten on this night of nights.

What matter, then, amidst all the joy that United just failed to retain their League Championship? Despite their adventures in Europe United had kept in touch with the contest for the Championship all the way through the 1967/68 season. It was an especially tight competition with United, Manchester City, Liverpool and Leeds all in contention right up to the final few games. But at the last it was City who edged ahead, with United close behind them.

1967–69

The all-conquering United team arrive back in Albert Square, Manchester, with the European Cup – acclaimed by hundreds of thousands of ecstatic supporters.

1968 **EUROPEAN CUP FINAL**

MANCHESTER UNITED 4 Charlton 2, Best, Kidd **BENFICA 1** Graca (after extra time)
29 MAY 1968 at Wembley • Referee: Lo Belly (Italy) • Attendance: 100,000

MANCHESTER UNITED

Stepney
Brennan
Dunne
Crerand
Foulkes
Stiles
Best
Kidd
Charlton
Sadler
Aston

BENFICA

Henrique
Adolfo
Humberto
Jacinto
Cruz
Graca
Jose Augusto
Coluna
Eusebio
Torres
Simoes

The memory can play tricks. When you think about the 1968 European Cup final it is easy to imagine United sweeping Benfica aside carelessly, playing attacking football of the highest order right from the first whistle. Surely Best bewitched the opposition every time he received the ball and didn't Charlton cut them to rags with run after devastating run from midfield? But watch a recording of the whole match over again now and it is surprising how edgy the first hour was. For much of the time the play was fractured and there were plenty of niggly fouls to wreck the flow of the game. United perhaps shaded possession, but their performance was cagey rather than cavalier. The result was not a foregone conclusion. If history had turned out only slightly differently they could have lost the match.

Alex Stepney said, 'There was history between the sides. We had pulverised them over there a couple of years before and won 5-1, the night when George was christened 'El Beatle'. And the previous summer we'd gone on a world tour and played them again in Los Angeles. There was trouble in that match and there was still some ill-feeling lingering.

'The football was not good in the first half. It was OK, but not brilliant. That's the way football is sometimes. It was 90 degrees in the stadium, which made playing football hard work, and Benfica were a very good team, so it was never going to be easy. They had something like 10 internationals in their line-up, so they could all play.'

Many miserable United fans were marooned outside Wembley without tickets for the match.

During the break, after a hot-tempered first-half, Busby again repeated the basics to his players. In their eagerness to push forward they were losing possession recklessly and making life difficult for themselves. Busby counselled, 'It is a warm night. Get hold of the ball and knock it around among yourselves. This is no pitch to give the ball away.'

United came out more composed in the second half and the first goal came early. Charlton leapt to guide a firm header from Sadler's cross inside the goalkeeper's left-hand post. He did not score many headers, but on this occasion his powerful leap and decisive finish put older supporters in mind of the sainted Tommy Taylor. But still United could not kill the game. They created many chances, and Aston had one of his greatest games on the

left to torment Benfica on numerous occasions, but the ball would not go in.

In the last 10 minutes Graca equalised when Torres finally beat Foulkes in the air, the ball running free for the Portuguese forward to score, and for the last moments of normal time the momentum lurched Benfica's way. Eusebio hit the bar, then could and should have won the game in the last minute as he bore down on Alex Stepney's goal with no defender in attendance. He looked certain to score the winning goal. As he pulled back his foot to deliver the blow United's manager turned his head away, unable to bear the anguish of seeing his dreams crumble another time. But Stepney made one of the greatest saves ever by a United keeper to stop the shot. Perhaps for the first and only time in his life Eusebio had lost his composure at the critical juncture. A shot placed either side of Stepney would have spelt the end for United. But the great man went for power and his blasted shot was close enough for the unblinking Stepney to clutch.

Bobby Charlton's superbly placed glancing header flies into the back of the Benfica net for United's first goal.

The keeper said, 'That is the save people remember, but I guarantee if I had made it four minutes into the match rather than four minutes from the end nobody would talk about it.

'I had a feeling Eusebio would go for power so I made sure I stood up. When he hit it, it was close enough for me to grasp to my chest and it stuck. If he had placed it he would have scored.'

Moments later the final whistle blew to herald extra-time. United's players were fatigued, but Busby instilled belief with a few well-chosen words. He kept it simple and reminded them of the principles of the game. 'If you pass the ball to each other you will beat them,' he urged. Nobby Stiles had been through a similar ordeal in the same place two years earlier, when the World Cup final went into extra-time. He was just as determined now that a victory would not elude him. Having been a groundstaff boy

at Old Trafford at the time of Munich, and a United fan from the cradle, the club was in his blood. The boy from Collyhurst knew what the next 30 minutes meant. He said, 'We were knackered but so were they. I remember thinking that British clubs always find something extra in these situations. I just didn't know where it would come from.'

It came from Best, of course.

It was in the final half hour that United, sparked by Best's ebullience and athleticism, really made their mark on the history of European football. It is hard to think of a more compelling 30 minutes as United ran through their full repertoire of skills to capture the European Cup for Busby. Stepney said, 'George was an unbelievably fit lad. By the end he was the only player still moving off the ball

George Best turns the game in United's favour in extra-time, sending the keeper the wrong way before scoring the second.

and making runs. Everybody else was knackered but George was still buzzing. He was the difference between the teams.'

After a couple of minutes of extra-time Stepney booted a long clearance down the field, which was glanced on by the head of Kidd. Best, full of running, was first to the ball. He set off on a run past a collection of jaded defenders, rounded the goalkeeper and rolled the ball over the line to give United the lead. Kidd added the third a minute later and how fitting it was that Charlton should finish the match with his side's fourth goal, set up by the irrepressible Kidd. He had every excuse for the tears that burst forth when the referee's whistle blew for time.

Stepney recalled, 'Usually when the final whistle goes in a big match and you have won, players will celebrate with their nearest team-mate. It is a strange thing, but we didn't do that. Almost to a man we went over to Matt and congratulated him first. It was an unconscious act and certainly unrehearsed. It felt like the right thing to do at the time. This was his dream and at last he had achieved everything he had set out to do since he lost that great team in 1958.'

The tears flowed from Busby, too, when Charlton received the enormous Champions Trophy and showed it off to the multitudes from Manchester dancing on Wembley's terraces. 'The moment when Bobby took the Cup... it cleansed me,' Busby said. 'It eased the pain of the guilt of going into Europe. It was my justification.'

It was an emotional moment for Bobby Charlton as he lifted the magnificent Champions Trophy in front of the Wembley masses.

On the last afternoon City required a win away to Newcastle to take the First Division trophy for the first time in 31 years and they pulled it off with a 4-3 victory. At one stage United had been five points ahead of the field, but the added strains of chasing the European Cup cost them points in the latter part of the season.

As the 1968/69 season came around the question was, how could United match the euphoria they had experienced on that magical May evening at Wembley? The answer was that they couldn't. As soon as Busby had realised his ambition of winning the European Cup, much of the purpose seemed to fizzle out of the club. The heroes of Wembley were ageing together and new faces were needed to reinvigorate the club. Perhaps Busby, who had already built three champion sides, lacked the energy to create an unprecedented fourth great team. But whatever the reason, United lacked the vim of old as the season kicked off and by Christmas they had slid towards the bottom of the table. A miserable 3-0 defeat at Highbury on Boxing Day 1968 had an end-of-the-road feeling about it and in January 1969 the newly-knighted Sir Matt announced he would step down at the end of the season. A new job as general manager, working with a head coach, beckoned. Stepney said, 'I don't think he wanted to retire, but his health was poor. The injuries he received at Munich still affected him and but for his health I don't think he would have decided to move upstairs at all.'

Busby could have made a clean break, and left United with the good wishes of the club and the whole footballing world to enjoy a peaceful retirement. He had no worlds left to conquer, but he could not cut his ties with the club that had been his life for a quarter of a century. In any case, he could not conceive of an existence not tied up with the game that had been his life's love as well as his livelihood for more than four decades. If he was no longer fit enough to take day-to-day control of Manchester United, he would stay to help a new man run the team. It made perfect sense in theory, but it flew in the face of an age-old football axiom: when it comes to management, two heads are never better than one.

Opposite United on the attack in the derby game at Maine Road on 30 September 1967. Bobby Charlton scored twice in a 2-1 away win.
Right Nobby Stiles, sent off in the violent World Club Championship clash with Argentine side Estudiantes.

Busby's last few months in sole charge were fractious and results were poor. Perhaps the nadir was the World Club Championship match against the Argentine side, Estudiantes, which should have been an enjoyable exhibition displaying the best of South American and European football. But the first leg in Buenos Aires degenerated into a kicking contest. Charlton sustained a deep head wound and needed stitches. Stiles was singled out for ill-treatment, headbutted and then sent off for retaliating. All over the field United players were booted, scratched and spat on. The travesty of a sporting contest ended 1-0 to Estudiantes.

The home leg finished with the same scoreline, but a forgettable match stays in the memory solely for the sending off of Best. For the whole match he had been subject to a series of brutal assaults by the Argentines, until he lashed out at one of his assailants. He was ordered off the field, mercifully, before he was carried off in the

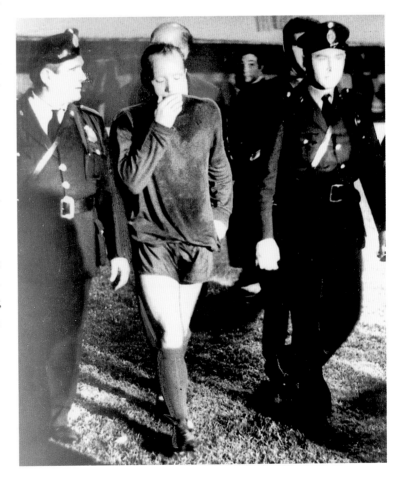

1967–69

St John Ambulance. Denis Law did not make it to the final whistle either. He was unable to continue after receiving a vicious kick in the leg. It was one of the most unpleasant encounters Old Trafford had ever seen.

United recovered slightly from their atrocious start to finish 11th in Division One and they reached the FA Cup quarter-finals before losing 1-0 at Everton. In the European Cup, too, United put in a brave showing, but they were not the irresistible side they had been the season before. After knocking out Waterford, Anderlecht

and Rapid Vienna, they were paired with AC Milan in the semi-finals and the Italians were too powerful for them. The tie was settled in the San Siro, where the Milanese won 2-0, and although Busby's men won the home leg 1-0 the visitors always looked favourites to hold their lead, even after Charlton had scored with 20 minutes left.

The comparison with the previous year's semi-final could not have been starker. Against Real Madrid, United were like a force of nature in the second leg. They dragged themselves into the final with an unbeatable mixture of footballing virtuosity and bottomless spirit. Against AC Milan, the same sense of belief was not apparent. They were also hamstrung by a series of bewildering refereeing decisions, which left many observers muttering about the honesty of what they had seen.

As the 1968/69 season wore on there was intense speculation about the identity of Busby's successor. The outgoing manager had the luxury afforded to few departing bosses – he was allowed the biggest say in choosing his successor. In the end Busby decided that continuity would best be served by appointing from within. He anointed the long-serving player and coach, 31-year-old Wilf McGuinness, as his heir. But McGuinness was not given the title of manager: he was head coach.

The Mancunian McGuinness was a popular figure around Old Trafford, revered for his long and loyal devotion to the United cause. He had signed for the club in 1953 and broke into the first team in October 1955, just in time to play his part in the rise of the Babes to footballing pre-eminence. He would have been with his pals on the plane at Munich, but for a knee injury which had detained him in Manchester.

When Jimmy Murphy and then Busby began the long task of rebuilding the team, McGuiness was an important figure. His dependability at half-back, and his example to the new players who were coming into the team, were valued highly by the

Left Wilf McGuinness attempted the impossible job of stepping into Matt Busby's place as United manager.

Opposite Bobby and Jack Charlton tussle for possession as United take on Leeds at Elland Road on 11 January 1969. Bobby scored, but Leeds won 2-1.

management team. McGuinness's playing career was cut short by a broken leg suffered while playing for the reserves against Stoke City in 1960. But United regarded McGuinness too highly to end his association with the club. He joined the coaching staff and in 1961 he was appointed reserve and youth team trainer. His ability to get the best out of players had impressed Busby and marked him out for future preferment.

McGuinness, though, did not have the authority to take on the rebuilding work that the United team needed. It was obvious the season after the European Cup had been won that change

was required. The team was growing old, but the club's dual leadership led to inertia at the top. Busby did not have the energy to embark on another overhaul; McGuinness did not have the stature. One man who saw the writing on the wall was George Best, a senior figure in the dressing room, even though he was still only in his early 20s. He pleaded with Busby to make him captain and revamp the team around him. But the old man who had gambled so heavily on youth a decade and a half before refused to do so now. The old guard stayed, and United limped towards a new decade with weak leadership and a fading team. Memories of May 1968 were already dwindling fast.

THE HEROES OF 1968

Statistics are for appearances and goals in all competitions while playing for United.

① ALEX STEPNEY 1966–78
GOALKEEPER • 539 Apps • 2 Gls

The Londoner became the world's most expensive keeper in September 1966 when Busby bought him from Chelsea for £55,000. Stepney had made his name at Millwall before moving to Stamford Bridge, but after just one appearance at his new club United swooped. It was an inspired purchase, as Stepney gave a dozen years' reliable service to the club.

He arrived at Old Trafford in time for the drive to the Championship in 1966/67 and Busby was in no doubt that Stepney's contribution was essential in the title-winning effort. 'The most important factor behind our Championship success was signing Alex Stepney,' he said. A year later Stepney had a sensational game in the European Cup final, denying Eusebio with a wondrous save from point-blank range in the dying seconds of the match to force extra time.

② TONY DUNNE 1960–73

RIGHT-BACK • 534 (1) Apps • 2 Gls

The Dubliner saved one of his best games out of the 535 he played for United for the European Cup final. He played his part to deny Benfica's multi-talented strikeforce more than a fleeting chance at goal.

His admirers insist that Tony Dunne ranks alongside Roger Byrne as one of the best full-backs ever to play for United. He was not a flamboyant player, but was skilled at breaking up attacks unfussily and using the ball constructively to set his side on the attack. Ever modest, Dunne said, 'I was just one of the players who got the ball for better players to play with.'

③ SHAY BRENAN 1957–70

LEFT-BACK • 358 (1) Apps • 6 Gls

Brennan was not a marquee name at United, but for a dozen years he did a valuable job as a solid if unspectacular defender. He joined United in the pre-Munich era and became a regular at either right-back or left-back through the difficult late 1950s and early 1960s era, and on into the mid-1960s renaissance, ending in the European Cup triumph of 1968.

Brennan was also highly regarded in the dressing room for his easy-going nature and self-deprecating charm. In a team rich with extravagant talents and world-famous names, Brennan was an important touchstone of humility. The Mancunian, who played for Ireland thanks to his parentage, never wanted any more than to pull on a red shirt and play for United. He said, 'The greatest time for me was always just turning up to train with the rest and to know I was a Manchester United footballer.'

④ PAT CRERAND 1962–71

RIGHT-HALF • 397 Apps • 15 Gls

The Glaswegian's performance against Benfica in 1968 was a typical Crerand effort: he never missed with a pass, never gave his midfield opponents a second's rest and never stopped trying his heart out for the team. His goals record was moderate and when Crerand hit top speed he still only reached sluggish, but he was the rock on which United's midfield was built. He formed a one-man barricade between the opposition and Alex Stepney's goal.

Crerand signed from Celtic in time to play in the 1963 FA Cup final victory over Leicester and he quit as a player in May 1971. In his post-playing days he managed Northampton Town and was also assistant manager under Tommy Docherty at Old Trafford, his spiritual home.

➎ BILL FOULKES 1952–70

CENTRE-HALF • 685 (3) Apps • 9 Gls

There were two survivors of Munich in the United team which beat Benfica: Charlton and the 36-year-old Foulkes. His accomplished team-mate recovered from the crash to become an England star and a world-famous footballer, but Foulkes dedicated the rest of his career to United – as low-key as you could get for a man with four Championship medals and a European Cup winner's medal to his credit.

In 18 years at the club, Foulkes, who came from St Helen's in the heart of the Lancashire coalfield, amassed over 680 appearances in all competitions. He played just once for England, in 1954, when he was still a part-time footballer. For the first few years of his United career Foulkes also worked shifts down the pit. He was revered at Old Trafford for his steadfast service in the middle of the defence, where he played most of his football, solid as a pit-prop.

Foulkes rarely ventured into the opposition half and his goals record is negligible – but one strike just happened to be among the most important in the club's history: the effort that beat Real Madrid in the 1968 European Cup semi-final.

After quitting as a player in 1970 he coached at United before managing teams in Norway, the USA and Japan.

➏ NOBBY STILES 1960–71

LEFT-HALF • 395 Apps • 19 Gls

Eusebio must have been sick of the sight of Norbert Stiles. In the 1966 World Cup semi-final at Wembley Stiles had shadowed Portugal's best player all over the park, nullifying his threat and putting Alf Ramsey's game plan into effect with perfection. Two years later they were together again at the same venue and Stiles was assiduous in his attentions once again. When it came to man-marking jobs Stiles was peerless.

Stiles was not famous for his silky skills, but he was nevertheless a vital component of the European Cup-winning side. He fought and ferreted his way through a mountain of unglamorous defensive duties so the more eye-catching players could do their work. Stiles certainly had the opposition rattled. The Benfica coach, Otto Gloria, complained, 'Stiles is a dangerous marker, tenacious and sometimes brutal. He takes recourse to anything to contain his man. Very badly intentioned. A bad sportsman.'

Stiles, who once took it as an enormous compliment when an opposition supporter hit him on the head with a bottle, could not have been happier with the tribute.

➐ GEORGE BEST 1963–74

FORWARD • 470 Apps • 179 Gls

(See also profile on pages 102–03)

The Irish genius saved one of the greatest performances of his career for a night when it was needed more than ever before – the 1968 European Cup final. United had only just been able to force the game into extra-time and Busby's leg-weary team must have wondered how they were going to dredge up a winner. But Best, a wonderfully fit athlete as well as a dazzling ball player, drew on all his reserves of energy and skill to provide the spark that gave United victory. It might have been the highwater mark of Best's achievement in the game – but what a performance to remember.

⑧ BRIAN KIDD **1967–74**
FORWARD • 257 (9) Apps • 70 Gls

Kidd burst into the United first team as a teenage tyro in the 1967/68 Charity Shield, and his youthful exuberance and eye for goals won him a regular place in the team. The local boy played 38 league games and scored 15 goals that season, but the strike for which he will be remembered most was the one he conjured up on his 19th birthday against Benfica.

His playing days at Old Trafford petered out disappointingly and he moved to Arsenal in 1974. But he returned to the club he supported as a boy and became a hugely influential youth coach, then assistant to Alex Ferguson, before leaving to manage Blackburn.

⑨ BOBBY CHARLTON **1956–73**
MIDFIELD • 757 (2) Apps • 249 Gls
(See also profile on pages 92-93)

Charlton was well known for scoring with fulminating shots from the edge of the area or even further out. He was less well known for his ability in the air. But he showed his heading ability to good effect against Benfica, when his precisely steered effort put United ahead against the Portuguese Champions. It was entirely fitting that Charlton should set United on the road to victory and appropriate that he should accept the trophy at the end of the night. No player had done more than Charlton to make sure that Busby's quest to win the greatest club prize of them all was realised.

⑩ DAVID SADLER **1963–74**
FORWARD • 328 (7) Apps • 27 Gls

Sadler was a versatile player who could operate as a commanding centre-half, pacy midfielder or handy striker. He had his first spell in the first-team as a replacement centre-forward for David Herd in 1963/64, but when he made his England debut in a 2-0 win against Northern Ireland at Wembley in 1967 he played as a centre-half. Against Benfica he was back in a forward role and his finely-flighted cross set up Charlton for United's first goal.

Sadler, originally from Kent, also won a Championship winner's medal in 1967. He left the club to join Preston for £25,000 in November 1973.

⑪ JOHN ASTON (Jnr) **1964–72**
FORWARD • 166 (21) Apps • 27 Gls

Aston played one of his best games for United against Benfica, probing at pace down the left flank and doubling back in defence when the game dictated. The clever winger who played so much of his career in the shadow of more dazzling team-mates, never gave the Portuguese a respite. The Benfica coach, Otto Gloria, said, 'I laid plans for coping with Best and Charlton and the other stars, but nobody warned me about this boy Aston.'

The Mancunian was never quite the same force for United after breaking a leg playing against Manchester City in August 1968 and he moved to Luton for £30,000 in 1972.

John Aston (right) in the thick of the fray during one of his best games for United – the 1968 European Cup final.

CHAPTER SEVEN

DECLINE AND FALL

1969-77

UNITED ENTERED THE 1970s IN SOME DISARRAY AS THE CLUB
WRESTLED WITH THE SUCCESSOR TO MATT BUSBY

Newly appointed 'manager' Wilf McGuinness lacked Busby's grip and gravitas, and United suffered a dreadful start to the 1969/70 season, drawing three and losing three of the first six games. McGuinness reacted, belatedly dropping some of the old guard briefly – Charlton, Dunne, Foulkes and Law were all rested during a turbulent late summer. Foulkes never played again and Brennan left the club the following August. But although the manager had shown the gumption to cut players from the side, he was less sure how to replace them.

He splashed out a club record £62,500 to bring in Scottish centre-half Ian Ure from Arsenal, but other transfer targets were missed. McGuinness was linked with big names, including Colin Todd, Malcolm Macdonald, Mick Mills and Ron Davies, but nothing came of the speculation. Supporters suspected that McGuinness was not given the full financial backing of the board.

The team's fortunes revived sufficiently to ensure an eighth-place finish and United also gave their fans cause to hope in the cup competitions. They reached the semi-finals of the League Cup, where they lost to City over two legs, and also enjoyed an exciting

run in the FA Cup, which featured some of the most memorable goals and individual performances in United's long association with the competition.

United won 1-0 at Ipswich in the third round with an own goal, which set up a fourth-round clash at home to City. Best missed the match through suspension (the punishment for a variety of disciplinary crimes) and Law was absent too through injury, but Brian Kidd stepped up to take responsibility for United's attacking effort. United went 1-0 up in the first half, when Charlton drew a foul from Glyn Pardoe, and Willie Morgan thrashed home the penalty. Kidd added United's second after the break, then topped a

---

Opposite Tommy Docherty consoles his desolate players after the shock 1-0 defeat to Southampton in the 1976 FA Cup final.
Right Paul Edwards scores against City in the 1969/70 League Cup semi-final first leg at Maine Road, which United lost 2-1.

brilliant performance with a beautifully judged lob over Ken Mulhearn in the City goal.

The fifth round produced one of the most remarkable displays ever seen in the Cup, as Best dismantled Northampton Town, a mid-table Fourth Division side, with a battery of goals. In the homely environs of the Cobblers' County Ground, which doubled up as Northants' cricket ground, United won 8-2 and Best scored six of them, as mixed a collection of goals as you will ever see. The Irishman appeared set on serving up a masterclass of the striker's art and, although the opposition weren't the strongest United had faced, Best's tour de force that day ranks high in many people's favourite memories of the genius's career.

United faced more stubborn opponents in the quarter-finals in Middlesbrough from Division Two. The Italian-Mancunian midfielder Carlo Sartori scored for United in a tight 1-1 draw at Ayresome Park, and Morgan and Charlton wrapped up a 2-1 replay win at Old Trafford.

Back in those pre-penalty shoot-out days, drawn Cup ties could be replayed so many times that the matches developed into little sagas. Clubs might be locked in bitter combat three or four times in the space of a couple of weeks before an exhausted winner emerged from the ordeal – and just such a mini-series unfolded as United went toe-to-toe with Leeds for a place in the final. Don Revie's Leeds were the reigning League Champions and the passing of time had done little to soften the Don's pragmatic view of how football should be played. His team were still unlovely and unloved outside the immediate vicinity of Elland Road. They were warm favourites to dispose of United in the semi-final at Hillsborough, but a grim encounter ended 0-0. It was the same story in the replay at Villa Park nine days later, when two hours of gruelling football produced plenty of fouls, but no goals. Finally, Leeds conjured up a goal three days later at Burnden Park. United had done most of the attacking

in the previous two semi-final slugfests, but it was Leeds who broke the stalemate. Billy Bremner cracked in a shot after 10 minutes and United lacked the firepower to beat Leeds's dogged defence. By now both teams were relieved to lay the semi-final to rest: they were heartily sick of the sight of each other.

McGuinness was finally given the title of manager in August 1970, but the change did not help the team. It was impossible for the youthful McGuinness to match Busby's eminence. Some of the players viewed McGuinness as an equal, if that, and he struggled to command respect.

United's league form sank back into mediocrity from the start of the 1970/71 season and McGuinness was relieved of his job in December. He had done his best in difficult circumstances and his demotion back to reserve team coach was a cruel blow for a man who had always strived to do his best for the club in any capacity. It was too much for McGuinness, a loyal servant and supporter of United, to endure and he quit the club in February 1971. He said, 'For 18 years I have been devoted to United. Now I must find a future away from Old Trafford.' That future took him first to Greece, with coaching spells at Aris Salonika and Panaraiki Patras, before he came back to England to manage York City. He also held staff jobs at Hull and Bury.

Busby resumed full control of the team and results picked up enough to guarantee another safe mid-table finish, but there was little sign of progress on the field. United looked a world away from challenging for major honours.

Opposite George Best powers home one of his six goals against Northampton in the FA Cup tie at the County Ground.
Right The United line-up before a Watney Cup tie against Derby County in the summer of 1970. The fading team struggled at the start of the season and Wilf McGuinness left the manager's job in December.

1969–77   More veterans shuffled towards the exit, with Stiles heading for Middlesbrough and Crerand joining the back-room staff in the summer of 1971, but there was no prospect of a fresh generation coming in to replace them. The once-fabled youth programme was no longer producing hungry and talented teenagers desperate to play in the first team. United made no significant signings, either. An air of lassitude hung about Old Trafford.

The shining jewel in the side had long been George Best. With 18 goals he finished as the club's top scorer in 1970/71, just as he had in the three seasons previously, but his rackety lifestyle was beginning to catch up with him. During that season he had more run-ins with Busby and in January he was suspended for two weeks for missing training repeatedly. He was also fined £250 by the FA for turning up over an hour late at another disciplinary hearing. Best, finally, was growing weary of carrying the team largely on his own shoulders and he was less and less inclined to hide his dissatisfaction. A fiercely proud man, he grew increasingly frustrated to see his team, which had once been the greatest in Europe, drift into mediocrity.

But Busby had more than Best to worry about. Once again he faced the task of finding and appointing his own successor and, not for the first time he took upon himself the task of shaping the club's future. Top of his list for the United manager's job was Jock Stein, who as Celtic boss had beaten him to the European Cup by a year. Busby used the ex-Celt, Pat Crerand, as his emissary to Stein, and for a while it appeared that United had their man. Stein met Busby, and the pair agreed a deal – but Stein had second thoughts and pulled out. Busby was bitter at what he perceived as a betrayal. He muttered that Stein had expressed interest in the United job merely as a bargaining tool to jack up his salary with Celtic. But that does not ring true with Stein's usual, highly principled way of conducting business. He was no less a stickler than Busby himself when it came to acting with honour and bringing dignity to the often-murky trade of football club management. It is more likely that Stein had a presentiment that he would never truly be manager of Manchester United while Busby remained at the club in an official capacity.

Chelsea's thoughtful manager, Dave Sexton, was also highly regarded by Busby. But Sexton appeared unwilling to move north. Busby finally found somebody prepared to take on the most difficult job in football. A little further down Busby's list of names was the former West Ham wing-half Frank O'Farrell who had impressed many observers by winning the Second Division Championship with Leicester City. He knew how gigantic his task was at Old Trafford, but he had the ambition to take it on and he accepted the offer.

O'Farrell arrived at Old Trafford well aware of how much he had to do. The job of rebuilding the team would take years rather than weeks or months, the dressing room was populated by disgruntled old pros who had seen and done it all, and in addition there were the increasingly zany antics of Best to cope with. In short, United were doing a good impression of a football club that refused to be managed and, to make matters worse for O'Farrell, the board showed no sign that they were prepared to be patient in allowing the new man time to turn the ship around.

George Best and Matt Busby in earnest conference at another
FA disciplinary hearing, January 1971.

Despite all that, O'Farrell began the job as he ended it – fired with enthusiasm – as the old football joke goes. On his first day in charge he said, 'Manchester United has rubbed off on me. I feel its glamour already. I feel, too, a great need to help the club back to its famed and feared reputation.' And for a while it looked like the team might live up to his brave words. United flew out of the blocks for the start of the 1971/72 season and O'Farrell seemed to have worked a miracle as his rejuvenated team raced to the top of the table. By the New Year they were five points clear of the field and odds-on to pick up their first Championship since 1967. Alas, the honeymoon ended in bitter recrimination as United went 11 matches without a win going into the spring, at one point enduring a spree of seven straight defeats.

At least O'Farrell reacted decisively, lashing out £200,000 to bring in the Forest winger Ian Storey-Moore and £125,000 on centre-half Martin Buchan from Aberdeen. The new signings helped to halt the slide as United finished the 1971/72 season in eighth place, for the third year on the trot. United's league form might have been inconsistent, but at least it was consistently inconsistent.

Below *New United manager Frank O'Farrell (left) with his head coach, Malcolm Musgrove.*

Overleaf *Alan Gowling goes for goal during a 0-0 draw with Everton at Old Trafford in March 1972. The result ended a run of seven straight defeats.*

The end of the season also saw Best's increasingly chaotic life unravelling further. At the start of the campaign Best had been in top form and at one point he reeled off 11 goals in a 10-match spell to drive United to the top of the table. But in the New Year he vanished for days and United's title hopes disappeared with him. Astonishingly, despite missing training on numerous occasions and going AWOL between games, Best still managed to play in 40 of United's 42 league matches and finished the club's top scorer yet again with 18 goals. In May 1972 he failed to turn up to play for Northern Ireland against Scotland and he admitted publicly that his drinking was out of control. He escaped to Spain, insisting that he had retired from professional football, aged 26. But his retirement lasted just a fortnight and he returned to Manchester in time for the start of the 1972/73 season. The messy end to his career, though, was in sight.

By now United had degenerated into something like anarchy, with the dressing room riven by discontent, Best in open revolt and results in freefall. United opened the new season abysmally, failing to win any of their first nine games and they were knocked out of the League Cup by Bristol Rovers. It was clear that O'Farrell, a mild-mannered man from Cork, was unable to keep a lid on the madness and he was relieved of his duties in December 1972, thanked for his services and paid off with a golden goodbye of about £50,000. He left Old Trafford feeling bitter about his treatment, frustrated that he had never been able to exert any authority while Busby was still around. Many of the players still called him Boss and O'Farrell felt he had been let down by him. 'I had never admired a man as much as Matt Busby,' O'Farrell said. 'But when I left Old Trafford I had never been let down by any man as much as by him.' Many of the players, who had not warmed to O'Farrell's self-effacing, low-key character, were glad to see O'Farrell leave. Denis Law said, 'He came a stranger and he left a stranger.'

His replacement was an altogether more abrasive, self-confident character – Tommy Docherty – who had learned his man-management skills on the streets of Glasgow's tough Gorbals district. As a player Docherty had been a combative wing-half for Celtic, Preston, Arsenal and Chelsea, and he took his uncompromising approach to the game into management. He moulded a collection of promising youngsters and veteran players into a formidable team at Chelsea in the 1960s, and also had spells in charge at Rotherham, QPR, Villa, Porto and the Scotland national side, before United hired him to banish the club's deep-seated malaise. He wasted no time in making his mark on the club. 'It was a disaster area,' Docherty said. 'Frank O'Farrell had come in and done a decent job in many ways, but there was still so much to do.

'The truth is the team which won the European Cup had gone on too long and it should have been broken up much sooner. There were lots of big names there long past their sell-by date and the rot had set in. A lot of it was down to Sir Matt staying on too long. He went upstairs, but he should really have left the club.

George Best tries a spot of fishing in Spain during his two-week retirement from football in the summer of 1972.

When Wilf McGuinness took over as coach Sir Matt was always there in the background and he never had a chance. It was the same story for Frank.

'Even by the time I arrived Sir Matt was still there, still with a big influence on the players. If I fell out with a player over something, and they felt they were getting no satisfaction, they were going to see Sir Matt. They called him "the old boss". That kind of thing isn't good for the stability of a club or for discipline. You can only have one boss.

'But the biggest disaster for United was letting Jimmy Murphy go. He never received half the credit he deserved for rebuilding the team after Munich and everything else he did for the club, and his knowledge was irreplaceable. He was a wonderful man.'

Above Tommy Docherty arrives at Ringway Airport, Manchester, prior to taking over as United's manager, with chairman Louis Edwards (centre).
Above right Bobby Charlton bids farewell to the supporters after his last match for United, a 1-0 defeat at Chelsea, 28 April 1973.

Docherty made it clear that a number of big names did not figure in his plans and a whole collection of them were destined to tumble out of the door in the summer of 1973. Among them was Charlton, who left at the end of the 1972/73 season to manage Preston. Law also went, moving across Manchester to play for City. The long-serving full-back Dunne signed for Bolton. Docherty's surgery enabled the team to avoid relegation in 1972/73 and United ended up in 18th place. But it was a wretched season all round, as the team could muster only 44 league goals. A distracted Best played less than half the season, scoring only four goals, and the side was toothless in attack without him. Charlton signed off his United career as top scorer, with just six goals. It felt like the nadir of United's fortunes, but there was one further indignity in store before the club could begin the long road back to success.

The new manager was not handed fortunes to spend, but he was busy enough with the funds which were granted to him as he strived to put a team together capable of climbing the First Division. During the 1973/74 season a slew of new names took their places in the side. Alex Forsyth joined from Partick Thistle

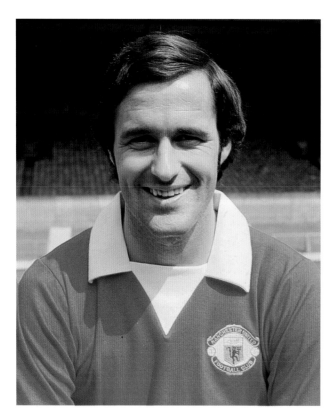

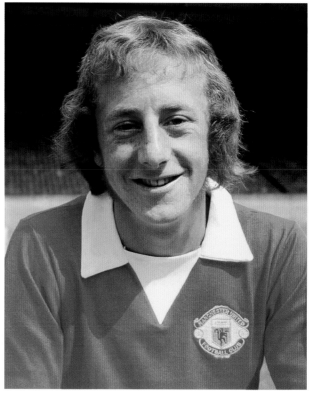

for £100,000, George Graham came from Arsenal for £120,000, Lou Macari arrived from Celtic for £200,000, Gerry Daly and Mick Martin cost a total of £45,000 from Bohemians, Stewart Houston signed from Brentford for £55,000, and Brian Greenhoff broke through from the youth team. Some famous names went the other way. Kidd was sold to Arsenal, Storey-Moore quit on medical grounds and David Sadler went to Preston. Best left for good after one last, abortive comeback. He played his last game for the club on New Year's Day 1974, in a 3-0 defeat at QPR. By then Best was desperate to leave and Docherty was desperate for him to go.

Amid all the activity Docherty was full of optimism that the corner had been turned. 'We thought we'd cracked it,' he said. 'We had some good new players coming in and I had revamped the youth policy, which had been allowed to fall into decline. I believed

we were heading in the right direction. But for a number of reasons we had to wait a while longer before we could say the club was on the way back. We couldn't get all the players we wanted into the club because there wasn't a lot of money about, and one or two signings didn't come off. The club was still recovering from years of neglect.'

United's seemingly inexorable decline had not quite bottomed out and in 1973/74 the club endured its worst season since before the war. Relegation is an ugly word, but United supporters had to come to terms with it now – for the first time in nearly four decades they plunged into the Second Division. All season long they struggled to score goals and at the turn of the year Alex Stepney was their joint top scorer with two penalties.

Weeks and months went by without United winning a game. From November all the way through to March they picked up just one victory, but a rally in the spring gave them a chance of survival. United's slim hope of staying up was still alive with two matches of the season to play, but they needed to win them both. The penultimate game was at Old Trafford on 27 April 1974, against

---

Above *George Graham joined United from Arsenal for £120,000.*

Above right *Mick Martin signed from Irish club Bohemians.*

City, and the death blow to their First Division existence was dealt by a ghost from the golden days of the 1960s – Denis Law.

The score was 0-0 and time was running out for United to find the winner, which might have granted them a stay of execution. But Law, lurking in the six-yard box with his back to goal, reacted instinctively when Francis Lee slipped a pass to him. He back-heeled the ball into the back of the net. It was the only goal he wished he'd never scored and he was distraught over the knowledge that he had turned out to be an instrument in his old club's demise. There was no celebration, just a sad walk off the field, head bowed. Eleven years earlier he had played in a United team that beat City to send them down. Now he had done the opposite and was full of remorse. 'I have seldom felt so depressed in my life as I did that weekend,' he said.

The referee was obliged to blow for time early because of a pitch invasion and United were doomed to the drop, sandwiched between Southampton and Norwich City. How United could have used a goalscorer of Law's calibre in that woeful season. Their defence was strong enough, but the strikers could not put the ball in the net. The new boy, Macari, ended the season as top scorer – but he had mustered only five goals.

United did not intend to slum it in the Second Division for long. They hit the top of the table before the end of August and stayed in front all the way until May, when the Second Division Championship was secured. Docherty used the season's sabbatical from the top division to build a hugely entertaining side that placed the accent on attack at all times. His key signing was Stuart Pearson,

Denis Law is surrounded by fans after the goal he wished he'd never scored at Old Trafford in April 1974.

Stuart Pearson gets off a shot against Fulham in October 1974, with Bobby Moore in attendance, during United's barnstorming Second Division campaign.

a striker from Hull City who cost £200,000. He lacked inches for a front man, but made up for that with a knack for getting in the right places to put the ball in the back of the net. He was exactly what the Doc had ordered: an unspectacular but steady taker of chances, and he top scored in his first season with 17 goals.

But far more important than that, for the first time in years United had a settled side. Week after week the team remained largely the same. In midfield Gerry Daly played 36 games and Sammy McIlroy only missed one; full-backs Stewart Houston and Alex Houston missed just five games between them; goalkeeper

Stepney played 40; Brian Greenhoff and Martin Buchan missed only four games between them in the centre of defence. Docherty said: 'Supporters still come up to me now and say, 'Thanks, you are the man who took us back into the First Division." I have to remind them that I was the man who had taken them down in the first place.'

Of course, it wasn't all joy for United. The promotion season also witnessed a sickening level of hooliganism all over the country, and thugs who associated themselves with United had the worst reputation of the lot. In December 1974 the FA and Football League held an emergency meeting to discuss the violence that followed United on their travels around the country's Second Division stadiums. They acted by making all United's away games all-ticket. In time the wave of football-related violence receded and, although the problem has never disappeared completely, mindless thuggery has not reached the same levels again at United games – largely thanks to supporters policing themselves. The majority had pride in the club's good name, and in their own reputation for being passionate and discerning football fans rather than knuckle-dragging street fighters.

United re-entered the First Division invigorated by their season's sojourn in the Second Division. It had done them no harm to take a break from the top-flight to visit venues that hadn't been on their schedule for many years, such as Orient, Oxford, Hull and York. Now they were back in the big time, and they began the 1975/76 season at a dash. Docherty's team won five and drew one of their first six matches to hit the top of the table, and Docherty had not diluted his attacking principles to get there. The highlight of the early season purple patch was a 5-1 demolition of Sheffield United at Old Trafford, in which the rampaging Pearson scored twice. All season long United stayed in touch with fellow title-chasers QPR

and Liverpool, but two defeats in their last three matches allowed their rivals to slip away. United eventually finished third just four points behind Champions Liverpool. Despite the disappointment of falling just short of the top prize, United could be satisfied that they had roared back into contention as one of England's top teams and they had done it playing a brand of football which thrilled their fans. Much of that was down to Docherty's tactic of using two old-fashioned wingers in Steve Coppell and Gordon Hill.

1969–77

Below left *Violence followed United as they toured the Second Division grounds of England in 1974/75. Fans were regularly arrested.*
Below *Steve Coppell set United's supporters alight with his dazzling wing play following his move from Tranmere Rovers in early 1975.*

Docherty said, 'People still say to me that that was the most entertaining United team they have ever seen. Later sides might have been more successful and won more trophies, but for sheer entertainment that team was top.

'Much of that was down to the wingers. I was brought up with teams who had great wingers and I always wanted them in my team. Hill and Coppell were terrific. They would raid down the touchline, hit the byline and get in crosses, and they were exciting to watch. There's no finer sight in football than to see a winger beat a defender for speed and skill, then put in a perfect cross for the strikers. I always had two weaknesses in life, wingers and women, although not necessarily in that order.

The flamboyant flank player Gordon Hill swings over another cross from the wing, against Coventry City in 1976.

'I was just as enthusiastic as the supporters. I loved watching that team play and I would be excited on a Friday night, just waiting for the next day's match to see what the boys would do. You always felt that we could win 5-0 or lose 5-0. The side was brilliant at times and unpredictable.'

United also treated their supporters to a swashbuckling run in the FA Cup. It began easily enough with home wins against Oxford United, a poor Second Division side, and Peterborough United from Division Three. The fifth round presented them with a much stiffer hurdle – United had to travel to Leicester City, who were thriving at the top end of the First Division. But goals from Gerry Daly and Lou Macari in a 2-1 win fired United into the quarter-finals for the first time in four seasons. United's sixth round opponents were Wolves, who at the time were fighting (unsuccessfully as it turned out) to stay in the First Division. United could only draw 1-1 at home, but goals from Brian Greenhoff,

Sammy McIlroy and Pearson earned them an exciting 3-2 win at Molineux and a place in the semi-finals.

Docherty's team went into the hat for the semi-final draw along with dangerous Derby County, and two lower league sides who were seen as makeweights in the competition – Southampton from Division Two and Crystal Palace from the Third Division. When United were drawn to play Derby, Docherty announced tactlessly that the real final would take place between his side and County at Hillsborough, implying that the semi-final between Palace and Saints was irrelevant, apart from deciding who would receive the runners-up medals. The words attributed to Docherty could not have been more incendiary: 'This is the first time that the FA Cup final will be played at Hillsborough. The other semi-final is a bit of a joke really.'

United reached Wembley by sweeping Derby aside with a 2-0 win, thanks to a sublime performance on the wing from Hill, which included two goals. Southampton won the other semi-final and the Saints manager, Lawrie McMenemy, shrewdly dusted down Docherty's quotes to motivate his men for the final. United were one of the shortest-priced favourites the FA Cup final had ever seen. They were flying high in the First Division and had reached Wembley on the back of some scintillating performances. Southampton, by contrast, were a middling Second Division side. Their line-up featured plenty of old pros – including the likes of Mick Channon, Peter Osgood, captain Peter Rodrigues and one-time United man Jim McCalliog, but surely they could not live with the pace and invention of Docherty's vibrant young side? In some quarters the match was cruelly dubbed Doc's Army v Dads' Army.

Yet on the day of the match the experienced old lags played at the top of their form while some of United's youngsters froze. It was McCalliog who picked out a perfect pass for Bobby Stokes to score the only goal of the game, in the closing minutes, to take the trophy to the Dell. Ten days earlier United still had a chance of winning their first-ever League-Cup Double. Now they had ended the season empty-handed.

Docherty said, 'Southampton were 7/1 outsiders and I would have put my mortgage on us winning that match, but it wasn't to be. It felt horrible to lose the final, but if I had to lose I'm glad it was against nice people. Southampton were a nice club and I was happy for them, although obviously I'd rather we had beaten them.'

The 1976/77 season began with a rare treat – United's re-entry into European competition for the first time since they had defended their European Cup eight years earlier. Their third-place league finish put them into the UEFA Cup and they could not have faced a much tougher welcome back to continental football. Docherty, though, was unperturbed when United were paired with Ajax, who had won the European Cup three times in a row earlier in the decade and remained a mighty side. 'I did not fear them,' said Docherty. 'I knew they were a fine team, but I fancied us against anybody because we were building a very good team of our own. I felt that the winners of the competition could come out of the tie.'

United lost the first leg 1-0 in Amsterdam, but they had not forgotten how to come back from behind in these two-legged ties. McIlroy and Macari scored the goals in United's 2-0 win to send them through to the next round. But their next opponents were just as tough and United hosted the powerful Juventus at Old Trafford in the first leg. McIlroy grabbed the only goal of the game, but the lead was too slight to defend in the Stadio Communale. United were blown away 3-0 in Turin. 'They were too good for us in Turin,' Docherty said. 'They had a team full of internationals, and others who were about to be internationals, and they deserved to go through.'

United had shown flashes of the old brilliance in their brief UEFA Cup adventure, but their inconsistency let them down. Docherty had not yet built a side resilient enough to gouge out results in any circumstances and that unreliability cost them in the League. After a promising start to the 1976/77 First Division season, United had a horrid couple of months from mid-October, failing to win any of their eight matches. Then the side clicked and they remained unbeaten from January through to April, winning eight and drawing two in a giddy 10-match run in which the team looked unbeatable. United had been given a lift by the signing of Brian Greenhoff's big brother, Jimmy, from Stoke City, and the new striker scored eight goals in the run-in to help United to a sixth-place finish. United also took that irresistible form into the FA Cup, as they set off once again on a sensational run to Wembley.

The campaign began with two 1-0 wins at Old Trafford against Third Division Walsall and QPR, before United faced their old

1969–77 pals, Southampton, in the fifth round at The Dell. United escaped from the south coast with a 2-2 draw and two goals from Jimmy Greenhoff saw them edge the replay with a tense 2-1 win at Old Trafford. Docherty's team now faced a strong Villa side, who were involved in four-way tussle for the title with Liverpool, City and Ipswich. Once again, United scrambled into the next round with victory by one goal, as Houston and Macari scored in another 2-1 win. Jimmy Armfield's Leeds were United's opposition for the semi-final at Hillsborough and another 2-1 victory took United to Wembley. The Yorkshire side were overwhelmed by United's attacking brio and were always likely losers after Jimmy Greenhoff

Jimmy Greenhoff (right) scores in the FA Cup fifth round replay at Southampton as United return to Wembley in 1977.

and Steve Coppell scored in a devastating opening 10-minute burst. Leeds pulled a goal back with an Allan Clarke penalty, but United always looked like emerging the victors.

Their opponents at Wembley were Bob Paisley's Liverpool, who had just won the league and were also looking forward to a European Cup final against Borussia Moenchengladbach four days after the FA Cup final. Victory over United would have given Liverpool the second leg of what would have been a historic Treble. But United had other ideas and ended Liverpool's dreams by winning the Cup with yet another 2-1 victory. It would be another 22 years before an English team captured that particular Treble.

After the final whistle Docherty cavorted with his players around a sunlit Wembley, enjoying the greatest day of his managerial career. Nobody could have guessed it then, but it was also destined to be the day of his last match as United's manager. Six weeks later, on 4 July

1977, Docherty was sacked by the board 10 days after announcing he was leaving his wife and family to live with the wife of the club's physio, Laurie Brown. At any other club the Cup-winning manager who had restored a failing team to the elite of English football after several years in the doldrums might have survived with his job. But United weren't like other clubs. The club was still hugely influenced by Busby's religious principles and, whether he had any direct involvement in Docherty's sacking or not, his beliefs certainly did. Manchester United existed in Busby's moral universe. Docherty's affair with another employee's wife was worse than a disciplinary infringement: it was a sin and he had to go. Docherty said, 'I have been punished for falling in love. What I have done has got nothing to do with my track record as a manager.'

He was quite right. Docherty had taken the hollow shell of a fading football club and built a thrilling team that was once again battling for honours at home and abroad. His buoyant personality had helped dispel the lethargy that had afflicted the club since 1968. United were the FA Cup holders for the first time in 14 years and they were back in Europe. In Docherty United had found a man with a personality big enough to fill the most demanding job in club football, and he was obliged to leave just at the point where he was ready to take the team to the next level and challenge the new kings of English football, Liverpool, for the Championship. But that task would fall to another, altogether quieter character.

Tommy Docherty revels in the moment as his delighted players crown him with the FA Cup following victory over Liverpool at Wembley in May 1977.

1977 **FA CUP FINAL**

MANCHESTER UNITED 2 Pearson, J Greenhoff **LIVERPOOL 1** Case

21 MAY 1977 at Wembley • Referee: R Matthewson • Attendance: 100,000

MANCHESTER UNITED

Stepney
Nicholl
Albiston
McIlroy
B Greenhoff
Buchan
Coppell
J Greenhoff
Pearson
Macari
Hill (McCreery)

LIVERPOOL

Clemence
Neal
Jones
Smith
Kennedy
Hughes
Keegan
Case
Heighway
Johnson (Callaghan)
McDermott

Twelve months before this match Tommy Docherty had risen to his feet to make a speech at United's post-FA Cup final banquet/wake and vowed, 'We will be back at Wembley next year. And we will win.' The 1-0 defeat against Second Division Southampton in May 1976 had rocked Old Trafford hard and the club were desperate to make amends. 'I have to admit, those words were spoken more in hope than expectation,' said Docherty. 'You can never say for sure you are going to win the Cup, because it's too unpredictable. But as that season went on I felt sure we could do it. I am a strong believer that there are some seasons when your name is on the Cup. I am sure that was the case with United that season.'

It certainly seemed as though most of the luck ran United's way at Wembley. There was no score at half-time, but then three came in a five-minute burst. Pearson gave United the lead five minutes into the second half. Jimmy Greenhoff lobbed the ball over Emlyn Hughes in the Liverpool defence and Pearson sprinted through to guide it into the net. More often than not Ray Clemence would have saved the effort, but on this occasion he allowed Pearson's precise but hardly thunderous shot to slide through his grasp. Liverpool equalised through Jimmy Case, before Dame Fortune once

Tommy Docherty leads his men out purposefully for the 1977 Wembley showdown against Liverpool.

again winked outrageously at United. Lou Macari let fly with a shot that was sailing furlongs wide, until it veered off Jimmy Greenhoff's torso. The spinning ball eluded both Clemence and Joey Jones before rolling over the goalline.

'Even now Lou and Jimmy argue over whose goal it was,' said Docherty. 'But I didn't care then and I don't care now. We had set out to win the Cup and we had won it. It made up for all the heartbreak of the year before.'

Above *Stuart Pearson shoots United into the lead at Wembley as Ray Clemence fails to gather his effort early in the second half.*
Right *The Greenhoff brothers have plenty to smile about as they show off the famous old trophy.*

THE CLASS OF '77

Statistics are for total appearances and goals while playing for United.

❶ ALEX STEPNEY 1966–78

GOALKEEPER • 539 Apps • 2 Gls

(See also Heroes of 1968 on page 126)

Stepney was the only survivor from the 1968 European Cup-winning side to play in the 1977 FA Cup final. He had arrived at Old Trafford from Chelsea more than a decade earlier, but after the victory over Liverpool his reputation as one of United's best-ever keepers was secure.

❷ JIMMY NICHOLL 1975–82

RIGHT-BACK • 235 (13) Apps • 6 Gls

Canadian-born Nicholl was a footballer first and a defender second, and his eye for a pass was a valuable weapon in United's arsenal. Nicholl also starred for Northern Ireland and won 73 caps, including appearances for his country at the 1982 and 1986 World Cups.

❸ ARTHUR ALBISTON 1974–88

LEFT-BACK • 467 (18) Apps • 7 Gls

The Scotland international chose a good day to make his FA Cup debut – in front of 100,000 spectators as United beat Liverpool 2-1. The 19-year-old had a late call-up to replace the injured Stewart Houston and his assured performance on such a daunting stage marked him down as a worthy first-team regular. Ever a modest team man, he offered his winner's medal to the unlucky Houston. The older man let the kid keep it: he deserved it.

Year after year Albiston provided reliable service in the United defence, before moving to West Brom on a free transfer. He also played 14 times for his country.

❹ SAMMY McILROY 1971–82

MIDFIELDER • 391 (28) Apps • 71 Gls

The Belfast boy was the last player Busby signed for the club before he gave up the full-time manager's job and it was one of the shrewdest pieces of business he ever conducted. McIlroy began his career as a striker, then went on to be the heartbeat of the United midfield for the best part of a decade. His all-action style, neat passing ability and knack for scoring vital goals made him a key member of the team.

He was lucky ever to play again after suffering severe injuries in a car crash in 1973, but the tough-minded McIlroy bounced back within months to play at the top level for another 10 years and to amass 88 caps for Northern Ireland.

❺ BRIAN GREENHOFF 1973–79

CENTRE-HALF • 268 (3) Apps • 17 Gls

The younger Greenhoff's United career began inauspiciously in relegation. But he survived the trauma of 1974 with his reputation unharmed and he was a cornerstone of the team that won promotion at the first attempt.

He started out as a midfielder, but became a dependable centre-half under Docherty – good enough to win 18 England caps. Greenhoff was not a lavishly gifted footballer, but he formed a solid central defensive partnership with Martin Buchan and was prepared to fill any role in the service of United.

⑥ MARTIN BUCHAN 1971–83
CENTRE-HALF • 456 Apps • 4 Gls

The Aberdonian was famously the man who mounted the 39 steps to the Royal Box to collect the FA Cup in 1977 and he had certainly earned the accolade. Through the difficult years of the early 1970s, including relegation, Buchan laboured to hold the United defence together. Now he could enjoy some reward for the difficult years, with an FA Cup winner's medal to go with the SFA equivalent he had won at Aberdeen.

Buchan never appeared to be hurried in his defensive duties, and his ability to read a game and anticipate a striker's next move were important qualities. They were to the fore in the 1977 final, when Buchan turned out despite an injury that had made him a doubt on the morning of the game. He turned in his customary impeccable performance and did as much as anyone to make sure that the Cup would come back to Manchester.

Buchan never claimed to be one of the greats and was happy to be thought of as a solid player who did his job. He said, 'If my name is mentioned in football circles in the future, I just hope they say, "He was a good professional."'

⑦ STEVE COPPELL 1975–83
WINGER • 393 (3) Apps • 70 Gls

Football supporters' wit can sometimes be a blunt instrument, but a banner flown by United fans at Wembley in 1977 told the truth, 'Stevie Gives The Kop 'ell,' it announced. And he did.

Coppell had been rousing spectators with his direct wing play since signing for United from Tranmere Rovers for £40,000 while he was still a student at Liverpool University. Docherty was desperate to play an old-fashioned attacking game with wingers marauding down both flanks and he found a wide-man after his own heart in Coppell. For those seasons before the Doc's departure Coppell played like a throwback to the days when every team turned out with an orthodox outside-right and an outside-left, running at the opposing full-back at every opportunity. His role changed slightly under Sexton, but he remained a hugely effective midfield player until a knee injury curtailed his playing days.

The fans had loved him for his unquenchable appetite for attack and because he was clearly in love with playing for United. He said, 'They were great days. I had to keep pinching myself. My only dream was to play until I dropped.'

⑧ JIMMY GREENHOFF 1976–81
STRIKER • 119 (4) Apps • 36 Gls

Towards the end of 1976 Docherty was concerned that United were losing some of their zip in attack. The manager had made his reputation by giving young players their chance, but this time he decided the man for the job was 30-year-old Jimmy Greenhoff from Stoke.

The Doc's £120,000 purchase did the trick for his jaded strike-force. Greenhoff scored three valuable goals on the way to Wembley in 1977 and he added another in the final – even if it did come off his upper body while he tried to avoid Lou Macari's shot.

Greenhoff played on for United until he was 34, when he signed for Crewe following Garry Birtles' £1 million arrival from Forest.

⑨ STUART PEARSON 1974–79

STRIKER • 179 (1) Apps • 66 Gls

The man they called Pancho loved scoring goals. You could tell that by his reaction after every single one of the 66 he netted in all competitions for United: the raised forearm and bunched fist, the gamecock strut and the 100-watt, face-splitting smile. His abundant zest for his job was obvious and his attitude to the game chimed with the team's spirit of enterprising attacking play.

'They were the best years of my life,' he said. 'We used to just go out and attack teams. If somebody scored three against us we knew we'd get four. It was great just going out on the pitch. We knew we'd enjoy it.'

⑪ GORDON HILL 1975–78

WINGER • 133 (1) Apps • 51 Gls

Hill had one of his best games for United in the 1977 FA Cup semi-final, when he destroyed Derby County almost single-handedly, scoring both goals in a 2-0 win. His performance that day said everything about the qualities Hill brought to the United team: surging runs down the flank, an insatiable relish for taking on defenders and a devastating shot.

He was seldom little more than a bystander when the opposition had the ball, which made him seem like a luxury in the post-Docherty era when teamwork held sway over individual brilliance. But at his best he was one of the most exciting players Old Trafford ever saw.

⑫ DAVID McCREERY 1975–79

MIDFIELDER • 57 (53) Apps • 8 Gls

McCreery, yet another Belfast boy made good at Old Trafford, was a regular substitute at United who never quite nailed down a starting place of his own. He was a valuable member of Docherty's squad and the manager would use him to replace tiring legs in the second-half. Despite his devotion to attack Docherty could be a pragmatist and McCreery was an option to stiffen up the centre of midfield when necessary, especially if United were ahead and he perceived a need to rein in excessive flamboyance. In the 1976 and 1977 FA Cup finals, McCreery came on in place of Hill.

His willingness to flog himself into the ground in the interests of the side was valued highly by team-mates and supporters, and earned him the affectionate nickname, 'Roadrunner'.

⑩ LOU MACARI 1972–84

MIDFIELDER • 374 (27) Apps • 97 Gls

Luigi Macari joined United from Celtic for £200,000, which made him one of the most expensive footballers in Britain. At first he was employed as a striker, even though at 5ft 6in he was one of the tiniest around. But Docherty turned him into a canny midfield operator, when he failed to make it as an out-and-out goalscorer in the First Division, and his ability to get forward from deep positions made him a potent penalty-area presence. He scored three goals on the way to Wembley in 1977 and he claimed at least a part-share in the winner against Liverpool. It was the little Scot's shot which flew off Greenhoff and past keeper Ray Clemence.

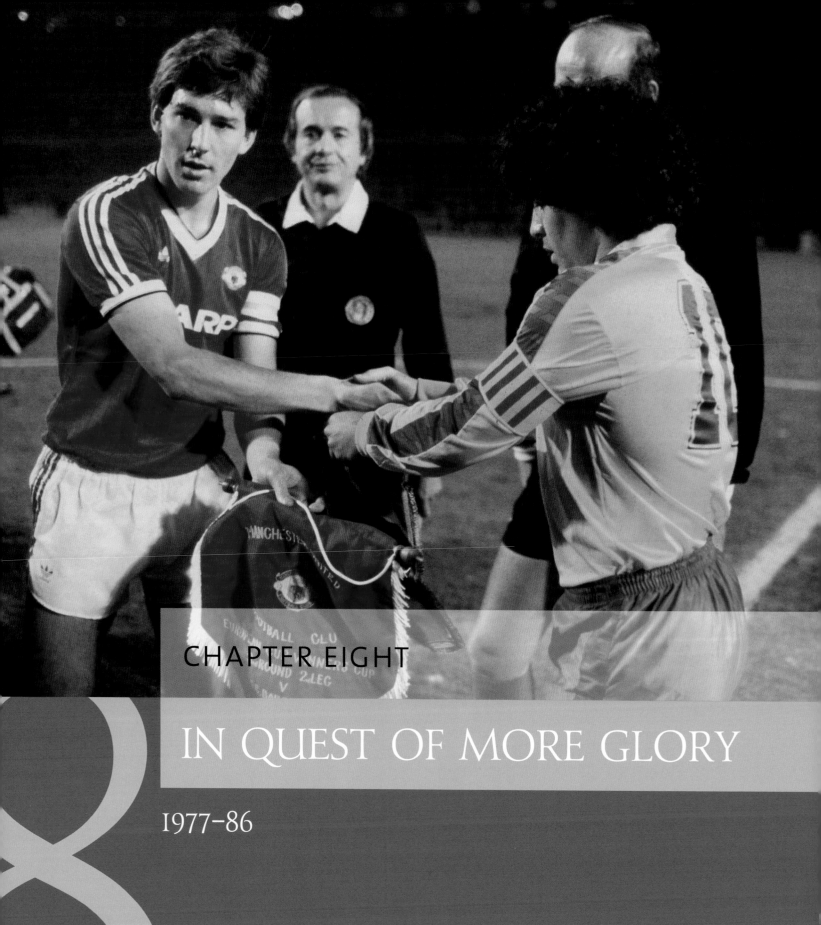

CHAPTER EIGHT

IN QUEST OF MORE GLORY

1977–86

THE SUMMER OF 1977 SAW UNITED AS FA CUP HOLDERS
AND BACK IN EUROPE – TOMMY DOCHERTY LEFT THE
CLUB IN GOOD SHAPE FOR HIS SUCCESSOR

After Tommy Docherty was sacked, United went back to the man they had identified as the perfect replacement for Busby years before: Dave Sexton was top of their list again. His CV was impeccable, especially as a coach, and his record of success stretched all the way back to his first job as an assistant at Chelsea in 1962. The man who had given him his first staff job at Stamford Bridge was, of course, T. Docherty Esq.

But there were one or two doubts about Sexton. Most obviously, he was very much a London man and had spent his entire coaching career at London clubs. From Stamford Bridge he had gone to Orient as manager, where he suffered his only comparative failure. Next stop was Fulham, where he saved the team from relegation against steep odds. Sexton then switched to Arsenal as assistant manager and coach under Bertie Mee, before replacing Docherty as Chelsea boss in 1967. It was there that Sexton was propelled into the front rank of English managers, winning a reputation as one of the most forward-thinking men in football. In a more hide-bound era of the game he was fascinated by the tactical aspect of football and was ready to switch formations during a match to confound the opposition.

His Chelsea team were an intriguing blend of graft and artistry, and those qualities saw them win a bruising 1970 FA Cup final against Leeds United after a replay. His crowning glory at the Bridge was the Cup-Winners' Cup triumph of the following season, when Chelsea beat Real Madrid in the final. When the club nearly went bust Sexton decamped to QPR and took the unheralded west London club to their best-ever League finish in second place in 1976.

But by the summer of 1977 Sexton was ready for a change and United came calling at just the right time: he finally agreed to

---

Opposite Bryan Robson and Maradona exchange greetings before one of the greatest matches Old Trafford has ever seen, the 3-0 win against Barcelona in the Cup-Winners' Cup on 21 March 1984.

Right Tommy Docherty's replacement, the urbane Dave Sexton.

1977–86

head north and take the United job. After all, the Islington-born ex-Crystal Palace and West Ham inside-forward had just about run out of clubs to work for in London.

It wasn't just his London roots that set Sexton apart. His character could not have been a greater contrast to Docherty's. The new man was quiet, studious and wary of attention. Docherty relished the spotlight and while he was in charge United were guaranteed a prominent place on the back pages. Sexton's instinct was to keep his cards close to his chest and give nothing away. The showman had given way to the shy man.

Arthur Albiston, the full-back who had signed for United as a teenager in 1974, said, 'Dave came in and he was a different character from Tommy, with a slightly different attitude to the job. Tommy's great strength was man-management and getting the best out of players by motivating them. Dave was more of a coach and interested in improving players' technique, and making them aware of their responsibilities on the field. I think that probably came as something of a shock to the players, but I enjoyed playing for him. He was a deep thinker about the game and I liked that about him.'

Sexton made it clear from the start that winning was paramount, even if it meant sacrificing some of the style and swagger United fans had come to expect. He said, 'I want to see the team winning and playing attractively. Which comes first? It must be winning.' Sexton was not against entertaining on principle, but any aesthetic pleasure his team provided would merely be a by-product of winning. Results in the new man's first season were patchy as he sought to rearrange the team to his own taste.

Stuart Pearson (far right) waits for the cross before scoring against St Etienne in the unlikely surroundings of Home Park, Plymouth. United won the Cup-Winners' Cup tie 2-0.

There were early exits in the FA Cup and League Cup, and United finished a mediocre 10th in the 1977/78 First Division campaign. There was disenchantment in Europe, too.

United had qualified for the Cup-Winners' Cup, and drew the strong French side St Etienne in the first round. Hill scored in the Stade Geoffrey Guichard to earn United a 1-1 draw, but a riot featuring United fans meant the club was barred from playing the home leg at Old Trafford. At first UEFA expelled United from the competition, but the punishment was reduced on appeal: an exclusion zone was thrown around Old Trafford and United were ordered to stage the second leg at least 300 kilometres away. That left only a handful of English league grounds available to host the tie and United found themselves in the unlikely position of hosting a European game at Home Park, Plymouth. They still managed to win 2-0. The run, though, came to an end in the next round against Porto. United were hammered 5-0 in Portugal and then went out, despite staging a thrilling rally back at Old Trafford, where a rousing 5-2 win was not quite good enough to see them go through.

Sexton broke up Docherty's side during the 1977/78 season and popular players were left out in the cold. Alex Stepney lost his place in goal to Paddy Roche and left to play for Dallas Tornado. Stuart Pearson was no longer an automatic choice and he moved to West Ham in due course. Alex Forsyth was sold to Rangers in the summer of 1978. But most traumatic of all for United fans, Gordon Hill left Old Trafford to join Docherty at Derby County. Hill had come to symbolise all that was good and exciting about United under Docherty. His reluctance to demean his talent by indulging in defence enraged team-mates at times, but to the fans on the terraces he could do no wrong. He brought panache, pace and a devil-may-care verve to the United team after years of sterility and they loved him for it. He in turn loved them.

The Cockney winger had arrived from Millwall for little money and in just three years he had become one of the most adored United players of his generation. Docherty gave him license to thrill, but he never fitted into Sexton's team template. The new manager was appalled by Hill's lack of application when United didn't have the ball and he told the distraught Hill he would have to go. The dismissal cost Sexton twice over. It lost him a huge amount of goodwill from the United supporters and he never replaced Hill's goals. The winger

might have been a liability when it came to stopping goals, but on the other hand he had been top scorer in two of his three seasons at the club. His best campaign was his last: from his wide position he scored 17 in 36 league games. Albiston said, 'Dave got a lot of criticism from the supporters over that. Gordon was a big favourite and he scored a lot of goals from out wide, but he didn't fit in with what the manager wanted. His replacement was Mickey Thomas, who was more of a work-horse and a very different player from Gordon.'

Sexton acted decisively to transform the team by buying in a couple of tried-and-tested Scotland internationals from Leeds to strengthen United's spine. In the New Year of 1978 he signed the centre-forward, Joe Jordan, for £300,000 – a record for English clubs that did not last long. A month later Gordon McQueen followed him down the M62 for £495,000. The centre-half could not hide his delight at joining the club. He said, 'Ask all the players in the country which club they would like to join and 99 per cent would say Manchester United. The other one per cent would be liars.' That one-eyed, pro-United bias made McQueen an instant darling of the Stretford End.

Gordon McQueen flanked by chairman Louis Edwards and Dave Sexton after signing for the club.

Gordon McQueen clears the danger during United's tricky 1-0 FA Cup fifth round victory at Colchester United on 20 February 1979.

Sexton's side continued to stutter in the league through the 1978/79 season, but they found form in the FA Cup once again in an electrifying run all the way to Wembley. Chelsea, by now well and truly skint and destined to finish bottom of the table in May 1979, were dispatched 3-0 at Old Trafford in the third round. Then Jimmy Greenhoff scored the only goal of the game in a fourth-round replay with Second Division Fulham at Old Trafford, after a fraught 1-1 draw at Craven Cottage. United made heavy weather of the fifth round too, winning 1-0 at Colchester United of the Third Division thanks again to Greenhoff, who had now scored in every game of United's peril-filled Cup campaign. They faced a third London team in the quarter finals, Tottenham away – but a goal from one of Sexton's new boys, Mickey Thomas, allowed them to escape with a 1-1 draw. The replay ended 2-0 and United were in the semi-finals.

Their opponents could not have been any tougher, as they faced that season's Champions and European Cup-holders, Liverpool, at Maine Road. It turned out to be one of the most eventful and memorable matches in the long history of the fixture. United tore

into Liverpool from the kick-off and it was an injustice when Kenny Dalglish put Bob Paisley's team in the lead after 20 minutes with a goal that even United supporters had to admit was extraordinary, featuring a jinking dribble through the defence and a cool finish past United's new keeper, Gary Bailey. United were level two minutes later when Jimmy Greenhoff crossed into the box and Jordan made the most of defensive indecision to steer a shot past Ray Clemence. Liverpool could have gone in at half-time in front when the referee awarded them a penalty for Buchan's push on Dalglish – but Terry McDermott hit the post. In the second half United continued to do most of the attacking and they were well worth another goal: Brian Greenhoff scored it as the Liverpool rearguard was caught dithering again. Now it was United's turn to defend as Liverpool poured forward in search of an equaliser. It finally came when Alan Hansen, of all people, arrived in the penalty area to shoot a loose ball past Bailey.

The replay at Goodison could hardly live up to the Maine Road classic, but it was close. Just as in the first game, United went at

Liverpool from the kick-off and shots rained in on Clemence's goal. After the early flurry Liverpool came back to threaten United, and by half-time both sets of goalposts and crossbars had been struck, and Bailey and Clemence were the busiest men on the park. But one goal in the second half settled the match. With ten minutes left Jordan passed to Thomas out on the left wing and the Welshman put the ball over to Jimmy Greenhoff in the area. The striker let the ball bounce and, as Clemence raced from his goal to intercept, placed his header inside the post. United were at Wembley for the third time in four years and for the second time in two years they had robbed Liverpool of the Double.

The 1979 United v Arsenal FA Cup final – the so-called 'Five-Minute final' – was instantly hailed as one of Wembley's greatest matches, but that came as scant comfort to United. They staged a

Jimmy Greenhoff steers his header past Liverpool keeper Ray Clemence in the semi-final replay at Goodison Park to take United to Wembley.

1977–86

remarkable comeback from two goals down to equalise in the last four minutes, only to see Arsenal snatch the Cup back again in the final seconds.

The Gunners went ahead in the first quarter of an hour through Brian Talbot and Frank Stapleton made it 2-0 just before half-time. When the 85th minute of the match ticked by with no change to the score, United were bereft of hope and thousands of disconsolate Mancunians began trooping to the exits. But then Coppell launched a free-kick in to Jordan and his knockdown was scrambled into the net by Gordon McQueen. Then, incredibly, United won possession from the restart, Sammy McIlroy accepted a pass from Coppell, danced past a couple of tired challenges and fired United's second. But straight from Arsenal's kick-off, a dagger through the heart... Liam Brady gathered the last of his strength and set off on a run, ghosting past a host of United players before switching a pass left to Graham Rix. His cross hurtled over to Alan Sunderland at the far post and the perma-frizzed front-man bundled the ball over the line, despite Arthur Albiston's desperate challenge. Arsenal had scored

the third goal of a mad four-minute spell and now it really was all over. Defeat following that brief glimpse of salvation was difficult to bear. McIlroy said, 'To lose after that was like winning the pools only to find you'd forgotten to post the coupon.' Albiston said, 'It was so disappointing. We hadn't played at our best, but we thought we had done enough to go into extra-time, and if we had I think we could have won it. But it was snatched away again in the last few seconds. We had wanted to win it for Dave, because he was under pressure to win something. But Cup finals can be like that.'

Undaunted, Sexton set about improving the team in the summer of 1979 and he paid a club-record £825,000 for Chelsea's midfield playmaker, Ray Wilkins. Wilkins became the second-most expensive player in Britain – Trevor Francis had moved from Birmingham to Nottingham Forest in the first £1 million transfer earlier in the year.

Sammy McIlroy gives United new hope, making the score 2-2, and extra-time seems possible. Arsenal snatched the match moments later.

Sexton had been a mentor for the teenage Wilkins in his early days at Stamford Bridge and the United boss gambled big money to provide the creative spark which his team had sorely lacked. For much of the 1979/80 season it looked like Sexton's hunch had paid off. The new man starred in a highly effective United side, which challenged Liverpool for top spot in the First Division all the way through the autumn, winter and into the spring. Sexton had the defence tighter than it had been for years. The South African keeper, Gary Bailey, was ever-present and ever dependable. Jimmy Nicholl and Albiston were solid full-backs, and Buchan and McQueen forged one of the best central defensive partnerships Old Trafford had seen in years. Further up the field United had a good blend of artistry and industry with Coppell, McIlroy, Macari, Wilkins and Thomas. But it was the goalscoring that let them down. Jordan top scored with 13 goals, but

he never found a reliable partner to share the burden up front and that is where United lost their chance of the title. Liverpool finished top of the table by two points from United in second, having scored 81 goals to United's 65.

Despite the valiant tilt at the title, it was a troubled season for United. In January 1980 their fans were at the fore again as football violence flared. Two Middlesbrough supporters died when a wall collapsed at Ayresome Park after the game against United and away fans were implicated in the tragedy. And there was change in the

Above left Ray Wilkins, who joined from Chelsea to breathe new life into United's midfield.

Above Gary Bailey, United's dependable South African goalkeeper.

1977–86   Old Trafford boardroom in February 1980 as Louis Edwards, who had been a director since 1958 and chairman for 15 years, died of a heart attack. At the time of his passing, Edwards was under investigation for alleged corruption and financial misdeeds at United and in his butchery business, following charges levelled by the TV programme, *World in Action*. The case died with him, and he was succeeded as chairman by his son, Martin.

Despite the high finishing position in the league, there was trouble on the park, too, and many United supporters were unhappy with the football their team was playing. They were winning most of the time, but the expected dash was missing. United were a highly effective team, but they missed the kinds of players who used to get the fans on the edge of their seats: United were functional, but predictable. There could not be a worse crime for United supporters, who craved flair and flamboyance.

needed in the leader of their attack. None of this was Birtles's fault, but the shy introvert was not cut out to be the focus of the team and United's scorer in chief. Watching him play for United, it was hard to shake off the feeling that he was the wrong man in the wrong place at the wrong time. He failed to score in any of the 25 league games he played before the end of the season came to end his, and Sexton's, torment. And it wasn't just the striker who was to blame for United's bloodless showing. For much of the time the service he received from midfield was threadbare and the team had been handicapped by the long-term absence of Wilkins, through injury, just as much as they had been by Birtles' impotence up front. When Wilkins came back for the final matches United ended the season with seven wins out of seven. But the late flourish could not mask the truth: United had gone backwards in the league and were fortunate to finish eighth. They had lost their first match

United began the 1980/81 season in a similar fashion to the previous campaign. They were certainly hard to beat and lost just once in the first 14 league games. On occasions they even turned on the razzmatazz, as they did when they thrashed Leicester 5-0 at Old Trafford in September 1980, and the little-remembered Yugoslavian import, Nikola Jovanovic, scored twice. But for the most part they lacked the attacking edge needed to excite the crowd and turn draws into victories. So it was that Sexton bet the farm on one big-money transfer: in October 1980 Garry Birtles joined the club from Forest for £1.25 million, as Sexton desperately sought a striker who could thrive alongside Jordan. It was the mistake that was to cost him his job.

Right from the start, Birtles never looked comfortable as a United player. He lacked the self-belief, arrogance even, which United

in the League Cup, lost in the first round of the UEFA Cup to Widzew Lodz, and lost in the fourth round of the FA Cup against Forest. The vast outlay on Birtles had called into question Sexton's judgement of a player. And to cap it all, United supporters were staying away from Old Trafford in their tens of thousands. Despite United's winning form, the last home game against Norwich City attracted a crowd that just edged past 40,000. For a club that had grown accustomed to gates in excess of 50,000 season after season, it was an unambiguous vote of no-confidence in Sexton's regime. Within a week of the end of the season he was sacked.

Nikola Jovanovich, the Yugoslav whose star shone briefly at Old Trafford.

Albiston said, 'We had gone close to winning the league under Dave, but we were not quite good enough. We had come second, but couldn't quite take the next step and it was unlucky for Dave. He had come in and changed the way the team played. Under Tommy the attitude was attack at all costs and Dave had a more organised approach, and less was left to chance. In the end he suffered because he wasn't as popular in the media. Tommy had a good relationship with the Press and was always good for a quote. Dave was more introverted and for that reason maybe his good qualities weren't as widely recognised as they should have been.'

Not for the first time in their recent history, United found that recruiting a new manager was not as simple as selecting the right candidate and picking up the phone. Several names at the top of the club's wish list declined to be considered for the post. Lawrie McMenemy, the Southampton manager and their nemesis from 1976, said no. Bobby Robson, who had wrought a small miracle by turning little Ipswich Town into Cup winners and First Division

contenders, was satisfied to stay in Suffolk. Ron Saunders, the taciturn Villa boss who made the reserved Sexton look like a song-and-dance man, also declined. Finally, United found a man willing to take on the manager's job. Ron Atkinson from West Bromwich Albion was installed. Not only was Atkinson not the first choice candidate: he wasn't even the first-choice candidate named Ron. But he quickly showed that he had the chutzpah to fill the role.

Left *Garry Birtles, the luckless striker who endured a difficult time at Old Trafford following his £1 million move from Forest.*
Above *Ron Atkinson, who allied himself with the United supporters from his first day at Old Trafford, salutes the crowd.*

In terms of character he was more in the mould of Docherty than Sexton. In playing style, too, he was deemed to be more adventurous than his predecessor. Atkinson had turned West Brom into one of the most enjoyable sides to watch in the country and he had a reputation for producing attractive, entertaining teams. He also had a refreshingly open attitude towards fans and the media, and right from the start he built a rapport with the public. He had the fans on-side from the first day. In one of his first statements after accepting the job he pledged to provide a team they could take pride in. He said, 'I will not just be United's manager. I will be an ardent fan. If the team bores me, it will be boring supporters who hero-worship the players. I will not allow these people to be betrayed.'

'It is time for action at Old Trafford. Others may have been frightened off before me but I have not.'

He also had an instinct for the kinds of displays the supporters wanted to see. He said, 'Old Trafford is a theatre for entertainment, drama and football spectacle. It's not a stadium where you should hear bellyaching or fans bickering about their own team. That just destroys the magic of the place.'

Albiston said, 'Ron projected this flash image that he lived up to, with all the champagne and the gold jewellery, but that was all nonsense. In reality he was like Dave, a serious thinker about the game. And he had an amazing memory for players and matches, which he could call on. He was so knowledgeable about the game.'

Atkinson had plenty of work to do after arriving at Old Trafford in June 1981. There were a number of glaring gaps in his squad, which needed filling as quickly as possible, and the new manager was given the cash he wanted. Joe Jordan left in July to join AC Milan. United had already lost Jimmy Greenhoff to Crewe and Andy Ritchie had been sold to Brighton, so Atkinson needed to ginger up his striking capability. It did not take him long to bring in the Irish centre-forward, Frank Stapleton, from Arsenal for £900,000. The re-building stretched into the autumn and in October 1981 Atkinson raided his old club to buy a ready-made midfield engine room. He bought Bryan Robson for a British-record £1.5 million and Remi Moses came with him for £500,000. Sexton had tried to buy Robson earlier, but the-then Baggies manager, Atkinson, wouldn't sell. Atkinson told Sexton at the time that the only way Robson would

join United was if he was the manager. Once the 24-year-old Robson was safely signed up, on the Old Trafford pitch in front of 50,000 supporters, Atkinson announced that he had just got the bargain of the century and promised that the boy would turn out to be the club's best midfield player since Duncan Edwards.

Results picked up in the 1981/82 season and a new, optimistic spirit blew through Old Trafford. Garry Birtles was even scoring goals – four in consecutive matches in October and November. United were good enough to finish a hugely encouraging third in the table, although a long way behind the Champions, Liverpool. The cups, though, were disappointing as United went out at the earliest possible stages against Watford in the FA Cup and Spurs in the League Cup.

The following year Atkinson set a cracking pace as he strived to fashion a squad strong enough to challenge Liverpool at the top of the table. One of his best signings in the summer of 1982 didn't cost a penny. Arnold Muhren, the classy left-sided midfielder, arrived from Ipswich Town on a free transfer. He was also able to sign the gifted young centre-half, Paul McGrath, for next to nothing from St Patrick's Athletic in Ireland. The revamped team continued to thrive in the league, finishing the 1982/83 season third for the second year in a row. There was a vast improvement in their cup form, too. United reached their first-ever League Cup final, which they lost 2-1 to Liverpool at Wembley. But the real thrills came in the FA Cup.

United beat West Ham 2-0 at Old Trafford in the third round and Luton 2-0 away in the fourth round, before Derby, a mid-table Second Division team, provided United with a stiff test at the Baseball Ground. United only just sneaked through with a winner from their new teenage hope from Northern Ireland, Norman Whiteside. By now United had the Twin Towers firmly in sight and a goal from Stapleton gave them victory over Everton at Old Trafford in the quarter-finals. That win set up a seismic semi-final with Arsenal, as United sought to erase the bitter memories of the 1979 final. This time the ball ran United's way. Tony Woodcock put

Remi Moses arrived at Old Trafford from West Brom with Bryan Robson
and provided fine service before injury curtailed his career.

the Gunners ahead at Villa Park, but second-half goals from Robson, and Whiteside with a vicious volley, sent them into the final.

Their opponents at Wembley were Brighton, who had been relegated from the First Division and were looking at the FA Cup as a consolation for losing their top-flight status. They arrived at the stadium, by helicopter, with the carefree attitude of a team who knew that the whole world expected them to lose by at least four goals.

Above Bryan Robson soars to put United in front against Arsenal in the 1983 FA Cup semi-final at Villa Park.
Left Norman Whiteside scores the second with a spectacular volley to book United's ticket to the FA Cup final.

But not for the first time the old arena laid on a gripping story in which a team of fearless underdogs threatened to turn over a red-hot favourite. For long stretches of the first match at Wembley it looked likely that the Cup was heading for Sussex.

Gordon Smith, who was destined to go down in Wembley folklore for one of its most memorable misses, put Brighton in front after a quarter of an hour. Half-time came and went with Brighton still in the lead. But United levelled early in the second half when Whiteside glanced on Mike Duxbury's cross and Stapleton was first to the ball to score. With 20 minutes left United went ahead when a delicious Muhren pass found Wilkins in space and his curling shot sailed into the net. Just as the celebrations were getting underway among the jubilant United hordes, Brighton equalised through Gary Stevens to set up an arduous half-hour of extra-time on the sodden, energy-sapping Wembley surface. Right at the end Smith had his chance of glory when he was clear through on goal, but his scuffed shot hit Gary Bailey's legs. United survived to force a replay and their greater class told in the rematch. United fans acclaimed their first trophy in six years with as much relief as joy.

With that elusive prize in the bag, United were ready to take their place once again as one of the top teams in the country. In the 1983/84 season they were a constant threat to Liverpool, until their title challenge evaporated over the final five matches when they failed to win once. In the end United finished fourth, six points behind Liverpool, with Southampton and Forest just ahead of them in second and third positions. The FA Cup provided an embarrassment with a 2-0 defeat away to Third Division Bournemouth in the third round. But United made up for that blow by enjoying their first significant run in Europe for 15 years, an adventure that featured one of the greatest games Old Trafford has ever seen.

The Cup-Winners' Cup campaign kicked off against the Czech side, Dukla Prague, and United's hopes of making any further progress so nearly came to grief on the banks of the Danube. Atkinson's side struggled to a 1-1 draw in the home leg, but a 2-2 draw in Prague gave them a narrow win on away goals. The second round was simple by comparison as they pulled off a 4-1 aggregate win over Spartak Varna of Bulgaria. But that victory set up a dazzling two-legged clash with Maradona's Barcelona.

It looked all over for United when they travelled to the Nou Camp and were outclassed in a 2-0 defeat. United faced likely elimination in the second leg, but 58,547 true believers turned up at Old Trafford to watch the denouement. The faithful were rewarded

Gordon Smith must score... but he doesn't, as United escape with a replay at Wembley.

167

1983 **FA CUP FINAL REPLAY**

MANCHESTER UNITED 4 Robson 2, Whiteside, Muhren (pen) **BRIGHTON & HOVE ALBION 0**

26 MAY 1983 at Wembley • Referee: A. Grey • Attendance: 92,000

MANCHESTER UNITED

Bailey
Duxbury
Albiston
Wilkins
Moran
McQueen
Robson
Muhren
Stapleton
Whiteside
Davies

**BRIGHTON &
HOVE ALBION**

Moseley
Gatting
Pearce
Grealish
Foster
Stevens
Case
Howlett
Robinson
Smith
Smillie

United were mightily fortunate to have a chance in a replay at all. In the last minute of extra-time five days earlier, with the score level at 2-2, Brighton's Gordon Smith had a chance to win the Cup, but fluffed an effort from close range. It was their last shot at glory, as United overwhelmed the Seagulls in the rematch.

Bryan Robson scored the first with a turf-skimming shot. Then Whiteside's subtle header made him the youngest man ever to score in an FA Cup final. He was 18 years and 19 days old. It was all over before half-time, when Robson made it 3-0 with a tap-in, and Arnold Muhren scored a second-half penalty to give United the biggest FA Cup final victory since 1903, when Bury beat Derby 6-0.

Arnold Muhren and Bryan Robson, the midfield duo who both scored in the 4-0 Cup final replay win against Brighton.

with one of the most extraordinary nights of footballing drama Old Trafford has ever witnessed. Albiston said, 'If you asked me to pick out one memory to cherish from all my years at Old Trafford, I would go for the night we beat Barcelona.

'There was always a terrific atmosphere at Old Trafford whoever the opposition were, or what the competition was. Even when there wasn't a soul in the place, the ground seemed to have a special aura about it. But this night took it to another level of noise and emotion. For a start there were hardly any away supporters in the ground, so it was jammed to the rafters with United fans. And Old Trafford seems even more alive when one of the great teams are the opposition, and Barcelona with Maradona and Bernd Schuster, were certainly that. So all that was enough in itself to create a special atmosphere. But as the comeback unfolded, the atmosphere grew and grew and grew until it felt like the place would explode.

'Sometimes when you are a player you take games for granted, even big games. Because you are playing Wednesday, Saturday,

Wednesday, month after month, season after season, they can blur into one. It's not until you retire, and you have time to reflect on the matches you've played in, that you realise how special those times were. And for me, there were none so special as that night.'

On the evening of 21 March 1984, United were magnificent against Barcelona and Robson played like a person possessed. He was a one-man wrecking ball in the midfield, destroying Barcelona attacks at their genesis and driving his team forward in turn. It was inevitable that he would score the first, with a flying header. Then he shot United level after the Barca keeper, visibly wilting in the crucible of fervour stoked by 58,000 Mancunian voices, dropped a cross. And Robson set up Stapleton for United's winner, the last act in a barely-believable drama.

Bryan Robson scores his first against Barcelona, in one of the greatest performances of his career.

1977–86 United could not top that effort and in the semi-finals they went out to Juventus. The Italians forced a 1-1 draw at Old Trafford and their 2-1 win in Turin was enough to put United out. But for that astounding victory over Barcelona, this Atkinson team had already achieved a measure of immortality. The Barcelona match came at just the right time to help United fans forget an episode that could have spelt disaster for their club. It came within an inch of falling into the crooked clutches of Robert Maxwell.

In February 1984 the *Daily Mirror* (owner: R. Maxwell) began banging the drum in support of a Maxwell takeover at United. The millionaire publishing tycoon's eye had alighted on football as a new area of commerce ripe for exploitation and he was keen to own the market-leading brand. Maxwell already owned Oxford United and was theoretically barred from seeking involvement in any other club, but rules were seldom taken into much consideration when Maxwell had set his heart on a deal. He offered £10 million for a controlling stake and the chairman, Martin Edwards, was tempted to sell out. Maxwell was informed that a bid of £15 million could be looked on favourably. Happily for the future prosperity of United, Maxwell jibbed at the cost and bought Derby County instead.

Against Barcelona United had shown that they could beat Europe's best on their day, but the real test remained the First Division: Atkinson still sought the kind of consistency that would sustain a title challenge. By the start of the 1984/85 season

a couple of leading players had moved on: Wilkins went to AC Milan for £1.5 million in the summer of 1984 and Macari quit to manage Swindon. Atkinson bolstered the midfield by bringing in Gordon Strachan from Aberdeen for £600,000 and the Danish international, Jesper Olsen, for £800,000 from Ajax. United also benefited from the emergence of a Welsh striker from the youth set-up, Mark Hughes.

The newly configured United side lost just once in the first nine games of the season and began to show the durability of potential Champions. It was like the old days under Docherty as United poured forward in quest of goals whatever the circumstances of the match. Supporters delighted in matchdays as Old Trafford became a daunting fortress once again. Newcastle were beaten 5-0. Arsenal came and lost 4-2. Villa were thumped 4-0. Stoke suffered another 5-0 hammering. But United were still beset by inconsistency and there were grim afternoons when the goals went in the other direction. There was a painful 0-5 at Goodison, and a 1-5 on the last day of the season at Watford, and in the end United were found wanting. They had plenty of firepower in their team, and the impressive Hughes top-scored with 16 goals, but they lacked the ruthlessness required of Champions. They finished the 1984/85 season in fourth place again and Everton ran away with the title. But not for the first time, United were about to stand in the way of a Merseyside team and the Double.

By a strange quirk United's FA Cup campaign began, for the second consecutive year, against Bournemouth. But this time they played the Cherries at home and won 3-0. United were at home again in the next round and a rare Paul McGrath goal contributed to a 2-1 win over Coventry. In the fifth round Atkinson's team travelled to play Second Division Blackburn and McGrath kept his scoring spree going in a 2-0 win. The quarter-final against West Ham at Old Trafford belonged to Whiteside, as his hat-trick sank the visitors in a 4-2 romp. United's opponents in the semi-final were the toughest side they had faced yet – Liverpool, at Goodison Park.

For 70 pulsating minutes at Everton's ground the teams tore into each other without being able to conjure a goal – until the mighty

Jesper Olsen looks impressed with this history of his new club as he arrives at Old Trafford from Dutch giants Ajax in summer 1984.

Robson finally made the breakthrough. He let fly with a ferocious shot that veered off Hughes and beat Bruce Grobbelaar. With two minutes left United had one foot in Wembley, before Liverpool's Irish midfielder, Ronnie Whelan, shot past Bailey to force extra-time.

United seized the upper hand in the added half-hour and, when Stapleton put them ahead again in the late stages of the first period, Liverpool looked buried. But frantic Liverpool pressure in the final seconds unnerved the United defence, and Liverpool striker Paul Walsh bundled in a second equaliser to force a replay at Maine Road.

This time it was United's turn to hit back after conceding. Late in the first half Steve Nicol pumped a ball into United's box and Paul McGrath headed it past Bailey for an own goal. United burst into action from the start of the second half, as Robson streaked forward from the halfway line and launched a long-range shot which surged beyond Grobbelaar's reach into the back of the net. Now United were in the ascendancy. After an hour Strachan played a precise through-ball for Hughes to chase and the Welshman held

off Mark Lawrenson to score. This time there was no way back for Liverpool and United were in the final.

Their opponents at Wembley, Everton, were already League Champions. They had also won the Cup-Winners' Cup, beating Rapid Vienna in Rotterdam three days earlier and were well fancied to capture the treble at Wembley. The odds lurched even more in Everton's favour following Kevin Moran's sending off, but the resilience of the United side came to the fore as the 10 men battled Everton to a standstill and Whiteside produced an extra-time finish to win United's sixth FA Cup.

_____

Above *Mark Hughes fires in the only goal Norman Whiteside didn't score in United's 4-2 win against West Ham in the FA Cup quarter-final at Old Trafford on 9 March 1985.*

Overleaf *The jubilant Manchester United team celebrate their 1-0 victory over Everton in the 1985 FA Cup final at Wembley.*

1985 **FA CUP FINAL**

MANCHESTER UNITED 1 Whiteside **EVERTON 0** (after extra-time)
18 MAY 1985 at Wembley • Referee: P. Willis • Attendance: 100,000

MANCHESTER UNITED

Bailey
Gidman
Albiston (Duxbury)
Whiteside
McGrath
Moran
Robson
Strachan
Hughes
Stapleton
Olsen

EVERTON

Southall
Stevens
Van Den Hauwe
Ratcliffe
Mountfield
Reid
Steven
Gray
Sharp
Bracewell
Sheedy

Kevin Moran would have chosen to enter the FA Cup record books for another reason, but you don't always choose how history remembers you. This would have to do: the big Irishman was the first player ever to be sent off in an FA Cup final. There was one, sweet consolation prize. Moran did not return to Manchester burdened with shame. Rather, he had a shiny Cup winner's medal around his neck instead.

The centre-half felt the long arm of the law when referee Peter Willis, a County Durham copper, dismissed him for a trip on Peter Reid. The harsh verdict sentenced his teammates to struggle on a hot, muggy day for 12 minutes of normal time, and another 30 minutes' extra-time, a man light, but they pulled it off in fine style and won the match against all the odds with a Whiteside wonder goal.

As is often the case, the sending off galvanised the disadvantaged team and United did most of the attacking after Moran went off. Olsen, especially, served his team by ceaselessly carrying the ball forward and tormenting Everton's tired defenders.

United looked the stronger team in extra-time and after five minutes Whiteside struck. Hughes played a pass out to the Irishman on the right and there appeared to be no imminent danger for Everton as their left-back, Pat Van Den Hauwe, ushered him inside. But the defender stood off Whiteside just enough to let him curl a long-range shot between Neville Southall's grasp and the far post.

Match-winner Norman Whiteside shows off the Cup at Wembley, with the unlucky Kevin Moran.

The Cup triumph was the cue for a huge party in Manchester, but still United craved the most important prize in English football – it was now 18 years since the club had won the Championship, and as each fruitless season came and went the desire to land the trophy grew more intense. As he prepared his squad for the 1985/86 season, Atkinson lost a couple of old stagers as McQueen left to coach in Hong Kong and Muhren went home to play for Ajax. But they were hardly missed as United raced off to their best ever start in a league season.

The campaign began with a coruscating display against Villa at Old Trafford and United won 4-0. Hughes, especially, was in unstoppable form and scored twice. That set the standard for the first 10 games of the season – every one of which United won. The highlight was a 5-1 annihilation of Atkinson's old team, West Brom, at the Hawthorns, but every match was like a carnival for United fans as their team played some of the brightest football the country had seen for years. After that 10-game opening burst United were already nine points clear of their nearest challengers. Their first defeat didn't come for 16 games, when they suffered a 0-3 aberration at Leicester. But that was just a blip. By Christmas United were so far ahead of the opposition at the top of the table it seemed certain that they would win the Championship by a record early date.

It was all so much hubris. United had been in sizzling form in the summer and autumn, but in the winter they froze with the Championship there for the taking. As Easter loomed United were reeled in by the eventual Champions, Liverpool, and Everton and West Ham raced past them as well. From looking like champions in waiting, United eventually finished fourth, 12 points behind Kenny Dalglish's team.

Albiston said, 'You can't put your finger on any one reason why we didn't do it. If it was possible to identify one thing we would have done it at the time and won the league. It's not the whole reason, but the team was heavily influenced by Bryan Robson and midway through the season he began to suffer from injuries.

Paul McGrath (second from left) celebrates with Bryan Robson (left), Norman Whiteside and Mark Hughes (right) after scoring in United's 2-1 win at Arsenal on 24 August 1985.

We badly missed him. But it really all comes down to the same thing: we weren't quite good enough or consistent enough over 42 games to win the league. You can do it over six games to win a cup, but over a whole season you will be found out.'

It also did not help United that Hughes, who had been United's most dynamic forward player in the first half of the season, had a dip in form after it was revealed in the New Year that he would join Barcelona in the summer. Despite the unsettling effect the transfer talk had on him, Hughes still finished the season as United's top scorer with 17 league goals. United's failure to close the deal for the Championship came as a blow, but few could have predicted that it would be fatal for Atkinson. Nor did early exits from the domestic cups amount to sackable offences and it was hardly Atkinson's fault that United were banned from playing in Europe along with all the other English teams after the carnage at Heysel. What really put the skids under Atkinson was his apparent lack of grip in the transfer market.

1977–86   After Hughes's departure was announced Atkinson splashed plenty of cash on players who turned out to be dubious investments. Among the new faces who never quite made the grade were John Sivebaek, Peter Barnes, Mark Higgins, Terry Gibson, Colin Gibson and Peter Davenport. There seemed to be little pattern to the spending, but Atkinson was given the benefit of the doubt – for a few months longer at any rate. His reign stretched into the 1986/87 season, but the writing was already on the wall and it read: Atkinson out.

The United squad, 1986/87, which ended Alex Ferguson's first season as manager in 11th place in the First Division.

United kicked off the campaign in miserable fashion. In stark contrast to the previous summer when they were unbeatable, a palsied United now lost their first three matches. They raised their game to beat Southampton 5-1 at home in the fifth game, but it was a false dawn. They lost their next three, and after 13 games United had mustered just three wins and were 19th in the First Division. The coup de grace came after a 4-1 League Cup replay defeat at Southampton on 4 November, where an insipid display was rated as the worst many supporters had ever seen from a United team. The manager put a brave face on defeat. Even now he talked a good game, explaining that United could climb out of the slough of despond and improve their league position. He said, 'We need to get some First Division respectability and I still believe that is possible with the staff we have got. I thought we could get a result at Southampton, but things didn't work out.' Within two days, Atkinson was out.

He was thanked for his services, sacked, and walked away with a six-figure sum in compensation. But the generous severance payment was no consolation for Atkinson. He said, 'It hurts deep down and the anguish of losing this job won't disappear in a long time. Nobody wants to leave United, whether they are the boss or the teaboy.'

When it came down to it, the reason Atkinson had lost his job was because United hadn't won the league. He had five years in which to achieve it and, despite lavish spending, the trophy had remained in other clubs' hands. At moments, especially in 1985/86, Atkinson looked like he might do it, but the title always ended up on Merseyside. Albiston said, 'Not winning the title was like a noose around the club's neck. Every year which went by without winning it, the noose got tighter.'

The search began all over again for the man who would fulfil United's historical mission to wrest the Championship from its Merseyside monopoly. They found the right person, but the struggle to the summit of English football – and eventually European football – would take in more than a few twists and turns. That long journey began in November 1986 when Alex Ferguson arrived from Aberdeen to start work as Manchester United's manager.

The new boss, Alex Ferguson, parades in full United regalia soon after his arrival at Old Trafford.

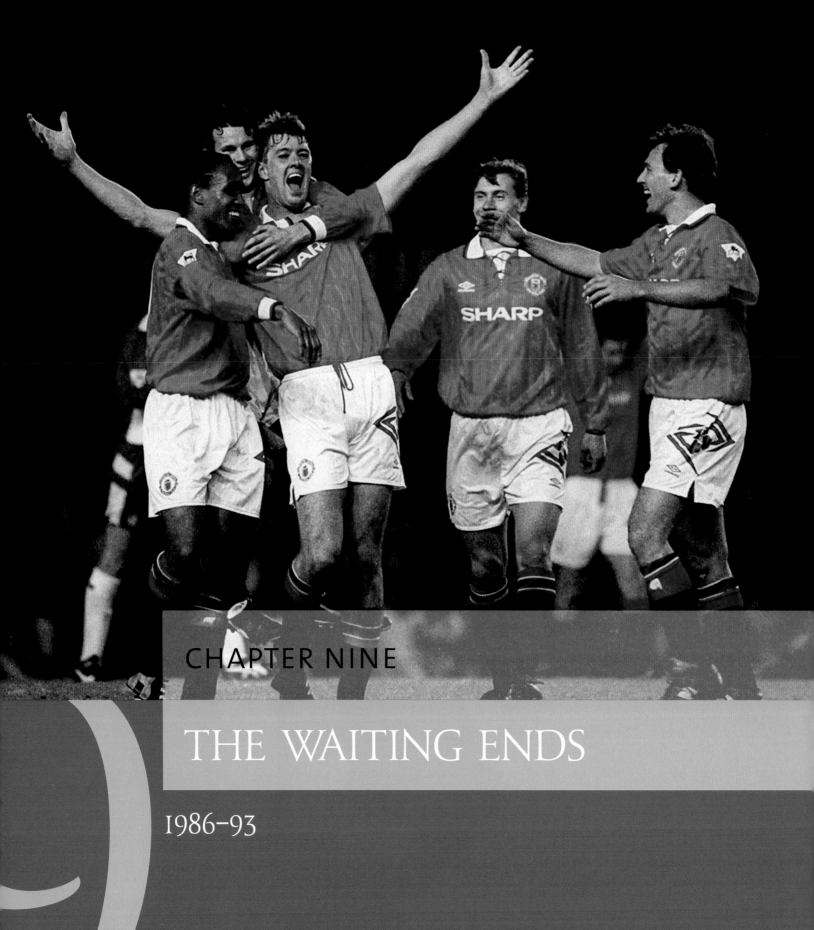

CHAPTER NINE

THE WAITING ENDS

1986–93

ALEX FERGUSON ARRIVED AT UNITED ON 7 NOVEMBER 1986
AND IMMEDIATELY BEGAN REBUILDING THE 'BIGGEST AND
MOST GLAMOROUS CLUB IN THE COUNTRY'

This time there would be no indecision when it came to selecting a new manager. The first choice was Ferguson and he accepted the job on the day Atkinson left. Other big-name managers had been wary of taking the United job in the past, and some had been put off by the magnitude of the challenge and its all-consuming nature. But Ferguson was ready for the task and when the call came from United he recalled the words of his mentor and predecessor as Scotland boss, Jock Stein, who had rejected a chance to manage the club. Ferguson said, 'Jock Stein once told me that he turned down the job with United and he regretted it all his life. I am determined not to miss the chance.'

United knew exactly what they were getting when they made their appointment. Ferguson was a widely experienced manager who had turned Aberdeen into the best team in Scotland and led them to success in Europe. He also had experience of international football, having managed Scotland at the 1986 World Cup finals. Neither were the players in any doubt about what to expect. Ferguson had made a reputation as a strong disciplinarian, who ate cheats and dilettantes for breakfast, and he promised a very different style

of management. Atkinson, in the main, had been the players' pal. Ferguson did not care whether the players liked him or not, just as long as they did their best for Manchester United.

Ferguson's priority for what was left of the 1986/87 season was simple: to save the team from relegation. The last few months under Atkinson had seen the side slip from title challengers to candidates

Opposite Jubilant United players mob Gary Pallister after he scores against Blackburn Rovers in May 1993.
Right Alex Ferguson has plenty to think about, watching his first match in charge of Manchester United.

1986–93 for the drop and Ferguson found himself in charge of a club in trouble. Crisis would be too strong a word, but there was little cohesion in the dressing room, an air of defeat hung about the place and discipline had been allowed to slide. Old Trafford was crying out for a firm hand on the tiller to set United back on the right course and improvement was needed at all levels of the club, right down to the youth set-up. But the radical overhaul would have to wait while Ferguson set about the arduous task of collecting enough points to make sure he would still be manager of a Division One team the following August.

There was no money to spend on new players, but Ferguson worked hard with the men at his disposal to make them a more formidable unit. Training was tougher and several players found themselves in disciplinary trouble as their social lives clashed with the new boss's work ethic. Results, though, improved sufficiently for United to end the season in 11th place and there was even the exciting distraction of a rare FA Cup clash with City to take the supporters' minds off the struggle for survival. Fate ordained that Ferguson's first FA Cup tie in charge of United should be the first Manchester derby in the competition since 1980 and United's victory put a lot of credit in Ferguson's account in only his second month at the club, as Whiteside scored in the 1-0 win at Old Trafford. The Cup run ended in the next round against Coventry, but that hardly mattered in the circumstances. Staying up meant everything and, considering the peril they had been in when Ferguson took over, it was a minor triumph that United finished the season so far up the table.

By necessity, Ferguson had to make changes gradually. If he had tackled the club's shortcomings head on, the manager would have set himself up in conflict with some of the club's biggest

for his subtle changes to have an effect. But keeping United in the First Division was a good start.

After six months at Old Trafford Ferguson had a good idea about the players who formed part of the club's future and about the ones who were dispensable. Terry Gibson was sold to Wimbledon in the summer of 1987, John Sivebaek was off-loaded to St Etienne, Frank Stapleton left for Ajax and the luckless Gary Bailey quit through injury. Peter Barnes had already returned to City in January 1987. Ferguson was granted funds to beef up his squad and among his first signings were some notable names who went on to become Old Trafford legends. Steve Bruce arrived from Norwich for £825,000 to shore up the back four; Celtic's prolific goalscorer, Brian McClair, who was Scotland's Player of the Year, signed for £850,000; and Ferguson also snapped up the highly-decorated England full-back Viv Anderson from Forest for £250,000.

Bruce said, 'It was a dream come true when United came calling to sign me. Chelsea and Tottenham were interested in signing me as well, and I think the Norwich chairman, Robert Chase, had just about done a deal with Spurs. But when I heard United were after me, I pleaded with the chairman to talk to United and when the deal went through I couldn't believe it.

'United might not have been champions for many a long year, but they were still the biggest and most glamorous club in the country. And the fact that I was able to go back north and sign for United meant so much to me. Alex Ferguson didn't need to sell the club to me. They only had to mention they were interested and I was there.'

Bruce made an immediate impact on the United defence, and McClair's prowess up front helped bring about a transformation in United's fortunes in the 1987/88 season. Gone were the jaded, below-par performances of the end of Atkinson's reign and the goals had begun to flow once again. McClair banged in 24 league goals – the biggest haul by a United player in a season since George Best. The midfield looked full of attacking intent too, as Robson scored 11, Strachan chipped in with eight and Whiteside bagged seven. United did, though, miss a productive partner to work with McClair. Peter Davenport, who had been one of Atkinson's last signings, scored five, but United still looked light up front. The new-look team was good enough to finished second in the table, although they were a long

names and most popular players, and a dressing room revolt would have helped nobody. Brian Clough had tried that at Leeds in 1974, but telling a room full of internationals that they would have to change their ways earned him the sack 44 days later following a mutiny. Ferguson was too canny for that. He said, 'You can't go into a club and tell people their fitness is terrible, that they're bevvying, they're playing too much golf and their ground is filthy. You simply have to improve things bit by bit.' It was a sound strategy, but also risky. Ferguson was presuming he would be allowed enough time

Opposite Alex Ferguson welcomes two key signings to Old Trafford, Viv Anderson and Brian McClair.

Above Steve Bruce joined United from Norwich City for £825,000.

way behind Liverpool, but the league performance in Ferguson's first full season was hugely encouraging. The way they ended the campaign suggested they might emerge as real rivals to Liverpool in the season to come: United did not lose any of their last 10 games in 1987/88, and won eight of them. United were back in business as title contenders, but Liverpool formed a colossal barrier to that ambition.

Bruce said, 'Sure, we finished second, and that was encouraging, but we weren't kidding ourselves. We were a million miles away from challenging for the title. It had been 20 years since the club had won it and it seemed like it might be another 20 years before we won it again. They were still really early days in United's rise back to the top under Alex Ferguson. The job had only just begun.'

Opposite Brian McClair holds off Alvin Martin of West Ham during a 1-1 draw at Upton Park, October 1987.

Below Liverpool's Steve Nicol rises to clear in the dramatic 3-3 draw at Anfield, April 1988.

Ferguson knew that if he wanted to bring the Championship back to Old Trafford he would have to dislodge Liverpool. United's fierce rivalry with the Anfield club fuelled Ferguson's desire to take the title. His ambition to knock Liverpool off the top spot, and restore United as champions, informed every minute of his working life. Ferguson admitted that the job of making United the best in the country kept him awake at night in his first years in the job. He was not the first United manager to find the job taking over his entire being and it was Liverpool's dominance which disturbed him most.

It was clear in 1987/88 that Ferguson was eager to fight Liverpool to a standstill and he was not prepared to cede an inch of ground in his struggle. In April 1988, when Liverpool had all-but sealed the Championship, United travelled to Anfield and came away with a point in a bitterly fought battle. United hit back from 3-1 down to draw 3-3, despite having Colin Gibson sent off after an hour. Ferguson, enraged at what he saw as blatant home bias on the referee's part, did not bother to disguise his anger: he was

not going to meekly accept that Liverpool were English football's untouchables. He gave Liverpool and footballing officialdom generally both barrels. He said, 'I can now understand why clubs come away from here having to bite their tongues knowing they have been done by referees. I am not getting at this referee. It is the whole intimidating atmosphere and the monopoly Liverpool have enjoyed here for years that gets to them eventually.' Liverpool's manager, Kenny Dalglish, was passing by with his infant daughter in his arms when Ferguson made his remarks and loudly suggested that the Press would get more sense from his six-week-old baby. The spat between the bosses did not help relations between the clubs. But Ferguson had thrown down a marker: it was his mission, bordering on a mania, to replace Liverpool at the summit of English football. The United-Liverpool duel would provide one of the English game's most gripping sub-plots for the next few seasons.

In 1988/89 Ferguson's refurbishment of the United squad continued. By the time the season kicked off Graeme Hogg had been sold to Portsmouth, Remi Moses had retired through injury, Kevin Moran left for Sporting Gijon in Spain and Arthur Albiston moved to West Brom. Soon after the season started the goalkeeper, Chris Turner, switched to Sheffield Wednesday and two months later two more Atkinson signings left: Jesper Olsen to Bordeaux and Peter Davenport headed for Middlesbrough. Gordon Strachan left for Leeds in the spring. Ferguson replenished his team with a couple of big money signings, with one in particular delighting the fans – Mark Hughes returned from the continent to lead the United attack once again. Ferguson also returned to Aberdeen to buy a new keeper, Jim Leighton, and he brought in a talented teenager from Torquay, Lee Sharpe.

Despite Ferguson's extensive surgery it was Arsenal, not United, who emerged as the chief contenders for Liverpool's crown and, in a season scarred by Hillsborough, the Gunners won the Championship in May 1989 with the last kick of the campaign at Anfield. United by contrast endured a frustrating season which saw the side's league form regress. Ferguson's organisational abilities ensured that

Jim Leighton was snapped up by Ferguson to take the keeper's jersey at United. He knew the keeper well from their days at Aberdeen.

United were difficult to beat, but his team was seldom able to string together sequences of victories. Draws, though, were another matter. In a remarkable eight-match run from October through to the end of November 1988 United drew seven times. By the end of the campaign United were rooted in a nondescript 11th place. The title looked further away than ever. They did, though, enjoy their best FA Cup run since winning the trophy in 1985, to reach the quarter-finals, where they lost 1-0 to Forest at Old Trafford.

Bruce said, 'That season was a step back in terms of league position and it was a tough year, I'll not deny it. It hurt badly that we were a long way behind the other teams. But it takes a long time to rebuild a club, to set it back on solid footings, and that was what Alex was doing. He was the new brush coming in to clean the place up and that was a long process. It was never going to be instant success, far from it. They were painful years and we struggled.

'As the seasons went by and we still hadn't won the league the players felt terrible. The expectations were so high. United were

the biggest, best-supported club in the land and the supporters craved the Championship like it was their right. It was like England and the World Cup. Everybody looks back to 1966, when we last won it, and the desire to win it again grows deeper every four years. That's what it was like at United year after year until we finally won it. It was agony for everybody at the club.'

The 1988/89 season had hardly been glorious and United still had some way to go before the tide turned. Ferguson spent the summer of 1989 on a lavish shopping spree to revamp his under-performing team and by the time he had finished the total transfer bill topped £8 million, which for the times was a hair-raising amount. Nearly £2.5 million went on West Ham's midfield hardman, Paul Ince. More than £2 million brought in Middlesbrough's Gary Pallister, as Ferguson sought a dependable partner for Steve Bruce in the centre of defence following the departure of Paul McGrath to Villa. Another £1.5 million brought Forest midfielder Neil Webb to Old Trafford. The Southampton striker Danny Wallace cost £1.5 million and the Norwich midfielder, Mike Phelan, was a £1.3 million buy.

The new signings, though, were far from immediate successes. A miserable start to the season gave way to a horrible autumn, as United's expensively assembled side spluttered through the first months. It began brightly enough on the first day of the season when Arsenal were overwhelmed 4-1 at Old Trafford, but form was patchy from then on, with brief flashes of brilliance giving way to inexplicable slumps. In September 1989 United thrashed Millwall 5-1 at home, with the resurgent Hughes scoring a hat-trick. Then seven days later they committed the ultimate crime of surrendering against City, who had just been promoted and were bottom of the First Division. United lost 5-1 in a humiliating episode and the cataclysm brought calls for Ferguson's head. It was United's biggest derby defeat for 34 years.

The team suffered a desperate lurch in form in November when they set off on a run of 11 league matches without a win. Demands from supporters for Ferguson's sacking intensified and by

Above right Neil Webb arrived at Old Trafford from Nottingham Forest for £1.5 million.

Right Gary Pallister came from Middlesbrough to add steel to United's back four alongside Steve Bruce.

1986–93 January 1990 thousands of the United faithful were in open revolt. Gates at Old Trafford had fallen bellow 40,000 – an alarming sight for Ferguson, especially as his costly new players were looking like flops. Falling gates and bad results combined with poor performance in the transfer market was the recipe that had ended Sexton's reign at Old Trafford. Now it looked as though Ferguson was on the same slippery slope to the sack. There were also ructions in the boardroom as another corporate predator eyed the club. This time the would-be purchaser was property magnate Michael Knighton, who posed as a potential saviour and a man of the people – not least when he showily took to the field before a match wearing football strip, headed a ball down to the Stretford End and hammered it into the net. At that stage Knighton's overtures appeared to have been successful and he was poised to take control for an outlay of £20 million. But by October 1989 all bets were off as the deal unravelled in the glare of hostile publicity.

The coup de grâce for Ferguson could so easily have come in the third round of the FA Cup. United were well down the league table and out of the League Cup, and if they had been eliminated from the FA Cup at the first stage Ferguson's prospects would have been bleak. United were handed a tricky third round draw away to Brian Clough's highly talented Nottingham Forest side, who had finished third in the First Division the previous season. But the match at the City Ground went down in United legend as the day when Ferguson's job was saved and the club began its rise back to the top. The only goal of the game in a fighting United display was scored by Mark Robins and it set United on the way to their first trophy under Ferguson, and the birth of a new United dynasty to rival that of Busby.

Bruce said, 'That was the start of the comeback right there. We needed a spark to ignite the whole thing and get the club going, and that FA Cup run in 1990 was exactly what we needed. You can trace everything that followed, all the titles and the trophies, the European

Below Michael Knighton posed as a would-be saviour at Old Trafford before his deal to buy the club unravelled.

Below right Mark Robins wheels away in triumph after scoring the goal at the City Ground which has been credited with saving Alex Ferguson's job.

Cup and the Treble back to Mark Robins's goal on that afternoon in Nottingham, because from that came the Cup run and our first trophy under Alex, and from then on we added success after success.'

By a strange accident of the draw United were destined to reach Wembley without playing a single game at Old Trafford. In the fourth round they went to Hereford United's quaint Edgar Street ground and Ferguson's team endured a torrid afternoon. The only difference between the First Division side and the struggling Fourth Division team was a Clayton Blackmore goal, and the midfielder's winner provided a lifeline for the manager. Robins's winner in Nottingham is always marked down as the one that saved the manager. But Blackmore's effort in Herefordshire saved Ferguson from a nightmare on Edgar Street and an early and embarassing exit from the competition.

United travelled to Newcastle, then in the Second Division, in the fifth round and pulled off a 3-2 victory, and another tense 1-0 win at Sheffield United took Ferguson's side into the semi-finals, where they met Oldham Athletic. The Latics were a mid-table Second Division side, but Joe Royle had turned them into a dangerous proposition in cup competitions. United needed all their resources of skill, nerve and sinew to emerge from the first game at Maine Road with a 3-3 draw. The replay was just as closely fought and once again Robins stepped up to help his manager out of a jam. The striker came off the bench to score his third goal of the Cup campaign as United won 2-1 to reach the final.

United might have expected Liverpool to be their opponents in the final, as the Merseysiders faced Crystal Palace in the second semi-final. Palace were languishing in the lower reaches of the First Division and had lost 9-0 at Anfield earlier in the season. But the south London side wreaked vengeance on Liverpool to fix a date with United at Wembley.

United had lived on their nerves every step of the way in the Cup run and it was no different in the final. Gary O'Reilly shot Palace ahead, before Bryan Robson equalised to make the half-time score 1-1. Hughes gave United the advantage after an hour, but Steve Coppell, Palace's manager, brought on his secret weapon with 10 minutes to go: Ian Wright. The striker equalised with his first real touch of the game to send the match into extra-time and Wright struck again early in the first period to put Palace ahead. The score remained at

3-2 as the final whistle loomed, but in the closing minutes Webb and Wallace combined to send Hughes through on goal and the Welshman scored to send the final into a replay. Five days later the young left-back, Lee Martin, wrote his name indelibly into the annals of Manchester United by scoring the only goal of the game. It was the first of many trophies United were to reap in the Ferguson era.

The Cup triumph earned the beleaguered Ferguson some respite and he used the breathing space to continue his reconstruction, as the dependable full-back, Denis Irwin, came to United from Oldham Athletic for £625,000. The next season showed a steady rather than spectacular improvement in United's league form, as they dragged themselves up to sixth position. Mark Hughes played well enough to be voted the Player of the Year by his fellow pros as he had been in 1989 – but he was not United's top league scorer. He was beaten by the unlikely figure of Steve Bruce, who netted 13 times in an extraordinary season, which also featured another six Bruce goals in cup competitions. The defender's goal-drenched campaign featured a three-match spell when he banged in five goals. The big Geordie scored twice in a 4-1 home win over Luton and got another two against his old club, Norwich, at Carrow Road a week later. He kept up the run with another goal in a 2-1 win against Wimbledon at Old Trafford.

United booked another day out at Wembley when they reached the 1991 League Cup final. They lost 1-0 against Sheffield Wednesday – to the enormous satisfaction of their manager, Ron Atkinson – but the season was lifted to sublime heights by a glorious run in the European Cup-Winners' Cup.

United played four two-legged ties on the way to the final and they pulled off a rare feat by winning every away leg. Their journey to the final in Rotterdam took in victories against Pecsi Munkas of Hungary, Wrexham, Montpellier and Legia Warsaw in the semi-finals and, not surprisingly in his golden season, Bruce was United's joint top-scorer in the cup run. The centre-half scored vital goals in United's 3-0 home leg victory against Wrexham, another in the 2-0 win at the Racecourse Ground, his third in the 2-0 win in Montpellier and a fourth in the 3-1 win away to Legia Warsaw.

United showed impressive form throughout the competition, but it was the away win in France which lodges most clearly in the memory. Ferguson's team had drawn the first leg 1-1 at Old Trafford and they were in severe peril of leaving the competition at the Stade

1986–93 de la Masson. Montpellier were a strong side and they had come through more difficult games than United to reach the quarter-finals, with victories over PSV Eindhoven and Steaua Bucharest to their credit. But United rocked the home side by taking the lead just before half-time as Clayton Blackmore scored from a free-kick. United made it 3-1 on aggregate early in the second half when Blackmore won a penalty and Bruce smacked the kick home. It was a victory to stand alongside the finest against-the-odds triumphs of United's European history.

McClair, like Bruce, also scored four in the early rounds as United set up their toughest task of the competition by far. Barcelona waited in the final and, although the Catalonians were clear favourites to lift the trophy, United enjoyed their first taste of European glory since 1968 with a stupendous 2-1 win. Ferguson was thrilled with the victory and not just for its own sake. His experience at Aberdeen taught him that success breeds more success, and trophies beget more trophies. One of the highpoints of his time at Pittodrie had been winning this same Cup-Winners' Cup against Real Madrid in May 1983. Seven years on he had recaptured it and the proud boss was inclined to look on it as the precursor

---

Below Mark Hughes scores against Crystal Palace in the FA Cup final draw in May 1990.

Overleaf Bryan Robson drives himself past Lauren Blanc in the stirring clash with French side Montpellier.

1990 **FA CUP FINAL REPLAY**

MANCHESTER UNITED 1 Martin **CRYSTAL PALACE 0**

12 MAY 1990 at Wembley • Referee: A. Gunn • Attendance: 80,000

Palace had had their chance to win the Cup on the Saturday and missed it. After a pulsating 3-3 draw, which could so easily have ended as a win for the south London side, the teams returned to Wembley the following Thursday and a single United goal was enough to take the trophy back to Old Trafford.

Steve Coppell's Palace went into the replay with a completely different tactical outlook. In the first game they had discomfited United by attacking at pace and by utilising the threat of their rocket-heeled substitute, Ian Wright, to devastating effect late in the game. Now their aims were baser: they seemed to kick everything above grass level. Oddly, the rougher approach against a more skilful side backfired on them, as United dealt quite comfortably with everything Palace could throw at them. After all, any team containing such martial spirits as Ince, Bruce, Pallister, Robson and Hughes was quite capable of

looking after itself. Despite the galaxy of stellar names in the United line-up, it was the unheralded left-back, Lee Martin, who scored the winner. He broke from deep to crash an unstoppable shot into the roof of the net and ensured himself a perpetual niche in the pantheon of United heroes.

There was one notable absentee from United's victorious team. Jim Leighton had been made the scapegoat for United's hesitant defensive showing in the first game and was replaced between the sticks by the idiosyncratic, shouting goalkeeper, Les Sealey. Ferguson had shown, as if he needed to, that he was not a sentimental man when it came to team selection.

Winning the final was a joyous experience, but there remained a nagging thought. Steve Bruce said, 'Winning the FA Cup was fantastic, but it wasn't the trophy we really wanted... The Championship was still our Holy Grail.'

MANCHESTER UNITED

Sealey
Ince
Martin
Bruce
Phelan
Pallister
Robson
Webb
McClair
Hughes
Wallace

CRYSTAL PALACE

Martyn
Pemberton
Shaw
Gray
O'Reilly
Thorn
Barber (Wright)
Thomas
Bright
Salako (Madden)
Pardew

1986–93   of many more triumphs. On the night United won the cup he said, 'We can use this as a platform. Having experienced this tonight, you need it all the time now. It becomes like a drug.'

United set off on the quest for their next fix of achievement with new weapons in their armoury. In the closing weeks of the 1990/91 season two flying wingers had made their United debuts: a 17-year-old Welsh/Mancunian named Ryan Giggs and Andrei Kanchelskis from the Ukraine. Two more key players joined in time for the start of the 1991/92 season – goalkeeper Peter Schmeichel came from Danish club Brondby for £500,000 and England defender Paul Parker arrived from QPR for £1.7 million. Ferguson had assembled a side which looked strong enough to finish above Liverpool and Arsenal. But as the season unfolded, a new threat emerged from a wholly unexpected source.

United's ambition to win the elusive Championship appeared jinxed. In a season when English football's dominant superpowers from Highbury and Anfield suffered a blip in their fortunes, a newly resurgent Leeds United arose to fight for the title. With Liverpool and Arsenal both out of contention, a newly potent United could have enjoyed a serene run-in to the long-awaited prize. It was not to be, as bad luck and some old failings surfaced to scupper their chances. Ferguson's team set the pace from the start, going unbeaten in their first dozen games and taking up residence at the top of the table by the end of the summer. They looked on course

United fans paint Rotterdam red for the 1991 Cup-Winners' Cup final against Barcelona.

1991 **EUROPEAN CUP-WINNERS' CUP FINAL**

MANCHESTER UNITED 2 Hughes 2 **BARCELONA 1** Koeman

15 MAY 1991 at De Kuip Stadium, Rotterdam • Referee: K. Karlson (Sweden) • Attendance:48,000

It turned out be a night of glorious vindication for Mark Hughes, the striker who returned home to Old Trafford after being spurned at Barcelona. The Welsh striker was told he was not good enough for the giant Catalan club, but he made his former employers rue those words as his two goals won the cup for United.

After a goalless first half United wrested control of the game in the second period. Midway through the second half Bryan Robson planted a free-kick on Steve Bruce's forehead and Hughes guided the goalbound effort over the line. Five minutes later Hughes scored the goal that, perhaps more than any other, stands out as the most memorable of the 163 he scored in his United career.

Hughes spearheaded a break towards the Barcelona area, but there appeared to be little chance of a goal as the striker was shepherded wide of the target. But Hughes put in a spurt to get clear of the cover and, from a wide position, launched a searing shot with the outside of his boot which found the net from the narrowest of angles. It was a goal worthy of winning any cup final and it sealed this match, despite Barcelona's late consolation.

The match-winner Mark Hughes brandishes the trophy in Rotterdam.

MANCHESTER UNITED

Sealey
Irwin
Bruce
Pallister
Blackmore
Phelan
Robson
Ince
Sharpe
Hughes
McClair

BARCELONA

Busquets
Alexanco (Pinilla)
Nando
Koeman
Ferrer
Goikotxea
Eusebio
Bakero
Beguiristain
Salinas
Laudrup

MARK HUGHES

FORWARD (1983–86, 1988–95) • 453 (14) APPEARANCES • 163 GOALS

Mark Hughes was one of those players whose off-field demeanour was completely at odds with his personality on the pitch. Away from the hurly-burly of a match he was softly spoken and undemonstrative. Yet throw him into the midst of a game and he became a warrior in the United cause. That's not to say that Hughes was a dirty player. Better to say he played the game with a will to win so fierce it was disconcerting and a ruthless streak a mile wide. Other less bellicose strikers could drift through games waiting for their chance to score beautiful goals. Hughes had to be involved in all aspects of the game, dropping deep to scrap for possession in midfield if the ball was not reaching him further up the field. He had an unquenchable will to succeed which, married to his abundance of talent, made him a vastly important player in his two spells at the club.

Hughes first grabbed the attention at United as a callow but classy snaffler of chances in 1984/85 and his goals fuelled the team's abortive tilt at the title the following season. But United unaccountably allowed Hughes to sign for Barcelona just as he was reaching maturity. Hughes had emerged from the youth ranks at Old Trafford, but the club's hierarchy chose to cash in their asset and accepted a £2 million bid for him. Happily for United Hughes was miserable abroad. He never fitted in at Barcelona, went on loan to Bayern Munich, and returned to Old Trafford a wiser and more complete footballer.

In the seasons to come he played an important role in the honours that followed. He scored his fair share of goals, among them occasional show-stopping Goal of the Season contenders, but much of his work was unglamorous. His strength in possession and faultless close ball skills made him a natural target man, and he provided the perfect conduit for countless United attacks. The team had plenty of flamboyant, forward-minded players who could destroy opponents with flashy dribbles and mesmerising tricks. Hughes gave them the option of knocking the ball early, safe in the knowledge that he would keep it for as long as it took for team-mates to flood forward in support.

Much of his play might have looked straightforward to the untrained eye, but his peers knew better. Twice, in 1989 and 1991, he was voted Players' Player of the Year, the individual prize which professionals crave above any other.

BRYAN ROBSON

MIDFIELDER (1981–94) • 437 (24) APPEARANCES • 99 GOALS

In his 13 years at Old Trafford Bryan Robson was less a midfield player and more a force of nature. His importance to the team rested not just on the fact that he was several players in one: ever-reliable defensive bulwark, creative livewire and regular goalscorer. Robson could do everything in the game, he could pass short and long, tackle, shoot, head, and he had the athleticism to run all day. Robson found his best position in central midfield, but he could equally as well have turned out at centre-half or centre-forward. His versatility drew favourable comparisons with another young lion from United's past: Duncan Edwards.

As well as all that, Robson was a driving force and inspirational captain, leading his men with a passionate intensity that presaged Roy Keane. Robson led from the front, brave to the point of recklessness and ever-ready to run through brick walls in the service of United – his men would always follow him into the breach.

Robson's presence was perhaps Ron Atkinson's most valuable legacy to United. Atkinson had been Robson's manager at West Bromwich and in the injury-prone youngster he correctly identified a future titan of the game. It cost him £1.5 million to prise him from the Hawthorns in October 1981, but that outlay was repaid many times over.

Robson's best days were beginning to fade just as a United golden era was beginning in the early 1990s, but the old maestro lingered long enough to hand the baton of excellence over to a new generation of United legends. He was far from an automatic choice in the breakthrough season of 1992/93, but he re-entered the arena for the closing stages and scored the final goal of the title-winning campaign, aged 36.

1986–93

for the Championship as early as Bonfire Night, but while all the usual suspects fell away in United's wake Leeds clung on doggedly. The two Uniteds fought a fascinating duel all the way through the autumn, winter and into the spring. It was just Ferguson's luck that Howard Wilkinson welded together a functional, efficient, point-harvesting machine of a side to disrupt the coronation, and it was a cruel rebuke to Ferguson that Gordon Strachan played an influential role in Leeds's powerful midfield quartet. Ferguson had considered Strachan surplus to requirements at Old Trafford and let him go to Elland Road for just £300,000. The little midfielder ended the season as Player of the Year and with a Championship winner's medal.

Even with Leeds in pursuit United could and should have won the league in May 1992. In April it was theirs to lose, and they went ahead and lost it. Over the final yards fixture congestion proved fatal to their hopes, as Ferguson's team were obliged to play their last six matches in a fortnight, and they ran out of gas. Leeds, by contrast, grew stronger over the final weeks, helped by a lavish sprinkling of magic dust strewn by their French striker, Eric Cantona.

With one week of the season left United were still two points ahead of Leeds with a game in hand, but then the jitters struck. They lost at home for the first time that season, 2-1 against Forest. Two days later they were beaten 1-0 at relegated West Ham. In another four days they lost 2-0 at Anfield, of all places, and now the title was in Leeds's hands if they could hold their nerve. The Yorkshire side had been in remorseless form all season and they did not slip up, and a 3-2 victory at Bramall Lane stole the title from United's clutches. It didn't take a mathematical genius to work out that United's title-less run had now stretched for a quarter-of-a-century.

United gained some consolation from their first-ever success in the League Cup, a competition which they had shunned in its early days. Brian McClair scored their winner in the final against Forest and they were glad of any trophy at all, because they had little joy elsewhere in a highly frustrating season. United had become the first top-flight side to lose an FA Cup tie on penalties, when they went out at Southampton in the fourth round. Their defence of the Cup-Winners' Cup ended early at the hands of Atlético Madrid.

United's ultimately fruitless chase for the Championship took place against a backdrop of frantic change in British football. The financial landscape of the sport was being transformed and United were in the vanguard of the revolution. For over a century most clubs had been run as small family businesses, often by well-meaning citizens with little interest in or knowledge of football. On a national scale the sport was largely in the hands of committees, staffed by time-serving worthies. At every level, all this was about to change.

Throughout the 1991/92 season the future of the game in England was shrouded in uncertainty as the Football League and the Football Association were locked in a battle for power. The root of the matter was, of course, money. Satellite TV wanted live football to lure subscribers to the new technology and it was prepared to pay big sums for exclusive access to the action. The leading First Division clubs wanted to keep most of the cash for themselves and their hard-

Mark Hughes (left) and Steve Bruce applaud the United fans after losing 2-0 at Anfield in April 1992, a result that sent their title challenge clattering off the rails.

headed logic was faultless: the big teams generated most of the money, therefore they should get most of it. The Football League, representing all 92 professional clubs, wanted the proceeds to be shared out more equally across the divisions. That prompted the best-supported sides to threaten a breakaway, which would have meant they could collar every penny the television companies were prepared to pay. In the end the traditional League system of English football was preserved – but compromise came at a huge cost for the lower league clubs. The FA Premier League was formed in time for the start of the 1992/93 season and the top flight teams began to bank television revenues vastly in excess of anything they had ever seen before. In May 1992 a deal was struck in which the BBC and Sky agreed to pay £300 million over five years for highlights and live games. That was just the start,

as television revenues continued to rocket and then went into orbit as the European Champions League took off.

United had geared up for football's brave new world by becoming a public limited company in the summer of 1991. The move brought benefits as well as drawbacks. Perhaps crucially, the initial injection of capital ensured that in the early days of the Premier League, the club would have the financial clout to compete for the best players available. Football had restructured itself in such a way that the most successful clubs would make the most money, giving them a head-start on the also-rans the following season. It was vitally important for ambitious clubs to climb aboard this gravy train at the start of the journey or they would be left standing at the station for a long time, perhaps forever. Failure in the early days would condemn lesser teams to a frustrating future of watching richer clubs contesting the big prizes, while they did their best to survive in the big league. The best most of them could hope for would be the occasional decent cup run and perhaps UEFA Cup qualification.

Goalscorer Brian McClair shows off the League Cup after United had beaten Forest 1-0 in the final at Wembley in April 1992.

These were the cold, hard facts of football in the early 1990s, and while United would go on to benefit from them, they were not of the club's making. In time they would capitalise on their position as Britain's biggest and best-supported club, but they were only able to do so because Ferguson created a team to match the club's stature.

The first, giant step towards the club's domination of British football in the 1990s came in the 1992/93 season, the first of the newly-created FA Premier League. It is odd how the memory can play tricks. Looking back on that history-changing campaign it is easy to imagine that United led the field from start to finish, blazing their way to a first Championship for 26 years on a non-stop glory ride. Not so. In the early skirmishes United were dismal. They lost the first match of the season 2-1 at Sheffield United, then went down 3-0 at home to Everton. They failed to win their third game, also at home, as they stumbled to a lacklustre 1-1 draw with Ipswich. They finally broke their duck in the fourth match, with a fortunate 1-0 win at Southampton, but already United were flirting with the relegation places rather than vying for top spot. But the team suddenly clicked into gear, reeling off five wins on the bounce to soar up the table. Old frustrations crept back, though, as they drew the next five, then lost two more. Then came the spark that ignited United's unstoppable drive for the title – and its name was Eric Cantona.

Brian Deane scores the first goal in Premiership history for Sheffield United as Alex Ferguson's side lose the first game of the 1992/93 season 2-1 at Bramall Lane.

The moody, magnificent Frenchman had already proved his genius as a footballing alchemist by turning Howard Wilkinson's base metal into pure gold at Elland Road. Ferguson coveted the player, knowing that he could be the difference between a good team and a great one, but he despaired of ever persuading Leeds to sell him. Then he took advantage of an almighty stroke of luck. One day Wilkinson called United to inquire about the availability of Denis Irwin. Ferguson rebuffed the approach for his full-back, but idly inquired whether Cantona might be for sale – fully expecting Wilkinson to laugh off the suggestion that Leeds might sell their best player to their biggest rivals. But it was an inspired hunch: Cantona was for sale and Ferguson could not believe that Wilkinson was handing him the chance to buy the player he wanted above all others. His incredulity deepened when he landed Cantona for £1.2 million. It ranked among the greatest transfer bargains of all time.

Cantona immediately brought a fresh dimension to United's attacking efforts. He scored vital goals, set up many more, but most of all his self-confidence, arrogance even, coursed through the players around him and lifted the spirit in the club to a new level. At once, the team was flying. Mark Hughes up front was energised, and Kanchelskis and Giggs tore down the flanks with new vigour. Paul Ince held the centre and Lee Sharpe played the most effective football of his life. The defence, too, looked impregnable with Pallister and Bruce forming a solid barrier in the middle, and Irwin and Parker snuffing out threats from the wings. Behind them all, Schmeichel was confirming his reputation as the best goalkeeper in the world.

team in the country. Manchester enjoyed the biggest party the city had seen for years when the new Premiership Champions played Blackburn at Old Trafford the next day. United marked the occasion by winning stylishly 3-1, in the benign presence of Sir Matt Busby. At last United had found a manager to emulate his title-winning exploits. Twenty-six years of hurt were banished on a sunlit evening at Old Trafford.

After Cantona's arrival United hauled in the long-time leaders, Norwich City, and opened up a gap at the top which widened as the season's end loomed in view. Only Villa clung on to any semblance of a hope of catching United, but this time there was to be no collapse – barring a worrying wobble in March when United lost at Oldham and then drew three on the spin. But United, suffused with self-belief, righted themselves and cruised to the title by a clear 10 points on the back of a blistering finish as they won their last seven matches.

They were confirmed as Premier League Champions on May Day Monday 1993, without kicking a ball, when their only possible challengers, Villa, lost to Oldham. Ferguson was not even watching the game. He was playing golf and had reached the 18th green when a man wandered over from the neighbouring fairway and said, 'Excuse me Mr Ferguson. You are the Champions.' It had taken him seven years, but he had finally pulled off the feat demanded of all United managers: he had made them into the top

Above *Alex Ferguson unveils one of his greatest ever signings, Eric Cantona, who arrived from Leeds United for a song.*
Right *Cantona in typically flamboyant action.*

SIR ALEX FERGUSON

MANAGER (1986–PRESENT)

Sir Alex Ferguson had to walk a long, hard road to become the most successful Manchester United manager of all time. He was born in Glasgow's shipbuilding district of Govan in 1941 and, after leaving school the teenage Ferguson joined the tens of thousands of men who laboured in the yards, as an apprentice welder. But the boy was also turning out for Glasgow's famous amateur club, Queen's Park, and his prowess as a centre-forward outshone his ability with a welder's torch, and he was soon signed on as a professional by Perth's St Johnstone in 1960. After four years there he was snapped up by Dunfermline Athletic, who were at the time one of Scotland's elite clubs. But a boyhood dream came true in 1967 when Rangers, the team he had supported all his life, paid £65,000 to take him to Ibrox.

The move did not work out well. Ferguson gained a reputation for truculence, a trait which landed him in trouble with team-mates, opponents, referees and the Rangers management. He was showing early signs of the single-mindedness that would make him such a formidable manager, but at this stage his intransigence saw him transferred to Falkirk, where he had a taste of coaching, and later to Ayr United.

Ferguson took his first steps as a fledgling manager at East Stirling in July 1974, but after making an early impact there he was given the chance to manage a bigger club, St Mirren, in Paisley on the outskirts of Glasgow. He took the Buddies to promotion into Scotland's top flight and also energised the club with his forceful personality. Ferguson was so determined to get the local community to back their team, he took to driving around the streets of Paisley with a loudspeaker system bolted to the roof

of his car before kick-off, and exhorted the populace to turn up at Love Street to see the game. Despite this level of commitment Ferguson fell victim of a boardroom coup and lost his job. But he had already done enough to come to the attention of a city club who were down on their luck and in need of a thrusting young leader. That club was Aberdeen and Ferguson piloted the Dons to an unprecedented list of honours: three Championships, four SFA Cups, a Scottish League Cup and a Cup-Winners' Cup final triumph over Real Madrid. In November 1986 he was the automatic choice of the Manchester United board to replace Ron Atkinson.

It took some time, but Ferguson vindicated their decision many times over as he turned United into Britain's team of the 1990s, made them kings of Europe once again and set them on the way to more glory in the 21st century.

At long last, Alex Ferguson grasps the Premier League trophy.

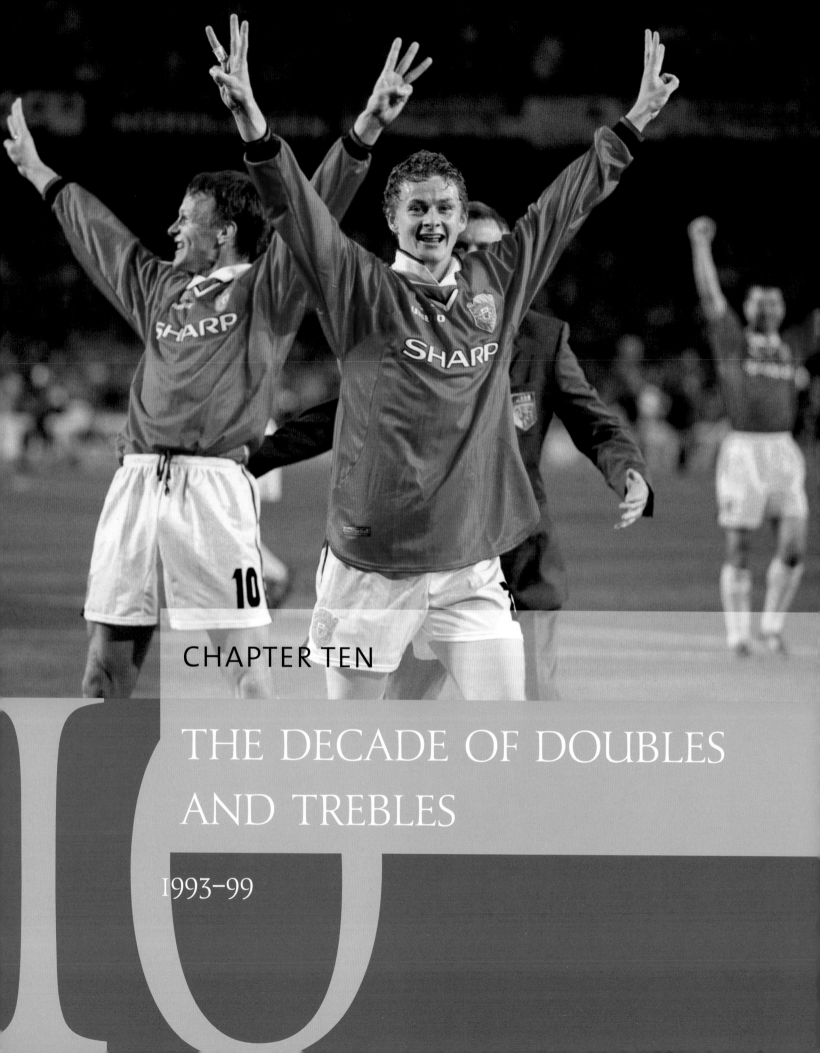

CHAPTER TEN

THE DECADE OF DOUBLES AND TREBLES

1993–99

IT WAS LIKE A DAM BURSTING. ONCE UNITED HAD WON THEIR
FIRST TITLE ALL THE PENT-UP DESIRE THAT HAD BEEN MASSING
FOR MORE THAN A QUARTER OF A CENTURY WAS UNLEASHED
AND FERGUSON'S MAGNIFICENT CHAMPIONS SET ABOUT
BOSSING ENGLISH FOOTBALL

The manager made the team even stronger by buying Nottingham Forest's accomplished Irish midfielder, Roy Keane, for £3.75 million and he slotted into a side which grew visibly more confident in its own ability with each victory. United seized leadership of the 1993/94 Premiership before summer was done with five wins and a draw in the first six games.

In seasons past encouraging sequences of wins such as these were followed by inexplicable blips as United lacked the consistency needed to win titles. Now Ferguson had added iron ruthlessness to the team's attacking zeal. Rare defeats sparked fresh determination to avoid further mishaps and any lingering doubts about the team's status as the best in the country were quickly banished. United slipped up in the seventh game of the season, losing 1-0 at Chelsea. But the team responded with a scintillating series of eight wins on the spin and from September 1993 they didn't lose a match until the following March.

The Premiership title should have been in the bag long before the Easter eggs were unwrapped, but United suffered a dip in form just as the finishing line came into view. In the past it might have proved fatal to their title drive. A rash of indiscipline broke out within the team: Cantona was sent off twice in a week, Schmeichel saw red in the FA Cup quarter-final with Charlton and Andrei Kanchelskis was ordered off in the League Cup final defeat to Villa. United also began to drop league points in March, allowing their nearest challengers, Blackburn Rovers, back into the contest.

Opposite The goalscorers Ole Gunnar Solskjaer (right) and Teddy Sheringham parade at the Nou Camp after United's heart-stopping, Treble-winning victory over Bayern Munich in May 1999.
Right The English Championship is back in United's hands for the first time since the 1960s.

But Ferguson's United weren't about to surrender and when it really mattered the team rediscovered its best form to pull away in the closing stages, eventually racing eight points clear of Kenny Dalglish's emerging side.

By April United were chasing an achievement that had always eluded them, even in the great years of the 1950s when the Busby Babes were the best team in the country: Ferguson's men were Champions, but they craved the League and Cup Double.

United won their first three FA Cup ties, all away from home, without conceding a goal – 1-0 at Sheffield United, 2-0 at Norwich and 3-0 at Wimbledon. They were finally given a home draw at the quarter-finals stage and they had little difficulty in beating Charlton 3-1. Now they faced familiar semi-final opponents, Oldham Athletic, at Wembley – and the Latics again proved tough adversaries. Joe Royle's team were winning 1-0 with moments to go when Mark Hughes dredged up an equaliser and United won the replay 4-1. Chelsea were their opponents in the final.

United had needed replays against unfancied opposition to win their previous two FA Cups, but now against a strong Chelsea

team, who had beaten them twice in the league, 90 minutes was all they needed. United turned on the style and won the match in the end with considerable ease after some early alarms. Eric Cantona scored two second-half penalties, Hughes got the third and Brian McClair came off the bench to add the fourth. McClair said, 'It was a good feeling to have the Double, but by that time we felt we were capable of winning every competition we were in. We were confident and that final against Chelsea was typical of our attitude.

'We had lost to Chelsea in the league a couple of times, but on the morning of the game we felt we would win. Even in the first half when they played well and hit the bar, and we weren't at our best, we believed we would win. That was the mark of that team.

'That was a big difference for players who had been at the club for a while, because they could remember the days when we were still waiting to win our first title and it never seemed to come. They could remember when we lost out to Leeds and some people wondered if we would ever win the Championship at all. But the first time we won it all those ghosts were exorcised. For the United teams which followed it was easier, because that burden had been removed, and they could get on with playing and winning without having to worry about history all the time.'

United were delighted with their Double, but they would have to wait another few years for a Treble, because as well as losing the League Cup final United also suffered an early exit from the revamped European Cup. Ferguson's team made their return to Europe's top competition by beating Kispest Honved of Hungary. But to reach the lucrative group stages they had to beat the dangerous Turkish team, Galatasaray. The task was beyond them in their first season back in the big time of continental football. The Turks fought, scratched and spat their way to a 3-3 draw in the first leg at Old Trafford, and their ugly tactics succeeded in rousing the ire of Cantona. As the players were leaving the field at half-time Cantona aimed a volley of well-chosen French invective at the referee. Cantona may well have got away with the tirade against an English referee, but unfortunately for Cantona, Kurt Rothlisberger was a

Mark Hughes shares a bath with the Football Association Challenge Cup.

1994 **FA CUP FINAL**

MANCHESTER UNITED 4 Cantona 2 pens, Hughes, McClair **CHELSEA 0**
14 MAY 1994 at Wembley • Referee: David Elleray • Attendance: 79,634

The final score was emphatic, but it disguised the fact that for an hour Chelsea looked the better team at a wet Wembley and United were clinging to the ropes for much of the time. Gavin Peacock hit the bar in the first half and a tide of blue shirts threatened to swamp Schmeichel's area. But this United side was made of durable material and they picked up their game in the final half-hour to pull away over the closing stages, inspired to a great extent by the strut and swagger of their French talisman, Cantona.

The breakthrough came after Eddie Newton fouled Denis Irwin in the box and Cantona nonchalantly sent Kharine the wrong way. Five minutes later Frank Sinclair fouled Kanchelskis close to goal and Cantona once again conned Kharine to score. Brian McClair said, 'Eric was such a great penalty-taker that we never doubted for a moment that he would score them both. We had been under some pressure earlier in the game, and it was a case of being patient and waiting for the game to turn our way, which it did.'

With United in charge and Chelsea in disarray Mark Hughes made it 3-0 a couple of minutes later, pouncing on an error by Sinclair before firing home. United had the luxury of a penalty miss as Cantona passed up on the chance of a hat-trick of spot-kick goals, but they still made it 4-0 in the late stages. Hughes sent Ince clear and the midfielder took the ball past Kharine before crossing for McClair to finish. McClair said, 'Paul Ince could have scored, but he was good enough to roll it to me and I miskicked the ball into an empty net.'

Eric Cantona makes no mistake from the penalty spot as United thrash Chelsea at Wembley.

MANCHESTER UNITED

Schmeichel
Parker
Irwin (Sharpe)
Bruce
Kanchelskis (McClair)
Pallister
Cantona
Ince
Keane
Hughes
Giggs

CHELSEA

Kharine
Clarke
Sinclair
Kjeldberg
Johnsen
Burley (Hoddle)
Spencer
Newton
Stein (Cascarino)
Peacock
Wise

processed slowly through the streets. The hearse came to a halt outside his beloved Old Trafford, the ground he had done so much to restore after the ravages of war, and a vast throng of mourners stood in the rain for two minutes in silent tribute to him.

Ferguson, the man who had restored United to the status they last enjoyed when Busby was in charge, paid an emotional tribute to his illustrious predecessor, naming him as the greatest manager Britain had seen. He said, 'He was the outstanding man of them all. Even Bill Shankly and Jock Stein sought his advice and experience.'

Busby had been a master at getting the best from a disparate collection of hugely gifted players. Ferguson had a big job on his hands dealing with just one singular talent.

Ferguson must have known when he bought Eric Cantona that he was bidding adieu to any chance of a quiet life. True, he had picked Leeds's pocket to land a footballing genius, one of the cleverest footballers ever to play in this country. But the devilish Frenchman also trailed clouds of sulphur wherever he went: you couldn't have the brilliance without the brimstone. Cantona's impetuosity made the 1994/95 season a torment for Ferguson and United.

In January 1995 United were aiming for an unprecedented back-to-back Double. Their form was good and Ferguson had spent £6 million to bring Newcastle United's free-scoring striker, Andy Cole, to Old Trafford. The prospect of Cantona's magical creative talent combined with Cole's goalscoring prowess was almost a guarantee of trophies. Sadly, a second of near-insanity from Cantona ended with the striker in a police cell and United's season veering off the rails.

On 25 January 1995, United were playing Crystal Palace at Selhurst Park and the match was what is often euphemistically described as a physical affair. Tempers boiled over and Cantona was sent off. As the Frenchman trudged back to the dressing room a Palace supporter lurched to the front row of the stand and let fly at the player with a foul-mouthed stream of abuse. The percentage play for Cantona would have been to ignore the cretin and continue on his way. But the television pictures of what happened next were destined to rival the Zapruder film of the Kennedy assassination as the most-replayed screen footage of all time. Cantona launched a flying kick into the chest of his tormentor and seemed keen to extend the exchange when team-mates intervened to end what

Francophone Swiss, and a French teacher by trade, and the thrust of Cantona's remarks were not lost on him. Cantona was sent off.

United's reception for the second leg in Istanbul was a hot one and the banners proclaiming 'Wellcome to the Hell' were appropriate. The 0-0 draw that followed was a deeply uncomfortable experience for United, and the players were jostled by armed paramilitary troops on their way off the field and both Robson and Cantona were punched by policemen in the tunnel. It was a brutal lesson that European football posed new problems that would have to be overcome if Ferguson was ever to realise his dream of emulating Busby by winning the greatest club trophy of them all.

Sadly, Matt Busby did not live to see United's re-emergence as a power in European football. The man who made the modern Manchester United died on 20 January 1994, aged 84. His passing provoked widespread grief in Manchester and beyond, and his funeral brought his adopted city to a standstill as the cortège

Turkish fans extend their customary warm welcome to the players, officials and supporters of Manchester United Football Club.

surely would have been a very messy episode. One United player in particular was distraught: David May had scored a rare goal in the match, which ended 1-1. Who would remember his strike now?

The full majesty of the law was brought to bear upon Cantona. He was charged with assault and for a few dreadful hours it seemed to be Strangeways here we come for the striker, as Croydon magistrates sentenced him to two weeks in jail. But while Cantona languished in a holding cell at the court waiting for an escort to cart him off to prison, United's legal team swung into action. They immediately lodged an appeal against the sentence and successfully applied for their man to be released on bail. The application was allowed and Cantona walked free. At a later hearing his sentence was commuted to 120 hours' community service, which he spent coaching delighted Manchester schoolchildren.

It's hard to say for certain to what extent the traumatic events scuppered United's chances of chasing another Double, but there

Above An emotional congregation show their respects outside Old Trafford on the day of Sir Matt Busby's funeral.

Right Eric Cantona trudges off the field at Selhurst Park, seconds before the assault that shocked the world.

1993–99   is no doubt the Cantona saga overshadowed the rest of the season. In addition to the justice meted out by Croydon magistrates, the FA also barred Cantona from playing until the following season. United were shorn of their most influential player for the remainder of the campaign. But despite those handicaps United went desperately close to another big haul of trophies and, in the immediate aftermath of the shock events at Selhurst Park, the team were still close to the peak of their form. Ipswich Town suffered an angry backlash as they got on the wrong end of a 9-0 hammering at Old Trafford in March. In the end, though, United finished the season with nothing.

The fight for the Premiership title went down to the last day. United needed to win at Upton Park and Blackburn had to lose at Anfield for United to take the Championship. Brian McClair said, 'We felt confident that Liverpool would beat Blackburn and as it turned out that's exactly what happened. So we had to beat West Ham. I scored to make it 1-1, and we had so many chances to win it, and we should have scored, but that's the way football goes sometimes. It doesn't work to plan.

'At the time we didn't think that the Cantona situation was a distraction. The manager and the coaching staff did their best to take our minds off that, but looking back it had to have an effect, even apart from losing Eric as a player through his suspension. Nobody will ever know why he decided to launch himself feet-first into the stand that night at Selhurst Park, but I'm sure now it had a massive effect on our season. You can't condone what Eric did, but you can understand it.'

United had the chance to make up for losing the Premiership title by winning another FA Cup final. At Wembley they came up against Everton, English football's self-styled dogs of war, but in a season that was physically and emotionally draining, it was a match too far for United. There was a sense of an era coming to a close as the team turned in a weak performance and lost 1-0 against Joe Royle's determined side. They possessed enough class to take the Toffees apart, but an oddly subdued United never imposed themselves on the game. Brian McClair said, 'We didn't play well. For whatever reason we couldn't get ourselves up for it.'

It felt like the end of an era and it was the end of an era. By the time the 1995/96 season kicked off a very different United took to the field. Ferguson indulged in a summer clear-out, perhaps influenced by the pale showing against Everton. Paul Ince, who had set himself up as the 'Guvnor' of Old Trafford, was sold by Ferguson – the only governor who mattered at United – to Internazionale for £7 million. Kanchelskis went to Everton for another £5 million and Hughes finally took his last bow, switching to Chelsea for £1.5 million. The surgery was drastic, but the manager felt he had ready-made replacements for the departees as a rich generation of young players emerged from United's vibrant youth programme. Great names of the future such as David Beckham, Paul Scholes and the Neville brothers were pushing for places in the first team, and Ferguson was prepared to give them their heads.

With a team full of youngsters, and Cantona's return from suspension still two months away, United struggled on the first day of the 1995/96 campaign with a 3-1 defeat at Villa Park. It was the game that prompted Alan Hansen to make a hasty remark on *Match of the Day* to the effect that no team ever won anything with kids. United supporters, steeped in the legend of the Busby Babes and raised on stories of the early exploits of Best, knew different. The Villa demise turned out to be nothing more serious than early season rustiness and the new-look side immediately embarked on a run of

Left *Andy Cole celebrates the third of his five-goal haul as United hammer Ipswich 9-0 at Old Trafford.*
Opposite *Paul Scholes doesn't bother to hide his delight after scoring against City in a 1-0 win at Old Trafford in October 1995.*

five consecutive wins. United did not lose another game until the day before Bonfire Night and even without Cantona the rejuvenated team were flying. Cantona's long-awaited return came on 1 October 1995, when the visitors to Old Trafford were Liverpool. The day embellished the Cantona fable even further, as the Frenchman turned in a sparkling display and scored a penalty in a 2-2 draw.

In an ordinary season United's form up to Christmas might have seen them way clear at the top of the table. But new adversaries had emerged from the north and their incredible form in the run-up to the turn of the year had left United trailing. Kevin Keegan's Newcastle had taken an iron grip on the top of the Premiership, spinning out victory after victory to lay waste to their rivals. In January 1996 the Geordies led United by 12 points and the rest of the season was shaping up into a coronation for Keegan's exciting team. But Newcastle suddenly, if not inexplicably, lost their way and United remorselessly reeled them in over the final months, chipping away at their ever-crumbling lead.

It was Cantona who fired the depth-charge that holed Newcastle below the waterline and the turning point came on a mild night in March at St James' Park where the top two met. For long periods of a torrid match Newcastle penned United back into their own half, but United defended valiantly, falling back to form an impenetrable

red cordon across the 18-yard line, refusing to let the black-and-white shirts pass. And once the Geordies had been repelled United caught them out with a classic goal on the break, and it was the cool Cantona who scored it to seal a 1-0 victory. Newcastle still held a substantial lead, but the momentum now lay with United. Keegan weakened his own team's chances in February by bringing in Faustino Asprilla. The Colombian was clearly a skilful striker capable of scoring wonder goals, but his arrival unbalanced the Newcastle team and they never looked the same.

As the two teams went head to head down the stretch it was the Newcastle novices who cracked under the pressure. Keegan memorably lost the plot after Ferguson had mischievously wondered whether Newcastle's opponents would be trying their hardest against them. The Newcastle manager wigged out live on Sky, in a bizarre anti-Ferguson rant. He said, 'We've never resorted to that. You simply don't say things like he did in this game. I have kept really quiet, but I tell you something, he went down in my estimation after that and I'll tell him this – we're still fighting for this title. He has got to go to Middlesbrough and get something. And I tell you honestly, I would love it if we beat them now – absolutely love it.' Of course, United did go to Middlesbrough and get something – it was the Premiership trophy. United's 3-0 win at the Riverside on the last day of the season was enough to give them the title by four points – a remarkable 16-point swing since January.

Six days later United had another significant date – the FA Cup final against Liverpool at Wembley, with a second Double on the line. The match provided the stage for Cantona to crown his season, scoring to give United victory in a match fraught with tension. It was a personal triumph for Cantona, who ended the season as the key player in United's Double-winning team. There was no doubt that Cantona was the outstanding player in the country. Two days before scoring the winner against Liverpool he accepted the Players' Player of the Year award – the first United player to win it since George Best in 1968. It was an amazing turnaround from the dark

The faces say it all as Kevin Keegan and Ferguson duel for the 1995/96 Championship, a rivalry that grew bitter as the finishing line hove into view.

days of January 1995, when newspapers were calling for Cantona to be deported and banned from football for life.

Cantona was the unassailable king of Old Trafford, but the new generation of United heroes continued to make huge strides. Chief among them was the young David Beckham, who presented his credentials as an England international with a goal from his own half in the 3-0 victory at Wimbledon on the first day of the 1996/97 Premiership season. United enjoyed a blistering start, but the wheels came off in spectacular fashion in October, beginning with a humiliating afternoon at St James' Park.

United had hammered the Geordies 4-0 in the Charity Shield just a couple of months earlier, but now Newcastle exacted revenge

with a 5-0 win. A week later United suffered another thrashing, this time going down 6-3 at Southampton. A woeful spell ended with a 2-1 home defeat against Chelsea. Not for the first or last time in his long reign at Old Trafford, some wondered whether Ferguson was losing his grip. But the obituaries were absurdly premature:

Below Brian Kidd, whose skilful coaching played such a big part in the development of young talent at Old Trafford, holds the Premiership trophy with Alex Ferguson.

Overleaf Eric Cantona scores the winning goal against Liverpool in the 1996 FA Cup final.

1996 **FA CUP FINAL**

MANCHESTER UNITED 1 Cantona **LIVERPOOL 0**

11 MAY 1996 at Wembley • Referee: Dermot Gallagher • Attendance: 79,007

MANCHESTER UNITED

Schmeichel
Irwin
P Neville
May
Keane
Pallister
Cantona
Beckham (G Neville)
Cole (Scholes)
Butt
Giggs

LIVERPOOL

James
McAteer
Jones (Thomas)
Scales
Wright
Babb
McManaman
Redknapp
Collymore (Rush)
Barnes
Fowler

United knew they would win the FA Cup final a full hour before the game had even kicked off. Brian McClair said, 'We saw Liverpool come out of the tunnel onto the pitch in their white suits and we knew we had won. They looked ridiculous, like they were on holiday rather than at the FA Cup final. Just looking at them was all the motivation we needed, as if we needed any anyway. You just looked at them strutting about Wembley and thought, "We have to beat them."'

The first FA Cup final since 1977 between the north-west rivals should have been a classic. United's exciting young team had just won the title and Liverpool's so-called Spice Boys had been playing attractive football all season. But the weight of expectation from both sets of supporters was difficult for the two teams to bear and the regional superpowers cancelled each out in a dull game riddled with errors. McClair said, 'They came out with a game plan to try to stifle us and it worked most of the time. In the end the match needed one piece of wonderful work to win it.'

For 86 minutes the match meandered along in search of some magic to turn it one way or the other – and it was Cantona who conjured up the match's defining moment. Both teams were tired and apparently resigned to extra-time when Beckham took a corner on the right. David James came out to push the ball away, but the clearance

was slowed down as it cannoned off Ian Rush. The ball fell to Cantona on the edge of the area, and he twisted his body to let fly with a half-volley which arrowed through a tangle of limbs before surging past James into the back of the net. It was a goal worthy to win a Cup final better than this one, but United did not care too much about the quality of the game.

McClair said, 'It was a terrific moment, because for Eric it meant he was back at the pinnacle after being down in the depths the year before. It was as if he felt he owed a debt to the club for its loyalty and he was able to repay it.' The Ferguson era had struck a new seam of success, with another Double added to the club's roll of honour.

The soberly-suited United players greet their more flamboyantly dressed Liverpool rivals before the match.

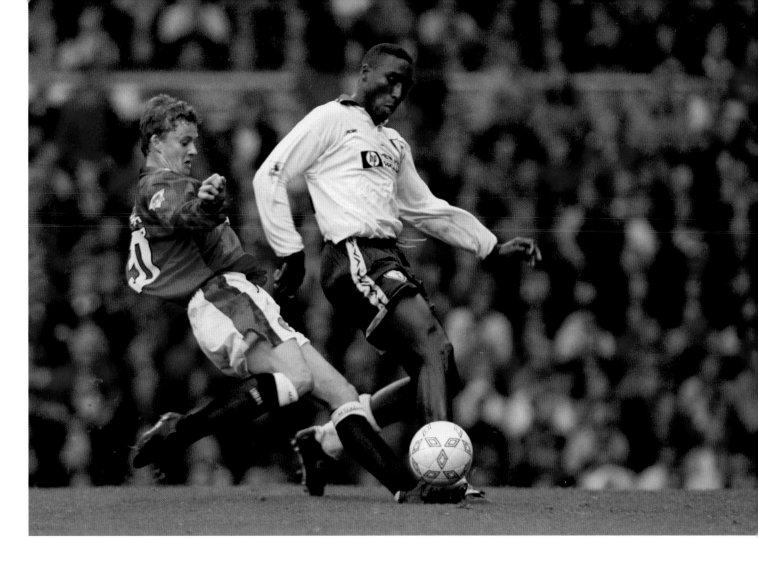

United went undefeated for the next 16 games and by March 1997 they were closing in on another title. They faced challenges from Arsenal, Liverpool and Newcastle, but by now United had got into the habit of winning Championships. They celebrated their fourth title in five seasons with a 2-0 win at home to West Ham on 11 May and ended the season seven points clear of Newcastle in second.

United had found the winning formula in the league, but they had yet to find their way in the Champions League. In 1996/97 they went into the group stage with Fenerbahce, Juventus and Rapid Vienna, and in a remarkably symmetrical six-game series they won all their home games 2-0 and lost all the away ties 1-0. Nine points were enough to send them into the knockout rounds and, when they opened up with a 4-0 massacre of Porto at Old Trafford to book their first-ever Champions League semi-final, they were rated potential winners of the competition. Sadly they were handed a lesson in playing two-legged European ties by Borussia Dortmund, who gouged out 1-0 wins home and away. Their trip to the last four had been hugely encouraging, but United were not yet quite ready to challenge in European football's big league. McClair said, 'We were so close and we could have beaten Dortmund. I think we were too cautious in our

approach in both legs. We lost 1-0 in Germany, but we still had a great chance in the second leg. But we lost an early goal and that made it difficult for us. I really believe that if we'd beaten Dortmund, as we could and should have done, we would have gone on to beat Juventus in the Champions League final, as Dortmund did.

'In Europe getting through the semi-final can be harder than winning the final itself. Because the final is a one-off game and, whoever the opposition are, you have an equal chance of winning.'

United were back for another tilt at the Champions League in 1997/98 – but they faced up to the challenge without Cantona. After five glorious years at Old Trafford he announced his retirement with a typically oblique parting statement. He told a bemused press conference, 'When the seagulls follow the trawler, it's because they think sardines will be thrown into the sea.'

Despite the void left by Cantona's absence, United furthered their Champions League education with another encouraging run

Ole Gunnar Solskjaer scores one of his two goals in a 2-0 win against Tottenham at Old Trafford in September 1996.

ERIC CANTONA

FORWARD (1992–97) • 184 (1) APPEARANCES • 82 GOALS

Alex Ferguson's wisdom was called into question when he raided Elland Road to buy Cantona in 1992. The Frenchman was widely regarded as the most gifted overseas player ever to perform in the English league and there was no doubting his skill on the ball or ability to turn a game with a moment of inspired genius. But he was also considered to be a disruptive influence, an upsetter of apple carts, and just plain wrong for a club like Manchester United and a manager like Ferguson.

Well, it is true that life was much livelier around Old Trafford after Cantona arrived. Along with his breathtaking ability he brought a disdain for authority and a contempt for convention which lesser players could not possibly have displayed. But Cantona, 'le roi', was forgiven all, because he provided the spark, the missing, magic ingredient that turned Manchester United into the best team in Britain for the first time in a generation.

Yes, Ferguson took a gamble and there were moments (like the martial arts demonstration at Selhurst Park and numerous other disciplinary outrages) when it looked like the manager had lost. But as another wise football person once said, it is the bad players who are the real gamble. And Ferguson made something of a Faustian pact with the devil that lurked in Cantona. He was prepared to put up with Cantona's sometimes-irrational acts, where another, less talented player might have been sent packing. Cantona, for his part, felt he had found a home at United – a place where his special skills and singular character would be accepted pretty much without question. He said, 'Nothing will ever make me wiser and there's nothing I need to be wise about. What I mean is there are bad sides to my character, but without them I wouldn't be what I am. You either accept me as I am or you don't. At Manchester they decided to accept me from the start and it's paid off.'

United were a good team struggling to find an extra gear when Cantona arrived in 1992/93. He immediately raised the team's attacking performance to a higher level, and in that first season he was the difference between his new club winning their first title since 1967 and falling just short yet again. If he'd quit in the summer of 1993 his place as a United legend would still be assured. But there was more, including the club's first-ever Double in 1994.

After returning from his ban for booting the Palace supporter in 1995 Ferguson showed his faith in Cantona by making him team captain. Touched by the gesture, Cantona did everything in his power to repay the debt he felt he owed Ferguson and United for their loyalty. The result was another Double, sealed with Cantona's winner against Liverpool in the 1996 FA Cup final at Wembley. But more than all his medals and honours, Cantona lives in the memory for the style in which he played the game. English football can be a rough old pastime and sometimes Cantona appeared to float above the melee, waiting for the chance to contribute something that transcended the mundanity around him. He had the temperament of an artist rather than a sportsman, a trait noticed by Michel Platini, his France national team manager. Platini, a man who knew something about the aesthetics of football, said, 'I have the impression that if he cannot score a beautiful goal he would rather not score at all.'

There was time for one last title win in 1996/97, before Cantona called a halt to his career just as he began to show the first faint traces of decline. United and football will never see his like again.

to the later rounds in 1997/98. This time their form in the group stage was exemplary, as they reeled off home wins against Kosice, Juventus and Feyenoord, and even overcame their recent failings away from home to beat Kosice and Feyenoord in their own backyards. Their only defeat on the way to the knockout rounds was a narrow 0-1 defeat in Juve's Stadio Delle Alpi.

United, though, came unstuck against Monaco, despite coming away from the first leg on the Riviera with a handy 0-0 draw. McClair said, 'It was another game we could have won, but David Trezeguet scored first at Old Trafford and we couldn't get into the game. They were a difficult team to play against. But although we were sorry to go out, all the time we were learning more and more about playing in Europe and it was experience which was to stand us in good stead.'

There had been signs that United were ready to take the next step in their development and make a real challenge in the Champions League, but nothing which had gone before suggested that United were about to embark on the most remarkable campaign that English football had ever seen. They waited until the last year of the century to turn in the greatest performance in their history – the season when they pulled off a clean sweep of Champions League, Premiership and FA Cup in a glorious culmination of decades of

United achievement. The heirs to the railway workers of Newton Heath Football Club, who had formed the club more than a century earlier, took United to undreamt of heights. After this staggering campaign, there would be no new worlds left to conquer.

As United's golden season unfolded the tension did not weaken for one moment. There were many times over the months when United came close to missing one, two or even all three of their targets. United fans needed nerves of steel to cope with all the twists and turns along the way, but the times of suffering, and the desperate passages when the Treble looked impossible, made the eventual triumph all the sweeter. As early as the first game of the season United put their followers through the mill, trailing 2-1 against Leicester at Old Trafford before Beckham found a 90th-minute equaliser to rescue a draw. Who could have guessed that that single point would make the difference between winning and losing the title, and the Treble, nine months later? In the second

Below *Andy Cole keeps up his impressive scoring record in Europe with a strike against Feyenoord.*

Opposite *David Beckham makes a name for himself with the United faithful.*

game of the campaign, too, United struggled to beat a less-talented team, drawing 0-0 at West Ham in a match they dominated. But that afternoon in east London was significant for the arrival of a player who would play a massive role in United's story of success. He was Dwight Yorke, who signed from Aston Villa for £12.6m. The Trinidadian scored twice in the next match, a 4-1 home win against Charlton, and never stopped scoring for the rest of the season, and ending it as United's top scorer.

United's poor early season form continued into September, with a worrying home defeat at the hands of Arsenal, which called their title chances into serious doubt. The Gunners cruised to a 3-0 win and, if you had asked a neutral which of the sides on show that day at Old Trafford were destined to win the Premiership, they would have named the north London team. The defeat saw United skitter further down the table and they moved into the autumn no higher than 10th in the table. United's attitude now was crucial. Even at this early point in the season they risked falling so far behind the leaders that they would have little chance to make up the lost ground. But they dragged themselves right back into the Championship picture by winning their next three matches impressively. First of all they put a big dent in Liverpool's hopes by beating them 2-0 at Old Trafford, with a Denis Irwin penalty and a late Paul Scholes goal. Then they won comfortably at Southampton, which had been a tricky venue for United down the years. Then United showed they really were back in business by whacking Wimbledon 5-1 at home.

But this was a season when United, frustratingly, found it impossible to pull away from the field. In December the team suffered a slump in results that would have been more appropriate for a side facing relegation. They drew at Villa and Spurs, then drew with Chelsea at home and rounded off a terrible four-match spell by losing to Middlesbrough at Old Trafford the week before Christmas. But United were lucky. None of the teams bunched at the top of the table could escape either, United went into the New Year still pitching for the title and it was now that Ferguson's side put in a supercharged spurt to put themselves in pole position for the Premiership. A 3-0 win against Forest at Old Trafford on Boxing Day triggered a 20-match unbeaten run that lasted all the way to the end of the season. Their performances through January 1999 were especially destructive. They beat West Ham 4-1 at home; larruped Leicester 6-2 a week later on the back of a Yorke hat-trick; and a run of five consecutive victories ended with an 8-1 blitz at Forest, which included four goals for Solskjaer in the last 10 minutes. The nippy Norwegian was getting some practice in for being a United hero.

United moved into February as table toppers, with Arsenal and Chelsea proving their most stubborn challengers. Over the final strides Chelsea fell away and United fought the Gunners for the title. Arsenal blinked first, losing 1-0 at Leeds in the penultimate game of the season to hand the advantage to United. It came down to the last act of the 38-match saga and the visit of Tottenham on 16 May, and after a fright when Spurs took the lead United hit back through Beckham and Cole to win the match and the Premiership title.

It was a league season when Roy Keane, more than ever, stirred himself to deeds of greatness. United chased trophies on three fronts in an arduous programme of demanding matches, but if United were

---

Opposite *Dwight Yorke powers home a spectacular header against Charlton Athletic to put United top of the table on the last day of January 1999.*

Right *Andy Cole lobs the ball over Tottenham keeper, Ian Walker, to clinch the Premiership title, the first trophy of United's glorious Treble.*

Roy Keane and Gary Neville both performed to the highest standards during United's best ever season.

ever tempted to take their foot off the gas along the way, Keane was there to set them on the right road. His driving presence in midfield proved to be the powerhouse of United's team and he missed only three league games. But if Keane was the general, he led a team of willing warriors. Schmeichel was at his imperious best in goal. Gary Neville was indomitable at right-back, his brother Phil filled in admirably wherever he was needed and Irwin was unflappable on the left. In Jaap Stam United had acquired one of the best central defenders ever to play for the club and Ronny Johnsen completed a strong partnership. The midfield was a fount of creativity, with Keane and Nicky Butt working as the central-midfield engine room, Giggs and Scholes providing the tricks and frills. Up front Yorke and

Cole formed one of the deadliest double acts Old Trafford had seen in years, and in reserve Ferguson could call on the subtle skills of Solskjaer and Sheringham – especially in the big games.

This multi-talented team was hunting down another FA Cup while the league was being won, and United had mixed blessings in the draw along the way. On the plus side, they were handed home ties at every stage through to the semi-finals. On the debit side, all their opponents, apart from emerging Fulham, came from the Premiership. But United took on and beat all-comers: 3-1 against Middlesbrough, 2-1 against Liverpool, 1-0 against Fullham, then 2-0 against Chelsea in a replay at Stamford Bridge after the first game ended 0-0. That sent United through to play Arsenal in the semi-final at Villa Park.

The two sides could not be separated in the first encounter, which ended 0-0. But the replay at the same venue has gone down into United legend as the match which made the Treble really possible. Beckham shot United into the lead after a quarter of an hour, but Arsenal equalised through Bergkamp midway through the second half. The Gunners had the chance to take the lead when they won a penalty – but Schmeichel saved Bergkamp's kick, one of the best and most vital stops of his whole Old Trafford career. Now the stage was set for Giggs to score one of the greatest United goals of all time. With 10 minutes left in the extra period Giggs found the energy and imagination to embark on a dribble which took him the length of the field, through most of the Arsenal team, culminating in a blistering finish past David Seaman. The extravagance of Giggs's celebration told you all you needed to know about the importance of the goal. The Welshman set off on a mad sprint around Villa Park, wheeling his jersey in the air as he ran, while jubilant team-mates tried to catch up with him. It was a goal that said, 'We are United. We are never beaten. The Treble is ours for the taking.'

The second leg of United's triple crown was captured against Newcastle in the FA Cup final on 22 May 1999. Far from being the exciting showpiece of the English season, United strolled to a 2-0 victory in a match that was as low-key as a Tuesday morning training session. Sheringham scored the first after 10 minutes and Scholes wrapped it up early in the second half. Newcastle hardly posed a threat all afternoon and of the three trophies United won in the season this one was by far the easiest to come by.

But if the FA Cup was a walk in the park, the Champions League was Everest. Their route was long and hazardous, and any number of times United could have succumbed short of the summit. But they were carried through the season as if gripped by a sense of destiny: there was a feeling that this was their season and the European Cup was waiting for them at the end of it. All they had to do was believe in their abilities, and reach out and grasp it. There was a messianic zeal about United's quest for the trophy that brought to mind Busby's grand obsession with the same competition in the 1950s and 1960s.

United kicked off their Champions League adventure with a second qualifying round game against Lodz of Poland. Fans with long memories could tell stories of the difficulties the team had encountered in the past with Polish opposition but this time there

Above Ryan Giggs finishes off one of the greatest goals in United's history to sink the Gunners in the FA Cup semi-final and keep the Treble dream alive.

Right The United bench hail the club's FA Cup final win against Newcastle in 1999 as they make it two trophies for the season.

was no slip up. United won 2-0 at home in the first leg and finished the job with an efficient 0-0 draw in eastern Europe.

Their task in the group stage, though, could hardly have been much tougher. Only two from Bayern Munich, Barcelona, Brondby and United could go through to the quarter-finals. And it was a close-run thing as three of Europe's greatest clubs battled for survival. The Danes fell out of contention early and from then on it was a slug-fest between the Big Three. United opened up with a 3-3 draw at home to Barca and followed that with a 2-2 draw in Munich – which could have been a United win except for a last-minute own-goal scored by Sheringham. He owed his team-mates a last-minute goal against Bayern for that one. United racked up goals against Brondby, 6-2 in Denmark and 5-0 at home, before facing the final two decisive matches. A defeat now could have ended United's chances, but they held their nerve to draw 3-3 again with Barca in the Nou Camp and 1-1 at home to Bayern to reach the last eight.

Internazionale were United's opponents in the quarter-finals, and most non-United observers made the Milanese the favourites for the tie. Inter's line-up was packed with world-class names such

as Zanetti, Bergomi, Simeone, Zamorano, Djorkaeff and Roberto Baggio – but United had no reason to fear such a star-studded side. They had grown increasingly confident in their own worth and with good reason. United did a masterly job in the first-leg at Old Trafford, stifling the Italians in defence and scoring twice themselves through Dwight Yorke. They had a scare in the second leg when Inter pulled one back midway through the second-half to ensure an edgy conclusion to the game, but Scholes put a chance away two minutes from time to confirm United's place in the last four.

United faced Italian opponents again in the semi-finals and the clash with Juventus turned out to be one of the most memorable European encounters United had ever experienced. Juve were even stronger than Inter, with the likes of Montero, Deschamps, Davids, Zidane and Filippo Inzaghi on their roster, and the team from Turin were odds on to reach their fourth successive Champions League final.

With a minute of the first leg at Old Trafford left, the Treble looked like an impossible dream for United. Conte had scored for Juve midway through the first half and there seemed a slim chance that United could drag themselves back into the tie. The shutters were pulled down and United hammered away at them to no avail. The prospect of going to the Stadio Delle Alpi a goal down was not appealing. But once again Giggs found the life-saving breakthrough, scoring in the 90th minute to give his team a shred of hope for the return. But even that small glimmer seemed to have disappeared 10 minutes into the second leg in Turin. Filippo Inzaghi scored twice to make the score 3-1 on aggregate and, in a season when the quest for the Treble never ran smooth, this was the rockiest section so far. Surely it was time to mourn what would have been the greatest feat in English football history. But United were not finished, and it was Roy Keane's powers of leadership and dynamic midfield skills that pulled the game out off the fire.

Keane himself scored midway through the second half, powering Beckham's corner into the net with an unstoppable header. Then 10 minutes later Yorke brought the scores level, taking advantage of

Roy Keane showed all of his leadership qualities by scoring a vital goal against Bayern Munich in the Champions League group stage.

Cole's perfectly flighted pass. United now led on away goals, but the advantage was slender. Juventus still looked dangerous and, roared on by their home crowd, were capable of pushing United over the precipice at any moment. But United dug in and refused to yield. Keane, especially, was an immovable force. Even after he was booked for a foul on Zidane, meaning he would miss the final through suspension, the Irishman never missed a beat. He knew he would have no part to play in the Nou Camp – but he strived mightily to ensure that his team-mates would take the field. Scholes, too, was denied his chance of a final appearance when he was booked.

Juve poured forward in search of the winning goal, but the United rearguard never buckled. Crucially, United were able to relieve the pressure by making forays of their own towards the Juve area and when another goal was scored in the final minutes it came from the visitors. Yorke made a thrusting run into the penalty area and was brought down by the keeper before he could shoot. United might have had a penalty, but before the referee could make his mind up Cole pounced on the loose ball and put it away. United were in the final against Bayern Munich in Barcelona.

It was typical of United's season that they should save the most dramatic performance to the last. There had been a sense of theatre about their progress at every point of the story and the ending could not been crafted better. At 1-0 down in the final minute against Bayern, United weren't just dead, they had already been been buried and mourners were comforting the grief-stricken next-of-kin prior to tucking into the ham buffet and climbing into the Scotch. But it took more than a mortal blow to kill off this United side. The team which had forgotten how to lose leapt out of its coffin and joined in the wake for Bayern Munich.

Ferguson hailed the victory with an oration which was no less eloquent for its brevity. He said to a stunned TV-watching nation seconds after the final whistle, 'Football, eh? Bloody hell!' It wasn't a bad way to sum up not just the astonishing Treble-winning season, but a whole decade's worth of achievement.

Dwight Yorke swoops to make it 2-2 with Juventus in a dramatic Champions League semi-final second leg in Turin.

1999 CHAMPIONS LEAGUE FINAL

MANCHESTER UNITED 2 Sheringham, Solskjaer **BAYERN MUNICH 1** Basler

26 MAY 1999 at Nou Camp, Barcelona • Referee: Pierluigi Collina (Italy) • Attendance: 90,000

MANCHESTER UNITED

Schmeichel
G Neville
Irwin
Johnsen
Butt
Stam
Beckham
Blomqvist (Sheringham)
Cole (Solskjaer)
Yorke
Giggs

BAYERN MUNICH

Kahn
Babbel
Tarnat
Linke
Matthaus (Fink)
Kuffour
Basler (Salihamidzic)
Effenberg
Jancker
Zickler (Scholl)
Jeremies

If this wasn't the greatest night in the history of Manchester United, it has to be in the top two. Perhaps nothing will ever usurp the night Busby and United found redemption at Wembley in May 1968, but if you ever wanted a textbook display of footballing courage, and a cliff-hanging, heart-stopping conclusion to 10 months of effort, this would be it. It wasn't just that United won the European Cup to capture the Treble. It was the fact that they did it in a fashion that epitomised all the values the club has strived to embody down the decades: they won it with style, unconquerable determination and a devotion to the importance of teamwork. The victory over Bayern Munich was the quintessence of Manchester United. And how odd that the stars should collide in such a way that the game would be played on the 90th anniversary of Busby's birth against a team from Munich.

Ferguson had to shuffle his team around in the absence of the suspended Keane and Scholes, so Giggs found himself on the right wing, Blomqvist was stationed on

Fergie's Army turned a corner of Catalonia into an enclave of Manchester for the night.

the left and Beckham joined Butt in the middle. Perhaps it was unsurprising that Bayern settled better and Basler scored from a free-kick after five minutes. For the rest of the match United played catch-up football and Bayern looked comfortable. United's new formation struggled to create chances and they were still trailing at half-time. Ferguson's team-talk was concise and a masterclass in motivation. He said, 'The cup will be only six feet away from you and if you lose you can't even touch it.'

Even so, as the last 10 minutes ticked by United looked nowhere near scoring a goal. Quite the opposite. Bayern pressed ahead and smacked United's post and bar. But Bayern made the fatal error of imagining that they had the game won. They took off their most influential figures, Basler and Matthaus, and threw on two defensive-minded players, in the belief that United's last push for an equaliser would be throttled. But Ferguson's substitutions were rather more effective.

The fourth official had already held up the board indicating three minutes of added time would be played when Sheringham swung into action for the equaliser. United won a corner and their captain, Schmeichel, playing his last game for the club, piled forward to cause mayhem in the area. The ball was half-cleared to Giggs near the edge of the penalty area and in his anxiety the winger scuffed his shot. The ball was bobbling wide – before Sheringham stuck his right foot at the ball and steered it past Oliver Kahn.

The game was now heading for extra-time and a golden goal decider, perhaps even penalties. But United did not want penalties, or a golden goal, or even extra-time. Solskjaer won a corner, Beckham hoisted it onto the head of Sheringham, and his knockdown was met by the

Teddy Sheringham is ecstatic after netting to make the score 1-1.

baby-faced Norwegian, Solskjaer, who hammered the ball into the roof of the net. United were Champions of Europe. It was a bizarre end to a deeply weird evening. Even Gary Neville, a man not often given to flights of fancy, said there was something 'supernatural' about the events which unfolded from the 89th minute onwards.

Ferguson, soon to be dubbed Sir Alex on the back of his team's exploits, said: 'The most important factor was the spirit of the team. They just never give in, they don't know how to. A manager can talk about tactics, but if the players can't bring that inner beast out of them then he's wasting his time. Well, they've got that beast inside them and they found it when it mattered.

'People will never forget this team. My 1994 Double-winning side had a mental toughness about them, but this crop is the best, they have proved that. They are legends.'

Above *Ole Gunnar Solskjaer meets his destiny by crashing home the winner in Barcelona to capture the Treble for United.*
Opposite *Captain for the night Peter Schmeichel leads the celebrations in the Nou Camp.*

CHAPTER ELEVEN

21ST CENTURY BOYS

1999–2006

IN THE EARLY YEARS OF THE 21ST CENTURY MANCHESTER UNITED
REMAIN ONE OF THE MOST FAMOUS CLUBS ON THE PLANET –
BUT, AS CHIEF EXECUTIVE DAVID GILL SAID, 'OUR PAST IS IMPORTANT
TO US. NO MATTER HOW BIG THE CLUB GETS, IT WILL ALWAYS
HAVE A HEART AND A SOUL, AND REMEMBER ITS HISTORY'

United moved into the new century as Champions of their country and their continent, and it might have been understandable if the team's level of performance had dropped in 1999/2000. After all, United had gorged themselves on success in 1999. Could they possibly be hungry for more? The answer was yes, as United ran away with the Premiership title again, their sixth in eight years. But there was no chance of United repeating their Treble, for the simple reason that they passed up on the chance to defend their FA Cup.

United pulled out of the competition under pressure, oddly enough, from the FA itself, which was in the midst of an ill-fated bid to host the 2006 World Cup. The FA wanted to ingratiate itself with FIFA by persuading the English and European Champions to compete in the new Club World Championship in Brazil. The new competition clashed with the third round of the FA Cup and United clearly couldn't be in two places at once, so they had to choose between the two. At first United were reluctant to attend the event in Brazil. It was hard to see what they could gain from travelling halfway across the world to chase a trophy of questionable prestige in the middle of the English season. But after some thought United booked their tickets to Rio.

They opened up with a 1-1 draw against Necaxa of Mexico, then lost 3-1 to Vasco da Gama and beat South Melbourne 2-0. The results weren't good enough to put United into the final, but FIFA's inter-continental club bunfight worked out well for United in the end. They enjoyed a welcome spell of warm weather mid-season training and the month's break from league matches did them no harm. When they flew out to South America in December they were a point behind Leeds at the top of the table with a match in hand. Four weeks later United, refreshed, returned to action no more than three points behind the Yorkshire club and with two games to spare. And they had few fears over fixture congestion, because there were no FA Cup ties to worry about. Far from being a debilitating distraction, the jaunt to Brazil could not have been planned much better for United's benefit.

Opposite More joy for United as the jubilant players cavort with their eighth Premiership title in 2003.

Right David Beckham enjoys a practice session with some local youths during United's jaunt to Brazil for the Club World Championship in 2000.

United overtook Leeds at the top with a late Beckham goal in a 1-0 home win over Middlesbrough on 29 January 2000 and they were never seriously troubled again on the way to the title. The killer blow came on 20 February, when Cole scored in United's 1-0 win at Elland Road. That was the start of an unbeaten run which lasted 14 matches, through to the end of the season, and United won their final 11 matches. The title was won five games early, on 22 April, when a 3-1 win at Southampton made United's advantage unassailable.

It was another fine all-round team performance that brought the title to Old Trafford, but some individuals stood out. Yorke, again, was the team's most prolific striker, finishing with 20 league goals. Cole chipped in with 19. But, again, it was Keane who embodied the team's will to win. If anything his performances topped those of the previous season and he picked up both the PFA and Football Writers' Player of the Year awards for his efforts. But the Irishman was honoured in spite of an ugly incident during the game with Boro, when a scared young ref, Andy D'Urso, was jostled by almost the entire United team as they disputed a decision. Keane led the

angry deputation and later memorably blamed D'Urso for the episode. He said, 'What happened was unfortunate. Although if he had stood still I don't think we would have been chasing him. But he kept running and we kept chasing.' After he had had time to see the incident again Keane confessed that the team might have gone too far in cornering the unhappy whistler. He vowed that United would not gang up on officials in the same way again.

For a long while it looked possible that United could successfully defend their European crown in the newly expanded Champions League. Ferguson's team now had to negotiate two group stages before reaching the knockout rounds and in the end the marathon wore them down. United came through the first stage without a hitch, going through as winners of their group, along with Marseille, while Sturm Graz of Austria and Croatia

Roy Keane bubbling over with enthusiasm after beating Spurs in the last home game of the 1999–2000 season.

Paul Scholes scores with a header in the 3-0 win against Valencia
at Old Trafford in the group stages of the Champions League.

Zagreb were eliminated. They also finished in first place in their much tougher second group – beating Valencia into second place, with Fiorentina and Bordeaux missing out on the quarter-finals. United were drawn to play their long-time rivals and old adversaries, Real Madrid, in the last eight.

United got off to an encouraging start in the tie, with a solid 0-0 draw in the Bernabeu. With the second home leg to come the United fans, who had enjoyed their taste of European glory in Barcelona, were already thinking about a night out in Paris for the final in May. But Real were a different and far more potent side in

Manchester than they had been in Madrid. Roy Keane's own goal put the visitors in front midway through the first half and two Raul goals early in the second half put the tie beyond United. Sir Alex's side staged a typically determined rally and pulled goals back through Beckham and a Scholes penalty, but the final narrow scoreline could not mask the truth. Madrid were the best team in Europe that season and it was no less than their due that they went on to beat Valencia in the final.

After such a sustained period of success United were in danger of running out of records to break as they embarked on football in the 21st century. But there were still pinnacles to be scaled and yet another club first was achieved in 2000/01 – a hat-trick of Premiership titles. The only major addition Sir Alex made to the squad before the season was Fabien Barthez, the World Cup-

with 15 goals. And for the second successive year a United player won both player of the year awards, as Sheringham revelled in a late flowering to his career. It is safe to assume that Andy Cole was not the first person to congratulate Sheringham on his accolades. Cole admitted, bizarrely, that he was not on speaking terms with his striking partner. He said, 'I'm pleased at the way my partnership with Teddy is going on the pitch, but it's fair to say that we don't have Sunday lunch together. We are still not talking.' The words cast an odd light on the spirit at a club that had prided itself on teamwork and the collective ethos.

But even though there was an unsettled air about the United team during a season when Ferguson used his squad to its full extent, they still kept all the pretenders to their crown at bay. United went top in October when they won 3-0 at Leicester and they led all the way to the line. Arsenal were their closest rivals, but the Londoners' hopes of pegging United back expired on 25 February 2001, when they came to Old Trafford and were tanked 6-1. Yorke scored a hat-trick in the first 22 minutes of the match and by half-time United were already 5-1 up. By the end of the season United were so far ahead of the field they could afford to lose their last three matches and still take the title 10 points ahead of Arsenal.

Once again United went out of the Champions League in the quarter-finals, this time at the hands of their old friends Bayern Munich. United looked doomed to defeat from the moment Sergio scored a late winner for Bayern in the first leg at Old Trafford and they lost 2-1 in Munich's Olympic Stadium to leave the competition. Just like the year before, United had the dubious consolation of having lost to the eventual Champions.

It was inevitable that at some time United's golden run should come to an end, even if it was just for a season. They had enjoyed the richest seam of success in their long history, but sooner or later they were bound to experience the jarring shock of a season without a trophy and it finally happened in 2001/02 as Arsenal enjoyed their place in the sun with a League and Cup Double. It was supposed to be Sir Alex's last season as manager of Manchester United. He had announced his decision to stand down at the end of the season in May 2002 and Sir Alex aimed to go out on a high – by recapturing the European Cup. As fate would have it, the final was scheduled to take place in his native Glasgow and there could be no

winning France goalkeeper. The season before the manager had tried to replace the sadly missed Schmeichel with Mark Bosnich, then Raimond van der Gouw, but neither keeper looked able to fill the great man's boots. It was hardly surprising, though, as the Great Dane had made an unanswerable case for being named the best United No.1 of all time – one of the rare automatic picks for that mythical team of Old Trafford immortals, along with Duncan Edwards. But now Barthez came into the team and made an immediate impact. If his approach to his job was sometimes eccentric, he did at least possess the strength of personality and character United needed to lead their defence.

In a season when Cole and Yorke could only muster 30 league starts between them, Sheringham emerged as United's top striker

Fabien Barthez, the French goalkeeper, came closer than anyone to filling Peter Schmeichel's large sized boots.

stronger motivation to succeed. With that in mind Sir Alex pepped up his team with two big-money buys during the summer: one of the newcomers was a resounding success who became a key Old Trafford figure for the next five years. The other was not.

Sir Alex had been keen to sign the PSV Eindhoven striker, Ruud van Nistelrooy, for years and he finally got his man for £19 million. The other new boy was the Argentina midfielder, Juan Sebastian Veron, who joined for an eye-watering £28 million from Lazio. Others were moving in the opposite direction. Jaap Stam found himself out in the cold after making some mild observations about life at Old Trafford in his autobiography and a slight loss of form. The talented defender was immediately transferred to Lazio after one game of the season. The speed of the move was stunning.

One minute Stam was a popular player at Old Trafford and apparently an important player in the club's plans. The next he was standing by the luggage carousel at Rome airport, about to begin a new life in Serie A. A bewildered Stam could scarcely believe what had happened to him. 'They sold me like a cow,' he said. His surprise replacement at Old Trafford was the 35-year-old French international, Laurent Blanc.

Van Nistelrooy was an instant hit and scored 23 league goals in his first season – a tally topped only by Arsenal's Thierry Henry. Yet despite his exploits United could only finish third in the table, the

Roy Keane bursts through the Arsenal defence to score in United's 6-1 demolition of closest rivals Arsenal in February 2001.

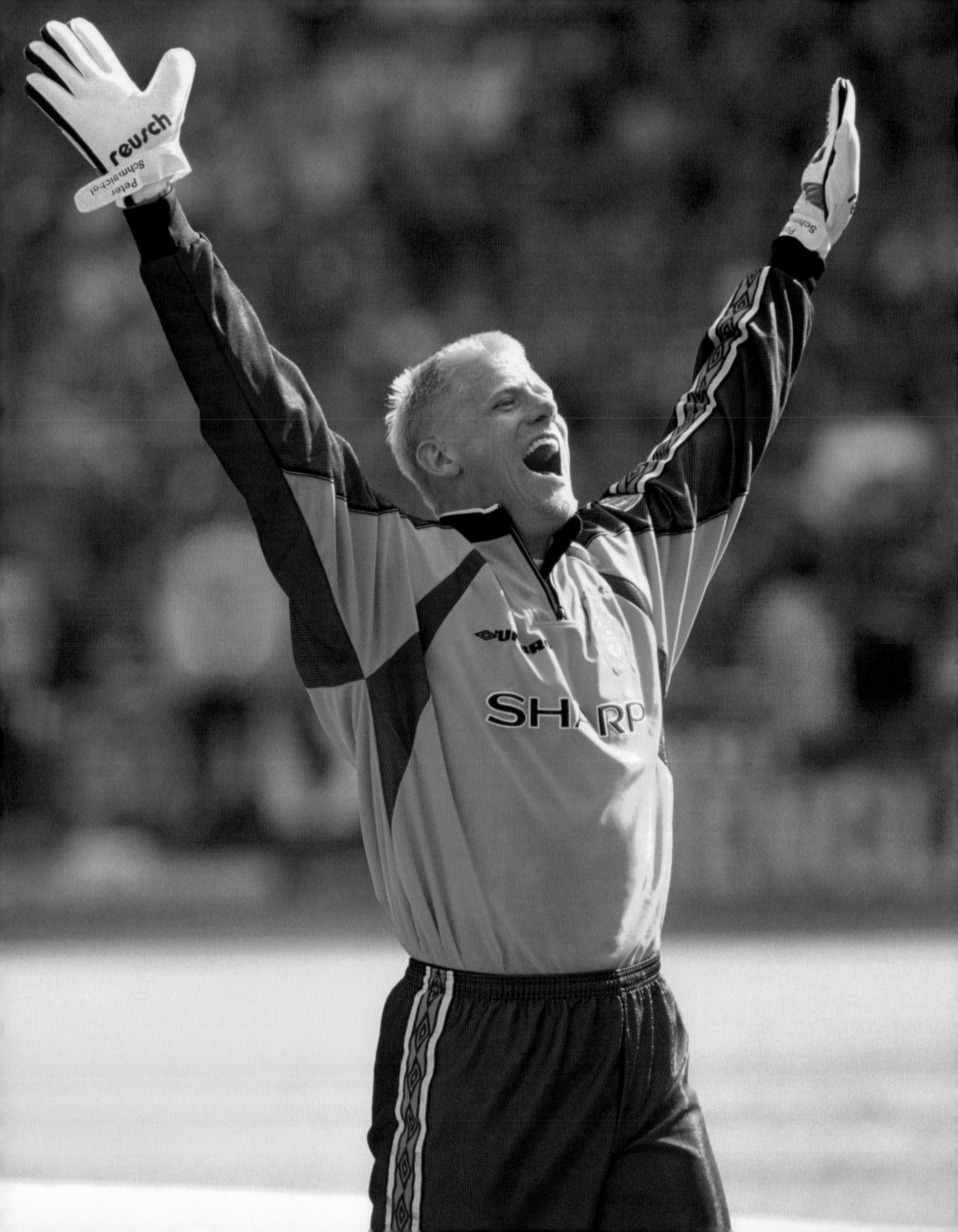
reusch
Peter Schmeichel
SHARP

PETER SCHMEICHEL

GOALKEEPER (1991–99) • 398 APPEARANCES • 1 GOAL

The great players are irreplaceable and, if you were pressed to name one former United player from the last 30 years whose absence mattered more than anybody's, it would be the giant Dane. Whisper it, but even the shock of King Cantona's abrupt departure was softened by the goals that flowed from the boots of Dwight Yorke. But almost a decade on from the time Schmeichel quit England to play in Portugal, United have yet to find anybody close to matching his skill or presence.

He did not arrive ready-made as the potentate of the United penalty area. When he joined from Brondby in August 1991 (at £500,000, another candidate for transfer bargain of all-time) Schmeichel displayed an uncertainty and rawness which only experience can cure. But as season followed season so Schmeichel's stature grew, until he was, for a spell, the best goalkeeper in the world.

There were no weaknesses in his game, but in some areas of the keeper's art he was especially brilliant: at one-on-ones with strikers, he out-psyched and outmanoeuvred even the coolest heads in the game and invariably came out on top. He dominated his area like no other keeper before or since and Schmeichel was just as happy bullying his own defenders as he was bossing opposing players. His agility was remarkable for a man with such a large frame and his handling skills were peerless (strange that a man with hands the size of JCB buckets should be an accomplished amateur pianist). In addition, his uncannily accurate throws gave countless United attacks early momentum, as he set his team on the way to the opposition goal. Alan Hodgkinson, United's goalkeeping coach and the man who scouted the young Schmeichel in Denmark, dubbed him 'the only playmaking keeper in the country'.

Ferguson knew Schmeichel's full worth, but he did not believe in building his keeper up too far. Instead of naming Schmeichel as the best buy of all time, he merely claimed he was the best of the century.

The pinnacle of Schmeichel's Old Trafford career came in May 1999, when he captained the team in place of the suspended Roy Keane in the Champions League final against Bayern in Barcelona. Schmeichel showed typical never-say-die spirit when he charged forward for a corner in the dying seconds, adding to the confusion in the Bayern box, which led to United's equaliser. Given his service to the club throughout the success-soaked 1990s, when he did so much to contribute to the United renaissance, it was entirely fitting that Schmeichel should be the first man to hold aloft the huge silver trophy. It couldn't have been in safer hands.

Peter Schmeichel, a safe choice for the greatest Manchester United goalkeeper of all time.

first time they had been out of the top two since 1991. There was no joy either in the cups. United's mix of youth team lads and reserve team old lags made their customary exit at the first possible stage of the League Cup – 4-0 to Arsenal – and the FA Cup trail went cold in the fourth round, with a 2-0 defeat at Middlesbrough.

United did at least enjoy a better run in the Champions League. They beat Deportivo La Coruña 5-2 on aggregate in the quarter-finals, but then lost out to German opposition once again. This time it was Bayer Leverkusen who halted their run, earning a 2-2 draw at Old Trafford before going through on away goals with a 1-1 draw in Germany. This disappointing end should have been Sir Alex's swansong as United boss. May 2002 was his scheduled retirement date – but he had had a change of heart by then and in February 2002 he rescinded his resignation. Faced with the prospect of life away from his beloved team, Sir Alex recoiled at the prospect and decided to stay to chase more trophies.

Opposite Ruud Van Nistelrooy leaps highest against Leicester City to head one of his 23 league goals in season 2001/02.
Above Ole Gunnar Solskjaer pounces to put the ball in the Real Madrid net in United's remarkable 4-3 victory at Old Trafford, but it was not enough as Real won 6-5 on aggregate.

Sir Alex, with a new lease of life following his close-brush with retirement, reinvigorated his team by splashing out a British-record £30 million to bring in Rio Ferdinand from Leeds United to beef up the defence. But despite the investment United began the 2002/03 season poorly and they had their worst start since the Premiership began. United were stuck in ninth place as summer turned into autumn. Arsenal already looked the team to beat again and United had ceded them a six-point head start after just half a dozen games. But this was a slow-burning United campaign, markedly different in character from the pillar-to-post charges they had specialised in over the last few years. Now Sir Alex's side were content to stay in touch as the season unfolded. They waited and watched patiently while other would-be Champions hit the top, only to fade and fall back into the pack.

After the Gunners' bright start Liverpool went clear, grinding out result after result, stitching together an unbeaten record that lasted into November. But from that highpoint they were never the same force again. Arsenal raced back into the reckoning playing attractive, attacking football that had commentators drooling. Newcastle, too, threatened the top places and eventually finished third. Chelsea also had a good season and ran on to finish fourth. But United were always lurking and on 12 April they hit the front decisively with a thrilling 6-2 win at Newcastle. They never looked like being toppled from that moment on and eventually won the 2002/03 Premiership title by five points from Arsenal.

As United closed in on their eighth Premiership triumph they were also embroiled in another Champions League campaign, knowing they would hold a big advantage over their opponents if they could reach the final: it was scheduled to be played at Old Trafford. Romantics suggested that it would be the perfect venue for Sir Alex to regain the trophy. But fairytales don't always come true, even for Manchester United. They came through a qualifying round and the first group stage unscathed, but Real Madrid proved to be their nemesis once again in the quarter-finals. United lost 3-1 in Madrid and they just failed to turn the tide of the tie in a remarkable 4-3 victory at Old Trafford, which saw the Spaniards go through 6-5. In the end United hosted an all-Italian final, with AC Milan beating Juventus on penalties after a dull 0-0 draw.

Sir Alex made some changes for the 2003/04 season: Veron was gone. So was Barthez. And, most significantly, so was Beckham, sold to Real Madrid after an unhappy final season which featured dressing room altercations with Sir Alex. In came a raft of new signings, including the world's most-expensive teenager, Cristiano Ronaldo, from Sporting Lisbon, David Bellion, the Sunderland striker, and Louis Saha, the Fulham forward. But the new blood failed to prevent Arsenal recapturing the Premiership title. Halfway through the season United looked well placed to finish top again as they held a three-point advantage over the Gunners. But their stability was undermined in a bizarre episode that saw them lose Ferdinand for eight months.

The defender had been singled out for a drugs test by inspectors who had called in for a spot check at the club's training ground. There was nothing sinister about the operation: it was common practice for random samples to be taken in this way. But Ferdinand left the Carrington complex before giving his sample and could not be contacted by club officials. The player said he forgot about the test and turned his mobile phone off while he was shopping. If the full weight of anti-doping law had been thrown at Ferdinand, he could have expected a ban in the vicinity of two years. In the event, the eight-month sanction was a gift. But without him United suffered and Arsenal sailed to the title. There was also more misery in the Champions League, as United lost 3-2 on aggregate against

Porto at the first knockout stage. But United saved the 2003/04 season by winning the FA Cup.

United began their run to Cardiff with victory at Aston Villa, where two Paul Scholes goals in the second-half gave them a 2-1 win. And there was plenty of nostalgia for the days of Best when United were drawn to play at Northampton in the fourth round. The maestro had enjoyed one his greatest triumphs at the old County Ground in an FA Cup tie and, although no modern United player could hope to match his goalscoring exploits, they did at least win 3-0. It was City next at Old Trafford and United swept their rivals

Above Rio Ferdinand in training at Carrington, the scene of the furore over his missed drugs test.

Opposite Cristiano Ronaldo hoists the ball into the back of the Manchester City net during United's fifth-round FA Cup win in 2004.

DAVID BECKHAM

MIDFIELDER (1992–2003) • 356 (38) APPEARANCES • 85 GOALS

Sometimes the gaudy publicity caravan which followed Beckham threatened to obscure his importance as a player. During his time at Old Trafford he grew from a homesick Leytonstone lad making his way in the youth team into the most-recognised footballer in the world. More, he became a fully-fledged international celebrity and a specimen of that strange breed of folk who are famous for being famous. But although the hype and hoopla surrounding his much-chronicled and photographed life became a distraction from his day job, his public profile failed to blot out completely his extravagant ability as a footballer.

He won a regular place in the United team in 1996 and the boyhood Cockney Red took his chance gleefully. Given an opportunity to shine in the Premiership, Beckham delivered in full. He first grabbed popular attention with his audacious halfway line goal against Wimbledon in August 1996 and he quickly showed he was not a one-trick pony. The gifts which would make him into one of the planet's best players were apparent even then: an uncanny knack for delivering long-range passes to a centimetre's accuracy; an astonishing virtuosity with a dead-ball; and an athleticism that enabled him to combine a high level of skill with a formidable work ethic. In those early days he was Ferguson's dream: a star player without the star mentality; an outrageously talented individual with the will to harness his gifts in the team's cause.

Beckham remained devoted to his craft as a footballer. Even towards the end of his United career, when a new Beckham haircut was a front-page story across the world, he was still putting in the hard hours of practice necessary to keep his skills razor sharp. But he no longer matched the usual image of a Manchester United footballer. The exposure he commanded on television and in the press made George Best look like a publicity-shunning hermit.

It wasn't all his fault. True, he married a pop star and moved in celebrity circles where paparazzi flash-guns go with the territory, but Beckham could not help being photogenic and famous in a celebrity-fixated culture. However, there can be little doubt that the glare of attention he received did not make his manager happy and a parting of the ways became inevitable. It was hastened by the notorious dressing room incident when a football boot propelled by Sir Alex struck Beckham on the head. Beckham had once viewed his manager as a second father. But it was time now for the son to strike out on his own and the move to Real Madrid was made.

All the magazine photo-shoots and tabloid exclusives may have diverted attention from what he did best, but the wisest judges in the game were not fooled. They knew a footballer when they saw one and Beckham was universally seen as one of the best England had ever produced. Sir Tom Finney, who knew a thing or two about operating down the right flank, said, 'When you see a footballer of that standard in any company, he is a class apart.' It will do as a last word on the quality Beckham brought to his work at Old Trafford.

aside with a 4-2 win, which featured a red card for Gary Neville's head butt on Steve McManaman and a couple of goals for van Nistelrooy. The Dutchman scored another couple in the 2-1 home win over Fulham, after an early fright when Steed Malbranque had given the Cottagers the lead from the spot. That earned United a match-up with Arsenal in the semi-finals at Villa Park and Scholes won it for United with a goal after half-an-hour.

United duly beat Millwall in Cardiff to chalk up their 11th win in the competition, on a strangely muted occasion. Millwall were perhaps lucky to be in the final, since they hadn't had to beat a Premiership team to make it to the Millennium Stadium, but that hardly accounted for the paucity of their ambition and lack of fight. The boys from Bermondsey prided themselves on their chippy, No One Likes Us We Don't Care mentality – but they seemed to face United with an inferiority complex. United expected Lions and came up against pussycats. It might have been a simple victory for United, but at least the afternoon provided a number of statistical landmarks for United fans to savour. Roy Keane approached the end of his Old Trafford career by winning his fourth FA Cup winner's medal in his sixth final. Sir Alex's fifth FA Cup was also an all-time best for a manager and United's keeper, Tim Howard, became the first US citizen to win the Cup.

Since United re-emerged as a title-winning force in the early 1990s, they had faced a number of rivals in their quest for honours. At first they needed to usurp Liverpool as the country's top club. Arsenal posed a perennial threat. And intermittent challenges also came from the likes of Leeds, Blackburn Rovers, Villa and Newcastle United. In 2004/05, though, a new and even more potent threat emerged from the south to question United's hegemony

in the Premiership. Chelsea had been developing into a Premier power for some years, under the managements of Glenn Hoddle, Ruud Gullit, Gianluca Vialli and Claudio Ranieri. Though they were a dangerous and successful cup team, and occasionally threatened to mount a challenge in the league, their efforts tended to peter out long before the business end of the season came around. Chelsea, it seemed, would always be Chelsea: entertaining at times,

Roy Keane proudly displays his fourth FA Cup
triumph in six attempts as United beat Millwall
in May 2004.

but ultimately flaky. That all changed practically overnight, as the Russian oil billionaire, Roman Abramovich, bought the club and began to pump a high proportion of Siberia's gross domestic product into Stamford Bridge.

United were used to this kind of attack. Nouveau riche clubs had risen up before, to dazzle briefly and enjoy some small success, and then burn out like a brilliant Catherine wheel. Blackburn took a title off them on the back of Jack Walker's steel millions and were relegated. Leeds, under David O'Leary, gambled their club's fortune and more on success and reached the Champions League semi-final, before one stumble put the skids under their challenge. The banks demanded their money back, and the famous old club was relegated and nearly went out of existence. But the Chelsea experience was different altogether.

It was clear that Abramovich's Chelsea revolution was no flash-in-the-pan phenomenon. Abramovich clearly intended to keep spending until success was achieved and the money would last as long as there was oil under the Arctic. Once the charismatic and idiosyncratic Portuguese, Jose Mourinho, took over as head coach, the blue touchpaper was lit and the sky was the limit for Chelsea – now the world's richest club. Even United, who could still afford to shell out upwards of £20 million on Everton's Wayne Rooney in 2005, could not match Chelsea's outlay on players.

The 2004/05 Premiership season turned into an unequal battle between Mourinho's team and the rest. They hit the top in November and stayed out on their own until they were confirmed as Champions. United never got back on terms following a slow start to the season and they ended up in third place, a scarcely credible 18 points behind the winners. There was disappointment, too, in the other competitions. The Champions League campaign ground to a halt in the first knockout round, as United lost 1-0 home and away to AC Milan. United were back in Cardiff for the FA Cup final, where they earned the unwanted distinction of becoming the first team in history to lose an FA Cup final on penalties. After having the better of the game against Arsenal for two, goalless hours, the

Wayne Rooney, United's £20 million wonderkid, on the charge against Liverpool.

Gunners held their nerve in the shoot-out and Patrick Vieira crashed in the winning kick to signal a trophyless season for United.

The headlines in the summer of 2005 were not monopolised, as usual, by transfer talk. Takeover talk dominated instead. The Florida-based Glazer family, owners of the Tampa Bay Buccaneers NFL franchise among an array of other commercial interests, took a decisive step towards a takeover of Manchester United. Their shareholding in United leapt to 70 per cent after they bought the 28 per cent stake of Irish tycoons J.P. McManus and John Magnier, and the Americans set about hoovering up the remaining shares they needed to own the club outright.

Despite the protests the Glazers quickly snapped up all the shares they needed to own United outright and the club became a private rather than a public company. Some diehard supporters insisted that Manchester United was no longer Manchester United and they broke away to form a new club, FC United, which began life at the bottom of the Football League pyramid. But the vast majority of

2004 **FA CUP FINAL**

MANCHESTER UNITED 3 Ronaldo, Van Nistelrooy 2 (1 pen) **MILLWALL 0**

22 MAY 2004 at Millennium Stadium, Cardiff • Referee: Jeff Winter • Attendance: 71,350

United never looked like losing a match against lower division opponents who treated the FA Cup final like a day trip to the seaside. The south Londoners were just happy to be in Cardiff at all and winning the game seemed to be the last thing on their minds. Even Dennis Wise, their player-manager and a notoriously spiky character, was on his best behaviour. He took on his familiar role of pantomime villain just long enough to receive the only booking of the afternoon, but you could tell his heart wasn't really in it.

Ronaldo, who went through his full repertoire of tricks, juggles and stepovers to dazzle the crowd, scored the first goal with a

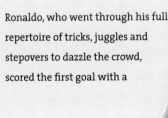

thumping header at the end of the first half. United could have run in many more in a risibly one-sided second period, but two goals from van Nistelrooy sufficed. The first after an hour was a penalty after Giggs had been fouled, his second a tap-in from Giggs's cross with ten minutes to go.

MANCHESTER UNITED

Howard (Carroll)
G Neville
Brown
Silvestre
O'Shea
Fletcher (Butt)
Keane
Ronaldo (Solskjaer)
Scholes
Giggs
Van Nistelrooy

MILLWALL

Marshall
Elliott
Lawrence
Ward
Ryan (Cogan)
Wise (Weston)
Ifill
Cahill
Livermore
Sweeney
Harris (McCammon)

Opposite *Ronaldo heads United into a first-half lead.*
Right *Wes Brown (left) and Ruud Van Nistelrooy show their delight after United's comfortable FA Cup final victory over Millwall.*

ROY KEANE

MIDFIELDER (1993–2005) • 458 (22) APPEARANCES • 51 GOALS

It's hard to think of a weakness in Roy Keane, unless you count his allergy to prawns. In the dozen years he was at Old Trafford the Irishman developed into the perfect central midfield player and one of the most inspirational captains ever to wear the red shirt. United fans know a player who shares their passion for their club when they see one and Keane came in that bracket. His commitment to his club was total.

Of course, there was a downside to the boy from Cork. He was no Corinthian. Keane could be nasty and he was no stranger to referees' notebooks or the august members of the FA's disciplinary committee. But his uncompromising approach to his trade just made the fans love him all the more. He may at times have been a hard-nosed, crude-tackling, ref-baiting felon – but he was their hard-nosed, crude-tackling, ref-baiting felon.

Keane was vital to United's cause for so long, because the team gained so many different players wrapped up in the one jersey. He was a midfield scrapper without equal, a man who went into challenges with such fierce determination that a 50:50 ball was more like 80:20 in his favour. His reputation saw to that. And once he had the ball, he was an effective passer. In his heyday, too, he could operate box-to-box in a manner reminiscent of Bryan Robson at his best. And although his goals ratio was not the greatest, he chipped in with important strikes.

Most important of all, he was possessed of a drive and a will to win that ensured United were always on the march forward and never beaten until the final whistle sounded. He spread his martial values to the rest of team and made certain that every player operated at full capacity all the time. The notion of United carrying any shirkers or dilettantes while Keane was on the same pitch was unthinkable.

The idea is enough to make United fans shudder, but Keane might have missed out on a move to the club. When Brian Clough was ready to let his rough diamond leave Forest in the summer of 1993, Arsenal and Blackburn were in the hunt to sign him.

But Ferguson, as he tends to do when a truly great player becomes available, did everything in his power to land Keane and he duly arrived for £3.75 million. It was the beginning of a truly rewarding relationship between player and club.

United fans came to accept the new owners. The waiting list for season tickets showed no sign of dwindling and, in the event, most United supporters were prepared to give the new management a chance – especially when they were prepared to back Sir Alex with cash for transfers.

Finding an answer to Chelsea's apparent invincibility was on top of Sir Alex's agenda for the 2005/06 season. But again, United waited in vain for a chink to appear in Chelsea's armour. United had what would normally have been an outstanding season in the league, with the kind of points total that would in previous seasons easily have been enough to win the title. But now it was only good enough to guarantee second place. Chelsea were simply too strong.

There was little joy in the other competitions to compensate for the dispiriting end to the league season, either. The FA Cup campaign ended 1-0 at Liverpool in the fifth round, an afternoon that was made all the blacker by Alan Smith's broken leg. And in the Champions League United committed the rare error of failing to get out of their group stage. Only a victory over Wigan in the final of the League Cup and the prospect of a late title challenge gave United fans something to smile about in a difficult season, when the club also bade farewell to Roy Keane. He quit the club in November 2005 to sign for Celtic, his ageing warrior's limbs no longer up to the job of leading the United midfield as they did in days of yore. And, in the same month, George Best died from illness related to his alcoholism. He was 59.

Above A disappointing result, a 4-1 defeat by Middlesbrough at the Riverside in October 2005, did however see a landmark as Ronaldo scored United's 1,000th goal in the Premiership.

Left Perhaps the best result of a league season during which United played well without much to show for it was a 1-0 win at home to eventual champions Chelsea in November. A tremendous team performance was rewarded when a looping header from Darren Fletcher proved to be the only goal of the game. Here Ji-sung Park takes on the Chelsea defence.

Opposite The only silverware of the 2005/06 season came in the Carling Cup. The Millennium Stadium provided the setting and the supporters enjoyed a superb day out courtesy of a brilliant performance and four goals without reply against Wigan Athletic.

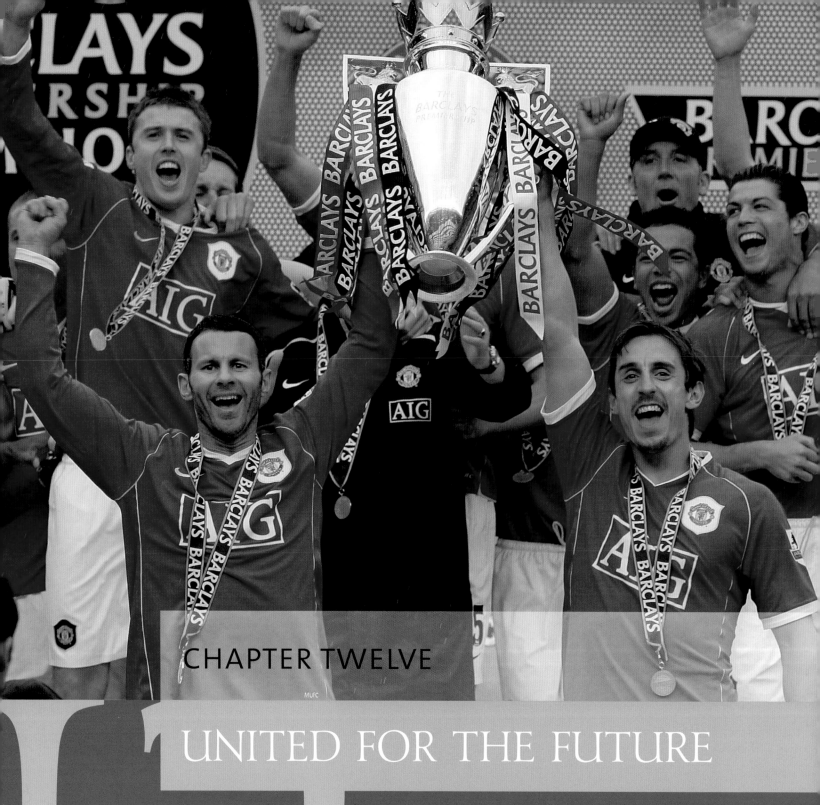

CHAPTER TWELVE

UNITED FOR THE FUTURE

2006–12

AS THE 21ST CENTURY DEVELOPED, CHELSEA REMAINED
UNITED'S HOTTEST RIVALS AT THE TOP OF THE ENGLISH
GAME, AND THE COUNTRY'S TWO BIGGEST CLUBS
CONTINUED THAT RIVALRY ON EUROPE'S GREATEST FOOTBALL
STAGE – IN THE CHAMPIONS LEAGUE.

Before the 2006/07 campaign started it might have been logical to assume that Chelsea would be the strongest contenders for the Premiership yet again. Roman Abramovich's cash-fuelled footballing juggernaut had, after all, acquired the title with conspicuous comfort the season before. And during the summer of 2006 they had apparently made the team even stronger, spending fortunes on two of Europe's best players – the Bayern Munich midfielder Michael Ballack and Andriy Shevchenko, the AC Milan striker.

But there was a quiet confidence around Old Trafford that United were building an exciting new side capable of wresting back the Premiership crown from the Londoners. Even though United had lost their most consistent goal-scorer of recent times, Ruud van Nistelrooy, to Real Madrid, there was still cause for quiet optimism. The biggest name to arrive at the club was Michael Carrick, the Tottenham midfielder. The Geordie's ball-playing skills and obvious class made him a welcome addition to the squad. In addition, Cristiano Ronaldo had been in sublime form at the World Cup. Paul Scholes and Ryan Giggs still bubbled with creativity,

Wayne Rooney was ready to build on the good start he had made at United, and there were signs that a solid defensive platform was developing.

But still for the first time since The Reds re-emerged as England's top team in the early 1990s, they began the season a long way from being favourites for the title.

There was a real fear, in the country at large if not around Old Trafford, that Chelsea were equipped to steamroll the opposition with their clout in the transfer market – not just for the 2006/07 season, but in the foreseeable future. This was the challenge facing Sir Alex as his team kicked off their campaign at home to Fulham.

The early signs for United were encouraging. They scored four times before the season was 20 minutes old, as Rooney netted twice and Ronaldo began his incredible scoring spree in a 5-1 victory. The pair combined perfectly in attack, to confound ideas that their

Opposite The victorious Manchester United team show off the Premiership trophy at the end of the successful 2006/07 campaign.
Right Michael Carrick, Sir Alex Ferguson's big summer signing who arrived from Tottenham Hotspur in 2006.

2006–12 · World Cup spat might have harmed their working relationship. It was also significant that Arsenal and Liverpool both failed to win their opening games: this was destined to be a straight fight between the deposed kings of the Premiership and José Mourinho's new champions. Sir Alex knew even then that his team were

good enough to throw down a serious challenge to Chelsea. He told reporters following the Fulham romp, 'That was a superb performance from a maturing team. We've never had a better start in my time here.'

United's league form confirmed them as real title contenders all through the late summer and into autumn. As early as October the title seemed certain to be a two-horse race, when Liverpool came to Old Trafford and were vanquished 2-0 with goals from a resurgent Scholes and Ferdinand. That win took United clear of Chelsea on goal difference at the top of the table, and opened up an 11-point lead over Liverpool. It was a carnival day all round for United, as Sir Bobby Charlton was honoured on the 50th anniversary of his arrival at Old Trafford, Scholes played his 500th game for United, and Rooney his 100th. For good measure, the 75,828 attendance was United's biggest ever, and the largest in the history of the Premiership. The confident display of a rampant United side lived up to the party atmosphere.

Sir Alex was too canny to indulge in hyperbole, but he was clearly pleased with the side's progress. 'There is a growing belief in the team,' he said. 'We started the season with hope and desire and intent and so far they have not let us down.' The following week Rooney celebrated his new six-year contract at United by scoring a dazzling hat-trick in a 4-0 win at Bolton, as United put together a sizzling run of seven wins in seven Premiership games.

At the end of November United faced the most critical moment of the season so far, as Chelsea came to Old Trafford. Louis Saha gave United the lead in the first half, but Mourinho's men rallied and Ricardo Carvalho equalised in the second half to leave the final score tied at 1-1. But in the circumstances United had more to celebrate than the Londoners. The draw ensured that Chelsea stayed three points in arrears, and even with half the season to play, United's form was good enough to suggest the gap would take some closing.

Top *Having missed much of the early part of 2006 with a serious eye injury, Paul Scholes returned to form for the new season. Here he scores United's first goal in their 2-0 home win against Liverpool, October 2006.*
Left *After ten games without a goal Wayne Rooney produced a masterclass in finishing during United's 4-0 win at Bolton. Here he surges past defender Nicky Hunt to score the first of his three goals.*

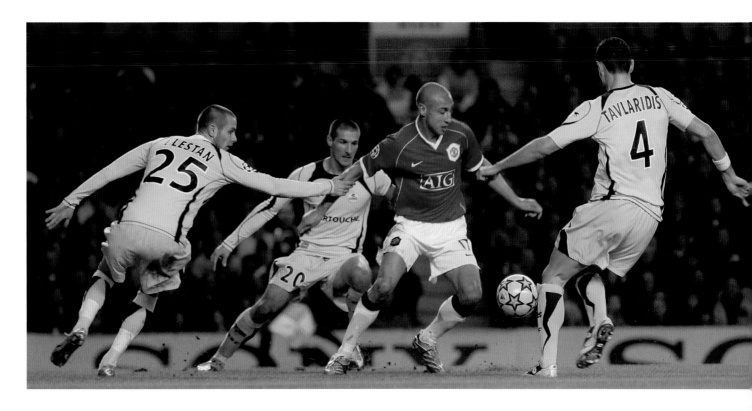

United put in a scintillating burst during Christmas week, reeling off three victories ending in a 3-2 victory against Reading at Old Trafford. It meant that United went into 2007 with a six-point lead over Chelsea. There appeared to be no sign of United slowing down in their pursuit of the title, and Chelsea were clinging on. That victory over Reading was also another personal triumph for Ronaldo. The troubles of the post-World Cup period, when every day brought fresh stories of his imminent departure, had long-since been forgotten. His growing maturity, as a footballer and as a team player, was one of the key factors in United's rise to the top, and another two goals against the Royals took his total for the season to 12. Sir Alex beamed, 'He's getting better all the time'.

United had not missed van Nistelrooy as the goals flew in – but the team did lack cover up front, especially as the Reds were about to embark on the later stages of the Champions League campaign. The lack of bodies prompted Sir Alex to make one of the shrewdest signings in recent years. Henrik Larsson joined the club in the January transfer window. The Swede might have been 35, but he was blessed with the fitness of a 25-year-old, and his arrival gave the club an immediate lift. The craft and guile he had learned in his goal-drenched years at Celtic and Barcelona gave United a new dimension up front, and any danger that they would run out of attacking options as the season wore on was removed.

Larsson made his debut in the 2-1 FA Cup third round win against Villa at Old Trafford, and he crowned the appearance with a goal. He scored only two more before his return to Helsingborgs in March, but his worth to the team was incalculable. In his 13-game cameo of a United career the Reds lost just once. After his last game at Old Trafford, where he scored in a 1-0 Champions League first knockout round game against Lille, Sir Alex paid a heartfelt tribute to the striker, saying, 'It was a great way for Henrik to sign off. He has been an absolute pleasure to work with. He has made an impact on the club.'

Henrik Larsson takes on the Lille defence in his last appearance at Old Trafford, March 2007. The Swede scored the only goal of the game to send United into the Champions League quarter-finals.

RUUD VAN NISTELROOY

STRIKER (2001–06) • 200 (19) APPEARANCES • 150 GOALS

The manner of van Nistelrooy's exit from Old Trafford could have been more dignified, but once the recriminations had died away, there was one inescapable verdict on his five years with United – he was the club's most natural goalscorer since Denis Law was King.

The Dutchman was a master of the finisher's trade, and dealt in all kinds of goals. Like Law, he loved scoring tap-ins just as much as Hollywood strikes from distance. In that sense he was a very different player from Eric Cantona when it came to scoring goals. Van Nistelrooy was happy to dwell among the muck and nettles of the six-yard box, and get his hands dirty in the pursuit of goals. His place of work was the penalty area, and an in-built striker's sat-nav system helped him home in on goal whenever the ball flew near. Strong in the air, accurate with either foot, and blessed with a determination that rivalled Roy Keane's, van Nistelrooy had the lot.

Sir Alex Ferguson knew exactly what he was getting for his cash when he paid PSV Eindhoven a British-record £19 million for the player in August 2001. He had long coveted van Nistelrooy, and was not deterred from signing him even after an earlier deal broke down when the player snapped cruciate ligaments hours before a transfer was completed.

Perhaps van Nistelrooy's best season for United was his second – 2002/03 – when United cruised to the title ahead of Arsenal. Van Nistelrooy was the Premiership's top scorer with 25 goals, and the 14 he scored in Europe also gave him the Champions League Golden Boot.

The goals kept on coming for van Nistelrooy in the following seasons, but injuries did too, and he never quite equalled his early brilliance. And it was sad that such a fond relationship with United should have curdled in his final season, when rows with management and team-mates spelt his inevitable departure. Sir Alex tested his resolve by leaving him out of the team for lengthy periods, and faced with a straight choice – fight or flight – van Nistelrooy chose the second option. He signed for Real Madrid in July 2006.

Despite the unhappy break, van Nistelrooy's place as a United great is secure. It was fitting that he ended his time at Old Trafford as United's all-time top goalscorer in Europe, with 38 goals.

That Larsson strike against Lille sent United into the Champions League quarter-finals, where United produced one of their greatest ever European displays. The Reds faced Roma in the last eight of the competition.

United came away from the first leg in Italy 2-1 down, and they were happy to settle for that after Scholes had been sent off for two bookings just 30 minutes into the game. It was a night when the football was overshadowed by sickening violence off the field, as United's fans were attacked by Roma Ultras and police.

United answered brutality with beauty in the second leg, as an imperious display of attacking football swept Roma out of the competition. United's stunning 7-1 win was the first time in 23 years they had overcome a first-leg deficit in Europe.

Sir Alex had made a typically bold selection for a European tie by naming Alan Smith in the team for his first start since he shattered his leg at Anfield. The decision paid off as Smith featured heavily in United's devastating start. The Reds went level on aggregate after 11 minutes when Carrick scored his first European goal. Smith scored

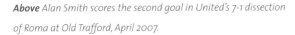

Above Alan Smith scores the second goal in United's 7-1 dissection of Roma at Old Trafford, April 2007.

Right United's goalscorer John O'Shea celebrates with Rio Ferdinand as United beat Liverpool 1-0 at Anfield, March 2007.

his first for a year and a half to put United ahead, and Rooney made it 3-0 soon after. By now the atmosphere inside Old Trafford was febrile, as the United crowd bayed for more goals. The team responded. It was 4-0 a minute before half-time when Ronaldo hit the target, and still United weren't finished. Five minutes after the restart Ronaldo scored his second. Carrick cracked home the sixth goal after an hour, and Patrice Evra made it seven. The performance ranked with anything seen in the great Treble-winning season.

It was United's biggest win in the competition since 1968. But that earlier hammering had come against the Irish part-timers of Waterford rather than a top-notch Serie A outfit. The man with the best view of the unfolding massacre was United's keeper, Edwin van der Sar. In his honour-strewn career with Ajax and Holland he had witnessed some handy displays, but nothing to equal this bravura showing. 'I have never seen a performance like this in my whole life,' he said with something approaching wonder after the final whistle.

'We were just very, very good,' said Gary Neville, who told reporters that the victory marked a return to the attacking traditions which had shaped the club's approach to playing the game since the days of Busby. 'From last year our style has changed,' Neville said. 'Ronaldo, Saha and Rooney started playing up front together and the

speed in our play, what I call the Manchester United way, returned. It's speed. Quick, counter-attacking football. Defending one minute and the ball in the back of the net 10 seconds later. We lost that for some reason over the previous couple of years, but we're getting back to it.'

The rampage against Roma proved to be the highwater mark of the European campaign, however. United were paired with AC Milan in the semi-finals, and after Ronaldo had given them an early lead in the home leg they were unpicked by the magic of Kaka, who scored twice before half-time. Rooney dragged the Reds back into the tie with an equaliser after an hour and a thunderous winner in the last seconds of the match, and United appeared well placed to reach the final in Athens. But it was not to be. In Italy Kaka scored again in the first quarter of an hour to rock United back on their heels, and the Reds were picked off twice more as Milan emerged comfortable 3-0 winners on a depressing night for United.

Despite that body blow in the San Siro United were still chasing a League/FA Cup Double. Right through the winter and early spring United stayed ahead of Chelsea with a string of victories. In most matches United's greater skill and firepower up-front were enough to sink the opposition. But they also showed an appetite for nicking victories and grinding out results when necessary.

They showed that cussed spirit at Anfield in March, when United came away with a 1-0 win thanks to a goal in injury time from one of their less-heralded performers, John O'Shea. United had been under the Liverpool cosh for lengthy periods of the match, and Scholes was sent off again late in the game. United surely would have been delighted with a draw to limit the damage to their title hopes. But O'Shea stepped up to complete a season double over Liverpool, pouncing in the six-yard box after Pepe Reina had failed to hold Ronaldo's free-kick. It was United's only serious effort on goal in the entire match – but they made it count.

That victory put United 12 points clear, at least for a few hours until Chelsea beat Portsmouth in the late kick-off game to reduce the gap to a still-daunting nine points. O'Shea knew the psychological importance of his late strike, too. 'This must be soul-destroying for Chelsea,' he told the press with barely concealed glee after the game. 'Watching with a couple of minutes to go, they must have thought we would drop two points, or even three if Liverpool had knocked

one in after we had been reduced to ten men.' More than ever before, the Premiership was now theirs to lose.

As the season swung into April, United stayed in control at the top of the table. While José Mourinho muttered about the inadequate size of his squad, and the effects of injuries, his Chelsea team lost the invincible aura that had built up when they were winning the title. There was just one brief moment when Chelsea glimpsed a sign of weakness in United, and that came on a crazy day at Goodison Park.

Everton, passions inflamed by the pre-match tributes to Alan Ball who had died that week, tore into United from the start of the match and carved open a 2-0 lead. They had chances to make it 3-0, which would surely have put the game beyond United. But Sir Alex's side dug in and staged a dramatic comeback.

Ronaldo, who began the game on the bench, emerged to put in one of his finest displays of the season, and his quality blew the Toffees off the park. O'Shea scored another vital goal to give United a chance after the goalkeeper had dropped the ball at his feet.

Cristiano Ronaldo and Rio Ferdinand celebrate United's unlikely victory at Everton as United close in on the Premiership crown. Two down with 20 minutes left, United stormed back to win 4-2.

Edwin van der Sar saves Darius Vassell's penalty as United win 1-0 at Manchester City during the title run-in, May 2007.

Then the equaliser came from an entirely unexpected source. The Everton captain Phil Neville, who did not score a huge volume of goals during his long career at Old Trafford (five in 11 years), gave a huge boost to the Reds' title chances when he hacked a clearance into the back of his own net. United ran Everton ragged in the hunt for a winner, with Ronaldo to the fore as attack after attack swept towards the home goal. It finally came when Rooney crashed in a shot with 10 minutes left. Chris Eagles added a fourth, and United had rescued three points on a day when defeat might have thrown the title back into the balance.

Sir Alex, for one, felt that United were almost over the line, 'The Champion feeling is there,' he said.

The day took on an even rosier hue for United fans when news came through of Bolton's 2-2 draw at Stamford Bridge. That meant the Reds were taking a five-point lead into the last three games of the season.

United were in no mood to slip up now. They won the next game 1-0 at City on 5 May, and the Premiership title was officially theirs when Chelsea could only draw 1-1 at Arsenal the following day.

Sir Alex hailed his young Champions with a glowing tribute. Written off at the start of the season, the emerging new side had outclassed Chelsea's expensive assembly of stars. 'This title is the team's greatest achievement to date simply because it's a relatively new team, and really it's their first attempt at winning a title together,' said Sir Alex. 'That's why we're all encouraged. I think this team will get better.'

Sir Alex also promised supporters that the squad would be strengthened, so United would be in a position to withstand the inevitable challenges that would come in 2007/08. From Chelsea, of course; from a freshly financed Liverpool; and from Arsenal, who threatened to emerge stronger from a transitional season.

Sir Alex also showered praise on individuals who had come into the club and made vital contributions to the title-winning effort. He said, 'We had a good foundation in players like Giggs, Scholes, Neville, Solskjaer and Ferdinand. Then we brought some new players in, like Heinze, Vidic, Evra, Carrick, Rooney, Ronaldo and Park. They gave us a far more balanced and powerful squad.

'Vidic has been the best centre-half in the country this season. He's been absolutely outstanding. You could see the difference his partnership with Rio Ferdinand made to us against Manchester City. That foundation of strength in the central defensive position is something we've been wanting for a long time, going back to Pallister and Bruce. We've had some good combinations but none lasted as long as hopefully these two will do.'

There was one man who stood out even in that stellar company. That was Ronaldo, who became the first player since Andy Gray 30 years ago to win the PFA Player of the Year and Young Player of the Year awards in the same season.

The 22-year-old was delighted with the double honour. He had begun the season with boos ringing in his ears wherever he played. Now he was ending it to cheers of acclaim from all fair-minded football lovers. 'My colleagues have voted for me and that is fantastic because the players know the qualities of players,' he said. 'I want to keep working hard and getting better because these trophies have now given me more motivation. This great team has helped me because when the team wins it is easier for us all to play with more confidence.'

Before the season began some supporters feared that United might be short on firepower up front in the absence of a big-name replacement for van Nistelrooy. Ronaldo went a long way to filling the void with his 17 league goals from midfield. Now some observers went further, and were ready to call Ronaldo the best footballer in the world on the back of his exploits for United. No less a person than the Chelsea and England captain, John Terry, backed the claim. 'I could watch United just to watch him,' Terry said. 'He does things no one else in the world is doing at the minute. He's the best in the world. At his best, not many people can stop him.'

Following the title triumph, United aimed to complete the Double. The story of the whole season had been about United's week to week duel with Chelsea, so it was fitting that the clubs met in the final match of the season, the FA Cup final, the first at the new Wembley since 2000.

After a long, hard season it was too much to hope that the sides would serve up a classic to suit the festive occasion. It was a scrappy, nervy anti-climax of a game which never quite burst into life. The 90 minutes came and went without a goal, and the match was finally put out of its misery five minutes before the end of extra-time, when Didier Drogba scored the winning goal.

Sir Alex admitted that his team's performance had an after the Lord Mayor's Show flavour about it. He acknowledged the defeat philosophically, and looked ahead to the next season. 'The players are too tired,' he said. 'I have seen it time and time again in football.

The important thing is to accept it and get on with it. I'll wake up in the morning and get on with life.'

That dropped the curtain on another dramatic season for the Reds. It had brought with it disappointments, like the FA Cup final defeat, elimination against AC Milan and the shock of defeat against Southend in the League Cup. But they were outweighed by the joy of ascending to the summit of the English game once more with the recapture of the Premiership title. And there was that never-to-be-forgotten night against Roma, when the Theatre of Dreams truly lived up to its name. Now United were ready for the next adventure.

Sir Alex, in Churchillian mode, told supporters they faced testing times ahead as United set out to consolidate their position back at the top of English football. More than ever before in the history of the Premiership, there was a real chance of a four-cornered title fight in 2007/08. The days of United rolling over the opposition and winning Championships at a canter were over, he warned. 'For us to dominate the League again will be a difficult task,' he said.

Paul Scholes sprays the champagne as the jubilant United side celebrate the Premiership trophy's return to Old Trafford for the first time since 2002/03.

2006–12

2006–12

No one doubted that it would be difficult to defend their title, but Sir Alex moved decisively in the summer to inject fresh talent into his squad, especially up front. He spent over £6.5 million, recruiting Carlos Tevez on loan, whose goals had saved West Ham from the drop the season before. He also brought the young attack-minded stars, Nani and Anderson, to Old Trafford. The midfield positions were bolstered by the addition of Owen Hargreaves, who arrived from Bayern Munich. But despite the mood of anticipation that gripped the club's supporters in August 2007, United didn't have it all their own way once the action started. Far from it. The season began with the new-look United team displaying patchy form, and the first three matches yielded just two points. Worse than that, they lost to Manchester City. But the tide certainly turned during September, never more so than in the home game against Chelsea, when United welcomed the Blues' new manager Avram Grant to the Premiership with a 2-0 victory. That came in a run of eight consecutive league wins which turbocharged United's race for the title.

The autumn was a period when United's defenders proved crucial to the club's cause. In a string of eight Premiership and

Champions League games they won 1-0 on six occasions. United were destined to end the season as the Premiership's top scorers, but they needed the obduracy of the back-four, especially the central pairing of Ferdinand and Vidic, to keep their ambitions alive.

The goals really began to pour into opposition nets as winter kicked in. There were four-goal hauls at home to Wigan, away to Villa, at Dynamo Kiev, then at home to Middlesbrough, Kiev again and Derby. There was no sentiment shown to an old friend as Roy Keane's Sunderland were also hit for four at the Stadium of Light. But the sternest punishment was reserved for Newcastle United. They were dispatched 6-0 at Old Trafford in January, as Ronaldo scored his sole hat-trick in a near-miraculous season of achievement. Then the Magpies unravelled to the tune of 5-1 at St James' Park the following month, Ronaldo scoring twice.

Above *Ronaldo side-foots home against Newcastle United, yet another strike in another goal-filled season.*
Left *Nemanja Vidic, staunch in United's rearguard alongside Rio Ferdinand, clears the danger against Arsenal.*

As a gripping campaign headed into the final stretch, there was one afternoon when the result of a match meant less than the soul of a club. It came in February, when the 50th anniversary of Munich coincided with United's home game against City. There had been fears that the minute's mute tribute before the match might be spoiled, but in the event it was observed with silence. For one afternoon the whole of Manchester, and the entire football world, came together to remember the tragedy of Munich. The emotional freight of the afternoon, and the memorials that had taken place in the preceding days, weighed heavily on the players, and it was a rare off-day for the side. The Reds lost, but for once it didn't seem to matter. United, and the City of Manchester, had emerged from a difficult ordeal with dignity intact.

As the campaign moved into spring, the Premiership title was increasingly a tight, two-horse race between United and Chelsea. There was no room for any slip-ups, and dropping points was a luxury neither team could afford. There were times when United's unsung squad players made key contributions to the cause. On one

harrowing day at Derby, United needed a succession of brilliant saves from their young reserve keeper, Ben Foster, to deny the relegation-haunted home team. It wasn't until late in the game that Ronaldo scored the only goal to avoid a potentially calamitous result. Foster showed the spirit and indomitable attitude that typified United's efforts right through the season. Those qualities

Above *Sir Alex Ferguson and Sven-Göran Eriksson lead the teams out before an emotion-charged Manchester Derby.*
Right *Ronaldo scores the only goal of the game at Pride Park to keep United's title challenge on course.*

were on show again at Middlesbrough in April, when United trailed 2-1 in the last quarter of an hour. Now it was Wayne Rooney's turn to step up for his team-mates with a vital equaliser.

In the final few matches United kept their nerve to edge ahead of Chelsea. The Londoners' hopes were dealt a terrific blow when they drew at home to Wigan, after Emile Heskey scored a 95th-minute equaliser. But United still needed to avoid defeats, and they looked certain to suffer a loss at Blackburn that would have plunged the Premiership race into greater doubt than ever. But Tevez scored a late equaliser to save a priceless point.

As it had done on several previous occasions in Sir Alex's United career, the championship was settled on the last day of the season. Chelsea could steal it if they beat Bolton at home and United slipped up at Wigan. But neither eventuality came to pass. Chelsea were held 1-1, and United eased to a 2-0 win at the JJB Stadium. Ronaldo, fittingly enough in his goal-strewn season, opened the scoring from the spot. And the club's faithful servant, 34-year-old supersub Ryan Giggs, made the game – and the Premiership title – safe in the second half.

Sir Alex was thrilled to win his 10th League title in 16 seasons. No one needed to tell him that winning the biggest prize in English football left United just one short of Liverpool's all-time tally of 18 top-flight titles. The manager backed his youthful team to overhaul

the mark sooner rather than later. 'I think it will come,' he told reporters in the jubilant aftermath of the Premiership-clinching win. 'This side is young. It's developing all the time. There are plenty of years left in them. They will do it in their own time.'

While the drama of the Premiership was unfolding, United had been making serene progress in the Champions League. Sir Alex's side had emerged from their opening group with some ease, beating Sporting Lisbon and Dynamo Kiev away from home, while overcoming Roma, Kiev and Lisbon at Old Trafford. That set up a testing First Knockout round tie against Lyon, which United were relieved to survive. They needed the substitute, Tevez, to force a 1-1 draw in France, and only Ronaldo's goal at Old Trafford put them in the quarter-finals.

The last-eight could have been fraught with peril for United, as they were paired once again with Roma. They had to travel to the Stadio Olimpico for the first leg, a venue that had caused so much grief for their supporters in the past. But United focused on their job on the field, and turned in a highly professional performance to win 2-0 in front of a hostile crowd topping 80,000. The 1-0 win at home was enough to put United into the semi-finals to meet Barcelona.

It was a season when United's cavaliers served up football that was adorned by ambition and attacking intent. But there was little of that in evidence for the first leg in the Nou Camp, when United dug deep to grind out a 0-0 draw after Ronaldo had missed from the spot.

Given that he had missed the 1999 Champions League final, it was appropriate that Paul Scholes should book his own ticket to the 2008 version. He scored with a sumptuous long-range strike to clinch the home leg and fix a date with Chelsea in Moscow, for the first-ever Champions League final contested by two English clubs.

Scholes duly collected his winner's medal, as United put the seal on one of the most memorable campaigns in their history. They were being hailed in some quarters as one of the best teams, if not the best, ever to grace Old Trafford. The test of their greatness would be their ability to build on their achievements, and exceed them, which Sir Alex knew would be difficult.

Rooney wheels away in triumph after a priceless goal salvages a result against Middlesbrough.

The 2008/09 season saw United leave their blocks slowly, as the team took time to hit its stride. In the first four matches, the Reds mustered a solitary victory in the Premier League. But the early-season ring-rustiness soon disappeared, as United set off in pursuit of another title. They lurked near the top of the table throughout the autumn, and finally hit first place in January 2009 after winning 1-0 at Bolton. That victory was engineered by a last-minute goal from Dimitar Berbatov.

The lavishly talented Bulgarian striker had joined United from Spurs the previous summer, with Sir Alex investing a sum reported to be around £30 million on his singular talents. For that outlay, United had gained a proven goalscorer, but also a player with the kind of wit and guile on the ball beloved of United fans. He wore

the No. 9 jersey, but he was a long way from being the orthodox target man.

Frank Stapleton, a man who filled that position with some distinction for United, commented, 'If you think about the

Above Tevez pounces late to earn United a precious point at Blackburn.

Right Ryan Giggs is submerged by his team-mates after scoring in United's title-clinching victory at Wigan.

2008 **CHAMPIONS LEAGUE FINAL**

MANCHESTER UNITED 1 Ronaldo **CHELSEA 1** Lampard (after extra-time) United won 6-5 on penalties
21 MAY 2008 at Luzhniki Stadium, Moscow • Referee: Lubos Michel (Slovakia) • Attendance: 69,552

MANCHESTER UNITED

Van der Sar
Brown (Anderson)
Ferdinand
Vidic
Evra
Hargreaves
Scholes (Giggs)
Carrick
Ronaldo
Tevez
Rooney (Nani)

CHELSEA

Cech
Essien
Carvalho
Terry
A Cole
Ballack
Makelele (Belletti)
Lampard
J Cole (Anelka)
Drogba
Malouda (Kalou)

Manchester United don't do dull Champions League finals. So it was always inevitable that the competition's first-ever all-English final would throw up enough twists and turns to rival the stirring events in Barcelona of nine years before.

After two hours of compelling action had failed to produce a winner, the drama came down to penalties – and whoever blinked first would lose out. History will probably remember the Chelsea and England captain, John Terry, as the hapless fall-guy who lost the cup. He had a kick to win it, but lost his footing on the rain-drenched pitch and hit the post. United were in no mood to miss out on that reprieve – and when Edwin van der Sar saved Nicolas Anelka's sudden-death effort, the celebrations could begin. United had conquered European football for the third time.

The spectre of penalties had been a long way from the minds of United supporters for most of the first half, as their team took a grip on the game. For most of that opening period it looked like United might win with something to spare, and when Cristiano Ronaldo scored with a header after 26 minutes, there was an air of predictability about it. The season had, after all, belonged to the Portuguese genius, and it was only right that he should score the goal that paved the way to glory. Yet the Londoners weren't about to lie down and die in Moscow. Belatedly, they rediscovered the high-tempo, powerful pressing game that had pushed United all the way in the Premiership, and their recovery made for a nerve-jangling spectacle. As the first half wore on, Chelsea began to take the upper hand, and it was no shock when Frank Lampard, appearing in the biggest game of his career days after the death of his mother, scored the equaliser just before the half-time whistle.

Ronaldo powers a header past Petr Cech after 26 minutes to give United the lead.

The celebrations begin as United display the Champions League trophy in Moscow.

Both teams threw every ounce of their strength and skill into a gripping second-half duel. United had bossed most of the first half, but the Londoners had the edge in the second period. Didier Drogba and Lampard hit the post, but neither side could find the killer strike.

As it so often does, extra-time proved an anticlimax, as two tiring sides began to show more caution. But what won the Cup for United, more than anything, was their greater concentration and discipline.

Seconds before the end of extra time, Drogba got himself sent off for a petulant slap at Nemanja Vidic. Chelsea's backroom staff later confirmed that Drogba would have taken the critical penalty rather than Terry, and you have to think that one of the world's greatest centre-forwards would have had a better chance of converting from 12 yards than the willing centre-back.

For United, Carlos Tevez and Michael Carrick kept their composure to score their team's first two kicks, before Ronaldo chose this moment of all moments to mislay his ruthlessness in front of goal. Owen Hargreaves and Nani kept United in the shoot-out with successful strikes, and when Terry missed his, United and Chelsea had both scored four out of five. Sudden death kicked in, and Anderson netted the first to put United 5-4 ahead.

Kalou struck back for the Blues, but then United's evergreen Welshman, Ryan Giggs, put his team ahead with a nerveless shot. That put a world of responsibility on the shoulders of the ex-Arsenal, Liverpool and Manchester City striker, Anelka, and his weak attempt was palmed away by van der Sar. The Dutchman was engulfed by his ecstatic team-mates, and the United fans who had made the long trek to Moscow celebrated in the stands. And so did the many millions more, watching on televisions all around the world. Fifty years after the tragedy of Munich, the trophy that means more to the club than any other was on its way home.

Moments after the triumph, a thrilled Sir Alex Ferguson told a packed press conference, 'When you win the European Cup it's a special occasion, you treasure these things. We have had to wait nine years to do it again, which proves it's not an easy tournament to win. It's now three [victories] and it has a far better ring to it, I must say.

'Hopefully we can build on that because, particularly for the younger players who had not been [to a final] before, you can't not relish an occasion like that.'

2006–12

traditional centre forwards United have had over the years, Berbatov is different to all of them. He's unpredictable, a player that, in a tight match, can open up the game at any point. And his touch is simply sublime.' It was the ability to change a game with a sudden flash of genius that Sir Alex was anxious to add to the squad. And Berbatov was able to supply that rare commodity at frequent intervals. The 14 goals he scored in the 2008/09 campaign were a priceless contribution to the club's trophy-winning effort.

Bulgarian striker Dimitar Berbatov's unpredictable skills and 14 goals played a big part in United's trophy-laden 2008/09 season.

That win at the Reebok Stadium came in the midst of a run of 11 victories on the trot, as United took command of the contest for the Premier League title. They stayed out in front all the way through to May, and in their penultimate game of the campaign, the Reds entertained Arsenal, with a point required to capture another Premier League crown. Despite one or two scares for the United defence, the match ended 0-0 and the celebrations could begin.

There was, after all, plenty to celebrate. It was United's third consecutive title, and their 18th in total. It escaped nobody in football that that figure put United level with Liverpool for top-flight titles. Sir Alex's vow, made all those years earlier when he first stepped across the threshold at Old Trafford, that his aim was

to 'knock Liverpool off their perch' had come a step closer. A tumult rocked the famous, century-old stadium as club captain Gary Neville hoisted the out-size trophy, and displayed it to all corners. Each player was introduced to the crowd in turn, and the cheers could be heard across Lancashire. The loudest shouts of acclamation were reserved for Sir Alex. But just moments after his emotional reception, the manager was already looking forward to the tasks ahead. 'The great challenge now is to try to win it next year because that would be something special,' he observed. 'A nineteenth league title would give us a special place in the club's history.'

The title wasn't the only trophy United landed in 2008/09. In December 2008 they travelled to Yokohama, Japan, for the FIFA Club World Cup. It might not have been at the top of every supporter's must-win list of honours – but United are nothing if not pioneers in the world game, and the club took the fledgling competition seriously. That was apparent in the semi-final, where they defeated local hopefuls Gamba Osaka 5-3. That set up a final against LDU Quito, of Ecuador, and United won the competition for the first time in their history, with Rooney scoring the only goal of the game.

Sir Alex Ferguson leads the players around Old Trafford after a draw with Arsenal had secured United's record-equalling 18th top-flight title on 18 May 2009.

United also advanced to the final of the League Cup at Wembley, where they faced Spurs. It was an afternoon when the Reds' reserve goalkeeper, Ben Foster, again proved his class, with a series of fine saves to keep the score tied at 0-0 through normal time and extra time. Foster kept his cool in the ensuing penalty shoot-out, which United won 4-1, to take the trophy for the third time in the club's history.

After collecting the man of the match award, Foster explained that he had done his homework ahead of a possible spot-kick contest by watching Spurs' penalty takers in action on his iPod! Foster told reporters, 'Just before the shoot-out I was looking at an iPod with goalkeeping coach Eric Steele and it contained images of Tottenham's players taking penalties. They told me for Jamie O'Hara that I should stand up and be strong and he would probably go the way he did. I had done a lot of research before, but this is an innovation we have brought in at the club.'

It was proof again that meticulous preparation on the training ground is the foundation of so much success. Foster, and United's coaching team, had proved that the old cliché is correct: you really do make your own luck.

Above Wayne Rooney volleys the ball past the Quito keeper for the only goal of the Club World Cup final in Yokohama.

Right Anderson in action during the League Cup final against Spurs. The Brazilian scored the final penalty in United's 4-1 shoot-out triumph.

Alas, even the most scrupulous preparations sometimes go awry, and footballing destiny conspires to grab prizes from a team's grasp. United were heading for an immortal Quintuple, by adding the FA Cup and Champions League to their Premier League, League Cup and Club World Cup haul. They reached the semi-finals of the FA Cup at Wembley, but lost out to Everton on penalties after a sterile two hours of football ended goalless. Former United keeper Tim Howard was on obdurate form between the sticks for the Toffees, and saved penalties from Ferdinand and Berbatov in the shoot-out.

Worse disappointment was to come in the Champions League. United eased through their group stage, remaining unbeaten and topping the pool ahead of Villarreal, Aalborg and Celtic. The matches against The Bhoys were the highlight of the section, with United winning 3-0 at home and escaping from the daunting fortress of Parkhead with a 1-1 draw, thanks to Giggs'

late goal. Their serene form took them through into the knockout stages – and their first tie was an intriguing match-up with Jose Mourinho's Internazionale.

The first leg in Milan was a pulsating contest, and both teams created enough chances to put the game to bed. But despite the free-flowing, nerve-jangling action, the game ended 0-0. It was a dangerous scoreline to take back to Old Trafford, in the knowledge that a single away goal for Inter would swing the tie decisively in their favour. But United took control of the tie in the opening minutes, when Vidic headed in Giggs' corner. While the score remained at 1-0 the tie rested on a razor's edge, as an Inter equaliser would take them through. But Ronaldo added a second early in the

Ryan Giggs heads United's 84th-minute equaliser against Celtic during their group stage match of the 2008/09 Champions League in Glasgow.

2006–12

second half, and that turned out to be the last goal of the game. United were in the quarter-finals.

They faced Porto at home in the first leg of their last-eight encounter, and United made hard work of a 2-2 draw. That meant they had to travel to the Estadio do Dragao and play as if they were the home team, in a winner-takes-all clash – and they didn't let their loyal travelling support down. Ronaldo stamped his class all over the occasion in the first few minutes, with a shot from outside the penalty area that flew past the home keeper in a blur. United lived

United taught Arsenal a lesson during the Champions League semi-finals, winning 1-0 at Old Trafford and then scoring two early goals, including this one from Ji-sung Park, in the second leg in London.

on their nerves for the rest of the game, as Porto had their chances to score, just as United did. But the match ended 1-0, and United were in the semi-finals – against Arsenal.

The tie with the Gunners was billed as a grudge match, as there had been little love lost between the clubs over the previous few years. The North-South rivalry had at times boiled over into bitterness, and football had sometimes come second behind score-settling when the sides met. But the first leg at Old Trafford was more of a celebration of the game, as both teams played their full part in an absorbing contest. John O'Shea grabbed the only goal of the game with a half volley in the first half, and it gave United a precarious lead to take to the Emirates Stadium.

Arsenal were highly fancied to overcome the deficit on their home ground, where they had built a formidable record since quitting

Highbury. But when the sides met again in North London, experience was the deciding factor, as United's seasoned campaigners bossed the Gunners' youngsters. United scored an early goal through Ji-sung Park, and a couple of minutes later Ronaldo steered a long-range free-kick into the back of the net to give United an impregnable 3-0 aggregate lead. Arsenal pressed forward, desperately seeking a way back into the game, but United never looked like buckling. Ronaldo piled on the misery with another goal after an hour. The Gunners struck back with a Robin van Persie penalty, but United strode into the final with a 4-1 aggregate victory. They had proved their class, and were worthy standard-bearers of English football going into the final.

The great showpiece of European club football pitted United against another of the continent's true footballing aristocrats – Barcelona – and the two great clubs faced each other in Rome's fabled Stadio Olimpico.

United started the better side, finding plenty of joy attacking down Barcelona's flanks. Twice in the opening minutes Ronaldo drifted into shooting range. Twice he was denied. For those first few heady minutes of the final it appeared that the English Champions might overrun the Catalan side, as United's white shirts poured forward and bore down on the Barca goal, but they could not breach the last defences. The failure to convert dominance into goals was penalised cruelly after 10 minutes, and the course of the match turned around, when Samuel Eto'o scored an opportunistic goal for Barca.

From that moment, Barcelona grew in composure, and kept the ball coolly while United grew frantic in their search for an equaliser. Sir Alex's gallant side conjured moments of threat, but much of their attacking sting had been drawn by Eto'o's sickening blow. He played his last attacking cards, pitching Ronaldo, Rooney, Tevez and Berbatov together in attack, but Barcelona's nerve held. Sir Alex's gamble was bold, but with 20 minutes remaining Lionel Messi scuppered United's chances with a goal on the break. United supporters have never seen their team give up on a game, and they had cause for real pride as their heroes strived manfully until time ran out. But there would be no Champions League triumph for them this time.

Sir Alex knew there was no shame in losing to a side as gifted as Barcelona. If United had converted a chance in the opening exchanges, history might have turned out a whole lot differently.

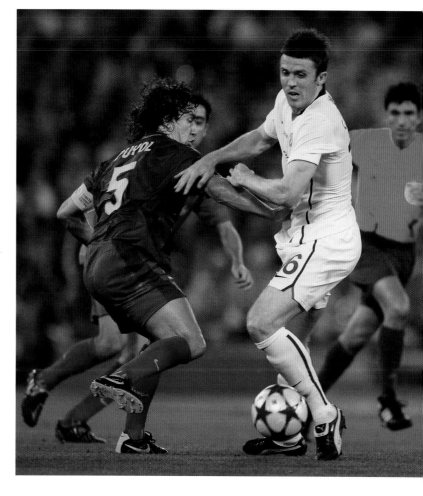

But he paid magnanimous tribute to Barcelona, who rode out the opening storm, and then showed that they could also play a bit. 'We didn't play as well as we can, but you have to give Barcelona credit,' confessed Sir Alex. 'We started brightly and confidently and could have been in front in the first ten minutes but the goal was a killer. But we've done well. It's been a long season, we've had 66 games and you've got to give the players credit for their courage and resilience. Next season we'll be better.'

Despite United's bright start in the final, they could not find a way past the Barca defence. A goal by Samuel Eto'o after ten minutes gave the Catalans the upper hand and a second goal by Messi saw them wrest the trophy from the holders.

It did not take long for the dust to settle on a searing night in the Eternal City before Sir Alex began planning for the 2009/10 campaign. It was certain to be a new-look United side for the new season, as they lost their brightest star to Real Madrid. Ronaldo had yearned for a move to the Bernabeu for some time and he finally had his wish granted, as United reluctantly bade him farewell. The transfer fee was a world record £80 million, but there is no doubt that United would rather have kept the player who had lit up Old Trafford for half a decade. United also went into the new season without Tevez, as the Argentinian chose to join Manchester City. Sir Alex reinforced his squad with an audacious swoop for Michael Owen, and also bought exciting Wigan wide-man Antonio Valencia in to the squad. The scene was set for United's tilt at a fourth successive Premier League crown.

The goal seemed eminently possible when United stormed to the top of the table at the end of September, on the back of a 2-0 win at Stoke City. But they did not stay in first place for long. They duelled with Chelsea throughout the campaign, with United swapping top spot with the Londoners for a few weeks at a time, but neither club

Opposite *The evergreen Ryan Giggs, whose performances during the 2008/09 season helped United to the title, and won him the Footballer of the Year and BBC Sports Personality of the Year awards.*
Above *Flying winger Antonio Valencia settled in at Old Trafford straight away. Sir Alex was pleased with the purchase, 'He's got great balance, power and speed,' said the manager. 'He's immediately taken to the challenge well and with purpose.*

CRISTIANO RONALDO

MIDFIELD/STRIKER (2003–09) • 244 (48) APPEARANCES • 118 GOALS

It is a hallmark of a great player that their role in the team is difficult to define. Their brilliance defies a one- or two-word description. You could ask the question of legends like Puskas, Pele, Best, Cruyff, Cantona and Maradona – what was their position? Inside forward? Attacking midfield? Winger? Centre forward? All of them prove elusive when trying to pin them down to a single role, and Cristiano Ronaldo dos Santos Aveiro fits easily into that company.

It never mattered much what Ronaldo's nominal position in the Manchester United formation might have been: above anything else, he possessed a finely wrought genius for scoring goals and winning football matches. And that was his real purpose at Old Trafford.

There have been a handful of occasions during Sir Alex Ferguson's reign at United where he has spotted a young player, and knew he had to acquire him for the club, no matter what it took. The young Ryan Giggs was one. Wayne Rooney was certainly another, and it did not take him long to realise that Ronaldo was a must-have player. Sir Alex and his staff, as well as senior players, knew United must have Ronaldo in the summer of 2003, when they played a friendly match in Portugal against his club, Sporting Lisbon. The home side won, largely thanks to the attacking verve displayed by the 18-year-old.

'After we played Sporting, the lads in the dressing room talked about him constantly,' Sir Alex recalled. 'On the plane back from the game they urged me to sign him – that's how highly they rated him. He is one of the most exciting young players I've ever seen.'

It did not take long for Sir Alex to do the deal, and Ronaldo moved to England for a fee in the region of £12 million. It seemed like a lot for a teenager with hardly any track record. Unless you had seen him play. And it spoke volumes about Sir Alex's faith in the kid that he had no hesitation in handing him the fabled No. 7 shirt as soon as

he signed. It marked the start of a six-year spell at United that brought a raft of team and personal honours: the Champions League, three Premier League titles, the FA Cup, two League Cups, two PFA Player of the Year awards, two Football Writers' Footballer of the Year awards, and European and a World Player of the Year prize. In 2007/08, he scored an astonishing 42 goals in the campaign.

There was natural disappointment when Ronaldo chose to move on in 2009, but his departure was far from being an act of desertion. Much as he came to love the north-west of England, and training in the cold at Carrington, he always had a hankering to return to his Latin roots. Indeed, he might have moved much earlier, but for a real sense of loyalty to the club and the manager who had done so much to propel him into the front rank of the world's star players. But it shouldn't be forgotten that Ronaldo made nearly 200 league appearances for United, and scored 84 Premier League goals. Numbers don't tell the whole story, but both figures are higher than those achieved by an unquestionable Old Trafford great such as Cantona.

George Best, who knew a fellow great when he saw one, was in no doubt where Ronaldo rated in the Old Trafford pantheon of legendary performers. 'There have been a few players described as the new George Best over the years,' said Best. 'But this is the first time it's been a compliment to me.'

2006–12

could build up a gap and pull away. The decisive few days came late in the season, when the Reds lost 2-1 at home to Carlo Ancelotti's team on 3 April, and could only draw 0-0 at Blackburn in their next game.

For a few hours United went back to the top of the table when they beat Spurs 3-1 in a lunchtime game at Old Trafford, just two matches before the end of the season. But Chelsea kept their cool and won their game in hand to regain top spot. The title, though, was still in the balance on the last day of the season. Sir Alex's valiant side gave themselves an outside chance of retaining their title by beating Stoke City 4-0 at home. But Chelsea snatched the honour from their grasp by easing to an 8-0 victory against Wigan

Athletic at Stamford Bridge, the prelude to the Londoners' first-ever League and Cup Double.

Sir Alex was in a philosophical, and gracious, mood as he conceded the title to Chelsea. 'You can't agonise over these things,' he said moments after the season's final whistle. 'Sometimes you get the breaks, on other occasions you don't. But we applaud Chelsea winning the title and I applaud Carlo Ancelotti. We know how hard it is to win the league.'

There had been similar disappointment, too, in the Champions League. The campaign began brightly, as United stormed into the knockout stages at the head of a tricky group that included Besiktas, CSKA Moscow and Wolfsburg. And the Reds underlined their status as favourites when they hammered the mighty AC Milan in the second round.

In one of the most emphatic drubbings the *Rossoneri* had ever experienced in European football, United beat them 3-2 in their own stadium, then took them apart in a 4-0 victory at Old Trafford. It was a highly charged night of raw passion, when an emotional crowd thrilled to Rooney's two-goal show – a performance which strengthened his credentials to be hailed as Europe's leading striker. It was an occasion that would also be remembered for the return of David Beckham, who was afforded a hero's reception by an appreciative audience, who recalled the peerless service he had given to the club. Beckham returned the applause, and was clearly touched by the display of affection towards him.

Sadly, United had peaked too early in the competition that still holds the club in its thrall. They went to Bayern Munich for the first leg of the quarter-final where, despite an early goal from Rooney, they lost 2-1. In the home leg, United scored another goal in the first five minutes, through Darron Gibson, and went on to lead 3-0 on the night, but the match ended 3-2 to United – giving Bayern victory on away goals. The Germans reckoned they still owed United for 1999. But United will always have that victory in Barcelona.

David Beckham's return to Old Trafford with AC Milan for a Champions League tie was a bittersweet occasion for the player. He received a rapturous reception shortly before the Rossoneri were put to the sword on the end of a 7-2 aggregate drubbing.

United's interest in the FA Cup was terminated by a 1-0 home defeat at the hands of their former rivals, Leeds United. But they were able to put some precious metal in the trophy cabinet thanks to the Carling Cup. The highlight of the competition was a thrilling two-legged semi-final with City. The clubs' age-old rivalry had been exacerbated by City's new found wealth and aggressive activity in the transfer market, which featured the signing of Tevez. That move was aggravated, in United's eyes, by what they saw as provocative marketing by City – who plastered posters of Tevez on billboards, bearing the inflammatory legend 'Welcome to Manchester'.

Earlier in the season, United had won a dramatic derby at Old Trafford by 4-3, with Owen scoring in the sixth minute of added time. It all made for a febrile atmosphere when the first game kicked off at Eastlands. City won that encounter 2-1, but United showed all

Darron Gibson celebrates after his fifth-minute goal had levelled up the Champions League quarter-final tie against Bayern Munich. However, two late strikes for the Germans saw United crash out on the away-goals rule.

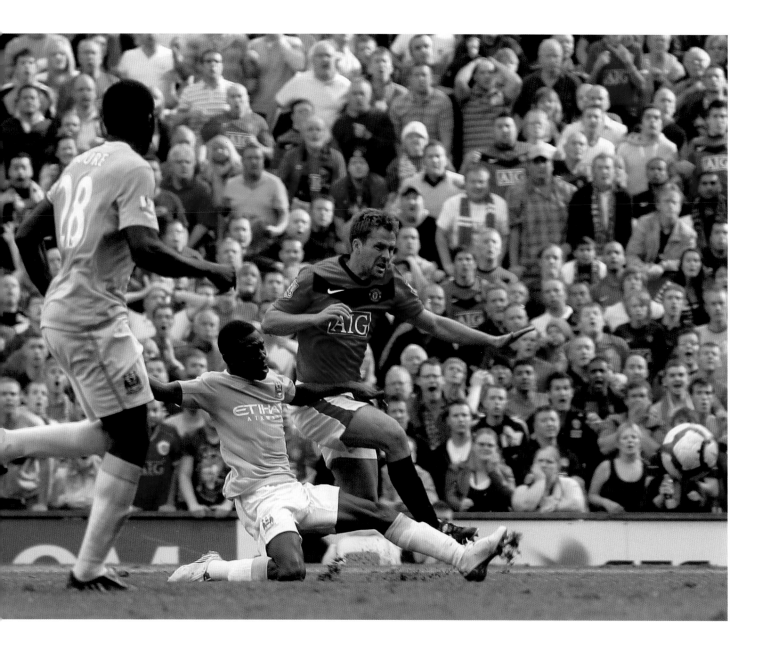

their experience and savvy in the second leg, and reached the final with a 3-1 victory. Just to complete City's misery, United would also win the return Premier League fixture in added time, thanks to a Paul Scholes goal.

Michael Owen steers the ball home to give United a dramatic 4-3 win in the Manchester derby at Old Trafford in September 2009.

Sir Alex's team then dispatched Aston Villa in the final at Wembley, with goals from Owen and Rooney. It had been a campaign that included great moments, many of them featuring the extraordinary talents of Rooney, who capped a remarkable season by being crowned the PFA Player of the Year and the Football Writers' Footballer of the Year. But the fact that the game's biggest trophies went elsewhere was a cause of deep regret for the United faithful across the world.

The 2010/11 season saw four teams battling it out at the top of the Premier League in an exciting, topsy-turvy tussle that lasted nine tension-filled months. Throughout the campaign Chelsea, Arsenal and Manchester City all jostled with United for top spot, and the destination of the championship trophy was in doubt right through to May.

On the first afternoon of the campaign, Chelsea threw down a marker when they thrashed West Bromwich Albion 6-0. United kicked off their season a couple of days later and answered in style with a classy 3-0 demolition of Newcastle United. The opening salvoes set the scene for the enthralling exchanges to come.

United kept their convincing form going through the first months of the campaign, as they built a daunting sequence of unbeaten results. Autumn came and went, and no one could get the better of the Red Devils. Into winter, through Christmas and the New Year, and still United kept a zero in the losses column. There were many highlights along the way as United threw down the gauntlet to their title rivals. On 19 September, Dimitar Berbatov re-wrote the history of United–Liverpool clashes by grabbing a hat-trick as United defeated their Lancashire neighbours 3-2 at Old Trafford. The Bulgarian hit-man's treble was the first by a United player against Liverpool since Stan Pearson's in 1946.

Berbatov set another new landmark at the end of November when he netted five in United's 7-1 dismantling of Blackburn

One of the major highlights of the 2009/10 campaign was the brilliant form of Wayne Rooney – his tally of 34 goals, four of which came in the Champions League ties against AC Milan, put him firmly on the list of the world's best footballers.

Rovers at Old Trafford. The result was even more significant in that it saw United hit the summit of the Premier League for the first time in the season ahead of Arsenal and Chelsea.

United did their chances of regaining the title the world of good when they beat the Gunners 1-0 at Old Trafford on 13 December, after the Londoners had retaken top spot in the league while United's schedule was disrupted by the weather. Ji-sung Park's first-half strike put United back in charge of the title race, but still the chasing pack nibbled at their heels. City deposed United from first place after beating Villa, but United restored their advantage and went into the New Year in pole position with a 1-1 draw at Birmingham City.

Though United stayed strong through the worst of the winter, they couldn't open a significant gap over their dogged pursuers. However, there was cause for great satisfaction on the first day in February, when Sir Alex's team equalled United's record of unbeaten league games. The 3-1 home win over Villa was their 29th match undefeated on the trot. But the joy was tempered with sadness, as Gary Neville announced his retirement from football in the aftermath of the victory. The full-back had not been an automatic choice for some while after a series of injuries, and his decision to bow out with dignity earned him even greater respect and affection around Old Trafford.

Sadly, United weren't able to extend their record run, as they lost on their next outing. Relegation-haunted Wolves ran out 2-1 winners at Molineux, and the defeat gave fresh heart to the clubs behind United, who were on the lookout for any hint of weakness or self-doubt. In the circumstances, the next fixture couldn't have been more daunting – a game against City, who for the first time in a generation had serious thoughts about capturing the title themselves.

Above *Dimitar Berbatov finishes his masterclass in the striker's art as he climbs above Jamie Carragher to glance home John O'Shea's cross and complete his hat-trick ten minutes from the end of the 3-2 win over rivals Liverpool.*

Left *Patrice Evra and Rio Ferdinand congratulate Nemanja Vidic as his goal wraps up United's 3-1 win over Aston Villa. Although scoring freely at one end of the pitch, United's continuing challenge for domestic and European honours owed much to the rock-solid defending of this trio.*

The scene was set for a United hero to stamp his class all over the occasion. The match was tied at 1-1 as it ticked towards the final ten minutes, when Wayne Rooney unleashed an audacious overhead shot from the edge of the box. It was many viewers' idea of the goal of the season. In some quarters it was instantly dubbed the greatest goal in the history of the Premier League. It proved if any proof were needed that Rooney remained United's match-winner par excellence, and a striker capable of conjuring a wonder goal from nothing.

In the first week of March, United's title push was halted by away defeats at Chelsea and Liverpool, results that served only to ratchet up the pressure. But United took a fresh grip on proceedings with a 1-0 win at home to Bolton that took them five points clear at the top. They owed their win to a last-minute goal from Berbatov,

2006–12

The most important goals are not always the most spectacular, but Wayne Rooney's overhead bicycle kick that put United 2-1 ahead against City minutes from the end of a pulsating derby had all the ingredients necessary to ensure it was voted the best goal in the history of the Premier League.

GARY NEVILLE

RIGHT-BACK (1992–2011) • 566 (36) APPEARANCES • 7 GOALS

Football supporters can spot an impostor from a mile away. They know at a glance the difference between a badge-kissing dilettante and a true club servant – and there was never any doubt around Old Trafford about the strength of Gary Neville's United allegiance. He was a Red Devil to the core, all the way through his career, and even in retirement he vowed he always would be. Neville was the real deal, and the fans loved him for it.

Neville took the first steps of his long, illustrious United career in the ridiculously talented team that won the FA Youth Cup in 1992. Other graduates from that precocious band included Beckham, Butt and Giggs. Despite that auspicious introduction, it took Neville until 1995 to establish a regular place in Alex Ferguson's starting line-up, but once he did, he showed a maturity and ability beyond his years. After fewer than 20 Premier League appearances, he made his England debut in a friendly against Japan – the first of 85 caps for his country, a record number for an England right-back. At the end of the season he collected his first Premier League winner's medal and his first FA Cup winner's medal – the first items of what was destined to be a weighty collection of silver.

As Sir Alex built a series of trophy-winning sides through the latter half of the 1990s and into the 2000s, Neville remained a dependable and valuable fixture at right-back. There was nothing grandstanding about his style of play. In his own half of the field, he was quick into the tackle, good in the air for a sub-6ft defender, and blessed with an unerring positional sense. Going forward,

he forged a productive alliance with David Beckham, especially, on United's right flank, which contributed immensely to United's attacking potency. Through the years, he was consistency personified.

The only opponent Neville couldn't keep out was time itself, and in 2011 he announced his retirement. He had the dignity to realise that his best days were behind him, and bade farewell with good grace, and with a heartfelt tribute to the club he loves: 'I don't want to become a passenger,' he said. 'Everybody would say – play football for as long as you possibly can. Everybody would say that, because you can't go back to it. But there's more to it than that for me. For me to go and play at another football club just won't happen. I won't dilute my memories of football. I know that would happen for me. My colours are so firmly nailed to the mast at this club, for me to go and run out in a different shirt, I just wouldn't enjoy that.'

He left a rich legacy – the vast haul of honours he helped United amass in his near-two decades at Old Trafford, of which his personal tally was one Champions League, eight Premier League titles, three FA Cups and two League Cups.

2006–12

who was threatening to run away with the Premier League's Golden Boot prize.

The margin grew to seven points as a Rooney hat-trick sank West Ham at Upton Park, as United hit back from 2-0 down. Suddenly, United were surging ahead while their rivals stuttered,

and what had been an attritional battle for the title was turning into a parade, though it was still too early to book the open-topped bus.

Although the Gunners' own ambitions of overtaking United had dwindled, their 1-0 win against Sir Alex's men at the Emirates, with three games of the campaign remaining, gave Chelsea a chance of retaining their crown. It was a dramatic moment for United to host a title showdown against Chelsea, with the Premier League trophy up for grabs.

In a feverish atmosphere at Old Trafford, United took control of their own destiny with a goal in the first minute. It came from Mexican striker Javier 'Chicharito' Hernandez, who had become an instant favourite at the club since his summer move from Guadalajara. Vidic added a second midway through the first half, and Frank Lampard's reply wasn't even a consolation. United's 2-1 win left them needing just a single point from their last two games of the campaign.

They didn't put their supporters through any unnecessary suffering, completing the job at the first time of asking with a 1-1 draw at Blackburn on 14 May, sealed with Rooney's equalising 73rd-minute penalty. The match ended in surreal fashion, as both teams declared a kind of footballing armistice for the final 10 minutes. Rovers were content with their point. United's was the one that gave them the title. While the non-aggression pact saw both teams stroll around the pitch, United's travelling support threw an impromptu and noisy party in the Ewood Park stands. No one had to explain to them that the Premier League triumph was their 19th top-flight title: Liverpool's long-standing record had been shattered.

Sir Alex, who had vowed a quarter of a century earlier that he would 'knock Liverpool off their perch', had done just that. 'It was a long day, it was agony watching at times, but we got there in the

Javier Hernandez is ecstatic after scoring in the first minute of the showdown against Premier League title holders Chelsea. Attracted by his goalscoring instincts and aerial ability, Sir Alex moved quickly to sign the Mexican from Chivas Guadalajara before the 2010 World Cup. It was to prove an astute signing.

end,' he said. The landmark title was another adornment to the list of honours he had amassed at Old Trafford in a career that was now longer than even the great Sir Matt Busby's. He had passed his illustrious predecessor's stint of 24 years one month and 13 days back in December. This was a day to revel in the achievement of another great United side. 'I was a bit disappointed in the performance today, to be honest, but I'm not particularly bothered by that,' said Sir Alex. 'It is a great achievement to win a nineteenth title.'

It was United's sole domestic trophy for the season. Their FA Cup ambitions had been thwarted with defeat against Manchester City in the semi-finals, and their interest in the League Cup ended at West Ham in the quarter-finals. But all through the season, United kept their sights on the Champions League.

The campaign began with United facing Rangers, Valencia and Bursaspor of Turkey in the group stages. On the face of it,

Manchester United 19, Liverpool 18 – United's players celebrate their landmark league title on the Old Trafford pitch after the final match of the season against Blackpool.

it looked a comfortable draw for United, but the first match proved that qualification for the knockout rounds would not be so straightforward.

Rangers were their first opponents, and a stubborn defensive display saw Scotland's finest return to Glasgow with a point after a combative 0-0 draw. It meant that United couldn't afford too many slip-ups in the rest of the games, and Sir Alex's men responded, showing they were in a determined mood to go all the way to the final. Three wins on the spin away to Valencia, at home to Bursaspor and then in Turkey left United needing just one more point to qualify for the sudden-death stages. It was secured as Rooney's late penalty gave United a 1-0 win at Ibrox. United confirmed their status as group winners with a 1-1 draw with Valencia in the sixth and final match.

United were drawn to play the dangerous French side, Marseille, in the round of 16, and it was an encounter that nearly ended in defeat. The first leg in France was a nervy 0-0 draw with few chances for either team, which meant United faced a tense night at Old Trafford in the second leg, with the outcome on a knife-edge. Hernandez showed the goal-stealing skills that made him such a quick favourite with the fans to put United 1-0 up in the early minutes, but they played the rest of the match on the brink of a precipice. A single Marseille goal would have spelt disaster. United had no room to breathe until 75 minutes had ticked by, when Hernandez pounced again to make the score 2-0. Even then United weren't quite home. A Wes Brown own goal put the visitors within a goal of going through themselves – but at last the final whistle blew and United were in the last eight.

By this stage of the competition, only the Continent's elite sides were left in, and in a totally open draw United could have been paired with any of Internazionale, Barcelona, Real Madrid or the other remaining English clubs – Tottenham or Chelsea. In the event, the draw set up a re-match of the heart-stoppingly tense 2008 final, with United set to play Chelsea.

The first leg was staged at Stamford Bridge, and Sir Alex's side fought their way to a priceless 1-0 victory. Once again, they owed much to Rooney, who netted the only goal of the game. It had been a fraught campaign for the Scouse striker, and for his relationship with the club. A mid-season transfer wrangle threatened to end his

association with United, but in the end reason had prevailed and Rooney re-dedicated himself to the United cause. It was nights like the Champions League quarter-final at the Bridge that made United fans breathe a big sigh of relief that he had.

United had done the hard part by carving out an advantage away from home. But they still had to finish the job at Old Trafford. Hernandez made the task slightly simpler by snaffling a chance just before half time, which left Chelsea needing to score twice to go through on away goals. Their chances of doing that receded when Ramires was sent off in the second half, but it still seemed possible when Drogba netted for the Londoners. Home celebrations could really begin when Park put United 3-1 up on aggregate with a dozen minutes left on the clock. It was enough to take United into the semi-finals, where they faced the emergent German power, Schalke 04.

United played with great style at the Veltins Arena, turning in an extravagantly attacking performance that had the Germans on the back foot from the start. Only a series of unlikely saves and a desperate rearguard action kept United out, until the evergreen Giggs scored midway through the second half. Rooney added a second to make sure that the home leg would most likely see a stately progress into the final for United. So it came to pass. Strikes from Antonio Valencia and Darron Gibson put the match well beyond Schalke, and even though the Germans pulled a goal back, United's third Champions League final appearance in four years was never really in doubt. Anderson wrapped it all up with two goals in five second-half minutes, and United eased to a 6-1 aggregate victory.

United's opponents in the final at Wembley were Barcelona, in a repeat of the 2009 showpiece. Of course, United had warm memories of European Cup finals at the national stadium – 1968

Opposite *In two years Chris Smalling went from non-league Maidstone United to Premier League champions Manchester United. Not that you would have guessed from the form shown by the defender during his debut season at Old Trafford. Given an extended run in the side due to an injury to Rio Ferdinand, he fitted in perfectly, showing speed, composure and strength in abundance.*

2006–12

and all that wasn't such a distant memory. But the same was true for Barca. They won their first-ever European Cup crown at Wembley against Sampdoria in 1992. In the event, the force was with Barca, who turned out to be good value for a 3-1 victory. Pedro gave them the lead in the first half, and even though Rooney scored a sumptuous equaliser, the champions of Spain pulled away in the second half with goals from the sublime Messi and a clincher from David Villa. There was to be no reprise of 1968.

Sir Alex gracefully conceded that the stronger side won on the night, and he also paid full tribute to the virtuosity of Barcelona. Moments after the final whistle he swallowed his disappointment to say: 'I expected us to do better, but we have to acknowledge that we were beaten by a better team. The best team we have ever faced. It has been a good season for us with two Wembley appearances – it's just a shame it ends on such a disappointing note. But there is no shame in losing to Barcelona. We have proved that we are a good European side, but every now and again you come up against a team that are better than you, and this is that night.'

There was change in the air around Old Trafford as the 2011/12 season dawned. Sir Alex moved decisively to freshen up his squad for the challenges to come, and a parade of exciting new talents arrived at the club as old favourites bade their farewells. Among the players to make their exits was Edwin van der Sar, who hung up his goalkeeping gloves after years of distinguished service between the sticks. The big Dutchman had emerged as one of the finest keepers

Two of the new faces at Old Trafford at the start of the 2011/12 season – keeper David De Gea and Phil Jones – celebrate the first silverware of their United careers after beating Manchester City 3-2 in the Community Shield at Wembley.

ever to play for the club, worthy to be mentioned in the same breath as Peter Schmeichel. His replacement was the promising Atlético Madrid goalkeeper, 20-year-old David De Gea, who had caught the attention of United's vigilant scouts with a string of impressive displays in La Liga.

Sir Alex also swooped to snap up the versatile Blackburn Rovers star, Phil Jones. United fans could see immediately that Jones possessed maturity beyond his 19 years. Even in his debut season, he looked composed and assured whether slotting into the back four or stiffening the midfield. No greater compliment could be paid to the youngster than the observation that he already looked every inch a Manchester United footballer.

Ashley Young arrived from Aston Villa, and the England international boosted United's attacking options at a stroke. He offered thrust and threat down the flanks, as well as menace and

an eye for goal in a more central position. The squad roster was also strengthened considerably by the return of striker Danny Welbeck from a useful spell on loan at Sunderland, while midfielder Tom Cleverley had also developed his game during a season at Wigan Athletic. With former Fulham defender Chris Smalling starting his second season at the club, Sir Alex had a young and vibrant squad at his disposal.

Sir Alex would need all the reinforcements he could muster in a challenging campaign. His mission was to defend the title against the incursions of a free-spending Manchester City, as well as all the other usual suspects. He was also aiming to compete at the pinnacle of the Continental game with a side in transition.

United began the league season in effervescent style, winning the first five games, including a barnstorming 8-2 victory against Arsenal at Old Trafford. Rooney scored a hat-trick in the

dismantling of Arsène Wenger's side, but the performance was a testament to the ability of United's new boys: Welbeck opened the scoring, De Gea saved a penalty and Young scored twice. On the evidence of this showing it looked as though United's future was in safe hands.

Rooney added another treble in the next game, a 5-0 win at Bolton, and by the end of September United were established at the top of the table. But, before autumn was out, it was clear that United

The start of something special. Danny Welbeck leaps to head home United's first goal against Arsenal at Old Trafford. A hat-trick from Wayne Rooney, a brace from Ashley Young and other goals from Ji-sung Park and Nani completed an astonishing 8-2 victory, the Gunners' worst defeat since 1896.

2006–12 weren't going to lead a procession to another title. Not even close. That much was made obvious on a bleak October day at Old Trafford when they lost 6-1 to Manchester City, and ceded the leadership of the league to their cross-city rivals. It was a freak result, which was defined more than anything by the sending off of Jonny Evans. But it was obvious to anyone with sound judgement that the challenge thrown down by this City side would be of a different, more enduring, quality than any witnessed since their last title triumph in 1968.

All the way through the rest of 2011 and into the New Year, United pursued City doggedly. They showed flashes of brilliance, including a 5-0 demolition of Wigan Athletic, which featured a hat-trick from Berbatov, who had found himself on the edge of things in the new campaign. United's pursuit was given added impetus in January when Sir Alex made a surprise signing... a young prospect named Paul Scholes! Scholes had officially retired in the summer, and even enjoyed a testimonial match against the New York

Cosmos before the season began. But, just like Sir Alex himself all those years before, Scholes soon realised that he had packed it in too soon. He still had plenty to offer, and Sir Alex was only too glad to recapture his services.

It was immediately clear that United had been missing a singular talent. Scholes never appeared to miss a pass. He was perfection personified, whether delivering the ball a few yards to his nearest teammate, or picking out an audacious cross-field ball and sending

it with laser-guided precision. Ever ready to collect the ball from his own back four, he was the link in every United attack. Scholes, incredibly enough at his veteran stage, was the signing of the season.

In February, City finally began to display some nerves in the front-runner's role, and United pounced to take advantage. Halfway through the month, Liverpool visited Old Trafford for a match where victory would see United regain top spot. The game was overshadowed somewhat by an ugly scene before the kick-off when Liverpool striker Luis Suarez refused to shake Patrice Evra's hand. The incident occurred after the Uruguayan had been disciplined for making racist remarks to the United player. But all United really cared about was earning the three points. They took the lead early in the second half through Rooney's volley. Rooney added a second minutes later, and Liverpool could muster only a consolation goal as United emerged 2-1 winners.

As winter gave way to spring, it looked like United might turn the Premier League season into a parade after all. On 8 April, they beat QPR 2-0 while City lost 1-0 to Arsenal. Eight points clear with only a month of the season to run, United could see the Premier League trophy in front of them for the taking... but it was just a mirage. United lost their next match 1-0 at Wigan. A few days later, they drew 4-4 with Everton, after leading by two goals within reach of the final whistle. The defensive solidity that had been in evidence in the first half of the season had suddenly gone missing.

If you wanted to pinpoint a moment when United's challenge was fatally compromised, you could argue that came on the evening of 7 December 2011 – the night when United lost 2-1 in Basel during their ill-fated Champions League campaign. After 44 minutes of the game, Nemanja Vidic limped out of the action with a cruciate knee ligament injury. He was not to return for the rest of the campaign. The dominant Serb had forged an indomitable central defensive

Paul Scholes' return to Old Trafford in January 2012 marked a significant improvement in United's results. From his 'debut' at Eastlands until the visit of QPR on 8 April, United won every Premier League game apart from the 3-3 draw at Chelsea. QPR too were duly beaten, thanks in part to this screamer from Scholes, a result that put United eight points ahead of City with six games to go.

2006–12

partnership with Rio Ferdinand, one of the doughtiest pairings in the club's history. United missed him sorely and, in a season when Sir Alex added a host of exciting new recruits to his squad, it was the cruel loss of Vidic that might have been the crucial factor in the destiny of the league title, as well as seeing the Reds fail to deliver a successful run in any of the cup competitions.

United's worst fears were realised when they travelled across the city to the Etihad Stadium on 30 April for what amounted to a title decider. City needed a victory to draw level on points with

All eyes are on the handshake that didn't happen as Liverpool's Luis Suarez refuses to shake Patrice Evra's hand. The incident created a feverish atmosphere inside Old Trafford, and provided an undercurrent throughout a bad-tempered game. However, two second-half goals from Wayne Rooney ensured the points stayed in Manchester following United's 2-1 victory.

United – but with a crushingly superior goal difference. City edged a taut encounter by a single goal, seizing the title initiative with only two games remaining.

Despite this setback, the destination of the Premier League trophy was still in doubt on the last day of the season. United needed to win at Sunderland while hoping that City dropped points at home against relegation-threatened QPR. Before the games kicked off, Sir Alex expressed the hope that 'something stupid' might happen. United kept their part of the bargain by beating Sunderland while on a mad afternoon at Eastlands plenty of stupid things did indeed happen. City were losing 2-1 to Rangers as injury time kicked in. But somehow they conjured up the two goals they needed to wrest the crown from United's disbelieving grasp.

It was a bitter blow for United, a club who knew all about winning trophies against the odds in time added-on. Sir Alex graciously congratulated City on their title, but even in the immediate emotional aftermath of an incredible finale to a pulsating season, he had an eye on the future, and paid tribute to a young United team that had a golden future ahead of it.

'This is a good experience for them, even if it's a bad one,' he said. 'We have a lot of young players and they will be around in five, six or ten years at United. We have a rich history, better than anyone, and it will take them a century to get to our level of history. This is a challenge for us, and we're good at challenges.'

Sir Bobby Charlton echoed his thoughts: 'In football you learn you have to be prepared for surprises. We have an unbelievable club. The club without question is the best in the world. We have fantastic players, fantastic staff and I'm ever so proud. There'll be a lot of pressure put on the lads to do the best they can, but they've always done that and we will survive. We have the tools and we have the desire, and with that desire we're capable of doing anything, as we've already proved.'

United's two great knights spoke the truth. The emergence of City had given United a new mission: to regain their status at the summit of English football, and to compete at the top of the European game once more.

It would be difficult, certainly, but United had faced tougher tests in their long history. This was, after all, the club that had emerged from the chrysalis of a working men's sports and social society to become a professional football club; survived bankruptcy on numerous occasions in its early days; endured player revolts, fan rebellions, match-fixing scandals, relegations and boardroom ructions many times over; saw its ground bombed almost into oblivion in wartime; suffered the destruction of its greatest-ever team at Munich; coped with the indignity of relegation a handful of years after conquering Europe, before setting out on the long, slow climb back to the top of continental football. And in the last few years United had come to terms with the swiftly changing, often bewildering realities of football's new financial landscape.

United were ready to do what they always have done: to look to the future with confidence that there will be new heroes to honour, glories to be won and many more stirring chapters to be written in the greatest sporting story ever told.

Antonio Valencia's superb form during the spring saw him scoop all the major awards at Manchester United's end-of-season prize-giving, with both the players and the supporters voting him Player of the Year. He also won the prize for Goal of the Season for his right-foot piledriver that broke the deadlock against Blackburn at Ewood Park on 2 April – a goal he celebrated in style.

CLUB STATISTICS

CONTENTS

The following section contains the details of every match played by Manchester United in League, FA Cup, League Cup and European cup competitions. There is also a separate page which details five other competitions in which matches are classified by the club as 'competitive' – The FA Charity (Community) Shield, the Club World Cup, the Inter-Continental Club Cup, the European Super Cup and the Club World Championship.

The results are catalogued in individual seasons together with scorers and match attendances for every game ever played. There is also a final league table and a complete summary of appearances and goalscorers for each season.

Following the main results section there is a comprehensive player roll call, which lists every player who has appeared for the club in one of these competitive matches, detailing each player's appearance and goalscoring record in each of the competitions. The details from this roll call are then summarised in a 'Top 10' section, which lists the top 10 appearance-makers and goalscorers both overall and in each of the individual mainstream competitions.

QUIRKY FACTS ABOUT THE STATS

In a history spanning one hundred and twenty-six years of competition there have inevitably been matches which have given rise to quirky facts; here are just some of them.

United have 'lost' cup ties on TWELVE occasions without 'losing' the ties; in the FA Cup in 2009, losing to Everton in the semi-final on penalty kicks; in 2005, losing the final to Arsenal on penalty kicks; in 1992, losing in the 4th Round to Southampton on penalty kicks; and in 1886, losing in the 1st Round to Fleetwood Rangers in perhaps the most bizarre circumstances of all (see FA Cup 1886/87 below). In the Champions League (European Cup) in 2010, losing to Bayern Munich on away goals; similarly in 2002 to Bayer Leverkusen, in 1998 to Monaco and in 1993 to Galatasaray. In the UEFA Cup in 1995 to Rotor Volgograd (away goals, despite Peter Schmeichel's header), in 1992 to Torpedo Moscow (penalty kicks), in 1985 to Videoton (penalty kicks) and in 1980 to Widzew Lodz (away goals). United have only ever once won a cup tie on away goals, against Dukla Prague in the 1984 European Cup-Winners' Cup.

United once lost a cup-tie yet played another match in the competition. In 1970, having lost the FA Cup semi-final to Leeds United after two replays, United played Watford in a third place play-off, winning 2-0.

In 1893 Newton Heath played an entire match with ten men. Regular goalkeeper Jimmy Warner was injured during the journey to the Victoria Ground to play a fixture against Stoke City and no reserves had been taken along. So only ten men took the field with centre-half Willie Stewart deputising in goal. Sadly he was a better defender than goalkeeper – Newton Heath lost 7-1.

TEAM NAMES

In common with Manchester United, many football clubs changed their names in the years following their formation in the late 19th and early 20th centuries. In the same way that Newton Heath became Manchester United; Ardwick, formed in 1887, became Manchester City in 1894, and more elaborately Dial Square, formed in 1886, became Royal Arsenal, then Woolwich Arsenal before becoming simply Arsenal in 1913. For the purposes of continuity, current club names have been used throughout this section.

VENUES

Where a match has been designated as a home fixture, the opposing team's name is shown in capitals.

ABBREVIATIONS

The following abbreviations are used in the listings for the various cup competitions:

IntRd	Intermediate Round	Rd2L2	2nd Round 2nd Leg
IntRdR	Intermediate Round Replay	Rd2R	2nd Round Replay
IntRdR2	Intermediate Round 2nd Replay	Rd3	3rd Round
IntRdR3	Intermediate Round 3rd Replay	Rd3L1	3rd Round 1st Leg
P1	Champions League Phase 1	Rd3L2	3rd Round 2nd Leg
P2	Champions League Phase 2	Rd3R	3rd Round Replay
PRdL1	Preliminary Round 1st Leg	Rd3R2	3rd Round 2nd Round Replay
PRdL2	Preliminary Round 2nd Leg	Rd32L1	Round of 32 1st Leg
QFL1	Quarter-Final 1st Leg	Rd32L2	Round of 32 2nd Leg
QFL2	Quarter-Final 2nd Leg	Rd4	4th Round
QRd1	1st Qualifying Round	Rd4L1	4th Round 1st Leg
QRd2	2nd Qualifying Round	Rd4L2	4th Round 2nd Leg
QRd3	3rd Qualifying Round	Rd4R	4th Round Replay
QRd4	4th Qualifying Round	Rd4R2	4th Round 2nd Replay
QRd5	5th Qualifying Round	Rd5	5th Round
QRd5R	5th Qualifying Round Replay	Rd5R	5th Round Replay
QRdL1	Qualifying Round 1st Leg	Rd6	6th Round
QRdL2	Qualifying Round 2nd Leg	Rd6R	6th Round Replay
Rd1	1st Round	Rd6R2	6th Round 2nd Replay
Rd1L1	1st Round 1st Leg	SF	Semi-Final
Rd1L2	1st Round 2nd Leg	SFL1	Semi-Final 1st Leg
Rd1R	1st Round Replay	SFL2	Semi-Final 2nd Leg
Rd16L1	Round of 16 1st Leg	SFR	Semi-Final Replay
Rd16L2	Round of 16 2nd Leg	SFR2	Semi-Final 2nd Replay
Rd2	2nd Round	SupRd	Supplementary Round
Rd2L1	2nd Round 1st Leg		

CLUB HONOURS

COMPETITION	YEARS WON
FA PREMIER LEAGUE	1993, 1994, 1996, 1997, 1999, 2000, 2001, 2003, 2007, 2008, 2009, 2011
FOOTBALL LEAGUE DIVISION ONE	1908, 1911, 1952, 1956, 1957, 1965, 1967
FOOTBALL LEAGUE DIVISION TWO	1936, 1975
FA CUP	1909, 1948, 1963, 1977, 1983, 1985, 1990, 1994, 1996, 1999, 2004
FOOTBALL LEAGUE CUP	1992, 2006, 2009, 2010

COMPETITION	YEARS WON
EUROPEAN CHAMPIONS CLUBS' CUP	1968, 1999, 2008
EUROPEAN CUP-WINNERS' CUP	1991
CLUB WORLD CUP	2008
INTER-CONTINENTAL CUP	1999
EUROPEAN SUPER CUP	1991
FA CHARITY SHIELD/ COMMUNITY SHIELD	1908, 1911, 1952, 1956, 1957, 1965*, 1967*, 1977*, 1983, 1990*, 1993, 1994, 1997, 2003, 2007, 2008, 2010, 2011
FA YOUTH CUP	1953, 1954, 1955, 1956, 1957, 1964, 1992, 1995, 2003, 2011

* Joint holders

THE EARLY YEARS

Newton Heath were not admitted to the Football League until season 1892/93 but competed in the FA Cup on four occasions between 1886 and 1892 as detailed below.

Their very first entry into the FA Cup resulted in a first round exit at the hands of Fleetwood Rangers. The match ended 2-2 after 90 minutes and the referee asked the two clubs to play a period of extra-time in the hope of settling the tie. Newton Heath refused and the tie was consequently awarded to their opponents.

1886/87

FA CUP

DATE	OPPONENTS	SCORE	GOALSCORERS	ATTENDANCE
Oct 30	Fleetwood Rangers (Rd1)	2-2	Doughty J 2	2,000

1889/90

FA CUP

DATE	OPPONENTS	SCORE	GOALSCORERS	ATTENDANCE
Jan 18	Preston North End (Rd1)	1-6	Craig	7,900

1890/91

FA CUP

DATE	OPPONENTS	SCORE	GOALSCORERS	ATTENDANCE
Oct 4	HIGHER WALTON (QRd1)	2-0	Evans, Farman	3,000
Oct 25	Bootle Reserves (QRd2)	0-1		500

1891/92

FA CUP

DATE	OPPONENTS	SCORE	GOALSCORERS	ATTENDANCE
Oct 3	MANCHESTER CITY (QRd1)	5-1	Farman 2, Doughty R, Edge, Sneddon	11,000
Oct 24	Heywood (QRd2) *			
Nov 14	South Shore (QRd3)	2-0	Doughty J, Farman	2,000
Dec 5	BLACKPOOL (QRd4)	3-4	Edge 2, Farman	4,000

* Heywood scratched. Tie awarded to Newton Heath.

APPEARANCES

PLAYER	LGE	FAC	TOT	PLAYER	LGE	FAC	TOT
Owen J	–	6	6	Davies L	–	1	1
Doughty R	–	5	5	Denman	–	1	1
Farman	–	5	5	Donnelly	–	1	1
Powell	–	4	4	Earp	–	1	1
Slater	–	4	4	Evans	–	1	1
Stewart	–	4	4	Felton	–	1	1
Clements	–	3	3	Gotheridge	–	1	1
Doughty J	–	3	3	Gyves	–	1	1
Edge	–	3	3	Harrison	–	1	1
Henrys	–	3	3	Hay	–	1	1
McFarlane	–	3	3	Howells	–	1	1
Mitchell	–	3	3	Longton	–	1	1
Sneddon	–	3	3	Milarvie	–	1	1
Craig	–	2	2	O'Shaughnessy	–	1	1
Davies J	–	2	2	Owen G	–	1	1
Sharpe	–	2	2	Ramsay	–	1	1
Beckett	–	1	1	Rattigan	–	1	1
Burke	–	1	1	Turner	–	1	1
Dale	–	1	1	Wilson	–	1	1

GOALSCORERS

PLAYER	LGE	FAC	TOT
Farman	–	5	5
Doughty J	–	3	3
Edge	–	3	3
Craig	–	1	1
Doughty R	–	1	1
Evans	–	1	1
Sneddon	–	1	1

1892/93

FOOTBALL LEAGUE DIVISION ONE

DATE	OPPONENTS	SCORE	GOALSCORERS	ATTENDANCE
Sep 3	Blackburn Rovers	3-4	Coupar, Donaldson, Farman	8,000
Sep 10	BURNLEY	1-1	Donaldson	10,000
Sep 17	Burnley	1-4	Donaldson	7,000
Sep 24	Everton	0-6		10,000
Oct 1	West Bromwich Albion	0-0		4,000
Oct 8	WEST BROMWICH ALBION	2-4	Donaldson, Hood	9,000
Oct 15	WOLVERHAMPTON W.	10-1	Donaldson 3, Stewart 3, Carson, Farman, Hendry, Hood	4,000
Oct 19	EVERTON	3-4	Donaldson, Farman, Hood	4,000
Oct 22	Sheffield Wednesday	0-1		6,000
Oct 29	Nottingham Forest	1-1	Farman	6,000
Nov 5	BLACKBURN ROVERS	4-4	Farman 2, Carson, Hood	12,000
Nov 12	NOTTS COUNTY	1-3	Carson	8,000
Nov 19	ASTON VILLA	2-0	Coupar, Fitzsimmons	7,000
Nov 26	Accrington Stanley	2-2	Colville, Fitzsimmons	3,000
Dec 3	Bolton Wanderers	1-4	Coupar	3,000
Dec 10	BOLTON WANDERERS	1-0	Donaldson	4,000
Dec 17	Wolverhampton W.	0-2		5,000
Dec 24	SHEFFIELD WEDNESDAY	1-5	Hood	4,000
Dec 26	Preston North End	1-2	Coupar	4,000
Dec 31	DERBY COUNTY	7-1	Donaldson 3, Farman 3, Fitzsimmons	3,000
Jan 7	Stoke City	1-7	Coupar	1,000
Jan 14	NOTTINGHAM FOREST	1-3	Donaldson	8,000
Jan 26	Notts County	0-4		1,000
Feb 11	Derby County	1-5	Fitzsimmons	5,000
Mar 4	SUNDERLAND	0-5		15,000
Mar 6	Aston Villa	0-2		4,000
Mar 31	STOKE CITY	1-0	Farman	10,000
Apr 1	PRESTON NORTH END	2-1	Donaldson 2	9,000
Apr 4	Sunderland	0-6		3,500
Apr 8	ACCRINGTON STANLEY	3-3	Donaldson, Fitzsimmons, Stewart	3,000

FA CUP

DATE	OPPONENTS	SCORE	GOALSCORERS	ATTENDANCE
Jan 21	Blackburn Rovers (Rd1)	0-4		7,000

		P	W	D	L	F	A	Pts
1	Sunderland	30	22	4	4	100	36	48
2	Preston North End	30	17	3	10	57	39	37
3	Everton	30	16	4	10	74	51	36
4	Aston Villa	30	16	3	11	73	62	35
5	Bolton Wanderers	30	13	6	11	56	55	32
6	Burnley	30	13	4	13	51	44	30
7	Stoke City	30	12	5	13	58	48	29
8	West Bromwich Albion	30	12	5	13	58	69	29
9	Blackburn Rovers	30	8	13	9	47	56	29
10	Nottingham Forest	30	10	8	12	48	52	28
11	Wolverhampton Wanderers	30	12	4	14	47	68	28
12	Sheffield Wednesday	30	12	3	15	55	65	27
13	Derby County	30	9	9	12	52	64	27
14	Notts County	30	10	4	16	53	61	24
15	Accrington Stanley	30	6	11	13	57	81	23
16	NEWTON HEATH	30	6	6	18	50	85	18

By season 1892/93 formal promotion and relegation had not yet been introduced, so the team at the bottom of the First Division played a 'Test Match' against the team at the top of the Second Division. Newton Heath finished the season in bottom place in Division One but managed to win their 'Test' and keep their top-flight status for the following season. Details of these matches can be found in the 'OTHER COMPETITIVE MATCHES' section on page 324.

APPEARANCES

PLAYER	LGE	FAC	TOT
Erentz	29	1	30
Mitchell	29	1	30
Stewart	29	1	30
Farman	28	1	29
Perrins	28	1	29
Donaldson	26	1	27
Clements	24	1	25
Hood	21	1	22
Warner	22	–	22
Coupar	21	–	21
Fitzsimmons	18	1	19
Carson	13	–	13
Colville	9	1	10
Davies	7	1	8
Mathieson	8	–	8
Brown	7	–	7
Cassidy	4	–	4
Henrys	3	–	3
Hendry	2	–	2
Kinloch	1	–	1

GOALSCORERS

PLAYER	LGE	FAC	TOT
Donaldson	16	–	16
Farman	10	–	10
Coupar	5	–	5
Fitzsimmons	5	–	5
Hood	5	–	5
Stewart	4	–	4
Carson	3	–	3
Colville	1	–	1
Hendry	1	–	1

1893/94

FOOTBALL LEAGUE DIVISION ONE

DATE	OPPONENTS	SCORE	GOALSCORERS	ATTENDANCE
Sep 2	BURNLEY	3-2	Farman 3	10,000
Sep 9	West Bromwich Albion	1-3	Donaldson	4,500
Sep 16	Sheffield Wednesday	1-0	Farman	7,000
Sep 23	NOTTINGHAM FOREST	1-1	Donaldson	10,000
Sep 30	Darwen	0-1		4,000
Oct 7	Derby County	0-2		7,000
Oct 14	WEST BROMWICH ALBION	4-1	Peden 2, Donaldson, Erentz	8,000
Oct 21	Burnley	1-4	Hood	7,000
Oct 28	Wolverhampton W.	0-2		4,000
Nov 4	DARWEN	0-1		8,000
Nov 11	WOLVERHAMPTON W.	1-0	Davidson	5,000
Nov 25	Sheffield United	1-3	Fitzsimmons	2,000
Dec 2	EVERTON	0-3		6,000
Dec 6	Sunderland	1-4	Campbell	5,000
Dec 9	Bolton Wanderers	0-2		5,000
Dec 16	ASTON VILLA	1-3	Peden	8,000
Dec 23	Preston North End	0-2		5,000
Jan 6	Everton	0-2		8,000
Jan 13	SHEFFIELD WEDNESDAY	1-2	Peden	9,000
Feb 3	Aston Villa	1-5	Mathieson	5,000
Mar 3	SUNDERLAND	2-4	McNaught, Peden	10,000
Mar 10	SHEFFIELD UNITED	0-2		5,000
Mar 12	BLACKBURN ROVERS	5-1	Donaldson 3, Clarkin, Farman	5,000
Mar 17	DERBY COUNTY	2-6	Clarkin 2	8,000
Mar 23	STOKE CITY	6-2	Farman 2, Peden 2, Clarkin, Erentz	8,000
Mar 24	BOLTON WANDERERS	2-2	Donaldson, Farman	10,000
Mar 26	Blackburn Rovers	0-4		5,000
Mar 31	Stoke City	1-3	Clarkin	4,000
Apr 7	Nottingham Forest	0-2		4,000
Apr 14	PRESTON NORTH END	1-3	Mathieson	4,000

FA CUP

DATE	OPPONENTS	SCORE	GOALSCORERS	ATTENDANCE
Jan 27	MIDDLESBROUGH (Rd1)	4-0	Donaldson 2, Farman, Peden	5,000
Feb 10	BLACKBURN ROVERS (Rd2)	0-0		18,000
Feb 17	Blackburn Rovers (Rd2R)	1-5	Donaldson	5,000

FINAL LEAGUE TABLE

		P	W	D	L	F	A	Pts
1	Aston Villa	30	19	6	5	84	42	44
2	Sunderland	30	17	4	9	72	44	38
3	Derby County	30	16	4	10	73	62	36
4	Blackburn Rovers	30	16	2	12	69	53	34
5	Burnley	30	15	4	11	61	51	34
6	Everton	30	15	3	12	90	57	33
7	Nottingham Forest	30	14	4	12	57	48	32
8	West Bromwich Albion	30	14	4	12	66	59	32
9	Wolverhampton Wanderers	30	14	3	13	52	63	31
10	Sheffield United	30	13	5	12	47	61	31
11	Stoke City	30	13	3	14	65	79	29
12	Sheffield Wednesday	30	9	8	13	48	57	26
13	Bolton Wanderers	30	10	4	16	38	52	24
14	Preston North End	30	10	3	17	44	56	23
15	Darwen	30	7	5	18	37	83	19
16	NEWTON HEATH	30	6	2	22	36	72	14

Formal promotion and relegation had still not been introduced, so Newton Heath were again required to play a 'Test Match' against the team at the top of the Second Division. This time they were unsuccessful and lost their Division One status. Details of this match can be found in the 'OTHER COMPETITIVE MATCHES' section on page 324.

APPEARANCES

PLAYER	LGE	FAC	TOT
Davidson	28	3	31
Peden	28	3	31
Perrins	27	3	30
McNaught	26	3	29
Mitchell	25	3	28
Stewart	25	3	28
Donaldson	24	3	27
Fall	23	3	26
Erentz	22	3	25
Farman	18	1	19
Clarkin	12	2	14
Hood	12	2	14
Clements	12	–	12
Parker	11	1	12
Fitzsimmons	9	–	9
Douglas	7	–	7
Campbell	5	–	5
Graham	4	–	4
Thompson	3	–	3
Dow	2	–	2
Mathieson	2	–	2
Prince	2	–	2
Stone	2	–	2
Rothwell	1	–	1

GOALSCORERS

PLAYER	LGE	FAC	TOT
Donaldson	7	3	10
Farman	8	1	9
Peden	7	1	8
Clarkin	5	–	5
Erentz	2	–	2
Mathieson	2	–	2
Campbell	1	–	1
Davidson	1	–	1
Fitzsimmons	1	–	1
Hood	1	–	1
McNaught	1	–	1

1894/95

FOOTBALL LEAGUE DIVISION TWO

DATE	OPPONENTS	SCORE	GOALSCORERS	ATTENDANCE
Sep 8	Burton Wanderers	0–1		3,000
Sep 15	CREWE ALEXANDRA	6–1	Dow 2, Smith 2, Clarkin, McCartney	6,000
Sep 22	Leicester City	3–2	Dow 2, Smith	6,000
Oct 6	Darwen	1–1	Donaldson	6,000
Oct 13	ARSENAL	3–3	Donaldson 2, Clarkin	4,000
Oct 20	Burton Swifts	2–1	Donaldson 2	5,000
Oct 27	LEICESTER CITY	2–2	McNaught, Smith	3,000
Nov 3	Manchester City	5–2	Smith 4, Clarkin	14,000
Nov 10	ROTHERHAM UNITED	3–2	Davidson, Donaldson, Peters	4,000
Nov 17	Grimsby Town	1–2	Clarkin	3,000
Nov 24	DARWEN	1–1	Donaldson	5,000
Dec 1	Crewe Alexandra	2–0	Clarkin, Smith	600
Dec 8	BURTON SWIFTS	5–1	Peters 2, Smith 2, Dow	4,000
Dec 15	Notts County	1–1	Donaldson	5,000
Dec 22	LINCOLN CITY	3–0	Donaldson, Millar, Smith	2,000
Dec 24	Port Vale	5–2	Clarkin, Donaldson, McNaught, Millar, Smith	1,000
Dec 26	Walsall	2–1	Millar, Stewart	1,000
Dec 29	Lincoln City	0–3		3,000
Jan 1	PORT VALE	3–0	Millar 2, Rothwell	5,000
Jan 5	MANCHESTER CITY	4–1	Clarkin 2, Donaldson, Smith	12,000
Jan 12	Rotherham United	1–2	Erentz	2,000
Mar 2	BURTON WANDERERS	1–1	Peters	6,000
Mar 23	GRIMSBY TOWN	2–0	Cassidy 2	9,000
Mar 30	Arsenal	2–3	Clarkin, Donaldson	6,000
Apr 3	WALSALL	9–0	Cassidy 2, Donaldson 2, Peters 2, Smith 2, Clarkin	6,000
Apr 6	NEWCASTLE UNITED	5–1	Cassidy 2, Smith 2, og	5,000
Apr 12	BURY	2–2	Cassidy, Donaldson	15,000
Apr 13	Newcastle United	0–3		4,000
Apr 15	Bury	1–2	Peters	10,000
Apr 20	NOTTS COUNTY	3–3	Cassidy, Clarkin, Smith	12,000

FA CUP

DATE	OPPONENTS	SCORE	GOALSCORERS	ATTENDANCE
Feb 2	STOKE CITY (Rd1)	2–3	Smith, Peters	7,000

FINAL LEAGUE TABLE

		P	W	D	L	F	A	Pts
1	Bury	30	23	2	5	78	33	48
2	Notts County	30	17	5	8	75	45	39
3	NEWTON HEATH	30	15	8	7	78	44	38
4	Leicester City	30	15	8	7	72	53	38
5	Grimsby Town	30	18	1	11	79	52	37
6	Darwen	30	16	4	10	74	43	36
7	Burton Wanderers	30	14	7	9	67	39	35
8	Arsenal	30	14	6	10	75	58	34
9	Manchester City	30	14	3	13	82	72	31
10	Newcastle United	30	12	3	15	72	84	27
11	Burton Swifts	30	11	3	16	52	74	25
12	Rotherham United	30	11	2	17	55	62	24
13	Lincoln City	30	10	0	20	52	92	20
14	Walsall	30	10	0	20	47	92	20
15	Port Vale	30	7	4	19	39	77	18
16	Crewe Alexandra	30	3	4	23	26	103	10

As Newton Heath finished in third place in Division Two, this season's 'Test Match' was against the team third from bottom in Division One, Stoke City. Newton Heath lost the match and so remained in Division Two for the following season. Details of this match can be found in the 'OTHER COMPETITIVE MATCHES' section on page 324.

APPEARANCES

PLAYER	LGE	FAC	TOT
Douglas	30	1	31
Peters	30	1	31
Clarkin	29	1	30
Smith	29	1	30
Erentz	28	1	29
Donaldson	27	1	28
Dow	27	–	27
McNaught	26	1	27
Perrins	25	1	26
Stewart	22	1	23
McCartney	18	1	19
Davidson	12	–	12
Cassidy	8	–	8
Millar	6	1	7
Farman	5	–	5
Stone	4	–	4
Cairns	1	–	1
Longair	1	–	1
McFetteridge	1	–	1
Rothwell	1	–	1

GOALSCORERS

PLAYER	LGE	FAC	TOT
Smith	19	1	20
Donaldson	15	–	15
Clarkin	11	–	11
Cassidy	8	–	8
Peters	7	1	8
Dow	5	–	5
Millar	5	–	5
McNaught	2	–	2
Davidson	1	–	1
Erentz	1	–	1
McCartney	1	–	1
Rothwell	1	–	1
Stewart	1	–	1
own goal	1	–	1

1895/96

FOOTBALL LEAGUE DIVISION TWO

DATE	OPPONENTS	SCORE	GOALSCORERS	ATTENDANCE
Sep 7	CREWE ALEXANDRA	5–0	Cassidy 2, Aitken, Kennedy, Smith	6,000
Sep 14	Loughborough Town	3–3	Cassidy 2, McNaught	3,000
Sep 21	BURTON SWIFTS	5–0	Cassidy 2, Donaldson 2, Kennedy	9,000
Sep 28	Crewe Alexandra	2–0	Smith 2	2,000
Oct 5	MANCHESTER CITY	1–1	Clarkin	12,000
Oct 12	Liverpool	1–7	Cassidy	7,000
Oct 19	NEWCASTLE UNITED	2–1	Cassidy, Peters	8,000
Oct 26	Newcastle United	1–2	Kennedy	8,000
Nov 2	LIVERPOOL	5–2	Peters 3, Clarkin, Smith	10,000
Nov 9	Arsenal	1–2	Cassidy	9,000
Nov 16	LINCOLN CITY	5–5	Clarkin 2, Cassidy, Collinson, Peters	8,000
Nov 23	Notts County	2–0	Cassidy, Kennedy	3,000
Nov 30	ARSENAL	5–1	Cartwright 2, Clarkin, Kennedy, Peters	6,000
Dec 7	Manchester City	1–2	Cassidy	18,000
Dec 14	NOTTS COUNTY	3–0	Cassidy, Clarkin, Donaldson	3,000
Dec 21	Darwen	0–3		3,000
Jan 1	GRIMSBY TOWN	3–2	Cassidy 3	8,000
Jan 4	Leicester City	0–3		7,000
Jan 11	ROTHERHAM UNITED	3–0	Donaldson 2, Stephenson	3,000
Feb 3	LEICESTER CITY	2–0	Kennedy, Smith	1,000
Feb 8	Burton Swifts	1–4	Vance	2,000
Feb 29	BURTON WANDERERS	1–2	McNaught	1,000
Mar 7	Rotherham United	3–2	Donaldson, Kennedy, Smith	1,500
Mar 14	Grimsby Town	2–4	Kennedy, Smith	2,000
Mar 18	Burton Wanderers	1–5	Dow	2,000
Mar 23	Port Vale	0–3		3,000
Apr 3	DARWEN	4–0	Kennedy 3, McNaught	1,000
Apr 4	LOUGHBOROUGH TOWN	2–0	Donaldson, Smith	4,000
Apr 6	PORT VALE	2–1	Clarkin, Smith	5,000
Apr 11	Lincoln City	0–2		2,000

FA CUP

DATE	OPPONENTS	SCORE	GOALSCORERS	ATTENDANCE
Feb 1	KETTERING (Rd1)	2–1	Donaldson, Smith	6,000
Feb 15	DERBY COUNTY (Rd2)	1–1	Kennedy	20,000
Feb 19	Derby County (Rd2R)	1–5	Donaldson	6,000

FINAL LEAGUE TABLE

		P	W	D	L	F	A	Pts
1	Liverpool	30	22	2	6	106	32	46
2	Manchester City	30	21	4	5	63	38	46
3	Grimsby Town	30	20	2	8	82	38	42
4	Burton Wanderers	30	19	4	7	69	40	42
5	Newcastle United	30	16	2	12	73	50	34
6	NEWTON HEATH	30	15	3	12	66	57	33
7	Arsenal	30	14	4	12	59	42	32
8	Leicester City	30	14	4	12	57	44	32
9	Darwen	30	12	6	12	72	67	30
10	Notts County	30	12	2	16	57	54	26
11	Burton Swifts	30	10	4	16	39	69	24
12	Loughborough Town	30	9	5	16	40	67	23
13	Lincoln City	30	9	4	17	53	75	22
14	Port Vale	30	7	4	19	43	78	18
15	Rotherham United	30	7	3	20	34	97	17
16	Crewe Alexandra	30	5	3	22	30	95	13

APPEARANCES

PLAYER	LGE	FAC	TOT
Kennedy	29	3	32
Smith	28	3	31
Cartwright	27	3	30
McNaught	28	2	30
Fitzsimmons	26	3	29
Clarkin	26	2	28
Erentz	24	2	26
Cassidy	19	1	20
Donaldson	17	3	20
Dow	19	1	20
Peters	16	3	19
Douglas	18	–	18
Collinson	13	3	16
Perrins	12	1	13
Vance	10	–	10
Ridgway	6	3	9
Stafford	4	–	4
Whittaker	3	–	3
Aitken	2	–	2
Whitney	2	–	2
Stephenson	1	–	1

GOALSCORERS

PLAYER	LGE	FAC	TOT
Cassidy	16	–	16
Kennedy	11	1	12
Smith	9	1	10
Donaldson	7	2	9
Clarkin	7	–	7
Peters	6	–	6
McNaught	3	–	3
Cartwright	2	–	2
Aitken	1	–	1
Collinson	1	–	1
Dow	1	–	1
Stephenson	1	–	1
Vance	1	–	1

1896/97

FOOTBALL LEAGUE DIVISION TWO

DATE	OPPONENTS	SCORE	GOALSCORERS	ATTENDANCE
Sep 1	GAINSBOROUGH TRINITY	2–0	McNaught 2	4,000
Sep 5	Burton Swifts	5–3	Brown, Bryant, Cassidy, Draycott, McNaught	3,000
Sep 7	WALSALL	2–0	Cassidy, Donaldson	7,000
Sep 12	LINCOLN CITY	3–1	Cassidy 2, Donaldson	7,000
Sep 19	Grimsby Town	0–2		3,000
Sep 21	Walsall	3–2	Brown, Draycott, McNaught	7,000
Sep 26	NEWCASTLE UNITED	4–0	Cassidy 3, Donaldson	7,000
Oct 3	Manchester City	0–0		20,000
Oct 10	BIRMINGHAM CITY	1–1	Draycott	7,000
Oct 17	Blackpool	2–4	Bryant, Draycott	5,000
Oct 21	Gainsborough Trinity	0–2		4,000
Oct 24	BURTON WANDERERS	3–0	Cassidy 3	4,000
Nov 7	GRIMSBY TOWN	4–2	Cassidy 2, Donaldson, Jenkyns	5,000
Nov 28	Birmingham City	0–1		4,000
Dec 19	Notts County	0–3		5,000
Dec 25	MANCHESTER CITY	2–1	Donaldson, Smith	18,000
Dec 26	BLACKPOOL	2–0	Cassidy 2	9,000
Dec 28	Leicester City	0–1		8,000
Jan 1	Newcastle United	0–2		17,000
Jan 9	BURTON SWIFTS	1–1	Donaldson	3,000
Feb 6	LOUGHBOROUGH TOWN	6–0	Smith 2, Boyd, Donaldson, Draycott, Jenkyns	5,000
Feb 20	LEICESTER CITY	2–1	Boyd, Donaldson	8,000
Mar 2	DARWEN	3–1	Cassidy 2, Boyd	3,000
Mar 13	Darwen	2–0	Cassidy, Gillespie	2,000
Mar 20	Burton Wanderers	2–1	Gillespie, og	3,000
Mar 22	ARSENAL	1–1	Boyd	10,000
Mar 27	NOTTS COUNTY	1–1	Bryant	1,000
Apr 1	Lincoln City	3–1	Jenkyns 3	1,000
Apr 3	Arsenal	2–0	Boyd, Donaldson	6,000
Apr 10	Loughborough Town	0–2		3,000

FA CUP

DATE	OPPONENTS	SCORE	GOALSCORERS	ATTENDANCE
Dec 12	WEST MANCHESTER (QRd3)	7–0	Cassidy 2, Gillespie 2, Rothwell 2, Bryant	6,000
Jan 2	NELSON (QRd4)	3–0	Cassidy, Donaldson, Gillespie	5,000
Jan 16	BLACKPOOL (QRd5)	2–2	Donaldson, Gillespie	1,500
Jan 20	Blackpool (QRd5R)	2–1	Boyd, Cassidy	5,000
Jan 30	KETTERING (Rd1)	5–1	Cassidy 3, Donaldson 2	1,500
Feb 13	Southampton (Rd2)	1–1	Donaldson	8,000
Feb 17	SOUTHAMPTON (Rd2R)	3–1	Bryant 2, Cassidy	7,000
Feb 27	Derby County (Rd3)	0–2		12,000

FINAL LEAGUE TABLE

		P	W	D	L	F	A	Pts
1	Notts County	30	19	4	7	92	43	42
2	NEWTON HEATH	30	17	5	8	56	34	39
3	Grimsby Town	30	17	4	9	66	45	38
4	Birmingham City	30	16	5	9	69	47	37
5	Newcastle United	30	17	1	12	56	52	35
6	Manchester City	30	12	8	10	58	50	32
7	Gainsborough Trinity	30	12	7	11	50	47	31
8	Blackpool	30	13	5	12	59	56	31
9	Leicester City	30	13	4	13	59	56	30
10	Arsenal	30	13	4	13	68	70	30
11	Darwen	30	14	0	16	67	61	28
12	Walsall	30	11	4	15	53	69	26
13	Loughborough Town	30	12	1	17	50	64	25
14	Burton Swifts	30	9	6	15	46	61	24
15	Burton Wanderers	30	9	2	19	31	67	20
16	Lincoln City	30	5	2	23	27	85	12

After finishing in second place in Division Two, Newton Heath were required to play 'Test Matches' against Burnley and Sunderland. They were ultimately unsuccessful and were required to remain in Division Two for the following season. Details of these matches can be found in the 'OTHER COMPETITIVE MATCHES' section on page 324.

APPEARANCES

PLAYER	LGE	FAC	TOT
McNaught	30	8	38
Bryant	29	8	37
Donaldson	29	8	37
Cassidy	28	8	36
Jenkyns	27	8	35
Draycott	29	5	34
Erentz	27	6	33
Stafford	24	8	32
Barrett	23	8	31
Cartwright	25	5	30
Gillespie	17	8	25
Smith	14	3	17
Boyd	10	4	14
Brown	7	–	7
Ridgway	5	–	5
Morgan	2	–	2
Wetherell	2	–	2
Kennedy	1	–	1
Rothwell	–	1	1
Vance	1	–	1

GOALSCORERS

PLAYER	LGE	FAC	TOT
Cassidy	17	8	25
Donaldson	9	5	14
Boyd	5	1	6
Bryant	3	3	6
Gillespie	2	4	6
Draycott	5	–	5
Jenkyns	5	–	5
Smith	3	–	3
Brown	2	–	2
Rothwell	–	2	2
own goal	1	–	1

1897/98

FOOTBALL LEAGUE DIVISION TWO

DATE	OPPONENTS	SCORE	GOALSCORERS	ATTENDANCE
Sep 4	LINCOLN CITY	5–0	Boyd 3, Bryant, Cassidy	5,000
Sep 11	Burton Swifts	4–0	Boyd 3, Cassidy	2,000
Sep 18	LUTON TOWN	1–2	Cassidy	8,000
Sep 25	Blackpool	1–0	Smith	2,000
Oct 2	LEICESTER CITY	2–0	Boyd 2	6,000
Oct 9	Newcastle United	0–2		12,000
Oct 16	MANCHESTER CITY	1–1	Gillespie	20,000
Oct 23	Birmingham City	1–2	Bryant	6,000
Oct 30	WALSALL	6–0	Cassidy 2, Donaldson 2, Bryant, Gillespie	6,000
Nov 6	Lincoln City	0–1		2,000
Nov 13	NEWCASTLE UNITED	0–1		7,000
Nov 20	Leicester City	1–1	Wedge	6,000
Nov 27	GRIMSBY TOWN	2–1	Bryant, Wedge	5,000
Dec 11	Walsall	1–1	Boyd	2,000
Dec 25	Manchester City	1–0	Cassidy	16,000
Dec 27	Gainsborough Trinity	1–2	Boyd	3,000
Jan 1	BURTON SWIFTS	4–0	Boyd, Bryant, Carman, McNaught	6,000
Jan 8	Arsenal	1–5	Erentz F	8,000
Jan 12	BURNLEY	0–0		7,000
Jan 15	BLACKPOOL	4–0	Boyd 2, Cartwright, Cassidy	4,000
Feb 26	ARSENAL	5–1	Bryant 2, Boyd, Cassidy, Collinson	6,000
Mar 7	Burnley	3–6	Bryant 2, Collinson	3,000
Mar 19	Darwen	3–2	Boyd 2, McNaught	2,000
Mar 21	Luton Town	2–2	Boyd, Cassidy	2,000
Mar 29	LOUGHBOROUGH TOWN	5–1	Boyd 3, Cassidy 2	2,000
Apr 2	Grimsby Town	3–1	Cassidy 2, Boyd	5,000
Apr 8	GAINSBOROUGH TRINITY	1–0	Cassidy	4,000
Apr 9	BIRMINGHAM CITY	3–1	Boyd, Gillespie, Morgan	4,000
Apr 16	Loughborough Town	0–0		1,000
Apr 23	DARWEN	3–2	Collinson 2, Bryant	4,000

FA CUP

DATE	OPPONENTS	SCORE	GOALSCORERS	ATTENDANCE
Jan 29	WALSALL (Rd1)	1–0	og	6,000
Feb 12	LIVERPOOL (Rd2)	0–0		12,000
Feb 16	Liverpool (Rd2R)	1–2	Collinson	6,000

FINAL LEAGUE TABLE

		P	W	D	L	F	A	Pts
1	Burnley	30	20	8	2	80	24	48
2	Newcastle United	30	21	3	6	64	32	45
3	Manchester City	30	15	9	6	66	36	39
4	NEWTON HEATH	30	16	6	8	64	35	38
5	Arsenal	30	16	5	9	69	49	37
6	Birmingham City	30	16	4	10	58	50	36
7	Leicester City	30	13	7	10	46	35	33
8	Luton Town	30	13	4	13	68	50	30
9	Gainsborough Trinity	30	12	6	12	50	54	30
10	Walsall	30	12	5	13	58	58	29
11	Blackpool	30	10	5	15	49	61	25
12	Grimsby Town	30	10	4	16	52	62	24
13	Burton Swifts	30	8	5	17	38	69	21
14	Lincoln City	30	6	5	19	43	82	17
15	Darwen	30	6	2	22	31	76	14
16	Loughborough Town	30	6	2	22	24	87	14

APPEARANCES

PLAYER	LGE	FAC	TOT
Boyd	30	3	33
Cassidy	30	3	33
McNaught	30	3	33
Bryant	29	3	32
Erentz F	28	3	31
Barrett	27	3	30
Cartwright	27	3	30
Stafford	25	–	25
Draycott	21	3	24
Gillespie	19	1	20
Collinson	10	3	13
Dunn	10	2	12
Erentz H	6	3	9
Morgan	9	–	9
Donaldson	8	–	8
Jenkyns	8	–	8
Smith	5	–	5
Carman	3	–	3
Ridgway	3	–	3
Wedge	2	–	2

GOALSCORERS

PLAYER	LGE	FAC	TOT
Boyd	22	–	22
Cassidy	14	–	14
Bryant	10	–	10
Collinson	4	1	5
Gillespie	3	–	3
Donaldson	2	–	2
McNaught	2	–	2
Wedge	2	–	2
Carman	1	–	1
Cartwright	1	–	1
Erentz F	1	–	1
Morgan	1	–	1
Smith	1	–	1
own goal	–	1	1

1898/99

FOOTBALL LEAGUE DIVISION TWO

DATE	OPPONENTS	SCORE	GOALSCORERS	ATTENDANCE
Sep 3	Gainsborough Trinity	2–0	Bryant, Cassidy	2,000
Sep 10	MANCHESTER CITY	3–0	Boyd, Cassidy, Collinson	20,000
Sep 17	Glossop	2–1	Bryant, Cassidy	6,000
Sep 24	WALSALL	1–0	Gillespie	8,000
Oct 1	Burton Swifts	1–5	Boyd	2,000
Oct 8	PORT VALE	2–1	Bryant, Cassidy	10,000
Oct 15	Birmingham City	1–4	Cassidy	5,000
Oct 22	LOUGHBOROUGH TOWN	6–1	Brooks 2, Cassidy 2, Collinson 2	2,000
Nov 5	GRIMSBY TOWN	3–2	Brooks, Cassidy, Gillespie	5,000
Nov 12	BARNSLEY	0–0		5,000
Nov 19	New Brighton Tower	3–0	Collinson 2, Cassidy	5,000
Nov 26	LINCOLN CITY	1–0	Bryant	4,000
Dec 3	Arsenal	1–5	Collinson	7,000
Dec 10	BLACKPOOL	3–1	Cassidy, Collinson, Cunningham	5,000
Dec 17	Leicester City	0–1		8,000
Dec 24	DARWEN	9–0	Bryant 3, Cassidy 3, Gillespie 2, og	2,000
Dec 26	Manchester City	0–4		25,000
Dec 31	GAINSBOROUGH TRINITY	6–1	Collinson 2, Bryant, Boyd, Cartwright, Draycott	2,000
Jan 2	BURTON SWIFTS	2–2	Boyd, Cassidy	6,000
Jan 14	GLOSSOP	3–0	Cunningham, Erentz, Gillespie	12,000
Jan 21	Walsall	0–2		3,000
Feb 4	Port Vale	0–1		6,000
Feb 18	Loughborough Town	1–0	Bryant	1,500
Feb 25	BIRMINGHAM CITY	2–0	Boyd, Roberts	12,000
Mar 4	Grimsby Town	0–3		4,000
Mar 18	NEW BRIGHTON TOWER	1–2	Cassidy	20,000
Mar 25	Lincoln City	0–2		3,000
Apr 1	ARSENAL	2–2	Bryant, Cassidy	5,000
Apr 3	Blackpool	1–0	Cassidy	3,000
Apr 4	Barnsley	2–0	Lee 2	4,000
Apr 8	Luton Town	1–0	Lee	1,000
Apr 12	LUTON TOWN	5–0	Cartwright, Cassidy, Gillespie, Lee, Morgan	3,000
Apr 15	LEICESTER CITY	2–2	Cassidy, Gillespie	6,000
Apr 22	Darwen	1–1	Morgan	1,000

FA CUP

DATE	OPPONENTS	SCORE	GOALSCORERS	ATTENDANCE
Jan 28	Tottenham Hotspur (Rd1)	1–1	Cassidy	15,000
Feb 1	TOTTENHAM HOTSPUR (Rd1R)	3–5	Bryant 3	6,000

FINAL LEAGUE TABLE

		P	W	D	L	F	A	Pts
1	Manchester City	34	23	6	5	92	35	52
2	Glossop	34	20	6	8	76	38	46
3	Leicester City	34	18	9	7	64	42	45
4	NEWTON HEATH	34	19	5	10	67	43	43
5	New Brighton Tower	34	18	7	9	71	52	43
6	Walsall	34	15	12	7	79	36	42
7	Arsenal	34	18	5	11	72	41	41
8	Birmingham City	34	17	7	10	85	50	41
9	Port Vale	34	17	5	12	56	34	39
10	Grimsby Town	34	15	5	14	71	60	35
11	Barnsley	34	12	7	15	52	56	31
12	Lincoln City	34	12	7	15	51	56	31
13	Burton Swifts	34	10	8	16	51	70	28
14	Gainsborough Trinity	34	10	5	19	56	72	25
15	Luton Town	34	10	3	21	51	95	23
16	Blackpool	34	8	4	22	49	90	20
17	Loughborough Town	34	6	6	22	38	92	18
18	Darwen	34	2	5	27	22	141	9

APPEARANCES

PLAYER	LGE	FAC	TOT
Barrett	34	2	36
Cassidy	34	2	36
Stafford	33	2	35
Bryant	32	2	34
Cartwright	33	1	34
Erentz	32	2	34
Draycott	31	2	33
Gillespie	28	2	30
Morgan	24	2	26
Collinson	21	2	23
Cunningham	15	2	17
Boyd	12	–	12
Pepper	7	1	8
Griffiths	7	–	7
Lee	7	–	7
Connachan	4	–	4
Brooks	3	–	3
Roberts	3	–	3
Turner J	3	–	3
Jones	2	–	2
Turner R	2	–	2
Walker	2	–	2
Cairns	1	–	1
Gourlay	1	–	1
Hopkins	1	–	1
Owen	1	–	1
Radcliffe	1	–	1

GOALSCORERS

PLAYER	LGE	FAC	TOT
Cassidy	19	1	20
Bryant	10	3	13
Collinson	9	–	9
Boyd	5	–	5
Lee	4	–	4
Brooks	3	–	3
Cartwright	2	–	2
Cunningham	2	–	2
Morgan	2	–	2
Draycott	1	–	1
Erentz	1	–	1
Roberts	1	–	1
own goal	1	–	1

1899/1900

FOOTBALL LEAGUE DIVISION TWO

DATE	OPPONENTS	SCORE	GOALSCORERS	ATTENDANCE
Sep 2	GAINSBOROUGH TRINITY	2–2	Cassidy, Lee	8,000
Sep 9	Bolton Wanderers	1–2	Ambler	5,000
Sep 16	LOUGHBOROUGH TOWN	4–0	Bain, Cassidy, Griffiths, og	6,000
Sep 23	Burton Swifts	0–0		2,000
Sep 30	Sheffield Wednesday	1–2	Bryant	8,000
Oct 7	LINCOLN CITY	1–0	Cassidy	5,000
Oct 14	Birmingham City	0–1		10,000
Oct 21	NEW BRIGHTON TOWER	2–1	Cassidy 2	5,000
Nov 4	ARSENAL	2–0	Jackson, Roberts	5,000
Nov 11	Barnsley	0–0		3,000
Nov 25	Luton Town	1–0	Jackson	3,000
Dec 2	PORT VALE	3–0	Cassidy 2, Jackson	5,000
Dec 16	MIDDLESBROUGH	2–1	Erentz, Parkinson	4,000
Dec 23	Chesterfield	1–2	Griffiths	2,000
Dec 26	Grimsby Town	7–0	Bryant 2, Cassidy 2, Jackson, Parkinson, og	2,000
Dec 30	Gainsborough Trinity	1–0	Parkinson	2,000
Jan 6	BOLTON WANDERERS	1–2	Parkinson	5,000
Jan 13	Loughborough Town	2–0	Jackson, Parkinson	1,000
Jan 20	BURTON SWIFTS	4–0	Gillespie 3, Parkinson	4,000
Feb 3	SHEFFIELD WEDNESDAY	1–0	Bryant	10,000
Feb 10	Lincoln City	0–1		2,000
Feb 17	BIRMINGHAM CITY	3–2	Cassidy, Godsmark, Parkinson	10,000
Feb 24	New Brighton Tower	4–1	Collinson 2, Godsmark, Smith	8,000
Mar 3	GRIMSBY TOWN	1–0	Smith	4,000
Mar 10	Arsenal	1–2	Cassidy	3,000
Mar 17	BARNSLEY	3–0	Cassidy 2, Leigh	6,000
Mar 24	Leicester City	0–2		8,000
Mar 31	LUTON TOWN	5–0	Cassidy 3, Godsmark 2	6,000
Apr 7	Port Vale	0–1		3,000
Apr 13	LEICESTER CITY	3–2	Gillespie, Griffiths, og	10,000
Apr 14	WALSALL	5–0	Jackson 2, Erentz, Foley, Gillespie	4,000
Apr 17	Walsall	0–0		3,000
Apr 21	Middlesbrough	0–2		8,000
Apr 28	CHESTERFIELD	2–1	Holt, Grundy	6,000

FA CUP

DATE	OPPONENTS	SCORE	GOALSCORERS	ATTENDANCE
Oct 28	South Shore (QRd3)	1–3	Jackson	3,000

FINAL LEAGUE TABLE

		P	W	D	L	F	A	Pts
1	Sheffield Wednesday	34	25	4	5	84	22	54
2	Bolton Wanderers	34	22	8	4	79	25	52
3	Birmingham City	34	20	6	8	78	38	46
4	NEWTON HEATH	34	20	4	10	63	27	44
5	Leicester City	34	17	9	8	53	36	43
6	Grimsby Town	34	17	6	11	67	46	40
7	Chesterfield	34	16	6	12	65	60	38
8	Arsenal	34	16	4	14	61	43	36
9	Lincoln City	34	14	8	12	46	43	36
10	New Brighton Tower	34	13	9	12	66	58	35
11	Port Vale	34	14	6	14	39	49	34
12	Walsall	34	12	8	14	50	55	32
13	Gainsborough Trinity	34	9	7	18	47	75	25
14	Middlesbrough	34	8	8	18	39	69	24
15	Burton Swifts	34	9	6	19	43	84	24
16	Barnsley	34	8	7	19	46	79	23
17	Luton Town	34	5	8	21	40	75	18
18	Loughborough Town	34	1	6	27	18	100	8

APPEARANCES

PLAYER	LGE	FAC	TOT
Barrett	34	1	35
Erentz	34	1	35
Griffiths	33	1	34
Jackson	32	1	33
Stafford	31	1	32
Morgan	30	1	31
Cassidy	29	1	30
Cartwright	25	1	26
Bryant	19	1	20
Parkinson	15	–	15
Smith	12	–	12
Gillespie	10	–	10
Ambler	9	–	9
Clark	9	–	9
Godsmark	9	–	9
Leigh	9	–	9
Collinson	7	–	7
Foley	7	–	7
Roberts	6	1	7
Lee	4	–	4
Bain	2	–	2
Blackmore	1	1	2
Fitzsimmons	2	–	2
Sawyer	2	–	2
Grundy	1	–	1
Heathcote	1	–	1
Holt	1	–	1

GOALSCORERS

PLAYER	LGE	FAC	TOT
Cassidy	16	–	16
Jackson	7	1	8
Parkinson	7	–	7
Gillespie	5	–	5
Bryant	4	–	4
Godsmark	4	–	4
Griffiths	3	–	3
Collinson	2	–	2
Erentz	2	–	2
Smith	2	–	2
Ambler	1	–	1
Bain	1	–	1
Foley	1	–	1
Grundy	1	–	1
Holt	1	–	1
Leigh	1	–	1
Roberts	1	–	1
own goals	3	–	3

1900/01

FOOTBALL LEAGUE DIVISION TWO

DATE	OPPONENTS	SCORE	GOALSCORERS	ATTENDANCE
Sep 1	Glossop	0-1		8,000
Sep 8	MIDDLESBROUGH	4-0	Griffiths, Grundy, Jackson, Leigh	5,500
Sep 15	Burnley	0-1		4,000
Sep 22	PORT VALE	4-0	Grundy, Leigh, Schofield, Smith	6,000
Sep 29	Leicester City	0-1		6,000
Oct 6	NEW BRIGHTON TOWER	1-0	Jackson	5,000
Oct 13	Gainsborough Trinity	1-0	Leigh	2,000
Oct 20	WALSALL	1-1	Schofield	8,000
Oct 27	Burton Swifts	1-3	Leigh	2,000
Nov 10	Arsenal	1-2	Jackson	8,000
Nov 24	Stockport County	0-1		5,000
Dec 1	BIRMINGHAM CITY	0-1		5,000
Dec 8	Grimsby Town	0-2		4,000
Dec 15	LINCOLN CITY	4-1	Leigh 2, Morgan H, Schofield	4,000
Dec 22	Chesterfield	1-2	og	4,000
Dec 26	BLACKPOOL	4-0	Griffiths, Leigh, Morgan B, Schofield	10,000
Dec 29	GLOSSOP	3-0	Leigh 2, Morgan H	8,000
Jan 1	Middlesbrough	2-1	Schofield 2	12,000
Jan 12	BURNLEY	0-1		10,000
Jan 19	Port Vale	0-2		1,000
Feb 16	GAINSBOROUGH TRINITY	0-0		7,000
Feb 19	New Brighton Tower	0-2		2,000
Feb 25	Walsall	1-1	Morgan B	2,000
Mar 2	BURTON SWIFTS	1-1	Leigh	5,000
Mar 13	BARNSLEY	1-0	Leigh	6,000
Mar 16	ARSENAL	1-0	Leigh	5,000
Mar 20	LEICESTER CITY	2-3	Fisher, Jackson	2,000
Mar 23	Blackpool	2-1	Griffiths 2	2,000
Mar 30	STOCKPORT COUNTY	3-1	Leigh, Morgan H, Schofield	4,000
Apr 5	Lincoln City	0-2		5,000
Apr 6	Birmingham City	0-1		6,000
Apr 9	Barnsley	2-6	Jackson, Morgan B	3,000
Apr 13	GRIMSBY TOWN	1-0	Morgan H	3,000
Apr 27	CHESTERFIELD	1-0	Leigh	1,000

FA CUP

DATE	OPPONENTS	SCORE	GOALSCORERS	ATTENDANCE
Jan 5	PORTSMOUTH (SupRd)	3-0	Griffiths, Jackson, Stafford	5,000
Feb 9	BURNLEY (Rd1)	0-0		8,000
Feb 13	Burnley (Rd1R)	1-7	Schofield	4,000

FINAL LEAGUE TABLE

		P	W	D	L	F	A	Pts
1	Grimsby Town	34	20	9	5	60	33	49
2	Birmingham City	34	19	10	5	57	24	48
3	Burnley	34	20	4	10	53	29	44
4	New Brighton Tower	34	17	8	9	57	38	42
5	Glossop	34	15	8	11	51	33	38
6	Middlesbrough	34	15	7	12	50	40	37
7	Arsenal	34	15	6	13	39	35	36
8	Lincoln City	34	13	7	14	43	39	33
9	Port Vale	34	11	11	12	45	47	33
10	NEWTON HEATH	34	14	4	16	42	38	32
11	Leicester City	34	11	10	13	39	37	32
12	Blackpool	34	12	7	15	33	58	31
13	Gainsborough Trinity	34	10	10	14	45	60	30
14	Chesterfield	34	9	10	15	46	58	28
15	Barnsley	34	11	5	18	47	60	27
16	Walsall	34	7	13	14	40	56	27
17	Stockport County	34	11	3	20	38	68	25
18	Burton Swifts	34	8	4	22	34	66	20

APPEARANCES

PLAYER	LGE	FAC	TOT
Leigh	34	3	37
Morgan B	33	3	36
Cartwright	31	3	34
Erentz	31	3	34
Griffiths	31	2	33
Stafford	30	3	33
Schofield	29	3	32
Whitehouse	29	3	32
Jackson	29	2	31
Fisher	25	3	28
Morgan H	20	3	23
Collinson	11	1	12
Grundy	10	–	10
Garvey	6	–	6
Smith	5	–	5
Heathcote	3	1	4
Sawyer	4	–	4
Greenwood	3	–	3
Lawson	3	–	3
Booth	2	–	2
Ambler	1	–	1
Hayes	1	–	1
Johnson	1	–	1
Lappin	1	–	1
Whitney	1	–	1

GOALSCORERS

PLAYER	LGE	FAC	TOT
Leigh	14	–	14
Schofield	7	1	8
Jackson	5	1	6
Griffiths	4	1	5
Morgan H	4	–	4
Morgan B	3	–	3
Grundy	2	–	2
Smith	1	–	1
Stafford	–	1	1
own goal	1	–	1

1901/02

FOOTBALL LEAGUE DIVISION TWO

DATE	OPPONENTS	SCORE	GOALSCORERS	ATTENDANCE
Sep 7	GAINSBOROUGH TRINITY	3-0	Preston 2, Lappin	3,000
Sep 14	Middlesbrough	0-5		12,000
Sep 21	BRISTOL CITY	1-0	Griffiths	5,000
Sep 28	Blackpool	4-2	Preston 2, Schofield, og	3,000
Oct 5	STOCKPORT COUNTY	3-3	Schofield 2, Preston	5,000
Oct 12	Burton United	0-0		3,000
Oct 19	Glossop	0-0		7,000
Oct 26	DONCASTER ROVERS	6-0	Coupar 3, Griffiths, Preston, og	7,000
Nov 9	WEST BROMWICH ALBION	1-2	Fisher	13,000
Nov 16	Arsenal	0-2		3,000
Nov 23	BARNSLEY	1-0	Griffiths	4,000
Nov 30	Leicester City	2-3	Cartwright, Preston	4,000
Dec 7	Preston North End	1-5	Preston	2,000
Dec 21	PORT VALE	1-0	Richards	3,000
Dec 26	Lincoln City	0-2		4,000
Jan 1	PRESTON NORTH END	0-2		10,000
Jan 4	Gainsborough Trinity	1-1	Lappin	2,000
Jan 18	Bristol City	0-4		6,000
Jan 25	BLACKPOOL	0-1		2,500
Feb 1	Stockport County	0-1		2,000
Feb 11	BURNLEY	2-0	Lappin, Preston	1,000
Feb 15	GLOSSOP	1-0	Erentz	5,000
Feb 22	Doncaster Rovers	0-4		3,000
Mar 1	LINCOLN CITY	0-0		6,000
Mar 8	West Bromwich Albion	0-4		10,000
Mar 15	ARSENAL	0-1		4,000
Mar 17	Chesterfield	0-3		2,000
Mar 22	Barnsley	2-3	Cartwright, Higson	2,500
Mar 28	Burnley	0-1		3,000
Mar 29	LEICESTER CITY	2-0	Griffiths, Hayes	2,000
Apr 7	MIDDLESBROUGH	1-2	Erentz	2,000
Apr 19	Port Vale	1-1	Schofield	2,000
Apr 21	BURTON UNITED	3-1	Cartwright, Griffiths, Preston	500
Apr 23	CHESTERFIELD	2-0	Coupar, Preston	2,000

FA CUP

DATE	OPPONENTS	SCORE	GOALSCORERS	ATTENDANCE
Dec 14	LINCOLN CITY (IntRd)	1-2	Fisher	4,000

FINAL LEAGUE TABLE

		P	W	D	L	F	A	Pts
1	West Bromwich Albion	34	25	5	4	82	29	55
2	Middlesbrough	34	23	5	6	90	24	51
3	Preston North End	34	18	6	10	71	32	42
4	Arsenal	34	18	6	10	50	26	42
5	Lincoln City	34	14	13	7	45	35	41
6	Bristol City	34	17	6	11	52	35	40
7	Doncaster Rovers	34	13	8	13	49	58	34
8	Glossop	34	10	12	12	36	40	32
9	Burnley	34	10	10	14	41	45	30
10	Burton United	34	11	8	15	46	54	30
11	Barnsley	34	12	6	16	51	63	30
12	Port Vale	34	10	9	15	43	59	29
13	Blackpool	34	11	7	16	40	56	29
14	Leicester City	34	12	5	17	38	56	29
15	NEWTON HEATH	34	11	6	17	38	53	28
16	Chesterfield	34	11	6	17	47	68	28
17	Stockport County	34	8	7	19	36	72	23
18	Gainsborough Trinity	34	4	11	19	30	80	19

APPEARANCES

PLAYER	LGE	FAC	TOT
Morgan	33	1	34
Cartwright	29	1	30
Griffiths	29	1	30
Preston	29	1	30
Schofield	29	1	30
Banks	27	1	28
Stafford	26	1	27
Erentz	25	1	26
Whitehouse	23	1	24
Lappin	21	–	21
Fisher	17	1	18
Smith	16	1	17
Hayes	16	–	16
Coupar	11	–	11
Saunders	11	–	11
Higgins	10	–	10
Richards	9	–	9
Higson	5	–	5
Williams	4	–	4
Heathcote	3	–	3
O'Brien	1	–	1

GOALSCORERS

PLAYER	LGE	FAC	TOT
Preston	11	–	11
Griffiths	5	–	5
Coupar	4	–	4
Schofield	4	–	4
Cartwright	3	–	3
Lappin	3	–	3
Erentz	2	–	2
Fisher	1	1	2
Hayes	1	–	1
Higson	1	–	1
Richards	1	–	1
own goals	2	–	2

1902/03

FOOTBALL LEAGUE DIVISION TWO

DATE	OPPONENTS	SCORE	GOALSCORERS	ATTENDANCE
Sep 6	Gainsborough Trinity	1–0	Richards	4,000
Sep 13	BURTON UNITED	1–0	Hurst	15,000
Sep 20	Bristol City	1–3	Hurst	6,000
Sep 27	GLOSSOP	1–1	Hurst	12,000
Oct 4	CHESTERFIELD	2–1	Preston 2	12,000
Oct 11	Stockport County	1–2	Pegg	6,000
Oct 25	Arsenal	1–0	Beadsworth	12,000
Nov 8	Lincoln City	3–1	Peddie 2, Hurst	3,000
Nov 15	BIRMINGHAM CITY	0–1		25,000
Nov 22	Leicester City	1–1	Downie	5,000
Dec 6	Burnley	2–0	Pegg, og	4,000
Dec 20	Port Vale	1–1	Peddie	4,000
Dec 25	MANCHESTER CITY	1–1	Pegg	40,000
Dec 26	BLACKPOOL	2–2	Downie, Morrison	10,000
Dec 27	BARNSLEY	2–1	Lappin, Peddie	9,000
Jan 3	GAINSBOROUGH TRINITY	3–1	Downie, Peddie, Pegg	8,000
Jan 10	Burton United	1–3	Peddie	3,000
Jan 17	BRISTOL CITY	1–2	Preston	12,000
Jan 24	Glossop	3–1	Downie, Griffiths, Morrison	5,000
Jan 31	Chesterfield	0–2		6,000
Feb 14	Blackpool	0–2		3,000
Feb 28	Doncaster Rovers	2–2	Morrison 2	4,000
Mar 7	LINCOLN CITY	1–2	Downie	4,000
Mar 9	ARSENAL	3–0	Arkesden, Peddie, Pegg	5,000
Mar 21	LEICESTER CITY	5–1	Fitchett, Griffiths, Morrison, Pegg, Smith	8,000
Mar 23	STOCKPORT COUNTY	0–0		2,000
Mar 30	PRESTON NORTH END	0–1		3,000
Apr 4	BURNLEY	4–0	Peddie 2, Griffiths, Morrison	3,000
Apr 10	Manchester City	2–0	Peddie, Schofield	30,000
Apr 11	Preston North End	1–3	Pegg	7,000
Apr 13	DONCASTER ROVERS	4–0	Arkesden, Bell, Griffiths, Morrison	6,000
Apr 18	PORT VALE	2–1	Schofield 2	8,000
Apr 20	Birmingham City	1–2	Peddie	6,000
Apr 25	Barnsley	0–0		2,000

FA CUP

DATE	OPPONENTS	SCORE	GOALSCORERS	ATTENDANCE
Nov 1	ACCRINGTON STANLEY (QRd3)	7–0	Williams 3, Morgan, Richards, Peddie, Pegg	6,000
Nov 13	OSWALDTWISTLE ROVERS (QRd4)	3–2	Beadsworth, Pegg, Williams	5,000
Nov 29	SOUTHPORT CENTRAL (QRd5)	4–1	Pegg 3, Banks	6,000
Dec 13	BURTON UNITED (IntRd)	1–1	Griffiths	6,000
Dec 17	Burton United (IntRdR)	3–1	Peddie, Pegg, Schofield	7,000
Feb 7	LIVERPOOL (Rd1)	2–1	Peddie 2	15,000
Feb 21	Everton (Rd2)	1–3	Griffiths	15,000

FINAL LEAGUE TABLE

		P	W	D	L	F	A	Pts
1	Manchester City	34	25	4	5	95	29	54
2	Birmingham City	34	24	3	7	74	36	51
3	Arsenal	34	20	8	6	66	30	48
4	Bristol City	34	17	8	9	59	38	42
5	MANCHESTER UNITED	34	15	8	11	53	38	38
6	Chesterfield	34	14	9	11	67	40	37
7	Preston North End	34	13	10	11	56	40	36
8	Barnsley	34	13	8	13	55	51	34
9	Port Vale	34	13	8	13	57	62	34
10	Lincoln City	34	12	6	16	46	53	30
11	Glossop	34	11	7	16	43	58	29
12	Gainsborough Trinity	34	11	7	16	41	59	29
13	Burton United	34	11	7	16	39	59	29
14	Blackpool	34	9	10	15	44	59	28
15	Leicester City	34	10	8	16	41	65	28
16	Doncaster Rovers	34	9	7	18	35	72	25
17	Stockport County	34	7	6	21	39	74	20
18	Burnley	34	6	8	20	30	77	20

APPEARANCES

PLAYER	LGE	FAC	TOT
Peddie	30	6	36
Pegg	28	7	35
Read	27	6	33
Griffiths	25	7	32
Birchenough	25	5	30
Rothwell	22	6	28
Downie	22	5	27
Cartwright	22	4	26
Hurst	16	5	21
Morrison	20	–	20
Schofield	16	4	20
Banks	13	3	16
Morgan	12	2	14
Beadsworth	9	3	12
Stafford	10	2	12
Richards	8	3	11
Smith	8	2	10
Williams	8	2	10
Arkesden	9	–	9
Whitehouse	7	1	8
Marshall	6	–	6
Bell	5	–	5
Fitchett	5	–	5
Lappin	5	–	5
Ball	4	–	4
Preston	4	–	4
Street	1	2	3
Bunce	2	–	2
Hayes	2	–	2
Saunders	1	1	2
Christie	1	–	1
Cleaver	1	–	1
Turner	–	1	1

GOALSCORERS

PLAYER	LGE	FAC	TOT
Peddie	11	4	15
Pegg	7	6	13
Morrison	7	–	7
Griffiths	4	2	6
Downie	5	–	5
Hurst	4	–	4
Schofield	3	1	4
Williams	–	4	4
Preston	3	–	3
Arkesden	2	–	2
Beadsworth	1	1	2
Richards	1	1	2
Bell	1	–	1
Fitchett	1	–	1
Lappin	1	–	1
Smith	1	–	1
Banks	–	1	1
Morgan	–	1	1
own goal	1	–	1

1903/04

FOOTBALL LEAGUE DIVISION TWO

DATE	OPPONENTS	SCORE	GOALSCORERS	ATTENDANCE
Sep 5	BRISTOL CITY	2–2	Griffiths 2	40,000
Sep 7	Burnley	0–2		5,000
Sep 12	Port Vale	0–1		3,000
Sep 19	Glossop	5–0	Griffiths 2, Arkesden, Downie, Robertson A	3,000
Sep 26	BRADFORD CITY	3–1	Pegg 3	30,000
Oct 3	Arsenal	0–4		20,000
Oct 10	BARNSLEY	4–0	Pegg 2, Griffiths, Robertson A	20,000
Oct 17	Lincoln City	0–0		5,000
Oct 24	STOCKPORT COUNTY	3–1	Arkesden, Grassam, Schofield A	15,000
Nov 7	BOLTON WANDERERS	0–0		30,000
Nov 21	PRESTON NORTH END	0–2		15,000
Dec 19	GAINSBOROUGH TRINITY	4–2	Arkesden, Duckworth, Grassam, Robertson A	6,000
Dec 25	CHESTERFIELD	3–1	Arkesden 2, Robertson A	15,000
Dec 26	Burton United	2–2	Arkesden 2	4,000
Jan 2	Bristol City	1–1	Griffiths	8,000
Jan 9	PORT VALE	2–0	Arkesden, Grassam	10,000
Jan 16	GLOSSOP	3–1	Arkesden 2, Downie	10,000
Jan 23	Bradford City	3–3	Griffiths 2, Downie	12,000
Jan 30	ARSENAL	1–0	Robertson A	40,000
Feb 13	LINCOLN CITY	2–0	Downie, Griffiths	8,000
Mar 9	Blackpool	1–2	Grassam	3,000
Mar 12	BURNLEY	3–1	Grassam 2, Griffiths	14,000
Mar 19	Preston North End	1–1	Arkesden	7,000
Mar 26	GRIMSBY TOWN	2–0	Robertson A 2	12,000
Mar 28	Stockport County	3–0	Hall, Pegg, Schofield A	2,500
Apr 1	Chesterfield	2–0	Bell, Hall	5,000
Apr 2	Leicester City	1–0	McCartney	4,000
Apr 5	Barnsley	2–0	Grassam, Schofield A	5,000
Apr 9	BLACKPOOL	3–1	Grassam 2, Schofield A	10,000
Apr 12	Grimsby Town	1–3	Grassam	8,000
Apr 16	Gainsborough Trinity	1–0	Robertson A	4,000
Apr 23	BURTON UNITED	2–0	Grassam, Robertson A	8,000
Apr 25	Bolton Wanderers	0–0		10,000
Apr 30	LEICESTER CITY	5–2	Schofield A 2, Bonthron, Griffiths, Robertson A	7,000

FA CUP

DATE	OPPONENTS	SCORE	GOALSCORERS	ATTENDANCE
Dec 12	BIRMINGHAM CITY (IntRd)	1–1	Schofield A	10,000
Dec 16	Birmingham City (IntRdR)	1–1	Arkesden	5,000
Dec 21	Birmingham City (IntRdR2) (at Bramall Lane, Sheffield)	1–1	Schofield A	3,000
Jan 11	Birmingham City (IntRdR3) (at Hyde Road, Manchester)	3–1	Arkesden 2, Grassam	9,372
Feb 6	Notts County (Rd1)	3–3	Arkesden, Downie, Schofield A	12,000
Feb 10	NOTTS COUNTY (Rd1R)	2–1	Morrison, Pegg	18,000
Feb 20	Sheffield Wednesday (Rd2)	0–6		22,051

FINAL LEAGUE TABLE

		P	W	D	L	F	A	Pts
1	Preston North End	34	20	10	4	62	24	50
2	Arsenal	34	21	7	6	91	22	49
3	MANCHESTER UNITED	34	20	8	6	65	33	48
4	Bristol City	34	18	6	10	73	41	42
5	Burnley	34	15	9	10	50	55	39
6	Grimsby Town	34	14	8	12	50	49	36
7	Bolton Wanderers	34	12	10	12	59	41	34
8	Barnsley	34	11	10	13	38	57	32
9	Gainsborough Trinity	34	14	3	17	53	60	31
10	Bradford City	34	12	7	15	45	59	31
11	Chesterfield	34	11	8	15	37	45	30
12	Lincoln City	34	11	8	15	41	58	30
13	Port Vale	34	10	9	15	54	52	29
14	Burton United	34	11	7	16	45	61	29
15	Blackpool	34	11	5	18	40	67	27
16	Stockport County	34	8	11	15	40	72	27
17	Glossop	34	10	6	18	57	64	26
18	Leicester City	34	6	10	18	42	82	22

APPEARANCES

PLAYER	LGE	FAC	TOT
Bonthron	33	7	40
Griffiths	30	7	37
Downie	29	6	35
Schofield A	26	7	33
Arkesden	26	6	32
Robertson A	27	5	32
Grassam	23	5	28
Sutcliffe	21	7	28
Robertson S	24	2	26
Hayes	21	3	24
Morrison	9	7	16
Pegg	13	3	16
Cartwright	9	6	15
McCartney	13	–	13
Moger	13	–	13
Blackstock	7	3	10
Read	8	1	9
Wilkinson	8	1	9
Gaudie	7	1	8
Hall	8	–	8
Bell	6	–	6
Robertson T	3	–	3
Kerr	2	–	2
Lyons	2	–	2
Roberts	2	–	2
Schofield J	2	–	2
Duckworth	1	–	1
Hartwell	1	–	1

GOALSCORERS

PLAYER	LGE	FAC	TOT
Arkesden	11	4	15
Grassam	11	1	12
Griffiths	11	–	11
Robertson A	10	–	10
Schofield A	6	3	9
Pegg	6	1	7
Downie	4	1	5
Bell	1	–	1
Bonthron	1	–	1
Duckworth	1	–	1
McCartney	1	–	1
Morrison	–	1	1

1904/05

FOOTBALL LEAGUE DIVISION TWO

DATE	OPPONENTS	SCORE	GOALSCORERS	ATTENDANCE
Sep 3	Port Vale	2-2	Allan 2	4,000
Sep 10	BRISTOL CITY	4-1	Peddie, Robertson S, Schofield, Williams	20,000
Sep 17	BOLTON WANDERERS	1-2	Mackie	25,000
Sep 24	Glossop	2-1	Allan, Roberts	6,000
Oct 8	Bradford City	1-1	Arkesden	12,000
Oct 15	LINCOLN CITY	2-0	Arkesden, Schofield	15,000
Oct 22	Leicester City	3-0	Arkesden, Peddie, Schofield A	7,000
Oct 29	BARNSLEY	4-0	Allan, Downie, Peddie, Schofield	15,000
Nov 5	West Bromwich Albion	2-0	Arkesden, Williams	5,000
Nov 12	BURNLEY	1-0	Arkesden	15,000
Nov 19	Grimsby Town	1-0	Bell	4,000
Dec 3	Doncaster Rovers	1-0	Peddie	10,000
Dec 10	GAINSBOROUGH TRINITY	3-1	Arkesden 2, Allan	12,000
Dec 17	Burton United	3-2	Peddie 3	3,000
Dec 24	LIVERPOOL	3-1	Arkesden, Roberts, Williams	40,000
Dec 26	CHESTERFIELD	3-0	Allan 2, Williams	20,000
Dec 31	PORT VALE	6-1	Allan 3, Arkesden, Hayes, Roberts	8,000
Apr 1	DONCASTER ROVERS	6-0	Arkesden 2, Roberts 2, Allan, Peddie, og	6,000
Jan 3	Bolton Wanderers	4-2	Allan 2, Peddie, Williams	35,000
Jan 7	Bristol City	1-1	Arkesden	12,000
Jan 21	GLOSSOP	4-1	Mackie 2, Arkesden, Grassam	20,000
Feb 11	Lincoln City	0-3		2,000
Feb 18	LEICESTER CITY	4-1	Peddie 3, Allan	7,000
Feb 25	Barnsley	0-0		5,000
Mar 4	WEST BROMWICH ALBION	2-0	Peddie, Williams	8,000
Mar 11	Burnley	0-2		7,000
Mar 18	GRIMSBY TOWN	2-1	Allan, Duckworth	12,000
Mar 25	Blackpool	1-0	Grassam	6,000
Jan 2	BRADFORD CITY	7-0	Duckworth 3, Beddow, Peddie, Wombwell	10,000
Apr 8	Gainsborough Trinity	0-0		6,000
Apr 15	BURTON UNITED	5-0	Duckworth 2, Peddie 2, Arkesden	16,000
Apr 21	Chesterfield	0-2		10,000
Apr 22	Liverpool	0-4		28,000
Apr 24	BLACKPOOL	3-1	Allan, Arkesden, Peddie	4,000

FA CUP

DATE	OPPONENTS	SCORE	GOALSCORERS	ATTENDANCE
Jan 14	FULHAM (IntRd)	2-2	Arkesden, Mackie	17,000
Jan 18	Fulham (IntRdR)	0-0		15,000
Jan 23	Fulham (IntRdR2) (at Villa Park)	0-1		6,000

FINAL LEAGUE TABLE

		P	W	D	L	F	A	Pts
1	Liverpool	34	27	4	3	93	25	58
2	Bolton Wanderers	34	27	2	5	87	32	56
3	MANCHESTER UNITED	34	24	5	5	81	30	53
4	Bristol City	34	19	4	11	66	45	42
5	Chesterfield	34	14	11	9	44	35	39
6	Gainsborough Trinity	34	14	8	12	61	58	36
7	Barnsley	34	14	5	15	38	56	33
8	Bradford City	34	12	8	14	45	49	32
9	Lincoln City	34	12	7	15	42	40	31
10	West Bromwich Albion	34	13	4	17	56	48	30
11	Burnley	34	12	6	16	43	52	30
12	Glossop	34	10	10	14	37	46	30
13	Grimsby Town	34	11	8	15	33	46	30
14	Leicester City	34	11	7	16	40	55	29
15	Blackpool	34	9	10	15	36	48	28
16	Port Vale	34	10	7	17	47	72	27
17	Burton United	34	8	4	22	30	84	20
18	Doncaster Rovers	34	3	2	29	23	81	8

APPEARANCES

PLAYER	LGE	FAC	TOT
Bonthron	32	3	35
Downie	32	3	35
Moger	32	3	35
Bell	29	3	32
Peddie	32	–	32
Arkesden	28	3	31
Roberts	28	–	28
Allan	27	–	27
Schofield	24	3	27
Hayes	22	3	25
Williams	22	2	24
Fitchett	11	2	13
Beddow	9	–	9
Grassam	6	3	9
Duckworth	8	–	8
Robertson S	8	–	8
Wombwell	8	–	8
Mackie	5	2	7
Blackstock	3	–	3
Hartwell	2	1	3
Griffiths	2	–	2
Robertson A	1	1	2
Valentine	2	–	2
Holden	1	–	1
Lyons	–	1	1

GOALSCORERS

PLAYER	LGE	FAC	TOT
Peddie	17	–	17
Allan	16	–	16
Arkesden	15	1	16
Duckworth	6	–	6
Williams	6	–	6
Roberts	5	–	5
Schofield	4	–	4
Grassam	2	–	2
Beddow	1	–	1
Bell	1	–	1
Downie	1	–	1
Hayes	1	–	1
Robertson S	1	–	1
Wombwell	1	–	1
own goal	1	–	1

1905/06

FOOTBALL LEAGUE DIVISION TWO

DATE	OPPONENTS	SCORE	GOALSCORERS	ATTENDANCE
Sep 2	BRISTOL CITY	5-1	Sagar 3, Beddow, Picken	25,000
Sep 4	BLACKPOOL	2-1	Peddie 2	7,000
Sep 9	Grimsby Town	1-0	Sagar	6,000
Sep 16	Glossop	2-1	Beddow, Bell	7,000
Sep 23	STOCKPORT COUNTY	3-1	Peddie 2, Sagar	15,000
Sep 30	Blackpool	1-0	Roberts	7,000
Oct 7	BRADFORD CITY	0-0		17,000
Oct 14	West Bromwich Albion	0-1		15,000
Oct 21	LEICESTER CITY	3-2	Peddie 2, Sagar	12,000
Oct 25	Gainsborough Trinity	2-2	Bonthron 2	4,000
Oct 28	Hull City	1-0	Picken	14,000
Nov 4	LINCOLN CITY	2-1	Picken, Roberts	15,000
Nov 11	Chesterfield	0-1		3,000
Nov 18	PORT VALE	3-0	Beddow, Peddie, og	8,000
Nov 25	Barnsley	3-0	Beddow, Picken, og	3,000
Dec 2	LEYTON ORIENT	4-0	Peddie 2, Picken 2	12,000
Dec 9	Burnley	3-1	Beddow, Peddie, Picken	8,000
Dec 23	Burton United	2-0	Schofield 2	5,000
Dec 25	CHELSEA	0-0		35,000
Dec 30	Bristol City	1-1	Roberts	18,000
Jan 6	GRIMSBY TOWN	5-0	Beddow 3, Picken 2	10,000
Jan 15	LEEDS UNITED	0-3		15,000
Jan 20	GLOSSOP	5-2	Picken 2, Beddow, Peddie, Williams	7,000
Jan 27	Stockport County	1-0	Peddie	15,000
Feb 10	Bradford City	5-1	Beddow 2, Roberts, Schofield, Wombwell	8,000
Feb 17	WEST BROMWICH ALBION	0-0		30,000
Mar 3	HULL CITY	5-0	Picken 2, Peddie, Sagar, Schofield	16,000
Mar 17	CHESTERFIELD	4-1	Picken 3, Sagar	16,000
Mar 24	Port Vale	0-1		3,000
Mar 29	Leicester City	5-2	Peddie 3, Picken, Sagar	5,000
Mar 31	BARNSLEY	5-1	Sagar 3, Bell, Picken	15,000
Apr 7	Leyton Orient	1-0	Wall	8,000
Apr 13	Chelsea	1-1	Sagar	60,000
Apr 14	BURNLEY	1-0	Sagar	12,000
Apr 16	GAINSBOROUGH TRINITY	2-0	Allan 2	20,000
Apr 21	Leeds United	3-1	Allan, Peddie, Wombwell	15,000
Apr 25	Lincoln City	3-2	Allan 2, Wall	1,500
Apr 28	BURTON UNITED	6-0	Picken 2, Sagar 2, Peddie, Wall	16,000

FA CUP

DATE	OPPONENTS	SCORE	GOALSCORERS	ATTENDANCE
Jan 13	STAPLE HILL (Rd1)	7-2	Beddow 3, Picken 2, Allan, Williams	7,560
Feb 3	NORWICH CITY (Rd2)	3-0	Downie, Peddie, Sagar	10,000
Feb 24	ASTON VILLA (Rd3)	5-1	Picken 3, Sagar 2	35,500
Mar 10	ARSENAL (Rd4)	2-3	Peddie, Sagar	26,500

FINAL LEAGUE TABLE

		P	W	D	L	F	A	Pts
1	Bristol City	38	30	6	2	83	28	66
2	MANCHESTER UNITED	38	28	6	4	90	28	62
3	Chelsea	38	22	9	7	90	37	53
4	West Bromwich Albion	38	22	8	8	79	36	52
5	Hull City	38	19	6	13	67	54	44
6	Leeds United	38	17	9	12	59	47	43
7	Leicester City	38	15	12	11	53	48	42
8	Grimsby Town	38	15	10	13	46	46	40
9	Burnley	38	15	8	15	42	53	38
10	Stockport County	38	13	9	16	44	56	35
11	Bradford City	38	13	8	17	46	60	34
12	Barnsley	38	12	9	17	60	62	33
13	Lincoln City	38	12	6	20	69	72	30
14	Blackpool	38	10	9	19	37	62	29
15	Gainsborough Trinity	38	12	4	22	44	57	28
16	Glossop	38	10	8	20	49	71	28
17	Port Vale	38	12	4	22	49	82	28
18	Chesterfield	38	10	8	20	40	72	28
19	Burton United	38	10	6	22	34	67	26
20	Leyton Orient	38	7	7	24	35	78	21

APPEARANCES

PLAYER	LGE	FAC	TOT
Bell	36	4	40
Downie	34	4	38
Roberts	34	4	38
Peddie	34	3	37
Picken	33	4	37
Holden	27	4	31
Moger	27	4	31
Bonthron	26	4	30
Schofield	23	4	27
Wombwell	25	2	27
Sagar	20	3	23
Beddow	21	1	22
Blackstock	21	–	21
Williams	10	2	12
Duckworth	10	–	10
Valentine	8	–	8
Arkesden	7	–	7
Allan	5	1	6
Wall	6	–	6
Donaghy	3	–	3
Montgomery	3	–	3
Lyons	2	–	2
Blew	1	–	1
Dyer	1	–	1
Robertson	1	–	1

GOALSCORERS

PLAYER	LGE	FAC	TOT
Picken	20	5	25
Peddie	18	2	20
Sagar	16	4	20
Beddow	11	3	14
Allan	5	1	6
Roberts	4	–	4
Schofield	4	–	4
Wall	3	–	3
Bell	2	–	2
Bonthron	2	–	2
Wombwell	2	–	2
Williams	1	1	2
Downie	–	1	1
own goals	2	–	2

1906/07

FOOTBALL LEAGUE DIVISION ONE

DATE	OPPONENTS	SCORE	GOALSCORERS	ATTENDANCE
Sep 1	Bristol City	2–1	Picken, Roberts	5,000
Sep 3	Derby County	2–2	Schofield 2	5,000
Sep 8	NOTTS COUNTY	0–0		30,000
Sep 15	Sheffield United	2–0	Bell, Downie	12,000
Sep 22	BOLTON WANDERERS	1–2	Peddie	45,000
Sep 29	DERBY COUNTY	1–1	Bell	25,000
Oct 6	Stoke City	2–1	Duckworth 2	7,000
Oct 13	BLACKBURN ROVERS	1–1	Wall	20,000
Oct 20	Sunderland	1–4	Peddie	18,000
Oct 27	BIRMINGHAM CITY	2–1	Peddie 2	14,000
Nov 3	Everton	0–3		20,000
Nov 10	ARSENAL	1–0	Downie	20,000
Nov 17	Sheffield Wednesday	2–5	Menzies, Peddie	7,000
Nov 24	BURY	2–4	Peddie, Wall	30,000
Dec 1	Manchester City	0–3		40,000
Dec 8	MIDDLESBROUGH	3–1	Wall 2, Sagar	12,000
Dec 15	Preston North End	0–2		9,000
Dec 22	NEWCASTLE UNITED	1–3	Menzies	18,000
Dec 25	LIVERPOOL	0–0		20,000
Dec 26	Aston Villa	0–2		20,000
Dec 29	BRISTOL CITY	0–0		10,000
Jan 1	ASTON VILLA	1–0	Turnbull	40,000
Jan 5	Notts County	0–3		10,000
Jan 19	SHEFFIELD UNITED	2–0	Turnbull, Wall	15,000
Jan 26	Bolton Wanderers	1–0	Turnbull	25,000
Feb 2	Newcastle United	0–5		30,000
Feb 9	STOKE CITY	4–1	Picken 2, Meredith, og	15,000
Feb 16	Blackburn Rovers	4–2	Meredith 2, Sagar, Wall	5,000
Feb 23	PRESTON NORTH END	3–0	Wall 2, Sagar	16,000
Mar 2	Birmingham City	1–1	Menzies	20,000
Mar 16	Arsenal	0–4		6,000
Mar 25	SUNDERLAND	2–0	Turnbull, Williams	12,000
Mar 30	Bury	2–1	Menzies, Meredith	25,000
Apr 1	Liverpool	1–0	Turnbull	20,000
Apr 6	MANCHESTER CITY	1–1	Roberts	40,000
Apr 10	SHEFFIELD WEDNESDAY	5–0	Wall 3, Picken, Sagar	10,000
Apr 13	Middlesbrough	0–2		15,000
Apr 22	EVERTON	3–0	Bannister, Meredith, Turnbull	10,000

FA CUP

DATE	OPPONENTS	SCORE	GOALSCORERS	ATTENDANCE
Jan 12	Portsmouth (Rd1)	2–2	Picken, Wall	24,329
Jan 16	PORTSMOUTH (Rd1R)	1–2	Wall	8,000

FINAL LEAGUE TABLE

		P	W	D	L	F	A	Pts
1	Newcastle United	38	22	7	9	74	46	51
2	Bristol City	38	20	8	10	66	47	48
3	Everton	38	20	5	13	70	46	45
4	Sheffield United	38	17	11	10	57	55	45
5	Aston Villa	38	19	6	13	78	52	44
6	Bolton Wanderers	38	18	8	12	59	47	44
7	Arsenal	38	20	4	14	66	59	44
8	MANCHESTER UNITED	38	17	8	13	53	56	42
9	Birmingham City	38	15	8	15	52	52	38
10	Sunderland	38	14	9	15	65	66	37
11	Middlesbrough	38	15	6	17	56	63	36
12	Blackburn Rovers	38	14	7	17	56	59	35
13	Sheffield Wednesday	38	12	11	15	49	60	35
14	Preston North End	38	14	7	17	44	57	35
15	Liverpool	38	13	7	18	64	65	33
16	Bury	38	13	6	19	58	68	32
17	Manchester City	38	10	12	16	53	77	32
18	Notts County	38	8	15	15	46	50	31
19	Derby County	38	9	9	20	41	59	27
20	Stoke City	38	8	10	20	41	64	26

APPEARANCES

PLAYER	LGE	FAC	TOT
Moger	38	2	40
Wall	38	2	40
Bell	35	2	37
Roberts	31	1	32
Duckworth	28	2	30
Bonthron	28	1	29
Holden	27	2	29
Picken	26	2	28
Downie	19	1	20
Menzies	17	2	19
Meredith	16	2	18
Burgess	17	–	17
Peddie	16	–	16
Wombwell	14	2	16
Turnbull	15	–	15
Sagar	10	–	10
Schofield	10	–	10
Berry	9	–	9
Bannister	4	–	4
Blackstock	3	1	4
Allan	3	–	3
Beddow	3	–	3
Buckley	3	–	3
Williams	3	–	3
Yates	3	–	3
Young	2	–	2

GOALSCORERS

PLAYER	LGE	FAC	TOT
Wall	11	2	13
Peddie	6	–	6
Turnbull	6	–	6
Meredith	5	–	5
Picken	4	1	5
Menzies	4	–	4
Sagar	4	–	4
Bell	2	–	2
Downie	2	–	2
Duckworth	2	–	2
Roberts	2	–	2
Schofield	2	–	2
Bannister	1	–	1
Williams	1	–	1
own goal	1	–	1

1907/08

FOOTBALL LEAGUE DIVISION ONE

DATE	OPPONENTS	SCORE	GOALSCORERS	ATTENDANCE
Sep 2	Aston Villa	4–1	Meredith 2, Bannister, Wall	20,000
Sep 7	LIVERPOOL	4–0	Turnbull A 3, Wall	24,000
Sep 9	MIDDLESBROUGH	2–1	Turnbull A 2	20,000
Sep 14	Middlesbrough	1–2	Bannister	18,000
Sep 21	SHEFFIELD UNITED	2–1	Turnbull A 2	25,000
Sep 28	Chelsea	4–1	Meredith 2, Bannister, Turnbull A	40,000
Oct 5	NOTTINGHAM FOREST	4–0	Bannister, Turnbull J, Wall, og	20,000
Oct 12	Newcastle United	6–1	Wall 2, Meredith, Roberts, Turnbull A, Turnbull J	25,000
Oct 19	Blackburn Rovers	5–1	Turnbull A 3, Turnbull J 2	30,000
Oct 26	BOLTON WANDERERS	2–1	Turnbull A, Turnbull J	35,000
Nov 2	Birmingham City	4–3	Meredith 2, Turnbull J, Wall	20,000
Nov 9	EVERTON	4–3	Wall 2, Meredith, Roberts	30,000
Nov 16	Sunderland	2–1	Turnbull A 2	30,000
Nov 23	ARSENAL	4–2	Turnbull A 4	10,000
Nov 30	Sheffield Wednesday	0–2		40,000
Dec 7	BRISTOL CITY	2–1	Wall 2	20,000
Dec 14	Notts County	1–1	Meredith	11,000
Dec 21	MANCHESTER CITY	3–1	Turnbull A 2, Wall	35,000
Dec 25	BURY	2–1	Meredith, Turnbull J	45,000
Dec 28	Preston North End	0–0		12,000
Jan 1	Bury	1–0	Wall	29,500
Jan 18	Sheffield United	0–2		17,000
Jan 25	CHELSEA	1–0	Turnbull J	20,000
Feb 8	NEWCASTLE UNITED	1–1	Turnbull J	50,000
Feb 15	BLACKBURN ROVERS	1–2	Turnbull A	15,000
Feb 29	BIRMINGHAM CITY	1–0	Turnbull A	12,000
Mar 14	SUNDERLAND	3–0	Bell, Berry, Wall	15,000
Mar 21	Arsenal	0–1		20,000
Mar 25	Liverpool	4–7	Wall 2, Bannister, Turnbull J	10,000
Mar 28	SHEFFIELD WEDNESDAY	4–1	Wall 2, Halse, Turnbull A	30,000
Apr 4	Bristol City	1–1	Wall	12,000
Apr 8	Everton	3–1	Halse, Turnbull A, Wall	17,000
Apr 11	NOTTS COUNTY	0–1		20,000
Apr 17	Nottingham Forest	0–2		22,000
Apr 18	Manchester City	0–0		40,000
Apr 20	ASTON VILLA	1–2	Picken	10,000
Apr 22	Bolton Wanderers	2–2	Halse, Stacey	18,000
Apr 25	PRESTON NORTH END	2–1	Halse, og	8,000

FA CUP

DATE	OPPONENTS	SCORE	GOALSCORERS	ATTENDANCE
Jan 11	BLACKPOOL (Rd1)	3–1	Wall 2, Bannister	11,747
Feb 1	CHELSEA (Rd2)	1–0	Turnbull A	25,184
Feb 22	Aston Villa (Rd3)	2–0	Wall, Turnbull A	12,777
Mar 7	Fulham (Rd4)	1–2	Turnbull J	41,000

FINAL LEAGUE TABLE

		P	W	D	L	F	A	Pts
1	MANCHESTER UNITED	38	23	6	9	81	48	52
2	Aston Villa	38	17	9	12	77	59	43
3	Manchester City	38	16	11	11	62	54	43
4	Newcastle United	38	15	12	11	65	54	42
5	Sheffield Wednesday	38	19	4	15	73	64	42
6	Middlesbrough	38	17	7	14	54	45	41
7	Bury	38	14	11	13	58	61	39
8	Liverpool	38	16	6	16	68	61	38
9	Nottingham Forest	38	13	11	14	59	62	37
10	Bristol City	38	12	12	14	58	61	36
11	Everton	38	15	6	17	58	64	36
12	Preston North End	38	12	12	14	47	53	36
13	Chelsea	38	14	8	16	53	62	36
14	Blackburn Rovers	38	12	12	14	51	63	36
15	Arsenal	38	12	12	14	51	63	36
16	Sunderland	38	16	3	19	78	75	35
17	Sheffield United	38	12	11	15	52	58	35
18	Notts County	38	13	8	17	39	51	34
19	Bolton Wanderers	38	14	5	19	52	58	33
20	Birmingham City	38	9	12	17	40	60	30

APPEARANCES

PLAYER	LGE	FAC	TOT
Meredith	37	4	41
Bannister	36	4	40
Wall	36	4	40
Bell	35	4	39
Duckworth	35	3	38
Roberts	32	3	35
Turnbull A	30	4	34
Moger	29	4	33
Burgess	27	3	30
Holden	26	3	29
Turnbull J	26	3	29
Stacey	18	3	21
Downie	10	–	10
Broomfield	9	–	9
Picken	8	–	8
Halse	6	–	6
Menzies	6	–	6
Berry	3	1	4
Thomson	3	–	3
McGillivray	1	1	2
Dalton	1	–	1
Hulme	1	–	1
Whiteside	1	–	1
Williams	1	–	1
Wilson	1	–	1

GOALSCORERS

PLAYER	LGE	FAC	TOT
Turnbull A	25	2	27
Wall	19	3	22
Turnbull J	10	1	11
Meredith	10	–	10
Bannister	5	1	6
Halse	4	–	4
Roberts	2	–	2
Bell	1	–	1
Berry	1	–	1
Picken	1	–	1
Stacey	1	–	1
own goals	2	–	2

1908/09

FOOTBALL LEAGUE DIVISION ONE

DATE	OPPONENTS	SCORE	GOALSCORERS	ATTENDANCE
Sep 5	Preston North End	3–0	Turnbull J 2, Halse	18,000
Sep 7	BURY	2–1	Turnbull J 2	16,000
Sep 12	MIDDLESBROUGH	6–3	Turnbull J 4, Halse, Wall	25,000
Sep 19	Manchester City	2–1	Halse, Turnbull J	40,000
Sep 26	LIVERPOOL	3–2	Halse 2, Turnbull J	25,000
Oct 3	Bury	2–2	Halse, Wall	25,000
Oct 10	SHEFFIELD UNITED	2–1	Bell 2	14,000
Oct 17	Aston Villa	1–3	Halse	40,000
Oct 24	NOTTINGHAM FOREST	2–2	Turnbull A 2	20,000
Oct 31	Sunderland	1–6	Turnbull A	30,000
Nov 7	CHELSEA	0–1		15,000
Nov 14	Blackburn Rovers	3–1	Halse, Turnbull J, Wall	25,000
Nov 21	BRADFORD CITY	2–0	Picken, Wall	15,000
Nov 28	SHEFFIELD WEDNESDAY	3–1	Halse, Picken, Turnbull J	20,000
Dec 5	Everton	2–3	Bannister, Halse	35,000
Dec 12	LEICESTER CITY	4–2	Wall 3, Picken	10,000
Dec 19	Arsenal	1–0	Halse	10,000
Dec 25	Newcastle United	1–2	Wall	35,000
Dec 26	NEWCASTLE UNITED	1–0	Halse	40,000
Jan 1	NOTTS COUNTY	4–3	Halse 2, Roberts, Turnbull A	15,000
Jan 2	PRESTON NORTH END	0–2		18,000
Jan 9	Middlesbrough	0–5		15,000
Jan 23	MANCHESTER CITY	3–1	Livingstone 2, Wall	40,000
Jan 30	Liverpool	1–3	Turnbull A	30,000
Feb 13	Sheffield United	0–0		12,000
Feb 27	Nottingham Forest	0–2		7,000
Mar 13	Chelsea	1–1	Wall	30,000
Mar 15	SUNDERLAND	2–2	Payne, Turnbull J	10,000
Mar 20	BLACKBURN ROVERS	0–3		11,000
Mar 31	ASTON VILLA	0–2		10,000
Apr 3	Sheffield Wednesday	0–2		15,000
Apr 9	BRISTOL CITY	0–1		18,000
Apr 10	EVERTON	2–2	Turnbull J 2	8,000
Apr 12	Bristol City	0–0		18,000
Apr 13	Notts County	1–0	Livingstone	7,000
Apr 17	Leicester City	2–3	Turnbull J, Wall	8,000
Apr 27	ARSENAL	1–4	Turnbull J	10,000
Apr 29	Bradford City	0–1		30,000

FA CUP

DATE	OPPONENTS	SCORE	GOALSCORERS	ATTENDANCE
Jan 16	BRIGHTON (Rd1)	1–0	Halse	8,300
Feb 6	EVERTON (Rd2)	1–0	Halse	35,217
Feb 20	BLACKBURN ROVERS (Rd3)	6–1	Turnbull A 3, Turnbull J 3	38,500
Mar 10	Burnley (Rd4)	3–2	Turnbull J 2, Halse	16,850
Mar 27	Newcastle United (SF) (at Bramall Lane, Sheffield)	1–0	Halse	40,118
Apr 24	Bristol City (Final) (at Crystal Palace)	1–0	Turnbull A	71,401

FINAL LEAGUE TABLE

		P	W	D	L	F	A	Pts
1	Newcastle United	38	24	5	9	65	41	53
2	Everton	38	18	10	10	82	57	46
3	Sunderland	38	21	2	15	78	63	44
4	Blackburn Rovers	38	14	13	11	61	50	41
5	Sheffield Wednesday	38	17	6	15	67	61	40
6	Arsenal	38	14	10	14	52	49	38
7	Aston Villa	38	14	10	14	58	56	38
8	Bristol City	38	13	12	13	45	58	38
9	Middlesbrough	38	14	9	15	59	53	37
10	Preston North End	38	13	11	14	48	44	37
11	Chelsea	38	14	9	15	56	61	37
12	Sheffield United	38	14	9	15	51	59	37
13	MANCHESTER UNITED	38	15	7	16	58	68	37
14	Nottingham Forest	38	14	8	16	66	57	36
15	Notts County	38	14	8	16	51	48	36
16	Liverpool	38	15	6	17	57	65	36
17	Bury	38	14	8	16	63	77	36
18	Bradford City	38	12	10	16	47	47	34
19	Manchester City	38	15	4	19	67	69	34
20	Leicester City	38	8	9	21	54	102	25

APPEARANCES

PLAYER	LGE	FAC	TOT
Moger	36	6	42
Wall	34	6	40
Duckworth	33	6	39
Meredith	34	4	38
Stacey	32	6	38
Halse	29	6	35
Roberts	27	6	33
Hayes	22	6	28
Turnbull J	22	6	28
Bell	20	6	26
Turnbull A	19	6	25
Downie	23	–	23
Bannister	16	–	16
Livingstone	11	2	13
Picken	13	–	13
Linkson	10	–	10
Curry	8	–	8
Burgess	4	–	4
Ford	4	–	4
Hardman	4	–	4
Hulme	3	–	3
Christie	2	–	2
Holden	2	–	2
McGillivray	2	–	2
Payne	2	–	2
Wilcox	2	–	2
Berry	1	–	1
Donnelly	1	–	1
Quinn	1	–	1
Thomson	1	–	1

GOALSCORERS

PLAYER	LGE	FAC	TOT
Turnbull J	17	5	22
Wall	11	–	11
Halse	5	4	9
Livingstone	3	–	3
Picken	3	–	3
Bell	2	–	2
Bannister	1	–	1
Payne	1	–	1
Roberts	1	–	1

1909/10

FOOTBALL LEAGUE DIVISION ONE

DATE	OPPONENTS	SCORE	GOALSCORERS	ATTENDANCE
Sep 1	BRADFORD CITY	1–0	Wall	12,000
Sep 4	BURY	2–0	Turnbull J 2	12,000
Sep 6	NOTTS COUNTY	2–1	Turnbull J, Wall	6,000
Sep 11	Tottenham Hotspur	2–2	Turnbull J, Wall	40,000
Sep 18	PRESTON NORTH END	1–1	Roberts	13,000
Sep 25	Notts County	2–3	Turnbull A 2	11,000
Oct 2	NEWCASTLE UNITED	1–1	Wall	30,000
Oct 9	Liverpool	2–3	Turnbull A 2	30,000
Oct 16	ASTON VILLA	2–0	Halse, Turnbull A	20,000
Oct 23	Sheffield United	1–0	Wall	30,000
Oct 30	ARSENAL	1–0	Wall	20,000
Nov 6	Bolton Wanderers	3–2	Homer 2, Halse	20,000
Nov 13	CHELSEA	2–0	Turnbull A, Wall	10,000
Nov 20	Blackburn Rovers	2–3	Homer 2	40,000
Nov 27	NOTTINGHAM FOREST	2–6	Halse, Wall	12,000
Dec 4	Sunderland	0–3		12,000
Dec 18	Middlesbrough	2–1	Homer, Turnbull A	10,000
Dec 25	SHEFFIELD WEDNESDAY	0–3		25,000
Dec 27	Sheffield Wednesday	1–4	Wall	37,000
Jan 1	Bradford City	2–0	Turnbull A, Wall	25,000
Jan 8	Bury	1–1	Homer	10,000
Jan 22	TOTTENHAM HOTSPUR	5–0	Roberts 2, Connor, Hooper, Meredith	7,000
Feb 5	Preston North End	0–1		4,000
Feb 12	Newcastle United	4–3	Turnbull A 2, Blott, Roberts	20,000
Feb 19	LIVERPOOL	3–4	Homer, Turnbull A, Wall	45,000
Feb 26	Aston Villa	1–7	Meredith	20,000
Mar 5	SHEFFIELD UNITED	1–0	Picken	40,000
Mar 12	Arsenal	0–0		4,000
Mar 19	BOLTON WANDERERS	5–0	Halse, Meredith, Picken, Turnbull J, Wall	20,000
Mar 25	BRISTOL CITY	2–1	Turnbull J, Picken	50,000
Mar 26	Chelsea	1–1	Turnbull J	25,000
Mar 28	Bristol City	1–2	Meredith	18,000
Apr 2	BLACKBURN ROVERS	2–0	Halse 2	20,000
Apr 6	EVERTON	3–2	Turnbull J 2, Meredith	5,500
Apr 9	Nottingham Forest	0–2		7,000
Apr 16	SUNDERLAND	2–0	Turnbull A, Wall	12,000
Apr 23	Everton	3–3	Homer, Turnbull A, Wall	10,000
Apr 30	MIDDLESBROUGH	4–1	Picken 4	10,000

FA CUP

DATE	OPPONENTS	SCORE	GOALSCORERS	ATTENDANCE
Jan 15	Burnley (Rd1)	0–2		16,628

FINAL LEAGUE TABLE

		P	W	D	L	F	A	Pts
1	Aston Villa	38	23	7	8	84	42	53
2	Liverpool	38	21	6	11	78	57	48
3	Blackburn Rovers	38	18	9	11	73	55	45
4	Newcastle United	38	19	7	12	70	56	45
5	MANCHESTER UNITED	38	19	7	12	69	61	45
6	Sheffield United	38	16	10	12	62	41	42
7	Bradford City	38	17	8	13	64	47	42
8	Sunderland	38	18	5	15	66	51	41
9	Notts County	38	15	10	13	67	59	40
10	Everton	38	16	8	14	51	56	40
11	Sheffield Wednesday	38	15	9	14	60	63	39
12	Preston North End	38	15	5	18	52	58	35
13	Bury	38	12	9	17	62	66	33
14	Nottingham Forest	38	11	11	16	54	72	33
15	Tottenham Hotspur	38	11	10	17	53	69	32
16	Bristol City	38	12	8	18	45	60	32
17	Middlesbrough	38	11	9	18	56	73	31
18	Arsenal	38	11	9	18	37	67	31
19	Chelsea	38	11	7	20	47	70	29
20	Bolton Wanderers	38	9	6	23	44	71	24

APPEARANCES

PLAYER	LGE	FAC	TOT
Moger	36	1	37
Stacey	32	1	33
Wall	32	1	33
Meredith	31	1	32
Hayes	30	1	31
Duckworth	29	1	30
Roberts	28	1	29
Halse	27	1	28
Bell	27	–	27
Turnbull A	26	1	27
Picken	19	1	20
Turnbull J	19	–	19
Homer	17	–	17
Livingstone	16	–	16
Blott	10	–	10
Whalley	9	–	9
Connor	8	–	8
Holden	7	–	7
Donnelly	4	–	4
Downie	3	–	3
Hooper	2	–	2
Round	2	–	2
Bannister	1	–	1
Burgess	1	–	1
Curry	–	1	1
Ford	1	–	1
Quinn	1	–	1

GOALSCORERS

PLAYER	LGE	FAC	TOT
Wall	14	–	14
Turnbull A	13	–	13
Turnbull J	9	–	9
Homer	8	–	8
Picken	7	–	7
Halse	6	–	6
Meredith	5	–	5
Roberts	4	–	4
Connor	1	–	1
Hooper	1	–	1

1910/11

FOOTBALL LEAGUE DIVISION ONE

DATE	OPPONENTS	SCORE	GOALSCORERS	ATTENDANCE
Sep 1	Arsenal	2-1	Halse, West	15,000
Sep 3	BLACKBURN ROVERS	3-2	Meredith, Turnbull, West	40,000
Sep 10	Nottingham Forest	1-2	Turnbull	20,000
Sep 17	MANCHESTER CITY	2-1	Turnbull, West	60,000
Sep 24	Everton	1-0	Turnbull	25,000
Oct 1	SHEFFIELD WEDNESDAY	3-2	Wall 2, West	20,000
Oct 8	Bristol City	1-0	Halse	20,000
Oct 15	NEWCASTLE UNITED	2-0	Halse, Turnbull	50,000
Oct 22	Tottenham Hotspur	2-2	West 2	30,000
Oct 29	MIDDLESBROUGH	1-2	Turnbull	35,000
Nov 5	Preston North End	2-0	Turnbull, West	13,000
Nov 12	NOTTS COUNTY	0-0		13,000
Nov 19	Oldham Athletic	3-1	Turnbull 2, Wall	25,000
Nov 26	Liverpool	2-3	Roberts, Turnbull	8,000
Dec 3	BURY	3-2	Homer 2, Turnbull	7,000
Dec 10	Sheffield United	0-2		8,000
Dec 17	ASTON VILLA	2-0	Turnbull, West	20,000
Dec 24	Sunderland	2-1	Meredith, Turnbull	30,000
Dec 26	ARSENAL	5-0	Picken 2, West 2, Meredith	40,000
Dec 27	Bradford City	0-1		35,000
Dec 31	Blackburn Rovers	0-1		20,000
Jan 2	BRADFORD CITY	1-0	Meredith	40,000
Jan 7	NOTTINGHAM FOREST	4-2	Homer, Picken, Wall, og	10,000
Jan 21	Manchester City	1-1	Turnbull	40,000
Jan 28	EVERTON	2-2	Duckworth, Wall	45,000
Feb 11	BRISTOL CITY	3-1	Homer, Picken, West	14,000
Feb 18	Newcastle United	1-0	Halse	45,000
Mar 4	Middlesbrough	2-2	Turnbull, West	8,000
Mar 11	PRESTON NORTH END	5-0	West 2, Connor, Duckworth, Turnbull	25,000
Mar 15	TOTTENHAM HOTSPUR	3-2	Meredith, Turnbull, West	10,000
Mar 18	Notts County	0-1		12,000
Mar 25	OLDHAM ATHLETIC	0-0		35,000
Apr 1	LIVERPOOL	2-0	West 2	20,000
Apr 8	Bury	3-0	Homer 2, Halse	20,000
Apr 15	SHEFFIELD UNITED	1-1	West	22,000
Apr 17	Sheffield Wednesday	0-0		25,000
Apr 22	Aston Villa	2-4	Halse 2	50,000
Apr 29	SUNDERLAND	5-1	Halse 2, Turnbull, West, og	10,000

FA CUP

DATE	OPPONENTS	SCORE	GOALSCORERS	ATTENDANCE
Jan 14	Blackpool (Rd1)	2-1	Picken, West	12,000
Feb 4	ASTON VILLA (Rd2)	2-1	Halse, Wall	65,101
Feb 25	West Ham United (Rd3)	1-2	Turnbull	26,000

FINAL LEAGUE TABLE

		P	W	D	L	F	A	Pts
1	MANCHESTER UNITED	38	22	8	8	72	40	52
2	Aston Villa	38	22	7	9	69	41	51
3	Sunderland	38	15	15	8	67	48	45
4	Everton	38	19	7	12	50	36	45
5	Bradford City	38	20	5	13	51	42	45
6	Sheffield Wednesday	38	17	8	13	47	48	42
7	Oldham Athletic	38	16	9	13	44	41	41
8	Newcastle United	38	15	10	13	61	43	40
9	Sheffield United	38	15	8	15	49	43	38
10	Arsenal	38	13	12	13	41	49	38
11	Notts County	38	14	10	14	37	45	38
12	Blackburn Rovers	38	13	11	14	62	54	37
13	Liverpool	38	15	7	16	53	53	37
14	Preston North End	38	12	11	15	40	49	35
15	Tottenham Hotspur	38	13	6	19	52	63	32
16	Middlesbrough	38	11	10	17	49	63	32
17	Manchester City	38	9	13	16	43	58	31
18	Bury	38	9	11	18	43	71	29
19	Bristol City	38	11	5	22	43	66	27
20	Nottingham Forest	38	9	7	22	55	75	25

APPEARANCES

PLAYER	LGE	FAC	TOT
Stacey	36	3	39
Meredith	35	3	38
Turnbull	35	3	38
West	35	3	38
Roberts	33	3	36
Bell	27	3	30
Wall	26	3	29
Moger	25	2	27
Duckworth	22	3	25
Halse	23	2	25
Donnelly	15	3	18
Picken	14	1	15
Whalley	15	–	15
Edmonds	13	1	14
Livingstone	10	–	10
Hofton	9	–	9
Holden	8	–	8
Connor	7	–	7
Homer	7	–	7
Linkson	7	–	7
Curry	5	–	5
Sheldon	5	–	5
Hodge	2	–	2
Hooper	2	–	2
Blott	1	–	1
Hayes	1	–	1

GOALSCORERS

PLAYER	LGE	FAC	TOT
West	19	1	20
Turnbull	18	1	19
Halse	9	1	10
Homer	6	–	6
Wall	5	1	6
Meredith	5	–	5
Picken	4	1	5
Duckworth	2	–	2
Connor	1	–	1
Roberts	1	–	1
own goals	2	–	2

1911/12

FOOTBALL LEAGUE DIVISION ONE

DATE	OPPONENTS	SCORE	GOALSCORERS	ATTENDANCE
Sep 2	Manchester City	0-0		35,000
Sep 9	EVERTON	2-1	Halse, Turnbull	20,000
Sep 16	West Bromwich Albion	0-1		35,000
Sep 23	SUNDERLAND	2-2	Stacey 2	20,000
Sep 30	Blackburn Rovers	2-2	West 2	30,000
Oct 7	SHEFFIELD WEDNESDAY	3-1	Halse 2, West	30,000
Oct 14	Bury	1-0	Turnbull	18,000
Oct 21	MIDDLESBROUGH	3-4	Halse, Turnbull, West	20,000
Oct 28	Notts County	1-0	Turnbull	15,000
Nov 4	TOTTENHAM HOTSPUR	1-0	West	20,000
Nov 11	PRESTON NORTH END	0-0		10,000
Nov 18	Liverpool	2-3	Roberts, West	15,000
Nov 25	ASTON VILLA	3-1	West 2, Roberts	20,000
Dec 2	Newcastle United	3-2	West 2, Halse	40,000
Dec 9	SHEFFIELD UNITED	1-0	Halse	12,000
Dec 16	Oldham Athletic	2-2	Turnbull, West	20,000
Dec 23	BOLTON WANDERERS	2-0	Halse, Turnbull	20,000
Dec 25	BRADFORD CITY	0-1		50,000
Dec 26	Bradford City	1-0	West	40,000
Dec 30	MANCHESTER CITY	0-0		50,000
Jan 1	ARSENAL	2-0	Meredith, West	20,000
Jan 6	Everton	0-4		12,000
Jan 20	WEST BROMWICH ALBION	1-2	Wall	8,000
Jan 27	Sunderland	0-5		12,000
Feb 10	Sheffield Wednesday	0-3		25,000
Feb 17	BURY	0-0		6,000
Mar 2	NOTTS COUNTY	2-0	West 2	10,000
Mar 16	Preston North End	0-0		7,000
Mar 23	LIVERPOOL	1-1	Nuttall	10,000
Mar 30	Aston Villa	0-6		15,000
Apr 5	Arsenal	1-2	Turnbull	14,000
Apr 6	NEWCASTLE UNITED	0-2		14,000
Apr 9	Tottenham Hotspur	1-1	Wall	20,000
Apr 13	Sheffield United	1-6	Nuttall	7,000
Apr 17	Middlesbrough	0-3		5,000
Apr 20	OLDHAM ATHLETIC	3-1	West 2, Wall	15,000
Apr 27	Bolton Wanderers	1-1	Meredith	20,000
Apr 29	BLACKBURN ROVERS	3-1	Hamill, Meredith, West	20,000

FA CUP

DATE	OPPONENTS	SCORE	GOALSCORERS	ATTENDANCE
Jan 13	HUDDERSFIELD TOWN (Rd1)	3-1	West 2, Halse	19,579
Feb 3	Coventry City (Rd2)	5-1	Halse 2, Turnbull, Wall, West	17,130
Feb 24	Reading (Rd3)	1-1	West	24,069
Feb 29	READING (Rd3R)	3-0	Turnbull 2, Halse	29,511
Mar 9	BLACKBURN ROVERS (Rd4)	1-1	og	59,300
Mar 14	Blackburn Rovers (Rd4R)	2-4	West 2	39,296

FINAL LEAGUE TABLE

		P	W	D	L	F	A	Pts
1	Blackburn Rovers	38	20	9	9	60	43	49
2	Everton	38	20	6	12	46	42	46
3	Newcastle United	38	18	8	12	64	50	44
4	Bolton Wanderers	38	20	3	15	54	43	43
5	Sheffield Wednesday	38	16	9	13	69	49	41
6	Aston Villa	38	17	7	14	76	63	41
7	Middlesbrough	38	16	8	14	56	45	40
8	Sunderland	38	14	11	13	58	51	39
9	West Bromwich Albion	38	15	9	14	43	47	39
10	Arsenal	38	15	8	15	55	59	38
11	Bradford City	38	15	8	15	46	50	38
12	Tottenham Hotspur	38	14	9	15	53	53	37
13	MANCHESTER UNITED	38	13	11	14	45	60	37
14	Sheffield United	38	13	10	15	63	56	36
15	Manchester City	38	13	9	16	56	58	35
16	Notts County	38	14	7	17	46	63	35
17	Liverpool	38	12	10	16	49	55	34
18	Oldham Athletic	38	12	10	16	46	54	34
19	Preston North End	38	13	7	18	40	57	33
20	Bury	38	6	9	23	32	59	21

APPEARANCES

PLAYER	LGE	FAC	TOT
Meredith	35	6	41
Wall	33	6	39
Bell	32	6	38
West	32	6	38
Roberts	32	5	37
Edmonds	30	6	36
Turnbull	30	6	36
Stacey	29	6	35
Duckworth	26	6	32
Halse	24	6	30
Linkson	21	4	25
Hamill	16	–	16
Donnelly	13	–	13
Hodge	10	–	10
Holden	6	2	8
Hofton	7	–	7
Knowles	7	–	7
Blott	6	–	6
Moger	6	–	6
Nuttall	6	–	6
Whalley	5	1	6
Sheldon	5	–	5
Royals	2	–	2
Anderson	1	–	1
Capper	1	–	1
Homer	1	–	1
Livingstone	1	–	1
McCarthy	1	–	1

GOALSCORERS

PLAYER	LGE	FAC	TOT
West	17	6	23
Halse	8	4	12
Turnbull	7	3	10
Wall	3	1	4
Meredith	3	–	3
Roberts	2	–	2
Stacey	2	–	2
Hamill	1	–	1
own goal	–	1	1

1912/13

FOOTBALL LEAGUE DIVISION ONE

DATE	OPPONENTS	SCORE	GOALSCORERS	ATTENDANCE
Sep 2	Arsenal	0-0		11,000
Sep 7	MANCHESTER CITY	0-1		40,000
Sep 14	West Bromwich Albion	2-1	Livingstone, Turnbull	25,000
Sep 21	EVERTON	2-0	West 2	40,000
Sep 28	Sheffield Wednesday	3-3	West 2, Turnbull	30,000
Oct 5	BLACKBURN ROVERS	1-1	Wall	45,000
Oct 12	Derby County	1-2	Turnbull	15,000
Oct 19	TOTTENHAM HOTSPUR	2-0	Turnbull, West	12,000
Oct 26	Middlesbrough	2-3	Nuttall 2	10,000
Nov 2	NOTTS COUNTY	2-1	Anderson, Meredith	12,000
Nov 9	Sunderland	1-3	West	20,000
Nov 16	Aston Villa	2-4	Wall, West	20,000
Nov 23	LIVERPOOL	3-1	Anderson 2, Wall	8,000
Nov 30	Bolton Wanderers	1-2	Wall	25,000
Dec 7	SHEFFIELD UNITED	4-0	Anderson, Turnbull, Wall, West	12,000
Dec 14	Newcastle United	3-1	West 3	20,000
Dec 21	OLDHAM ATHLETIC	0-0		30,000
Dec 25	Chelsea	4-1	West 2, Anderson, Whalley	33,000
Dec 26	CHELSEA	4-2	Turnbull 2, Anderson, Wall	20,000
Dec 28	Manchester City	2-0	West 2	38,000
Jan 1	BRADFORD CITY	2-0	Anderson 2	30,000
Jan 4	WEST BROMWICH ALBION	1-1	Roberts	25,000
Jan 18	Everton	1-4	Hamill	20,000
Jan 25	SHEFFIELD WEDNESDAY	2-0	West, Whalley	45,000
Feb 8	Blackburn Rovers	0-0		38,000
Feb 15	DERBY COUNTY	4-0	West 2, Anderson, Turnbull	30,000
Mar 1	MIDDLESBROUGH	2-3	Meredith, Whalley	15,000
Mar 8	Notts County	2-1	Anderson, Turnbull	10,000
Mar 15	SUNDERLAND	1-3	Sheldon	15,000
Mar 21	ARSENAL	2-0	Anderson, Whalley	20,000
Mar 22	ASTON VILLA	4-0	Stacey, Turnbull, Wall, West	30,000
Mar 25	Bradford City	0-1		25,000
Mar 29	Liverpool	2-0	Wall, West	12,000
Mar 31	Tottenham Hotspur	1-1	Blott	12,000
Apr 5	BOLTON WANDERERS	2-1	Anderson, Wall	30,000
Apr 12	Sheffield United	1-2	Wall	12,000
Apr 19	NEWCASTLE UNITED	3-0	Hunter 2, West	10,000
Apr 26	Oldham Athletic	0-0		3,000

FA CUP

DATE	OPPONENTS	SCORE	GOALSCORERS	ATTENDANCE
Jan 11	COVENTRY CITY (Rd1)	1-1	Wall	11,500
Jan 16	Coventry City (Rd1R)	2-1	Anderson, Roberts	20,042
Feb 1	Plymouth Argyle (Rd2)	2-0	Anderson, Wall	21,700
Feb 22	Oldham Athletic (Rd3)	0-0		26,932
Feb 26	OLDHAM ATHLETIC (Rd3R)	1-2	West	31,180

FINAL LEAGUE TABLE

		P	W	D	L	F	A	Pts
1	Sunderland	38	25	4	9	86	43	54
2	Aston Villa	38	19	12	7	86	52	50
3	Sheffield Wednesday	38	21	7	10	75	55	49
4	MANCHESTER UNITED	38	19	8	11	69	43	46
5	Blackburn Rovers	38	16	13	9	79	43	45
6	Manchester City	38	18	8	12	53	37	44
7	Derby County	38	17	8	13	69	66	42
8	Bolton Wanderers	38	16	10	12	62	63	42
9	Oldham Athletic	38	14	14	10	50	55	42
10	West Bromwich Albion	38	13	12	13	57	50	38
11	Everton	38	15	7	16	48	54	37
12	Liverpool	38	16	5	17	61	71	37
13	Bradford City	38	12	11	15	50	60	35
14	Newcastle United	38	13	8	17	47	47	34
15	Sheffield United	38	14	6	18	56	70	34
16	Middlesbrough	38	11	10	17	55	69	32
17	Tottenham Hotspur	38	12	6	20	45	72	30
18	Chelsea	38	11	6	21	51	73	28
19	Notts County	38	7	9	22	28	56	23
20	Arsenal	38	3	12	23	26	74	18

APPEARANCES

PLAYER	LGE	FAC	TOT
Beale	37	5	42
Stacey	36	5	41
Wall	36	5	41
West	36	4	40
Turnbull	35	4	39
Whalley	26	5	31
Anderson	24	5	29
Duckworth	24	5	29
Roberts	24	5	29
Meredith	22	5	27
Bell	26	–	26
Hodge	19	5	24
Hamill	15	2	17
Linkson	17	–	17
Sheldon	16	–	16
Nuttall	10	–	10
Hunter	3	–	3
Blott	2	–	2
Gipps	2	–	2
Holden	2	–	2
Knowles	2	–	2
Livingstone	2	–	2
Donnelly	1	–	1
Mew	1	–	1

GOALSCORERS

PLAYER	LGE	FAC	TOT
West	21	1	22
Anderson	12	2	14
Wall	10	2	12
Turnbull	10	–	10
Whalley	4	–	4
Hunter	2	–	2
Meredith	2	–	2
Nuttall	2	–	2
Roberts	1	1	2
Blott	1	–	1
Hamill	1	–	1
Livingstone	1	–	1
Sheldon	1	–	1
Stacey	1	–	1

1913/14

FOOTBALL LEAGUE DIVISION ONE

DATE	OPPONENTS	SCORE	GOALSCORERS	ATTENDANCE
Sep 6	Sheffield Wednesday	3-1	Turnbull, West, og	32,000
Sep 8	SUNDERLAND	3-1	Anderson, Turnbull, Whalley	25,000
Sep 13	BOLTON WANDERERS	0-1		45,000
Sep 20	Chelsea	2-0	Anderson, Wall	40,000
Sep 27	OLDHAM ATHLETIC	4-1	West 2, Anderson, Wall	55,000
Oct 4	TOTTENHAM HOTSPUR	3-1	Stacey, Wall, Whalley	25,000
Oct 11	Burnley	2-1	Anderson 2	30,000
Oct 18	PRESTON NORTH END	3-0	Anderson 3	30,000
Oct 25	Newcastle United	1-0	West	35,000
Nov 1	LIVERPOOL	3-0	Wall 2, West	30,000
Nov 8	Aston Villa	1-3	Woodcock	20,000
Nov 15	MIDDLESBROUGH	0-1		15,000
Nov 22	Sheffield United	0-2		30,000
Nov 29	DERBY COUNTY	3-3	Turnbull 2, Meredith	20,000
Dec 6	Manchester City	2-0	Anderson 2	40,000
Dec 13	BRADFORD CITY	1-1	Knowles	18,000
Dec 20	Blackburn Rovers	1-0	og	35,000
Dec 25	EVERTON	0-1		25,000
Dec 26	Everton	0-5		40,000
Dec 27	SHEFFIELD WEDNESDAY	2-1	Meredith, Wall	10,000
Jan 1	WEST BROMWICH ALBION	1-0	Wall	35,000
Jan 3	Bolton Wanderers	1-6	West	35,000
Jan 17	CHELSEA	0-1		20,000
Jan 24	OLDHAM ATHLETIC	2-2	Wall, Woodcock	10,000
Feb 7	Tottenham Hotspur	1-2	Wall	22,000
Feb 14	BURNLEY	0-1		35,000
Feb 21	Middlesbrough	1-3	Anderson	12,000
Feb 28	NEWCASTLE UNITED	2-2	Anderson, Potts	30,000
Mar 5	Preston North End	2-4	Travers, Wall	12,000
Mar 14	ASTON VILLA	0-6		30,000
Apr 4	Derby County	2-4	Anderson, Travers	7,000
Apr 10	Sunderland	0-2		20,000
Apr 11	MANCHESTER CITY	0-1		36,000
Apr 13	West Bromwich Albion	1-2	Travers	20,000
Apr 15	Liverpool	2-1	Travers, Wall	28,000
Apr 18	Bradford City	1-1	Thomson	10,000
Apr 22	SHEFFIELD UNITED	2-1	Anderson 2	4,500
Apr 25	BLACKBURN ROVERS	0-0		20,000

FA CUP

DATE	OPPONENTS	SCORE	GOALSCORERS	ATTENDANCE
Jan 10	Swindon Town (Rd1)	0-1		18,187

FINAL LEAGUE TABLE

		P	W	D	L	F	A	Pts
1	Blackburn Rovers	38	20	11	7	78	42	51
2	Aston Villa	38	19	6	13	65	50	44
3	Middlesbrough	38	19	5	14	77	60	43
4	Oldham Athletic	38	17	9	12	55	45	43
5	West Bromwich Albion	38	15	13	10	46	42	43
6	Bolton Wanderers	38	16	10	12	65	52	42
7	Sunderland	38	17	6	15	63	52	40
8	Chelsea	38	16	7	15	46	55	39
9	Bradford City	38	12	14	12	40	40	38
10	Sheffield United	38	16	5	17	63	60	37
11	Newcastle United	38	13	11	14	39	48	37
12	Burnley	38	12	12	14	61	53	36
13	Manchester City	38	14	8	16	51	53	36
14	MANCHESTER UNITED	38	15	6	17	52	62	36
15	Everton	38	12	11	15	46	55	35
16	Liverpool	38	14	7	17	46	62	35
17	Tottenham Hotspur	38	12	10	16	50	62	34
18	Sheffield Wednesday	38	13	8	17	53	70	34
19	Preston North End	38	12	6	20	52	69	30
20	Derby County	38	8	11	19	55	71	27

APPEARANCES

PLAYER	LGE	FAC	TOT
Meredith	34	1	35
Stacey	34	1	35
Anderson	32	–	32
Beale	31	1	32
West	30	1	31
Wall	29	1	30
Hodge, James	28	1	29
Hamill	26	–	26
Knowles	18	1	19
Whalley	18	1	19
Turnbull	17	1	18
Haywood	14	–	14
Travers	13	–	13
Woodcock	11	1	12
Gipps	11	–	11
Duckworth	9	–	9
Hudson	9	–	9
Norton	8	–	8
Hunter	7	–	7
Potts	6	–	6
Thomson	6	–	6
Royals	5	–	5
Chorlton	4	–	4
Hodge, John	4	–	4
Livingstone	3	1	4
Cashmore	3	–	3
Hooper	3	–	3
Mew	2	–	2
Roberts	2	–	2
Rowe	1	–	1

GOALSCORERS

PLAYER	LGE	FAC	TOT
Anderson	15	–	15
Wall	11	–	11
West	6	–	6
Travers	4	–	4
Turnbull	4	–	4
Meredith	2	–	2
Whalley	2	–	2
Woodcock	2	–	2
Knowles	1	–	1
Potts	1	–	1
Stacey	1	–	1
Thomson	1	–	1
own goals	2	–	2

1914/15

FOOTBALL LEAGUE DIVISION ONE

DATE	OPPONENTS	SCORE	GOALSCORERS	ATTENDANCE
Sep 2	OLDHAM ATHLETIC	1-3	O'Connell	13,000
Sep 5	MANCHESTER CITY	0-0		20,000
Sep 12	Bolton Wanderers	0-3		10,000
Sep 19	BLACKBURN ROVERS	2-0	West 2	15,000
Sep 26	Notts County	2-4	Turnbull, Wall	12,000
Oct 3	SUNDERLAND	3-0	Anderson, Stacey, West	16,000
Oct 10	Sheffield Wednesday	0-1		19,000
Oct 17	WEST BROMWICH ALBION	0-0		18,000
Oct 24	Everton	2-4	Anderson, Wall	15,000
Oct 31	CHELSEA	2-2	Anderson, Hunter	15,000
Nov 7	Bradford City	2-4	Hunter, West	12,000
Nov 14	BURNLEY	0-2		12,000
Nov 21	Tottenham Hotspur	0-2		12,000
Nov 28	NEWCASTLE UNITED	1-0	West	5,000
Dec 5	Middlesbrough	1-1	Anderson	7,000
Dec 12	SHEFFIELD UNITED	1-2	Anderson	8,000
Dec 19	Aston Villa	3-3	Norton 2, Anderson	10,000
Dec 26	Liverpool	1-1	Stacey	25,000
Jan 1	BRADFORD PARK AVENUE	1-2	Anderson	8,000
Jan 2	Manchester City	1-1	West	30,000
Jan 16	BOLTON WANDERERS	4-1	Potts 2, Stacey, Woodcock	8,000
Jan 23	Blackburn Rovers	3-3	Woodcock 2, og	7,000
Jan 30	NOTTS COUNTY	2-2	Potts, Stacey	7,000
Feb 6	Sunderland	0-1		5,000
Feb 13	SHEFFIELD WEDNESDAY	2-0	West, Woodcock	7,000
Feb 20	West Bromwich Albion	0-0		10,000
Feb 27	EVERTON	1-2	Woodcock	10,000
Mar 13	BRADFORD CITY	1-0	Potts	14,000
Mar 20	Burnley	0-3		12,000
Mar 27	TOTTENHAM HOTSPUR	1-1	Woodcock	15,000
Apr 2	LIVERPOOL	2-0	Anderson 2	18,000
Apr 3	Newcastle United	0-2		12,000
Apr 5	Bradford Park Avenue	0-5		15,000
Apr 6	Oldham Athletic	0-1		2,000
Apr 10	MIDDLESBROUGH	2-2	O'Connell, Turnbull	15,000
Apr 17	Sheffield United	1-3	West	14,000
Apr 19	Chelsea	3-1	Norton, West, Woodcock	13,000
Apr 26	ASTON VILLA	1-0	Anderson	8,000

FA CUP

DATE	OPPONENTS	SCORE	GOALSCORERS	ATTENDANCE
Jan 9	Sheffield Wednesday (Rd1)	0-1		23,248

FINAL LEAGUE TABLE

		P	W	D	L	F	A	Pts
1	Everton	38	19	8	11	76	47	46
2	Oldham Athletic	38	17	11	10	70	56	45
3	Blackburn Rovers	38	18	7	13	83	61	43
4	Burnley	38	18	7	13	61	47	43
5	Manchester City	38	15	13	10	49	39	43
6	Sheffield United	38	15	13	10	49	41	43
7	Sheffield Wednesday	38	15	13	10	61	54	43
8	Sunderland	38	18	5	15	81	72	41
9	Bradford Park Avenue	38	17	7	14	69	65	41
10	West Bromwich Albion	38	15	10	13	49	43	40
11	Bradford City	38	13	14	11	55	49	40
12	Middlesbrough	38	13	12	13	62	74	38
13	Liverpool	38	14	9	15	65	75	37
14	Aston Villa	38	13	11	14	62	72	37
15	Newcastle United	38	11	10	17	46	48	32
16	Notts County	38	9	13	16	41	57	31
17	Bolton Wanderers	38	11	8	19	68	84	30
18	MANCHESTER UNITED	38	9	12	17	46	62	30
19	Chelsea	38	8	13	17	51	65	29
20	Tottenham Hotspur	38	8	12	18	57	90	28

In the summer of 1915 the Football League and the FA Cup were suspended due to the increasing severity of the conflict in Europe. Though not encouraged by the authorities, wartime football was played but the matches were regarded as unofficial and therefore the appearance and goalscoring records were not recognised by the League and are not included in this volume.

APPEARANCES

PLAYER	LGE	FAC	TOT
Beale	37	1	38
O'Connell	34	1	35
West	33	1	34
Norton	29	–	29
Meredith	26	1	27
Hodge, John	26	–	26
Stacey	24	1	25
Anderson	23	1	24
Knowles	19	–	19
Woodcock	19	–	19
Potts	17	1	18
Wall	17	1	18
Hunter	15	1	16
Cookson	12	1	13
Turnbull	13	–	13
Allman	12	–	12
Haywood	12	–	12
Spratt	12	–	12
Montgomery	11	–	11
Gipps	10	–	10
Travers	8	–	8
Hodge, James	4	1	5
Hudson	2	–	2
Mew	1	–	1
Prince	1	–	1
Whalley	1	–	1

GOALSCORERS

PLAYER	LGE	FAC	TOT
Anderson	10	–	10
West	9	–	9
Woodcock	7	–	7
Potts	4	–	4
Stacey	4	–	4
Norton	3	–	3
Hunter	2	–	2
O'Connell	2	–	2
Turnbull	2	–	2
Wall	2	–	2
own goal	1	–	1

1919/20

FOOTBALL LEAGUE DIVISION ONE

DATE	OPPONENTS	SCORE	GOALSCORERS	ATTENDANCE
Aug 30	Derby County	1-1	Woodcock	12,000
Sep 1	SHEFFIELD WEDNESDAY	0-0		13,000
Sep 6	DERBY COUNTY	0-2		15,000
Sep 8	Sheffield Wednesday	3-1	Meehan, Spence, Woodcock	10,000
Sep 13	Preston North End	3-2	Spence 2, Meehan	15,000
Sep 20	PRESTON NORTH END	5-1	Spence 2, Woodcock 2, Montgomery	18,000
Sep 27	Middlesbrough	1-1	Woodcock	20,000
Oct 4	MIDDLESBROUGH	1-1	Woodcock	28,000
Oct 11	Manchester City	3-3	Hodge, Hopkin, Spence	30,000
Oct 18	MANCHESTER CITY	1-0	Spence	40,000
Oct 25	Sheffield United	2-2	Hopkin, Woodcock	18,000
Nov 1	SHEFFIELD UNITED	3-0	Hodges, Spence, Woodcock	24,500
Nov 8	Burnley	1-2	Hodge	15,000
Nov 15	BURNLEY	0-1		25,000
Nov 22	Oldham Athletic	3-0	Hodges, Hopkin, Spence	15,000
Dec 6	Aston Villa	0-2		40,000
Dec 13	ASTON VILLA	1-2	Hilditch	30,000
Dec 20	NEWCASTLE UNITED	2-1	Hodges, Spence	20,000
Dec 26	LIVERPOOL	0-0		45,000
Dec 27	Newcastle United	1-2	Hilditch	45,000
Jan 1	Liverpool	0-0		30,000
Jan 3	CHELSEA	0-2		25,000
Jan 17	Chelsea	0-1		40,000
Jan 24	West Bromwich Albion	1-2	Woodcock	20,000
Feb 7	Sunderland	0-3		25,000
Feb 11	OLDHAM ATHLETIC	1-1	Bissett	15,000
Feb 14	SUNDERLAND	2-0	Harris, Hodges	35,000
Feb 21	Arsenal	3-0	Spence 2, Hopkin	25,000
Feb 25	WEST BROMWICH ALBION	1-2	Spence	20,000
Feb 28	ARSENAL	0-1		20,000
Mar 6	EVERTON	1-0	Bissett	25,000
Mar 13	Everton	0-0		30,000
Mar 20	BRADFORD CITY	0-0		25,000
Mar 27	Bradford City	1-2	Bissett	18,000
Apr 2	BRADFORD PARK AVENUE	0-1		30,000
Apr 3	BOLTON WANDERERS	1-1	Toms	39,000
Apr 6	Bradford Park Avenue	4-1	Bissett, Grimwood, Toms, Woodcock	14,000
Apr 10	Bolton Wanderers	5-3	Bissett 2, Meredith, Toms, Woodcock	25,000
Apr 17	BLACKBURN ROVERS	1-1	Hopkin	40,000
Apr 24	Blackburn Rovers	0-5		30,000
Apr 26	NOTTS COUNTY	0-0		30,000
May 1	Notts County	2-0	Meredith, Spence	20,000

FA CUP

DATE	OPPONENTS	SCORE	GOALSCORERS	ATTENDANCE
Jan 10	Port Vale (Rd1)	1-0	Toms	14,549
Jan 31	ASTON VILLA (Rd2)	1-2	Woodcock	48,600

FINAL LEAGUE TABLE

		P	W	D	L	F	A	Pts
1	West Bromwich Albion	42	28	4	10	104	47	60
2	Burnley	42	21	9	12	65	59	51
3	Chelsea	42	22	5	15	56	51	49
4	Liverpool	42	19	10	13	59	44	48
5	Sunderland	42	22	4	16	72	59	48
6	Bolton Wanderers	42	19	9	14	72	65	47
7	Manchester City	42	18	9	15	71	62	45
8	Newcastle United	42	17	9	16	44	39	43
9	Aston Villa	42	18	6	18	75	73	42
10	Arsenal	42	15	12	15	56	58	42
11	Bradford Park Avenue	42	15	12	15	60	63	42
12	MANCHESTER UNITED	42	13	14	15	54	50	40
13	Middlesbrough	42	15	10	17	61	65	40
14	Sheffield United	42	16	8	18	59	69	40
15	Bradford City	42	14	11	17	54	63	39
16	Everton	42	12	14	16	69	68	38
17	Oldham Athletic	42	15	8	19	49	52	38
18	Derby County	42	13	12	17	47	57	38
19	Preston North End	42	14	10	18	57	73	38
20	Blackburn Rovers	42	13	11	18	64	77	37
21	Notts County	42	12	12	18	56	74	36
22	Sheffield Wednesday	42	7	9	26	28	64	23

APPEARANCES

PLAYER	LGE	FAC	TOT
Mew	42	2	44
Hopkin	39	2	41
Silcock	40	1	41
Meehan	36	2	38
Moore	36	2	38
Hilditch	32	2	34
Spence	32	1	33
Woodcock	28	2	30
Whalley	23	2	25
Grimwood	22	2	24
Bissett	22	–	22
Meredith	19	2	21
Hodges	18	–	18
Hodge	16	–	16
Montgomery	14	–	14
Toms	12	1	13
Barlow	7	–	7
Harris	7	–	7
Forster	5	–	5
Potts	4	1	5
Robinson	2	–	2
Sapsford	2	–	2
Williamson	2	–	2
Prentice	1	–	1
Spratt	1	–	1

GOALSCORERS

PLAYER	LGE	FAC	TOT
Spence	14	–	14
Woodcock	11	1	12
Bissett	6	–	6
Hopkin	5	–	5
Hodges	4	–	4
Toms	3	1	4
Hilditch	2	–	2
Hodge	2	–	2
Meehan	2	–	2
Grimwood	1	–	1
Harris	1	–	1
Montgomery	1	–	1

1920/21

FOOTBALL LEAGUE DIVISION ONE

DATE	OPPONENTS	SCORE	GOALSCORERS	ATTENDANCE
Aug 28	BOLTON WANDERERS	2–3	Hopkin, Meehan	50,000
Aug 30	Arsenal	0–2		40,000
Sep 4	Bolton Wanderers	1–1	Sapsford	35,000
Sep 6	ARSENAL	1–1	Spence	45,000
Sep 11	CHELSEA	3–1	Meehan 2, Leonard	40,000
Sep 18	Chelsea	2–1	Leonard 2	35,000
Sep 25	TOTTENHAM HOTSPUR	0–1		50,000
Oct 2	Tottenham Hotspur	1–4	Spence	45,000
Oct 9	OLDHAM ATHLETIC	4–1	Sapsford 2, Meehan, Miller	50,000
Oct 16	Oldham Athletic	2–2	Spence, og	20,000
Oct 23	PRESTON NORTH END	1–0	Miller	42,000
Oct 30	Preston North End	0–0		25,000
Nov 6	SHEFFIELD UNITED	2–1	Leonard 2	30,000
Nov 13	Sheffield United	0–0		18,000
Nov 20	MANCHESTER CITY	1–1	Miller	63,000
Nov 27	Manchester City	0–3		35,000
Dec 4	BRADFORD PARK AVENUE	5–1	Miller 2, Myerscough 2, Partridge	25,000
Dec 11	Bradford Park Avenue	4–2	Myerscough 2, Miller, Partridge	10,000
Dec 18	NEWCASTLE UNITED	2–0	Hopkin, Miller	40,000
Dec 25	Aston Villa	4–3	Grimwood 2, Harrison, Partridge	38,000
Dec 27	ASTON VILLA	1–3	Harrison	70,504
Jan 1	Newcastle United	3–6	Hopkin, Partridge, Silcock	40,000
Jan 15	WEST BROMWICH ALBION	1–4	Partridge	30,000
Jan 22	West Bromwich Albion	2–0	Myerscough, Partridge	30,000
Feb 5	LIVERPOOL	1–1	Grimwood	30,000
Feb 9	Liverpool	0–2		35,000
Feb 12	EVERTON	1–2	Meredith	30,000
Feb 20	SUNDERLAND	3–0	Harrison, Hilditch, Robinson	40,000
Mar 5	Sunderland	3–2	Sapsford 2, Goodwin	25,000
Mar 9	Everton	0–2		38,000
Mar 12	BRADFORD CITY	1–1	Robinson	30,000
Mar 19	Bradford City	1–1	Sapsford	25,000
Mar 25	Burnley	0–1		20,000
Mar 26	Huddersfield Town	2–5	Harris, Partridge	17,000
Mar 28	BURNLEY	0–3		28,000
Apr 2	HUDDERSFIELD TOWN	2–0	Bissett 2	30,000
Apr 9	Middlesbrough	4–2	Spence 2, Bissett, Grimwood	15,000
Apr 16	MIDDLESBROUGH	0–1		25,000
Apr 23	Blackburn Rovers	0–2		18,000
Apr 30	BLACKBURN ROVERS	0–1		20,000
May 2	Derby County	1–1	Bissett	8,000
May 7	DERBY COUNTY	3–0	Spence 2, Sapsford	10,000

FA CUP

DATE	OPPONENTS	SCORE	GOALSCORERS	ATTENDANCE
Jan 8	Liverpool (Rd1)	1–1	Miller	40,000
Jan 12	LIVERPOOL (Rd1R)	1–2	Partridge	30,000

FINAL LEAGUE TABLE

		P	W	D	L	F	A	Pts
1	Burnley	42	23	13	6	79	36	59
2	Manchester City	42	24	6	12	70	50	54
3	Bolton Wanderers	42	19	14	9	77	53	52
4	Liverpool	42	18	15	9	63	35	51
5	Newcastle United	42	20	10	12	66	45	50
6	Tottenham Hotspur	42	19	9	14	70	48	47
7	Everton	42	17	13	12	66	55	47
8	Middlesbrough	42	17	12	13	53	53	46
9	Arsenal	42	15	14	13	59	63	44
10	Aston Villa	42	18	7	17	63	70	43
11	Blackburn Rovers	42	13	15	14	57	59	41
12	Sunderland	42	14	13	15	57	60	41
13	MANCHESTER UNITED	42	15	10	17	64	68	40
14	West Bromwich Albion	42	13	14	15	54	58	40
15	Bradford City	42	12	15	15	61	63	39
16	Preston North End	42	15	9	18	61	65	39
17	Huddersfield Town	42	15	9	18	42	49	39
18	Chelsea	42	13	13	16	48	58	39
19	Oldham Athletic	42	9	15	18	49	86	33
20	Sheffield United	42	6	18	18	42	68	30
21	Derby County	42	5	16	21	32	58	26
22	Bradford Park Avenue	42	8	8	26	43	76	24

APPEARANCES

PLAYER	LGE	FAC	TOT
Mew	40	2	42
Silcock	37	2	39
Hilditch	34	–	34
Hopkin	31	2	33
Partridge	28	2	30
Harris	26	2	28
Forster	26	1	27
Grimwood	25	2	27
Miller	25	2	27
Moore	26	–	26
Harrison	23	2	25
Sapsford	21	–	21
Barlow	19	1	20
Meehan	15	–	15
Spence	15	–	15
Bissett	12	2	14
Meredith	14	–	14
Myerscough	13	–	13
Leonard	10	–	10
Robinson	7	–	7
Goodwin	5	–	5
Hodges	2	–	2
Hofton	1	1	2
Montgomery	2	–	2
Steward	2	–	2
Albinson	–	1	1
Radford	1	–	1
Schofield	1	–	1
Toms	1	–	1

GOALSCORERS

PLAYER	LGE	FAC	TOT
Miller	7	1	8
Partridge	7	1	8
Sapsford	7	–	7
Spence	7	–	7
Leonard	5	–	5
Myerscough	5	–	5
Bissett	4	–	4
Grimwood	4	–	4
Meehan	4	–	4
Harrison	3	–	3
Hopkin	3	–	3
Robinson	2	–	2
Goodwin	1	–	1
Harris	1	–	1
Hilditch	1	–	1
Meredith	1	–	1
Silcock	1	–	1
own goal	1	–	1

1921/22

FOOTBALL LEAGUE DIVISION ONE

DATE	OPPONENTS	SCORE	GOALSCORERS	ATTENDANCE
Aug 27	Everton	0–5		30,000
Aug 29	WEST BROMWICH ALBION	2–3	Partridge, Robinson	20,000
Sep 3	EVERTON	2–1	Harrison, Spence	25,000
Sep 7	West Bromwich Albion	0–0		15,000
Sep 10	Chelsea	0–0		35,000
Sep 17	CHELSEA	0–0		28,000
Sep 24	Preston North End	2–3	Lochhead, Partridge	25,000
Oct 1	PRESTON NORTH END	1–1	Spence	30,000
Oct 8	Tottenham Hotspur	2–2	Sapsford, Spence	35,000
Oct 15	TOTTENHAM HOTSPUR	2–1	Sapsford, Spence	30,000
Oct 22	Manchester City	1–4	Spence	24,000
Oct 29	MANCHESTER CITY	3–1	Spence 3	56,000
Nov 5	MIDDLESBROUGH	3–5	Lochhead, Sapsford, Spence	30,000
Nov 12	Middlesbrough	0–2		18,000
Nov 19	Aston Villa	1–3	Spence	30,000
Nov 26	ASTON VILLA	1–0	Henderson	33,000
Dec 3	Bradford City	1–2	Spence	15,000
Dec 10	BRADFORD CITY	1–1	Henderson	9,000
Dec 17	Liverpool	1–2	Sapsford	40,000
Dec 24	LIVERPOOL	0–0		30,000
Dec 26	BURNLEY	0–1		15,000
Dec 27	Burnley	2–4	Lochhead, Sapsford	10,000
Dec 31	Newcastle United	0–3		20,000
Jan 2	Sheffield United	0–3		18,000
Jan 14	NEWCASTLE UNITED	0–1		20,000
Jan 21	Sunderland	1–2	Sapsford	10,000
Jan 28	SUNDERLAND	3–1	Lochhead, Sapsford, Spence	18,000
Feb 11	HUDDERSFIELD TOWN	1–1	Spence	30,000
Feb 18	Birmingham City	1–0	Spence	20,000
Feb 25	BIRMINGHAM CITY	1–1	Sapsford	35,000
Feb 27	Huddersfield Town	1–1	Sapsford	30,000
Mar 11	ARSENAL	1–0	Spence	30,000
Mar 18	BLACKBURN ROVERS	0–1		30,000
Mar 25	Blackburn Rovers	0–3		15,000
Apr 1	BOLTON WANDERERS	0–1		28,000
Apr 5	Arsenal	1–3	Lochhead	25,000
Apr 8	Bolton Wanderers	0–1		28,000
Apr 15	OLDHAM ATHLETIC	0–3		30,000
Apr 17	SHEFFIELD UNITED	3–2	Lochhead, Harrison, Partridge	28,000
Apr 22	Oldham Athletic	1–1	Lochhead	30,000
Apr 29	CARDIFF CITY	1–1	Partridge	18,000
May 6	Cardiff City	1–3	Lochhead	16,000

FA CUP

DATE	OPPONENTS	SCORE	GOALSCORERS	ATTENDANCE
Jan 7	CARDIFF CITY (Rd1)	1–4	Sapsford	25,726

FINAL LEAGUE TABLE

		P	W	D	L	F	A	Pts
1	Liverpool	42	22	13	7	63	36	57
2	Tottenham Hotspur	42	21	9	12	65	39	51
3	Burnley	42	22	5	15	72	54	49
4	Cardiff City	42	19	10	13	61	53	48
5	Aston Villa	42	22	3	17	74	55	47
6	Bolton Wanderers	42	20	7	15	68	59	47
7	Newcastle United	42	18	10	14	59	45	46
8	Middlesbrough	42	16	14	12	79	69	46
9	Chelsea	42	17	12	13	40	43	46
10	Manchester City	42	18	9	15	65	70	45
11	Sheffield United	42	15	10	17	59	54	40
12	Sunderland	42	16	8	18	60	62	40
13	West Bromwich Albion	42	15	10	17	51	63	40
14	Huddersfield Town	42	15	9	18	53	54	39
15	Blackburn Rovers	42	13	12	17	54	57	38
16	Preston North End	42	13	12	17	42	65	38
17	Arsenal	42	15	7	20	47	56	37
18	Birmingham City	42	15	7	20	48	60	37
19	Oldham Athletic	42	13	11	18	38	50	37
20	Everton	42	12	12	18	57	55	36
21	Bradford City	42	11	10	21	48	72	32
22	MANCHESTER UNITED	42	8	12	22	41	73	28

APPEARANCES

PLAYER	LGE	FAC	TOT
Mew	41	1	42
Partridge	37	1	38
Silcock	36	–	36
Spence	35	1	36
Lochhead	31	1	32
Hilditch	29	1	30
Sapsford	29	1	30
Grimwood	28	–	28
Radford	26	1	27
Scott	23	1	24
McBain	21	1	22
Harrison	21	–	21
Bennion	15	–	15
Harris	13	1	14
Gibson	11	1	12
Robinson	12	–	12
Brett	10	–	10
Henderson	10	–	10
Myerscough	7	–	7
Bissett	6	–	6
Forster	4	–	4
Howarth	4	–	4
Barlow	3	–	3
Thomas	3	–	3
Goodwin	2	–	2
Haslam	1	–	1
Pugh	1	–	1
Schofield	1	–	1
Steward	1	–	1
Taylor	1	–	1

GOALSCORERS

PLAYER	LGE	FAC	TOT
Spence	15	–	15
Sapsford	9	1	10
Lochhead	8	–	8
Partridge	4	–	4
Harrison	2	–	2
Henderson	2	–	2
Robinson	1	–	1

1922/23

FOOTBALL LEAGUE DIVISION TWO

DATE	OPPONENTS	SCORE	GOALSCORERS	ATTENDANCE
Aug 26	CRYSTAL PALACE	2-1	Spence, Wood	30,000
Aug 28	Sheffield Wednesday	0-1		12,500
Sep 2	Crystal Palace	3-2	Spence 2, Williams	8,500
Sep 4	SHEFFIELD WEDNESDAY	1-0	Spence	22,000
Sep 9	Wolverhampton W.	1-0	Williams	18,000
Sep 16	WOLVERHAMPTON W.	1-0	Spence	28,000
Sep 23	Coventry City	0-2		19,000
Sep 30	COVENTRY CITY	2-1	Henderson, Spence	25,000
Oct 7	PORT VALE	1-2	Spence	25,000
Oct 14	Port Vale	0-1		16,000
Oct 21	FULHAM	1-1	Myerscough	18,000
Oct 28	Fulham	0-0		20,000
Nov 4	LEYTON ORIENT	0-0		16,500
Nov 11	Leyton Orient	1-1	Goldthorpe	11,000
Nov 18	Bury	2-2	Goldthorpe 2	21,000
Nov 25	BURY	0-1		28,000
Dec 2	ROTHERHAM UNITED	3-0	Lochhead, McBain, Spence	13,500
Dec 9	Rotherham United	1-1	Goldthorpe	7,500
Dec 16	STOCKPORT COUNTY	1-0	McBain	24,000
Dec 23	Stockport County	0-1		15,500
Dec 25	WEST HAM UNITED	1-2	Lochhead	17,500
Dec 26	West Ham United	2-0	Lochhead 2	25,000
Dec 30	Hull City	1-2	Lochhead	6,750
Jan 1	BARNSLEY	1-0	Lochhead	29,000
Jan 6	HULL CITY	3-2	Goldthorpe, Lochhead, og	15,000
Jan 20	LEEDS UNITED	0-0		25,000
Jan 27	Leeds United	1-0	Lochhead	24,500
Feb 10	Notts County	6-1	Goldthorpe 4, Myerscough 2	10,000
Feb 17	DERBY COUNTY	0-0		27,500
Feb 21	NOTTS COUNTY	1-1	Lochhead	12,100
Mar 3	SOUTHAMPTON	1-2	Lochhead	30,000
Mar 14	Derby County	1-1	MacDonald	12,000
Mar 17	Bradford City	1-1	Goldthorpe	10,000
Mar 21	BRADFORD CITY	1-1	Spence	15,000
Mar 30	SOUTH SHIELDS	3-0	Goldthorpe 2, Lochhead	26,000
Mar 31	Blackpool	0-1		21,000
Apr 2	South Shields	3-0	Goldthorpe, Hilditch, Spence	6,500
Apr 7	BLACKPOOL	2-1	Lochhead, Radford	20,000
Apr 11	Southampton	0-0		5,500
Apr 14	LEICESTER CITY	1-0	Bain	25,000
Apr 21	LEICESTER CITY	0-2		30,000
Apr 28	Barnsley	2-2	Lochhead, Spence	8,000

FA CUP

DATE	OPPONENTS	SCORE	GOALSCORERS	ATTENDANCE
Jan 13	Bradford City (Rd1)	1-1	Partridge	27,000
Jan 17	BRADFORD CITY (Rd1R)	2-0	Barber, Goldthorpe	27,791
Feb 3	Tottenham Hotspur (Rd2)	0-4		38,333

FINAL LEAGUE TABLE

		P	W	D	L	F	A	Pts
1	Notts County	42	23	7	12	46	34	53
2	West Ham United	42	20	11	11	63	38	51
3	Leicester City	42	21	9	12	65	44	51
4	MANCHESTER UNITED	42	17	14	11	51	36	48
5	Blackpool	42	18	11	13	60	43	47
6	Bury	42	18	11	13	55	46	47
7	Leeds United	42	18	11	13	43	36	47
8	Sheffield Wednesday	42	17	12	13	54	47	46
9	Barnsley	42	17	11	14	62	51	45
10	Fulham	42	16	12	14	43	32	44
11	Southampton	42	14	14	14	40	40	42
12	Hull City	42	14	14	14	43	45	42
13	South Shields	42	15	10	17	35	44	40
14	Derby County	42	14	11	17	46	50	39
15	Bradford City	42	12	13	17	41	45	37
16	Crystal Palace	42	13	11	18	54	62	37
17	Port Vale	42	14	9	19	39	51	37
18	Coventry City	42	15	7	20	46	63	37
19	Leyton Orient	42	12	12	18	40	50	36
20	Stockport County	42	14	8	20	43	58	36
21	Rotherham United	42	13	9	20	44	63	35
22	Wolverhampton Wanderers	42	9	9	24	42	77	27

APPEARANCES

PLAYER	LGE	FAC	TOT
Mew	41	3	44
Silcock	37	3	40
Grimwood	36	3	39
Lochhead	34	3	37
Radford	34	3	37
Spence	35	2	37
Hilditch	32	3	35
Barson	31	3	34
Partridge	30	3	33
Goldthorpe	22	3	25
McBain	21	–	21
Thomas	18	–	18
Wood	15	1	16
Bennion	14	–	14
Myerscough	13	1	14
Moore	12	–	12
Mann	10	–	10
Williams	5	–	5
Bain	4	–	4
Barber	2	1	3
Cartman	3	–	3
Lievesley	2	1	3
Lyner	3	–	3
Henderson	2	–	2
MacDonald	2	–	2
Broome	1	–	1
Pugh	1	–	1
Sarvis	1	–	1
Steward	1	–	1

GOALSCORERS

PLAYER	LGE	FAC	TOT
Goldthorpe	13	1	14
Lochhead	13	–	13
Spence	11	–	11
Myerscough	3	–	3
McBain	2	–	2
Williams	2	–	2
Bain	1	–	1
Henderson	1	–	1
Hilditch	1	–	1
MacDonald	1	–	1
Radford	1	–	1
Wood	1	–	1
Barber	–	1	1
Partridge	–	1	1
own goal	1	–	1

1923/24

FOOTBALL LEAGUE DIVISION TWO

DATE	OPPONENTS	SCORE	GOALSCORERS	ATTENDANCE
Aug 25	Bristol City	2-1	Lochhead, MacDonald	20,500
Aug 27	SOUTHAMPTON	1-0	Goldthorpe	21,750
Sep 1	BRISTOL CITY	2-1	Lochhead, Spence	21,000
Sep 3	Southampton	0-0		11,500
Sep 8	Bury	0-2		19,000
Sep 15	BURY	0-1		43,000
Sep 22	South Shields	0-1		9,750
Sep 29	SOUTH SHIELDS	1-1	Lochhead	22,250
Oct 6	Oldham Athletic	2-3	og 2	12,250
Oct 13	OLDHAM ATHLETIC	2-0	Bain 2	26,000
Oct 20	STOCKPORT COUNTY	3-0	Mann 2, Bain	31,500
Oct 27	Stockport County	2-3	Barber, Lochhead	16,500
Nov 3	Leicester City	2-2	Lochhead 2	17,000
Nov 10	LEICESTER CITY	3-0	Lochhead, Mann, Spence	20,000
Nov 17	Coventry City	1-1	og	13,580
Dec 1	Leeds United	0-0		20,000
Dec 8	LEEDS UNITED	3-1	Lochhead 2, Spence	22,250
Dec 15	Port Vale	1-0	Grimwood	7,500
Dec 22	PORT VALE	5-0	Bain 3, Lochhead, Spence	11,750
Dec 25	BARNSLEY	1-2	Grimwood	34,000
Dec 26	Barnsley	0-1		12,000
Dec 29	Bradford City	0-0		11,500
Jan 2	COVENTRY CITY	1-2	Bain	7,000
Jan 5	BRADFORD CITY	3-0	Bain, Lochhead, McPherson	18,000
Jan 19	Fulham	1-3	Lochhead	15,500
Jan 26	FULHAM	0-0		25,000
Feb 6	Blackpool	0-1		6,000
Feb 9	BLACKPOOL	0-0		13,000
Feb 16	Derby County	0-3		12,000
Feb 23	DERBY COUNTY	0-0		25,000
Mar 1	Nelson	2-0	Kennedy, Spence	2,750
Mar 8	NELSON	0-1		8,500
Mar 15	HULL CITY	1-1	Lochhead	13,000
Mar 22	Hull City	1-1	Miller	6,250
Mar 29	STOKE CITY	2-2	Smith 2	13,000
Apr 5	Stoke City	0-3		11,000
Apr 12	CRYSTAL PALACE	5-1	Spence 4, Smith	8,000
Apr 18	Leyton Orient	0-1		18,000
Apr 19	Crystal Palace	1-1	Spence	7,000
Apr 21	LEYTON ORIENT	2-2	Evans 2	11,000
Apr 26	SHEFFIELD WEDNESDAY	2-0	Lochhead, Smith	7,500
May 3	Sheffield Wednesday	0-2		7,250

FA CUP

DATE	OPPONENTS	SCORE	GOALSCORERS	ATTENDANCE
Jan 12	PLYMOUTH ARGYLE (Rd1)	1-0	McPherson	35,700
Feb 2	HUDDERSFIELD TOWN (Rd2)	0-3		66,673

FINAL LEAGUE TABLE

		P	W	D	L	F	A	Pts
1	Leeds United	42	21	12	9	61	35	54
2	Bury	42	21	9	12	63	35	51
3	Derby County	42	21	9	12	75	42	51
4	Blackpool	42	18	13	11	72	47	49
5	Southampton	42	17	14	11	52	31	48
6	Stoke City	42	14	18	10	44	42	46
7	Oldham Athletic	42	14	17	11	45	52	45
8	Sheffield Wednesday	42	16	12	14	54	51	44
9	South Shields	42	17	10	15	49	50	44
10	Leyton Orient	42	14	15	13	40	36	43
11	Barnsley	42	16	11	15	57	61	43
12	Leicester City	42	17	8	17	64	54	42
13	Stockport County	42	13	16	13	44	52	42
14	MANCHESTER UNITED	42	13	14	15	52	44	40
15	Crystal Palace	42	13	13	16	53	65	39
16	Port Vale	42	13	12	17	50	66	38
17	Hull City	42	10	17	15	46	51	37
18	Bradford City	42	11	15	16	35	48	37
19	Coventry City	42	11	13	18	52	68	35
20	Fulham	42	10	14	18	45	56	34
21	Nelson	42	10	13	19	40	74	33
22	Bristol City	42	7	15	20	32	65	29

APPEARANCES

PLAYER	LGE	FAC	TOT
Moore	42	2	44
Hilditch	41	2	43
Lochhead	40	2	42
Spence	36	2	38
Bennion	34	2	36
McPherson	34	2	36
Steward	30	2	32
Radford	30	1	31
Mann	25	2	27
Grimwood	22	–	22
Bain	18	1	19
Barson	17	2	19
Mew	12	–	12
Smith	12	–	12
Ellis	11	–	11
Silcock	8	1	9
Haslam	7	–	7
MacDonald	7	–	7
Evans	6	–	6
Kennedy	6	–	6
Thomas	6	–	6
Partridge	5	–	5
Goldthorpe	4	–	4
Miller	4	–	4
Dennis	3	–	3
Barber	1	–	1
Henderson	–	1	1
Tyler	1	–	1

GOALSCORERS

PLAYER	LGE	FAC	TOT
Lochhead	14	–	14
Spence	10	–	10
Bain	8	–	8
Smith	4	–	4
Mann	3	–	3
Evans	2	–	2
Grimwood	2	–	2
McPherson	1	1	2
Barber	1	–	1
Goldthorpe	1	–	1
Kennedy	1	–	1
MacDonald	1	–	1
Miller	1	–	1
own goals	3	–	3

1924/25

FOOTBALL LEAGUE DIVISION TWO

DATE	OPPONENTS	SCORE	GOALSCORERS	ATTENDANCE
Aug 30	LEICESTER CITY	1-0	Goldthorpe	21,250
Sep 1	Stockport County	1-2	Lochhead	12,500
Sep 6	Stoke City	0-0		15,250
Sep 8	BARNSLEY	1-0	Henderson	9,500
Sep 13	COVENTRY CITY	5-1	Henderson 2, Lochhead, McPherson, Spence	12,000
Sep 20	Oldham Athletic	3-0	Henderson 3	14,500
Sep 27	SHEFFIELD WEDNESDAY	2-0	McPherson, Smith	29,500
Oct 4	Leyton Orient	1-0	Lochhead	15,000
Oct 11	CRYSTAL PALACE	1-0	Lochhead	27,750
Oct 18	Southampton	2-0	Lochhead 2	10,000
Oct 25	Wolverhampton W.	0-0		17,500
Nov 1	FULHAM	2-0	Henderson, Lochhead	24,000
Nov 8	Portsmouth	1-1	Smith	19,500
Nov 15	HULL CITY	2-0	Hanson, McPherson	29,750
Nov 22	Blackpool	1-1	Hanson	9,500
Nov 29	DERBY COUNTY	1-1	Hanson	59,500
Dec 6	South Shields	2-1	Henderson, McPherson	6,500
Dec 13	BRADFORD CITY	3-0	Henderson 2, McPherson	18,250
Dec 20	Port Vale	1-2	Lochhead	11,000
Dec 25	Middlesbrough	1-1	Henderson	18,500
Dec 26	MIDDLESBROUGH	2-0	Henderson, Smith	44,000
Dec 27	Leicester City	0-3		18,250
Jan 1	CHELSEA	1-0	Grimwood	30,500
Jan 3	STOKE CITY	2-0	Henderson 2	24,500
Jan 17	Coventry City	0-1		9,000
Jan 24	OLDHAM ATHLETIC	0-1		20,000
Feb 7	LEYTON ORIENT	4-2	Kennedy 2, McPherson, Pape	18,250
Feb 14	Crystal Palace	1-2	Lochhead	11,250
Feb 23	Sheffield Wednesday	1-1	Pape	3,000
Feb 28	WOLVERHAMPTON W.	3-0	Spence 2, Kennedy	21,250
Mar 7	Fulham	0-1		16,000
Mar 14	PORTSMOUTH	2-0	Lochhead, Spence	22,000
Mar 21	Hull City	1-0	Lochhead	6,250
Mar 28	BLACKPOOL	0-0		26,250
Apr 4	Derby County	0-1		24,000
Apr 10	STOCKPORT COUNTY	2-0	Pape 2	43,500
Apr 11	SOUTH SHIELDS	1-0	Lochhead	24,000
Apr 13	Chelsea	0-0		16,500
Apr 18	Bradford City	1-0	Smith	13,250
Apr 22	SOUTHAMPTON	1-1	Pape	26,500
Apr 25	PORT VALE	4-0	Lochhead, McPherson, Smith, Spence	33,500
May 2	Barnsley	0-0		11,250

FA CUP

DATE	OPPONENTS	SCORE	GOALSCORERS	ATTENDANCE
Jan 10	Sheffield Wednesday (Rd1)	0-2		35,079

FINAL LEAGUE TABLE

		P	W	D	L	F	A	Pts
1	Leicester City	42	24	11	7	90	32	59
2	MANCHESTER UNITED	42	23	11	8	57	23	57
3	Derby County	42	22	11	9	71	36	55
4	Portsmouth	42	15	18	9	58	50	48
5	Chelsea	42	16	15	11	51	37	47
6	Wolverhampton Wanderers	42	20	6	16	55	51	46
7	Southampton	42	13	18	11	40	36	44
8	Port Vale	42	17	8	17	48	56	42
9	South Shields	42	12	17	13	42	38	41
10	Hull City	42	15	11	16	50	49	41
11	Leyton Orient	42	14	12	16	42	42	40
12	Fulham	42	15	10	17	41	56	40
13	Middlesbrough	42	10	19	13	36	44	39
14	Sheffield Wednesday	42	15	8	19	50	56	38
15	Barnsley	42	13	12	17	46	59	38
16	Bradford City	42	13	12	17	37	50	38
17	Blackpool	42	14	9	19	65	61	37
18	Oldham Athletic	42	13	11	18	35	51	37
19	Stockport County	42	13	11	18	37	57	37
20	Stoke City	42	12	11	19	34	46	35
21	Crystal Palace	42	12	10	20	38	54	34
22	Coventry City	42	11	9	22	45	84	31

APPEARANCES

PLAYER	LGE	FAC	TOT
Spence	42	1	43
Steward	42	1	43
Moore	40	1	41
Grimwood	39	1	40
McPherson	38	1	39
Lochhead	37	–	37
Mann	32	1	33
Barson	32	–	32
Smith	31	1	32
Silcock	29	–	29
Henderson	22	1	23
Bennion	17	–	17
Jones	15	1	16
Pape	16	–	16
Kennedy	11	1	12
Hilditch	4	1	5
Rennox	4	–	4
Hanson	3	–	3
Thomas	3	–	3
Bain	1	–	1
Goldthorpe	1	–	1
Haslam	1	–	1
Partridge	1	–	1
Taylor	1	–	1

GOALSCORERS

PLAYER	LGE	FAC	TOT
Henderson	14	–	14
Lochhead	13	–	13
McPherson	7	–	7
Pape	5	–	5
Smith	5	–	5
Spence	5	–	5
Hanson	3	–	3
Kennedy	3	–	3
Goldthorpe	1	–	1
Grimwood	1	–	1

1925/26

FOOTBALL LEAGUE DIVISION ONE

DATE	OPPONENTS	SCORE	GOALSCORERS	ATTENDANCE
Aug 29	West Ham United	0-1		25,630
Sep 2	ASTON VILLA	3-0	Barson, Lochhead, Spence	41,717
Sep 5	ARSENAL	0-1		32,288
Sep 7	Aston Villa	2-2	Hanson, Rennox	27,701
Sep 12	Manchester City	1-1	Rennox	62,994
Sep 16	LEICESTER CITY	3-2	Rennox 2, Lochhead	21,275
Sep 19	Liverpool	0-5		18,824
Sep 26	BURNLEY	6-1	Rennox 3, Hanson, Hilditch, Smith	17,259
Oct 3	Leeds United	0-2		26,265
Oct 10	NEWCASTLE UNITED	2-1	Rennox, Thomas	39,651
Oct 17	TOTTENHAM HOTSPUR	0-0		26,496
Oct 24	Cardiff City	2-0	McPherson 2	15,846
Oct 31	HUDDERSFIELD TOWN	1-1	Thomas	37,213
Nov 7	Everton	3-1	McPherson, Rennox, Spence	12,387
Nov 14	BIRMINGHAM CITY	3-1	Barson, Spence, Thomas	23,559
Nov 21	Bury	3-1	McPherson 2, Spence	16,591
Nov 28	BLACKBURN ROVERS	2-0	McPherson, Thomas	33,660
Dec 5	Sunderland	1-2	Rennox	25,507
Dec 12	SHEFFIELD UNITED	1-2	McPherson	31,132
Dec 19	West Bromwich Albion	1-5	McPherson	17,651
Dec 25	BOLTON WANDERERS	2-1	Hanson, Spence	38,503
Dec 28	Leicester City	3-1	McPherson 3	28,367
Jan 2	WEST HAM UNITED	2-1	Rennox 2	29,612
Jan 16	Arsenal	2-3	McPherson, Spence	25,252
Jan 23	MANCHESTER CITY	1-6	Rennox	48,657
Feb 6	Burnley	1-0	McPherson	17,141
Feb 13	LEEDS UNITED	2-1	McPherson, Sweeney	29,584
Feb 27	Tottenham Hotspur	1-0	Smith	25,466
Mar 10	LIVERPOOL	3-3	Hanson, Rennox, Spence	9,214
Mar 13	Huddersfield Town	0-5		27,842
Mar 17	Bolton Wanderers	1-3	McPherson	10,794
Mar 20	EVERTON	0-0		30,058
Apr 2	Notts County	3-0	Rennox 2, McPherson	18,453
Apr 3	BURY	0-1		41,085
Apr 5	NOTTS COUNTY	0-1		19,606
Apr 10	Blackburn Rovers	0-7		15,870
Apr 14	Newcastle United	1-4	Hanson	9,829
Apr 19	Birmingham City	1-2	Rennox	8,948
Apr 21	SUNDERLAND	5-1	Taylor 3, Smith, Thomas	10,918
Apr 24	Sheffield United	0-2		15,571
Apr 28	CARDIFF CITY	1-0	Inglis	9,116
May 1	WEST BROMWICH ALBION	3-2	Taylor 3	9,974

FA CUP

DATE	OPPONENTS	SCORE	GOALSCORERS	ATTENDANCE
Jan 9	Port Vale (Rd3)	3-2	Spence 2, McPherson	14,841
Jan 30	Tottenham Hotspur (Rd4)	2-2	Spence, Thomas	40,000
Feb 3	TOTTENHAM HOTSPUR (Rd4R)	2-0	Rennox, Spence	45,000
Feb 20	Sunderland (Rd5)	3-3	Smith 2, McPherson	50,500
Feb 24	SUNDERLAND (Rd5R)	2-1	McPherson, Smith	58,661
Mar 6	Fulham (Rd6)	2-1	McPherson, Smith	28,699
Mar 27	Manchester City (SF) (at Bramall Lane, Sheffield)	0-3		46,450

FINAL LEAGUE TABLE

		P	W	D	L	F	A	Pts
1	Huddersfield Town	42	23	11	8	92	60	57
2	Arsenal	42	22	8	12	87	63	52
3	Sunderland	42	21	6	15	96	80	48
4	Bury	42	20	7	15	85	77	47
5	Sheffield United	42	19	8	15	102	82	46
6	Aston Villa	42	16	12	14	86	76	44
7	Liverpool	42	14	16	12	70	63	44
8	Bolton Wanderers	42	17	10	15	75	76	44
9	MANCHESTER UNITED	42	19	6	17	66	73	44
10	Newcastle United	42	16	10	16	84	75	42
11	Everton	42	12	18	12	72	70	42
12	Blackburn Rovers	42	15	11	16	91	80	41
13	West Bromwich Albion	42	16	8	18	79	78	40
14	Birmingham City	42	16	8	18	66	81	40
15	Tottenham Hotspur	42	15	9	18	66	79	39
16	Cardiff City	42	16	7	19	61	76	39
17	Leicester City	42	14	10	18	70	80	38
18	West Ham United	42	15	7	20	63	76	37
19	Leeds United	42	14	8	20	64	76	36
20	Burnley	42	13	10	19	85	108	36
21	Manchester City	42	12	11	19	89	100	35
22	Notts County	42	13	7	22	54	74	33

APPEARANCES

PLAYER	LGE	FAC	TOT
Spence	39	7	46
Mann	34	7	41
Rennox	34	7	41
Moore	33	7	40
Silcock	33	7	40
Steward	35	2	37
McPherson	29	7	36
Smith	30	5	35
Thomas	29	6	35
Barson	28	4	32
Hilditch	28	3	31
Hanson	24	2	26
McCrae	9	4	13
Haslam	9	2	11
Mew	6	5	11
Jones	10	–	10
Grimwood	7	1	8
Bennion	7	–	7
Inglis	7	–	7
Taylor	6	–	6
Hannaford	4	1	5
Lochhead	5	–	5
Hall	3	–	3
Partridge	3	–	3
Sweeney	3	–	3
Bain	2	–	2
Pape	2	–	2
Astley	1	–	1
Iddon	1	–	1
Richardson	1	–	1

GOALSCORERS

PLAYER	LGE	FAC	TOT
McPherson	16	4	20
Rennox	17	1	18
Spence	7	4	11
Smith	3	4	7
Taylor	6	–	6
Thomas	5	1	6
Hanson	5	–	5
Barson	2	–	2
Lochhead	2	–	2
Hilditch	1	–	1
Inglis	1	–	1
Sweeney	1	–	1

1926/27

FOOTBALL LEAGUE DIVISION ONE

DATE	OPPONENTS	SCORE	GOALSCORERS	ATTENDANCE
Aug 28	Liverpool	2–4	McPherson 2	34,795
Aug 30	Sheffield United	2–2	McPherson 2	14,844
Sep 4	LEEDS UNITED	2–2	McPherson 2	26,338
Sep 11	Newcastle United	2–4	McPherson, Spence	28,050
Sep 15	ARSENAL	2–2	Hanson, Spence	15,259
Sep 18	BURNLEY	2–1	Spence 2	32,593
Sep 25	Cardiff City	2–0	Rennox, Spence	17,267
Oct 2	ASTON VILLA	2–1	Barson, Rennox	31,234
Oct 9	Bolton Wanderers	0–4		17,869
Oct 16	Bury	3–0	Spence 2, McPherson	22,728
Oct 23	BIRMINGHAM CITY	0–1		32,010
Oct 30	West Ham United	0–4		19,733
Nov 6	SHEFFIELD WEDNESDAY	0–0		16,166
Nov 13	Leicester City	3–2	McPherson 2, Rennox	18,521
Nov 20	EVERTON	2–1	Rennox 2	24,361
Nov 27	Blackburn Rovers	1–2	Spence	17,280
Dec 4	HUDDERSFIELD TOWN	0–0		33,135
Dec 11	Sunderland	0–6		15,385
Dec 18	WEST BROMWICH ALBION	2–0	Sweeney 2	18,585
Dec 25	Tottenham Hotspur	1–1	Spence	37,287
Dec 27	TOTTENHAM HOTSPUR	2–1	McPherson 2	50,665
Dec 28	Arsenal	0–1		30,111
Jan 1	SHEFFIELD UNITED	5–0	McPherson 2, Barson, Rennox, Sweeney	33,593
Jan 15	LIVERPOOL	0–1		30,304
Jan 22	Leeds United	3–2	McPherson, Rennox, Spence	16,816
Feb 5	Burnley	0–1		22,010
Feb 9	NEWCASTLE UNITED	3–1	Hanson, Harris, Spence	25,402
Feb 12	CARDIFF CITY	1–1	Hanson	26,213
Feb 19	Aston Villa	0–2		32,467
Feb 26	BOLTON WANDERERS	0–0		29,618
Mar 5	BURY	1–2	Smith A	14,709
Mar 12	Birmingham City	0–4		14,392
Mar 19	WEST HAM UNITED	0–3		18,347
Mar 26	Sheffield Wednesday	0–2		11,997
Apr 2	LEICESTER CITY	1–0	Spence	17,119
Apr 9	Everton	0–0		22,564
Apr 15	DERBY COUNTY	2–2	Spence 2	31,110
Apr 16	BLACKBURN ROVERS	2–0	Hanson, Spence	24,845
Apr 18	Derby County	2–2	Spence 2	17,306
Apr 23	Huddersfield Town	0–0		13,870
Apr 30	SUNDERLAND	0–0		17,300
May 7	West Bromwich Albion	2–2	Hanson, Spence	6,668

FA CUP

DATE	OPPONENTS	SCORE	GOALSCORERS	ATTENDANCE
Jan 8	Reading (Rd3)	1–1	Bennion	28,918
Jan 12	READING (Rd3R)	2–2	Spence, Sweeney	29,122
Jan 17	Reading (Rd3R2) (at Villa Park)	1–2	McPherson	16,500

FINAL LEAGUE TABLE

		P	W	D	L	F	A	Pts
1	Newcastle United	42	25	6	11	96	58	56
2	Huddersfield Town	42	17	17	8	76	60	51
3	Sunderland	42	21	7	14	98	70	49
4	Bolton Wanderers	42	19	10	13	84	62	48
5	Burnley	42	19	9	14	91	80	47
6	West Ham United	42	19	8	15	86	70	46
7	Leicester City	42	17	12	13	85	70	46
8	Sheffield United	42	17	10	15	74	86	44
9	Liverpool	42	18	7	17	69	61	43
10	Aston Villa	42	18	7	17	81	83	43
11	Arsenal	42	17	9	16	77	86	43
12	Derby County	42	17	7	18	86	73	41
13	Tottenham Hotspur	42	16	9	17	76	78	41
14	Cardiff City	42	16	9	17	55	65	41
15	MANCHESTER UNITED	42	13	14	15	52	64	40
16	Sheffield Wednesday	42	15	9	18	75	92	39
17	Birmingham City	42	17	4	21	64	73	38
18	Blackburn Rovers	42	15	8	19	77	96	38
19	Bury	42	12	12	18	68	77	36
20	Everton	42	12	10	20	64	90	34
21	Leeds United	42	11	8	23	69	88	30
22	West Bromwich Albion	42	11	8	23	65	86	30

APPEARANCES

PLAYER	LGE	FAC	TOT
Steward	42	3	45
Spence	40	3	43
Bennion	37	3	40
McPherson	32	3	35
Moore	30	3	33
Silcock	26	3	29
Barson	21	3	24
Rennox	22	1	23
Hanson	21	1	22
Jones	21	–	21
Wilson	21	–	21
Hilditch	16	3	19
Partridge	16	3	19
Chapman	17	–	17
Grimwood	17	–	17
Sweeney	13	3	16
Thomas	16	–	16
Mann	14	–	14
Smith T	10	1	11
Hannaford	7	–	7
Inglis	6	–	6
Smith A	5	–	5
Harris	4	–	4
Haslam	4	–	4
Haworth	2	–	2
Astley	1	–	1
Iddon	1	–	1

GOALSCORERS

PLAYER	LGE	FAC	TOT
Spence	18	1	19
McPherson	15	1	16
Rennox	7	–	7
Hanson	5	–	5
Sweeney	3	1	4
Barson	2	–	2
Harris	1	–	1
Smith A	1	–	1
Bennion	–	1	1

1927/28

FOOTBALL LEAGUE DIVISION ONE

DATE	OPPONENTS	SCORE	GOALSCORERS	ATTENDANCE
Aug 27	MIDDLESBROUGH	3–0	Spence 2, Hanson	44,957
Aug 29	Sheffield Wednesday	2–0	Hanson, Partridge	17,944
Sep 3	Birmingham City	0–0		25,863
Sep 7	SHEFFIELD WEDNESDAY	1–1	McPherson	18,759
Sep 10	NEWCASTLE UNITED	1–7	Spence	50,217
Sep 17	Huddersfield Town	2–4	Spence 2	17,307
Sep 19	Blackburn Rovers	0–3		18,243
Sep 24	TOTTENHAM HOTSPUR	3–0	Hanson 2, Spence	13,952
Oct 1	Leicester City	0–1		22,385
Oct 8	Everton	2–5	Bennion, Spence	40,080
Oct 15	CARDIFF CITY	2–2	Spence, Sweeney	31,090
Oct 22	DERBY COUNTY	5–0	Spence 3, Johnston, McPherson	18,304
Oct 29	West Ham United	2–1	McPherson, og	21,972
Nov 5	PORTSMOUTH	2–0	McPherson, og	13,119
Nov 12	Sunderland	1–4	Spence	13,319
Nov 19	ASTON VILLA	5–1	Partridge 2, Johnston, McPherson, Spence	25,991
Nov 26	Burnley	0–4		18,509
Dec 3	BURY	0–1		23,581
Dec 10	Sheffield United	1–2	Spence	11,984
Dec 17	ARSENAL	4–1	Hanson, McPherson, Partridge, Spence	18,120
Dec 24	Liverpool	0–2		14,971
Dec 26	BLACKBURN ROVERS	1–1	Spence	31,131
Dec 31	Middlesbrough	2–1	Hanson, Johnston	19,652
Jan 7	BIRMINGHAM CITY	1–1	Hanson	16,853
Jan 21	Newcastle United	1–4	Partridge	25,912
Feb 4	Tottenham Hotspur	1–4	Johnston	23,545
Feb 11	LEICESTER CITY	5–2	Nicol 2, Spence 2, Hanson	16,640
Feb 25	Cardiff City	0–2		15,579
Mar 7	HUDDERSFIELD TOWN	0–0		35,413
Mar 10	WEST HAM UNITED	1–1	Johnston	21,577
Mar 14	EVERTON	1–0	Rawlings	25,667
Mar 17	Portsmouth	0–1		25,400
Mar 28	Derby County	0–5		8,323
Mar 31	Aston Villa	1–3	Rawlings	24,691
Apr 6	Bolton Wanderers	2–3	Spence, Thomas	23,795
Apr 7	BURNLEY	4–3	Rawlings 3, Williams	28,311
Apr 9	BOLTON WANDERERS	2–1	Johnston, Rawlings	28,590
Apr 14	Bury	3–4	Johnston, McLenahan, Williams	17,440
Apr 21	SHEFFIELD UNITED	2–3	Rawlings, Thomas	27,137
Apr 25	SUNDERLAND	2–1	Hanson, Johnston	9,545
Apr 28	Arsenal	1–0	Rawlings	22,452
May 5	LIVERPOOL	6–1	Spence 3, Rawlings 2, Hanson	30,625

FA CUP

DATE	OPPONENTS	SCORE	GOALSCORERS	ATTENDANCE
Jan 14	BRENTFORD (Rd3)	7–1	Hanson 4, Johnston, McPherson, Spence	18,538
Jan 28	Bury (Rd4)	1–1	Johnston	25,000
Feb 1	BURY (Rd4R)	1–0	Spence	48,001
Feb 18	BIRMINGHAM CITY (Rd5)	1–0	Johnston	52,568
Mar 3	Blackburn Rovers (Rd6)	0–2		42,312

FINAL LEAGUE TABLE

		P	W	D	L	F	A	Pts
1	Everton	42	20	13	9	102	66	53
2	Huddersfield Town	42	22	7	13	91	68	51
3	Leicester City	42	18	12	12	96	72	48
4	Derby County	42	17	10	15	96	83	44
5	Bury	42	20	4	18	80	80	44
6	Cardiff City	42	17	10	15	70	80	44
7	Bolton Wanderers	42	16	11	15	81	66	43
8	Aston Villa	42	17	9	16	78	73	43
9	Newcastle United	42	15	13	14	79	81	43
10	Arsenal	42	13	15	14	82	86	41
11	Birmingham City	42	13	15	14	70	75	41
12	Blackburn Rovers	42	16	9	17	66	78	41
13	Sheffield United	42	15	10	17	79	86	40
14	Sheffield Wednesday	42	13	13	16	81	78	39
15	Sunderland	42	15	9	18	74	76	39
16	Liverpool	42	13	13	16	84	87	39
17	West Ham United	42	14	11	17	81	88	39
18	MANCHESTER UNITED	42	16	7	19	72	80	39
19	Burnley	42	16	7	19	82	98	39
20	Portsmouth	42	16	7	19	66	90	39
21	Tottenham Hotspur	42	15	8	19	74	86	38
22	Middlesbrough	42	11	15	16	81	88	37

APPEARANCES

PLAYER	LGE	FAC	TOT
Spence	38	5	43
Bennion	36	5	41
Jones	33	5	38
Wilson	33	5	38
Johnston	31	5	36
Richardson	32	4	36
Hanson	30	5	35
Mann	26	5	31
Silcock	26	4	30
McPherson	25	1	26
Moore	25	1	26
Partridge	23	3	26
Williams	13	3	16
Thomas	13	–	13
Rawlings	12	–	12
Barson	11	–	11
Steward	10	1	11
McLenahan	10	–	10
Chapman	9	–	9
Hilditch	5	–	5
Nicol	4	1	5
Ferguson	4	–	4
Sweeney	4	–	4
Haslam	3	–	3
Ramsden	2	–	2
Taylor	2	–	2
Bain	1	–	1

GOALSCORERS

PLAYER	LGE	FAC	TOT
Spence	22	2	24
Hanson	10	4	14
Johnston	8	3	11
Rawlings	10	–	10
McPherson	6	1	7
Partridge	5	–	5
Nicol	2	–	2
Thomas	2	–	2
Williams	2	–	2
Bennion	1	–	1
McLenahan	1	–	1
Sweeney	1	–	1
own goals	2	–	2

1928/29

FOOTBALL LEAGUE DIVISION ONE

DATE	OPPONENTS	SCORE	GOALSCORERS	ATTENDANCE
Aug 25	LEICESTER CITY	1-1	Rawlings	20,129
Aug 27	Aston Villa	0-0		30,356
Sep 1	Manchester City	2-2	Johnston, Wilson	61,007
Sep 8	Leeds United	2-3	Johnston, Spence	28,723
Sep 15	LIVERPOOL	2-2	Hanson, Silcock	24,077
Sep 22	West Ham United	1-3	Rawlings	20,788
Sep 29	NEWCASTLE UNITED	5-0	Rawlings 2, Hanson, Johnston, Spence	25,243
Oct 6	Burnley	4-3	Hanson 2, Spence 2	17,493
Oct 13	CARDIFF CITY	1-1	Johnston	26,010
Oct 20	BIRMINGHAM CITY	1-0	Johnston	17,522
Oct 27	Huddersfield Town	2-1	Hanson, Spence	13,648
Nov 3	BOLTON WANDERERS	1-1	Hanson	31,185
Nov 10	Sheffield Wednesday	1-2	Hanson	18,113
Nov 17	DERBY COUNTY	0-1		26,122
Nov 24	Sunderland	1-5	Rowley	15,932
Dec 1	BLACKBURN ROVERS	1-4	Ramsden	19,589
Dec 8	Arsenal	1-3	Hanson	18,923
Dec 15	EVERTON	1-1	Hanson	17,080
Dec 22	Portsmouth	0-3		12,836
Dec 25	SHEFFIELD UNITED	1-1	Ramsden	22,202
Dec 26	Sheffield United	1-6	Rawlings	34,696
Dec 29	Leicester City	1-2	Hanson	21,535
Jan 1	ASTON VILLA	2-2	Hilditch, Rowley	25,935
Jan 5	MANCHESTER CITY	1-2	Rawlings	42,555
Jan 19	LEEDS UNITED	1-2	Sweeney	21,995
Feb 2	WEST HAM UNITED	2-3	Reid, Rowley	12,020
Feb 9	Newcastle United	0-5		34,134
Feb 16	Liverpool	3-2	Reid 2, Thomas	8,852
Feb 16	BURNLEY	1-0	Rowley	12,516
Feb 23	Cardiff City	2-2	Hanson, Reid	13,070
Mar 2	Birmingham City	1-1	Hanson	16,738
Mar 9	HUDDERSFIELD TOWN	1-0	Hanson	28,183
Mar 16	Bolton Wanderers	1-1	Hanson	17,354
Mar 23	SHEFFIELD WEDNESDAY	2-1	Reid, Rowley	27,095
Mar 29	Bury	3-1	Reid 2, Thomas	27,167
Mar 30	Derby County	1-6	Hanson	14,619
Apr 1	BURY	1-0	Thomas	29,742
Apr 6	SUNDERLAND	3-0	Hanson, Mann, Reid	27,772
Apr 13	Blackburn Rovers	3-0	Reid 2, Ramsden	8,193
Apr 20	ARSENAL	4-1	Reid 2, Hanson, Thomas	22,858
Apr 27	Everton	4-2	Hanson 2, Reid 2	19,442
May 4	PORTSMOUTH	0-0		17,728

FA CUP

DATE	OPPONENTS	SCORE	GOALSCORERS	ATTENDANCE
Jan 12	Port Vale (Rd3)	3-0	Hanson, Spence, Taylor	17,519
Jan 26	BURY (Rd4)	0-1		40,558

FINAL LEAGUE TABLE

		P	W	D	L	F	A	Pts
1	Sheffield Wednesday	42	21	10	11	86	62	52
2	Leicester City	42	21	9	12	96	67	51
3	Aston Villa	42	23	4	15	98	81	50
4	Sunderland	42	20	7	15	93	75	47
5	Liverpool	42	17	12	13	90	64	46
6	Derby County	42	18	10	14	86	71	46
7	Blackburn Rovers	42	17	11	14	72	63	45
8	Manchester City	42	18	9	15	95	86	45
9	Arsenal	42	16	13	13	77	72	45
10	Newcastle United	42	19	6	17	70	72	44
11	Sheffield United	42	15	11	16	86	85	41
12	MANCHESTER UNITED	42	14	13	15	66	76	41
13	Leeds United	42	16	9	17	71	84	41
14	Bolton Wanderers	42	14	12	16	73	80	40
15	Birmingham City	42	15	10	17	68	77	40
16	Huddersfield Town	42	14	11	17	70	61	39
17	West Ham United	42	15	9	18	86	96	39
18	Everton	42	17	4	21	63	75	38
19	Burnley	42	15	8	19	81	103	38
20	Portsmouth	42	15	6	21	56	80	36
21	Bury	42	12	7	23	62	99	31
22	Cardiff City	42	8	13	21	43	59	29

APPEARANCES

PLAYER	LGE	FAC	TOT
Hanson	42	1	43
Moore	37	2	39
Steward	37	2	39
Spence	36	2	38
Spencer	36	2	38
Bennion	34	–	34
Silcock	27	2	29
Mann	25	2	27
Rowley	25	–	25
Wilson	19	2	21
Rawlings	19	1	20
Thomas	19	1	20
Dale	19	–	19
Williams	18	1	19
Reid	17	–	17
Johnston	12	–	12
Hilditch	11	–	11
Sweeney	6	2	8
Partridge	5	–	5
Ramsden	5	–	5
Richardson	5	–	5
Taylor	3	1	4
Nicol	2	–	2
Boyle	1	–	1
Inglis	1	–	1
McLenahan	1	–	1
Thomson	–	1	1

GOALSCORERS

PLAYER	LGE	FAC	TOT
Hanson	19	1	20
Reid	14	–	14
Rawlings	6	–	6
Spence	5	1	6
Johnston	5	–	5
Rowley	5	–	5
Thomas	4	–	4
Ramsden	3	–	3
Hilditch	1	–	1
Mann	1	–	1
Silcock	1	–	1
Sweeney	1	–	1
Wilson	1	–	1
Taylor	–	1	1

1929/30

FOOTBALL LEAGUE DIVISION ONE

DATE	OPPONENTS	SCORE	GOALSCORERS	ATTENDANCE
Aug 31	Newcastle United	1-4	Spence	43,489
Sep 2	Leicester City	1-4	Rowley	20,490
Sep 7	BLACKBURN ROVERS	1-0	Mann	22,362
Sep 11	LEICESTER CITY	2-1	Ball, Spence	16,445
Sep 14	Middlesbrough	3-2	Rawlings 3	26,428
Sep 21	LIVERPOOL	1-2	Spence	20,788
Sep 28	West Ham United	1-2	Hanson	20,695
Oct 5	MANCHESTER CITY	1-3	Thomas	57,201
Oct 7	Sheffield United	1-3	Boyle	7,987
Oct 12	GRIMSBY TOWN	2-5	Ball, Rowley	21,494
Oct 19	Portsmouth	0-3		18,070
Oct 26	ARSENAL	1-0	Ball	12,662
Nov 2	Aston Villa	0-1		24,292
Nov 9	DERBY COUNTY	3-2	Ball, Hanson, Rowley	15,174
Nov 16	Sheffield Wednesday	2-7	Ball, Hanson	14,264
Nov 23	BURNLEY	1-0	Rowley	9,060
Nov 30	Sunderland	4-2	Spence 2, Ball, Hanson	11,508
Dec 7	BOLTON WANDERERS	1-1	Ball	5,656
Dec 14	Everton	0-0		18,182
Dec 21	LEEDS UNITED	3-1	Ball 2, Hanson	15,054
Dec 25	BIRMINGHAM CITY	0-0		18,626
Dec 26	Birmingham City	1-0	Rowley	35,682
Dec 28	NEWCASTLE UNITED	5-0	Boyle 2, McLachlan, Rowley, Spence	14,862
Jan 4	Blackburn Rovers	4-5	Boyle 2, Ball, Rowley	23,923
Jan 18	MIDDLESBROUGH	0-3		21,028
Jan 25	Liverpool	0-1		28,592
Feb 1	WEST HAM UNITED	4-2	Spence 4	15,424
Feb 8	Manchester City	1-0	Reid	64,472
Feb 15	Grimsby Town	2-2	Reid, Rowley	9,337
Feb 22	PORTSMOUTH	3-0	Reid 2, Boyle	17,317
Mar 1	Bolton Wanderers	1-4	Reid	17,714
Mar 8	ASTON VILLA	2-3	McLachlan, Warburton	25,407
Mar 12	Arsenal	2-4	Ball, Wilson	18,082
Mar 15	Derby County	1-1	Rowley	9,102
Mar 29	Burnley	0-4		11,659
Apr 5	SUNDERLAND	2-1	McLenahan 2	13,230
Apr 14	SHEFFIELD WEDNESDAY	2-2	McLenahan, Rowley	12,806
Apr 18	HUDDERSFIELD TOWN	1-0	McLenahan	26,496
Apr 19	EVERTON	3-3	McLenahan, Rowley, Spence	13,320
Apr 22	Huddersfield Town	2-2	Hilditch, McLenahan	20,716
Apr 26	Leeds United	1-3	Spence	10,596
May 3	SHEFFIELD UNITED	1-5	Rowley	15,268

FA CUP

DATE	OPPONENTS	SCORE	GOALSCORERS	ATTENDANCE
Jan 11	SWINDON TOWN (Rd3)	0-2		33,226

FINAL LEAGUE TABLE

		P	W	D	L	F	A	Pts
1	Sheffield Wednesday	42	26	8	8	105	57	60
2	Derby County	42	21	8	13	90	82	50
3	Manchester City	42	19	9	14	91	81	47
4	Aston Villa	42	21	5	16	92	83	47
5	Leeds United	42	20	6	16	79	63	46
6	Blackburn Rovers	42	19	7	16	99	93	45
7	West Ham United	42	19	5	18	86	79	43
8	Leicester City	42	17	9	16	86	90	43
9	Sunderland	42	18	7	17	76	80	43
10	Huddersfield Town	42	17	9	16	63	69	43
11	Birmingham City	42	16	9	17	67	62	41
12	Liverpool	42	16	9	17	63	79	41
13	Portsmouth	42	15	10	17	66	62	40
14	Arsenal	42	14	11	17	78	66	39
15	Bolton Wanderers	42	15	9	18	74	74	39
16	Middlesbrough	42	16	6	20	82	84	38
17	MANCHESTER UNITED	42	15	8	19	67	88	38
18	Grimsby Town	42	15	7	20	73	89	37
19	Newcastle United	42	15	7	20	71	92	37
20	Sheffield United	42	15	6	21	91	96	36
21	Burnley	42	14	8	20	79	97	36
22	Everton	42	12	11	19	80	92	35

APPEARANCES

PLAYER	LGE	FAC	TOT
Spence	42	1	43
Rowley	40	1	41
Steward	39	1	40
Moore	28	1	29
Wilson	28	1	29
Bennion	28	–	28
Hilditch	27	1	28
Ball	23	1	24
McLachlan	23	1	24
Silcock	21	–	21
Thomas	21	–	21
Dale	19	–	19
Hanson	18	–	18
Jones	16	1	17
Taylor	16	1	17
Boyle	15	1	16
Mann	14	–	14
Reid	13	–	13
McLenahan	10	–	10
Spencer	10	–	10
Rawlings	4	–	4
Chesters	3	–	3
Warburton	2	–	2
Sweeney	1	–	1
Thomson	1	–	1

GOALSCORERS

PLAYER	LGE	FAC	TOT
Rowley	12	–	12
Spence	12	–	12
Ball	11	–	11
Boyle	6	–	6
McLenahan	6	–	6
Hanson	5	–	5
Reid	5	–	5
Rawlings	3	–	3
McLachlan	2	–	2
Hilditch	1	–	1
Mann	1	–	1
Thomas	1	–	1
Warburton	1	–	1
Wilson	1	–	1

1930/31

FOOTBALL LEAGUE DIVISION ONE

DATE	OPPONENTS	SCORE	GOALSCORERS	ATTENDANCE
Aug 30	ASTON VILLA	3–4	Reid, Rowley, Warburton	18,004
Sep 3	Middlesbrough	1–3	Rowley	15,712
Sep 6	Chelsea	2–6	Reid, Spence	68,648
Sep 10	HUDDERSFIELD TOWN	0–6		11,836
Sep 13	NEWCASTLE UNITED	4–7	Reid 3, Rowley	10,907
Sep 15	Huddersfield Town	0–3		14,028
Sep 20	Sheffield Wednesday	0–3		18,705
Sep 27	GRIMSBY TOWN	0–2		14,695
Oct 4	Manchester City	1–4	Spence	41,757
Oct 11	West Ham United	1–5	Reid	20,003
Oct 18	ARSENAL	1–2	McLachlan	23,406
Oct 25	Portsmouth	1–4	Rowley	19,262
Nov 1	BIRMINGHAM CITY	2–0	Gallimore, Rowley	11,479
Nov 8	Leicester City	4–5	Bullock 3, McLachlan	17,466
Nov 15	BLACKPOOL	0–0		14,765
Nov 22	Sheffield United	1–3	Gallimore	12,698
Nov 29	SUNDERLAND	1–1	Gallimore	10,971
Dec 6	Blackburn Rovers	1–4	Rowley	10,802
Dec 13	DERBY COUNTY	2–1	Reid, Spence	9,701
Dec 20	Leeds United	0–5		11,282
Dec 25	Bolton Wanderers	1–3	Reid	22,662
Dec 26	BOLTON WANDERERS	1–1	Reid	12,741
Dec 27	Aston Villa	0–7		32,505
Jan 1	LEEDS UNITED	0–0		9,875
Jan 3	CHELSEA	1–0	Warburton	8,966
Jan 17	Newcastle United	3–4	Warburton 2, Reid	24,835
Jan 28	SHEFFIELD WEDNESDAY	4–1	Hopkinson, Reid, Spence, Warburton	6,077
Jan 31	Grimsby Town	1–2	Reid	9,305
Feb 7	MANCHESTER CITY	1–3	Spence	39,876
Feb 14	WEST HAM UNITED	1–0	Gallimore	9,745
Feb 21	Arsenal	1–4	Thomson	41,510
Mar 7	Birmingham City	0–0		17,678
Mar 16	PORTSMOUTH	0–1		4,808
Mar 21	Blackpool	1–5	Hopkinson	13,162
Mar 25	LEICESTER CITY	0–0		3,679
Mar 28	SHEFFIELD UNITED	1–2	Hopkinson	5,420
Apr 3	Liverpool	1–1	Wilson	27,782
Apr 4	Sunderland	2–1	Hopkinson, Reid	13,590
Apr 6	LIVERPOOL	4–1	Reid 2, McLenahan, Rowley	8,058
Apr 11	BLACKBURN ROVERS	0–1		6,414
Apr 18	Derby County	1–6	Spence	6,610
May 2	MIDDLESBROUGH	4–4	Reid 2, Bennion, Gallimore	3,969

FA CUP

DATE	OPPONENTS	SCORE	GOALSCORERS	ATTENDANCE
Jan 10	Stoke City (Rd3)	3–3	Reid 3	23,415
Jan 14	STOKE CITY (Rd3R)	0–0		22,013
Jan 19	Stoke City (Rd3R2) (at Anfield)	4–2	Hopkinson 2, Gallimore, Spence	11,788
Jan 24	Grimsby Town (Rd4)	0–1		15,000

FINAL LEAGUE TABLE

		P	W	D	L	F	A	Pts
1	Arsenal	42	28	10	4	127	59	66
2	Aston Villa	42	25	9	8	128	78	59
3	Sheffield Wednesday	42	22	8	12	102	75	52
4	Portsmouth	42	18	13	11	84	67	49
5	Huddersfield Town	42	18	12	12	81	65	48
6	Derby County	42	18	10	14	94	79	46
7	Middlesbrough	42	19	8	15	98	90	46
8	Manchester City	42	18	10	14	75	70	46
9	Liverpool	42	15	12	15	86	85	42
10	Blackburn Rovers	42	17	8	17	83	84	42
11	Sunderland	42	16	9	17	89	85	41
12	Chelsea	42	15	10	17	64	67	40
13	Grimsby Town	42	17	5	20	82	87	39
14	Bolton Wanderers	42	15	9	18	68	81	39
15	Sheffield United	42	14	10	18	78	84	38
16	Leicester City	42	16	6	20	80	95	38
17	Newcastle United	42	15	6	21	78	87	36
18	West Ham United	42	14	8	20	79	94	36
19	Birmingham City	42	13	10	19	55	70	36
20	Blackpool	42	11	10	21	71	125	32
21	Leeds United	42	12	7	23	68	81	31
22	**MANCHESTER UNITED**	42	7	8	27	53	115	22

APPEARANCES

PLAYER	LGE	FAC	TOT
McLachlan	42	4	46
Steward	38	4	42
Bennion	36	4	40
Mellor	35	4	39
Spence	35	2	37
Reid	30	3	33
Gallimore	28	4	32
Hilditch	25	4	29
Rowley	29	–	29
Dale	22	4	26
Silcock	25	–	25
Warburton	18	4	22
Wilson	20	2	22
McLenahan	21	–	21
Hopkinson	17	2	19
Bullock	10	–	10
Parker	9	–	9
Ramsden	7	2	9
Jones	5	–	5
Chesters	4	–	4
Thomson	2	1	3
Williams	3	–	3
Lydon	1	–	1

GOALSCORERS

PLAYER	LGE	FAC	TOT
Reid	17	3	20
Rowley	7	–	7
Spence	6	1	7
Gallimore	5	1	6
Hopkinson	4	2	6
Warburton	5	–	5
Bullock	3	–	3
McLachlan	2	–	2
Bennion	1	–	1
McLenahan	1	–	1
Thomson	1	–	1
Wilson	1	–	1

1931/32

FOOTBALL LEAGUE DIVISION TWO

DATE	OPPONENTS	SCORE	GOALSCORERS	ATTENDANCE
Aug 29	Bradford Park Avenue	1–3	Reid	16,239
Sep 2	SOUTHAMPTON	2–3	Ferguson, Johnston	3,507
Sep 5	SWANSEA CITY	2–1	Hopkinson, Reid	6,763
Sep 7	Stoke City	0–3		10,518
Sep 12	TOTTENHAM HOTSPUR	1–1	Johnston	9,557
Sep 16	STOKE CITY	1–1	Spence	5,025
Sep 19	Nottingham Forest	1–2	Gallimore	10,166
Sep 26	CHESTERFIELD	3–1	Warburton 2, Johnston	10,834
Oct 3	Burnley	0–2		9,719
Oct 10	PRESTON NORTH END	3–2	Gallimore, Johnston, Spence	8,496
Oct 17	Barnsley	0–0		4,052
Oct 24	NOTTS COUNTY	3–3	Gallimore, Mann, Spence	6,694
Oct 31	Plymouth Argyle	1–3	Johnston	22,555
Nov 7	LEEDS UNITED	2–5	Spence 2	9,512
Nov 14	Oldham Athletic	5–1	Johnston 2, Spence 2, Mann	10,922
Nov 21	BURY	1–2	Spence	11,745
Nov 28	Port Vale	2–1	Spence 2	6,955
Dec 5	MILLWALL	2–0	Gallimore, Spence	6,396
Dec 12	Bradford City	3–4	Spence 2, Johnston	13,215
Dec 19	BRISTOL CITY	0–1		4,697
Dec 25	WOLVERHAMPTON W.	3–2	Hopkinson, Reid, Spence	33,123
Dec 26	Wolverhampton W.	0–7		37,207
Jan 2	BRADFORD PARK AVENUE	0–2		6,056
Jan 16	Swansea City	1–3	Warburton	5,888
Jan 23	Tottenham Hotspur	1–4	Reid	19,139
Jan 30	NOTTINGHAM FOREST	3–2	Reid 3	11,152
Feb 6	Chesterfield	3–1	Reid 2, Spence	9,457
Feb 17	BURNLEY	5–1	Johnston 2, Ridding 2, Gallimore	11,036
Feb 20	Preston North End	0–0		13,353
Feb 27	BARNSLEY	3–0	Hopkinson 2, Gallimore	18,223
Mar 5	Notts County	2–1	Hopkinson, Reid	10,817
Mar 12	PLYMOUTH ARGYLE	2–1	Spence 2	24,827
Mar 19	Leeds United	4–1	Reid 2, Johnston, Ridding	13,644
Mar 25	CHARLTON ATHLETIC	0–2		37,012
Mar 26	OLDHAM ATHLETIC	5–1	Reid 3, Fitton, Spence	17,886
Mar 28	Charlton Athletic	0–1		16,256
Apr 2	Bury	0–0		12,592
Apr 9	PORT VALE	2–0	Reid, Spence	10,916
Apr 16	Millwall	1–1	Reid	9,087
Apr 23	BRADFORD CITY	1–0	Fitton	17,765
Apr 30	Bristol City	1–2	Black	5,874
May 7	Southampton	1–1	Black	6,128

FA CUP

DATE	OPPONENTS	SCORE	GOALSCORERS	ATTENDANCE
Jan 9	Plymouth Argyle (Rd3)	1–4	Reid	28,000

FINAL LEAGUE TABLE

		P	W	D	L	F	A	Pts
1	Wolverhampton Wanderers	42	24	8	10	115	49	56
2	Leeds United	42	22	10	10	78	54	54
3	Stoke City	42	19	14	9	69	48	52
4	Plymouth Argyle	42	20	9	13	100	66	49
5	Bury	42	21	7	14	70	58	49
6	Bradford Park Avenue	42	21	7	14	72	63	49
7	Bradford City	42	16	13	13	80	61	45
8	Tottenham Hotspur	42	16	11	15	87	78	43
9	Millwall	42	17	9	16	61	61	43
10	Charlton Athletic	42	17	9	16	61	66	43
11	Nottingham Forest	42	16	10	16	77	72	42
12	MANCHESTER UNITED	42	17	8	17	71	72	42
13	Preston North End	42	16	10	16	75	77	42
14	Southampton	42	17	7	18	66	77	41
15	Swansea City	42	16	7	19	73	75	39
16	Notts County	42	13	12	17	75	75	38
17	Chesterfield	42	13	11	18	64	86	37
18	Oldham Athletic	42	13	10	19	62	84	36
19	Burnley	42	13	9	20	59	87	35
20	Port Vale	42	13	7	22	58	89	33
21	Barnsley	42	12	9	21	55	91	33
22	Bristol City	42	6	11	25	39	78	23

APPEARANCES

PLAYER	LGE	FAC	TOT
Spence	37	1	38
Silcock	35	1	36
Mellor	33	1	34
Steward	32	1	33
Bennion	28	1	29
Johnston	28	1	29
McLachlan	28	1	29
Reid	25	1	26
Gallimore	25	–	25
Hopkinson	19	–	19
Hilditch	17	1	18
Vincent	16	–	16
Ridding	14	1	15
Mann	13	–	13
Jones	12	–	12
McLenahan	11	1	12
Robinson	10	–	10
Page	9	–	9
Wilson	9	–	9
Ferguson	8	–	8
Fitton	8	–	8
Moody	8	–	8
Parker	8	–	8
Warburton	7	–	7
Dale	4	–	4
Black	3	–	3
Manley	3	–	3
Chesters	2	–	2
Dean	2	–	2
Lievesley	2	–	2
Lydon	2	–	2
McDonald	2	–	2
Rowley	1	–	1
Whittle	1	–	1

GOALSCORERS

PLAYER	LGE	FAC	TOT
Spence	19	–	19
Reid	17	1	18
Johnston	11	–	11
Gallimore	6	–	6
Hopkinson	5	–	5
Ridding	3	–	3
Warburton	3	–	3
Black	2	–	2
Fitton	2	–	2
Mann	2	–	2
Ferguson	1	–	1

1932/33

FOOTBALL LEAGUE DIVISION TWO

DATE	OPPONENTS	SCORE	GOALSCORERS	ATTENDANCE
Aug 27	STOKE CITY	0-2		24,996
Aug 29	Charlton Athletic	1-0	Spence	12,946
Sep 3	Southampton	2-4	Reid, og	7,978
Sep 7	CHARLTON ATHLETIC	1-1	McLenahan	9,480
Sep 10	Tottenham Hotspur	1-6	Ridding	23,333
Sep 17	GRIMSBY TOWN	1-1	Brown	17,662
Sep 24	Oldham Athletic	1-1	Spence	14,403
Oct 1	PRESTON NORTH END	0-0		20,800
Oct 8	Burnley	3-2	Brown, Gallimore, Spence	5,314
Oct 15	BRADFORD PARK AVENUE	2-1	Reid 2	18,918
Oct 22	MILLWALL	7-1	Reid 3, Brown 2, Gallimore, Spence	15,860
Oct 29	Port Vale	3-3	Ridding 2, Brown	7,138
Nov 5	NOTTS COUNTY	2-0	Gallimore, Ridding	24,178
Nov 12	Bury	2-2	Brown, Ridding	21,663
Nov 19	FULHAM	4-3	Gallimore, Brown, Ridding	28,803
Nov 26	Chesterfield	1-1	Ridding	10,277
Dec 3	BRADFORD CITY	0-1		28,513
Dec 10	West Ham United	1-3	Ridding	13,435
Dec 17	LINCOLN CITY	4-1	Reid 3, og	18,021
Dec 24	Swansea City	1-2	Brown	10,727
Dec 26	Plymouth Argyle	3-2	Spence 2, Reid	33,776
Dec 31	Stoke City	0-0		14,115
Jan 2	PLYMOUTH ARGYLE	4-0	Ridding 2, Chalmers, Spence	30,257
Jan 7	SOUTHAMPTON	1-2	McDonald	21,364
Jan 21	TOTTENHAM HOTSPUR	2-1	Frame, McDonald	20,661
Jan 31	Grimsby Town	1-1	Stewart	4,020
Feb 4	OLDHAM ATHLETIC	2-0	Ridding, Stewart	15,275
Feb 11	Preston North End	3-3	Dewar, Hopkinson, Stewart	15,662
Feb 22	BURNLEY	2-1	McDonald, Warburton	18,533
Mar 4	Millwall	0-2		22,587
Mar 11	PORT VALE	1-1	Hine	24,690
Mar 18	Notts County	0-1		13,018
Mar 25	BURY	1-3	McLenahan	27,687
Apr 1	Fulham	1-3	Dewar	21,477
Apr 5	Bradford Park Avenue	1-1	Vincent	6,314
Apr 8	CHESTERFIELD	2-1	Dewar, Frame	16,031
Apr 14	Nottingham Forest	2-3	Brown, Dewar	12,963
Apr 15	Bradford City	2-1	Brown, Hine	11,195
Apr 17	NOTTINGHAM FOREST	2-1	Hine, McDonald	16,849
Apr 22	WEST HAM UNITED	1-2	Dewar	14,958
Apr 29	Lincoln City	2-3	Dewar, Hine	8,507
May 6	SWANSEA CITY	1-1	Hine	65,988

FA CUP

DATE	OPPONENTS	SCORE	GOALSCORERS	ATTENDANCE
Jan 14	MIDDLESBROUGH (Rd3)	1-4	Spence	36,991

FINAL LEAGUE TABLE

		P	W	D	L	F	A	Pts
1	Stoke City	42	25	6	11	78	39	56
2	Tottenham Hotspur	42	20	15	7	96	51	55
3	Fulham	42	20	10	12	78	65	50
4	Bury	42	20	9	13	84	59	49
5	Nottingham Forest	42	17	15	10	67	59	49
6	MANCHESTER UNITED	42	15	13	14	71	68	43
7	Millwall	42	16	11	15	59	57	43
8	Bradford Park Avenue	42	17	8	17	77	71	42
9	Preston North End	42	16	10	16	74	70	42
10	Swansea City	42	19	4	19	50	54	42
11	Bradford City	42	14	13	15	65	61	41
12	Southampton	42	18	5	19	66	66	41
13	Grimsby Town	42	14	13	15	79	84	41
14	Plymouth Argyle	42	16	9	17	63	67	41
15	Notts County	42	15	10	17	67	78	40
16	Oldham Athletic	42	15	8	19	67	80	38
17	Port Vale	42	14	10	18	66	79	38
18	Lincoln City	42	12	13	17	72	87	37
19	Burnley	42	11	14	17	67	79	36
20	West Ham United	42	13	9	20	75	93	35
21	Chesterfield	42	12	10	20	61	84	34
22	Charlton Athletic	42	12	7	23	60	91	31

APPEARANCES

PLAYER	LGE	FAC	TOT
Moody	42	1	43
Mellor	40	1	41
Vincent	40	1	41
Frame	33	1	34
Silcock	27	1	28
Brown	25	–	25
McLenahan	24	1	25
Ridding	23	1	24
Chalmers	22	1	23
Stewart	21	1	22
McDonald	21	–	21
Spence	19	1	20
Manley	19	–	19
McLachlan	17	–	17
Dewar	16	–	16
Hine	14	–	14
Gallimore	12	–	12
Reid	11	1	12
Jones	10	–	10
Hopkinson	6	–	6
Warburton	6	–	6
Topping	5	–	5
Fitton	4	–	4
Page	3	–	3
Black	1	–	1
Heywood	1	–	1
Mitchell	1	–	1

GOALSCORERS

PLAYER	LGE	FAC	TOT
Ridding	11	–	11
Brown	10	–	10
Reid	10	–	10
Spence	7	1	8
Dewar	6	–	6
Gallimore	5	–	5
Hine	5	–	5
McDonald	4	–	4
Stewart	3	–	3
Frame	2	–	2
McLenahan	2	–	2
Chalmers	1	–	1
Hopkinson	1	–	1
Vincent	1	–	1
Warburton	1	–	1
own goals	2	–	2

1933/34

FOOTBALL LEAGUE DIVISION TWO

DATE	OPPONENTS	SCORE	GOALSCORERS	ATTENDANCE
Aug 26	Plymouth Argyle	0-4		25,700
Aug 30	NOTTINGHAM FOREST	0-1		16,934
Sep 2	LINCOLN CITY	1-1	Green	16,987
Sep 7	Nottingham Forest	1-1	Stewart	10,650
Sep 9	BOLTON WANDERERS	1-5	Stewart	21,779
Sep 16	Brentford	4-3	Brown 2, Frame, Hine	17,180
Sep 23	BURNLEY	5-2	Dewar 4, Brown	18,411
Sep 30	Oldham Athletic	0-2		22,736
Oct 7	PRESTON NORTH END	1-0	Hine	22,303
Oct 14	Bradford Park Avenue	1-6	Hine	11,033
Oct 21	Bury	1-2	Byrne	15,008
Oct 28	HULL CITY	4-1	Heywood 2, Green, Hine	16,269
Nov 4	Fulham	2-0	Stewart, og	17,049
Nov 11	SOUTHAMPTON	1-0	Manley	18,149
Nov 18	Blackpool	1-3	Brown	14,384
Nov 25	BRADFORD CITY	2-1	Dewar, og	20,902
Dec 2	Port Vale	3-2	Black, Brown, Dewar	10,316
Dec 9	NOTTS COUNTY	1-2	Dewar	15,564
Dec 16	Swansea City	1-2	Hine	6,591
Dec 23	MILLWALL	1-1	Dewar	12,043
Dec 25	GRIMSBY TOWN	1-3	Vose	29,443
Dec 26	Grimsby Town	3-7	Byrne 2, Frame	15,801
Dec 30	PLYMOUTH ARGYLE	0-3		12,206
Jan 6	Lincoln City	1-5	Brown	6,075
Jan 20	Bolton Wanderers	1-3	Ball	11,887
Jan 27	BRENTFORD	1-3	Ball	16,891
Feb 3	Burnley	4-1	Cape 2, Green, Stewart	9,906
Feb 10	OLDHAM ATHLETIC	2-3	Cape, Green	24,480
Feb 21	Preston North End	2-3	Gallimore 2	9,173
Feb 24	BRADFORD PARK AVENUE	0-4		13,389
Mar 3	BURY	2-1	Ball, Gallimore	11,176
Mar 10	Hull City	1-4	Ball	5,771
Mar 17	FULHAM	1-0	Ball	17,565
Mar 24	Southampton	0-1		4,840
Mar 30	WEST HAM UNITED	0-1		29,114
Mar 31	BLACKPOOL	2-0	Cape, Hine	20,038
Apr 2	West Ham United	1-2	Cape	20,085
Apr 7	Bradford City	1-1	Cape	9,258
Apr 14	PORT VALE	2-0	Brown, McMillen	14,777
Apr 21	Notts County	0-0		9,645
Apr 28	SWANSEA CITY	1-1	Topping	16,678
May 5	Millwall	2-0	Cape, Manley	24,003

FA CUP

DATE	OPPONENTS	SCORE	GOALSCORERS	ATTENDANCE
Jan 13	PORTSMOUTH (Rd3)	1-1	McLenahan	23,283
Jan 17	Portsmouth (Rd3R)	1-4	Ball	18,748

FINAL LEAGUE TABLE

		P	W	D	L	F	A	Pts
1	Grimsby Town	42	27	5	10	103	59	59
2	Preston North End	42	23	6	13	71	52	52
3	Bolton Wanderers	42	21	9	12	79	55	51
4	Brentford	42	22	7	13	85	60	51
5	Bradford Park Avenue	42	23	3	16	86	67	49
6	Bradford City	42	20	6	16	73	67	46
7	West Ham United	42	17	11	14	78	70	45
8	Port Vale	42	19	7	16	60	55	45
9	Oldham Athletic	42	17	10	15	72	60	44
10	Plymouth Argyle	42	15	13	14	69	70	43
11	Blackpool	42	15	13	14	62	64	43
12	Bury	42	17	9	16	70	73	43
13	Burnley	42	18	6	18	60	72	42
14	Southampton	42	15	8	19	54	58	38
15	Hull City	42	13	12	17	52	68	38
16	Fulham	42	15	7	20	48	67	37
17	Nottingham Forest	42	13	9	20	73	74	35
18	Notts County	42	12	11	19	53	62	35
19	Swansea City	42	10	15	17	51	60	35
20	MANCHESTER UNITED	42	14	6	22	59	85	34
21	Millwall	42	11	11	20	39	68	33
22	Lincoln City	42	9	8	25	44	75	26

APPEARANCES

PLAYER	LGE	FAC	TOT
Jones	39	2	41
Hine	33	2	35
Manley	30	2	32
Stewart	25	2	27
Hall	23	2	25
McMillen	23	2	25
McLenahan	22	2	24
Dewar	21	–	21
Ball	18	2	20
Vose	17	2	19
Frame	18	–	18
Cape	17	–	17
Silcock	16	1	17
Brown	15	1	16
Chalmers	12	–	12
Griffiths	10	–	10
Hacking	10	–	10
McKay	10	–	10
Robertson	10	–	10
Green	9	–	9
Hopkinson	9	–	9
McGillivray	8	1	9
Hillam	8	–	8
Vincent	8	–	8
Gallimore	7	–	7
Topping	6	–	6
Mellor	5	–	5
Nevin	4	1	5
Ridding	5	–	5
Black	4	–	4
Byrne	4	–	4
McDonald	4	–	4
Heywood	3	–	3
Ainsworth	2	–	2
Manns	2	–	2
Newton	2	–	2
Warburton	2	–	2
Behan	1	–	1

GOALSCORERS

PLAYER	LGE	FAC	TOT
Dewar	8	–	8
Brown	7	–	7
Cape	7	–	7
Hine	6	–	6
Ball	5	1	6
Green	4	–	4
Stewart	4	–	4
Byrne	3	–	3
Gallimore	3	–	3
Frame	2	–	2
Heywood	2	–	2
Manley	2	–	2
Black	1	–	1
McMillen	1	–	1
Topping	1	–	1
Vose	1	–	1
McLenahan	–	1	1
own goals	2	–	2

1934/35

FOOTBALL LEAGUE DIVISION TWO

DATE	OPPONENTS	SCORE	GOALSCORERS	ATTENDANCE
Aug 25	BRADFORD CITY	2–0	Manley 2	27,573
Sep 1	Sheffield United	2–3	Ball, Manley	18,468
Sep 3	Bolton Wanderers	1–3	og	16,238
Sep 8	BARNSLEY	4–1	Mutch 3, Manley	22,315
Sep 12	BOLTON WANDERERS	0–3		24,760
Sep 15	Port Vale	2–3	Jones (Tommy), Mutch	9,307
Sep 22	NORWICH CITY	5–0	Cape, Jones (Tommy), McLenahan, Mutch, Owen	13,052
Sep 29	SWANSEA CITY	3–1	Cape 2, Mutch	14,865
Oct 6	Burnley	2–1	Cape, Manley	16,757
Oct 13	OLDHAM ATHLETIC	4–0	Manley 2, McKay, Mutch	29,143
Oct 20	Newcastle United	1–0	Bamford	24,752
Oct 27	WEST HAM UNITED	3–1	Mutch 2, McKay	31,950
Nov 3	Blackpool	2–1	Bryant, McKay	15,663
Nov 10	BURY	1–0	Mutch	41,415
Nov 17	Hull City	2–3	Bamford 2	6,494
Nov 24	NOTTINGHAM FOREST	3–2	Mutch 2, Hine	27,192
Dec 1	Brentford	1–3	Bamford	21,744
Dec 8	FULHAM	1–0	Mutch	25,706
Dec 15	Bradford Park Avenue	2–1	Manley, Mutch	8,405
Dec 22	PLYMOUTH ARGYLE	3–1	Bamford, Bryant, Rowley	24,896
Dec 25	NOTTS COUNTY	2–1	Mutch, Rowley	32,965
Dec 26	Notts County	0–1		24,599
Dec 29	Bradford City	0–2		11,908
Jan 1	SOUTHAMPTON	3–0	Cape 2, Rowley	15,174
Jan 5	SHEFFIELD UNITED	3–3	Bryant, Mutch, Rowley	28,300
Jan 19	Barnsley	2–0	Bryant, Jones (Tommy)	10,177
Feb 2	Norwich City	2–3	Manley, Rowley	14,260
Feb 6	PORT VALE	2–1	Rowley, Jones (Tommy)	7,372
Feb 9	Swansea City	0–1		8,876
Feb 23	Oldham Athletic	1–3	Mutch	14,432
Mar 2	NEWCASTLE UNITED	0–1		20,728
Mar 9	West Ham United	0–0		19,718
Mar 16	BLACKPOOL	3–2	Bamford, Mutch, Rowley	25,704
Mar 23	Bury	1–0	Cape	7,229
Mar 27	BURNLEY	3–4	Boyd, Cape, McMillen	10,247
Mar 30	HULL CITY	3–0	Boyd 3	15,358
Apr 6	Nottingham Forest	2–2	Bryant 2	8,618
Apr 13	BRENTFORD	0–0		32,969
Apr 20	Fulham	1–3	Bamford	11,059
Apr 22	Southampton	0–1		12,458
Apr 27	BRADFORD PARK AVENUE	2–0	Bamford, Robertson	8,606
May 4	Plymouth Argyle	2–0	Bamford, Rowley	10,767

FA CUP

DATE	OPPONENTS	SCORE	GOALSCORERS	ATTENDANCE
Jan 12	Bristol Rovers (Rd3)	3–1	Bamford 2, Mutch	20,400
Jan 26	Nottingham Forest (Rd4)	0–0		32,862
Jan 30	NOTTINGHAM FOREST (Rd4R)	0–3		33,851

FINAL LEAGUE TABLE

		P	W	D	L	F	A	Pts
1	Brentford	42	26	9	7	93	48	61
2	Bolton Wanderers	42	26	4	12	96	48	56
3	West Ham United	42	26	4	12	80	63	56
4	Blackpool	42	21	11	10	79	57	53
5	MANCHESTER UNITED	42	23	4	15	76	55	50
6	Newcastle United	42	22	4	16	89	68	48
7	Fulham	42	17	12	13	76	56	46
8	Plymouth Argyle	42	19	8	15	75	64	46
9	Nottingham Forest	42	17	8	17	76	70	42
10	Bury	42	19	4	19	62	73	42
11	Sheffield United	42	16	9	17	79	70	41
12	Burnley	42	16	9	17	63	73	41
13	Hull City	42	16	8	18	63	74	40
14	Norwich City	42	14	11	17	71	61	39
15	Bradford Park Avenue	42	11	16	15	55	63	38
16	Barnsley	42	13	12	17	60	83	38
17	Swansea City	42	14	8	20	56	67	36
18	Port Vale	42	11	12	19	55	74	34
19	Southampton	42	11	12	19	46	75	34
20	Bradford City	42	12	8	22	50	68	32
21	Oldham Athletic	42	10	6	26	56	95	26
22	Notts County	42	9	7	26	46	97	25

APPEARANCES

PLAYER	LGE	FAC	TOT
Griffiths	40	3	43
Mutch	40	3	43
Vose	39	3	42
McKay	38	3	41
Robertson	36	3	39
Manley	30	1	31
Jones, Tom	27	2	29
Rowley	24	3	27
Bryant	24	2	26
Hacking	22	2	24
Bamford	19	3	22
Cape	21	1	22
Jones, Tommy	20	2	22
Porter	15	1	16
Owen	15	–	15
Langford	12	–	12
McLenahan	10	–	10
Hall	8	1	9
Ball	6	–	6
Boyd	6	–	6
Hine	4	–	4
McMillen	4	–	4
Mellor	1	–	1
Topping	1	–	1

GOALSCORERS

PLAYER	LGE	FAC	TOT
Mutch	18	1	19
Bamford	9	2	11
Manley	9	–	9
Cape	8	–	8
Rowley	8	–	8
Bryant	6	–	6
Boyd	4	–	4
Jones, Tommy	4	–	4
McKay	3	–	3
Ball	1	–	1
Hine	1	–	1
McLenahan	1	–	1
McMillen	1	–	1
Owen	1	–	1
Robertson	1	–	1
own goal	1	–	1

1935/36

FOOTBALL LEAGUE DIVISION TWO

DATE	OPPONENTS	SCORE	GOALSCORERS	ATTENDANCE
Aug 31	Plymouth Argyle	1–3	Bamford	22,366
Sep 4	CHARLTON ATHLETIC	3–0	Bamford, Cape, Chester	21,211
Sep 7	BRADFORD CITY	3–1	Bamford 2, Mutch	30,754
Sep 9	Charlton Athletic	0–0		13,178
Sep 14	Newcastle United	2–0	Bamford, Rowley	28,520
Sep 18	HULL CITY	2–0	Bamford 2	15,739
Sep 21	TOTTENHAM HOTSPUR	0–0		34,718
Sep 28	Southampton	1–2	Rowley	17,678
Oct 5	Port Vale	3–0	Mutch 2, Bamford	9,703
Oct 12	FULHAM	1–0	Rowley	22,723
Oct 19	SHEFFIELD UNITED	3–1	Cape, Mutch, Rowley	18,636
Oct 26	Bradford Park Avenue	0–1		12,216
Nov 2	LEICESTER CITY	0–1		39,074
Nov 9	Swansea City	1–2	Bamford	9,731
Nov 16	WEST HAM UNITED	2–3	Rowley 2	24,440
Nov 23	Norwich City	5–3	Rowley 3, Manley 2	17,266
Nov 30	DONCASTER ROVERS	0–0		23,569
Dec 7	Blackpool	1–4	Mutch	13,218
Dec 14	NOTTINGHAM FOREST	5–0	Bamford 2, Manley, Mutch, Rowley	15,284
Dec 26	BARNSLEY	1–1	Mutch	20,993
Dec 28	PLYMOUTH ARGYLE	3–2	Mutch 2, Manley	20,894
Jan 1	Barnsley	3–0	Gardner, Manley, Mutch	20,957
Jan 4	Bradford City	0–1		11,286
Jan 18	NEWCASTLE UNITED	3–1	Mutch 2, Rowley	22,968
Feb 1	SOUTHAMPTON	4–0	Mutch 2, Bryant, og	23,205
Feb 5	Tottenham Hotspur	0–0		20,085
Feb 8	PORT VALE	7–2	Manley 4, Rowley 2, Mutch	22,265
Feb 22	Sheffield United	1–1	Manley	25,852
Feb 29	BLACKPOOL	3–2	Bryant, Manley, Mutch	18,423
Mar 7	West Ham United	2–1	Bryant, Mutch	29,684
Mar 14	SWANSEA CITY	3–0	Manley, Mutch, Rowley	27,580
Mar 21	Leicester City	1–1	Bryant	18,200
Mar 28	NORWICH CITY	2–1	Rowley 2	31,596
Apr 1	Fulham	2–2	Bryant, Griffiths	11,137
Apr 4	Doncaster Rovers	0–0		13,474
Apr 10	Burnley	2–2	Bamford 2	27,245
Apr 11	BRADFORD PARK AVENUE	4–0	Mutch 2, Bamford, Bryant	33,517
Apr 13	BURNLEY	4–0	Bryant 2, Rowley 2	39,855
Apr 18	Nottingham Forest	1–1	Bamford	12,156
Apr 25	BURY	2–1	Lang, Rowley	35,027
Apr 29	Bury	3–2	Manley 2, Mutch	31,562
May 2	Hull City	1–1	Bamford	4,540

FA CUP

DATE	OPPONENTS	SCORE	GOALSCORERS	ATTENDANCE
Jan 11	Reading (Rd3)	3–1	Mutch 2, Manley	25,844
Jan 25	Stoke City (Rd4)	0–0		32,286
Jan 29	STOKE CITY (Rd4R)	0–2		34,440

FINAL LEAGUE TABLE

		P	W	D	L	F	A	Pts
1	MANCHESTER UNITED	42	22	12	8	85	43	56
2	Charlton Athletic	42	22	11	9	85	58	55
3	Sheffield United	42	20	12	10	79	50	52
4	West Ham United	42	22	8	12	90	68	52
5	Tottenham Hotspur	42	18	13	11	91	55	49
6	Leicester City	42	19	10	13	79	57	48
7	Plymouth Argyle	42	20	8	14	71	57	48
8	Newcastle United	42	20	6	16	88	79	46
9	Fulham	42	15	14	13	76	52	44
10	Blackpool	42	18	7	17	93	72	43
11	Norwich City	42	17	9	16	72	65	43
12	Bradford City	42	15	13	14	55	65	43
13	Swansea City	42	15	9	18	67	76	39
14	Bury	42	13	12	17	66	84	38
15	Burnley	42	12	13	17	50	59	37
16	Bradford Park Avenue	42	14	9	19	62	84	37
17	Southampton	42	14	9	19	47	65	37
18	Doncaster Rovers	42	14	9	19	51	71	37
19	Nottingham Forest	42	12	11	19	69	76	35
20	Barnsley	42	12	9	21	54	80	33
21	Port Vale	42	12	8	22	56	106	32
22	Hull City	42	5	10	27	47	111	20

APPEARANCES

PLAYER	LGE	FAC	TOT
Mutch	42	3	45
Porter	42	3	45
Griffiths	41	3	44
Vose	41	3	44
Brown	40	3	43
Rowley	37	3	40
Hall	36	3	39
McKay	35	3	38
Manley	31	3	34
Bamford	27	2	29
Bryant	21	1	22
Cape	17	–	17
Gardner	12	2	14
Chester	13	–	13
Ferrier	7	1	8
Lang	4	–	4
Breedon	3	–	3
Langford	3	–	3
Owen	2	–	2
Wassall	2	–	2
Whalley	2	–	2
Morton	1	–	1
Redwood	1	–	1
Robbie	1	–	1
Robertson	1	–	1

GOALSCORERS

PLAYER	LGE	FAC	TOT
Mutch	21	2	23
Rowley	19	–	19
Bamford	16	–	16
Manley	14	1	15
Bryant	8	–	8
Cape	2	–	2
Chester	1	–	1
Gardner	1	–	1
Griffiths	1	–	1
Lang	1	–	1
own goal	1	–	1

1936/37

FOOTBALL LEAGUE DIVISION ONE

DATE	OPPONENTS	SCORE	GOALSCORERS	ATTENDANCE
Aug 29	WOLVERHAMPTON W.	1-1	Bamford	42,731
Sep 2	Huddersfield Town	1-3	Manley	12,612
Sep 5	Derby County	4-5	Bamford 3, Wassall	21,194
Sep 9	HUDDERSFIELD TOWN	3-1	Bamford, Bryant, Mutch	26,839
Sep 12	MANCHESTER CITY	3-2	Bamford, Bryant, Manley	68,796
Sep 19	SHEFFIELD WEDNESDAY	1-1	Bamford	40,933
Sep 26	Preston North End	1-3	Bamford	24,149
Oct 3	ARSENAL	2-0	Bryant, Rowley	55,884
Oct 10	Brentford	0-4		28,019
Oct 17	Portsmouth	1-2	Manley	19,845
Oct 24	CHELSEA	0-0		29,859
Oct 31	Stoke City	0-3		22,464
Nov 7	CHARLTON ATHLETIC	0-0		26,084
Nov 14	Grimsby Town	2-6	Bryant, Mutch	9,844
Nov 21	LIVERPOOL	2-5	Manley, Thompson	26,419
Nov 28	Leeds United	1-2	Bryant	17,610
Dec 5	BIRMINGHAM CITY	1-2	Mutch	16,544
Dec 12	Middlesbrough	2-3	Halton, Manley	11,970
Dec 19	WEST BROMWICH ALBION	2-2	McKay, Mutch	21,051
Dec 25	BOLTON WANDERERS	1-0	Bamford	47,658
Dec 26	Wolverhampton W.	1-3	McKay	41,525
Dec 28	Bolton Wanderers	4-0	Bryant 2, McKay 2	11,801
Jan 1	SUNDERLAND	2-1	Bryant, Mutch	46,257
Jan 2	DERBY COUNTY	2-2	Rowley 2	31,883
Jan 9	Manchester City	0-1		64,862
Jan 23	Sheffield Wednesday	0-1		8,658
Feb 3	PRESTON NORTH END	1-1	Wrigglesworth	13,225
Feb 6	Arsenal	1-1	Rowley	37,236
Feb 13	Brentford	1-3	Baird	31,942
Feb 20	PORTSMOUTH	0-1		19,416
Feb 27	Chelsea	2-4	Bamford, Gladwin	16,382
Mar 6	STOKE CITY	2-1	Baird, McClelland	24,660
Mar 13	Charlton Athletic	0-3		25,943
Mar 20	GRIMSBY TOWN	1-1	Cape	26,636
Mar 26	EVERTON	2-1	Baird, Mutch	30,071
Mar 27	Liverpool	0-2		25,319
Mar 29	Everton	3-2	Bryant, Ferrier, Mutch	28,395
Apr 3	LEEDS UNITED	0-0		34,429
Apr 10	Birmingham City	2-2	Bamford 2	19,130
Apr 17	MIDDLESBROUGH	2-1	Bamford, Bryant	17,656
Apr 21	Sunderland	1-1	Bamford	12,876
Apr 24	West Bromwich Albion	0-1		16,234

FA CUP

DATE	OPPONENTS	SCORE	GOALSCORERS	ATTENDANCE
Jan 16	READING (Rd3)	1-0	Bamford	36,668
Jan 30	Arsenal (Rd4)	0-5		45,637

FINAL LEAGUE TABLE

		P	W	D	L	F	A	Pts
1	Manchester City	42	22	13	7	107	61	57
2	Charlton Athletic	42	21	12	9	58	49	54
3	Arsenal	42	18	16	8	80	49	52
4	Derby County	42	21	7	14	96	90	49
5	Wolverhampton Wanderers	42	21	5	16	84	67	47
6	Brentford	42	18	10	14	82	78	46
7	Middlesbrough	42	19	8	15	74	71	46
8	Sunderland	42	19	6	17	89	87	44
9	Portsmouth	42	17	10	15	62	66	44
10	Stoke City	42	15	12	15	72	57	42
11	Birmingham City	42	13	15	14	64	60	41
12	Grimsby Town	42	17	7	18	86	81	41
13	Chelsea	42	14	13	15	52	55	41
14	Preston North End	42	14	13	15	56	67	41
15	Huddersfield Town	42	12	15	15	62	64	39
16	West Bromwich Albion	42	16	6	20	77	98	38
17	Everton	42	14	9	19	81	78	37
18	Liverpool	42	12	11	19	62	84	35
19	Leeds United	42	15	4	23	60	80	34
20	Bolton Wanderers	42	10	14	18	43	66	34
21	MANCHESTER UNITED	42	10	12	20	55	78	32
22	Sheffield Wednesday	42	9	12	21	53	69	30

APPEARANCES

PLAYER	LGE	FAC	TOT
Bryant	37	2	39
Roughton	33	2	35
Brown	31	2	33
Bamford	29	2	31
Manley	31	–	31
McKay	29	2	31
Mutch	28	2	30
Breen	26	2	28
Vose	26	1	27
Winterbottom	21	2	23
Redwood	21	1	22
Griffiths	21	–	21
Whalley	19	2	21
Rowley	17	–	17
John	15	–	15
Baird	14	–	14
Lang	8	1	9
Gladwin	8	–	8
Wrigglesworth	7	1	8
Wassall	7	–	7
Ferrier	6	–	6
McClelland	5	–	5
Cape	4	–	4
Gardner	4	–	4
Halton	4	–	4
McLenahan	3	–	3
Mellor	2	–	2
Porter	2	–	2
Thompson	2	–	2
Breedon	1	–	1
Jones	1	–	1

GOALSCORERS

PLAYER	LGE	FAC	TOT
Bamford	14	1	15
Bryant	10	–	10
Mutch	7	–	7
Manley	5	–	5
McKay	4	–	4
Rowley	4	–	4
Baird	3	–	3
Cape	1	–	1
Ferrier	1	–	1
Gladwin	1	–	1
Halton	1	–	1
McClelland	1	–	1
Thompson	1	–	1
Wrigglesworth	1	–	1

1937/38

FOOTBALL LEAGUE DIVISION TWO

DATE	OPPONENTS	SCORE	GOALSCORERS	ATTENDANCE
Aug 28	NEWCASTLE UNITED	3-0	Manley 2, Bryant	29,446
Aug 30	Coventry City	0-1		30,575
Sep 4	Luton Town	0-1		20,610
Sep 8	COVENTRY CITY	2-2	Bamford, Bryant	17,455
Sep 11	BARNSLEY	4-1	Bamford 3, Manley	22,934
Sep 13	Bury	2-1	Ferrier 2	9,954
Sep 18	Stockport County	0-1		24,386
Sep 25	SOUTHAMPTON	1-2	Manley	22,729
Oct 2	SHEFFIELD UNITED	0-1		20,105
Oct 9	Tottenham Hotspur	1-0	Manley	31,189
Oct 16	Blackburn Rovers	1-1	Bamford	19,580
Oct 23	SHEFFIELD WEDNESDAY	1-0	Ferrier	16,379
Oct 30	Fulham	0-1		17,350
Nov 6	PLYMOUTH ARGYLE	0-0		18,359
Nov 13	Chesterfield	7-1	Bamford 4, Baird, Bryant, Manley	17,407
Nov 20	ASTON VILLA	3-1	Bamford, Manley, Pearson	33,193
Nov 27	Norwich City	3-2	Baird, Bryant, Pearson	17,397
Dec 4	SWANSEA CITY	5-1	Rowley 4, Bryant	17,782
Dec 11	Bradford Park Avenue	0-4		12,004
Dec 27	NOTTINGHAM FOREST	4-3	Baird 2, McKay, Wrigglesworth	30,778
Dec 28	Nottingham Forest	3-2	Bamford, Bryant, Carey	19,283
Jan 1	Newcastle United	2-2	Bamford, Rowley	40,088
Jan 15	LUTON TOWN	4-2	Bamford, Bryant, Carey, McKay	16,845
Jan 29	STOCKPORT COUNTY	3-1	Bamford, Bryant, McKay	31,852
Feb 2	Barnsley	2-2	Rowley, Smith	7,859
Feb 5	Southampton	3-3	Redwood 2, Baird	20,354
Feb 17	Sheffield United	2-1	Bryant, Smith	17,754
Feb 19	TOTTENHAM HOTSPUR	0-1		34,631
Feb 23	WEST HAM UNITED	4-0	Baird 2, Smith, Wassall	14,572
Feb 26	BLACKBURN ROVERS	2-1	Baird, Bryant	30,892
Mar 5	Sheffield Wednesday	3-1	Baird, Brown, Rowley	37,156
Mar 12	FULHAM	1-0	Baird	30,636
Mar 19	Plymouth Argyle	1-1	Rowley	20,311
Mar 26	CHESTERFIELD	4-1	Smith 2, Bryant, Carey	27,311
Apr 2	Aston Villa	0-3		54,654
Apr 9	NORWICH CITY	0-0		25,879
Apr 15	Burnley	0-1		28,459
Apr 16	Swansea City	2-2	Rowley, Smith	13,811
Apr 18	BURNLEY	4-0	McKay 2, Baird, Bryant	35,808
Apr 23	BRADFORD PARK AVENUE	3-1	Baird, McKay, Smith	28,919
Apr 30	West Ham United	0-1		14,816
May 7	BURY	2-0	McKay, Smith	53,604

FA CUP

DATE	OPPONENTS	SCORE	GOALSCORERS	ATTENDANCE
Jan 8	YEOVIL TOWN (Rd3)	3-0	Baird, Bamford, Pearson	49,004
Jan 22	Barnsley (Rd4)	2-2	Baird, Carey	35,549
Jan 26	BARNSLEY (Rd4R)	1-0	Baird	33,601
Feb 12	Brentford (Rd5)	0-2		24,147

FINAL LEAGUE TABLE

		P	W	D	L	F	A	Pts
1	Aston Villa	42	25	7	10	73	35	57
2	MANCHESTER UNITED	42	22	9	11	82	50	53
3	Sheffield United	42	22	9	11	73	56	53
4	Coventry City	42	20	12	10	66	45	52
5	Tottenham Hotspur	42	19	6	17	76	54	44
6	Burnley	42	17	10	15	54	54	44
7	Bradford Park Avenue	42	17	9	16	69	56	43
8	Fulham	42	16	11	15	61	57	43
9	West Ham United	42	14	14	14	53	52	42
10	Bury	42	18	5	19	63	60	41
11	Chesterfield	42	16	9	17	63	63	41
12	Luton Town	42	15	10	17	89	86	40
13	Plymouth Argyle	42	14	12	16	57	65	40
14	Norwich City	42	14	11	17	56	75	39
15	Southampton	42	15	9	18	55	77	39
16	Blackburn Rovers	42	14	10	18	71	80	38
17	Sheffield Wednesday	42	14	10	18	49	56	38
18	Swansea City	42	13	12	17	45	73	38
19	Newcastle United	42	14	8	20	51	58	36
20	Nottingham Forest	42	14	8	20	47	60	36
21	Barnsley	42	11	14	17	50	64	36
22	Stockport County	42	11	9	22	43	70	31

APPEARANCES

PLAYER	LGE	FAC	TOT
Bryant	39	4	43
Roughton	39	4	43
McKay	37	3	40
Baird	35	4	39
Breen	33	4	37
Vose	33	4	37
Redwood	29	4	33
Brown	28	3	31
Rowley	25	4	29
Bamford	23	4	27
Manley	21	1	22
Carey	16	3	19
Griffiths	18	–	18
Smith	17	–	17
Pearson	11	1	12
Breedon	9	–	9
Wassall	9	–	9
Gladwin	7	–	7
Whalley	6	–	6
Ferrier	5	–	5
Savage	4	1	5
Murray	4	–	4
Winterbottom	4	–	4
Wrigglesworth	4	–	4
Mutch	2	–	2
Porter	2	–	2
Jones	1	–	1
Thompson	1	–	1

GOALSCORERS

PLAYER	LGE	FAC	TOT
Bamford	14	1	15
Baird	12	3	15
Bryant	12	–	12
Rowley	9	–	9
Smith	8	–	8
Manley	7	–	7
McKay	7	–	7
Carey	3	1	4
Ferrier	3	–	3
Pearson	2	1	3
Redwood	2	–	2
Brown	1	–	1
Wassall	1	–	1
Wrigglesworth	1	–	1

317

1938/39

FOOTBALL LEAGUE DIVISION ONE

DATE	OPPONENTS	SCORE	GOALSCORERS	ATTENDANCE
Aug 27	Middlesbrough	1-3	Smith	25,539
Aug 31	BOLTON WANDERERS	2-2	Craven, og	37,950
Sep 3	BIRMINGHAM CITY	4-1	Smith 2, Bryant, Craven	22,228
Sep 7	Liverpool	0-1		25,070
Sep 10	Grimsby Town	0-1		14,077
Sep 17	Stoke City	1-1	Smith	21,526
Sep 24	CHELSEA	5-1	Carey, Manley, Redwood, Rowley, Smith	34,557
Oct 1	Preston North End	1-1	Bryant	25,964
Oct 8	CHARLTON ATHLETIC	0-2		35,730
Oct 15	BLACKPOOL	0-0		39,723
Oct 22	Derby County	1-5	Smith	26,612
Oct 29	SUNDERLAND	0-1		33,565
Nov 5	Aston Villa	2-0	Rowley, Wrigglesworth	38,357
Nov 12	WOLVERHAMPTON W.	1-3	Rowley	32,821
Nov 19	Everton	0-3		31,809
Nov 26	HUDDERSFIELD TOWN	1-1	Hanlon	23,164
Dec 3	Portsmouth	0-0		18,692
Dec 10	ARSENAL	1-0	Bryant	42,008
Dec 17	Brentford	5-2	Hanlon 2, Bryant, Manley, Rowley	14,919
Dec 24	MIDDLESBROUGH	1-1	Wassall	33,235
Dec 26	LEICESTER CITY	3-0	Wrigglesworth 2, Carey	26,332
Dec 27	Leicester City	1-1	Hanlon	21,434
Dec 31	Birmingham City	3-3	Hanlon, McKay, Pearson	20,787
Jan 14	GRIMSBY TOWN	3-1	Rowley 2, Wassall	25,654
Jan 21	STOKE CITY	0-1		37,384
Jan 28	Chelsea	1-0	Bradbury	31,265
Feb 4	PRESTON NORTH END	1-1	Rowley	41,061
Feb 11	Charlton Athletic	1-7	Hanlon	23,721
Feb 18	Blackpool	5-3	Hanlon 3, Bryant, Carey	15,253
Feb 25	DERBY COUNTY	1-1	Carey	37,166
Mar 4	Sunderland	2-5	Manley, Rowley	11,078
Mar 11	ASTON VILLA	1-1	Wassall	28,292
Mar 18	Wolverhampton W.	0-3		31,498
Mar 29	EVERTON	0-2		18,438
Apr 1	Huddersfield Town	1-1	Rowley	14,007
Apr 7	LEEDS UNITED	0-0		35,564
Apr 8	PORTSMOUTH	1-1	Rowley	25,457
Apr 10	Leeds United	1-3	Carey	13,771
Apr 15	Arsenal	1-2	Hanlon	25,741
Apr 22	BRENTFORD	3-0	Bryant, Carey, Wassall	15,353
Apr 29	Bolton Wanderers	0-0		10,314
May 6	LIVERPOOL	2-0	Hanlon 2	12,073

FA CUP

DATE	OPPONENTS	SCORE	GOALSCORERS	ATTENDANCE
Jan 7	West Bromwich Albion (Rd3)	0-0		23,900
Jan 11	WEST BROMWICH ALBION (Rd3R)	1-5	Redwood	17,641

FINAL LEAGUE TABLE

		P	W	D	L	F	A	Pts
1	Everton	42	27	5	10	88	52	59
2	Wolverhampton Wanderers	42	22	11	9	88	39	55
3	Charlton Athletic	42	22	6	14	75	59	50
4	Middlesbrough	42	20	9	13	93	74	49
5	Arsenal	42	19	9	14	55	41	47
6	Derby County	42	19	8	15	66	55	46
7	Stoke City	42	17	12	13	71	68	46
8	Bolton Wanderers	42	15	15	12	67	58	45
9	Preston North End	42	16	12	14	63	59	44
10	Grimsby Town	42	16	11	15	61	69	43
11	Liverpool	42	14	14	14	62	63	42
12	Aston Villa	42	15	11	16	71	60	41
13	Leeds United	42	16	9	17	59	67	41
14	MANCHESTER UNITED	42	11	16	15	57	65	38
15	Blackpool	42	12	14	16	56	68	38
16	Sunderland	42	13	12	17	54	67	38
17	Portsmouth	42	12	13	17	47	70	37
18	Brentford	42	14	8	20	53	74	36
19	Huddersfield Town	42	12	11	19	58	64	35
20	Chelsea	42	12	9	21	64	80	33
21	Birmingham City	42	12	8	22	62	84	32
22	Leicester City	42	9	11	22	48	82	29

APPEARANCES

PLAYER	LGE	FAC	TOT
Vose	39	1	40
Rowley	38	1	39
Griffiths	35	2	37
Redwood	35	2	37
Carey	32	2	34
Warner	29	2	31
Hanlon	27	2	29
Wassall	27	2	29
Bryant	27	–	27
Manley	23	–	23
Breedon	22	–	22
McKay	20	2	22
Smith	19	1	20
Tapken	14	2	16
Roughton	14	–	14
Wrigglesworth	12	2	14
Gladwin	12	1	13
Craven	11	–	11
Pearson	9	–	9
Breen	6	–	6
Dougan	4	–	4
Brown	3	–	3
Bradbury	2	–	2
Whalley	2	–	2

GOALSCORERS

PLAYER	LGE	FAC	TOT
Hanlon	12	–	12
Rowley	10	–	10
Bryant	6	–	6
Carey	6	–	6
Smith	6	–	6
Wassall	4	–	4
Manley	3	–	3
Wrigglesworth	3	–	3
Craven	2	–	2
Redwood	1	1	2
Bradbury	1	–	1
McKay	1	–	1
Pearson	1	–	1
own goal	1	–	1

1939/40

FOOTBALL LEAGUE DIVISION ONE

DATE	OPPONENTS	SCORE	GOALSCORERS	ATTENDANCE
Aug 26	GRIMSBY TOWN	4-0	Bryant, Carey, Pearson, Wrigglesworth	22,537
Aug 30	Chelsea	1-1	Bryant	15,157
Sep 2	Charlton Athletic	0-2		8,608

The Football League was suspended in September 1939 following the outbreak of the Second World War. Three matches had already been played but the details were expunged from League records following the suspension of the competition. The details appear here for informative purposes only and the appearance and goalscoring records are not included in the overall player records in this volume.

1945/46

FA CUP

DATE	OPPONENTS	SCORE	GOALSCORERS	ATTENDANCE
3rd Round 1st Leg				
Jan 5	Accrington Stanley	2-2	Smith, Wrigglesworth	9,968
3rd Round 2nd Leg				
Jan 9	ACCRINGTON STANLEY	5-1	Rowley 2, Bainbridge, Wrigglesworth, og	15,339
4th Round 1st Leg				
Jan 26	PRESTON NORTH END	1-0	Hanlon	36,237
4th Round 2nd Leg				
Jan 30	Preston North End	1-3	Hanlon	21,000

As the Second World War only finished in the early autumn of 1945, league football did not restart until the beginning of the 1946/47 season. However, the FA Cup restarted in January 1946 with the ties being played over two legs for the only time in its history.

Old Trafford was severely damaged by bombing during the war, so United played all their home matches at Maine Road until the end of the 1948/49 season; the only exceptions being their home FA Cup ties in season 1947/48 which were staged at various venues. Details of the venues for these games can be found with the respective matches.

APPEARANCES

PLAYER	LGE	FAC	TOT
Carey	–	4	4
Cockburn	–	4	4
Crompton	–	4	4
Hanlon	–	4	4
Rowley	–	4	4
Smith	–	4	4
Warner	–	4	4
Whalley	–	4	4
Wrigglesworth	–	4	4
Chilton	–	3	3
Roach	–	2	2
Walton	–	2	2
Bainbridge	–	1	1

GOALSCORERS

PLAYER	LGE	FAC	TOT
Hanlon	–	2	2
Rowley	–	2	2
Wrigglesworth	–	2	2
Bainbridge	–	1	1
Smith	–	1	1
own goal	–	1	1

1946/47

FOOTBALL LEAGUE DIVISION ONE

DATE	OPPONENTS	SCORE	GOALSCORERS	ATTENDANCE
Aug 31	GRIMSBY TOWN	2-1	Mitten, Rowley	41,025
Sep 4	Chelsea	3-0	Mitten, Pearson, Rowley	27,750
Sep 7	Charlton Athletic	3-1	Hanlon, Rowley, og	44,088
Sep 11	LIVERPOOL	5-0	Pearson 3, Mitten, Rowley	41,657
Sep 14	MIDDLESBROUGH	1-0	Rowley	65,112
Sep 18	CHELSEA	1-1	Chilton	30,275
Sep 21	Stoke City	2-3	Delaney, Hanlon	41,699
Sep 28	ARSENAL	5-2	Hanlon, Rowley 2, Wrigglesworth	62,718
Oct 5	PRESTON NORTH END	1-1	Wrigglesworth	55,395
Oct 12	Sheffield United	2-2	Rowley 2	35,543
Oct 19	Blackpool	1-3	Delaney	26,307
Oct 26	Sunderland	0-3		48,385
Nov 2	Aston Villa	0-0		53,668
Nov 9	DERBY COUNTY	4-1	Pearson 2, Mitten, Rowley	57,340
Nov 16	Everton	2-2	Pearson, Rowley	45,832
Nov 23	HUDDERSFIELD TOWN	5-2	Mitten 2, Morris 2, Rowley	39,216
Nov 30	Wolverhampton W.	2-3	Delaney, Hanlon	46,704
Dec 7	BRENTFORD	4-1	Rowley 3, Mitten	31,962
Dec 14	Blackburn Rovers	1-2	Morris	21,455
Dec 25	Bolton Wanderers	2-2	Rowley 2	28,505
Dec 26	BOLTON WANDERERS	1-0	Pearson	57,186
Dec 28	Grimsby Town	0-0		17,183
Jan 4	CHARLTON ATHLETIC	4-1	Burke 2, Buckle, Pearson	43,406
Jan 18	Middlesbrough	4-2	Pearson 2, Buckle, Morris	37,435
Feb 1	Arsenal	2-6	Morris, Pearson	29,415
Feb 5	STOKE CITY	1-1	Buckle	8,456
Feb 22	BLACKPOOL	3-0	Rowley 2, Hanlon	29,993
Mar 1	Sunderland	1-1	Delaney	25,038
Mar 8	ASTON VILLA	2-1	Burke, Pearson	36,965
Mar 15	Derby County	3-4	Burke 2, Pearson	19,579
Mar 22	EVERTON	3-0	Burke, Delaney, Warner	43,441
Mar 29	Huddersfield Town	2-2	Delaney, Pearson	18,509
Apr 5	WOLVERHAMPTON W.	3-1	Rowley 2, Hanlon	66,967
Apr 7	LEEDS UNITED	3-1	Burke 2, Delaney	41,772
Apr 8	Leeds United	2-0	Burke, McGlen	15,528
Apr 12	Brentford	0-0		21,714
Apr 19	BLACKBURN ROVERS	4-0	Pearson 2, Rowley, og	46,196
Apr 26	Portsmouth	1-0	Delaney	30,623
May 3	Liverpool	0-1		48,800
May 10	Preston North End	1-1	Pearson	23,278
May 17	PORTSMOUTH	3-0	Mitten, Morris, Rowley	37,614
May 26	SHEFFIELD UNITED	6-2	Rowley 3, Morris 2, Pearson	34,059

FA CUP

DATE	OPPONENTS	SCORE	GOALSCORERS	ATTENDANCE
Jan 11	Bradford Park Avenue (Rd3)	3-0	Rowley 2, Buckle	26,990
Jan 25	NOTTINGHAM FOREST (Rd4)	0-2		34,059

FINAL LEAGUE TABLE

		P	W	D	L	F	A	Pts
1	Liverpool	42	25	7	10	84	52	57
2	MANCHESTER UNITED	42	22	12	8	95	54	56
3	Wolverhampton Wanderers	42	25	6	11	98	56	56
4	Stoke City	42	24	7	11	90	53	55
5	Blackpool	42	22	6	14	71	70	50
6	Sheffield United	42	21	7	14	89	75	49
7	Preston North End	42	18	11	13	76	74	47
8	Aston Villa	42	18	9	15	67	53	45
9	Sunderland	42	18	8	16	65	66	44
10	Everton	42	17	9	16	62	67	43
11	Middlesbrough	42	17	8	17	73	68	42
12	Portsmouth	42	16	9	17	66	60	41
13	Arsenal	42	16	9	17	72	70	41
14	Derby County	42	18	5	19	73	79	41
15	Chelsea	42	16	7	19	69	84	39
16	Grimsby Town	42	13	12	17	61	82	38
17	Blackburn Rovers	42	14	8	20	45	53	36
18	Bolton Wanderers	42	13	8	21	57	69	34
19	Charlton Athletic	42	11	12	19	57	71	34
20	Huddersfield Town	42	13	7	22	53	79	33
21	Brentford	42	9	7	26	45	88	25
22	Leeds United	42	6	6	30	45	90	18

APPEARANCES

PLAYER	LGE	FAC	TOT
Pearson	42	2	44
Chilton	41	2	43
Delaney	37	2	39
Rowley	37	2	39
Warner	34	2	36
McGlen	33	2	35
Carey	31	2	33
Cockburn	32	–	32
Crompton	29	1	30
Hanlon	27	–	27
Morris	24	2	26
Aston	21	2	23
Mitten	20	–	20
Walton	15	–	15
Burke	13	–	13
Buckle	5	2	7
Collinson	7	–	7
Fielding	6	1	7
Wrigglesworth	4	–	4
Whalley	3	–	3
Worrall	1	–	1

GOALSCORERS

PLAYER	LGE	FAC	TOT
Rowley	26	2	28
Pearson	19	–	19
Burke	9	–	9
Delaney	8	–	8
Mitten	8	–	8
Morris	8	–	8
Hanlon	7	–	7
Buckle	3	1	4
Wrigglesworth	2	–	2
Chilton	1	–	1
McGlen	1	–	1
Warner	1	–	1
own goals	2	–	2

1947/48

FOOTBALL LEAGUE DIVISION ONE

DATE	OPPONENTS	SCORE	GOALSCORERS	ATTENDANCE
Aug 23	Middlesbrough	2-2	Rowley 2	39,554
Aug 27	LIVERPOOL	2-0	Morris, Pearson	52,385
Aug 30	CHARLTON ATHLETIC	6-2	Rowley 4, Morris, Pearson	52,659
Sep 3	Liverpool	2-2	Mitten, Pearson	48,081
Sep 6	Arsenal	1-2	Morris	64,905
Sep 8	Burnley	0-0		37,517
Sep 13	SHEFFIELD UNITED	0-1		49,808
Sep 20	Manchester City	0-0		71,364
Sep 27	Preston North End	1-2	Morris	34,372
Oct 4	STOKE CITY	1-1	Hanlon	45,745
Oct 11	GRIMSBY TOWN	3-4	Mitten, Morris, Rowley	40,035
Oct 18	Sunderland	0-1		37,148
Oct 25	ASTON VILLA	2-0	Delaney, Rowley	47,078
Nov 1	Wolverhampton W.	6-2	Morris 2, Pearson 2, Delaney, Mitten	44,309
Nov 8	HUDDERSFIELD TOWN	4-4	Rowley 4	59,772
Nov 15	Derby County	1-1	Carey	32,990
Nov 22	EVERTON	2-2	Cockburn, Morris	35,509
Nov 29	Chelsea	4-0	Morris 3, Rowley	43,617
Dec 6	BLACKPOOL	1-1	Pearson	63,683
Dec 13	Blackburn Rovers	1-1	Morris	22,784
Dec 20	MIDDLESBROUGH	2-1	Pearson 2	46,666
Dec 25	PORTSMOUTH	3-2	Morris 2, Rowley	42,776
Dec 27	Portsmouth	3-1	Morris 2, Delaney	27,674
Jan 1	BURNLEY	5-0	Rowley 3, Mitten 2	59,838
Jan 3	Charlton Athletic	2-1	Morris, Pearson	40,484
Jan 17	ARSENAL	1-1	Rowley	81,962
Jan 31	Sheffield United	1-2	Rowley	45,189
Feb 14	PRESTON NORTH END	1-1	Delaney	61,765
Feb 21	Stoke City	2-0	Buckle, Pearson	36,794
Mar 6	SUNDERLAND	3-1	Delaney, Mitten, Rowley	55,160
Mar 17	Grimsby Town	1-1	Rowley	12,284
Mar 20	WOLVERHAMPTON W.	3-2	Delaney, Mitten, Morris	50,667
Mar 22	Aston Villa	1-0	Pearson	52,368
Mar 26	BOLTON WANDERERS	0-2		71,623
Mar 27	Huddersfield Town	2-0	Burke, Pearson	38,266
Mar 29	Bolton Wanderers	1-0	Anderson	44,225
Apr 3	DERBY COUNTY	1-0	Pearson	49,609
Apr 7	MANCHESTER CITY	1-1	Rowley	71,690
Apr 10	Everton	0-2		44,198
Apr 17	CHELSEA	5-0	Pearson 2, Delaney, Mitten, Rowley	43,225
Apr 28	Blackpool	0-1		32,236
May 1	BLACKBURN ROVERS	4-1	Pearson 3, Delaney	44,439

FA CUP

DATE	OPPONENTS	SCORE	GOALSCORERS	ATTENDANCE
Jan 10	Aston Villa (Rd3)	6-4	Morris 2, Pearson 2, Delaney, Rowley	58,683
Jan 24	LIVERPOOL (Rd4) (at Goodison Park)	3-0	Mitten, Morris, Rowley	74,000
Feb 7	CHARLTON ATHLETIC (Rd5) (at Leeds Road, Huddersfield)	2-0	Mitten, Warner	33,312
Feb 28	PRESTON NORTH END (Rd6) (at Maine Road)	4-2	Pearson 2, Rowley, Mitten	74,213
Mar 13	Derby County (SF) (at Hillsborough)	3-1	Pearson 3	60,000
Apr 24	Blackpool (Final) (at Wembley)	4-2	Rowley 2, Anderson, Pearson	99,000

FINAL LEAGUE TABLE

		P	W	D	L	F	A	Pts
1	Arsenal	42	23	13	6	81	32	59
2	MANCHESTER UNITED	42	19	14	9	81	48	52
3	Burnley	42	20	12	10	56	43	52
4	Derby County	42	19	12	11	77	57	50
5	Wolverhampton Wanderers	42	19	9	14	83	70	47
6	Aston Villa	42	19	9	14	65	57	47
7	Preston North End	42	20	7	15	67	68	47
8	Portsmouth	42	19	7	16	68	50	45
9	Blackpool	42	17	10	15	57	41	44
10	Manchester City	42	15	12	15	52	47	42
11	Liverpool	42	16	10	16	65	61	42
12	Sheffield United	42	16	10	16	65	70	42
13	Charlton Athletic	42	17	6	19	57	66	40
14	Everton	42	17	6	19	52	66	40
15	Stoke City	42	14	10	18	41	55	38
16	Middlesbrough	42	14	9	19	71	73	37
17	Bolton Wanderers	42	16	5	21	46	58	37
18	Chelsea	42	14	9	19	53	71	37
19	Huddersfield Town	42	12	12	18	51	60	36
20	Sunderland	42	13	10	19	56	67	36
21	Blackburn Rovers	42	11	10	21	54	72	32
22	Grimsby Town	42	8	6	28	45	111	22

APPEARANCES

PLAYER	LGE	FAC	TOT
Aston	42	6	48
Chilton	41	6	47
Pearson	40	6	46
Rowley	39	6	45
Mitten	38	6	44
Morris	38	6	44
Carey	37	6	43
Crompton	37	6	43
Delaney	36	6	42
Cockburn	26	6	32
Anderson	18	5	23
Warner	15	1	16
McGlen	13	–	13
Hanlon	8	–	8
Burke	6	–	6
Walton	6	–	6
Worrall	5	–	5
Brown	3	–	3
Buckle	3	–	3
Lynn	3	–	3
Dale	2	–	2
Lowrie	2	–	2
Pegg	2	–	2
Ball	1	–	1
Cassidy	1	–	1

GOALSCORERS

PLAYER	LGE	FAC	TOT
Rowley	23	5	28
Pearson	18	8	26
Morris	18	3	21
Mitten	8	3	11
Delaney	8	1	9
Anderson	1	1	2
Buckle	1	–	1
Burke	1	–	1
Carey	1	–	1
Cockburn	1	–	1
Hanlon	1	–	1
Warner	–	1	1

1948/49

FOOTBALL LEAGUE DIVISION ONE

DATE	OPPONENTS	SCORE	GOALSCORERS	ATTENDANCE
Aug 21	DERBY COUNTY	1–2	Pearson	52,620
Aug 23	Blackpool	3–0	Rowley 2, Mitten	36,880
Aug 28	Arsenal	1–0	Mitten	64,150
Sep 1	BLACKPOOL	3–4	Delaney, Mitten, Morris	51,187
Sep 4	HUDDERSFIELD TOWN	4–1	Pearson 2, Delaney, Mitten	57,714
Sep 8	Wolverhampton W.	2–3	Morris, Rowley	42,617
Sep 11	Manchester City	0–0		64,502
Sep 15	WOLVERHAMPTON W.	2–0	Buckle, Pearson	33,871
Sep 18	Sheffield United	2–2	Buckle, Pearson	36,880
Sep 25	ASTON VILLA	3–1	Mitten 2, Pearson	53,820
Oct 2	Sunderland	1–2	Rowley	54,419
Oct 9	CHARLTON ATHLETIC	1–1	Burke	46,964
Oct 16	Stoke City	1–2	Morris	45,830
Oct 23	BURNLEY	1–1	Mitten	47,093
Oct 30	Preston North End	6–1	Mitten 2, Pearson 2, Morris, Rowley	37,372
Nov 6	EVERTON	2–0	Delaney, Morris	42,789
Nov 13	Chelsea	1–1	Rowley	62,542
Nov 20	BIRMINGHAM CITY	3–0	Morris, Pearson, Rowley	45,482
Nov 27	Middlesbrough	4–1	Rowley 3, Delaney	31,331
Dec 4	NEWCASTLE UNITED	1–1	Mitten	70,787
Dec 11	Portsmouth	2–2	McGlen, Mitten	29,966
Dec 18	Derby County	3–1	Burke 2, Pearson	31,498
Dec 25	LIVERPOOL	0–0		47,788
Dec 26	Liverpool	2–0	Burke, Pearson	53,325
Jan 1	ARSENAL	2–0	Burke, Mitten	58,688
Jan 22	MANCHESTER CITY	0–0		66,485
Feb 19	Aston Villa	1–2	Rowley	68,354
Mar 5	Charlton Athletic	3–2	Pearson 2, Downie	55,291
Mar 12	STOKE CITY	3–0	Downie, Mitten, Rowley	55,949
Mar 19	Birmingham City	0–1		46,819
Apr 6	Huddersfield Town	1–2	Rowley	17,256
Apr 9	CHELSEA	1–1	Mitten	27,304
Apr 15	Bolton Wanderers	1–0	Carey	44,999
Apr 16	Burnley	2–0	Rowley 2	37,722
Apr 18	BOLTON WANDERERS	3–0	Rowley 2	47,653
Apr 21	SUNDERLAND	1–2	Mitten	30,640
Apr 23	PRESTON NORTH END	2–2	Downie 2	43,214
Apr 27	Everton	0–2		39,106
Apr 30	Newcastle United	1–0	Burke	38,266
May 2	MIDDLESBROUGH	1–0	Rowley	20,158
May 4	SHEFFIELD UNITED	3–2	Downie, Mitten, Pearson	20,880
May 7	PORTSMOUTH	3–2	Rowley 2, Mitten	49,808

FA CUP

DATE	OPPONENTS	SCORE	GOALSCORERS	ATTENDANCE
Jan 8	BOURNEMOUTH (Rd3)	6–0	Burke 2, Rowley 2, Mitten, Pearson	55,012
Jan 29	BRADFORD P.A. (Rd4)	1–1	Mitten	82,771
Feb 5	Bradford P.A. (Rd4R)	1–1	Mitten	30,000
Feb 7	BRADFORD P.A. (Rd4R2)	5–0	Burke 2, Rowley 2, Pearson	70,434
Feb 12	YEOVIL TOWN (Rd5)	8–0	Rowley 5, Burke 2, Mitten	81,565
Feb 26	Hull City (Rd6)	1–0	Pearson	55,000
Mar 26	Wolverhampton W. (SF) (at Hillsborough)	1–1	Mitten	62,250
Apr 2	Wolverhampton W. (SFR) (at Goodison Park)	0–1		73,000

FINAL LEAGUE TABLE

		P	W	D	L	F	A	Pts
1	Portsmouth	42	25	8	9	84	42	58
2	MANCHESTER UNITED	42	21	11	10	77	44	53
3	Derby County	42	22	9	11	74	55	53
4	Newcastle United	42	20	12	10	70	56	52
5	Arsenal	42	18	13	11	74	44	49
6	Wolverhampton Wanderers	42	17	12	13	79	66	46
7	Manchester City	42	15	15	12	47	51	45
8	Sunderland	42	13	17	12	49	58	43
9	Charlton Athletic	42	15	12	15	63	67	42
10	Aston Villa	42	16	10	16	60	76	42
11	Stoke City	42	16	9	17	66	68	41
12	Liverpool	42	13	14	15	53	43	40
13	Chelsea	42	12	14	16	69	68	38
14	Bolton Wanderers	42	14	10	18	59	68	38
15	Burnley	42	12	14	16	43	50	38
16	Blackpool	42	11	16	15	54	67	38
17	Birmingham City	42	11	15	16	36	38	37
18	Everton	42	13	11	18	41	63	37
19	Middlesbrough	42	11	12	19	46	57	34
20	Huddersfield Town	42	12	10	20	40	69	34
21	Preston North End	42	11	11	20	62	75	33
22	Sheffield United	42	11	11	20	57	78	33

APPEARANCES

PLAYER	LGE	FAC	TOT
Chilton	42	8	50
Mitten	42	8	50
Crompton	41	8	49
Carey	41	7	48
Aston	39	8	47
Pearson	39	8	47
Rowley	39	8	47
Cockburn	36	8	44
Delaney	36	6	42
McGlen	23	8	31
Morris	21	1	22
Anderson	15	1	16
Burke	9	6	15
Downie	12	–	12
Ball	8	1	9
Lowrie	8	–	8
Buckle	5	2	7
Warner	3	–	3
Brown	1	–	1
Cassidy	1	–	1
Hanlon	1	–	1

GOALSCORERS

PLAYER	LGE	FAC	TOT
Rowley	20	9	29
Mitten	18	5	23
Pearson	14	3	17
Burke	6	6	12
Morris	6	–	6
Downie	5	–	5
Delaney	4	–	4
Buckle	2	–	2
Carey	1	–	1
McGlen	1	–	1

1949/50

FOOTBALL LEAGUE DIVISION ONE

DATE	OPPONENTS	SCORE	GOALSCORERS	ATTENDANCE
Aug 20	Derby County	1–0	Rowley	35,687
Aug 24	BOLTON WANDERERS	3–0	Mitten, Rowley, og	41,748
Aug 27	WEST BROMWICH ALBION	1–1	Pearson	44,655
Aug 31	Bolton Wanderers	2–1	Mitten, Pearson	36,277
Sep 3	MANCHESTER CITY	2–1	Pearson 2	47,760
Sep 7	Liverpool	1–1	Mitten	51,587
Sep 10	Chelsea	1–1	Rowley	61,357
Sep 17	STOKE CITY	2–2	Rowley 2	43,532
Sep 24	Burnley	0–1		41,072
Oct 1	SUNDERLAND	1–3	Pearson	49,260
Oct 8	CHARLTON ATHLETIC	3–2	Mitten 2, Rowley	43,809
Oct 15	Aston Villa	4–0	Mitten 2, Bogan, Rowley	47,483
Oct 22	WOLVERHAMPTON W.	3–0	Pearson 2, Bogan	51,427
Oct 29	Portsmouth	1–1	Pearson	41,098
Nov 5	HUDDERSFIELD TOWN	6–0	Pearson 2, Rowley 2, Delaney, Mitten	40,295
Nov 12	Everton	0–0		46,672
Nov 19	MIDDLESBROUGH	2–0	Pearson, Rowley	42,626
Nov 26	Blackpool	3–3	Pearson 2, Bogan	27,742
Dec 3	NEWCASTLE UNITED	1–1	Mitten	30,343
Dec 10	Fulham	0–1		35,362
Dec 17	DERBY COUNTY	0–1		33,753
Dec 24	West Bromwich Albion	2–1	Bogan, Rowley	46,973
Dec 26	ARSENAL	2–0	Pearson 2	53,928
Dec 27	Arsenal	0–0		65,133
Dec 31	Manchester City	2–1	Delaney, Pearson	63,704
Jan 14	CHELSEA	1–0	Mitten	46,954
Jan 21	Stoke City	1–3	Mitten	38,877
Feb 4	BURNLEY	3–2	Rowley 2, Mitten	46,702
Feb 18	Sunderland	2–2	Chilton, Rowley	63,251
Feb 25	Charlton Athletic	2–1	Carey, Rowley	44,920
Mar 8	ASTON VILLA	7–0	Mitten 4, Downie 2, Rowley	22,149
Mar 11	Middlesbrough	3–2	Downie 2, Rowley	46,702
Mar 15	LIVERPOOL	0–0		43,456
Mar 18	BLACKPOOL	1–2	Delaney	53,688
Mar 25	Huddersfield Town	1–3	Downie	34,348
Apr 1	EVERTON	1–1	Delaney	35,381
Apr 7	BIRMINGHAM CITY	0–2		47,170
Apr 8	Wolverhampton W.	1–1	Rowley	54,296
Apr 10	Birmingham City	0–0		35,863
Apr 15	PORTSMOUTH	0–2		44,908
Apr 22	Newcastle United	1–2	Downie	52,203
Apr 29	FULHAM	3–0	Rowley 2, Cockburn	11,968

FA CUP

DATE	OPPONENTS	SCORE	GOALSCORERS	ATTENDANCE
Jan 7	WEYMOUTH TOWN (Rd3)	4–0	Rowley 2, Delaney, Pearson	38,284
Jan 28	Watford (Rd4)	1–0	Rowley	32,800
Feb 11	PORTSMOUTH (Rd5)	3–3	Mitten 2, Pearson	53,688
Feb 15	Portsmouth (Rd5R)	3–1	Downie, Mitten	49,962
Mar 4	Chelsea (Rd6)	0–2		70,362

FINAL LEAGUE TABLE

		P	W	D	L	F	A	Pts
1	Portsmouth	42	22	9	11	74	38	53
2	Wolverhampton Wanderers	42	20	13	9	76	49	53
3	Sunderland	42	21	10	11	83	62	52
4	MANCHESTER UNITED	42	18	14	10	69	44	50
5	Newcastle United	42	19	12	11	77	55	50
6	Arsenal	42	19	11	12	79	55	49
7	Blackpool	42	17	15	10	46	35	49
8	Liverpool	42	17	14	11	64	54	48
9	Middlesbrough	42	20	7	15	59	48	47
10	Burnley	42	16	13	13	40	40	45
11	Derby County	42	17	10	15	69	61	44
12	Aston Villa	42	15	12	15	61	61	42
13	Chelsea	42	12	16	14	58	65	40
14	West Bromwich Albion	42	14	12	16	47	53	40
15	Huddersfield Town	42	14	9	19	52	73	37
16	Bolton Wanderers	42	10	14	18	45	59	34
17	Fulham	42	10	14	18	41	54	34
18	Everton	42	10	14	18	42	66	34
19	Stoke City	42	11	12	19	45	75	34
20	Charlton Athletic	42	13	6	23	53	65	32
21	Manchester City	42	8	13	21	36	68	29
22	Birmingham City	42	7	14	21	31	67	28

APPEARANCES

PLAYER	LGE	FAC	TOT
Delaney	42	5	47
Mitten	42	5	47
Aston	40	5	45
Pearson	41	4	45
Rowley	39	5	44
Carey	38	5	43
Chilton	35	5	40
Cockburn	35	5	40
Crompton	27	1	28
Warner	21	4	25
Bogan	18	4	22
Downie	18	2	20
Feehan	12	2	14
McGlen	13	1	14
Ball	13	–	13
Lynn	10	–	10
Buckle	7	–	7
Lancaster	2	2	4
Lowrie	3	–	3
McNulty	2	–	2
Birch	1	–	1
Clempson	1	–	1
Whitefoot	1	–	1
Wood	1	–	1

GOALSCORERS

PLAYER	LGE	FAC	TOT
Rowley	20	3	23
Mitten	16	3	19
Pearson	15	2	17
Downie	6	1	7
Delaney	4	2	6
Bogan	4	–	4
Carey	1	–	1
Chilton	1	–	1
Cockburn	1	–	1
own goal	1	–	1

1950/51

FOOTBALL LEAGUE DIVISION ONE

DATE	OPPONENTS	SCORE	GOALSCORERS	ATTENDANCE
Aug 19	FULHAM	1-0	Pearson	44,042
Aug 23	Liverpool	1-2	Rowley	30,211
Aug 26	Bolton Wanderers	0-1		40,431
Aug 30	LIVERPOOL	1-0	Downie	34,835
Sep 2	BLACKPOOL	1-0	Bogan	53,260
Sep 4	Aston Villa	3-1	Rowley 2, Pearson	42,724
Sep 9	Tottenham Hotspur	0-1		60,621
Sep 13	ASTON VILLA	0-0		33,021
Sep 16	CHARLTON ATHLETIC	3-0	Delaney, Pearson, Rowley	36,619
Sep 23	Middlesbrough	2-1	Pearson 2	48,051
Sep 30	Wolverhampton W.	0-0		45,898
Oct 7	SHEFFIELD WEDNESDAY	3-1	Downie, McShane, Rowley	40,651
Oct 14	Arsenal	0-3		66,150
Oct 21	PORTSMOUTH	0-0		41,842
Oct 28	Everton	4-1	Rowley 2, Aston, Pearson	51,142
Nov 4	BURNLEY	1-1	McShane	39,454
Nov 11	Chelsea	0-1		51,882
Nov 18	STOKE CITY	0-0		30,031
Nov 25	West Bromwich Albion	1-0	Birch	28,146
Dec 2	NEWCASTLE UNITED	1-2	Birch	34,502
Dec 9	Huddersfield Town	3-2	Aston 2, Birkett	26,713
Dec 16	Fulham	2-2	Pearson 2	19,649
Dec 23	BOLTON WANDERERS	2-3	Aston, Pearson	35,382
Dec 25	Sunderland	1-2	Aston	41,215
Dec 26	SUNDERLAND	3-5	Bogan 2, Aston	35,176
Jan 13	TOTTENHAM HOTSPUR	2-1	Birch, Rowley	43,283
Jan 20	Charlton Athletic	2-1	Aston, Birkett	31,978
Feb 3	MIDDLESBROUGH	1-0	Pearson	44,633
Feb 17	WOLVERHAMPTON W.	2-1	Birch, Rowley	42,022
Feb 26	Sheffield Wednesday	4-0	Downie, McShane, Rowley, Pearson	25,693
Mar 3	ARSENAL	3-1	Aston 2, Downie	46,202
Mar 10	Portsmouth	0-0		33,148
Mar 17	EVERTON	3-0	Aston, Downie, Pearson	29,317
Mar 23	DERBY COUNTY	2-0	Aston, Downie	42,009
Mar 24	Burnley	2-1	Aston, McShane	36,656
Mar 26	Derby County	4-2	Aston, Downie, Pearson, Rowley	25,860
Mar 31	CHELSEA	4-1	Pearson 3, McShane	25,779
Apr 7	Stoke City	0-2		25,690
Apr 14	WEST BROMWICH ALBION	3-0	Downie, Pearson, Rowley	24,764
Apr 21	Newcastle United	2-0	Pearson, Rowley	45,209
Apr 28	HUDDERSFIELD TOWN	6-0	Aston 2, McShane 2, Downie, Rowley	25,560
May 5	Blackpool	1-1	Downie	22,864

FA CUP

DATE	OPPONENTS	SCORE	GOALSCORERS	ATTENDANCE
Jan 6	OLDHAM ATHLETIC (Rd3)	4-1	Aston, Birch, Pearson, og	37,161
Jan 27	LEEDS UNITED (Rd4)	4-0	Pearson 3, Rowley	55,434
Feb 10	ARSENAL (Rd5)	1-0	Pearson	55,058
Feb 24	Birmingham City (Rd6)	0-1		50,000

FINAL LEAGUE TABLE

		P	W	D	L	F	A	Pts
1	Tottenham Hotspur	42	25	10	7	82	44	60
2	MANCHESTER UNITED	42	24	8	10	74	40	56
3	Blackpool	42	20	10	12	79	53	50
4	Newcastle United	42	18	13	11	62	53	49
5	Arsenal	42	19	9	14	73	56	47
6	Middlesbrough	42	18	11	13	76	65	47
7	Portsmouth	42	16	15	11	71	68	47
8	Bolton Wanderers	42	19	7	16	64	61	45
9	Liverpool	42	16	11	15	53	59	43
10	Burnley	42	14	14	14	48	43	42
11	Derby County	42	16	8	18	81	75	40
12	Sunderland	42	12	16	14	63	73	40
13	Stoke City	42	13	14	15	50	59	40
14	Wolverhampton Wanderers	42	15	8	19	74	61	38
15	Aston Villa	42	12	13	17	66	68	37
16	West Bromwich Albion	42	13	11	18	53	61	37
17	Charlton Athletic	42	14	9	19	63	80	37
18	Fulham	42	13	11	18	52	68	37
19	Huddersfield Town	42	15	6	21	64	92	36
20	Chelsea	42	12	8	22	53	65	32
21	Sheffield Wednesday	42	12	8	22	64	83	32
22	Everton	42	12	8	22	48	86	32

APPEARANCES

PLAYER	LGE	FAC	TOT
Aston	41	4	45
Allen	40	4	44
Carey	39	4	43
Pearson	39	4	43
Chilton	38	4	42
Rowley	39	3	42
Cockburn	35	4	39
Gibson	32	3	35
McShane	30	1	31
Downie	29	–	29
McGlen	26	1	27
Redman	16	2	18
Birkett	9	4	13
Delaney	13	–	13
Birch	8	4	12
Bogan	11	–	11
McNulty	4	1	5
Jones	4	–	4
Clempson	2	–	2
Crompton	2	–	2
McIlvenny	2	–	2
Whitefoot	2	–	2
Cassidy	1	–	1
Lowrie	–	1	1

GOALSCORERS

PLAYER	LGE	FAC	TOT
Pearson	18	5	23
Aston	15	1	16
Rowley	14	1	15
Downie	10	–	10
McShane	7	–	7
Birch	4	1	5
Bogan	3	–	3
Birkett	2	–	2
Delaney	1	–	1
own goal	–	1	1

1951/52

FOOTBALL LEAGUE DIVISION ONE

DATE	OPPONENTS	SCORE	GOALSCORERS	ATTENDANCE
Aug 18	West Bromwich Albion	3-3	Rowley 3	27,486
Aug 22	MIDDLESBROUGH	4-2	Rowley 3, Pearson	37,339
Aug 25	NEWCASTLE UNITED	2-1	Downie, Rowley	51,850
Aug 29	Middlesbrough	4-1	Pearson 2, Rowley 2	44,212
Sep 1	Bolton Wanderers	0-1		52,239
Sep 5	CHARLTON ATHLETIC	3-2	Rowley 2, Downie	26,773
Sep 8	STOKE CITY	4-0	Rowley 3, Pearson	48,660
Sep 12	Charlton Athletic	2-2	Downie 2	28,806
Sep 15	Manchester City	2-1	Berry, McShane	52,571
Sep 22	Tottenham Hotspur	0-2		70,882
Sep 29	PRESTON NORTH END	1-2	Aston	53,454
Oct 6	DERBY COUNTY	2-1	Berry, Pearson	39,767
Oct 13	Aston Villa	5-2	Pearson 2, Rowley 2, Bond	47,795
Oct 20	SUNDERLAND	0-1		40,915
Oct 27	Wolverhampton W.	2-0	Pearson, Rowley	46,167
Nov 3	HUDDERSFIELD TOWN	1-1	Pearson	25,616
Nov 10	Chelsea	2-4	Pearson, Rowley	48,960
Nov 17	PORTSMOUTH	1-3	Downie	35,914
Nov 24	Liverpool	0-0		42,378
Dec 1	BLACKPOOL	3-1	Downie 2, Rowley	34,154
Dec 8	Arsenal	3-1	Pearson, Rowley, og	55,451
Dec 15	WEST BROMWICH ALBION	5-1	Downie 2, Pearson 2, Berry	27,584
Dec 22	Newcastle United	2-2	Bond, Cockburn	45,414
Dec 25	FULHAM	3-2	Berry, Bond, Rowley	33,802
Dec 26	Fulham	3-3	Bond, Pearson, Rowley	32,671
Dec 29	BOLTON WANDERERS	1-0	Pearson	53,205
Jan 5	Stoke City	0-0		36,389
Jan 19	MANCHESTER CITY	1-1	Carey	54,245
Jan 26	TOTTENHAM HOTSPUR	2-0	Pearson, og	40,845
Feb 9	Preston North End	2-1	Aston, Berry	38,792
Feb 16	Derby County	3-0	Aston, Pearson, Rowley	27,693
Mar 1	ASTON VILLA	1-1	Berry	38,910
Mar 8	Sunderland	2-1	Cockburn, Rowley	48,078
Mar 15	WOLVERHAMPTON W.	2-0	Aston, Clempson	45,109
Mar 22	Huddersfield Town	2-3	Clempson, Pearson	30,316
Apr 5	Portsmouth	0-1		25,522
Apr 11	Burnley	1-1	Byrne	38,907
Apr 12	LIVERPOOL	4-0	Byrne 2, Downie, Rowley	42,970
Apr 14	BURNLEY	6-1	Byrne 2, Carey, Downie, Pearson, Rowley	44,508
Apr 19	Blackpool	2-2	Byrne, Rowley	29,118
Apr 21	CHELSEA	3-0	Carey, Pearson, og	37,436
Apr 26	ARSENAL	6-1	Rowley 3, Pearson 2, Byrne	53,651

FA CUP

DATE	OPPONENTS	SCORE	GOALSCORERS	ATTENDANCE
Jan 12	HULL CITY (Rd3)	0-2		43,517

FINAL LEAGUE TABLE

		P	W	D	L	F	A	Pts
1	MANCHESTER UNITED	42	23	11	8	95	52	57
2	Tottenham Hotspur	42	22	9	11	76	51	53
3	Arsenal	42	21	11	10	80	61	53
4	Portsmouth	42	20	8	14	68	58	48
5	Bolton Wanderers	42	19	10	13	65	61	48
6	Aston Villa	42	19	9	14	79	70	47
7	Preston North End	42	17	12	13	74	54	46
8	Newcastle United	42	18	9	15	98	73	45
9	Blackpool	42	18	9	15	64	64	45
10	Charlton Athletic	42	17	10	15	68	63	44
11	Liverpool	42	12	19	11	57	61	43
12	Sunderland	42	15	12	15	70	61	42
13	West Bromwich Albion	42	14	13	15	74	77	41
14	Burnley	42	15	10	17	56	63	40
15	Manchester City	42	13	13	16	58	61	39
16	Wolverhampton Wanderers	42	12	14	16	73	73	38
17	Derby County	42	15	7	20	63	80	37
18	Middlesbrough	42	15	6	21	64	88	36
19	Chelsea	42	14	8	20	52	72	36
20	Stoke City	42	12	7	23	49	88	31
21	Huddersfield Town	42	10	8	24	49	82	28
22	Fulham	42	8	11	23	58	77	27

APPEARANCES

PLAYER	LGE	FAC	TOT
Chilton	42	1	43
Pearson	41	1	42
Rowley	40	1	41
Carey	38	1	39
Cockburn	38	1	39
Berry	36	1	37
Allen	33	1	34
Downie	31	1	32
Byrne	24	1	25
McNulty	24	1	25
Bond	19	1	20
Aston	18	–	18
Redman	18	–	18
Gibson	17	–	17
McShane	12	–	12
Crompton	9	–	9
Clempson	8	–	8
Jones	3	–	3
Whitefoot	3	–	3
Birch	2	–	2
McGlen	2	–	2
Walton	2	–	2
Blanchflower	1	–	1
Cassidy	1	–	1

GOALSCORERS

PLAYER	LGE	FAC	TOT
Rowley	30	–	30
Pearson	22	–	22
Downie	11	–	11
Byrne	7	–	7
Berry	6	–	6
Aston	4	–	4
Bond	4	–	4
Carey	3	–	3
Clempson	2	–	2
Cockburn	2	–	2
McShane	1	–	1
own goals	3	–	3

1952/53

FOOTBALL LEAGUE DIVISION ONE

DATE	OPPONENTS	SCORE	GOALSCORERS	ATTENDANCE
Aug 23	CHELSEA	2-0	Berry, Downie	43,629
Aug 27	Arsenal	1-2	Rowley	58,831
Aug 30	Manchester City	1-2	Downie	56,140
Sep 3	ARSENAL	0-0		39,193
Sep 6	Portsmouth	0-2		37,278
Sep 10	Derby County	3-2	Pearson 3	20,226
Sep 13	BOLTON WANDERERS	1-0	Berry	40,531
Sep 20	Aston Villa	3-3	Rowley 2, Downie	43,490
Sep 27	SUNDERLAND	0-1		28,967
Oct 4	Wolverhampton W.	2-6	Rowley 2	40,132
Oct 11	STOKE CITY	0-2		28,968
Oct 18	Preston North End	5-0	Aston 2, Pearson 2, Rowley	33,502
Oct 25	BURNLEY	1-3	Aston	36,913
Nov 1	Tottenham Hotspur	2-1	Berry 2	44,300
Nov 8	SHEFFIELD WEDNESDAY	1-1	Pearson	48,571
Nov 15	Cardiff City	2-1	Aston, Pearson	40,096
Nov 22	NEWCASTLE UNITED	2-2	Aston, Pearson	33,528
Nov 29	West Bromwich Albion	1-3	Lewis	23,499
Dec 6	MIDDLESBROUGH	3-2	Pearson 2, Aston	27,617
Dec 13	Liverpool	2-1	Aston, Pearson	34,450
Dec 20	Chelsea	3-2	Doherty 2, Aston	23,261
Dec 25	Blackpool	0-0		27,778
Dec 26	BLACKPOOL	2-1	Carey, Lewis	48,077
Jan 1	DERBY COUNTY	1-0	Lewis	34,813
Jan 3	MANCHESTER CITY	1-1	Pearson	47,883
Jan 17	PORTSMOUTH	1-0	Lewis	32,341
Jan 24	Bolton Wanderers	1-2	Lewis	43,638
Feb 7	ASTON VILLA	3-1	Rowley 2, Lewis	34,339
Feb 18	Sunderland	2-2	Lewis, Pegg	24,263
Feb 21	WOLVERHAMPTON W.	0-3		38,269
Feb 28	Stoke City	1-3	Berry	30,219
Mar 7	PRESTON NORTH END	5-2	Pegg 2, Taylor 2, Rowley	52,590
Mar 14	Burnley	1-2	Byrne	45,682
Mar 25	TOTTENHAM HOTSPUR	3-2	Pearson 2, Pegg	18,384
Mar 28	Sheffield Wednesday	0-0		36,509
Apr 3	Charlton Athletic	2-2	Berry, Taylor	41,814
Apr 4	CARDIFF CITY	1-4	Byrne	37,163
Apr 6	CHARLTON ATHLETIC	3-2	Taylor 2, Rowley	30,105
Apr 11	Newcastle United	2-1	Taylor 2	38,970
Apr 18	WEST BROMWICH ALBION	2-2	Pearson, Viollet	31,380
Apr 20	LIVERPOOL	3-1	Berry, Pearson, Rowley	20,869
Apr 25	Middlesbrough	0-5		34,344

FA CUP

DATE	OPPONENTS	SCORE	GOALSCORERS	ATTENDANCE
Jan 10	Millwall (Rd3)	1-0	Pearson	35,652
Jan 31	WALTHAMSTOW AVE. (Rd4)	1-1	Lewis	34,748
Feb 5	Walthamstow Ave. (Rd4R) (at Highbury)	5-2	Rowley 2, Byrne, Lewis, Pearson	49,119
Feb 14	Everton (Rd5)	1-2	Rowley	77,920

FINAL LEAGUE TABLE

		P	W	D	L	F	A	Pts
1	Arsenal	42	21	12	9	97	64	54
2	Preston North End	42	21	12	9	85	60	54
3	Wolverhampton Wanderers	42	19	13	10	86	63	51
4	West Bromwich Albion	42	21	8	13	66	60	50
5	Charlton Athletic	42	19	11	12	77	63	49
6	Burnley	42	18	12	12	67	52	48
7	Blackpool	42	19	9	14	71	70	47
8	MANCHESTER UNITED	42	18	10	14	69	72	46
9	Sunderland	42	15	13	14	68	82	43
10	Tottenham Hotspur	42	15	11	16	78	69	41
11	Aston Villa	42	14	13	15	63	61	41
12	Cardiff City	42	14	12	16	54	46	40
13	Middlesbrough	42	14	11	17	70	77	39
14	Bolton Wanderers	42	15	9	18	61	69	39
15	Portsmouth	42	14	10	18	74	83	38
16	Newcastle United	42	14	9	19	59	70	37
17	Liverpool	42	14	8	20	61	82	36
18	Sheffield Wednesday	42	12	11	19	62	72	35
19	Chelsea	42	12	11	19	56	66	35
20	Manchester City	42	14	7	21	72	87	35
21	Stoke City	42	12	10	20	53	66	34
22	Derby County	42	11	10	21	59	74	32

APPEARANCES

PLAYER	LGE	FAC	TOT
Chilton	42	4	46
Aston	40	4	44
Berry	40	4	44
Byrne	40	4	44
Pearson	39	4	43
Carey	32	4	36
Rowley	26	4	30
Cockburn	22	4	26
Crompton	25	–	25
McNulty	23	–	23
Downie	20	2	22
Pegg	19	2	21
Gibson	20	–	20
Wood	12	4	16
Lewis	10	4	14
Taylor	11	–	11
Whitefoot	10	–	10
Doherty	5	–	5
McShane	5	–	5
Clempson	4	–	4
Viollet	3	–	3
Allen	2	–	2
Foulkes	2	–	2
Jones	2	–	2
Olive	2	–	2
Scott	2	–	2
Blanchflower	1	–	1
Bond	1	–	1
Edwards	1	–	1
Redman	1	–	1

GOALSCORERS

PLAYER	LGE	FAC	TOT
Pearson	16	2	18
Rowley	11	3	14
Lewis	7	2	9
Aston	8	–	8
Berry	7	–	7
Taylor	7	–	7
Pegg	4	–	4
Downie	3	–	3
Byrne	2	1	3
Doherty	2	–	2
Carey	1	–	1
Viollet	1	–	1

1953/54

FOOTBALL LEAGUE DIVISION ONE

DATE	OPPONENTS	SCORE	GOALSCORERS	ATTENDANCE
Aug 19	CHELSEA	1-1	Pearson	28,936
Aug 22	Liverpool	4-4	Byrne, Lewis, Rowley, Taylor	48,422
Aug 26	WEST BROMWICH ALBION	1-3	Taylor	31,806
Aug 29	NEWCASTLE UNITED	1-1	Chilton	27,837
Sep 2	West Bromwich Albion	0-2		28,892
Sep 5	Manchester City	0-2		53,097
Sep 9	MIDDLESBROUGH	2-2	Rowley 2	18,161
Sep 12	Bolton Wanderers	0-0		43,544
Sep 16	Middlesbrough	4-1	Taylor 2, Byrne, Rowley	23,607
Sep 19	PRESTON NORTH END	1-0	Byrne	41,171
Sep 26	Tottenham Hotspur	1-1	Rowley	52,837
Oct 3	BURNLEY	1-2	Pearson	37,696
Oct 10	SUNDERLAND	1-0	Rowley	34,617
Oct 17	Wolverhampton W.	1-3	Taylor	40,084
Oct 24	ASTON VILLA	1-0	Berry	30,266
Oct 31	Huddersfield Town	0-0		34,175
Nov 7	ARSENAL	2-2	Blanchflower, Rowley	28,141
Nov 14	Cardiff City	6-1	Viollet 2, Berry, Blanchflower, Rowley, Taylor	26,844
Nov 21	BLACKPOOL	4-1	Taylor 3, Viollet	49,853
Nov 28	Portsmouth	1-1	Taylor	29,233
Dec 5	SHEFFIELD UNITED	2-2	Blanchflower 2	31,693
Dec 12	Chelsea	1-3	Berry	37,153
Dec 19	LIVERPOOL	5-1	Blanchflower 2, Taylor 2, Viollet	26,074
Dec 25	SHEFFIELD WEDNESDAY	5-2	Taylor 3, Blanchflower, Viollet	27,123
Dec 26	Sheffield Wednesday	1-0	Viollet	44,196
Jan 2	Newcastle United	2-1	Blanchflower, Foulkes	55,780
Jan 16	MANCHESTER CITY	1-1	Berry	46,379
Jan 23	BOLTON WANDERERS	1-5	Taylor	46,663
Feb 6	Preston North End	3-1	Blanchflower, Rowley, Taylor	30,064
Feb 13	TOTTENHAM HOTSPUR	2-0	Rowley, Taylor	35,485
Feb 20	Burnley	0-2		29,576
Feb 27	Sunderland	2-0	Blanchflower, Taylor	58,440
Mar 6	WOLVERHAMPTON W.	1-0	Berry	38,939
Mar 13	Aston Villa	2-2	Taylor 2	26,023
Mar 20	HUDDERSFIELD TOWN	3-1	Blanchflower, Rowley, Viollet	40,181
Mar 27	Arsenal	1-3	Taylor	42,753
Apr 3	CARDIFF CITY	2-3	Rowley, Viollet	22,832
Apr 10	Blackpool	0-2		25,996
Apr 16	CHARLTON ATHLETIC	2-0	Aston, Viollet	31,876
Apr 17	PORTSMOUTH	2-0	Blanchflower, Viollet	29,663
Apr 19	Charlton Athletic	0-1		19,111
Apr 24	Sheffield United	3-1	Aston, Blanchflower, Viollet	29,189

FA CUP

DATE	OPPONENTS	SCORE	GOALSCORERS	ATTENDANCE
Jan 9	Burnley (Rd3)	3-5	Blanchflower, Taylor, Viollet	54,000

FINAL LEAGUE TABLE

		P	W	D	L	F	A	Pts
1	Wolverhampton Wanderers	42	25	7	10	96	56	57
2	West Bromwich Albion	42	22	9	11	86	63	53
3	Huddersfield Town	42	20	11	11	78	61	51
4	MANCHESTER UNITED	42	18	12	12	73	58	48
5	Bolton Wanderers	42	18	12	12	75	60	48
6	Blackpool	42	19	10	13	80	69	48
7	Burnley	42	21	4	17	78	67	46
8	Chelsea	42	16	12	14	74	68	44
9	Charlton Athletic	42	19	6	17	75	77	44
10	Cardiff City	42	18	8	16	51	71	44
11	Preston North End	42	19	5	18	87	58	43
12	Arsenal	42	15	13	14	75	73	43
13	Aston Villa	42	16	9	17	70	68	41
14	Portsmouth	42	14	11	17	81	89	39
15	Newcastle United	42	14	10	18	72	77	38
16	Tottenham Hotspur	42	16	5	21	65	76	37
17	Manchester City	42	14	9	19	62	77	37
18	Sunderland	42	14	8	20	81	89	36
19	Sheffield Wednesday	42	15	6	21	70	91	36
20	Sheffield United	42	11	11	20	69	90	33
21	Middlesbrough	42	10	10	22	60	91	30
22	Liverpool	42	9	10	23	68	97	28

APPEARANCES

PLAYER	LGE	FAC	TOT
Chilton	42	1	43
Byrne	41	1	42
Whitefoot	38	1	39
Berry	37	1	38
Rowley	36	1	37
Taylor	35	1	36
Foulkes	32	1	33
Viollet	29	1	30
Blanchflower	27	1	28
Wood	27	1	28
Edwards	24	1	25
Cockburn	18	–	18
Crompton	15	–	15
Aston	12	–	12
Pearson	11	–	11
McShane	9	–	9
Pegg	9	–	9
Gibson	7	–	7
Lewis	6	–	6
McNulty	4	–	4
McFarlane	1	–	1
Redman	1	–	1
Webster	1	–	1

GOALSCORERS

PLAYER	LGE	FAC	TOT
Taylor	22	1	23
Blanchflower	13	1	14
Rowley	12	–	12
Viollet	11	1	12
Berry	5	–	5
Byrne	3	–	3
Aston	2	–	2
Pearson	2	–	2
Chilton	1	–	1
Foulkes	1	–	1
Lewis	1	–	1

1954/55

FOOTBALL LEAGUE DIVISION ONE

DATE	OPPONENTS	SCORE	GOALSCORERS	ATTENDANCE
Aug 21	PORTSMOUTH	1-3	Rowley	38,203
Aug 23	Sheffield Wednesday	4-2	Blanchflower 2, Viollet 2	38,118
Aug 28	Blackpool	4-2	Webster 2, Blanchflower, Viollet	31,855
Sep 1	SHEFFIELD WEDNESDAY	2-0	Viollet 2	31,371
Sep 4	CHARLTON ATHLETIC	3-1	Rowley 2, Taylor	38,105
Sep 8	Tottenham Hotspur	2-0	Berry, Webster	35,162
Sep 11	Bolton Wanderers	1-1	Webster	44,661
Sep 15	TOTTENHAM HOTSPUR	2-1	Rowley, Viollet	29,212
Sep 18	HUDDERSFIELD TOWN	1-1	Viollet	45,648
Sep 25	Manchester City	2-3	Blanchflower, Taylor	54,105
Oct 2	Wolverhampton W.	2-4	Rowley, Viollet	39,617
Oct 9	CARDIFF CITY	5-2	Taylor 4, Viollet	39,378
Oct 16	Chelsea	6-5	Viollet 3, Taylor 2, Blanchflower	55,966
Oct 23	NEWCASTLE UNITED	2-2	Taylor, Viollet	29,217
Oct 30	Everton	2-4	Rowley, Taylor	63,021
Nov 6	PRESTON NORTH END	2-1	Viollet 2	30,063
Nov 13	Sheffield United	0-3		26,257
Nov 20	ARSENAL	2-1	Blanchflower, Taylor	33,373
Nov 27	West Bromwich Albion	0-2		33,931
Dec 4	LEICESTER CITY	3-1	Rowley, Viollet, Webster	19,369
Dec 11	Burnley	4-2	Webster 3, Viollet	24,977
Dec 18	Portsmouth	0-0		26,019
Dec 27	ASTON VILLA	0-1		49,136
Dec 28	Aston Villa	1-2	Taylor	48,718
Jan 1	BLACKPOOL	4-1	Blanchflower 2, Edwards, Viollet	51,918
Jan 22	BOLTON WANDERERS	1-1	Taylor	39,873
Feb 5	Huddersfield Town	3-1	Berry, Edwards, Pegg	31,408
Feb 12	MANCHESTER CITY	0-5		47,914
Feb 23	WOLVERHAMPTON W.	2-4	Edwards, Taylor	15,679
Feb 26	Cardiff City	0-3		16,329
Mar 5	BURNLEY	1-0	Edwards	31,729
Mar 19	EVERTON	1-2	Scanlon	32,295
Mar 26	Preston North End	2-0	Byrne, Scanlon	13,327
Apr 2	SHEFFIELD UNITED	5-0	Taylor 2, Berry, Viollet, Whelan	21,158
Apr 8	Sunderland	3-4	Edwards 2, Scanlon	43,882
Apr 9	Leicester City	0-1		34,362
Apr 11	SUNDERLAND	2-2	Byrne, Taylor	36,013
Apr 16	WEST BROMWICH ALBION	3-0	Taylor 2, Viollet	24,765
Apr 18	Newcastle United	0-2		35,540
Apr 23	Arsenal	3-2	Blanchflower 2, og	42,754
Apr 26	Charlton Athletic	1-1	Viollet	18,149
Apr 30	CHELSEA	2-1	Scanlon, Taylor	34,933

FA CUP

DATE	OPPONENTS	SCORE	GOALSCORERS	ATTENDANCE
Jan 8	Reading (Rd3)	1-1	Webster	26,000
Jan 12	READING (Rd3R)	4-1	Webster 2, Rowley, Viollet	24,578
Feb 19	Manchester City (Rd4)	0-2		75,000

FINAL LEAGUE TABLE

		P	W	D	L	F	A	Pts
1	Chelsea	42	20	12	10	81	57	52
2	Wolverhampton Wanderers	42	19	10	13	89	70	48
3	Portsmouth	42	18	12	12	74	62	48
4	Sunderland	42	15	18	9	64	54	48
5	MANCHESTER UNITED	42	20	7	15	84	74	47
6	Aston Villa	42	20	7	15	72	73	47
7	Manchester City	42	18	10	14	76	69	46
8	Newcastle United	42	17	9	16	89	77	43
9	Arsenal	42	17	9	16	69	63	43
10	Burnley	42	17	9	16	51	48	43
11	Everton	42	16	10	16	62	68	42
12	Huddersfield Town	42	14	13	15	63	68	41
13	Sheffield United	42	17	7	18	70	86	41
14	Preston North End	42	16	8	18	83	64	40
15	Charlton Athletic	42	15	10	17	76	75	40
16	Tottenham Hotspur	42	16	8	18	72	73	40
17	West Bromwich Albion	42	16	8	18	76	96	40
18	Bolton Wanderers	42	13	13	16	62	69	39
19	Blackpool	42	14	10	18	60	64	38
20	Cardiff City	42	13	11	18	62	76	37
21	Leicester City	42	12	11	19	74	86	35
22	Sheffield Wednesday	42	8	10	24	63	100	26

APPEARANCES

PLAYER	LGE	FAC	TOT
Foulkes	41	3	44
Berry	40	3	43
Byrne	39	3	42
Wood	37	3	40
Viollet	34	3	37
Edwards	33	3	36
Gibson	32	3	35
Blanchflower	29	3	32
Chilton	29	3	32
Taylor	30	1	31
Rowley	22	3	25
Whitefoot	24	–	24
Webster	17	2	19
Scanlon	14	–	14
Jones	13	–	13
Whelan	7	–	7
Pegg	6	–	6
Crompton	5	–	5
Goodwin	5	–	5
Bent	2	–	2
Cockburn	1	–	1
Greaves	1	–	1
Kennedy	1	–	1

GOALSCORERS

PLAYER	LGE	FAC	TOT
Viollet	20	1	21
Taylor	20	–	20
Webster	8	3	11
Blanchflower	10	–	10
Rowley	7	1	8
Edwards	6	–	6
Scanlon	4	–	4
Berry	3	–	3
Byrne	2	–	2
Pegg	1	–	1
Whelan	1	–	1
own goals	2	–	2

1955/56

FOOTBALL LEAGUE DIVISION ONE

DATE	OPPONENTS	SCORE	GOALSCORERS	ATTENDANCE
Aug 20	Birmingham City	2-2	Viollet 2	37,994
Aug 24	TOTTENHAM HOTSPUR	2-2	Berry, Webster	25,406
Aug 27	WEST BROMWICH ALBION	3-1	Lewis, Scanlon, Viollet	31,996
Aug 31	Tottenham Hotspur	2-1	Edwards 2	27,453
Sep 3	Manchester City	0-1		59,162
Sep 7	EVERTON	2-1	Blanchflower, Edwards	27,843
Sep 10	Sheffield United	0-1		28,241
Sep 14	Everton	2-4	Blanchflower, Webster	34,897
Sep 17	PRESTON NORTH END	3-2	Pegg, Taylor, Viollet	33,078
Sep 24	Burnley	0-0		26,873
Oct 1	LUTON TOWN	3-1	Taylor 2, Webster	34,409
Oct 8	WOLVERHAMPTON W.	4-3	Taylor 2, Doherty, Pegg	48,638
Oct 15	Aston Villa	4-4	Pegg 2, Blanchflower, Webster	29,478
Oct 22	HUDDERSFIELD TOWN	3-0	Berry, Pegg, Taylor	34,150
Oct 29	Cardiff City	1-0	Taylor	27,795
Nov 5	ARSENAL	1-1	Taylor	41,586
Nov 12	Bolton Wanderers	1-3	Taylor	38,109
Nov 19	CHELSEA	3-0	Taylor 2, Byrne	22,192
Nov 26	Blackpool	0-0		26,240
Dec 3	SUNDERLAND	2-1	Doherty, Viollet	39,901
Dec 10	Portsmouth	2-3	Pegg, Taylor	24,594
Dec 17	BIRMINGHAM CITY	2-1	Jones, Viollet	27,704
Dec 24	West Bromwich Albion	4-1	Viollet 3, Taylor	25,168
Dec 26	CHARLTON ATHLETIC	5-1	Viollet 2, Byrne, Doherty, Taylor	44,611
Dec 27	Charlton Athletic	0-3		42,040
Dec 31	MANCHESTER CITY	2-1	Taylor, Viollet	60,956
Jan 14	SHEFFIELD UNITED	3-1	Berry, Pegg, Taylor	30,162
Jan 21	Preston North End	1-3	Whelan	28,047
Feb 4	BURNLEY	2-0	Taylor, Viollet	27,342
Feb 11	Luton Town	2-0	Viollet, Whelan	16,354
Feb 18	Wolverhampton W.	2-0	Taylor 2	40,014
Feb 25	ASTON VILLA	1-0	Whelan	36,277
Mar 3	Chelsea	4-2	Viollet 2, Pegg, Taylor	32,050
Mar 10	CARDIFF CITY	1-1	Byrne	44,693
Mar 17	Arsenal	1-1	Viollet	50,758
Mar 24	BOLTON WANDERERS	1-0	Taylor	46,114
Mar 30	NEWCASTLE UNITED	5-2	Viollet 2, Doherty, Pegg, Taylor	58,994
Mar 31	Huddersfield Town	2-0	Taylor 2	37,780
Apr 2	Newcastle United	0-0		37,395
Apr 7	BLACKPOOL	2-1	Berry, Taylor	62,277
Apr 14	Sunderland	2-2	McGuinness, Whelan	19,865
Apr 21	PORTSMOUTH	1-0	Viollet	38,417

FA CUP

DATE	OPPONENTS	SCORE	GOALSCORERS	ATTENDANCE
Jan 7	Bristol Rovers (Rd3)	0-4		35,872

FINAL LEAGUE TABLE

		P	W	D	L	F	A	Pts
1	MANCHESTER UNITED	42	25	10	7	83	51	60
2	Blackpool	42	20	9	13	86	62	49
3	Wolverhampton Wanderers	42	20	9	13	89	65	49
4	Manchester City	42	18	10	14	82	69	46
5	Arsenal	42	18	10	14	60	61	46
6	Birmingham City	42	18	9	15	75	57	45
7	Burnley	42	18	8	16	64	54	44
8	Bolton Wanderers	42	18	7	17	71	58	43
9	Sunderland	42	17	9	16	80	95	43
10	Luton Town	42	17	8	17	66	64	42
11	Newcastle United	42	17	7	18	85	70	41
12	Portsmouth	42	16	9	17	78	85	41
13	West Bromwich Albion	42	18	5	19	58	70	41
14	Charlton Athletic	42	17	6	19	75	81	40
15	Everton	42	15	10	17	55	69	40
16	Chelsea	42	14	11	17	64	77	39
17	Cardiff City	42	15	9	18	55	69	39
18	Tottenham Hotspur	42	15	7	20	61	71	37
19	Preston North End	42	14	8	20	73	72	36
20	Aston Villa	42	11	13	18	52	69	35
21	Huddersfield Town	42	14	7	21	54	83	35
22	Sheffield United	42	12	9	21	63	77	33

APPEARANCES

PLAYER	LGE	FAC	TOT
Jones	42	1	43
Wood	41	1	42
Byrne	39	1	40
Pegg	35	1	36
Berry	34	1	35
Viollet	34	1	35
Taylor	33	1	34
Edwards	33	–	33
Foulkes	26	1	27
Colman	25	1	26
Blanchflower	18	–	18
Doherty	16	1	17
Whitefoot	15	1	16
Greaves	15	–	15
Webster	15	–	15
Whelan	13	–	13
Goodwin	8	–	8
Scanlon	6	–	6
Bent	4	–	4
Lewis	4	–	4
McGuinness	3	–	3
Crompton	1	–	1
Scott	1	–	1
Whitehurst	1	–	1

GOALSCORERS

PLAYER	LGE	FAC	TOT
Taylor	25	–	25
Viollet	20	–	20
Pegg	9	–	9
Berry	4	–	4
Doherty	4	–	4
Webster	4	–	4
Whelan	4	–	4
Blanchflower	3	–	3
Byrne	3	–	3
Edwards	3	–	3
Jones	1	–	1
Lewis	1	–	1
McGuinness	1	–	1
Scanlon	1	–	1

1956/57

FOOTBALL LEAGUE DIVISION ONE

DATE	OPPONENTS	SCORE	GOALSCORERS	ATTENDANCE
Aug 18	BIRMINGHAM CITY	2-2	Viollet 2	32,752
Aug 20	Preston North End	3-1	Taylor 2, Whelan	32,569
Aug 25	West Bromwich Albion	3-2	Taylor, Viollet, Whelan	26,387
Aug 29	PRESTON NORTH END	3-2	Viollet 3	32,515
Sep 1	PORTSMOUTH	3-0	Berry, Pegg, Viollet	40,369
Sep 5	Chelsea	2-1	Taylor, Whelan	29,082
Sep 8	Newcastle United	1-1	Whelan	50,130
Sep 15	SHEFFIELD WEDNESDAY	4-1	Berry, Taylor, Viollet, Whelan	48,078
Sep 22	MANCHESTER CITY	2-0	Viollet, Whelan	53,525
Sep 29	Arsenal	2-1	Berry, Whelan	62,479
Oct 6	CHARLTON ATHLETIC	4-2	Charlton 2, Berry, Whelan	41,439
Oct 13	Sunderland	3-1	Viollet, Whelan, og	49,487
Oct 20	EVERTON	2-5	Charlton, Whelan	43,151
Oct 27	Blackpool	2-2	Taylor 2	32,632
Nov 3	WOLVERHAMPTON W.	3-0	Pegg, Taylor, Whelan	59,835
Nov 10	Bolton Wanderers	0-2		39,922
Nov 17	LEEDS UNITED	3-2	Whelan 2, Charlton	51,131
Nov 24	Tottenham Hotspur	2-2	Berry, Colman	57,724
Dec 1	LUTON TOWN	3-1	Edwards, Pegg, Taylor	34,736
Dec 8	Aston Villa	3-1	Taylor 2, Viollet	42,530
Dec 15	Birmingham City	1-3	Whelan	36,146
Dec 26	CARDIFF CITY	3-1	Taylor, Viollet, Whelan	28,607
Dec 29	Portsmouth	3-1	Edwards, Pegg, Viollet	32,147
Jan 1	CHELSEA	3-0	Taylor 2, Whelan	42,116
Jan 12	NEWCASTLE UNITED	6-1	Pegg 2, Viollet 2, Whelan 2	44,911
Jan 19	Sheffield Wednesday	1-2	Taylor	51,068
Feb 2	Manchester City	4-2	Edwards, Taylor, Viollet, Whelan	63,872
Feb 9	ARSENAL	6-2	Whelan 2, Berry 2, Edwards, Taylor	60,384
Feb 18	Charlton Athletic	5-1	Charlton 3, Taylor 2	16,308
Feb 23	BLACKPOOL	0-2		42,602
Mar 6	Everton	2-1	Webster 2	34,029
Mar 9	ASTON VILLA	1-1	Charlton	55,484
Mar 16	Wolverhampton W.	1-1	Charlton	53,228
Mar 25	BOLTON WANDERERS	0-2		60,862
Mar 30	Leeds United	2-1	Berry, Charlton	47,216
Apr 6	TOTTENHAM HOTSPUR	0-0		60,349
Apr 13	Luton Town	2-0	Taylor 2	21,227
Apr 19	Burnley	3-1	Whelan 3	41,321
Apr 20	SUNDERLAND	4-0	Whelan 2, Edwards, Taylor	58,725
Apr 22	BURNLEY	2-0	Dawson, Webster	41,321
Apr 27	Cardiff City	3-2	Scanlon 2, Dawson	17,708
Apr 29	WEST BROMWICH ALBION	1-1	Dawson	20,357

FA CUP

DATE	OPPONENTS	SCORE	GOALSCORERS	ATTENDANCE
Jan 5	Hartlepool United (Rd3)	4-3	Whelan 2, Berry, Taylor	17,264
Jan 26	Wrexham (Rd4)	5-0	Taylor 2, Whelan 2, Byrne	34,445
Feb 16	EVERTON (Rd5)	1-0	Edwards	61,803
Mar 2	Bournemouth (Rd6)	2-1	Berry 2	28,799
Mar 23	Birmingham City (SF) (at Hillsborough)	2-0	Berry, Charlton	65,107
May 4	Aston Villa (Final) (at Wembley)	1-2	Taylor	100,000

EUROPEAN CUP

DATE	OPPONENTS	SCORE	GOALSCORERS	ATTENDANCE
Sep 12	Anderlecht (PRdL1)	2-0	Taylor, Viollet	35,000
Sep 26	ANDERLECHT (PRdL2) (at Maine Road)	10-0	Viollet 4, Taylor 3, Whelan 2, Berry	40,000
Oct 17	BOR. DORTMUND (Rd1L1) (at Maine Road)	3-2	Viollet 2, Pegg	75,598
Nov 21	Bor. Dortmund (Rd1L2)	0-0		44,570
Jan 16	Athletic Bilbao (QFL1)	3-5	Taylor, Viollet, Whelan	60,000
Feb 6	ATHLETIC BILBAO (QFL2) (at Maine Road)	3-0	Berry, Taylor, Viollet	70,000
Apr 11	Real Madrid (SFL1)	1-3	Taylor	135,000
Apr 25	REAL MADRID (SFL2) (at Maine Road)	2-2	Charlton, Taylor	65,000

FINAL LEAGUE TABLE

		P	W	D	L	F	A	Pts
1	MANCHESTER UNITED	42	28	8	6	103	54	64
2	Tottenham Hotspur	42	22	12	8	104	56	56
3	Preston North End	42	23	10	9	84	56	56
4	Blackpool	42	22	9	11	93	65	53
5	Arsenal	42	21	8	13	85	69	50
6	Wolverhampton Wanderers	42	20	8	14	94	70	48
7	Burnley	42	18	10	14	56	50	46
8	Leeds United	42	15	14	13	72	63	44
9	Bolton Wanderers	42	16	12	14	65	65	44
10	Aston Villa	42	14	15	13	65	55	43
11	West Bromwich Albion	42	14	14	14	59	61	42
12	Birmingham City	42	15	9	18	69	69	39
13	Chelsea	42	13	13	16	73	73	39
14	Sheffield Wednesday	42	16	6	20	82	88	38
15	Everton	42	14	10	18	61	79	38
16	Luton Town	42	14	9	19	58	76	37
17	Newcastle United	42	14	8	20	67	87	36
18	Manchester City	42	13	9	20	78	88	35
19	Portsmouth	42	10	13	19	62	92	33
20	Sunderland	42	12	8	22	67	88	32
21	Cardiff City	42	10	9	23	53	88	29
22	Charlton Athletic	42	9	4	29	62	120	22

APPEARANCES

PLAYER	LGE	FAC	EC	TOT
Berry	40	5	8	53
Foulkes	39	6	8	53
Whelan	39	6	8	53
Wood	39	6	8	53
Pegg	37	6	8	51
Byrne	36	6	8	50
Colman	36	6	8	50
Edwards	34	6	7	47
Taylor	32	4	8	44
Jones	29	4	6	39
Viollet	27	5	6	38
Charlton	14	2	1	17
Blanchflower	11	2	3	16
McGuinness	13	1	1	15
Bent	6	–	–	6
Goodwin	6	–	–	6
Webster	5	1	–	6
Scanlon	5	–	–	5
Dawson	3	–	–	3
Doherty	3	–	–	3
Greaves	3	–	–	3
Clayton	2	–	–	2
Cope	2	–	–	2
Hawksworth	1	–	–	1

GOALSCORERS

PLAYER	LGE	FAC	EC	TOT
Taylor	22	4	8	34
Whelan	26	4	3	33
Viollet	16	–	9	25
Berry	8	4	2	14
Charlton	10	1	1	12
Pegg	6	–	1	7
Edwards	5	1	–	6
Dawson	3	–	–	3
Webster	3	–	–	3
Scanlon	2	–	–	2
Colman	1	–	–	1
Byrne	–	1	–	1
own goal	1	–	–	1

1957/58

FOOTBALL LEAGUE DIVISION ONE

DATE	OPPONENTS	SCORE	GOALSCORERS	ATTENDANCE
Aug 24	Leicester City	3-0	Whelan 3	40,214
Aug 28	EVERTON	3-0	Taylor T, Viollet, og	59,103
Aug 31	MANCHESTER CITY	4-1	Berry, Edwards, Taylor T, Viollet	63,347
Sep 4	Everton	3-3	Berry, Viollet, Whelan	72,077
Sep 7	LEEDS UNITED	5-0	Berry 2, Taylor T 2, Viollet	50,842
Sep 9	Blackpool	4-1	Viollet 2, Whelan 2	34,181
Sep 14	Bolton Wanderers	0-4		48,003
Sep 18	BLACKPOOL	1-2	Edwards	40,763
Sep 21	ARSENAL	4-2	Whelan 2, Pegg, Taylor T	47,142
Sep 28	Wolverhampton W.	1-3	Doherty	48,825
Oct 5	ASTON VILLA	4-1	Taylor T 2, Pegg, og	43,102
Oct 12	Nottingham Forest	2-1	Viollet, Whelan	47,654
Oct 19	PORTSMOUTH	0-3		38,253
Oct 26	West Bromwich Albion	3-4	Taylor T 2, Whelan	52,160
Nov 2	BURNLEY	1-0	Taylor T	49,449
Nov 9	Preston North End	1-1	Whelan	39,063
Nov 16	SHEFFIELD WEDNESDAY	2-1	Webster 2	40,366
Nov 23	Newcastle United	2-1	Edwards, Taylor T	53,890
Nov 30	TOTTENHAM HOTSPUR	3-4	Pegg 2, Whelan	43,077
Dec 7	Birmingham City	3-3	Viollet 2, Taylor T	35,791
Dec 14	CHELSEA	0-1		36,853
Dec 21	LEICESTER CITY	4-0	Viollet 2, Charlton, Scanlon	41,631
Dec 25	LUTON TOWN	3-0	Charlton, Edwards, Taylor T	39,444
Dec 26	Luton Town	2-2	Scanlon, Taylor T	26,458
Dec 28	Manchester City	2-2	Charlton, Viollet	70,483
Jan 11	Leeds United	1-1	Viollet	39,401
Jan 18	BOLTON WANDERERS	7-2	Charlton 3, Viollet 2, Edwards, Scanlon	41,141
Feb 1	Arsenal	5-4	Taylor T 2, Charlton, Edwards, Viollet	63,578
Feb 22	NOTTINGHAM FOREST	1-1	Dawson	66,124
Mar 8	WEST BROMWICH ALBION	0-4		63,278
Mar 15	Burnley	0-3		37,247
Mar 29	Sheffield Wednesday	0-1		35,608
Mar 31	Aston Villa	2-3	Dawson, Webster	16,631
Apr 4	SUNDERLAND	2-2	Charlton, Dawson	47,421
Apr 5	PRESTON NORTH END	0-0		47,816
Apr 7	Sunderland	2-1	Webster 2	51,302
Apr 12	Tottenham Hotspur	0-1		59,836
Apr 16	Portsmouth	3-3	Dawson, Taylor E, Webster	39,975
Apr 19	BIRMINGHAM CITY	0-2		38,991
Apr 21	WOLVERHAMPTON W.	0-4		33,267
Apr 23	NEWCASTLE UNITED	1-1	Dawson	28,393
Apr 26	Chelsea	1-2	Taylor E	45,011

FA CUP

DATE	OPPONENTS	SCORE	GOALSCORERS	ATTENDANCE
Jan 4	Workington (Rd3)	3-1	Viollet 3	21,000
Jan 25	IPSWICH TOWN (Rd4)	2-0	Charlton 2	53,550
Feb 19	SHEFFIELD WEDNESDAY (Rd5)	3-0	Brennan 2, Dawson	59,848
Mar 1	West Bromwich Albion (Rd6)	2-2	Dawson, Taylor E	58,250
Mar 5	WEST BROMWICH ALBION (Rd6R)	1-0	Webster	60,000
Mar 22	Fulham (SF) (at Villa Park)	2-2	Charlton 2	69,745
Mar 26	Fulham (SFR) (at Highbury)	5-3	Dawson 3, Brennan, Charlton	38,000
May 3	Bolton Wanderers (Final) (at Wembley)	0-2		100,000

EUROPEAN CUP

DATE	OPPONENTS	SCORE	GOALSCORERS	ATTENDANCE
Sep 25	Shamrock Rovers (PRdL1)	6-0	Taylor T 2, Whelan 2, Berry, Pegg	45,000
Oct 2	SHAMROCK ROVERS (PRdL2)	3-2	Viollet 2, Pegg	33,754
Nov 20	DUKLA PRAGUE (Rd1L1)	3-0	Pegg, Taylor, Webster	60,000
Dec 4	Dukla Prague (Rd1L2)	0-1		35,000
Jan 14	RED STAR BELGRADE (QFL1)	2-1	Charlton, Colman	60,000
Feb 5	Red Star Belgrade (QFL2)	3-3	Charlton 2, Viollet	55,000
May 8	AC MILAN (SFL1)	2-1	Taylor E, Viollet	44,880
May 14	AC Milan (SFL2)	0-4		80,000

FINAL LEAGUE TABLE

		P	W	D	L	F	A	Pts
1	Wolverhampton Wanderers	42	28	8	6	103	47	64
2	Preston North End	42	26	7	9	100	51	59
3	Tottenham Hotspur	42	21	9	12	93	77	51
4	West Bromwich Albion	42	18	14	10	92	70	50
5	Manchester City	42	22	5	15	104	100	49
6	Burnley	42	21	5	16	80	74	47
7	Blackpool	42	19	6	17	80	67	44
8	Luton Town	42	19	6	17	69	63	44
9	MANCHESTER UNITED	42	16	11	15	85	75	43
10	Nottingham Forest	42	16	10	16	69	63	42
11	Chelsea	42	15	12	15	83	79	42
12	Arsenal	42	16	7	19	73	85	39
13	Birmingham City	42	14	11	17	76	89	39
14	Aston Villa	42	16	7	19	73	86	39
15	Bolton Wanderers	42	14	10	18	65	87	38
16	Everton	42	13	11	18	65	75	37
17	Leeds United	42	14	9	19	51	63	37
18	Leicester City	42	14	5	23	91	112	33
19	Newcastle United	42	12	8	22	73	81	32
20	Portsmouth	42	12	8	22	73	88	32
21	Sunderland	42	10	12	20	54	97	32
22	Sheffield Wednesday	42	12	7	23	69	92	31

APPEARANCES

PLAYER	LGE	FAC	EC	TOT
Foulkes	42	8	8	58
Byrne	26	2	6	34
Edwards	26	2	5	33
Taylor T	25	2	6	33
Colman	24	2	5	31
Gregg	19	8	4	31
Viollet	22	3	6	31
Webster	20	6	5	31
Charlton	21	7	2	30
Goodwin	16	6	3	25
Pegg	21	–	4	25
Wood	20	–	4	24
Berry	20	–	3	23
Whelan	20	–	3	23
Cope	13	6	2	21
Blanchflower	18	–	2	20
Greaves	12	6	2	20
Morgans	13	2	4	19
Taylor E	11	6	2	19
Crowther	11	5	2	18
Dawson	12	6	–	18
Jones	10	2	4	16
Pearson	8	4	2	14
Scanlon	9	2	3	14
McGuinness	7	–	1	8
Brennan	5	2	–	7
Harrop	5	1	–	6
Gaskell	3	–	–	3
Doherty	1	–	–	1
Heron	1	–	–	1
Jones	1	–	–	1

GOALSCORERS

PLAYER	LGE	FAC	EC	TOT
Viollet	16	3	4	23
Taylor T	16	–	3	19
Charlton	8	5	3	16
Whelan	12	–	2	14
Dawson	5	5	–	10
Webster	6	1	1	8
Pegg	4	–	3	7
Edwards	6	–	–	6
Berry	4	–	1	5
Taylor E	2	1	1	4
Scanlon	3	–	–	3
Brennan	–	3	–	3
Doherty	1	–	–	1
Colman	–	–	1	1
own goals	2	–	–	2

1958/59

FOOTBALL LEAGUE DIVISION ONE

DATE	OPPONENTS	SCORE	GOALSCORERS	ATTENDANCE
Aug 23	CHELSEA	5–2	Charlton 3, Dawson 2	52,382
Aug 27	Nottingham Forest	3–0	Charlton 2, Scanlon	44,971
Aug 30	Blackpool	1–2	Viollet	26,719
Sep 3	NOTTINGHAM FOREST	1–1	Charlton	51,880
Sep 6	BLACKBURN ROVERS	6–1	Charlton 2, Viollet 2, Scanlon, Webster	65,187
Sep 8	West Ham United	2–3	McGuinness, Webster	35,672
Sep 13	Newcastle United	1–1	Charlton	60,670
Sep 17	WEST HAM UNITED	4–1	Scanlon 3, Webster	53,276
Sep 20	TOTTENHAM HOTSPUR	2–2	Webster 2	62,277
Sep 27	Manchester City	1–1	Charlton	62,912
Oct 4	Wolverhampton W.	0–4		36,840
Oct 8	PRESTON NORTH END	0–2		46,163
Oct 11	ARSENAL	1–1	Viollet	56,148
Oct 18	Everton	2–3	Cope 2	64,079
Oct 25	WEST BROMWICH ALBION	1–2	Goodwin	51,721
Nov 1	Leeds United	2–1	Goodwin, Scanlon	48,574
Nov 8	BURNLEY	1–3	Quixall	48,509
Nov 15	Bolton Wanderers	3–6	Dawson 2, Charlton	33,358
Nov 22	LUTON TOWN	2–1	Charlton, Viollet	42,428
Nov 29	Birmingham City	4–0	Charlton 2, Bradley, Scanlon	28,658
Dec 6	LEICESTER CITY	4–1	Bradley, Charlton, Scanlon, Viollet	38,482
Dec 13	Preston North End	4–3	Bradley, Charlton, Scanlon, Viollet	26,290
Dec 20	Chelsea	3–2	Charlton, Goodwin, og	48,550
Dec 26	ASTON VILLA	2–1	Quixall, Viollet	63,098
Dec 27	Aston Villa	2–0	Pearson, Viollet	56,450
Jan 3	BLACKPOOL	3–1	Charlton 2, Viollet	61,961
Jan 31	NEWCASTLE UNITED	4–4	Charlton, Quixall, Scanlon, Viollet	49,008
Feb 7	Tottenham Hotspur	3–1	Charlton 2, Scanlon	48,401
Feb 16	MANCHESTER CITY	4–1	Bradley 2, Goodwin, Scanlon	59,846
Feb 21	WOLVERHAMPTON W.	2–1	Charlton, Viollet	62,794
Feb 28	Arsenal	2–3	Bradley, Viollet	67,162
Mar 2	Blackburn Rovers	3–1	Bradley 2, Scanlon	40,401
Mar 7	EVERTON	2–1	Goodwin, Scanlon	51,254
Mar 14	West Bromwich Albion	3–1	Bradley, Scanlon, Viollet	35,463
Mar 21	LEEDS UNITED	4–0	Viollet 3, Charlton	45,473
Mar 27	PORTSMOUTH	6–1	Charlton 2, Viollet 2, Bradley, og	52,004
Mar 28	Burnley	2–4	Goodwin, Viollet	44,577
Mar 30	Portsmouth	3–1	Charlton 2, Bradley	29,359
Apr 4	BOLTON WANDERERS	3–0	Charlton, Scanlon, Viollet	61,528
Apr 11	Luton Town	0–0		27,025
Apr 18	BIRMINGHAM CITY	1–0	Quixall	43,006
Apr 25	Leicester City	1–2	Bradley	38,466

FA CUP

DATE	OPPONENTS	SCORE	GOALSCORERS	ATTENDANCE
Jan 10	Norwich City (Rd3)	0–3		38,000

FINAL LEAGUE TABLE

		P	W	D	L	F	A	Pts
1	Wolverhampton Wanderers	42	28	5	9	110	49	61
2	MANCHESTER UNITED	42	24	7	11	103	66	55
3	Arsenal	42	21	8	13	88	68	50
4	Bolton Wanderers	42	20	10	12	79	66	50
5	West Bromwich Albion	42	18	13	11	88	68	49
6	West Ham United	42	21	6	15	85	70	48
7	Burnley	42	19	10	13	81	70	48
8	Blackpool	42	18	11	13	66	49	47
9	Birmingham City	42	20	6	16	84	68	46
10	Blackburn Rovers	42	17	10	15	76	70	44
11	Newcastle United	42	17	7	18	80	80	41
12	Preston North End	42	17	7	18	70	77	41
13	Nottingham Forest	42	17	6	19	71	74	40
14	Chelsea	42	18	4	20	77	98	40
15	Leeds United	42	15	9	18	57	74	39
16	Everton	42	17	4	21	71	87	38
17	Luton Town	42	12	13	17	68	71	37
18	Tottenham Hotspur	42	13	10	19	85	95	36
19	Leicester City	42	11	10	21	67	98	32
20	Manchester City	42	11	9	22	64	95	31
21	Aston Villa	42	11	8	23	58	87	30
22	Portsmouth	42	6	9	27	64	112	21

APPEARANCES

PLAYER	LGE	FAC	TOT
Goodwin	42	1	43
Scanlon	42	1	43
Gregg	41	1	42
McGuinness	39	1	40
Charlton	38	1	39
Viollet	37	1	38
Greaves	34	–	34
Quixall	33	1	34
Cope	32	1	33
Foulkes	32	1	33
Bradley	24	1	25
Carolan	23	1	24
Dawson	11	–	11
Taylor	11	–	11
Webster	7	–	7
Harrop	5	–	5
Pearson	4	–	4
Crowther	2	–	2
Morgans	2	–	2
Brennan	1	–	1
Hunter	1	–	1
Wood	1	–	1

GOALSCORERS

PLAYER	LGE	FAC	TOT
Charlton	29	–	29
Viollet	21	–	21
Scanlon	16	–	16
Bradley	12	–	12
Goodwin	6	–	6
Webster	5	–	5
Dawson	4	–	4
Quixall	4	–	4
Cope	2	–	2
McGuinness	1	–	1
Pearson	1	–	1
own goals	2	–	2

1959/60

FOOTBALL LEAGUE DIVISION ONE

DATE	OPPONENTS	SCORE	GOALSCORERS	ATTENDANCE
Aug 22	West Bromwich Albion	2–3	Viollet 2	40,076
Aug 26	CHELSEA	0–1		57,674
Aug 29	NEWCASTLE UNITED	3–2	Viollet 2, Charlton	53,257
Sep 2	Chelsea	6–3	Bradley 2, Viollet 2, Charlton, Quixall	66,579
Sep 5	Birmingham City	1–1	Quixall	38,220
Sep 9	LEEDS UNITED	6–0	Bradley 2, Charlton 2, Scanlon, Viollet	48,407
Sep 12	Tottenham Hotspur	1–5	Viollet	55,402
Sep 16	Leeds United	2–2	Charlton, og	34,048
Sep 19	Manchester City	0–3		58,300
Sep 26	Preston North End	0–4		35,016
Oct 3	LEICESTER CITY	4–1	Viollet 2, Charlton, Quixall	41,637
Oct 10	ARSENAL	4–2	Charlton, Quixall, Viollet, og	51,626
Oct 17	Wolverhampton W.	2–3	Viollet, og	45,451
Oct 24	SHEFFIELD WEDNESDAY	3–1	Viollet 2, Bradley	39,259
Oct 31	Blackburn Rovers	1–1	Quixall	39,621
Nov 7	FULHAM	3–3	Charlton, Scanlon, Viollet	44,063
Nov 14	Bolton Wanderers	1–1	Dawson	37,892
Nov 21	LUTON TOWN	4–1	Viollet 2, Goodwin, Quixall	40,572
Nov 28	Everton	1–2	Viollet	46,095
Dec 5	BLACKPOOL	3–1	Viollet 2, Pearson	45,558
Dec 12	Nottingham Forest	5–1	Viollet 3, Dawson, Scanlon	31,666
Dec 19	WEST BROMWICH ALBION	2–3	Dawson, Quixall	33,667
Dec 26	BURNLEY	1–2	Quixall	62,376
Dec 28	Burnley	4–1	Scanlon 2, Viollet 2	47,253
Jan 2	Newcastle United	3–7	Quixall 2, Dawson	57,200
Jan 16	BIRMINGHAM CITY	2–1	Quixall, Viollet	47,361
Jan 23	Tottenham Hotspur	1–2	Bradley	62,602
Feb 6	MANCHESTER CITY	0–0		59,450
Feb 13	PRESTON NORTH END	1–1	Viollet	44,014
Feb 24	Leicester City	1–3	Scanlon	33,191
Feb 27	Blackpool	6–0	Charlton 3, Viollet 2, Scanlon	23,996
Mar 5	WOLVERHAMPTON W.	0–2		60,560
Mar 19	NOTTINGHAM FOREST	3–1	Charlton 2, Dawson	35,269
Mar 26	Fulham	5–0	Viollet 2, Dawson, Giles, Pearson	38,250
Mar 30	Sheffield Wednesday	2–4	Charlton, Viollet	26,821
Apr 2	BOLTON WANDERERS	2–0	Charlton 2	45,298
Apr 9	Luton Town	3–2	Dawson 2, Bradley	21,242
Apr 15	West Ham United	1–2	Dawson	34,969
Apr 16	BLACKBURN ROVERS	1–0	Dawson	45,945
Apr 18	WEST HAM UNITED	5–3	Charlton 2, Dawson 2, Quixall	34,676
Apr 23	Arsenal	2–5	Giles, Pearson	41,057
Apr 30	EVERTON	5–0	Dawson 3, Bradley, Quixall	43,823

FA CUP

DATE	OPPONENTS	SCORE	GOALSCORERS	ATTENDANCE
Jan 9	Derby County (Rd3)	4–2	Charlton, Goodwin, Scanlon, og	33,297
Jan 30	Liverpool (Rd4)	3–1	Charlton 2, Bradley	56,736
Feb 20	SHEFFIELD WEDNESDAY (Rd5)	0–1		66,350

FINAL LEAGUE TABLE

		P	W	D	L	F	A	Pts
1	Burnley	42	24	7	11	85	61	55
2	Wolverhampton Wanderers	42	24	6	12	106	67	54
3	Tottenham Hotspur	42	21	11	10	86	50	53
4	West Bromwich Albion	42	19	11	12	83	57	49
5	Sheffield Wednesday	42	19	11	12	80	59	49
6	Bolton Wanderers	42	20	8	14	59	51	48
7	MANCHESTER UNITED	42	19	7	16	102	80	45
8	Newcastle United	42	18	8	16	82	78	44
9	Preston North End	42	16	12	14	79	76	44
10	Fulham	42	17	10	15	73	80	44
11	Blackpool	42	15	10	17	59	71	40
12	Leicester City	42	13	13	16	66	75	39
13	Arsenal	42	15	9	18	68	80	39
14	West Ham United	42	16	6	20	75	91	38
15	Everton	42	13	11	18	73	78	37
16	Manchester City	42	17	3	22	78	84	37
17	Blackburn Rovers	42	16	5	21	60	70	37
18	Chelsea	42	14	9	19	76	91	37
19	Birmingham City	42	13	10	19	63	80	36
20	Nottingham Forest	42	13	9	20	50	74	35
21	Leeds United	42	12	10	20	65	92	34
22	Luton Town	42	9	12	21	50	73	30

APPEARANCES

PLAYER	LGE	FAC	TOT
Foulkes	42	3	45
Carolan	41	3	44
Cope	40	3	43
Charlton	37	3	40
Viollet	36	3	39
Gregg	33	3	36
Quixall	33	3	36
Scanlon	31	3	34
Brennan	29	3	32
Bradley	29	2	31
Dawson	22	1	23
Goodwin	18	1	19
McGuinness	19	–	19
Setters	17	2	19
Giles	10	–	10
Pearson	10	–	10
Gaskell	9	–	9
Lawton	3	–	3
Greaves	2	–	2
Heron	1	–	1

GOALSCORERS

PLAYER	LGE	FAC	TOT
Viollet	32	–	32
Charlton	18	3	21
Dawson	15	–	15
Quixall	13	–	13
Bradley	8	1	9
Scanlon	7	1	8
Pearson	3	–	3
Giles	2	–	2
Goodwin	1	1	2
own goals	3	1	4

1960/61

FOOTBALL LEAGUE DIVISION ONE

DATE	OPPONENTS	SCORE	GOALSCORERS	ATTENDANCE
Aug 20	BLACKBURN ROVERS	1–3	Charlton	47,778
Aug 24	Everton	0–4		51,602
Aug 31	EVERTON	4–0	Dawson 2, Charlton, Nicholson	51,818
Sep 3	Tottenham Hotspur	1–4	Viollet	55,445
Sep 5	West Ham United	1–2	Quixall	30,506
Sep 10	LEICESTER CITY	1–1	Giles	35,493
Sep 14	WEST HAM UNITED	6–1	Charlton 2, Viollet 2, Scanlon, Quixall	33,695
Sep 17	Aston Villa	1–3	Viollet	43,593
Sep 24	WOLVERHAMPTON W.	1–3	Charlton	44,458
Oct 1	Bolton Wanderers	1–1	Giles	39,197
Oct 15	Burnley	3–5	Viollet 3	32,011
Oct 22	NEWCASTLE UNITED	3–2	Dawson, Setters, Stiles	37,516
Oct 24	NOTTINGHAM FOREST	2–1	Viollet 2	23,628
Oct 29	Arsenal	1–2	Quixall	45,715
Nov 5	SHEFFIELD WEDNESDAY	0–0		36,855
Nov 12	Birmingham City	1–3	Charlton	31,549
Nov 19	WEST BROMWICH ALBION	3–0	Dawson, Quixall, Viollet	32,756
Nov 26	Cardiff City	0–3		21,122
Dec 3	PRESTON NORTH END	1–0	Dawson	24,904
Dec 10	Fulham	4–4	Quixall 2, Charlton, Dawson	23,625
Dec 17	Blackburn Rovers	2–1	Pearson 2	17,285
Dec 24	Chelsea	2–1	Charlton, Dawson	37,601
Dec 26	CHELSEA	6–0	Dawson 3, Nicholson 2, Charlton	50,164
Dec 31	MANCHESTER CITY	5–1	Dawson 3, Charlton 2	61,213
Jan 14	TOTTENHAM HOTSPUR	2–0	Pearson, Stiles	65,295
Jan 21	Leicester City	0–6		31,308
Feb 4	ASTON VILLA	1–1	Charlton	33,525
Feb 11	Wolverhampton W.	1–2	Nicholson	38,526
Feb 18	BOLTON WANDERERS	3–1	Dawson 2, Quixall	37,558
Feb 25	Nottingham Forest	2–3	Charlton, Quixall	26,850
Mar 4	Manchester City	3–1	Charlton, Dawson, Pearson	50,479
Mar 11	Newcastle United	1–1	Charlton	28,870
Mar 18	ARSENAL	1–1	Moir	29,732
Mar 25	Sheffield Wednesday	1–5	Charlton	35,901
Mar 31	Blackpool	0–2		30,835
Apr 1	FULHAM	3–1	Charlton, Quixall, Viollet	24,654
Apr 3	BLACKPOOL	2–0	Nicholson, og	39,169
Apr 8	West Bromwich Albion	1–1	Pearson	27,750
Apr 12	BURNLEY	6–0	Quixall 3, Viollet 3	25,019
Apr 15	BIRMINGHAM CITY	4–1	Pearson 2, Quixall, Viollet	28,376
Apr 22	Preston North End	4–2	Charlton 2, Setters 2	21,252
Apr 29	CARDIFF CITY	3–3	Charlton 2, Setters	30,320

FA CUP

DATE	OPPONENTS	SCORE	GOALSCORERS	ATTENDANCE
Jan 7	MIDDLESBROUGH (Rd3)	3–0	Dawson 2, Cantwell	49,184
Jan 28	Sheffield Wednesday (Rd4)	1–1	Cantwell	58,000
Feb 1	SHEFFIELD WEDNESDAY (Rd4R)	2–7	Dawson, Pearson	65,243

LEAGUE CUP

DATE	OPPONENTS	SCORE	GOALSCORERS	ATTENDANCE
Oct 19	Exeter City (Rd1)	1–1	Dawson	14,494
Oct 26	EXETER CITY (Rd1R)	4–1	Quixall 2, Giles, Pearson	15,662
Nov 2	Bradford City (Rd2)	1–2	Viollet	4,670

FINAL LEAGUE TABLE

		P	W	D	L	F	A	Pts
1	Tottenham Hotspur	42	31	4	7	115	55	66
2	Sheffield Wednesday	42	23	12	7	78	47	58
3	Wolverhampton Wanderers	42	25	7	10	103	75	57
4	Burnley	42	22	7	13	102	77	51
5	Everton	42	22	6	14	87	69	50
6	Leicester City	42	18	9	15	87	70	45
7	MANCHESTER UNITED	42	18	9	15	88	76	45
8	Blackburn Rovers	42	15	13	14	77	76	43
9	Aston Villa	42	17	9	16	78	77	43
10	West Bromwich Albion	42	18	5	19	67	71	41
11	Arsenal	42	15	11	16	77	85	41
12	Chelsea	42	15	7	20	98	100	37
13	Manchester City	42	13	11	18	79	90	37
14	Nottingham Forest	42	14	9	19	62	78	37
15	Cardiff City	42	13	11	18	60	85	37
16	West Ham United	42	13	10	19	77	88	36
17	Fulham	42	14	8	20	72	95	36
18	Bolton Wanderers	42	12	11	19	58	73	35
19	Birmingham City	42	14	6	22	62	84	34
20	Blackpool	42	12	9	21	68	73	33
21	Newcastle United	42	11	10	21	86	109	32
22	Preston North End	42	10	10	22	43	71	30

APPEARANCES

PLAYER	LGE	FAC	LC	TOT
Brennan	41	3	2	46
Foulkes	40	3	2	45
Setters	40	3	2	45
Charlton	39	3	–	42
Quixall	38	2	1	41
Nicholson	31	3	3	37
Dawson	28	3	3	34
Pearson	27	3	3	33
Stiles	26	3	2	31
Gregg	27	1	2	30
Cantwell	24	3	–	27
Viollet	24	1	2	27
Giles	23	–	2	25
Gaskell	10	–	1	11
Scanlon	8	–	3	11
Moir	8	–	–	8
Cope	6	–	1	7
Bradley	4	–	–	4
Dunne	3	–	1	4
Haydock	4	–	–	4
Pinner	4	–	–	4
Briggs	1	2	–	3
Carolan	2	–	1	3
Lawton	1	–	1	2
Morgans	2	–	–	2
Bratt	–	–	1	1
Heron	1	–	–	1

GOALSCORERS

PLAYER	LGE	FAC	LC	TOT
Charlton	21	–	–	21
Dawson	16	3	1	20
Viollet	15	–	1	16
Quixall	13	–	2	15
Pearson	7	1	1	9
Nicholson	5	–	–	5
Setters	4	–	–	4
Giles	2	–	1	3
Stiles	2	–	–	2
Cantwell	–	2	–	2
Moir	1	–	–	1
Scanlon	1	–	–	1
own goal	1	–	–	1

1961/62

FOOTBALL LEAGUE DIVISION ONE

DATE	OPPONENTS	SCORE	GOALSCORERS	ATTENDANCE
Aug 19	West Ham United	1–1	Stiles	32,628
Aug 23	CHELSEA	3–2	Herd, Pearson, Viollet	45,847
Aug 26	BLACKBURN ROVERS	6–1	Herd 2, Quixall 2, Charlton, Setters	45,302
Aug 30	Chelsea	0–2		42,248
Sep 2	Blackpool	3–2	Viollet 2, Charlton	28,156
Sep 9	TOTTENHAM HOTSPUR	1–0	Quixall	57,135
Sep 16	Cardiff City	2–1	Dawson, Quixall	29,251
Sep 18	Aston Villa	1–1	Stiles	38,837
Sep 23	MANCHESTER CITY	3–2	Stiles, Viollet, og	56,345
Sep 30	WOLVERHAMPTON W.	2–0		39,457
Oct 7	West Bromwich Albion	1–1	Dawson	25,645
Oct 14	BIRMINGHAM CITY	0–2		30,674
Oct 21	Arsenal	1–5	Viollet	54,245
Oct 28	BOLTON WANDERERS	0–3		31,442
Nov 4	Sheffield Wednesday	1–3	Viollet	35,998
Nov 11	LEICESTER CITY	2–2	Giles, Viollet	21,567
Nov 18	Ipswich Town	1–4	McMillan	25,755
Nov 25	BURNLEY	1–4	Herd	41,029
Dec 2	Everton	1–5	Herd	48,099
Dec 9	FULHAM	3–0	Herd 2, Lawton	22,193
Dec 16	WEST HAM UNITED	1–2	Herd	29,472
Dec 26	NOTTINGHAM FOREST	6–3	Lawton 3, Brennan, Charlton, Herd	30,822
Jan 13	BLACKPOOL	0–1		26,999
Jan 15	ASTON VILLA	2–0	Charlton, Quixall	20,807
Jan 20	Tottenham Hotspur	2–2	Charlton, Stiles	55,225
Feb 3	CARDIFF CITY	3–0	Giles, Lawton, Stiles	29,200
Feb 10	Manchester City	2–0	Chisnall, Herd	49,959
Feb 24	WEST BROMWICH ALBION	4–1	Charlton 2, Quixall, Setters	32,456
Feb 28	Wolverhampton W.	2–2	Herd, Lawton	27,565
Mar 3	Birmingham City	1–1	Herd	25,812
Mar 17	Bolton Wanderers	0–1		34,366
Mar 20	Nottingham Forest	0–1		27,833
Mar 24	SHEFFIELD WEDNESDAY	1–1	Charlton	31,322
Apr 4	Leicester City	3–4	McMillan 2, Quixall	15,318
Apr 7	IPSWICH TOWN	5–0	Quixall 3, Setters, Stiles	24,976
Apr 10	Blackburn Rovers	0–3		14,623
Apr 14	Burnley	3–1	Brennan, Cantwell, Herd	36,240
Apr 16	ARSENAL	2–3	Cantwell, McMillan	24,258
Apr 21	EVERTON	1–1	Herd	31,926
Apr 23	SHEFFIELD UNITED	0–1		30,073
Apr 24	Sheffield United	3–2	McMillan 2, Stiles	25,324
Apr 28	Fulham	0–2		40,113

FA CUP

DATE	OPPONENTS	SCORE	GOALSCORERS	ATTENDANCE
Jan 6	BOLTON WANDERERS (Rd3)	2–1	Herd, Nicholson	42,202
Jan 31	ARSENAL (Rd4)	1–0	Setters	54,082
Feb 17	SHEFFIELD WEDNESDAY (Rd5)	0–0		59,553
Feb 21	Sheffield Wednesday (Rd5R)	2–0	Charlton, Giles	62,969
Mar 10	Preston North End (Rd6)	0–0		37,521
Mar 14	PRESTON NORTH END (Rd6R)	2–1	Charlton, Herd	63,468
Mar 31	Tottenham Hotspur (SF) (at Hillsborough)	1–3	Viollet	65,000

FINAL LEAGUE TABLE

		P	W	D	L	F	A	Pts
1	Ipswich Town	42	24	8	10	93	67	56
2	Burnley	42	21	11	10	101	67	53
3	Tottenham Hotspur	42	21	10	11	88	69	52
4	Everton	42	20	11	11	88	54	51
5	Sheffield United	42	19	9	14	61	69	47
6	Sheffield Wednesday	42	20	6	16	72	58	46
7	Aston Villa	42	18	8	16	65	56	44
8	West Ham United	42	17	10	15	76	82	44
9	West Bromwich Albion	42	15	13	14	83	67	43
10	Arsenal	42	16	11	15	71	72	43
11	Bolton Wanderers	42	16	10	16	62	66	42
12	Manchester City	42	17	7	18	78	81	41
13	Blackpool	42	15	11	16	70	75	41
14	Leicester City	42	17	6	19	72	71	40
15	MANCHESTER UNITED	42	15	9	18	72	75	39
16	Blackburn Rovers	42	14	11	17	50	58	39
17	Birmingham City	42	14	10	18	65	81	38
18	Wolverhampton Wanderers	42	13	10	19	73	86	36
19	Nottingham Forest	42	13	10	19	63	79	36
20	Fulham	42	13	7	22	66	74	33
21	Cardiff City	42	9	14	19	50	81	32
22	Chelsea	42	9	10	23	63	94	28

APPEARANCES

PLAYER	LGE	FAC	TOT
Brennan	41	6	47
Foulkes	40	7	47
Setters	38	7	45
Charlton	37	6	43
Stiles	34	4	38
Giles	30	7	37
Dunne	28	7	35
Herd	27	5	32
Gaskell	21	7	28
Lawton	20	7	27
Quixall	21	3	24
Nicholson	17	4	21
Cantwell	17	2	19
Pearson	17	–	17
Chisnall	9	4	13
Gregg	13	–	13
Viollet	13	–	13
McMillan	11	–	11
Moir	9	–	9
Briggs	8	–	8
Bradley	6	1	7
Dawson	4	–	4
Haydock	1	–	1

GOALSCORERS

PLAYER	LGE	FAC	TOT
Herd	14	3	17
Quixall	10	–	10
Charlton	8	2	10
Stiles	7	–	7
Viollet	7	–	7
Lawton	6	–	6
McMillan	6	–	6
Setters	3	1	4
Giles	2	1	3
Brennan	2	–	2
Cantwell	2	–	2
Dawson	2	–	2
Pearson	1	–	1
Nicholson	–	1	1
own goal	1	–	1

1962/63

FOOTBALL LEAGUE DIVISION ONE

DATE	OPPONENTS	SCORE	GOALSCORERS	ATTENDANCE
Aug 18	WEST BROMWICH ALBION	2-2	Herd, Law	51,685
Aug 22	Everton	1-3	Moir	69,501
Aug 25	Arsenal	3-1	Herd 2, Chisnall	62,308
Aug 29	EVERTON	0-1		63,437
Sep 1	BIRMINGHAM CITY	2-0	Giles, Herd	39,847
Sep 5	Bolton Wanderers	0-3		44,859
Sep 8	Leyton Orient	0-1		24,901
Sep 12	BOLTON WANDERERS	3-0	Herd 2, Cantwell	37,721
Sep 15	MANCHESTER CITY	2-3	Law 2	49,193
Sep 22	BURNLEY	2-5	Law, Stiles	45,954
Sep 29	Sheffield Wednesday	0-1		40,520
Oct 6	Blackpool	2-2	Herd 2	33,242
Oct 13	BLACKBURN ROVERS	0-3		42,252
Oct 24	Tottenham Hotspur	2-6	Herd, Quixall	51,314
Oct 27	WEST HAM UNITED	3-1	Quixall 2, Law	29,204
Nov 3	Ipswich Town	5-3	Law 4, Herd	18,483
Nov 10	LIVERPOOL	3-3	Giles, Herd, Quixall	43,810
Nov 17	Wolverhampton W.	3-2	Law 2, Herd	27,305
Nov 24	ASTON VILLA	2-2	Quixall 2	36,852
Dec 1	Sheffield United	1-1	Charlton	25,173
Dec 8	NOTTINGHAM FOREST	5-1	Herd 2, Charlton, Giles, Law	27,496
Dec 15	West Bromwich Albion	0-3		18,113
Dec 26	Fulham	1-0	Charlton	23,928
Feb 23	BLACKPOOL	1-1	Herd	43,121
Mar 2	Blackburn Rovers	2-2	Charlton, Law	27,924
Mar 9	TOTTENHAM HOTSPUR	0-2		53,416
Mar 18	West Ham United	1-3	Herd	28,950
Mar 23	IPSWICH TOWN	0-1		32,792
Apr 1	FULHAM	0-2		28,124
Apr 9	Aston Villa	2-1	Charlton, Stiles	26,867
Apr 13	Liverpool	0-1		51,529
Apr 15	LEICESTER CITY	2-2	Charlton, Herd	50,005
Apr 16	Leicester City	3-4	Law 3	37,002
Apr 20	SHEFFIELD UNITED	1-1	Law	31,179
Apr 22	WOLVERHAMPTON W.	2-1	Law, Herd	36,147
May 1	SHEFFIELD WEDNESDAY	1-3	Setters	31,878
May 4	Burnley	1-0	Law	30,266
May 6	ARSENAL	2-3	Law 2	35,999
May 10	Birmingham City	1-2	Law	21,814
May 15	Manchester City	1-1	Quixall	52,424
May 18	LEYTON ORIENT	3-1	Charlton, Law, og	32,759
May 20	Nottingham Forest	2-3	Giles, Herd	16,130

FA CUP

DATE	OPPONENTS	SCORE	GOALSCORERS	ATTENDANCE
Mar 4	HUDDERSFIELD TOWN (Rd3)	5-0	Law 3, Giles, Quixall	47,703
Mar 11	ASTON VILLA (Rd4)	1-0	Quixall	52,265
Mar 16	CHELSEA (Rd5)	2-1	Law, Quixall	48,298
Mar 30	Coventry City (Rd6)	3-1	Charlton 2, Quixall	44,000
Apr 27	Southampton (SF) (at Villa Park)	1-0	Law	65,000
May 25	Leicester City (Final) (at Wembley)	3-1	Herd 2, Law	100,000

FINAL LEAGUE TABLE

		P	W	D	L	F	A	Pts
1	Everton	42	25	11	6	84	42	61
2	Tottenham Hotspur	42	23	9	10	111	62	55
3	Burnley	42	22	10	10	78	57	54
4	Leicester City	42	20	12	10	79	53	52
5	Wolverhampton Wanderers	42	20	10	12	93	65	50
6	Sheffield Wednesday	42	19	10	13	77	63	48
7	Arsenal	42	18	10	14	86	77	46
8	Liverpool	42	17	10	15	71	59	44
9	Nottingham Forest	42	17	10	15	67	69	44
10	Sheffield United	42	16	12	14	58	60	44
11	Blackburn Rovers	42	15	12	15	79	71	42
12	West Ham United	42	14	12	16	73	69	40
13	Blackpool	42	13	14	15	58	64	40
14	West Bromwich Albion	42	16	7	19	71	79	39
15	Aston Villa	42	15	8	19	62	68	38
16	Fulham	42	14	10	18	50	71	38
17	Ipswich Town	42	12	11	19	59	78	35
18	Bolton Wanderers	42	15	5	22	55	75	35
19	MANCHESTER UNITED	42	12	10	20	67	81	34
20	Birmingham City	42	10	13	19	63	90	33
21	Manchester City	42	10	11	21	58	102	31
22	Leyton Orient	42	6	9	27	37	81	21

APPEARANCES

PLAYER	LGE	FAC	TOT
Foulkes	41	6	47
Law	38	6	44
Herd	37	6	43
Giles	36	6	42
Brennan	37	4	41
Quixall	31	5	36
Stiles	31	4	35
Charlton	28	6	34
Setters	27	6	33
Cantwell	25	5	30
Dunne	25	3	28
Gregg	24	4	28
Crerand	19	3	22
Gaskell	18	2	20
Lawton	12	–	12
Nicholson	10	–	10
Moir	9	–	9
Chisnall	6	–	6
McMillan	4	–	4
Pearson	2	–	2
Haydock	1	–	1
Walker	1	–	1

GOALSCORERS

PLAYER	LGE	FAC	TOT
Law	23	6	29
Herd	19	2	21
Quixall	7	4	11
Charlton	7	2	9
Giles	4	1	5
Stiles	2	–	2
Cantwell	1	–	1
Chisnall	1	–	1
Moir	1	–	1
Setters	1	–	1
own goal	1	–	1

1963/64

FOOTBALL LEAGUE DIVISION ONE

DATE	OPPONENTS	SCORE	GOALSCORERS	ATTENDANCE
Aug 24	Sheffield Wednesday	3-3	Charlton 2, Moir	32,177
Aug 28	IPSWICH TOWN	2-0	Law 2	39,921
Aug 31	EVERTON	5-1	Chisnall 2, Law 2, Sadler	62,965
Sep 3	Ipswich Town	7-2	Law 3, Chisnall, Moir, Sadler, Setters	28,113
Sep 7	Birmingham City	1-1	Chisnall	36,874
Sep 11	BLACKPOOL	3-0	Charlton 2, Law	47,400
Sep 14	WEST BROMWICH ALBION	1-0	Sadler	50,453
Sep 16	Blackpool	0-1		29,806
Sep 21	Arsenal	1-2	Herd	56,776
Sep 28	LEICESTER CITY	3-1	Herd 2, Setters	41,374
Oct 2	Chelsea	1-1	Setters	45,351
Oct 5	Bolton Wanderers	1-0	Herd	35,872
Oct 19	Nottingham Forest	2-1	Chisnall, Quixall	41,426
Oct 26	WEST HAM UNITED	0-1		45,120
Oct 28	BLACKBURN ROVERS	2-2	Quixall 2	41,169
Nov 2	Wolverhampton W.	0-2		34,159
Nov 9	TOTTENHAM HOTSPUR	4-1	Law 3, Herd	57,413
Nov 16	Aston Villa	0-4		36,276
Nov 23	LIVERPOOL	0-1		54,654
Nov 30	Sheffield United	2-1	Law 2	30,615
Dec 7	STOKE CITY	5-2	Law 4, Herd	52,232
Dec 14	SHEFFIELD WEDNESDAY	3-1	Herd 3	35,139
Dec 21	Everton	0-4		48,027
Dec 26	Burnley	1-6	Herd	35,764
Dec 28	BURNLEY	5-1	Herd 2, Moore 2, Best	47,834
Jan 11	BIRMINGHAM CITY	1-2	Sadler	44,695
Jan 18	West Bromwich Albion	4-1	Law 2, Best, Charlton	25,624
Feb 1	ARSENAL	3-1	Herd, Law, Setters	48,340
Feb 8	Leicester City	2-3	Herd, Law	35,538
Feb 19	BOLTON WANDERERS	5-0	Best 2, Herd 2, Charlton	33,926
Feb 22	Blackburn Rovers	3-1	Law 2, Chisnall	36,726
Mar 7	West Ham United	2-0	Herd, Sadler	27,027
Mar 21	Tottenham Hotspur	3-2	Charlton, Law, Moore	56,392
Mar 23	CHELSEA	1-1	Law	42,931
Mar 27	Fulham	2-2	Herd, Law	41,769
Mar 28	WOLVERHAMPTON W.	2-2	Charlton, Herd	44,470
Mar 30	FULHAM	3-0	Crerand, Foulkes, Herd	42,279
Apr 4	Liverpool	0-3		52,559
Apr 6	ASTON VILLA	1-0	Law	25,848
Apr 13	SHEFFIELD UNITED	2-1	Law, Moir	27,587
Apr 18	Stoke City	1-3	Charlton	45,670
Apr 25	NOTTINGHAM FOREST	3-1	Law 2, Moore	31,671

FA CUP

DATE	OPPONENTS	SCORE	GOALSCORERS	ATTENDANCE
Jan 4	Southampton (Rd3)	3-2	Crerand, Herd, Moore	29,164
Jan 25	BRISTOL ROVERS (Rd4)	4-1	Law 3, Herd	55,772
Feb 15	Barnsley (Rd5)	4-0	Law 2, Best, Herd	38,076
Feb 29	SUNDERLAND (Rd6)	3-3	Best, Charlton, og	63,700
Mar 4	Sunderland (Rd6R)	2-2	Charlton, Law	68,000
Mar 9	Sunderland (Rd6R2) (at Leeds Road, Huddersfield)	5-1	Law 3, Chisnall, Herd	54,952
Mar 14	West Ham United (SF) (at Hillsborough)	1-3	Law	65,000

EUROPEAN CUP-WINNERS' CUP

DATE	OPPONENTS	SCORE	GOALSCORERS	ATTENDANCE
Sep 25	Willem II (Rd1L1)	1-1	Herd	20,000
Oct 15	WILLEM II (Rd1L2)	6-1	Law 3, Charlton, Chisnall, Setters	46,272
Dec 3	Tottenham Hotspur (Rd2L1)	0-2		57,447
Dec 10	TOTTENHAM HOTSPUR (Rd2L2)	4-1	Charlton 2, Herd 2	50,000
Feb 26	SPORTING LISBON (QFL1)	4-1	Law 3, Charlton	60,000
Mar 18	Sporting Lisbon (QFL2)	0-5		40,000

FINAL LEAGUE TABLE

		P	W	D	L	F	A	Pts
1	Liverpool	42	26	5	11	92	45	57
2	MANCHESTER UNITED	42	23	7	12	90	62	53
3	Everton	42	21	10	11	84	64	52
4	Tottenham Hotspur	42	22	7	13	97	81	51
5	Chelsea	42	20	10	12	72	56	50
6	Sheffield Wednesday	42	19	11	12	84	67	49
7	Blackburn Rovers	42	18	10	14	89	65	46
8	Arsenal	42	17	11	14	90	82	45
9	Burnley	42	17	10	15	71	64	44
10	West Bromwich Albion	42	16	11	15	70	61	43
11	Leicester City	42	16	11	15	61	58	43
12	Sheffield United	42	16	11	15	61	64	43
13	Nottingham Forest	42	16	9	17	64	68	41
14	West Ham United	42	14	12	16	69	74	40
15	Fulham	42	13	13	16	58	65	39
16	Wolverhampton Wanderers	42	12	15	15	70	80	39
17	Stoke City	42	14	10	18	77	78	38
18	Blackpool	42	13	9	20	52	73	35
19	Aston Villa	42	11	12	19	62	71	34
20	Birmingham City	42	11	7	24	54	92	29
21	Bolton Wanderers	42	10	8	24	48	80	28
22	Ipswich Town	42	9	7	26	56	121	25

APPEARANCES

PLAYER	LGE	FAC	ECWC	TOT
Crerand	41	7	6	54
Foulkes	41	7	6	54
Charlton	40	7	6	53
Dunne	40	7	6	53
Setters	32	7	6	45
Herd	30	7	6	43
Law	30	6	5	41
Cantwell	28	2	4	34
Chisnall	20	4	4	28
Gaskell	17	7	4	28
Gregg	25	–	2	27
Best	17	7	2	26
Brennan	17	5	2	24
Sadler	19	–	2	21
Stiles	17	2	2	21
Moore	18	1	–	19
Moir	18	–	–	18
Quixall	9	–	3	12
Anderson	2	1	–	3
Tranter	1	–	–	1

GOALSCORERS

PLAYER	LGE	FAC	ECWC	TOT
Law	30	10	6	46
Herd	20	4	3	27
Charlton	9	2	4	15
Chisnall	6	1	1	8
Best	4	2	–	6
Sadler	5	–	–	5
Moore	4	1	–	5
Setters	4	–	1	5
Moir	3	–	–	3
Quixall	3	–	–	3
Crerand	1	1	–	2
Foulkes	1	–	–	1
own goal	–	1	–	1

1964/65

FOOTBALL LEAGUE DIVISION ONE

DATE	OPPONENTS	SCORE	GOALSCORERS	ATTENDANCE
Aug 22	WEST BROMWICH ALBION	2-2	Charlton, Law	52,007
Aug 24	West Ham United	1-3	Law	37,070
Aug 29	Leicester City	2-2	Law, Sadler	32,373
Sep 2	WEST HAM UNITED	3-1	Best, Connelly, Law	45,123
Sep 5	Fulham	1-2	Connelly	36,291
Sep 8	Everton	3-3	Connelly, Herd, Law	63,024
Sep 12	NOTTINGHAM FOREST	3-0	Herd 2, Connelly	45,012
Sep 16	EVERTON	2-1	Best, Law	49,968
Sep 19	Stoke City	2-1	Connelly, Herd	40,031
Sep 26	TOTTENHAM HOTSPUR	4-1	Crerand 2, Law 2	53,058
Sep 30	Chelsea	2-0	Best, Law	60,769
Oct 3	Burnley	0-0		30,761
Oct 10	SUNDERLAND	1-0	Herd	48,577
Oct 17	Wolverhampton W.	4-2	Law 2, Herd, og	26,763
Oct 24	ASTON VILLA	7-0	Law 4, Herd 2, Connelly	35,807
Oct 31	Liverpool	2-0	Crerand, Herd	52,402
Nov 7	SHEFFIELD WEDNESDAY	1-0	Herd	50,178
Nov 14	Blackpool	2-1	Connelly, Herd	31,129
Nov 21	BLACKBURN ROVERS	3-0	Best, Connelly, Herd	49,633
Nov 28	Arsenal	3-2	Law 2, Connelly	59,627
Dec 5	LEEDS UNITED	0-1		53,374
Dec 12	West Bromwich Albion	1-1	Law	28,126
Dec 16	BIRMINGHAM CITY	1-1	Charlton	25,721
Dec 26	Sheffield United	1-0	Best	37,295
Dec 28	SHEFFIELD UNITED	1-1	Herd	42,219
Jan 16	Nottingham Forest	2-2	Law 2	43,009
Jan 23	STOKE CITY	1-1	Law	50,392
Feb 6	Tottenham Hotspur	0-1		58,639
Feb 13	BURNLEY	3-2	Best, Charlton, Herd	38,865
Feb 24	Sunderland	0-1		51,336
Feb 27	WOLVERHAMPTON W.	3-0	Charlton 2, Connelly	37,018
Mar 13	CHELSEA	4-0	Herd 2, Best, Law	56,261
Mar 15	FULHAM	4-1	Connelly 2, Herd 2	45,402
Mar 20	Sheffield Wednesday	0-1		33,549
Mar 22	BLACKPOOL	2-0	Law 2	42,318
Apr 3	Blackburn Rovers	5-0	Charlton 3, Connelly, Herd	29,363
Apr 12	LEICESTER CITY	1-0	Herd	34,114
Apr 17	Leeds United	1-0	Connelly	52,368
Apr 19	Birmingham City	4-2	Best 2, Cantwell, Charlton	28,907
Apr 24	LIVERPOOL	3-0	Law 2, Connelly	55,772
Apr 26	ARSENAL	3-1	Law 2, Best	51,625
Apr 28	Aston Villa	1-2	Charlton	36,081

FA CUP

DATE	OPPONENTS	SCORE	GOALSCORERS	ATTENDANCE
Jan 9	CHESTER CITY (Rd3)	2-1	Best, Kinsey	40,000
Jan 30	Stoke City (Rd4)	0-0		53,009
Feb 3	STOKE CITY (Rd4R)	1-0	Herd	50,814
Feb 20	BURNLEY (Rd5)	2-1	Crerand, Law	54,000
Mar 10	Wolverhampton W. (Rd6)	5-3	Law 2, Best, Crerand, Herd	53,581
Mar 27	Leeds United (SF) (at Hillsborough)	0-0		65,000
Mar 31	Leeds United (SFR) (at City Ground, Nottingham)	0-1		46,300

INTER-CITIES' FAIRS CUP

DATE	OPPONENTS	SCORE	GOALSCORERS	ATTENDANCE
Sep 23	Djurgardens (Rd1L1)	1-1	Herd	6,537
Oct 27	DJURGARDENS (Rd1L2)	6-1	Law 3, Charlton 2, Best	38,437
Nov 11	Bor. Dortmund (Rd2L2)	6-1	Charlton 3, Best, Herd, Law	25,000
Dec 2	BOR. DORTMUND (Rd2L2)	4-0	Charlton 2, Connelly, Law	31,896
Jan 20	EVERTON (Rd3L1)	1-1	Connelly	50,000
Feb 9	Everton (Rd3L2)	2-1	Connelly, Herd	54,397
May 12	Strasbourg (QFL1)	5-0	Law 2, Charlton, Connelly, Herd	30,000
May 19	STRASBOURG (QFL2)	0-0		34,188
May 31	FERENCVAROS (SFL1)	3-2	Herd 2, Law	39,902
Jun 6	Ferencvaros (SFL2)	0-1		50,000
Jun 16	Ferencvaros (SFR)	1-2	Connelly	60,000

FINAL LEAGUE TABLE

		P	W	D	L	F	A	Pts
1	MANCHESTER UNITED	42	26	9	7	89	39	61
2	Leeds United	42	26	9	7	83	52	61
3	Chelsea	42	24	8	10	89	54	56
4	Everton	42	17	15	10	69	60	49
5	Nottingham Forest	42	17	13	12	71	67	47
6	Tottenham Hotspur	42	19	7	16	87	71	45
7	Liverpool	42	17	10	15	67	73	44
8	Sheffield Wednesday	42	16	11	15	57	55	43
9	West Ham United	42	19	4	19	82	71	42
10	Blackburn Rovers	42	16	10	16	83	79	42
11	Stoke City	42	16	10	16	67	66	42
12	Burnley	42	16	10	16	70	70	42
13	Arsenal	42	17	7	18	69	75	41
14	West Bromwich Albion	42	13	13	16	70	65	39
15	Sunderland	42	14	9	19	64	74	37
16	Aston Villa	42	16	5	21	57	82	37
17	Blackpool	42	12	11	19	67	78	35
18	Leicester City	42	11	13	18	69	85	35
19	Sheffield United	42	12	11	19	50	64	35
20	Fulham	42	11	12	19	60	78	34
21	Wolverhampton Wanderers	42	13	4	25	59	89	30
22	Birmingham City	42	8	11	23	64	96	27

APPEARANCES

PLAYER	LGE	FAC	ICFC	TOT
Brennan	42	7	11	60
Connelly	42	7	11	60
Dunne A	42	7	11	60
Foulkes	42	7	11	60
Best	41	7	11	59
Charlton	41	7	11	59
Stiles	41	7	11	59
Crerand	39	7	11	57
Dunne P	37	7	11	55
Herd	37	7	11	55
Law	36	6	10	52
Sadler	6	–	–	6
Setters	5	–	1	6
Gaskell	5	–	–	5
Cantwell	2	–	–	2
Fitzpatrick	2	–	–	2
Aston	1	–	–	1
Kinsey	–	1	–	1
Moir	1	–	–	1

GOALSCORERS

PLAYER	LGE	FAC	ICFC	TOT
Law	28	3	8	39
Herd	20	2	6	28
Connelly	15	–	5	20
Charlton	10	–	8	18
Best	10	2	2	14
Crerand	3	2	–	5
Cantwell	1	–	–	1
Sadler	1	–	–	1
Kinsey	–	1	–	1
own goal	1	–	–	1

1965/66

FOOTBALL LEAGUE DIVISION ONE

DATE	OPPONENTS	SCORE	GOALSCORERS	ATTENDANCE
Aug 21	SHEFFIELD WEDNESDAY	1-0	Herd	37,524
Aug 24	Nottingham Forest	2-4	Aston, Best	33,744
Aug 28	Northampton Town	1-1	Connelly	21,140
Sep 1	NOTTINGHAM FOREST	0-0		38,777
Sep 4	STOKE CITY	1-1	Herd	37,603
Sep 8	Newcastle United	2-1	Herd, Law	57,380
Sep 11	Burnley	0-3		30,235
Sep 15	NEWCASTLE UNITED	1-1	Stiles	30,401
Sep 18	CHELSEA	4-1	Law 3, Charlton	37,917
Sep 25	Arsenal	2-4	Aston, Charlton	56,757
Oct 9	LIVERPOOL	2-0	Best, Law	58,161
Oct 16	Tottenham Hotspur	1-5	Charlton	58,051
Oct 23	FULHAM	4-1	Herd 3, Charlton	32,716
Oct 30	Blackpool	2-1	Herd 2	24,703
Nov 6	BLACKBURN ROVERS	2-2	Charlton, Law	38,823
Nov 13	Leicester City	5-0	Herd 2, Best, Charlton, Connelly	34,551
Nov 20	SHEFFIELD UNITED	3-1	Best 2, Law	37,922
Dec 4	WEST HAM UNITED	0-0		32,924
Dec 11	Sunderland	3-2	Best 2, Herd	37,417
Dec 15	EVERTON	3-0	Best, Charlton, Herd	32,624
Dec 18	TOTTENHAM HOTSPUR	5-1	Law 2, Charlton, Herd, og	39,270
Dec 27	WEST BROMWICH ALBION	1-1	Law	54,102
Jan 1	Liverpool	1-2	Law	53,790
Jan 8	SUNDERLAND	1-1	Best	39,162
Jan 12	Leeds United	1-1	Herd	49,672
Jan 15	Fulham	1-0	Charlton	33,018
Jan 29	Sheffield Wednesday	0-0		39,281
Feb 5	NORTHAMPTON TOWN	6-2	Charlton 3, Law 2, Connelly	34,986
Feb 19	Stoke City	2-2	Connelly, Herd	36,667
Feb 26	BURNLEY	4-2	Herd 3, Charlton	49,892
Mar 12	Chelsea	0-2		60,269
Mar 19	ARSENAL	2-1	Law, Stiles	47,246
Apr 6	Aston Villa	1-1	Cantwell	28,211
Apr 9	LEICESTER CITY	1-2	Connelly	42,593
Apr 16	Sheffield United	1-3	Sadler	22,330
Apr 25	Everton	0-0		50,843
Apr 27	BLACKPOOL	2-1	Charlton, Law	26,953
Apr 30	West Ham United	2-3	Aston, Cantwell	36,416
May 4	West Bromwich Albion	3-3	Aston, Dunne A, Herd	22,609
May 7	Blackburn Rovers	4-1	Herd 2, Charlton, Sadler	14,513
May 9	ASTON VILLA	6-1	Herd 2, Sadler 2, Charlton, Ryan	23,039
May 19	LEEDS UNITED	1-1	Herd	35,008

FA CUP

DATE	OPPONENTS	SCORE	GOALSCORERS	ATTENDANCE
Jan 22	Derby County (Rd3)	5-2	Best 2, Law 2, Herd	33,827
Feb 12	ROTHERHAM UNITED (Rd4)	0-0		54,263
Feb 15	Rotherham United (Rd4R)	1-0	Connelly	23,500
Mar 5	Wolverhampton W. (Rd5)	4-2	Law 2, Best, Herd	53,500
Mar 26	Preston North End (Rd6)	1-1	Herd	37,876
Mar 30	PRESTON NORTH END (Rd6R)	3-1	Law 2, Connelly	60,433
Apr 23	Everton (SF) (at Burnden Park, Bolton)	0-1		60,000

EUROPEAN CUP

DATE	OPPONENTS	SCORE	GOALSCORERS	ATTENDANCE
Sep 22	HJK Helsinki (PRdL1)	3-2	Connelly, Herd, Law	25,000
Oct 6	HJK HELSINKI (PRdL2)	6-0	Connelly 3, Best 2, Charlton	30,388
Nov 17	ASK Vorwaerts (Rd1L1)	2-0	Connelly, Law	40,000
Dec 1	ASK VORWAERTS (Rd1L2)	3-1	Herd 3	30,082
Feb 2	BENFICA (QFL1)	3-2	Foulkes, Herd, Law	64,035
Mar 9	Benfica (QFL2)	5-1	Best 2, Charlton, Crerand, Connelly	75,000
Apr 13	Partizan Belgrade (SFL1)	0-2		60,000
Apr 20	PARTIZAN BELGRADE (SFL2)	1-0	Stiles	62,500

FINAL LEAGUE TABLE

		P	W	D	L	F	A	Pts
1	Liverpool	42	26	9	7	79	34	61
2	Leeds United	42	23	9	10	79	38	55
3	Burnley	42	24	7	11	79	47	55
4	MANCHESTER UNITED	42	18	15	9	84	59	51
5	Chelsea	42	22	7	13	65	53	51
6	West Bromwich Albion	42	19	12	11	91	69	50
7	Leicester City	42	21	7	14	80	65	49
8	Tottenham Hotspur	42	16	12	14	75	66	44
9	Sheffield United	42	16	11	15	56	59	43
10	Stoke City	42	15	12	15	65	64	42
11	Everton	42	15	11	16	56	62	41
12	West Ham United	42	15	9	18	70	83	39
13	Blackpool	42	14	9	19	55	65	37
14	Arsenal	42	12	13	17	62	75	37
15	Newcastle United	42	14	9	19	50	63	37
16	Aston Villa	42	15	6	21	69	80	36
17	Sheffield Wednesday	42	14	8	20	56	66	36
18	Nottingham Forest	42	14	8	20	56	72	36
19	Sunderland	42	14	8	20	51	72	36
20	Fulham	42	14	7	21	67	85	35
21	Northampton Town	42	10	13	19	55	92	33
22	Blackburn Rovers	42	8	4	30	57	88	20

APPEARANCES

PLAYER	LGE	FAC	EC	TOT
Crerand	41	7	7	55
Dunne A	40	7	8	55
Stiles	39	7	8	54
Charlton	38	7	8	53
Herd	36 (1)	7	7	50 (1)
Foulkes	33	7	8	48
Law	33	7	8	48
Connelly	31 (1)	6	8	45 (1)
Best	31	5	6	42
Brennan	28	5	5	38
Gregg	26	7	5	38
Cantwell	23	2	3	28
Aston	23	2	2	27
Dunne P	8	–	2	10
Sadler	10	–	–	10
Gaskell	8	–	1	9
Anderson	5 (1)	1	1	7 (1)
Fitzpatrick	3 (1)	–	1	4 (1)
Ryan	4	–	–	4
Noble	2	–	–	2

GOALSCORERS

PLAYER	LGE	FAC	EC	TOT
Herd	24	3	5	32
Law	15	6	3	24
Charlton	16	–	2	18
Best	9	3	4	16
Connelly	5	2	6	13
Aston	4	–	–	4
Sadler	4	–	–	4
Stiles	2	–	1	3
Cantwell	2	–	–	2
Dunne A	1	–	–	1
Ryan	1	–	–	1
Crerand	–	–	1	1
Foulkes	–	–	1	1
own goals	1	–	–	1

1966/67

FOOTBALL LEAGUE DIVISION ONE

DATE	OPPONENTS	SCORE	GOALSCORERS	ATTENDANCE
Aug 20	WEST BROMWICH ALBION	5–3	Law 2, Best, Herd, Stiles	41,343
Aug 23	Everton	2–1	Law 2	60,657
Aug 27	Leeds United	1–3	Best	45,092
Aug 31	EVERTON	3–0	Connelly, Foulkes, Law	61,114
Sep 3	NEWCASTLE UNITED	3–2	Connelly, Herd, Law	44,448
Sep 7	Stoke City	0–3		44,337
Sep 10	Tottenham Hotspur	1–2	Law	56,295
Sep 17	MANCHESTER CITY	1–0	Law	62,085
Sep 24	BURNLEY	4–1	Crerand, Herd, Law, Sadler	52,697
Oct 1	Nottingham Forest	1–4	Charlton	41,854
Oct 8	Blackpool	2–1	Law 2	33,555
Oct 15	CHELSEA	1–1	Law	56,789
Oct 29	ARSENAL	1–0	Sadler	45,387
Nov 5	Chelsea	3–1	Aston 2, Best	55,958
Nov 12	SHEFFIELD WEDNESDAY	2–0	Charlton, Herd	46,942
Nov 19	Southampton	2–1	Charlton 2	29,458
Nov 26	SUNDERLAND	5–0	Herd 4, Law	44,687
Nov 30	Leicester City	2–1	Best, Law	39,014
Dec 3	Aston Villa	1–2	Herd	39,937
Dec 10	LIVERPOOL	2–2	Best 2	61,768
Dec 17	West Bromwich Albion	4–3	Herd 3, Law	32,080
Dec 26	Sheffield United	1–2	Herd	42,752
Dec 27	SHEFFIELD UNITED	2–0	Crerand, Herd	59,392
Dec 31	LEEDS UNITED	0–0		53,486
Jan 14	TOTTENHAM HOTSPUR	1–0	Herd	57,366
Jan 21	Manchester City	1–1	Foulkes	62,983
Feb 4	Blackpool	1–1	Sadler	40,165
Feb 11	NOTTINGHAM FOREST	1–0	Law	62,727
Feb 25	BLACKPOOL	4–0	Charlton 2, Law, og	47,158
Mar 3	Arsenal	1–1	Aston	63,363
Mar 11	Newcastle United	0–0		37,430
Mar 18	LEICESTER CITY	5–2	Aston, Charlton, Herd, Law, Sadler	50,281
Mar 25	Liverpool	0–0		53,813
Mar 27	Fulham	2–2	Best, Stiles	47,290
Mar 28	FULHAM	2–1	Foulkes, Stiles	51,673
Apr 1	WEST HAM UNITED	3–0	Best, Charlton, Law	61,308
Apr 10	Sheffield Wednesday	2–2	Charlton 2	51,101
Apr 18	SOUTHAMPTON	3–0	Charlton, Law, Sadler	54,291
Apr 22	Sunderland	0–0		43,570
Apr 29	ASTON VILLA	3–1	Aston, Best, Law	55,782
May 6	West Ham United	6–1	Law 2, Best, Charlton, Crerand, Foulkes	38,424
May 13	STOKE CITY	0–0		61,071

FA CUP

DATE	OPPONENTS	SCORE	GOALSCORERS	ATTENDANCE
Jan 28	STOKE CITY (Rd3)	2–0	Herd, Law	63,500
Feb 18	NORWICH CITY (Rd4)	1–2	Law	63,409

LEAGUE CUP

DATE	OPPONENTS	SCORE	GOALSCORERS	ATTENDANCE
Sep 14	Blackpool (Rd2)	1–5	Herd	15,570

FINAL LEAGUE TABLE

		P	W	D	L	F	A	Pts
1	MANCHESTER UNITED	42	24	12	6	84	45	60
2	Nottingham Forest	42	23	10	9	64	41	56
3	Tottenham Hotspur	42	24	8	10	71	48	56
4	Leeds United	42	22	11	9	62	42	55
5	Liverpool	42	19	13	10	64	47	51
6	Everton	42	19	10	13	65	46	48
7	Arsenal	42	16	14	12	58	47	46
8	Leicester City	42	18	8	16	78	71	44
9	Chelsea	42	15	14	13	67	62	44
10	Sheffield United	42	16	10	16	52	59	42
11	Sheffield Wednesday	42	14	13	15	56	47	41
12	Stoke City	42	17	7	18	63	58	41
13	West Bromwich Albion	42	16	7	19	77	73	39
14	Burnley	42	15	9	18	66	76	39
15	Manchester City	42	12	15	15	43	52	39
16	West Ham United	42	14	8	20	80	84	36
17	Sunderland	42	14	8	20	58	72	36
18	Fulham	42	11	12	19	71	83	34
19	Southampton	42	14	6	22	74	92	34
20	Newcastle United	42	12	9	21	39	81	33
21	Aston Villa	42	11	7	24	54	85	29
22	Blackpool	42	6	9	27	41	76	21

APPEARANCES

PLAYER	LGE	FAC	LC	TOT
Best	42	2	1	45
Charlton	42	2	–	44
Dunne A	40	2	1	43
Crerand	39	2	1	42
Stiles	37	2	1	40
Sadler	35 (1)	2	1	38 (1)
Law	36	2	–	38
Stepney	35	2	–	37
Foulkes	33	1	1	35
Herd	28	2	1	31
Noble	29	2	–	31
Aston	26 (4)	–	1	27 (4)
Brennan	16	–	1	17
Connelly	6	–	1	7
Ryan	4 (1)	1	–	5 (1)
Gaskell	5	–	–	5
Cantwell	4	–	–	4
Fitzpatrick	3	–	–	3
Gregg	2	–	–	2
Dunne P	–	–	1	1
Anderson	– (1)	–	–	– (1)

GOALSCORERS

PLAYER	LGE	FAC	LC	TOT
Law	23	2	–	25
Herd	16	1	1	18
Charlton	12	–	–	12
Best	10	–	–	10
Aston	5	–	–	5
Sadler	5	–	–	5
Foulkes	4	–	–	4
Crerand	3	–	–	3
Stiles	3	–	–	3
Connelly	2	–	–	2
own goal	1	–	–	1

1967/68

FOOTBALL LEAGUE DIVISION ONE

DATE	OPPONENTS	SCORE	GOALSCORERS	ATTENDANCE
Aug 19	Everton	1–3	Charlton	61,452
Aug 23	LEEDS UNITED	1–0	Charlton	53,016
Aug 26	LEICESTER CITY	1–1	Foulkes	51,256
Sep 2	West Ham United	3–1	Kidd, Ryan, Sadler	36,562
Sep 6	Sunderland	1–1	Kidd	51,527
Sep 9	BURNLEY	2–2	Burns, Crerand	55,809
Sep 16	Sheffield Wednesday	1–1	Best	47,274
Sep 23	TOTTENHAM HOTSPUR	3–1	Best 2, Law	58,779
Sep 30	Manchester City	2–1	Charlton 2	62,942
Oct 7	ARSENAL	1–0	Aston	60,197
Oct 14	Sheffield United	3–0	Aston, Kidd, Law	29,170
Oct 25	COVENTRY CITY	4–0	Aston 2, Best, Charlton	54,253
Oct 28	Nottingham Forest	1–3	Best	49,946
Nov 4	STOKE CITY	1–0	Charlton	51,041
Nov 8	Leeds United	0–1		43,999
Nov 11	Liverpool	2–1	Best 2	54,515
Nov 18	SOUTHAMPTON	3–2	Aston, Charlton, Kidd	48,732
Nov 25	Chelsea	1–1	Kidd	54,712
Dec 2	WEST BROMWICH ALBION	2–1	Best 2	52,568
Dec 9	Newcastle United	2–2	Dunne, Kidd	48,639
Dec 16	EVERTON	3–1	Aston, Law, Sadler	60,736
Dec 23	Leicester City	2–2	Charlton, Law	40,104
Dec 26	WOLVERHAMPTON W.	4–0	Best 2, Charlton, Kidd	63,450
Dec 30	Wolverhampton W.	3–2	Aston, Charlton, Kidd	53,940
Jan 6	WEST HAM UNITED	3–1	Aston, Best, Charlton	54,498
Jan 20	SHEFFIELD WEDNESDAY	4–2	Best 2, Charlton, Kidd	55,254
Feb 3	Tottenham Hotspur	2–1	Best, Charlton	57,790
Feb 17	Burnley	1–2	Best	31,965
Feb 24	Arsenal	2–0	Best, og	46,417
Mar 2	CHELSEA	1–3	Kidd	62,978
Mar 16	Coventry City	0–2		47,110
Mar 23	NOTTINGHAM FOREST	3–0	Brennan, Burns, Herd	61,978
Mar 27	MANCHESTER CITY	1–3	Best	63,004
Mar 30	Stoke City	4–2	Aston, Best, Gowling, Ryan	30,141
Apr 6	LIVERPOOL	1–2	Best	63,059
Apr 12	Fulham	4–0	Best 2, Kidd, Law	40,152
Apr 13	Southampton	2–2	Best, Charlton	30,079
Apr 15	FULHAM	3–0	Aston, Best, Charlton	60,465
Apr 20	SHEFFIELD UNITED	1–0	Law	55,033
Apr 27	West Bromwich Albion	3–6	Kidd 2, Law	43,412
May 4	NEWCASTLE UNITED	6–0	Best 3, Kidd 2, Sadler	59,976
May 11	SUNDERLAND	1–2	Best	62,963

FA CUP

DATE	OPPONENTS	SCORE	GOALSCORERS	ATTENDANCE
Jan 27	TOTTENHAM HOTSPUR (Rd3)	2–2	Best, Charlton	63,500
Jan 31	Tottenham Hotspur (Rd3R)	0–1		57,200

EUROPEAN CUP

DATE	OPPONENTS	SCORE	GOALSCORERS	ATTENDANCE
Sep 20	HIBERNIANS MALTA (Rd1L1)	4–0	Law 2, Sadler 2	43,912
Sep 27	Hibernians Malta (Rd1L2)	0–0		25,000
Nov 15	Sarajevo (Rd2L1)	0–0		45,000
Nov 29	SARAJEVO (Rd2L2)	2–1	Aston, Best	62,801
Feb 28	GORNIK ZABRZE (QFL1)	2–0	Kidd, og	63,456
Mar 13	Gornik Zabrze (QFL2)	0–1		105,000
Apr 24	REAL MADRID (SFL1)	1–0	Best	63,500
May 15	Real Madrid (SFL2)	3–3	Foulkes, Sadler, og	125,000
May 29	Benfica (Final) (at Wembley)	4–1	Charlton 2, Best, Kidd	100,000

FINAL LEAGUE TABLE

		P	W	D	L	F	A	Pts
1	Manchester City	42	26	6	10	86	43	58
2	MANCHESTER UNITED	42	24	8	10	89	55	56
3	Liverpool	42	22	11	9	71	40	55
4	Leeds United	42	22	9	11	71	41	53
5	Everton	42	23	6	13	67	40	52
6	Chelsea	42	18	12	12	62	68	48
7	Tottenham Hotspur	42	19	9	14	70	59	47
8	West Bromwich Albion	42	17	12	13	75	62	46
9	Arsenal	42	17	10	15	60	56	44
10	Newcastle United	42	13	15	14	54	67	41
11	Nottingham Forest	42	14	11	17	52	64	39
12	West Ham United	42	14	10	18	73	69	38
13	Leicester City	42	13	12	17	64	69	38
14	Burnley	42	14	10	18	64	71	38
15	Sunderland	42	13	11	18	51	61	37
16	Southampton	42	13	11	18	66	83	37
17	Wolverhampton Wanderers	42	14	8	20	66	75	36
18	Stoke City	42	14	7	21	50	73	35
19	Sheffield Wednesday	42	11	12	19	51	63	34
20	Coventry City	42	9	15	18	51	71	33
21	Sheffield United	42	11	10	21	49	70	32
22	Fulham	42	10	7	25	56	98	27

APPEARANCES

PLAYER	LGE	FAC	EC	TOT
Best	41	2	9	52
Charlton	41	2	9	52
Crerand	41	2	9	52
Stepney	41	2	9	52
Sadler	40 (1)	2	9	51 (1)
Kidd	38	2	9	49
Dunne	37	2	9	48
Burns	36	2	7	45
Aston	34 (3)	2	6	42 (3)
Foulkes	24	–	6	30
Law	23	1	3	27
Stiles	20	–	7	27
Fitzpatrick	14 (3)	2	2	18 (3)
Brennan	13	–	3	16
Ryan	7 (1)	–	1	8 (1)
Herd	6	1	1	8
Gowling	4 (1)	–	–	4 (1)
Kopel	1 (1)	–	–	1 (1)
Rimmer	1	–	–	1

GOALSCORERS

PLAYER	LGE	FAC	EC	TOT
Best	28	1	3	32
Charlton	15	1	2	18
Kidd	15	–	2	17
Aston	10	–	1	11
Law	7	–	2	9
Sadler	3	–	3	6
Burns	2	–	–	2
Ryan	2	–	–	2
Foulkes	1	–	1	2
Brennan	1	–	–	1
Crerand	1	–	–	1
Dunne	1	–	–	1
Gowling	1	–	–	1
Herd	1	–	–	1
own goals	1	–	2	3

1968/69

FOOTBALL LEAGUE DIVISION ONE

DATE	OPPONENTS	SCORE	GOALSCORERS	ATTENDANCE
Aug 10	EVERTON	2-1	Best, Charlton	61,311
Aug 14	West Bromwich Albion	1-3	Charlton	38,299
Aug 17	Manchester City	0-0		63,052
Aug 21	COVENTRY CITY	1-0	Ryan	51,201
Aug 24	CHELSEA	0-4		55,114
Aug 28	TOTTENHAM HOTSPUR	3-1	Fitzpatrick 2, og	62,689
Aug 31	Sheffield Wednesday	4-5	Law 2, Best, Charlton	50,490
Sep 7	WEST HAM UNITED	1-1	Law	63,274
Sep 14	Burnley	0-1		32,935
Sep 21	NEWCASTLE UNITED	3-1	Best 2, Law	47,262
Oct 5	ARSENAL	0-0		61,843
Oct 9	Tottenham Hotspur	2-2	Crerand, Law	56,205
Oct 12	Liverpool	0-2		53,392
Oct 19	SOUTHAMPTON	1-2	Best	46,526
Oct 26	Queens Park Rangers	3-2	Best 2, Law	31,138
Nov 2	LEEDS UNITED	0-0		53,839
Nov 9	Sunderland	1-1	og	33,151
Nov 16	IPSWICH TOWN	0-0		45,796
Nov 23	Stoke City	0-0		30,562
Nov 30	WOLVERHAMPTON W.	2-0	Best, Law	50,165
Dec 7	Leicester City	1-2	Law	36,303
Dec 14	LIVERPOOL	1-0	Law	55,354
Dec 21	Southampton	0-2		26,194
Dec 26	Arsenal	0-3		62,300
Jan 11	Leeds United	1-2	Charlton	48,145
Jan 18	SUNDERLAND	4-1	Law 3, Best	45,670
Feb 1	Ipswich Town	0-1		30,837
Feb 15	Wolverhampton W.	2-2	Best, Charlton	44,023
Mar 8	MANCHESTER CITY	0-1		63,264
Mar 10	Everton	0-0		57,514
Mar 15	Chelsea	2-3	James, Law	60,436
Mar 19	QUEENS PARK RANGERS	8-1	Morgan 3, Best 2, Aston, Kidd, Stiles	36,638
Mar 22	SHEFFIELD WEDNESDAY	1-0	Best	45,527
Mar 24	STOKE CITY	1-1	Aston	39,931
Mar 29	West Ham United	0-0		41,546
Mar 31	Nottingham Forest	1-0	Best	41,892
Apr 2	WEST BROMWICH ALBION	2-1	Best 2	38,846
Apr 5	NOTTINGHAM FOREST	3-1	Morgan 2, Best	51,952
Apr 8	Coventry City	1-2	Fitzpatrick	45,402
Apr 12	Newcastle United	0-2		46,379
Apr 19	BURNLEY	2-0	Best, og	52,626
May 17	LEICESTER CITY	3-2	Best, Law, Morgan	45,860

FA CUP

DATE	OPPONENTS	SCORE	GOALSCORERS	ATTENDANCE
Jan 4	Exeter City (Rd3)	3-1	Fitzpatrick, Kidd, og	18,500
Jan 25	WATFORD (Rd4)	1-1	Law	63,498
Feb 3	Watford (Rd4R)	2-0	Law 2	34,000
Feb 8	Birmingham City (Rd5)	2-2	Best, Law	52,500
Feb 24	BIRMINGHAM CITY (Rd5R)	6-2	Law 3, Crerand, Kidd, Morgan	61,932
Mar 1	EVERTON (Rd6)	0-1		63,464

EUROPEAN CUP

DATE	OPPONENTS	SCORE	GOALSCORERS	ATTENDANCE
Sep 18	Waterford (Rd1L1)	3-1	Law 3	48,000
Oct 2	WATERFORD (Rd1L2)	7-1	Law 4, Burns, Charlton, Stiles	41,750
Nov 13	ANDERLECHT (Rd2L1)	3-0	Law 2, Kidd	51,000
Nov 27	Anderlecht (Rd2L2)	1-3	Sartori	40,000
Feb 26	RAPID VIENNA (QFL1)	3-0	Best 2, Morgan	61,932
Mar 5	Rapid Vienna (QFL2)	0-0		52,000
Apr 23	AC Milan (SFL1)	0-2		80,000
May 15	AC MILAN (SFL2)	1-0	Charlton	63,103

FINAL LEAGUE TABLE

		P	W	D	L	F	A	Pts
1	Leeds United	42	27	13	2	66	26	67
2	Liverpool	42	25	11	6	63	24	61
3	Everton	42	21	15	6	77	36	57
4	Arsenal	42	22	12	8	56	27	56
5	Chelsea	42	20	10	12	73	53	50
6	Tottenham Hotspur	42	14	17	11	61	51	45
7	Southampton	42	16	13	13	57	48	45
8	West Ham United	42	13	18	11	66	50	44
9	Newcastle United	42	15	14	13	61	55	44
10	West Bromwich Albion	42	16	11	15	64	67	43
11	MANCHESTER UNITED	42	15	12	15	57	53	42
12	Ipswich Town	42	15	11	16	59	60	41
13	Manchester City	42	15	10	17	64	55	40
14	Burnley	42	15	9	18	55	82	39
15	Sheffield Wednesday	42	10	16	16	41	54	36
16	Wolverhampton Wanderers	42	10	15	17	41	58	35
17	Sunderland	42	11	12	19	43	67	34
18	Nottingham Forest	42	10	13	19	45	57	33
19	Stoke City	42	9	15	18	40	63	33
20	Coventry City	42	10	11	21	46	64	31
21	Leicester City	42	9	12	21	39	68	30
22	Queens Park Rangers	42	4	10	28	39	95	18

APPEARANCES

PLAYER	LGE	FAC	EC	TOT
Stiles	41	6	8	55
Best	41	6	6	53
Stepney	38	5	6	49
Crerand	35	4	8	47
Charlton	32	6	8	46
Dunne	33	6	6	45
Law	30	6	7	43
Kidd	28 (1)	5	7	40 (1)
Fitzpatrick	28 (2)	6	4	38 (2)
Morgan	29	5	4	38
Sadler	26 (3)	- (1)	5	31 (4)
James	21	6	2	29
Burns	14 (2)	1	3 (1)	18 (3)
Brennan	13	-	3	16
Foulkes	10 (3)	-	5	15 (3)
Sartori	11 (2)	2	2	15 (2)
Aston	13	-	-	13
Kopel	7 (1)	1	1	9 (1)
Rimmer	4	1	2 (1)	7 (1)
Ryan	6	-	1	7
Gowling	2	-	-	2

GOALSCORERS

PLAYER	LGE	FAC	EC	TOT
Law	14	7	9	30
Best	19	1	2	22
Morgan	6	1	1	8
Charlton	5	-	2	7
Fitzpatrick	3	1	-	4
Kidd	1	2	1	4
Aston	2	-	-	2
Crerand	1	1	-	2
Stiles	1	-	1	2
James	1	-	-	1
Ryan	1	-	-	1
Burns	-	-	1	1
Sartori	-	-	1	1
own goals	3	1	-	4

1969/70

FOOTBALL LEAGUE DIVISION ONE

DATE	OPPONENTS	SCORE	GOALSCORERS	ATTENDANCE
Aug 9	Crystal Palace	2-2	Charlton, Morgan	48,610
Aug 13	EVERTON	0-2		57,752
Aug 16	SOUTHAMPTON	1-4	Morgan	46,328
Aug 19	Everton	0-3		53,185
Aug 23	Wolverhampton W.	0-0		50,783
Aug 27	NEWCASTLE UNITED	0-0		52,774
Aug 30	SUNDERLAND	3-1	Best, Givens, Kidd	50,570
Sep 6	Leeds United	2-2	Best 2	44,271
Sep 13	LIVERPOOL	1-0	Morgan	56,509
Sep 17	Sheffield Wednesday	3-1	Best 2, Kidd	39,298
Sep 20	Arsenal	2-2	Best, Sadler	59,498
Sep 27	WEST HAM UNITED	5-2	Best 2, Burns, Charlton, Kidd	58,579
Oct 4	Derby County	0-2		40,724
Oct 8	Southampton	3-0	Best, Burns, Kidd	31,044
Oct 11	IPSWICH TOWN	2-1	Best, Kidd	52,281
Oct 18	NOTTINGHAM FOREST	1-1	Best	53,702
Oct 25	West Bromwich Albion	1-2	Kidd	45,120
Nov 1	STOKE CITY	1-1	Charlton	53,406
Nov 8	Coventry City	2-1	Aston, Law	43,446
Nov 15	Manchester City	0-4		63,013
Nov 22	TOTTENHAM HOTSPUR	3-1	Charlton 2, Burns	50,003
Nov 29	Burnley	1-1	Best	23,770
Dec 6	CHELSEA	0-2		49,344
Dec 13	Liverpool	4-1	Charlton, Morgan, Ure, og	47,682
Dec 26	WOLVERHAMPTON W.	0-0		50,806
Dec 27	Sunderland	1-1	Kidd	36,504
Jan 10	ARSENAL	2-1	Morgan, Sartori	41,055
Jan 17	West Ham United	0-0		41,643
Jan 26	LEEDS UNITED	2-2	Kidd, Sadler	59,879
Jan 31	DERBY COUNTY	1-0	Charlton	59,315
Feb 10	Ipswich Town	1-0	Kidd	29,755
Feb 14	CRYSTAL PALACE	1-1	Kidd	54,711
Feb 28	Stoke City	2-2	Morgan, Sartori	38,917
Mar 17	BURNLEY	3-3	Best, Crerand, Law	38,377
Mar 21	Chelsea	1-2	Morgan	61,479
Mar 28	MANCHESTER CITY	1-2	Kidd	59,777
Mar 30	COVENTRY CITY	1-1	Kidd	38,647
Mar 31	Nottingham Forest	2-1	Charlton, Gowling	39,228
Apr 4	Newcastle United	1-5	Charlton	43,094
Apr 8	WEST BROMWICH ALBION	7-0	Charlton 2, Fitzpatrick 2, Gowling 2, Best	26,582
Apr 13	Tottenham Hotspur	1-2	Fitzpatrick	41,808
Apr 15	SHEFFIELD WEDNESDAY	2-2	Best, Charlton	36,649

FA CUP

DATE	OPPONENTS	SCORE	GOALSCORERS	ATTENDANCE
Jan 3	Ipswich Town (Rd3)	1-0	og	29,552
Jan 24	MANCHESTER CITY (Rd4)	3-0	Kidd 2, Morgan	63,417
Feb 7	Northampton Town (Rd5)	8-2	Best 6, Kidd 2	21,771
Feb 21	Middlesbrough (Rd6)	1-1	Sartori	40,000
Feb 25	MIDDLESBROUGH (Rd6R)	2-1	Charlton, Morgan	63,418
Mar 14	Leeds United (SF) (at Hillsborough)	0-0		55,000
Mar 23	Leeds United (SFR) (at Villa Park)	0-0		62,500
Mar 26	Leeds United (SFR2) (at Burnden Park, Bolton)	0-1		56,000
Apr 10	Watford (3rd Place P/O) (at Highbury)	2-0	Kidd 2	15,105

LEAGUE CUP

DATE	OPPONENTS	SCORE	GOALSCORERS	ATTENDANCE
Sep 3	MIDDLESBROUGH (Rd2)	1-0	Sadler	38,938
Sep 23	WREXHAM (Rd3)	2-0	Best, Kidd	48,347
Oct 14	Burnley (Rd4)	0-0		27,959
Oct 20	BURNLEY (Rd4R)	1-0	Best	50,275
Nov 12	Derby County (Rd5)	0-0		38,895
Nov 19	DERBY COUNTY (Rd5R)	1-0	Kidd	57,393
Dec 3	Manchester City (SFL1)	1-2	Charlton	55,799
Dec 17	MANCHESTER CITY (SFL2)	2-2	Edwards, Law	63,418

FINAL LEAGUE TABLE

		P	W	D	L	F	A	Pts
1	Everton	42	29	8	5	72	34	66
2	Leeds United	42	21	15	6	84	49	57
3	Chelsea	42	21	13	8	70	50	55
4	Derby County	42	22	9	11	64	37	53
5	Liverpool	42	20	11	11	65	42	51
6	Coventry City	42	19	11	12	58	48	49
7	Newcastle United	42	17	13	12	57	35	47
8	MANCHESTER UNITED	42	14	17	11	66	61	45
9	Stoke City	42	15	15	12	56	52	45
10	Manchester City	42	16	11	15	55	48	43
11	Tottenham Hotspur	42	17	9	16	54	55	43
12	Arsenal	42	12	18	12	51	49	42
13	Wolverhampton Wanderers	42	12	16	14	55	57	40
14	Burnley	42	12	15	15	56	61	39
15	Nottingham Forest	42	10	18	14	50	71	38
16	West Bromwich Albion	42	14	9	19	58	66	37
17	West Ham United	42	12	12	18	51	60	36
18	Ipswich Town	42	10	11	21	40	63	31
19	Southampton	42	6	17	19	46	67	29
20	Crystal Palace	42	6	15	21	34	68	27
21	Sunderland	42	6	14	22	30	68	26
22	Sheffield United	42	8	9	25	40	71	25

APPEARANCES

PLAYER	LGE	FAC	LC	TOT
Charlton	40	9	8	57
Sadler	40	9	8	57
Stepney	37	9	8	54
Best	37	8	8	53
Morgan	35	9	5	49
Kidd	33 (1)	9	6	48 (1)
Dunne	33	7	8	48
Ure	34	7	7	48
Burns	30 (2)	3 (1)	6	39 (3)
Crerand	25	9	2	36
Aston	21 (1)	1 (1)	6	28 (2)
Edwards	18 (1)	7	2	27 (1)
Fitzpatrick	20	1	5	26
Sartori	13 (4)	7	1 (2)	21 (6)
Law	10 (1)	- (2)	3	13 (3)
Stiles	8	3	2	13
Brennan	8 (1)	1	1	10 (1)
Gowling	6 (1)	-	- (1)	6 (2)
Givens	4 (4)	-	1	5 (4)
Rimmer	5	-	-	5
Foulkes	3	-	-	3
James	2	-	1	3
Ryan	- (1)	-	-	- (1)

GOALSCORERS

PLAYER	LGE	FAC	LC	TOT
Best	15	6	2	23
Kidd	12	6	2	20
Charlton	12	1	1	14
Morgan	7	2	-	9
Burns	3	-	-	3
Fitzpatrick	3	-	-	3
Gowling	3	-	-	3
Law	2	-	1	3
Sadler	2	-	1	3
Sartori	2	1	-	3
Aston	1	-	-	1
Crerand	1	-	-	1
Givens	1	-	-	1
Ure	1	-	-	1
Edwards	-	-	1	1
own goals	1	1	-	2

1970/71

FOOTBALL LEAGUE DIVISION ONE

DATE	OPPONENTS	SCORE	GOALSCORERS	ATTENDANCE
Aug 15	LEEDS UNITED	0-1		59,365
Aug 19	CHELSEA	0-0		50,979
Aug 22	Arsenal	0-4		54,117
Aug 25	Burnley	2-0	Law 2	29,385
Aug 29	WEST HAM UNITED	1-1	Fitzpatrick	50,643
Sep 2	EVERTON	2-0	Best, Charlton	51,346
Sep 5	Liverpool	1-1	Kidd	52,542
Sep 12	COVENTRY CITY	2-0	Best, Charlton	48,939
Sep 19	Ipswich Town	0-4		27,776
Sep 26	BLACKPOOL	1-1	Best	46,647
Oct 3	Wolverhampton W.	2-3	Gowling, Kidd	38,629
Oct 10	CRYSTAL PALACE	0-1		42,979
Oct 17	Leeds United	2-2	Charlton, Fitzpatrick	50,190
Oct 24	WEST BROMWICH ALBION	2-1	Kidd, Law	43,278
Oct 31	Newcastle United	0-1		45,140
Nov 7	STOKE CITY	2-2	Law, Sadler	47,451
Nov 14	Nottingham Forest	2-1	Gowling, Sartori	36,364
Nov 21	Southampton	0-1		30,202
Nov 28	HUDDERSFIELD TOWN	1-1	Best	45,306
Dec 5	Tottenham Hotspur	2-2	Best, Law	55,693
Dec 12	MANCHESTER CITY	1-4	Kidd	52,636
Dec 19	ARSENAL	1-3	Sartori	33,182
Dec 26	Derby County	4-4	Law 2, Best, Kidd	34,068
Jan 9	Chelsea	2-1	Gowling, Morgan	53,482
Jan 16	BURNLEY	1-1	Aston	40,135
Jan 30	Huddersfield Town	2-1	Aston, Law	48,965
Feb 6	TOTTENHAM HOTSPUR	2-1	Best, Morgan	36,060
Feb 20	SOUTHAMPTON	5-1	Gowling 4, Morgan	52,544
Feb 23	Everton	0-1		52,544
Feb 27	NEWCASTLE UNITED	1-0	Kidd	41,902
Mar 6	West Bromwich Albion	3-4	Aston, Best, Kidd	41,112
Mar 13	NOTTINGHAM FOREST	2-0	Best, Law	40,473
Mar 20	Stoke City	2-1	Best 2	40,005
Apr 3	West Ham United	1-2	Best	38,507
Apr 10	DERBY COUNTY	1-2	Law	45,691
Apr 12	WOLVERHAMPTON W.	1-0	Gowling	41,886
Apr 13	Coventry City	1-2	Best	33,818
Apr 17	Crystal Palace	5-3	Law 3, Best 2	39,145
Apr 19	LIVERPOOL	0-2		44,004
Apr 24	IPSWICH TOWN	3-2	Best, Charlton, Kidd	33,566
May 1	Blackpool	1-1	Law	29,857
May 5	Manchester City	4-3	Best 2, Charlton, Law	43,626

FA CUP

DATE	OPPONENTS	SCORE	GOALSCORERS	ATTENDANCE
Jan 2	MIDDLESBROUGH (Rd3)	0-0		47,824
Jan 5	Middlesbrough (Rd3R)	1-2	Best	41,000

LEAGUE CUP

DATE	OPPONENTS	SCORE	GOALSCORERS	ATTENDANCE
Sep 9	Aldershot (Rd2)	3-1	Best, Kidd, Law	18,509
Oct 7	PORTSMOUTH (Rd3)	1-0	Charlton	32,068
Oct 28	CHELSEA (Rd4)	2-1	Best, Charlton	47,565
Nov 18	CRYSTAL PALACE (Rd5)	4-2	Kidd 2, Charlton, Fitzpatrick	48,961
Dec 16	ASTON VILLA (SFL1)	1-1	Kidd	48,889
Dec 23	Aston Villa (SFL2)	1-2	Kidd	58,667

FINAL LEAGUE TABLE

		P	W	D	L	F	A	Pts
1	Arsenal	42	29	7	6	71	29	65
2	Leeds United	42	27	10	5	72	30	64
3	Tottenham Hotspur	42	19	14	9	54	33	52
4	Wolverhampton Wanderers	42	22	8	12	64	54	52
5	Liverpool	42	17	17	8	42	24	51
6	Chelsea	42	18	15	9	52	42	51
7	Southampton	42	17	12	13	56	44	46
8	MANCHESTER UNITED	42	16	11	15	65	66	43
9	Derby County	42	16	10	16	56	54	42
10	Coventry City	42	16	10	16	37	38	42
11	Manchester City	42	12	17	13	47	42	41
12	Newcastle United	42	14	13	15	44	46	41
13	Stoke City	42	12	13	17	44	48	37
14	Everton	42	12	13	17	54	60	37
15	Huddersfield Town	42	11	14	17	40	49	36
16	Nottingham Forest	42	14	8	20	42	61	36
17	West Bromwich Albion	42	10	15	17	58	75	35
18	Crystal Palace	42	12	11	19	39	57	35
19	Ipswich Town	42	12	10	20	42	48	34
20	West Ham United	42	10	14	18	47	60	34
21	Burnley	42	7	13	22	29	63	27
22	Blackpool	42	4	15	23	34	66	23

APPEARANCES

PLAYER	LGE	FAC	LC	TOT
Charlton	42	2	6	50
Best	40	2	6	48
Fitzpatrick	35	2	6	43
Dunne	35	2	5	42
Sadler	32	2	5	39
Law	28	2	4	34
Edwards	29 (1)	1	2	32 (1)
Kidd	24 (1)	2	6	32 (1)
Morgan	25	2	2	29
Rimmer	20	2	6	28
Crerand	24	2	1	27
Aston	19 (1)	–	3 (1)	22 (2)
Stepney	22	–	–	22
Stiles	17	–	2	19
Gowling	17 (3)	– (1)	1	18 (4)
Burns	16 (4)	–	1 (1)	17 (5)
Ure	13	1	3	17
James	13	–	3 (1)	16 (1)
Watson	8	–	2	10
Sartori	2 (5)	–	1	3 (5)
Donald	–	–	1	1
O'Neil	1	–	–	1
Young	– (1)	–	–	– (1)

GOALSCORERS

PLAYER	LGE	FAC	LC	TOT
Best	18	1	2	21
Law	15	–	1	16
Kidd	8	–	5	13
Gowling	8	–	–	8
Charlton	5	–	3	8
Aston	3	–	–	3
Morgan	3	–	–	3
Fitzpatrick	2	–	1	3
Sartori	2	–	–	2
Sadler	1	–	–	1

1971/72

FOOTBALL LEAGUE DIVISION ONE

DATE	OPPONENTS	SCORE	GOALSCORERS	ATTENDANCE
Aug 14	Derby County	2-2	Gowling, Law	35,886
Aug 18	Chelsea	3-2	Charlton, Kidd, Morgan	54,763
Aug 20	ARSENAL (at Anfield)	3-1	Charlton, Gowling, Kidd	27,649
Aug 23	WEST BROMWICH ALBION (at Victoria Ground, Stoke)	3-1	Best 2, Gowling	23,146
Aug 28	Wolverhampton W.	1-1	Best	46,471
Aug 31	Everton	0-1		52,151
Sep 4	IPSWICH TOWN	1-0	Best	45,656
Sep 11	Crystal Palace	3-1	Law 2, Kidd	44,020
Sep 18	WEST HAM UNITED	4-2	Best 3, Charlton	55,339
Sep 25	Liverpool	2-2	Charlton, Law	55,684
Oct 2	SHEFFIELD UNITED	2-0	Best, Gowling	51,735
Oct 9	Huddersfield Town	3-0	Best, Charlton, Law	33,458
Oct 16	DERBY COUNTY	1-0	Best	53,247
Oct 23	Newcastle United	1-0	Best	52,411
Oct 30	LEEDS UNITED	0-1		53,960
Nov 6	Manchester City	3-3	Gowling, Kidd, McIlroy	63,326
Nov 13	TOTTENHAM HOTSPUR	3-1	Law 2, McIlroy	54,058
Nov 20	LEICESTER CITY	3-2	Law 2, Kidd	48,757
Nov 27	Southampton	5-2	Best 3, Kidd, McIlroy	30,323
Dec 4	NOTTINGHAM FOREST	3-2	Kidd 2, Law	45,411
Dec 11	Stoke City	1-1	Law	33,887
Dec 18	Ipswich Town	0-0		29,229
Dec 27	COVENTRY CITY	2-2	James, Law	52,117
Jan 1	West Ham United	0-3		41,892
Jan 8	WOLVERHAMPTON W.	1-3	McIlroy	46,781
Jan 22	CHELSEA	0-1		55,927
Jan 29	West Bromwich Albion	1-2	Kidd	47,012
Feb 12	NEWCASTLE UNITED	0-2		44,983
Feb 19	Leeds United	1-5	Burns	45,399
Mar 4	Tottenham Hotspur	0-2		54,814
Mar 8	EVERTON	0-0		38,415
Mar 11	HUDDERSFIELD TOWN	2-0	Best, Storey-Moore	53,581
Mar 25	CRYSTAL PALACE	4-0	Gowling, Charlton, Law, Storey-Moore	41,550
Apr 1	Coventry City	3-2	Best, Charlton, Storey-Moore	37,901
Apr 3	LIVERPOOL	0-3		53,826
Apr 4	Sheffield United	1-1	Sadler	45,045
Apr 8	Leicester City	0-2		35,970
Apr 12	MANCHESTER CITY	1-3	Buchan	56,362
Apr 15	SOUTHAMPTON	3-2	Best, Kidd, Storey-Moore	38,437
Apr 22	Nottingham Forest	0-0		35,063
Apr 25	Arsenal	0-3		49,125
Apr 29	STOKE CITY	3-0	Best, Charlton, Storey-Moore	34,959

FA CUP

DATE	OPPONENTS	SCORE	GOALSCORERS	ATTENDANCE
Jan 15	Southampton (Rd3)	1-1	Charlton	30,190
Jan 19	SOUTHAMPTON (Rd3R)	4-1	Best 2, Aston, Sadler	50,960
Feb 5	Preston North End (Rd4)	2-0	Gowling 2	27,025
Feb 26	MIDDLESBROUGH (Rd5)	0-0		53,850
Feb 29	Middlesbrough (Rd5R)	3-0	Best, Charlton, Morgan	39,683
Mar 18	STOKE CITY (Rd6)	1-1	Best	54,226
Mar 22	Stoke City (Rd6R)	1-2	Best	49,192

LEAGUE CUP

DATE	OPPONENTS	SCORE	GOALSCORERS	ATTENDANCE
Sep 7	Ipswich Town (Rd2)	3-1	Best 2, Morgan	28,143
Oct 6	BURNLEY (Rd3)	1-1	Charlton	44,600
Oct 18	Burnley (Rd3R)	1-0	Charlton	27,511
Oct 27	STOKE CITY (Rd4)	1-1	Gowling	47,062
Nov 8	Stoke City (Rd4R)	0-0		40,805
Nov 15	Stoke City (Rd4R2)	1-2	Best	42,249

FINAL LEAGUE TABLE

		P	W	D	L	F	A	Pts
1	Derby County	42	24	10	8	69	33	58
2	Leeds United	42	24	9	9	73	31	57
3	Liverpool	42	24	9	9	64	30	57
4	Manchester City	42	23	11	8	77	45	57
5	Arsenal	42	22	8	12	58	40	52
6	Tottenham Hotspur	42	19	13	10	63	42	51
7	Chelsea	42	18	12	12	58	49	48
8	MANCHESTER UNITED	42	19	10	13	69	61	48
9	Wolverhampton Wanderers	42	18	11	13	65	57	47
10	Sheffield United	42	17	12	13	61	60	46
11	Newcastle United	42	15	11	16	49	52	41
12	Leicester City	42	13	13	16	41	46	39
13	Ipswich Town	42	11	16	15	39	53	38
14	West Ham United	42	12	12	18	47	51	36
15	Everton	42	9	18	15	37	48	36
16	West Bromwich Albion	42	12	11	19	42	54	35
17	Stoke City	42	10	15	17	39	56	35
18	Coventry City	42	9	15	18	44	67	33
19	Southampton	42	12	7	23	52	80	31
20	Crystal Palace	42	8	13	21	39	65	29
21	Nottingham Forest	42	8	9	25	47	81	25
22	Huddersfield Town	42	6	13	23	27	59	25

APPEARANCES

PLAYER	LGE	FAC	LC	TOT
Best	40	7	6	53
Charlton	40	7	6	53
Stepney	39	7	6	52
O'Neil	37	7	6	50
Sadler	37	6	6	49
James	37	5	6	48
Morgan	35	7	6	48
Gowling	35 (2)	6 (1)	6	47 (3)
Kidd	34	4	5	43
Law	32 (1)	7	2	41 (1)
Dunne	34	4	3	41
Burns	15 (2)	5	3	23 (2)
Buchan	13	2	–	15
McIlroy	8 (8)	1 (2)	2	11 (10)
Storey-Moore	11	–	–	11
Edwards	4	2	–	6
Young	5 (2)	–	–	5 (2)
Aston	2 (7)	– (1)	2 (2)	4 (10)
Connaughton	3	–	–	3
Sartori	– (2)	–	1	1 (2)
Fitzpatrick	1	–	–	1

GOALSCORERS

PLAYER	LGE	FAC	LC	TOT
Best	18	5	3	26
Law	13	–	–	13
Charlton	8	2	2	12
Kidd	10	–	–	10
Gowling	6	2	1	9
Storey-Moore	5	–	–	5
McIlroy	4	–	–	4
Morgan	1	1	1	3
Sadler	1	1	–	2
Buchan	1	–	–	1
Burns	1	–	–	1
James	1	–	–	1
Aston	–	1	–	1

1972/73

FOOTBALL LEAGUE DIVISION ONE

DATE	OPPONENTS	SCORE	GOALSCORERS	ATTENDANCE
Aug 12	IPSWICH TOWN	1–2	Law	51,459
Aug 15	Liverpool	0–2		54,789
Aug 19	Everton	0–2		52,348
Aug 23	LEICESTER CITY	1–1	Best	40,067
Aug 26	ARSENAL	0–0		48,108
Aug 30	CHELSEA	0–0		44,482
Sep 2	West Ham United	2–2	Best, Storey-Moore	31,939
Sep 9	COVENTRY CITY	0–1		37,073
Sep 16	Wolverhampton W.	0–2		34,049
Sep 23	DERBY COUNTY	3–0	Davies, Morgan, Storey-Moore	48,255
Sep 30	Sheffield United	0–1		37,347
Oct 7	West Bromwich Albion	2–2	Best, Storey-Moore	32,909
Oct 14	BIRMINGHAM CITY	1–0	MacDougall	52,104
Oct 21	Newcastle United	1–2	Charlton	38,170
Oct 28	TOTTENHAM HOTSPUR	1–4	Charlton	52,497
Nov 4	Leicester City	2–2	Best, Davies	32,575
Nov 11	LIVERPOOL	2–0	Davies, MacDougall	53,944
Nov 18	Manchester City	0–3		52,050
Nov 25	SOUTHAMPTON	2–1	Davies, MacDougall	36,073
Dec 2	Norwich City	2–0	MacDougall, Storey-Moore	35,910
Dec 9	STOKE CITY	0–2		41,347
Dec 16	Crystal Palace	0–5		39,484
Dec 23	LEEDS UNITED	1–1	MacDougall	46,382
Dec 26	Derby County	1–3	Storey-Moore	35,098
Jan 6	Arsenal	1–3	Kidd	51,194
Jan 20	WEST HAM UNITED	2–2	Charlton, Macari	50,878
Jan 24	EVERTON	0–0		58,970
Jan 27	Coventry City	1–1	Holton	42,767
Feb 10	WOLVERHAMPTON W.	2–1	Charlton 2	52,089
Feb 17	Ipswich Town	1–4	Macari	31,918
Mar 3	WEST BROMWICH ALBION	2–1	Kidd, Macari	46,735
Mar 10	Birmingham City	1–3	Macari	51,278
Mar 17	NEWCASTLE UNITED	2–1	Holton, Martin	48,426
Mar 24	Tottenham Hotspur	1–1	Graham	49,751
Mar 31	Southampton	2–0	Charlton, Holton	23,161
Apr 7	NORWICH CITY	1–0	Martin	48,593
Apr 11	CRYSTAL PALACE	2–0	Kidd, Morgan	46,891
Apr 14	Stoke City	2–2	Macari, Morgan	37,051
Apr 18	Leeds United	1–0	Anderson	45,450
Apr 21	MANCHESTER CITY	0–0		61,676
Apr 23	SHEFFIELD UNITED	1–2	Kidd	57,280
Apr 28	Chelsea	0–1		44,184

FA CUP

DATE	OPPONENTS	SCORE	GOALSCORERS	ATTENDANCE
Jan 13	Wolverhampton W. (Rd3)	0–1		40,005

LEAGUE CUP

DATE	OPPONENTS	SCORE	GOALSCORERS	ATTENDANCE
Sep 6	Oxford United (Rd2)	2–2	Charlton, Law	16,560
Sep 12	OXFORD UNITED (Rd2R)	3–1	Best 2, Storey-Moore	21,486
Oct 3	Bristol Rovers (Rd3)	1–1	Morgan	33,957
Oct 11	BRISTOL ROVERS (Rd3R)	1–2	McIlroy	29,349

FINAL LEAGUE TABLE

		P	W	D	L	F	A	Pts
1	Liverpool	42	25	10	7	72	42	60
2	Arsenal	42	23	11	8	57	43	57
3	Leeds United	42	21	11	10	71	45	53
4	Ipswich Town	42	17	14	11	55	45	48
5	Wolverhampton Wanderers	42	18	11	13	66	54	47
6	West Ham United	42	17	12	13	67	53	46
7	Derby County	42	19	8	15	56	54	46
8	Tottenham Hotspur	42	16	13	13	58	48	45
9	Newcastle United	42	16	13	13	60	51	45
10	Birmingham City	42	15	12	15	53	54	42
11	Manchester City	42	15	11	16	57	60	41
12	Chelsea	42	13	14	15	49	51	40
13	Southampton	42	11	18	13	47	52	40
14	Sheffield United	42	15	10	17	51	59	40
15	Stoke City	42	14	10	18	61	56	38
16	Leicester City	42	10	17	15	40	46	37
17	Everton	42	13	11	18	41	49	37
18	MANCHESTER UNITED	42	12	13	17	44	60	37
19	Coventry City	42	13	9	20	40	55	35
20	Norwich City	42	11	10	21	36	63	32
21	Crystal Palace	42	9	12	21	41	58	30
22	West Bromwich Albion	42	9	10	23	38	62	28

APPEARANCES

PLAYER	LGE	FAC	LC	TOT
Buchan	42	1	4	47
Morgan	39	1	4	44
Stepney	38	1	4	43
Charlton	34 (2)	1	4	39 (2)
Young	28 (2)	1	3	32 (2)
Storey-Moore	26	–	4	30
Dunne	24	– (1)	3	27 (1)
James	22	–	4	26
Best	19	–	4	23
Sadler	19	1	2	22
Kidd	17 (5)	1	2	20 (5)
Graham	18	1	–	19
MacDougall	18	–	–	18
O'Neil	16	–	1	17
Davies	15 (1)	1	–	16 (1)
Macari	16	–	–	16
Holton	15	–	–	15
Martin	14 (2)	–	–	14 (2)
Law	9 (2)	1	2	12 (2)
Forsyth	8	1	–	9
Fitzpatrick	5	–	1	6
Donald	4	–	1	5
McIlroy	4 (6)	–	– (3)	4 (9)
Rimmer	4	–	–	4
Watson	3	–	1	4
Anderson	2 (5)	–	–	2 (5)
Sidebottom	2	–	–	2
Edwards	1	–	–	1
Fletcher	– (2)	–	–	– (2)

GOALSCORERS

PLAYER	LGE	FAC	LC	TOT
Charlton	6	–	1	7
Storey-Moore	5	–	1	6
Best	4	–	2	6
Macari	5	–	–	5
MacDougall	5	–	–	5
Davies	4	–	–	4
Kidd	4	–	–	4
Morgan	3	–	1	4
Holton	3	–	–	3
Martin	2	–	–	2
Law	1	–	1	2
Anderson	1	–	–	1
Graham	1	–	–	1
McIlroy	–	–	1	1

1973/74

FOOTBALL LEAGUE DIVISION ONE

DATE	OPPONENTS	SCORE	GOALSCORERS	ATTENDANCE
Aug 25	Arsenal	0–3		51,501
Aug 29	STOKE CITY	1–0	James	43,614
Sep 1	QUEENS PARK RANGERS	2–1	Holton, McIlroy	44,156
Sep 5	Leicester City	0–1		29,152
Sep 8	Ipswich Town	1–2	Anderson	22,023
Sep 12	LEICESTER CITY	1–2	Stepney	40,793
Sep 15	WEST HAM UNITED	3–1	Kidd 2, Storey-Moore	44,757
Sep 22	Leeds United	0–0		47,058
Sep 29	LIVERPOOL	0–0		53,862
Oct 6	Wolverhampton W.	1–2	McIlroy	32,962
Oct 13	DERBY COUNTY	0–1		43,724
Oct 20	BIRMINGHAM CITY	1–0	Stepney	48,937
Oct 27	Burnley	0–0		31,976
Nov 3	CHELSEA	2–2	Greenhoff, Young	48,036
Nov 10	Tottenham Hotspur	1–2	Best	42,756
Nov 17	Newcastle United	2–3	Graham, Macari	41,768
Nov 24	NORWICH CITY	0–0		36,338
Dec 8	SOUTHAMPTON	0–0		31,648
Dec 15	COVENTRY CITY	2–3	Best, Morgan	28,589
Dec 22	Liverpool	0–2		40,420
Dec 26	SHEFFIELD UNITED	1–2	Macari	38,653
Dec 29	IPSWICH TOWN	2–0	Macari, McIlroy	36,365
Jan 1	Queens Park Rangers	0–3		32,339
Jan 12	West Ham United	1–2	McIlroy	34,147
Jan 19	ARSENAL	1–1	James	38,589
Feb 2	Coventry City	0–1		25,313
Feb 9	LEEDS UNITED	0–2		60,025
Feb 16	Derby County	2–2	Greenhoff, Houston	29,987
Feb 23	WOLVERHAMPTON W.	0–0		39,260
Mar 2	Sheffield United	1–0	Macari	29,203
Mar 13	Manchester City	0–0		51,331
Mar 16	Birmingham City	0–1		37,768
Mar 23	TOTTENHAM HOTSPUR	0–1		36,278
Mar 30	Chelsea	3–1	Daly, McIlroy, Morgan	29,602
Apr 3	BURNLEY	3–3	Forsyth, Holton, McIlroy	33,336
Apr 6	Norwich City	2–0	Greenhoff, Macari	28,223
Apr 13	NEWCASTLE UNITED	1–0	McCalliog	44,751
Apr 15	EVERTON	3–0	McCalliog 2, Houston	48,424
Apr 20	Southampton	1–1	McCalliog	30,789
Apr 23	Everton	0–1		46,093
Apr 27	MANCHESTER CITY	0–1		56,996
Apr 29	Stoke City	0–1		27,392

FA CUP

DATE	OPPONENTS	SCORE	GOALSCORERS	ATTENDANCE
Jan 5	PLYMOUTH ARGYLE (Rd3)	1–0	Macari	31,810
Jan 26	IPSWICH TOWN (Rd4)	0–1		37,177

LEAGUE CUP

DATE	OPPONENTS	SCORE	GOALSCORERS	ATTENDANCE
Oct 8	MIDDLESBROUGH (Rd2)	0–1		23,906

FINAL LEAGUE TABLE

		P	W	D	L	F	A	Pts
1	Leeds United	42	24	14	4	66	31	62
2	Liverpool	42	22	13	7	52	31	57
3	Derby County	42	17	14	11	52	42	48
4	Ipswich Town	42	18	11	13	67	58	47
5	Stoke City	42	15	16	11	54	42	46
6	Burnley	42	16	14	12	56	53	46
7	Everton	42	16	12	14	50	48	44
8	Queens Park Rangers	42	13	17	12	56	52	43
9	Leicester City	42	13	16	13	51	41	42
10	Arsenal	42	14	14	14	49	51	42
11	Tottenham Hotspur	42	14	14	14	45	50	42
12	Wolverhampton Wanderers	42	13	15	14	49	49	41
13	Sheffield United	42	14	12	16	44	49	40
14	Manchester City	42	14	12	16	39	46	40
15	Newcastle United	42	13	12	17	49	48	38
16	Coventry City	42	14	10	18	43	54	38
17	Chelsea	42	12	13	17	56	60	37
18	West Ham United	42	11	15	16	55	60	37
19	Birmingham City	42	12	13	17	52	64	37
20	Southampton	42	11	14	17	47	68	36
21	MANCHESTER UNITED	42	10	12	20	38	48	32
22	Norwich City	42	7	15	20	37	62	29

APPEARANCES

PLAYER	LGE	FAC	LC	TOT
Buchan M	42	2	1	45
Stepney	42	2	1	45
Morgan	41	2	1	44
Greenhoff	36	2	1	39
Macari	34 (1)	2	1	37 (1)
Holton	34	2	1	37
Young	29	2	1	32
McIlroy	24 (5)	1 (1)	–	25 (6)
Graham	23 (1)	1	1	25 (1)
Kidd	21	1 (1)	1	23 (1)
James	21	1	1	23
Forsyth	18 (1)	2	–	20 (1)
Houston	20	–	–	20
Daly	14 (2)	–	1	15 (2)
Martin	12 (4)	2	–	14 (4)
Best	12	–	–	12
Anderson	11 (1)	–	–	11 (1)
McCalliog	11	–	–	11
Griffiths	7	–	–	7
Fletcher	2 (3)	–	–	2 (3)
Bielby	2 (2)	–	–	2 (2)
Sadler	2 (1)	–	–	2 (1)
Sidebottom	2	–	–	2
Storey-Moore	2	–	–	2
Buchan G	– (3)	–	– (1)	– (4)

GOALSCORERS

PLAYER	LGE	FAC	LC	TOT
McIlroy	6	–	–	6
Macari	5	1	–	6
McCalliog	4	–	–	4
Greenhoff	3	–	–	3
Best	2	–	–	2
Holton	2	–	–	2
Houston	2	–	–	2
James	2	–	–	2
Kidd	2	–	–	2
Morgan	2	–	–	2
Stepney	2	–	–	2
Anderson	1	–	–	1
Daly	1	–	–	1
Forsyth	1	–	–	1
Graham	1	–	–	1
Storey-Moore	1	–	–	1
Young	1	–	–	1

1974/75

FOOTBALL LEAGUE DIVISION TWO

DATE	OPPONENTS	SCORE	GOALSCORERS	ATTENDANCE
Aug 17	Leyton Orient	2-0	Houston, Morgan	17,772
Aug 24	MILLWALL	4-0	Daly 3, Pearson	44,756
Aug 28	PORTSMOUTH	2-1	Daly, McIlroy	42,547
Aug 31	Cardiff City	1-0	Daly	22,344
Sep 7	NOTTINGHAM FOREST	2-2	Greenhoff, McIlroy	40,671
Sep 14	West Bromwich Albion	1-1	Pearson	23,721
Sep 16	Millwall	1-0	Daly	16,988
Sep 21	BRISTOL ROVERS	2-0	Greenhoff, og	42,948
Sep 25	BOLTON WANDERERS	3-0	Houston, Macari, og	47,084
Sep 28	Norwich City	0-2		24,586
Oct 5	Fulham	2-1	Pearson 2	26,513
Oct 12	NOTTS COUNTY	1-0	McIlroy	46,565
Oct 15	Portsmouth	0-0		25,608
Oct 19	Blackpool	3-0	Forsyth, Macari, McCalliog	25,370
Oct 26	SOUTHAMPTON	1-0	Pearson	48,724
Nov 2	OXFORD UNITED	4-0	Pearson 3, Macari	41,909
Nov 9	Bristol City	0-1		28,104
Nov 16	ASTON VILLA	2-1	Daly 2	55,615
Nov 23	Hull City	0-2		23,287
Nov 30	SUNDERLAND	3-2	McIlroy, Morgan, Pearson	60,585
Dec 7	Sheffield Wednesday	4-4	Macari 2, Houston, Pearson	35,230
Dec 14	LEYTON ORIENT	0-0		41,200
Dec 21	York City	1-0	Pearson	15,567
Dec 26	WEST BROMWICH ALBION	2-1	Daly, McIlroy	51,104
Dec 28	Oldham Athletic	0-1		26,384
Jan 11	SHEFFIELD WEDNESDAY	2-0	McCalliog 2	45,662
Jan 18	Sunderland	0-0		45,976
Feb 1	BRISTOL CITY	0-1		47,118
Feb 8	Oxford United	0-1		15,959
Feb 15	HULL CITY	2-0	Houston, Pearson	44,712
Feb 22	Aston Villa	0-2		39,156
Mar 1	CARDIFF CITY	4-0	Houston, Macari, McIlroy, Pearson	43,601
Mar 8	Bolton Wanderers	1-0	Pearson	38,152
Mar 15	NORWICH CITY	1-1	Pearson	56,202
Mar 22	Nottingham Forest	1-0	Daly	21,893
Mar 28	Bristol Rovers	1-1	Macari	19,337
Mar 29	YORK CITY	2-1	Macari, Morgan	46,802
Mar 31	OLDHAM ATHLETIC	3-2	Coppell, Macari, McIlroy	56,618
Apr 5	Southampton	1-0	Macari	21,866
Apr 12	FULHAM	1-0	Daly	52,971
Apr 19	Notts County	2-2	Greenhoff, Houston	17,320
Apr 26	BLACKPOOL	4-0	Pearson 2, Greenhoff, Macari	58,769

FA CUP

DATE	OPPONENTS	SCORE	GOALSCORERS	ATTENDANCE
Jan 4	WALSALL (Rd3)	0-0		43,353
Jan 7	Walsall (Rd3R)	2-3	Daly, McIlroy	18,105

LEAGUE CUP

DATE	OPPONENTS	SCORE	GOALSCORERS	ATTENDANCE
Sep 11	CHARLTON ATHLETIC (Rd2)	5-1	Macari 2, Houston, McIlroy, og	21,616
Oct 9	MANCHESTER CITY (Rd3)	1-0	Daly	55,169
Nov 13	BURNLEY (Rd4)	3-2	Macari 2, Morgan	46,275
Dec 4	Middlesbrough (Rd5)	0-0		36,005
Dec 18	MIDDLESBROUGH (Rd5R)	3-0	Macari, McIlroy, Pearson	49,501
Jan 15	NORWICH CITY (SFL1)	2-2	Macari	58,010
Jan 22	Norwich City (SFL2)	0-1		31,621

FINAL LEAGUE TABLE

		P	W	D	L	F	A	Pts
1	MANCHESTER UNITED	42	26	9	7	66	30	61
2	Aston Villa	42	25	8	9	79	32	58
3	Norwich City	42	20	13	9	58	37	53
4	Sunderland	42	19	13	10	65	35	51
5	Bristol City	42	21	8	13	47	33	50
6	West Bromwich Albion	42	18	9	15	54	42	45
7	Blackpool	42	14	17	11	38	33	45
8	Hull City	42	15	14	13	40	53	44
9	Fulham	42	13	16	13	44	39	42
10	Bolton Wanderers	42	15	12	15	45	41	42
11	Oxford United	42	15	12	15	41	51	42
12	Leyton Orient	42	11	20	11	28	39	42
13	Southampton	42	15	11	16	53	54	41
14	Notts County	42	12	16	14	49	59	40
15	York City	42	14	10	18	51	55	38
16	Nottingham Forest	42	12	14	16	43	55	38
17	Portsmouth	42	12	13	17	44	54	37
18	Oldham Athletic	42	10	15	17	40	48	35
19	Bristol Rovers	42	12	11	19	42	64	35
20	Millwall	42	10	12	20	44	56	32
21	Cardiff City	42	9	14	19	36	62	32
22	Sheffield Wednesday	42	5	11	26	29	64	21

APPEARANCES

PLAYER	LGE	FAC	LC	TOT
McIlroy	41 (1)	2	7	50 (1)
Buchan	41	2	7	50
Stepney	40	2	7	49
Houston	40	2	6	48
Greenhoff	39 (2)	2	6	47 (2)
Daly	36 (1)	2	7	45 (1)
Forsyth	39	–	6	45
Macari	36 (2)	2	6 (1)	44 (3)
Morgan	32 (2)	1	6 (1)	39 (3)
Pearson	30 (1)	2	4	36 (1)
McCalliog	20	1	5 (1)	26 (1)
Holton	14	–	3	17
Sidebottom	12	2	2	16
James	13	–	2	15
Young	7 (8)	2	1 (4)	10(12)
Coppell	9 (1)	–	–	9 (1)
Martin	7 (1)	–	1	8 (1)
Albiston	2	–	1	3
Baldwin	2	–	–	2
Roche	2	–	–	2
Davies	– (8)	– (2)	–	–(10)
McCreery	– (2)	–	–	– (2)
Graham	– (1)	–	–	– (1)
Nicholl	– (1)	–	–	– (1)

GOALSCORERS

PLAYER	LGE	FAC	LC	TOT
Pearson	17	–	1	18
Macari	11	–	7	18
Daly	11	1	1	13
McIlroy	7	1	2	10
Houston	6	–	1	7
Greenhoff	4	–	–	4
Morgan	3	–	1	4
McCalliog	3	–	–	3
Coppell	1	–	–	1
Forsyth	1	–	–	1
own goals	2	–	1	3

1975/76

FOOTBALL LEAGUE DIVISION ONE

DATE	OPPONENTS	SCORE	GOALSCORERS	ATTENDANCE
Aug 16	Wolverhampton W.	2-0	Macari 2	32,348
Aug 19	Birmingham City	2-0	McIlroy 2	33,177
Aug 23	SHEFFIELD UNITED	5-1	Pearson 2, Daly, McIlroy, og	55,949
Aug 27	COVENTRY CITY	1-1	Pearson	52,169
Aug 30	Stoke City	1-0	og	33,092
Sep 6	TOTTENHAM HOTSPUR	3-2	Daly 2, og	51,641
Sep 13	Queens Park Rangers	0-1		29,237
Sep 20	IPSWICH TOWN	1-0	Houston	50,513
Sep 24	Derby County	1-2	Daly	33,187
Sep 27	Manchester City	2-2	Macari, McCreery	46,931
Oct 4	LEICESTER CITY	0-0		47,878
Oct 11	Leeds United	2-1	McIlroy 2	40,264
Oct 18	ARSENAL	3-1	Coppell 2, Pearson	53,885
Oct 25	West Ham United	1-2	Macari	38,528
Nov 1	NORWICH CITY	1-0	Pearson	50,587
Nov 8	Liverpool	1-3	Coppell	49,136
Nov 15	ASTON VILLA	2-0	Coppell, McIlroy	51,682
Nov 22	Arsenal	1-3	Pearson	40,102
Nov 29	NEWCASTLE UNITED	1-0	Daly	52,624
Dec 6	Middlesbrough	0-0		32,454
Dec 13	Sheffield United	4-1	Pearson 2, Hill, Macari	31,741
Dec 20	WOLVERHAMPTON W.	1-0	Hill	44,269
Dec 23	Everton	1-1	Macari	41,732
Dec 27	BURNLEY	2-1	Macari, McIlroy	59,726
Jan 10	QUEENS PARK RANGERS	2-1	Hill, McIlroy	58,302
Jan 17	Tottenham Hotspur	1-1	Hill	49,189
Jan 31	BIRMINGHAM CITY	3-1	Forsyth, Macari, McIlroy	50,724
Feb 7	Coventry City	1-1	Macari	33,922
Feb 18	LIVERPOOL	0-0		59,709
Feb 21	Aston Villa	1-2	Macari	50,094
Feb 25	DERBY COUNTY	1-1	Pearson	59,632
Feb 28	WEST HAM UNITED	4-0	Forsyth, Macari, McCreery, Pearson	57,220
Mar 13	LEEDS UNITED	3-2	Daly, Houston, Pearson	59,429
Mar 16	Norwich City	1-1	Hill	27,787
Mar 20	Newcastle United	4-3	Pearson 2, og 2	45,048
Mar 27	MIDDLESBROUGH	3-0	Daly, Hill, McCreery	58,527
Apr 10	Ipswich Town	0-3		34,886
Apr 17	EVERTON	2-1	McCreery, og	61,879
Apr 19	Burnley	1-0	Macari	27,418
Apr 21	STOKE CITY	0-1		53,879
Apr 24	Leicester City	1-2	Coyne	31,053
May 4	MANCHESTER CITY	2-0	Hill, McIlroy	59,517

FA CUP

DATE	OPPONENTS	SCORE	GOALSCORERS	ATTENDANCE
Jan 3	OXFORD UNITED (Rd3)	2-1	Daly 2	41,082
Jan 24	PETERBOROUGH UNITED (Rd4)	3-1	Forsyth, Hill, McIlroy	56,352
Feb 14	Leicester City (Rd5)	2-1	Daly, Macari	34,000
Mar 6	WOLVERHAMPTON W. (Rd6)	1-1	Daly	59,433
Mar 9	Wolverhampton W. (Rd6R)	3-2	Greenhoff, McIlroy, Pearson	44,373
Apr 3	Derby County (SF)	2-0	Hill 2	55,000
	(at Hillsborough)			
May 1	Southampton (Final)	0-1		100,000
	(at Wembley)			

LEAGUE CUP

DATE	OPPONENTS	SCORE	GOALSCORERS	ATTENDANCE
Sep 10	BRENTFORD (Rd2)	2-1	Macari, McIlroy	25,286
Oct 8	Aston Villa (Rd3)	2-1	Coppell, Macari	41,447
Nov 12	Manchester City (Rd4)	0-4		50,182

FINAL LEAGUE TABLE

		P	W	D	L	F	A	Pts
1	Liverpool	42	23	14	5	66	31	60
2	Queens Park Rangers	42	24	11	7	67	33	59
3	MANCHESTER UNITED	42	23	10	9	68	42	56
4	Derby County	42	21	11	10	75	58	53
5	Leeds United	42	21	9	12	65	46	51
6	Ipswich Town	42	16	14	12	54	48	46
7	Leicester City	42	13	19	10	48	51	45
8	Manchester City	42	16	11	15	64	46	43
9	Tottenham Hotspur	42	14	15	13	63	63	43
10	Norwich City	42	16	10	16	58	58	42
11	Everton	42	15	12	15	60	66	42
12	Stoke City	42	15	11	16	48	50	41
13	Middlesbrough	42	15	10	17	46	45	40
14	Coventry City	42	13	14	15	47	57	40
15	Newcastle United	42	15	9	18	71	62	39
16	Aston Villa	42	11	17	14	51	59	39
17	Arsenal	42	13	10	19	47	53	36
18	West Ham United	42	13	10	19	48	71	36
19	Birmingham City	42	13	7	22	57	75	33
20	Wolverhampton Wanderers	42	10	10	22	51	68	30
21	Burnley	42	9	10	23	43	66	28
22	Sheffield United	42	6	10	26	33	82	22

APPEARANCES

PLAYER	LGE	FAC	LC	TOT
Buchan	42	7	3	52
Houston	42	7	3	52
Daly	41	7	3	51
McIlroy	41	7	3	51
Greenhoff	40	7	3	50
Coppell	39	7	3	49
Pearson	39	7	3	49
Stepney	38	7	2	47
Macari	36	6	3	45
Forsyth	28	7	–	35
Hill	26	7	–	33
Jackson	16 (1)	–	3	19 (1)
Nicholl	15 (5)	– (2)	3	18 (7)
McCreery	12(16)	1 (2)	– (1)	13(19)
Roche	4	–	1	5
Albiston	2 (1)	–	–	2 (1)
Coyne	1 (1)	–	–	1 (1)
Grimshaw	– (1)	–	– (1)	– (2)
Kelly	– (1)	–	–	– (1)
Young	– (1)	–	–	– (1)

GOALSCORERS

PLAYER	LGE	FAC	LC	TOT
Macari	12	1	2	15
Pearson	13	1	–	14
McIlroy	10	2	1	13
Daly	7	4	–	11
Hill	7	3	–	10
Coppell	4	–	1	5
McCreery	4	–	–	4
Forsyth	2	1	–	3
Houston	2	–	–	2
Coyne	1	–	–	1
Greenhoff	–	1	–	1
own goals	6	–	–	6

1976/77

FOOTBALL LEAGUE DIVISION ONE

DATE	OPPONENTS	SCORE	GOALSCORERS	ATTENDANCE
Aug 21	BIRMINGHAM CITY	2-2	Coppell, Pearson	58,898
Aug 24	Coventry City	2-0	Hill, Macari	26,775
Aug 28	Derby County	0-0		30,054
Sep 4	TOTTENHAM HOTSPUR	2-3	Coppell, Pearson	60,723
Sep 11	Newcastle United	2-2	Greenhoff B, Pearson	39,037
Sep 18	MIDDLESBROUGH	2-0	Pearson, og	56,712
Sep 25	Manchester City	3-1	Coppell, Daly, McCreery	48,861
Oct 2	Leeds United	2-0	Coppell, Daly	44,512
Oct 16	West Bromwich Albion	0-4		36,615
Oct 23	NORWICH CITY	2-2	Daly, Hill	54,356
Oct 30	IPSWICH TOWN	0-1		57,416
Nov 6	Aston Villa	2-3	Hill, Pearson	44,789
Nov 10	SUNDERLAND	3-3	Greenhoff B, Hill, Pearson	42,685
Nov 20	Leicester City	1-1	Daly	26,421
Nov 27	WEST HAM UNITED	0-2		55,366
Dec 18	Arsenal	1-3	McIlroy	39,572
Dec 27	EVERTON	4-0	Greenhoff J, Hill, Macari, Pearson	56,786
Jan 1	ASTON VILLA	2-0	Pearson 2	55,446
Jan 3	Ipswich Town	1-2	Pearson	30,105
Jan 15	COVENTRY CITY	2-0	Macari 2	46,567
Jan 19	BRISTOL CITY	2-1	Greenhoff B, Pearson	43,051
Jan 22	Birmingham City	3-2	Greenhoff J, Houston, Pearson	35,316
Feb 5	DERBY COUNTY	3-1	Houston, Macari, og	54,044
Feb 12	Tottenham Hotspur	3-1	Hill, Macari, McIlroy	46,946
Feb 16	LIVERPOOL	0-0		57,487
Feb 19	NEWCASTLE UNITED	3-1	Greenhoff J 3	51,828
Mar 5	MANCHESTER CITY	3-1	Coppell, Hill, Pearson	58,595
Mar 12	LEEDS UNITED	1-0	og	60,612
Mar 23	WEST BROMWICH ALBION	2-2	Coppell, Hill	51,053
Apr 2	Norwich City	1-2	og	24,161
Apr 5	Everton	2-1	Hill 2	38,216
Apr 9	STOKE CITY	3-0	Houston, Macari, Pearson	53,102
Apr 11	Sunderland	1-2	Hill	38,785
Apr 16	LEICESTER CITY	1-1	Greenhoff J	49,161
Apr 19	Queens Park Rangers	0-4		28,848
Apr 26	Middlesbrough	0-3		21,744
Apr 30	QUEENS PARK RANGERS	1-0	Macari	50,788
May 3	Liverpool	0-1		53,046
May 7	Bristol City	1-1	Greenhoff J	28,864
May 11	Stoke City	3-3	Hill 2, McCreery	24,204
May 14	ARSENAL	3-2	Greenhoff J, Hill, Macari	53,232
May 16	West Ham United	2-4	Hill, Pearson	29,904

FA CUP

DATE	OPPONENTS	SCORE	GOALSCORERS	ATTENDANCE
Jan 8	WALSALL (Rd3)	1-0	Hill	48,870
Jan 29	QUEENS PARK RANGERS (Rd4)	1-0	Macari	57,422
Feb 26	Southampton (Rd5)	2-2	Hill, Macari	29,137
Mar 8	SOUTHAMPTON (Rd5R)	2-1	Greenhoff J 2	58,103
Mar 19	ASTON VILLA (Rd6)	2-1	Houston, Macari	57,089
Apr 23	Leeds United (SF) (at Hillsborough)	2-1	Coppell, Greenhoff J	55,000
May 21	Liverpool (Final) (at Wembley)	2-1	Greenhoff J, Pearson	100,000

LEAGUE CUP

DATE	OPPONENTS	SCORE	GOALSCORERS	ATTENDANCE
Sep 1	TRANMERE ROVERS (Rd2)	5-0	Daly 2, Hill, Macari, Pearson	37,586
Sep 22	SUNDERLAND (Rd3)	2-2	Pearson, og	46,170
Oct 4	Sunderland (Rd3R)	2-2	Daly, Greenhoff B	46,170
Oct 6	SUNDERLAND (Rd3R2)	1-0	Greenhoff B	47,689
Oct 27	NEWCASTLE UNITED (Rd4)	7-2	Hill 3, Coppell, Houston, Nicholl, Pearson	52,002
Dec 1	EVERTON (Rd5)	0-3		57,738

UEFA CUP

DATE	OPPONENTS	SCORE	GOALSCORERS	ATTENDANCE
Sep 15	Ajax (Rd1L1)	0-1		30,000
Sep 29	AJAX (Rd1L2)	2-0	Macari, McIlroy	58,918
Oct 20	JUVENTUS (Rd2L1)	1-0	Hill	59,000
Nov 3	Juventus (Rd2L2)	0-3		66,632

FINAL LEAGUE TABLE

		P	W	D	L	F	A	Pts
1	Liverpool	42	23	11	8	62	33	57
2	Manchester City	42	21	14	7	60	34	56
3	Ipswich Town	42	22	8	12	66	39	52
4	Aston Villa	42	22	7	13	76	50	51
5	Newcastle United	42	18	13	11	64	49	49
6	MANCHESTER UNITED	42	18	11	13	71	62	47
7	West Bromwich Albion	42	16	13	13	62	56	45
8	Arsenal	42	16	11	15	64	59	43
9	Everton	42	14	14	14	62	64	42
10	Leeds United	42	15	12	15	48	51	42
11	Leicester City	42	12	18	12	47	60	42
12	Middlesbrough	42	14	13	15	40	45	41
13	Birmingham City	42	13	12	17	63	61	38
14	Queens Park Rangers	42	13	12	17	47	52	38
15	Derby County	42	9	19	14	50	55	37
16	Norwich City	42	14	9	19	47	64	37
17	West Ham United	42	11	14	17	46	65	36
18	Bristol City	42	11	13	18	38	48	35
19	Coventry City	42	10	15	17	48	59	35
20	Sunderland	42	11	12	19	46	54	34
21	Stoke City	42	10	14	18	28	51	34
22	Tottenham Hotspur	42	12	9	21	48	72	33

APPEARANCES

PLAYER	LGE	FAC	LC	UC	TOT
Greenhoff B	40	7	6	4	57
Stepney	40	7	6	4	57
McIlroy	39 (1)	7	6	4	56 (1)
Coppell	40	7	5	4	56
Hill	38 (1)	7	6	4	55 (1)
Nicholl	39	7	5	4	55
Macari	38	7	4	4	53
Pearson	39	7	4	3	53
Houston	36	6	5	4	51
Buchan	33	7	4	2	46
Greenhoff J	27	7	–	–	34
Daly	16 (1)	– (1)	6	4	26 (2)
Albiston	14 (3)	1	2 (2)	2 (1)	19 (6)
McCreery	9 (16)	– (3)	3 (2)	1 (3)	13 (24)
Forsyth	3 (1)	–	1	–	4 (1)
Waldron	3	–	1	–	4
Paterson	2	–	1	– (2)	3 (2)
Jackson	2	–	1	–	3
McGrath	2 (4)	–	– (1)	–	2 (5)
Roche	2	–	–	–	2
Foggon	– (3)	–	–	–	– (3)
Clark	– (1)	–	–	–	– (1)

GOALSCORERS

PLAYER	LGE	FAC	LC	UC	TOT
Hill	15	2	4	1	22
Pearson	15	1	3	–	19
Macari	9	3	1	1	14
Greenhoff J	8	4	–	–	12
Coppell	6	1	1	–	8
Daly	4	–	3	–	7
Greenhoff B	3	–	2	–	5
Houston	3	1	1	–	5
McIlroy	2	–	–	1	3
McCreery	2	–	–	–	2
Nicholl	–	–	1	–	1
own goals	4	–	1	–	5

1977/78

FOOTBALL LEAGUE DIVISION ONE

DATE	OPPONENTS	SCORE	GOALSCORERS	ATTENDANCE
Aug 20	Birmingham City	4-1	Macari 3, Hill	28,005
Aug 24	COVENTRY CITY	2-1	Hill, McCreery	55,726
Aug 27	IPSWICH TOWN	0-0		57,904
Sep 3	Derby County	1-0	Macari	21,279
Sep 10	Manchester City	1-3	Nicholl	50,856
Sep 17	CHELSEA	0-1		54,951
Sep 24	Leeds United	1-1	Hill	33,517
Oct 1	LIVERPOOL	2-0	Macari, McIlroy	55,089
Oct 8	Middlesbrough	1-2	Coppell	26,882
Oct 15	NEWCASTLE UNITED	3-2	Coppell, Greenhoff J, Coppell	55,056
Oct 22	West Bromwich Albion	0-4		27,526
Oct 29	Aston Villa	1-2	Nicholl	39,144
Nov 5	ARSENAL	1-2	Hill	53,055
Nov 12	Nottingham Forest	1-2	Pearson	30,183
Nov 19	NORWICH CITY	1-0	Pearson	48,729
Nov 26	Queens Park Rangers	2-2	Hill 2	25,367
Dec 3	WOLVERHAMPTON W.	3-1	Greenhoff J, McIlroy, Pearson	48,874
Dec 10	West Ham United	1-2	McGrath	20,242
Dec 17	NOTTINGHAM FOREST	0-4		54,374
Dec 26	Everton	6-2	Macari 2, Coppell, Greenhoff J, Hill, McIlroy	48,335
Dec 27	LEICESTER CITY	3-1	Coppell, Greenhoff J, Hill	57,396
Dec 31	Coventry City	0-3		24,706
Jan 2	BIRMINGHAM CITY	1-2	Greenhoff J	53,501
Jan 14	Ipswich Town	2-1	McIlroy, Pearson	23,321
Jan 21	DERBY COUNTY	4-0	Hill 2, Buchan, Pearson	57,115
Feb 8	BRISTOL CITY	1-1	Hill	43,457
Feb 11	Chelsea	2-2	Hill, McIlroy	32,849
Feb 25	Liverpool	1-3	McIlroy	49,095
Mar 1	LEEDS UNITED	0-1		49,101
Mar 4	MIDDLESBROUGH	0-0		46,322
Mar 11	Newcastle United	2-2	Hill, Jordan	25,825
Mar 15	MANCHESTER CITY	2-2	Hill 2	58,398
Mar 18	WEST BROMWICH ALBION	1-1	McQueen	46,329
Mar 25	Leicester City	3-2	Greenhoff J, Hill, Pearson	20,299
Mar 27	EVERTON	1-2	Hill	55,277
Mar 29	ASTON VILLA	1-1	McIlroy	41,625
Apr 1	Arsenal	1-3	Jordan	40,829
Apr 8	QUEENS PARK RANGERS	3-1	Pearson 2, Grimes	42,677
Apr 15	Norwich City	3-1	Coppell, Jordan, McIlroy	19,778
Apr 22	WEST HAM UNITED	3-0	Grimes, McIlroy, Pearson	54,089
Apr 25	Bristol City	1-0	Pearson	26,035
Apr 29	Wolverhampton W.	1-2	Greenhoff B	24,774

FA CUP

DATE	OPPONENTS	SCORE	GOALSCORERS	ATTENDANCE
Jan 7	Carlisle United (Rd3)	1-1	Macari	21,710
Jan 11	CARLISLE UNITED (Rd3R)	4-2	Macari 2, Pearson 2	54,156
Jan 28	WEST BROMWICH ALBION (Rd4)	1-1	Coppell	57,056
Feb 1	West Bromwich Albion (Rd4R)	2-3	Hill, Pearson	37,086

LEAGUE CUP

DATE	OPPONENTS	SCORE	GOALSCORERS	ATTENDANCE
Aug 30	Arsenal (Rd2)	2-3	McCreery, Pearson	36,171

EUROPEAN CUP-WINNERS' CUP

DATE	OPPONENTS	SCORE	GOALSCORERS	ATTENDANCE
Sep 14	Saint Etienne (Rd1L1)	1-1	Hill	33,678
Oct 5	SAINT ETIENNE (Rd1L2) (at Home Park, Plymouth)	2-0	Coppell, Pearson	31,634
Oct 19	Porto (Rd2L1)	0-4		70,000
Nov 2	PORTO (Rd2L2)	5-2	Coppell 2, Nicholl, og 2	51,831

FINAL LEAGUE TABLE

		P	W	D	L	F	A	Pts
1	Nottingham Forest	42	25	14	3	69	24	64
2	Liverpool	42	24	9	9	65	34	57
3	Everton	42	22	11	9	76	45	55
4	Manchester City	42	20	12	10	74	51	52
5	Arsenal	42	21	10	11	60	37	52
6	West Bromwich Albion	42	18	14	10	62	53	50
7	Coventry City	42	18	12	12	75	62	48
8	Aston Villa	42	18	10	14	57	42	46
9	Leeds United	42	18	10	14	63	53	46
10	MANCHESTER UNITED	42	16	10	16	67	63	42
11	Birmingham City	42	16	9	17	55	60	41
12	Derby County	42	14	13	15	54	59	41
13	Norwich City	42	11	18	13	52	66	40
14	Middlesbrough	42	12	15	15	42	54	39
15	Wolverhampton Wanderers	42	12	12	18	51	64	36
16	Chelsea	42	11	14	17	46	69	36
17	Bristol City	42	11	13	18	49	53	35
18	Ipswich Town	42	11	13	18	47	61	35
19	Queens Park Rangers	42	9	15	18	47	64	33
20	West Ham United	42	12	8	22	52	69	32
21	Newcastle United	42	6	10	26	42	78	22
22	Leicester City	42	5	12	25	26	70	22

APPEARANCES

PLAYER	LGE	FAC	LC	ECWC	TOT
Coppell	42	4	1	4	51
McIlroy	39	4	–	4	47
Nicholl	37	4	1	4	46
Hill	36	3	1	4	44
Macari	32	4	1	2	39
Pearson	30	4	1	3	38
Buchan	28	4	1	4	37
Albiston	27 (1)	4	1	4	36 (1)
Houston	31	3	–	2 (1)	36 (1)
Greenhoff B	31	1	1	2	35
Stepney	23	–	1	4	28
Greenhoff J	22 (1)	2 (1)	–	1	25 (2)
Roche	19	4	–	–	23
McCreery	13 (4)	– (1)	1	3	17 (5)
Jordan	14	2	–	–	16
McQueen	14	–	–	–	14
McGrath	9 (9)	–	– (1)	3 (1)	12 (11)
Grimes	7 (6)	1	1	– (2)	9 (8)
Ritchie	4	–	–	–	4
Forsyth	3	–	–	– (1)	3 (1)
Rogers	1	–	–	–	1

GOALSCORERS

PLAYER	LGE	FAC	LC	ECWC	TOT
Hill	17	1	–	1	19
Pearson	10	3	1	1	15
Macari	8	3	–	–	11
McIlroy	9	–	–	–	9
Coppell	5	1	–	3	9
Greenhoff J	6	–	–	–	6
Jordan	3	–	–	–	3
Nicholl	2	–	–	1	3
Grimes	2	–	–	–	2
McCreery	1	–	1	–	2
Buchan	1	–	–	–	1
Greenhoff B	1	–	–	–	1
McGrath	1	–	–	–	1
McQueen	1	–	–	–	1
own goals	–	–	–	2	2

1978/79

FOOTBALL LEAGUE DIVISION ONE

DATE	OPPONENTS	SCORE	GOALSCORERS	ATTENDANCE
Aug 19	BIRMINGHAM CITY	1-0	Jordan	56,139
Aug 23	Leeds United	3-2	Macari, McIlroy, McQueen	36,845
Aug 26	Ipswich Town	0-3		21,802
Sep 2	EVERTON	1-1	Buchan	53,982
Sep 9	Queens Park Rangers	1-1	Greenhoff J	23,477
Sep 16	NOTTINGHAM FOREST	1-1	Greenhoff J	53,039
Sep 23	Arsenal	1-1	Coppell	45,393
Sep 30	MANCHESTER CITY	1-0	Jordan	55,301
Oct 7	MIDDLESBROUGH	3-2	Macari 2, Jordan	45,402
Oct 14	Aston Villa	2-2	Macari, McIlroy	36,204
Oct 21	BRISTOL CITY	1-3	Greenhoff J	47,211
Oct 28	Wolverhampton W.	4-2	Greenhoff J 2, Greenhoff B, Jordan	23,141
Nov 4	SOUTHAMPTON	1-1	Greenhoff J	46,259
Nov 11	Birmingham City	1-5	Jordan	23,550
Nov 18	IPSWICH TOWN	2-0	Coppell, Greenhoff J	42,109
Nov 21	Everton	0-3		42,126
Nov 25	Chelsea	1-0	Greenhoff J	28,162
Dec 9	Derby County	3-1	Ritchie 2, Greenhoff J	23,180
Dec 16	TOTTENHAM HOTSPUR	2-0	McIlroy, Ritchie	52,026
Dec 22	Bolton Wanderers	0-3		32,390
Dec 26	LIVERPOOL	0-3		54,910
Dec 30	WEST BROMWICH ALBION	3-5	Greenhoff B, McIlroy, McQueen	45,091
Feb 3	ARSENAL	0-2		45,460
Feb 10	Manchester City	3-0	Coppell 2, Ritchie	46,151
Feb 24	ASTON VILLA	1-1	Greenhoff J	44,437
Feb 28	QUEENS PARK RANGERS	2-0	Coppell, Greenhoff J	36,085
Mar 3	Bristol City	2-1	McQueen, Ritchie	24,583
Mar 20	Coventry City	3-4	Coppell 2, McIlroy	25,382
Mar 24	LEEDS UNITED	4-1	Ritchie 3, Thomas	51,191
Mar 27	Middlesbrough	2-2	Coppell, McQueen	20,138
Apr 7	Norwich City	2-2	Macari, McQueen	19,382
Apr 11	BOLTON WANDERERS	1-2	Buchan	49,617
Apr 14	Liverpool	0-2		46,608
Apr 16	COVENTRY CITY	0-0		46,035
Apr 18	Nottingham Forest	1-1	Jordan	33,074
Apr 21	Tottenham Hotspur	1-1	McQueen	36,665
Apr 25	NORWICH CITY	1-0	Macari	33,678
Apr 28	DERBY COUNTY	0-0		42,546
Apr 30	Southampton	1-1	Ritchie	21,616
May 5	West Bromwich Albion	0-1		27,960
May 7	WOLVERHAMPTON W.	3-2	Coppell 2, Ritchie	39,402
May 16	CHELSEA	1-1	Coppell	38,109

FA CUP

DATE	OPPONENTS	SCORE	GOALSCORERS	ATTENDANCE
Jan 15	CHELSEA (Rd3)	3-0	Coppell, Greenhoff J, Grimes	38,743
Jan 31	Fulham (Rd4)	1-1	Greenhoff J	25,229
Feb 12	FULHAM (Rd4R)	1-0	Greenhoff J	41,200
Feb 20	Colchester United (Rd5)	1-0	Greenhoff J	13,171
Mar 10	Tottenham Hotspur (Rd6)	1-1	Thomas	51,800
Mar 14	TOTTENHAM HOTSPUR (Rd6R)	2-0	Jordan, McIlroy	55,584
Mar 31	Liverpool (SF)	2-2	Greenhoff B, Jordan	52,524
	(at Maine Road)			
Apr 4	Liverpool (SFR)	1-0	Greenhoff J	53,069
	(at Goodison Park)			
May 12	Arsenal (Final)	2-3	McIlroy, McQueen	100,000
	(at Wembley)			

LEAGUE CUP

DATE	OPPONENTS	SCORE	GOALSCORERS	ATTENDANCE
Aug 30	Stockport County (Rd2)	3-2	Greenhoff J, Jordan, McIlroy	41,761
	(United drawn away – tie switched to Old Trafford)			
Oct 4	WATFORD (Rd3)	1-2	Jordan	40,534

FINAL LEAGUE TABLE

		P	W	D	L	F	A	Pts
1	Liverpool	42	30	8	4	85	16	68
2	Nottingham Forest	42	21	18	3	61	26	60
3	West Bromwich Albion	42	24	11	7	72	35	59
4	Everton	42	17	17	8	52	40	51
5	Leeds United	42	18	14	10	70	52	50
6	Ipswich Town	42	20	9	13	63	49	49
7	Arsenal	42	17	14	11	61	48	48
8	Aston Villa	42	15	16	11	59	49	46
9	MANCHESTER UNITED	42	15	15	12	60	63	45
10	Coventry City	42	14	16	12	58	68	44
11	Tottenham Hotspur	42	13	15	14	48	61	41
12	Middlesbrough	42	15	10	17	57	50	40
13	Bristol City	42	15	10	17	47	51	40
14	Southampton	42	12	16	14	47	53	40
15	Manchester City	42	13	13	16	58	56	39
16	Norwich City	42	7	23	12	51	57	37
17	Bolton Wanderers	42	12	11	19	54	75	35
18	Wolverhampton Wanderers	42	13	8	21	44	68	34
19	Derby County	42	10	11	21	44	71	31
20	Queens Park Rangers	42	6	13	23	45	73	25
21	Birmingham City	42	6	10	26	37	64	22
22	Chelsea	42	5	10	27	44	92	20

APPEARANCES

PLAYER	LGE	FAC	LC	TOT
Coppell	42	9	2	53
McIlroy	40	9	2	51
Buchan	37	9	2	48
McQueen	36	9	2	47
Greenhoff J	33	9	2	44
Albiston	32 (1)	7	2	41 (1)
Greenhoff B	32 (1)	5	2	39 (1)
Macari	31 (1)	5	1	37 (1)
Bailey	28	9		37
Jordan	30	4 (1)	2	36 (1)
Thomas	25	8		33
Nicholl	19 (2)	6 (2)		25 (4)
Houston	21 (1)	2	1	24 (1)
Ritchie	16 (1)	3 (1)		19 (2)
Roche	14	–	2	16
McCreery	14 (1)	–	– (1)	14 (2)
Grimes	5 (11)	3	2	10 (11)
Sloan	3 (1)	–	–	3 (1)
Connell	2	–	–	2
Pearson	–	2	–	2
Paterson	1 (2)	–	–	1 (2)
Moran	1	–	–	1
McGrath	– (2)	–	–	– (2)

GOALSCORERS

PLAYER	LGE	FAC	LC	TOT
Greenhoff J	11	5	1	17
Coppell	11	1		12
Ritchie	10	–		10
Jordan	6	2	2	10
McIlroy	5	2	1	8
McQueen	6	1		7
Macari	6	–		6
Greenhoff B	2	1		3
Buchan	2	–		2
Thomas	1	1		2
Grimes	–	1		1

1979/80

FOOTBALL LEAGUE DIVISION ONE

DATE	OPPONENTS	SCORE	GOALSCORERS	ATTENDANCE
Aug 18	Southampton	1-1	McQueen	21,768
Aug 22	WEST BROMWICH ALBION	2-0	Coppell, McQueen	53,377
Aug 25	Arsenal	0-0		44,380
Sep 1	MIDDLESBROUGH	2-1	Macari 2	51,015
Sep 8	Aston Villa	3-0	Coppell, Grimes, Thomas	34,859
Sep 15	DERBY COUNTY	1-0	Grimes	54,308
Sep 22	Wolverhampton W.	1-3	Macari	35,503
Sep 29	STOKE CITY	4-0	McQueen 2, McIlroy, Wilkins	52,596
Oct 6	BRIGHTON	2-0	Coppell, Macari	52,641
Oct 10	West Bromwich Albion	0-2		27,713
Oct 13	Bristol City	1-1	Macari	28,305
Oct 20	IPSWICH TOWN	1-0	Grimes	50,826
Oct 27	Everton	0-0		37,708
Nov 3	SOUTHAMPTON	1-0	Macari	50,215
Nov 10	Manchester City	0-2		50,067
Nov 17	CRYSTAL PALACE	1-1	Jordan	52,800
Nov 24	NORWICH CITY	5-0	Jordan 2, Coppell, Macari, Moran	46,540
Dec 1	Tottenham Hotspur	2-1	Coppell, Macari	51,389
Dec 8	LEEDS UNITED	1-1	Thomas	58,348
Dec 15	Coventry City	2-1	Macari, McQueen	25,541
Dec 22	NOTTINGHAM FOREST	3-0	Jordan 2, McQueen	54,607
Dec 26	Liverpool	0-2		51,073
Dec 29	ARSENAL	3-0	Jordan, McIlroy, McQueen	54,295
Jan 12	Middlesbrough	1-1	Thomas	30,587
Feb 2	Derby County	3-1	McIlroy, Thomas, og	27,783
Feb 9	WOLVERHAMPTON W.	0-1		51,568
Feb 16	Stoke City	1-1	Coppell	28,389
Feb 23	BRISTOL CITY	4-0	Jordan 2, McIlroy, og	43,329
Feb 27	BOLTON WANDERERS	2-0	Coppell, McQueen	47,546
Mar 1	Ipswich Town	0-6		30,229
Mar 12	EVERTON	0-0		45,515
Mar 15	Brighton	0-0		29,621
Mar 22	MANCHESTER CITY	1-0	Thomas	56,387
Mar 29	Crystal Palace	2-0	Jordan, Thomas	33,056
Apr 2	Nottingham Forest	0-2		31,417
Apr 5	LIVERPOOL	2-1	Greenhoff, Thomas	57,342
Apr 7	Bolton Wanderers	3-1	Coppell, McQueen, Thomas	31,902
Apr 12	TOTTENHAM HOTSPUR	4-1	Ritchie 3, Wilkins	53,151
Apr 19	Norwich City	2-0	Jordan 2	23,274
Apr 23	ASTON VILLA	2-1	Jordan 2	45,201
Apr 26	COVENTRY CITY	2-1	McIlroy 2	52,154
May 3	Leeds United	0-2		39,625

FA CUP

DATE	OPPONENTS	SCORE	GOALSCORERS	ATTENDANCE
Jan 5	Tottenham Hotspur (Rd3)	1-1	McIlroy	45,207
Jan 9	TOTTENHAM HOTSPUR (Rd3R)	0-1		53,762

LEAGUE CUP

DATE	OPPONENTS	SCORE	GOALSCORERS	ATTENDANCE
Aug 29	Tottenham Hotspur (Rd2L1)	1-2	Thomas	29,163
Sep 5	TOTTENHAM HOTSPUR (Rd2L2)	3-1	Coppell, Thomas, og	48,292
Sep 26	Norwich City (Rd3)	1-4	McIlroy	18,312

FINAL LEAGUE TABLE

		P	W	D	L	F	A	Pts
1	Liverpool	42	25	10	7	81	30	60
2	MANCHESTER UNITED	42	24	10	8	65	35	58
3	Ipswich Town	42	22	9	11	68	39	53
4	Arsenal	42	18	16	8	52	36	52
5	Nottingham Forest	42	20	8	14	63	43	48
6	Wolverhampton Wanderers	42	19	9	14	58	47	47
7	Aston Villa	42	16	14	12	51	50	46
8	Southampton	42	18	9	15	65	53	45
9	Middlesbrough	42	16	12	14	50	44	44
10	West Bromwich Albion	42	11	19	12	54	50	41
11	Leeds United	42	13	14	15	46	50	40
12	Norwich City	42	13	14	15	58	66	40
13	Crystal Palace	42	12	16	14	41	50	40
14	Tottenham Hotspur	42	15	10	17	52	62	40
15	Coventry City	42	16	7	19	56	66	39
16	Brighton & Hove Albion	42	11	15	16	47	57	37
17	Manchester City	42	12	13	17	43	66	37
18	Stoke City	42	13	10	19	44	58	36
19	Everton	42	9	17	16	43	51	35
20	Bristol City	42	9	13	20	37	66	31
21	Derby County	42	11	8	23	47	67	30
22	Bolton Wanderers	42	5	15	22	38	73	25

APPEARANCES

PLAYER	LGE	FAC	LC	TOT
Bailey	42	2	3	47
Buchan	42	2	3	47
Nicholl	42	2	3	47
Coppell	42	2	2	46
McIlroy	41	2	2	45
Macari	39	2	3	44
Wilkins	37	2	3	42
Thomas	35	2	3	40
McQueen	33	2	2	37
Jordan	32	2	2	36
Albiston	25	–	3	28
Grimes	20 (6)	–	1	21 (6)
Houston	14	2	1	17
Moran	9	–	–	9
Ritchie	3 (5)	–	1 (2)	4 (7)
Greenhoff	4 (1)	–	–	4 (1)
Sloan	1 (4)	–	–	1 (4)
Jovanovic	1 (1)	–	–	1 (1)
Paterson	– (1)	–	1	1 (1)
McGrath	– (1)	–	–	– (1)

GOALSCORERS

PLAYER	LGE	FAC	LC	TOT
Jordan	13	–	–	13
Thomas	8	–	2	10
Macari	9	–	–	9
McQueen	9	–	–	9
Coppell	8	–	1	9
McIlroy	6	1	1	8
Grimes	3	–	–	3
Ritchie	3	–	–	3
Wilkins	2	–	–	2
Greenhoff	1	–	–	1
Moran	1	–	–	1
own goals	2	–	1	3

1980/81

FOOTBALL LEAGUE DIVISION ONE

DATE	OPPONENTS	SCORE	GOALSCORERS	ATTENDANCE
Aug 16	MIDDLESBROUGH	3–0	Grimes, Macari, Thomas	54,394
Aug 19	Wolverhampton W.	0–1		31,955
Aug 23	Birmingham City	0–0		28,661
Aug 30	SUNDERLAND	1–1	Jovanovic	51,498
Sep 6	Tottenham Hotspur	0–0		40,995
Sep 13	LEICESTER CITY	5–0	Jovanovic 2, Coppell, Grimes, Macari	43,229
Sep 20	Leeds United	0–0		32,539
Sep 27	MANCHESTER CITY	2–2	Albiston, Coppell	55,918
Oct 4	Nottingham Forest	2–1	Coppell, Macari	29,801
Oct 8	ASTON VILLA	3–3	McIlroy 2, Coppell	38,831
Oct 11	ARSENAL	0–0		49,036
Oct 18	Ipswich Town	1–1	McIlroy	28,572
Oct 22	Stoke City	2–1	Jordan, Macari	24,534
Oct 25	EVERTON	2–0	Coppell, Jordan	54,260
Nov 1	Crystal Palace	0–1		31,449
Nov 8	COVENTRY CITY	0–0		42,794
Nov 12	WOLVERHAMPTON W.	0–0		37,959
Nov 15	Middlesbrough	1–1	Jordan	20,606
Nov 22	Brighton	4–1	Jordan 2, Duxbury, McIlroy	23,923
Nov 29	SOUTHAMPTON	1–1	Jordan	46,840
Dec 6	Norwich City	2–2	Coppell, og	18,780
Dec 13	STOKE CITY	2–2	Jordan, Macari	39,568
Dec 20	Arsenal	1–2	Macari	33,730
Dec 26	LIVERPOOL	0–0		57,049
Dec 27	West Bromwich Albion	1–3	Jovanovic	30,326
Jan 10	BRIGHTON	2–1	Macari, McQueen	42,208
Jan 28	Sunderland	0–2		31,910
Jan 31	BIRMINGHAM CITY	2–0	Jordan, Macari	39,081
Feb 7	Leicester City	0–1		26,085
Feb 17	TOTTENHAM HOTSPUR	0–0		40,642
Feb 21	Manchester City	0–1		50,114
Feb 28	LEEDS UNITED	0–1		45,733
Mar 7	Southampton	0–1		22,698
Mar 14	Aston Villa	3–3	Jordan 2, McIlroy	42,182
Mar 18	NOTTINGHAM FOREST	1–1	og	38,205
Mar 21	IPSWICH TOWN	2–1	Nicholl, Thomas	46,685
Mar 28	Everton	1–0	Jordan	25,856
Apr 4	CRYSTAL PALACE	1–0	Duxbury	37,954
Apr 11	Coventry City	2–0	Jordan 2	20,201
Apr 14	Liverpool	1–0	McQueen	31,276
Apr 18	WEST BROMWICH ALBION	2–1	Jordan, Macari	44,442
Apr 25	NORWICH CITY	1–0	Jordan	40,165

FA CUP

DATE	OPPONENTS	SCORE	GOALSCORERS	ATTENDANCE
Jan 3	BRIGHTON (Rd3)	2–2	Duxbury, Thomas	42,199
Jan 7	Brighton (Rd3R)	2–0	Birtles, Nicholl	26,915
Jan 24	Nottingham Forest (Rd4)	0–1		34,110

LEAGUE CUP

DATE	OPPONENTS	SCORE	GOALSCORERS	ATTENDANCE
Aug 27	COVENTRY CITY (Rd2L1)	0–1		31,656
Sep 2	Coventry City (Rd2L2)	0–1		18,946

UEFA CUP

DATE	OPPONENTS	SCORE	GOALSCORERS	ATTENDANCE
Sep 17	WIDZEW LODZ (Rd1L1)	1–1	McIlroy	38,037
Oct 1	Widzew Lodz (Rd1L2)	0–0		40,000
	(United lost the tie on away goals rule)			

FINAL LEAGUE TABLE

		P	W	D	L	F	A	Pts
1	Aston Villa	42	26	8	8	72	40	60
2	Ipswich Town	42	23	10	9	77	43	56
3	Arsenal	42	19	15	8	61	45	53
4	West Bromwich Albion	42	20	12	10	60	42	52
5	Liverpool	42	17	17	8	62	42	51
6	Southampton	42	20	10	12	76	56	50
7	Nottingham Forest	42	19	12	11	62	44	50
8	MANCHESTER UNITED	42	15	18	9	51	36	48
9	Leeds United	42	17	10	15	39	47	44
10	Tottenham Hotspur	42	14	15	13	70	68	43
11	Stoke City	42	12	18	12	51	60	42
12	Manchester City	42	14	11	17	56	59	39
13	Birmingham City	42	13	12	17	50	61	38
14	Middlesbrough	42	16	5	21	53	61	37
15	Everton	42	13	10	19	55	58	36
16	Coventry City	42	13	10	19	48	68	36
17	Sunderland	42	14	7	21	52	53	35
18	Wolverhampton Wanderers	42	13	9	20	43	55	35
19	Brighton & Hove Albion	42	14	7	21	54	67	35
20	Norwich City	42	13	7	22	49	73	33
21	Leicester City	42	13	6	23	40	67	32
22	Crystal Palace	42	6	7	29	47	83	19

APPEARANCES

PLAYER	LGE	FAC	LC	UC	TOT
Albiston	42	3	2	2	49
Coppell	42	3	2	2	49
Bailey	40	3	2	2	47
Macari	37 (1)	3	2	1	43 (1)
Nicholl	36	3	2	2	43
Jordan	33	3	–	1	37
Thomas	30	3	2	2	37
McIlroy	31 (1)	1	2	2	36 (1)
Moran	32	1	–	– (1)	33 (1)
Buchan	26	2	2	2	32
Duxbury	27 (6)	– (2)	–	1 (1)	28 (9)
Birtles	25	3	–	–	28
Jovanovic	19	1	2	2	24
Wilkins	11 (2)	2	–	–	13 (2)
McQueen	11	2	–	–	13
Greenhoff	8 (1)	–	2	1	11 (1)
Grimes	6 (2)	–	–	2	8 (2)
Ritchie	3 (1)	–	2	–	5 (1)
Roche	2	–	–	–	2
McGrath	1	–	–	–	1
Sloan	– (2)	–	– (1)	–	– (3)
McGarvey	– (2)	–	–	–	– (2)
Whelan	– (1)	–	–	–	– (1)

GOALSCORERS

PLAYER	LGE	FAC	LC	UC	TOT
Jordan	15	–	–	–	15
Macari	9	–	–	–	9
Coppell	6	–	–	–	6
McIlroy	5	–	–	1	6
Jovanovic	4	–	–	–	4
Duxbury	2	1	–	–	3
Thomas	2	1	–	–	3
Grimes	2	–	–	–	2
McQueen	2	–	–	–	2
Nicholl	1	1	–	–	2
Albiston	1	–	–	–	1
Birtles	–	1	–	–	1
own goals	2	–	–	–	2

1981/82

FOOTBALL LEAGUE DIVISION ONE

DATE	OPPONENTS	SCORE	GOALSCORERS	ATTENDANCE
Aug 29	Coventry City	1–2	Macari	19,329
Aug 31	NOTTINGHAM FOREST	0–0		51,496
Sep 5	IPSWICH TOWN	1–2	Stapleton	45,555
Sep 12	Aston Villa	1–1	Stapleton	37,661
Sep 19	SWANSEA CITY	1–0	Birtles	47,309
Sep 22	Middlesbrough	2–0	Birtles, Stapleton	19,895
Sep 26	Arsenal	0–0		39,795
Sep 30	LEEDS UNITED	1–0	Stapleton	47,019
Oct 3	WOLVERHAMPTON W.	5–0	McIlroy 3, Birtles, Stapleton	46,837
Oct 10	Manchester City	0–0		52,037
Oct 17	BIRMINGHAM CITY	1–1	Coppell	48,800
Oct 21	MIDDLESBROUGH	1–0	Moses	38,342
Oct 24	Liverpool	2–1	Albiston, Moran	41,438
Oct 31	NOTTS COUNTY	2–1	Birtles, Moses	45,928
Nov 7	Sunderland	5–1	Stapleton 2, Birtles, Moran, Robson	27,070
Nov 21	Tottenham Hotspur	1–3	Birtles	35,534
Nov 28	BRIGHTON	2–0	Birtles, Stapleton	41,911
Dec 5	Southampton	2–3	Robson, Stapleton	24,404
Jan 6	EVERTON	1–1	Stapleton	40,451
Jan 23	Stoke City	3–0	Birtles, Coppell, Stapleton	19,793
Jan 27	WEST HAM UNITED	1–0	Macari	41,291
Jan 30	Swansea City	0–2		24,115
Feb 6	ASTON VILLA	4–1	Moran 2, Coppell, Robson	43,184
Feb 13	Wolverhampton W.	1–0	Birtles	22,481
Feb 20	ARSENAL	0–0		43,833
Feb 27	MANCHESTER CITY	1–1	Moran	57,830
Mar 6	Birmingham City	1–0	Birtles	19,637
Mar 17	COVENTRY CITY	0–1		34,499
Mar 20	Notts County	3–1	Coppell 2, Stapleton	17,048
Mar 27	SUNDERLAND	0–0		40,776
Apr 3	Leeds United	0–0		30,953
Apr 7	LIVERPOOL	0–1		48,371
Apr 10	Everton	3–3	Coppell 2, Grimes	29,306
Apr 12	WEST BROMWICH ALBION	1–0	Moran	38,717
Apr 17	TOTTENHAM HOTSPUR	2–0	Coppell, McGarvey	50,724
Apr 20	Ipswich Town	1–2	Gidman	25,744
Apr 24	Brighton	1–0	Wilkins	20,750
May 1	SOUTHAMPTON	1–0	McGarvey	40,038
May 5	Nottingham Forest	1–0	Stapleton	18,449
May 8	West Ham United	1–1	Moran	26,337
May 12	West Bromwich Albion	3–0	Birtles, Coppell, Robson	19,707
May 15	STOKE CITY	2–0	Robson, Whiteside	43,072

FA CUP

DATE	OPPONENTS	SCORE	GOALSCORERS	ATTENDANCE
Jan 2	Watford (Rd3)	0–1		26,104

LEAGUE CUP

DATE	OPPONENTS	SCORE	GOALSCORERS	ATTENDANCE
Oct 7	Tottenham Hotspur (Rd2L1)	0–1		39,333
Oct 28	TOTTENHAM HOTSPUR (Rd2L2)	0–1		55,890

FINAL LEAGUE TABLE

		P	W	D	L	F	A	Pts
1	Liverpool	42	26	9	7	80	32	87
2	Ipswich Town	42	26	5	11	75	53	83
3	MANCHESTER UNITED	42	22	12	8	59	29	78
4	Tottenham Hotspur	42	20	11	11	67	48	71
5	Arsenal	42	20	11	11	48	37	71
6	Swansea City	42	21	6	15	58	51	69
7	Southampton	42	19	9	14	72	67	66
8	Everton	42	17	13	12	56	50	64
9	West Ham United	42	14	16	12	66	57	58
10	Manchester City	42	15	13	14	49	50	58
11	Aston Villa	42	15	12	15	55	53	57
12	Nottingham Forest	42	15	12	15	42	48	57
13	Brighton & Hove Albion	42	13	13	16	43	52	52
14	Coventry City	42	13	11	18	56	62	50
15	Notts County	42	13	8	21	61	69	47
16	Birmingham City	42	10	14	18	53	61	44
17	West Bromwich Albion	42	11	11	20	46	57	44
18	Stoke City	42	12	8	22	44	63	44
19	Sunderland	42	11	11	20	38	58	44
20	Leeds United	42	10	12	20	39	61	42
21	Wolverhampton Wanderers	42	10	10	22	32	63	40
22	Middlesbrough	42	8	15	19	34	52	39

APPEARANCES

PLAYER	LGE	FAC	LC	TOT
Albiston	42	1	2	45
Wilkins	42	1	2	45
Stapleton	41	1	2	44
Bailey	39	1	2	42
Gidman	36 (1)	1	2	39 (1)
Coppell	35 (1)	–	2	37 (1)
Birtles	32 (1)	1	2	35 (1)
Robson	32	1	2	35
Moran	30	1	2	33
Buchan	27	1	2	30
Moses	20 (1)	1	1	22 (1)
McQueen	21	–	–	21
Duxbury	19 (5)	–	– (1)	19 (6)
McIlroy	12	1	1	14
McGarvey	10 (6)	–	–	10 (6)
Macari	10 (1)	– (1)	–	10 (2)
Grimes	9 (2)	–	–	9 (2)
Roche	3	–	–	3
Whiteside	1 (1)	–	–	1 (1)
Davies	1	–	–	1
Nicholl	– (1)	–	–	– (1)

GOALSCORERS

PLAYER	LGE	FAC	LC	TOT
Stapleton	13	–	–	13
Birtles	11	–	–	11
Coppell	9	–	–	9
Moran	7	–	–	7
Robson	5	–	–	5
McIlroy	3	–	–	3
Macari	2	–	–	2
McGarvey	2	–	–	2
Moses	2	–	–	2
Albiston	1	–	–	1
Gidman	1	–	–	1
Grimes	1	–	–	1
Whiteside	1	–	–	1
Wilkins	1	–	–	1

1982/83

FOOTBALL LEAGUE DIVISION ONE

DATE	OPPONENTS	SCORE	GOALSCORERS	ATTENDANCE
Aug 28	BIRMINGHAM CITY	3-0	Coppell, Moran, Stapleton	48,673
Sep 1	Nottingham Forest	3-0	Robson, Whiteside, Wilkins	23,956
Sep 4	West Bromwich Albion	1-3	Robson	24,928
Sep 8	EVERTON	2-1	Robson, Whiteside	43,186
Sep 11	IPSWICH TOWN	3-1	Whiteside 2, Coppell	43,140
Sep 18	Southampton	1-0	Macari	21,700
Sep 25	ARSENAL	0-0		43,198
Oct 2	Luton Town	1-1	Grimes	17,009
Oct 9	STOKE CITY	1-0	Robson	43,132
Oct 16	Liverpool	0-0		40,853
Oct 23	MANCHESTER CITY	2-2	Stapleton 2	57,334
Oct 30	West Ham United	1-3	Moran	31,684
Nov 6	Brighton	0-1		18,379
Nov 13	TOTTENHAM HOTSPUR	1-0	Muhren	47,869
Nov 20	Aston Villa	1-2	Stapleton	35,487
Nov 27	NORWICH CITY	3-0	Robson 2, Muhren	34,579
Dec 4	Watford	1-0	Whiteside	25,669
Dec 11	NOTTS COUNTY	4-0	Duxbury, Robson, Stapleton, Whiteside	33,618
Dec 18	Swansea City	0-0		15,748
Dec 27	SUNDERLAND	0-0		47,783
Dec 28	Coventry City	0-3		18,945
Jan 1	ASTON VILLA	3-1	Stapleton 2, Coppell	41,545
Jan 3	WEST BROMWICH ALBION	0-0		39,123
Jan 15	Birmingham City	2-1	Robson, Whiteside	19,333
Jan 22	NOTTINGHAM FOREST	2-0	Coppell, Muhren	38,615
Feb 5	Ipswich Town	1-1	Stapleton	23,804
Feb 26	LIVERPOOL	1-1	Muhren	57,397
Mar 2	Stoke City	0-1		21,266
Mar 5	Manchester City	2-1	Stapleton 2	45,400
Mar 19	BRIGHTON	1-1	Albiston	36,264
Mar 22	WEST HAM UNITED	2-1	McGarvey, Stapleton	30,227
Apr 2	COVENTRY CITY	3-0	Macari, Stapleton, og	36,814
Apr 4	Sunderland	0-0		31,486
Apr 9	SOUTHAMPTON	1-1	Robson	37,120
Apr 19	Everton	0-2		21,715
Apr 23	WATFORD	2-0	Cunningham, Grimes	43,048
Apr 30	Norwich City	1-1	Whiteside	22,233
May 2	Arsenal	0-3		23,602
May 7	SWANSEA CITY	2-1	Robson, Stapleton	35,724
May 9	LUTON TOWN	3-0	McGrath 2, Stapleton	34,213
May 11	Tottenham Hotspur	0-2		32,803
May 14	Notts County	2-3	McGrath, Muhren	14,395

FA CUP

DATE	OPPONENTS	SCORE	GOALSCORERS	ATTENDANCE
Jan 8	WEST HAM UNITED (R3)	2-0	Coppell, Stapleton	44,143
Jan 29	Luton Town (R4)	2-0	Moran, Moses	20,516
Feb 19	Derby County (R5)	1-0	Whiteside	33,022
Mar 12	EVERTON (R6)	1-0	Stapleton	58,198
Apr 16	Arsenal (SF) (at Villa Park)	2-1	Robson, Whiteside	46,535

FA CUP

DATE	OPPONENTS	SCORE	GOALSCORERS	ATTENDANCE
May 21	Brighton (Final) (at Wembley)	2-2	Stapleton, Wilkins	100,000
May 26	Brighton (Final Replay) (at Wembley)	4-0	Robson 2, Muhren, Whiteside	92,000

LEAGUE CUP

DATE	OPPONENTS	SCORE	GOALSCORERS	ATTENDANCE
Oct 06	BOURNEMOUTH (R2L1)	2-0	Stapleton, og	22,091
Oct 26	Bournemouth (R2L2)	2-2	Coppell, Muhren	13,226
Nov 10	Bradford City (R3)	0-0		15,568
Nov 24	BRADFORD CITY (R3R)	4-1	Albiston, Coppell, Moran, Moses	24,507
Dec 1	SOUTHAMPTON (R4)	2-0	McQueen, Whiteside	28,378
Jan 19	NOTTINGHAM FOREST (R5)	4-0	McQueen 2, Coppell, Robson	44,413
Feb 15	Arsenal (SF1L)	4-2	Coppell 2, Whiteside, Stapleton	43,136
Feb 23	ARSENAL (SF2L)	2-1	Coppell, Moran	56,635
Mar 26	Liverpool (Final) (at Wembley)	1-2	Whiteside	100,000

UEFA CUP

DATE	OPPONENTS	SCORE	GOALSCORERS	ATTENDANCE
Sep 15	VALENCIA (R1L1)	0-0		46,588
Sep 29	Valencia (R1L2)	1-2	Robson	35,000

FINAL LEAGUE TABLE

		P	W	D	L	F	A	Pts
1	Liverpool	42	24	10	8	87	37	82
2	Watford	42	22	5	15	74	57	71
3	MANCHESTER UNITED	42	19	13	10	56	38	70
4	Tottenham Hotspur	42	20	9	13	65	50	69
5	Nottingham Forest	42	20	9	13	62	50	69
6	Aston Villa	42	21	5	16	62	50	68
7	Everton	42	18	10	14	66	48	64
8	West Ham United	42	20	4	18	68	62	64
9	Ipswich Town	42	15	13	14	64	50	58
10	Arsenal	42	16	10	16	58	56	58
11	West Bromwich Albion	42	15	12	15	51	49	57
12	Southampton	42	15	12	15	54	58	57
13	Stoke City	42	16	9	17	53	64	57
14	Norwich City	42	14	12	16	52	58	54
15	Notts County	42	15	7	20	55	71	52
16	Sunderland	42	12	14	16	48	61	50
17	Birmingham City	42	12	14	16	40	55	50
18	Luton Town	42	12	13	17	65	84	49
19	Coventry City	42	13	9	20	48	59	48
20	Manchester City	42	13	8	21	47	70	47
21	Swansea City	42	10	11	21	51	69	41
22	Brighton & Hove Albion	42	9	13	20	38	68	40

APPEARANCES

PLAYER	LGE	FAC	LC	UC	TOT
Duxbury	42	7	9	2	60
Stapleton	41	7	9	2	59
Albiston	38	7	9	2	56
Whiteside	39	7	7 (2)	2	55 (2)
Bailey	37	7	9	2	55
McQueen	37	7	8	1	53
Robson	33	6	8	2	49
Muhren	32	6	8	–	46
Moran	29	7	7	1	44
Moses	29	5	8	1	43
Coppell	29	4	8	1 (1)	42 (1)
Wilkins	26	4	3 (1)	2	35 (1)
Grimes	15 (1)	1	2	2	20 (1)
McGrath	14	– (1)	1	–	15 (1)
Buchan	3	–	1	2	6
Wealands	5	–	–	–	5
Davies	2 (1)	2	–	–	4 (1)
Macari	2 (7)	– (1)	1 (2)	– (1)	3 (11)
McGarvey	3 (4)	–	–	–	3 (4)
Cunningham	3 (2)	–	–	–	3 (2)
Gidman	3	–	–	–	3
Beardsley	–	–	1	–	1

GOALSCORERS

PLAYER	LGE	FAC	LC	UC	TOT
Stapleton	14	3	2	–	19
Robson	10	3	1	1	15
Whiteside	8	3	3	–	14
Coppell	4	1	6	–	11
Muhren	5	1	1	–	7
Moran	2	1	2	–	5
McGrath	3	–	–	–	3
McQueen	–	–	3	–	3
Grimes	2	–	–	–	2
Macari	2	–	–	–	2
Albiston	1	–	1	–	2
Wilkins	1	1	–	–	2
Moses	–	1	1	–	2
Cunningham	1	–	–	–	1
Duxbury	1	–	–	–	1
McGarvey	1	–	–	–	1
own goals	1	–	1	–	2

1983/84

FOOTBALL LEAGUE DIVISION ONE

DATE	OPPONENTS	SCORE	GOALSCORERS	ATTENDANCE
Aug 27	QUEENS PARK RANGERS	3-1	Muhren 2, Stapleton	48,742
Aug 29	NOTTINGHAM FOREST	1-2	Moran	43,005
Sep 3	Stoke City	1-0	Muhren	23,704
Sep 6	Arsenal	3-2	Moran, Robson, Stapleton	42,703
Sep 10	LUTON TOWN	2-0	Albiston, Muhren	41,013
Sep 17	Southampton	0-3		20,674
Sep 24	LIVERPOOL	1-0	Stapleton	56,121
Oct 1	Norwich City	3-3	Whiteside 2, Stapleton	19,290
Oct 15	WEST BROMWICH ALBION	3-0	Albiston, Graham, Whiteside	42,221
Oct 22	Sunderland	1-0	Wilkins	26,826
Oct 29	WOLVERHAMPTON W.	3-0	Stapleton 2, Robson	41,880
Nov 5	ASTON VILLA	1-2	Robson	45,077
Nov 12	Leicester City	1-1	Robson	24,409
Nov 19	WATFORD	4-1	Stapleton 3, Robson	43,111
Nov 27	West Ham United	1-1	Wilkins	23,355
Dec 3	EVERTON	0-1		43,664
Dec 10	Ipswich Town	2-0	Crooks, Graham	19,779
Dec 16	TOTTENHAM HOTSPUR	4-2	Graham 2, Moran 2	33,616
Dec 26	Coventry City	1-1	Muhren	21,553
Dec 27	NOTTS COUNTY	3-3	Crooks, McQueen, Moran	41,544
Dec 31	STOKE CITY	1-0	Graham	40,164
Jan 2	Liverpool	1-1	Whiteside	44,622
Jan 13	Queens Park Rangers	1-1	Robson	16,308
Jan 21	SOUTHAMPTON	3-2	Muhren, Robson, Stapleton	40,371
Feb 4	NORWICH CITY	0-0		36,851
Feb 7	Birmingham City	2-2	Hogg, Whiteside	19,957
Feb 12	Luton Town	5-0	Robson 2, Whiteside 2, Stapleton	11,265
Feb 18	Wolverhampton W.	1-1	Whiteside	20,676
Feb 25	SUNDERLAND	2-1	Moran 2	40,615
Mar 3	Aston Villa	3-0	Moses, Robson, Whiteside	32,874
Mar 10	LEICESTER CITY	2-0	Hughes, Moses	39,473
Mar 17	ARSENAL	4-0	Muhren 2, Robson, Stapleton	48,942
Mar 31	West Bromwich Albion	0-2		28,104
Apr 7	BIRMINGHAM CITY	1-0	Robson	39,896
Apr 14	Notts County	0-1		13,911
Apr 17	Watford	0-0		20,764
Apr 21	COVENTRY CITY	4-1	Hughes 2, McGrath, Wilkins	38,524
Apr 28	WEST HAM UNITED	0-0		44,124
May 5	Everton	1-1	Stapleton	28,802
May 7	IPSWICH TOWN	1-2	Hughes	44,257
May 12	Tottenham Hotspur	1-1	Whiteside	39,790
May 16	Nottingham Forest	0-2		23,651

FA CUP

DATE	OPPONENTS	SCORE	GOALSCORERS	ATTENDANCE
Jan 7	Bournemouth (Rd3)	0-2		14,782

LEAGUE CUP

DATE	OPPONENTS	SCORE	GOALSCORERS	ATTENDANCE
Oct 3	Port Vale (Rd2L1)	1-0	Stapleton	19,885
Oct 26	PORT VALE (Rd2L2)	2-0	Whiteside, Wilkins	23,589
Nov 8	Colchester United (Rd3)	2-0	McQueen, Moses	13,031
Nov 30	Oxford United (Rd4)	1-1	Hughes	13,739
Dec 7	OXFORD UNITED (Rd4R)	1-1	Stapleton	27,459
Dec 19	Oxford United (Rd4R2)	1-2	Graham	13,912

EUROPEAN CUP-WINNERS' CUP

DATE	OPPONENTS	SCORE	GOALSCORERS	ATTENDANCE
Sep 14	DUKLA PRAGUE (Rd1L1)	1-1	Wilkins	39,745
Sep 27	Dukla Prague (Rd1L2) (United won the tie on away goals rule)	2-2	Robson, Stapleton	28,850
Oct 19	Spartak Varna (Rd2L1)	2-1	Graham, Robson	40,000
Nov 2	SPARTAK VARNA (Rd2L2)	2-0	Stapleton 2	39,079
Mar 7	Barcelona (Rd3L1)	0-2		70,000
Mar 21	BARCELONA (Rd3L2)	3-0	Robson 2, Stapleton	58,547
Apr 11	JUVENTUS (SFL1)	1-1	Davies	58,171
Apr 25	Juventus (SFL2)	1-2	Whiteside	64,655

FINAL LEAGUE TABLE

		P	W	D	L	F	A	Pts
1	Liverpool	42	22	14	6	73	32	80
2	Southampton	42	22	11	9	66	38	77
3	Nottingham Forest	42	22	8	12	76	45	74
4	MANCHESTER UNITED	42	20	14	8	71	41	74
5	Queens Park Rangers	42	22	7	13	67	37	73
6	Arsenal	42	18	9	15	74	60	63
7	Everton	42	16	14	12	44	42	62
8	Tottenham Hotspur	42	17	10	15	64	65	61
9	West Ham United	42	17	9	16	60	55	60
10	Aston Villa	42	17	9	16	59	61	60
11	Watford	42	16	9	17	68	77	57
12	Ipswich Town	42	15	8	19	55	57	53
13	Sunderland	42	13	13	16	42	53	52
14	Norwich City	42	12	15	15	48	49	51
15	Leicester City	42	13	12	17	65	68	51
16	Luton Town	42	14	9	19	53	66	51
17	West Bromwich Albion	42	14	9	19	48	62	51
18	Stoke City	42	13	11	18	44	63	50
19	Coventry City	42	13	11	18	57	77	50
20	Birmingham City	42	12	12	18	39	50	48
21	Notts County	42	10	11	21	50	72	41
22	Wolverhampton Wanderers	42	6	11	25	27	80	29

APPEARANCES

PLAYER	LGE	FAC	LC	ECWC	TOT
Stapleton	42	1	6	8	57
Albiston	40	1	6	8	55
Wilkins	42	1	6	6	55
Bailey	40	1	5	8	54
Duxbury	39	1	6	8	54
Moran	38	–	5	8	51
Robson	33	1	6	6	46
Graham	33 (4)	1	5	6 (1)	45 (5)
Whiteside	30 (7)	1	6	5 (1)	42 (8)
Moses	31 (4)	1	5 (1)	5 (1)	42 (6)
Muhren	26	1	2	5	34
McQueen	20	–	4	4	28
Hogg	16	1	–	4	21
McGrath	9	–	1	2	12
Hughes	7 (4)	–	1 (1)	2 (2)	10 (7)
Crooks	6 (1)	–	–	–	6 (1)
Gidman	4	–	1	1 (1)	6 (1)
Davies	3	–	–	– (1)	3 (1)
Wealands	2	–	1	–	3
Macari	– (5)	– (1)	– (2)	2	2 (8)
Blackmore	1	–	–	–	1
Dempsey	–	–	–	– (1)	– (1)

GOALSCORERS

PLAYER	LGE	FAC	LC	ECWC	TOT
Stapleton	13	–	2	4	19
Robson	12	–	–	4	16
Whiteside	10	–	1	1	12
Muhren	8	–	–	–	8
Moran	7	–	–	–	7
Graham	5	–	1	1	7
Hughes	4	–	1	–	5
Wilkins	3	–	1	1	5
Moses	2	–	1	–	3
Albiston	2	–	–	–	2
Crooks	2	–	–	–	2
McQueen	1	–	1	–	2
Hogg	1	–	–	–	1
McGrath	1	–	–	–	1
Davies	–	–	–	1	1

1984/85

FOOTBALL LEAGUE DIVISION ONE

DATE	OPPONENTS	SCORE	GOALSCORERS	ATTENDANCE
Aug 25	WATFORD	1-1	Strachan	53,668
Aug 28	Southampton	0-0		22,183
Sep 1	Ipswich Town	1-1	Hughes	20,876
Sep 5	CHELSEA	1-1	Olsen	48,398
Sep 8	NEWCASTLE UNITED	5-0	Strachan 2, Hughes, Moses, Olsen	54,915
Sep 15	Coventry City	3-0	Whiteside 2, Robson	18,312
Sep 22	LIVERPOOL	1-1	Strachan	56,638
Sep 29	West Bromwich Albion	2-1	Robson, Strachan	26,292
Oct 6	Aston Villa	0-3		37,131
Oct 13	WEST HAM UNITED	5-1	Brazil, Hughes, McQueen, Moses, Strachan	47,559
Oct 20	TOTTENHAM HOTSPUR	1-0	Hughes	54,516
Oct 27	Everton	0-5		40,742
Nov 2	ARSENAL	4-2	Strachan 2, Hughes, Robson	32,279
Nov 10	Leicester City	3-2	Brazil, Hughes, Strachan	23,840
Nov 17	LUTON TOWN	2-0	Whiteside 2	41,630
Nov 24	Sunderland	2-3	Hughes, Robson	25,405
Dec 1	NORWICH CITY	2-0	Hughes, Robson	36,635
Dec 8	Nottingham Forest	2-3	Strachan 2	25,902
Dec 15	QUEENS PARK RANGERS	3-0	Brazil, Duxbury, Gidman	36,134
Dec 22	IPSWICH TOWN	3-0	Gidman, Robson, Strachan	35,168
Dec 26	Stoke City	1-2	Stapleton	20,985
Dec 29	Chelsea	3-1	Hughes, Moses, Stapleton	42,197
Jan 1	SHEFFIELD WEDNESDAY	1-2	Hughes	47,625
Jan 12	COVENTRY CITY	0-1		35,992
Feb 2	WEST BROMWICH ALBION	2-0	Strachan 2	36,681
Feb 9	Newcastle United	1-1	Moran	32,555
Feb 23	Arsenal	1-0	Whiteside	48,612
Mar 2	EVERTON	1-1	Olsen	51,150
Mar 12	Tottenham Hotspur	2-1	Hughes, Whiteside	42,908
Mar 15	West Ham United	2-2	Robson, Stapleton	16,674
Mar 23	ASTON VILLA	4-0	Hughes 3, Whiteside	40,941
Mar 31	Liverpool	1-0	Stapleton	34,886
Apr 3	LEICESTER CITY	2-1	Robson, Stapleton	35,950
Apr 6	STOKE CITY	5-0	Hughes 2, Olsen 2, Whiteside	42,940
Apr 9	Sheffield Wednesday	0-1		39,380
Apr 21	Luton Town	1-2	Whiteside	10,320
Apr 24	SOUTHAMPTON	0-0		31,291
Apr 27	SUNDERLAND	2-2	Moran, Robson	38,979
May 4	Norwich City	1-0	Moran	15,502
May 6	NOTTINGHAM FOREST	2-0	Gidman, Stapleton	41,775
May 11	Queens Park Rangers	3-1	Brazil 2, Strachan	20,483
May 13	Watford	1-5	Moran	20,500

FA CUP

DATE	OPPONENTS	SCORE	GOALSCORERS	ATTENDANCE
Jan 5	BOURNEMOUTH (Rd3)	3-0	McQueen, Stapleton, Strachan	32,080
Jan 26	COVENTRY CITY (Rd4)	2-1	Hughes, McGrath	38,039
Feb 15	Blackburn Rovers (Rd5)	2-0	McGrath, Strachan	22,692
Mar 9	WEST HAM UNITED (Rd6)	4-2	Whiteside 3, Hughes	46,769
Apr 13	Liverpool (SF) (at Goodison Park)	2-2	Robson, Stapleton	51,690
Apr 17	Liverpool (SFR) (at Maine Road)	2-1	Hughes, Robson	45,775
May 18	Everton (Final) (at Wembley)	1-0	Whiteside	100,000

LEAGUE CUP

DATE	OPPONENTS	SCORE	GOALSCORERS	ATTENDANCE
Sep 26	BURNLEY (Rd2L1)	4-0	Hughes 3, Robson	28,383
Oct 9	Burnley (Rd2L2)	3-0	Brazil 2, Olsen	12,690
Oct 30	EVERTON (Rd3)	1-2	Brazil	50,918

UEFA CUP

DATE	OPPONENTS	SCORE	GOALSCORERS	ATTENDANCE
Sep 19	RABA VASAS (Rd1L1)	3-0	Hughes, Muhren, Robson	33,119
Oct 3	Raba Vasas (Rd1L2)	2-2	Brazil, Muhren	26,000
Oct 24	PSV Eindhoven (Rd2L1)	0-0		27,500
Nov 7	PSV EINDHOVEN (Rd2L2)	1-0	Strachan	39,281
Nov 28	DUNDEE UNITED (Rd3L1)	2-2	Robson, Strachan	48,278
Dec 12	Dundee United (Rd3L2)	3-2	Hughes, Muhren, og	21,821
Mar 6	VIDEOTON (QFL1)	1-0	Stapleton	35,432
Mar 20	Videoton (QFL2)	0-1		25,000

(United lost the tie on penalty kicks)

FINAL LEAGUE TABLE

		P	W	D	L	F	A	Pts
1	Everton	42	28	6	8	88	43	90
2	Liverpool	42	22	11	9	68	35	77
3	Tottenham Hotspur	42	23	8	11	78	51	77
4	MANCHESTER UNITED	42	22	10	10	77	47	76
5	Southampton	42	19	11	12	56	47	68
6	Chelsea	42	18	12	12	63	48	66
7	Arsenal	42	19	9	14	61	49	66
8	Sheffield Wednesday	42	17	14	11	58	45	65
9	Nottingham Forest	42	19	7	16	56	48	64
10	Aston Villa	42	15	11	16	60	60	56
11	Watford	42	14	13	15	81	71	55
12	West Bromwich Albion	42	16	7	19	58	62	55
13	Luton Town	42	15	9	18	57	61	54
14	Newcastle United	42	13	13	16	55	70	52
15	Leicester City	42	15	6	21	65	73	51
16	West Ham United	42	13	12	17	51	68	51
17	Ipswich Town	42	13	11	18	46	57	50
18	Coventry City	42	15	5	22	47	64	50
19	Queens Park Rangers	42	13	11	18	53	72	50
20	Norwich City	42	13	10	19	46	64	49
21	Sunderland	42	10	10	22	40	62	40
22	Stoke City	42	3	8	31	24	91	17

APPEARANCES

PLAYER	LGE	FAC	LC	UC	TOT
Albiston	39	7	3	8	57
Strachan	41	7	2	6	56
Bailey	38	6	3	8	55
Hughes	38	7	2	8	55
Olsen	36	6	2	6 (1)	50 (1)
Robson	32 (1)	4	2	7	45 (1)
Hogg	29	5	3	6	43
Gidman	27	6	1	6 (1)	40 (1)
Moses	26	3	3	6	38
Duxbury	27 (3)	2 (1)	2	6	37 (4)
Whiteside	23 (4)	6	1	4 (1)	34 (5)
McGrath	23	7	–	2	32
Stapleton	21 (3)	5	1 (1)	4 (1)	31 (5)
Moran	19	3	2	4	28
Brazil	17 (3)	– (1)	2 (1)	2	21 (5)
McQueen	12	1	–	2	15
Muhren	7 (5)	1	1	3	12 (5)
Pears	4	1	–	–	5
Garton	2	–	1	– (1)	3 (1)
Blackmore	1	–	1	–	2
Graham	–	–	1	–	1

GOALSCORERS

PLAYER	LGE	FAC	LC	UC	TOT
Hughes	16	3	3	2	24
Strachan	15	2	–	2	19
Robson	9	2	1	2	14
Whiteside	9	4	–	–	13
Stapleton	6	2	–	1	9
Brazil	5	–	3	1	9
Olsen	5	–	1	–	6
Moran	4	–	–	–	4
Gidman	3	–	–	–	3
Moses	3	–	–	–	3
Muhren	–	–	–	3	3
McQueen	1	1	–	–	2
McGrath	–	2	–	–	2
Duxbury	1	–	–	–	1
own goal	–	–	–	1	1

1985/86

FOOTBALL LEAGUE DIVISION ONE

DATE	OPPONENTS	SCORE	GOALSCORERS	ATTENDANCE
Aug 17	ASTON VILLA	4-0	Hughes 2, Olsen, Whiteside	49,743
Aug 20	Ipswich Town	1-0	Robson	18,777
Aug 24	Arsenal	2-1	Hughes, McGrath	37,145
Aug 26	WEST HAM UNITED	2-0	Hughes, Strachan	50,773
Aug 31	Nottingham Forest	3-1	Barnes, Hughes, Stapleton	26,274
Sep 4	NEWCASTLE UNITED	3-0	Stapleton 2, Hughes	51,102
Sep 7	OXFORD UNITED	3-0	Barnes, Robson, Whiteside	51,820
Sep 14	Manchester City	3-0	Albiston, Duxbury, Robson	48,773
Sep 21	West Bromwich Albion	5-1	Brazil 2, Blackmore, Stapleton, Strachan	25,068
Sep 28	SOUTHAMPTON	1-0	Hughes	52,449
Oct 5	Luton Town	1-1	Hughes	17,454
Oct 12	QUEENS PARK RANGERS	2-0	Hughes, Olsen	48,845
Oct 19	LIVERPOOL	1-1	McGrath	54,492
Oct 26	Chelsea	2-1	Hughes, Olsen	42,485
Nov 2	COVENTRY CITY	2-0	Olsen 2	46,748
Nov 9	Sheffield Wednesday	0-1		48,105
Nov 16	TOTTENHAM HOTSPUR	0-0		54,575
Nov 23	Leicester City	0-3		22,008
Nov 30	WATFORD	1-1	Brazil	42,181
Dec 7	IPSWICH TOWN	1-0	Stapleton	37,981
Dec 14	Aston Villa	3-1	Blackmore, Hughes, Strachan	27,626
Dec 21	ARSENAL	0-1		44,386
Dec 26	Everton	1-3	Stapleton	42,551
Jan 1	BIRMINGHAM CITY	1-0	Gibson C	43,095
Jan 11	Oxford United	3-1	Gibson C, Hughes, Whiteside	13,280
Jan 18	NOTTINGHAM FOREST	2-3	Olsen 2	46,717
Feb 2	West Ham United	1-2	Robson	22,642
Feb 9	Liverpool	1-1	Gibson C	35,064
Feb 22	WEST BROMWICH ALBION	3-0	Olsen 3	45,193
Mar 1	Southampton	0-1		19,012
Mar 15	Queens Park Rangers	0-1		23,407
Mar 19	LUTON TOWN	2-0	Hughes, McGrath	33,668
Mar 22	MANCHESTER CITY	2-2	Gibson C, Strachan	51,274
Mar 29	Birmingham City	1-1	Robson	22,551
Mar 31	EVERTON	0-0		51,189
Apr 5	Coventry City	3-1	Gibson C, Robson, Strachan	17,160
Apr 9	CHELSEA	1-2	Olsen	45,355
Apr 13	SHEFFIELD WEDNESDAY	0-2		32,331
Apr 16	Newcastle United	4-2	Hughes 2, Robson, Whiteside	31,840
Apr 19	Tottenham Hotspur	0-0		32,357
Apr 26	LEICESTER CITY	4-0	Blackmore, Davenport, Hughes, Stapleton	38,840
May 3	Watford	1-1	Hughes	18,414

FA CUP

DATE	OPPONENTS	SCORE	GOALSCORERS	ATTENDANCE
Jan 9	ROCHDALE (Rd3)	2-0	Hughes, Stapleton	40,223
Jan 25	Sunderland (Rd4)	0-0		35,484
Jan 29	SUNDERLAND (Rd4R)	3-0	Olsen 2, Whiteside	43,402
Mar 5	West Ham United (Rd5)	1-1	Stapleton	26,441
Mar 9	WEST HAM UNITED (Rd5R)	0-2		30,441

LEAGUE CUP

DATE	OPPONENTS	SCORE	GOALSCORERS	ATTENDANCE
Sep 24	Crystal Palace (Rd2L1)	1-0	Barnes	21,507
Oct 9	CRYSTAL PALACE (Rd2L2)	1-0	Whiteside	26,118
Oct 29	WEST HAM UNITED (Rd3)	1-0	Whiteside	32,056
Nov 26	Liverpool (Rd4)	1-2	McGrath	41,291

FINAL LEAGUE TABLE

		P	W	D	L	F	A	Pts
1	Liverpool	42	26	10	6	89	37	88
2	Everton	42	26	8	8	87	41	86
3	West Ham United	42	26	6	10	74	40	84
4	MANCHESTER UNITED	42	22	10	10	70	36	76
5	Sheffield Wednesday	42	21	10	11	63	54	73
6	Chelsea	42	20	11	11	57	56	71
7	Arsenal	42	20	9	13	49	47	69
8	Nottingham Forest	42	19	11	12	69	53	68
9	Luton Town	42	18	12	12	61	44	66
10	Tottenham Hotspur	42	19	8	15	74	52	65
11	Newcastle United	42	17	12	13	67	72	63
12	Watford	42	16	11	15	69	62	59
13	Queens Park Rangers	42	15	7	20	53	64	52
14	Southampton	42	12	10	20	51	62	46
15	Manchester City	42	11	12	19	43	57	45
16	Aston Villa	42	10	14	18	51	67	44
17	Coventry City	42	11	10	21	48	71	43
18	Oxford United	42	10	12	20	62	80	42
19	Leicester City	42	10	12	20	54	76	42
20	Ipswich Town	42	11	8	23	32	55	41
21	Birmingham City	42	8	5	29	30	73	29
22	West Bromwich Albion	42	4	12	26	35	89	24

APPEARANCES

PLAYER	LGE	FAC	LC	TOT
McGrath	40	4	4	48
Whiteside	37	5	4	46
Albiston	37	5	3	45
Hughes	40	3	2	45
Stapleton	34 (7)	5	4	43 (7)
Strachan	27 (1)	5	1	33 (1)
Olsen	25 (3)	3 (2)	3	31 (5)
Bailey	25	2	4	31
Duxbury	21 (2)	3	3	27 (2)
Gidman	24	2	1	27
Robson	21	3	2	26
Moran	18 (1)	3	4	25 (1)
Gibson C	18	4	–	22
Turner	17	3	–	20
Hogg	17	–	2	19
Blackmore	12	2 (2)	2	16 (2)
Barnes	12 (1)	–	3	15 (1)
Davenport	11	–	–	11
Garton	10	1	–	11
Higgins	6	2	–	8
Brazil	1(10)	–	2 (2)	3(12)
Moses	4	–	–	4
Gibson T	2 (5)	–	–	2 (5)
Sivebaek	2 (1)	–	–	2 (1)
Dempsey	1	–	–	1
Wood	– (1)	–	–	– (1)

GOALSCORERS

PLAYER	LGE	FAC	LC	TOT
Hughes	17	1	–	18
Olsen	11	2	–	13
Stapleton	7	2	–	9
Robson	7	–	–	7
Whiteside	4	1	2	7
Gibson C	5	–	–	5
Strachan	5	–	–	5
McGrath	3	–	1	4
Blackmore	3	–	–	3
Brazil	3	–	–	3
Barnes	2	–	1	3
Albiston	1	–	–	1
Davenport	1	–	–	1
Duxbury	1	–	–	1

1986/87

FOOTBALL LEAGUE DIVISION ONE

DATE	OPPONENTS	SCORE	GOALSCORERS	ATTENDANCE
Aug 23	Arsenal	0–1		41,382
Aug 25	WEST HAM UNITED	2–3	Davenport, Stapleton	43,306
Aug 30	CHARLTON ATHLETIC	0–1		37,544
Sep 6	Leicester City	1–1	Whiteside	16,785
Sep 13	SOUTHAMPTON	5–1	Stapleton 2, Davenport, Olsen, Whiteside	40,135
Sep 16	Watford	0–1		21,650
Sep 21	Everton	1–3	Robson	25,843
Sep 28	CHELSEA	0–1		33,340
Oct 4	Nottingham Forest	1–1	Robson	34,828
Oct 11	SHEFFIELD WEDNESDAY	3–1	Davenport 2, Whiteside	45,890
Oct 18	LUTON TOWN	1–0	Stapleton	39,927
Oct 25	Manchester City	1–1	Stapleton	32,440
Nov 1	COVENTRY CITY	1–1	Davenport	36,946
Nov 8	Oxford United	0–2		13,545
Nov 15	Norwich City	0–0		22,684
Nov 22	QUEENS PARK RANGERS	1–0	Sivebaek	42,235
Nov 29	Wimbledon	0–1		12,112
Dec 7	TOTTENHAM HOTSPUR	3–3	Davenport 2, Whiteside	35,957
Dec 13	Aston Villa	3–3	Davenport 2, Whiteside	29,205
Dec 20	LEICESTER CITY	2–0	Gibson C, Stapleton	34,150
Dec 26	Liverpool	1–0	Whiteside	40,663
Dec 27	NORWICH CITY	0–1		44,610
Jan 1	NEWCASTLE UNITED	4–1	Olsen, Stapleton, Whiteside, og	43,334
Jan 3	Southampton	1–1	Olsen	20,409
Jan 24	ARSENAL	2–0	Gibson T, Strachan	51,367
Feb 7	Charlton Athletic	0–0		15,482
Feb 14	WATFORD	3–1	Davenport, McGrath, Strachan	35,763
Feb 21	Chelsea	1–1	Davenport	26,516
Feb 28	EVERTON	0–0		47,421
Mar 7	MANCHESTER CITY	2–0	Robson, og	48,619
Mar 14	Luton Town	1–2	Robson	12,509
Mar 21	Sheffield Wednesday	0–1		29,888
Mar 28	NOTTINGHAM FOREST	2–0	McGrath, Robson	39,182
Apr 4	OXFORD UNITED	3–2	Davenport 2, Robson	32,443
Apr 14	West Ham United	0–0		23,486
Apr 18	Newcastle United	1–2	Strachan	32,706
Apr 20	LIVERPOOL	1–0	Davenport	54,103
Apr 25	Queens Park Rangers	1–1	Strachan	17,414
May 2	WIMBLEDON	0–1		31,686
May 4	Tottenham Hotspur	0–4		36,692
May 6	Coventry City	1–1	Whiteside	23,407
May 9	ASTON VILLA	3–1	Blackmore, Duxbury, Robson	35,179

FA CUP

DATE	OPPONENTS	SCORE	GOALSCORERS	ATTENDANCE
Jan 10	MANCHESTER CITY (Rd3)	1–0	Whiteside	54,294
Jan 31	COVENTRY CITY (Rd4)	0–1		49,082

LEAGUE CUP

DATE	OPPONENTS	SCORE	GOALSCORERS	ATTENDANCE
Sep 24	PORT VALE (Rd2L1)	2–0	Stapleton, Whiteside	18,906
Oct 7	Port Vale (Rd2L2)	5–2	Moses 2, Barnes, Davenport, Stapleton	10,486
Oct 29	SOUTHAMPTON (Rd3)	0–0		23,639
Nov 4	Southampton (Rd3R)	1–4	Davenport	17,915

FINAL LEAGUE TABLE

		P	W	D	L	F	A	Pts
1	Everton	42	26	8	8	76	31	86
2	Liverpool	42	23	8	11	72	42	77
3	Tottenham Hotspur	42	21	8	13	68	43	71
4	Arsenal	42	20	10	12	58	35	70
5	Norwich City	42	17	17	8	53	51	68
6	Wimbledon	42	19	9	14	57	50	66
7	Luton Town	42	18	12	12	47	45	66
8	Nottingham Forest	42	18	11	13	64	51	65
9	Watford	42	18	9	15	67	54	63
10	Coventry City	42	17	12	13	50	45	63
11	MANCHESTER UNITED	42	14	14	14	52	45	56
12	Southampton	42	14	10	18	69	68	52
13	Sheffield Wednesday	42	13	13	16	58	59	52
14	Chelsea	42	13	13	16	53	64	52
15	West Ham United	42	14	10	18	52	67	52
16	Queens Park Rangers	42	13	11	18	48	64	50
17	Newcastle United	42	12	11	19	47	65	47
18	Oxford United	42	11	13	18	44	69	46
19	Charlton Athletic	42	11	11	20	45	55	44
20	Leicester City	42	11	9	22	54	76	42
21	Manchester City	42	8	15	19	36	57	39
22	Aston Villa	42	8	12	22	45	79	36

APPEARANCES

PLAYER	LGE	FAC	LC	TOT
Davenport	34 (5)	1 (1)	4	39 (6)
McGrath	34 (1)	– (1)	4	38 (2)
Strachan	33 (1)	2	2	37 (1)
Duxbury	32	2	3	37
Moran	32 (1)	2	2 (1)	36 (2)
Whiteside	31	2	3 (1)	36 (1)
Robson	29 (1)	–	3	32 (1)
Stapleton	25 (9)	2	4	31 (9)
Sivebaek	27 (1)	2	1	30 (1)
Turner	23	2	4	29
Gibson C	24	1	1	26
Olsen	22 (6)	2	1 (1)	25 (7)
Albiston	19 (3)	–	4	23 (3)
Moses	17 (1)	–	4	21 (1)
Walsh	14	–	–	14
Gibson T	12 (4)	1 (1)	– (2)	13 (7)
Hogg	11	–	2	13
Blackmore	10 (2)	1	–	11 (2)
Garton	9	2	–	11
O'Brien	9 (2)	–	–	9 (2)
Barnes	7	–	2	9
Bailey	5	–	–	5
Wood	2	–	– (1)	2 (1)
Gill	1	–	–	1

GOALSCORERS

PLAYER	LGE	FAC	LC	TOT
Davenport	14	–	2	16
Whiteside	8	1	1	10
Stapleton	7	–	2	9
Robson	7	–	–	7
Strachan	4	–	–	4
Olsen	3	–	–	3
McGrath	2	–	–	2
Moses	–	–	2	2
Blackmore	1	–	–	1
Duxbury	1	–	–	1
Gibson C	1	–	–	1
Gibson T	1	–	–	1
Sivebaek	1	–	–	1
Barnes	–	–	1	1
own goals	2	–	–	2

1987/88

FOOTBALL LEAGUE DIVISION ONE

DATE	OPPONENTS	SCORE	GOALSCORERS	ATTENDANCE
Aug 15	Southampton	2–2	Whiteside 2	21,214
Aug 19	ARSENAL	0–0		43,893
Aug 22	WATFORD	2–0	McClair, McGrath	38,769
Aug 29	Charlton Athletic	3–1	McClair, McGrath, Robson	14,046
Aug 31	CHELSEA	3–1	McClair, Strachan, Whiteside	46,616
Sep 5	Coventry City	0–0		27,125
Sep 12	NEWCASTLE UNITED	2–2	McClair, Olsen	45,619
Sep 19	Everton	1–2	Whiteside	38,439
Sep 26	TOTTENHAM HOTSPUR	1–0	McClair	48,087
Oct 3	Luton Town	1–1	McClair	9,137
Oct 10	Sheffield Wednesday	4–2	McClair 2, Blackmore, Robson	32,779
Oct 17	NORWICH CITY	2–1	Davenport, Robson	39,821
Oct 24	West Ham United	1–1	Gibson	19,863
Oct 31	NOTTINGHAM FOREST	2–2	Robson, Whiteside	44,669
Nov 15	LIVERPOOL	1–1	Whiteside	47,106
Nov 21	Wimbledon	1–2	Blackmore	11,532
Dec 5	Queens Park Rangers	2–0	Davenport, Robson	20,632
Dec 12	OXFORD UNITED	3–1	Strachan 2, Olsen	34,709
Dec 19	Portsmouth	2–1	McClair, Robson	22,207
Dec 26	Newcastle United	0–1		26,461
Dec 28	EVERTON	2–1	McClair 2	47,024
Jan 1	CHARLTON ATHLETIC	0–0		37,257
Jan 2	Watford	1–0	McClair	18,038
Jan 16	SOUTHAMPTON	0–2		35,716
Jan 24	Arsenal	2–1	McClair, Strachan	29,392
Feb 6	COVENTRY CITY	1–0	O'Brien	37,144
Feb 10	Derby County	2–1	Strachan, Whiteside	20,016
Feb 13	Chelsea	2–1	Bruce, O'Brien	25,014
Feb 23	Tottenham Hotspur	1–1	McClair	25,731
Mar 5	Norwich City	0–1		19,129
Mar 12	SHEFFIELD WEDNESDAY	4–1	McClair 2, Blackmore, Davenport	33,318
Mar 19	Nottingham Forest	0–0		27,598
Mar 26	WEST HAM UNITED	3–1	Anderson, Robson, Strachan	37,269
Apr 2	DERBY COUNTY	4–1	McClair 3, Gibson	40,146
Apr 4	Liverpool	3–3	Robson 2, Strachan	43,497
Apr 12	LUTON TOWN	3–0	Davenport, McClair, Robson	28,830
Apr 30	QUEENS PARK RANGERS	2–1	Bruce, og	35,733
May 2	Oxford United	2–0	Anderson, Strachan	8,966
May 7	PORTSMOUTH	4–1	McClair 2, Davenport, Robson	35,105
May 9	WIMBLEDON	2–1	McClair 2	28,040

FA CUP

DATE	OPPONENTS	SCORE	GOALSCORERS	ATTENDANCE
Jan 10	Ipswich Town (Rd3)	2–1	Anderson, og	23,012
Jan 30	CHELSEA (Rd4)	2–0	McClair, Whiteside	50,716
Feb 20	Arsenal (Rd5)	1–2	McClair	54,161

LEAGUE CUP

DATE	OPPONENTS	SCORE	GOALSCORERS	ATTENDANCE
Sep 23	HULL CITY (Rd2L1)	5–0	Davenport, McClair, McGrath, Strachan, Whiteside	25,041
Oct 7	Hull City (Rd2L2)	1–0	McClair	13,586
Oct 28	CRYSTAL PALACE (Rd3)	2–1	McClair 2	27,283
Nov 18	Bury (Rd4)	2–1	McClair, Whiteside	33,519
	(United drawn away – tie switched to Old Trafford)			
Jan 20	Oxford United (Rd5)	0–2		12,658

FINAL LEAGUE TABLE

		P	W	D	L	F	A	Pts
1	Liverpool	40	26	12	2	87	24	90
2	MANCHESTER UNITED	40	23	12	5	71	38	81
3	Nottingham Forest	40	20	13	7	67	39	73
4	Everton	40	19	13	8	53	27	70
5	Queens Park Rangers	40	19	10	11	48	38	67
6	Arsenal	40	18	12	10	58	39	66
7	Wimbledon	40	14	15	11	58	47	57
8	Newcastle United	40	14	14	12	55	53	56
9	Luton Town	40	14	11	15	57	58	53
10	Coventry City	40	13	14	13	46	53	53
11	Sheffield Wednesday	40	15	8	17	52	66	53
12	Southampton	40	12	14	14	49	53	50
13	Tottenham Hotspur	40	12	11	17	38	48	47
14	Norwich City	40	12	9	19	40	52	45
15	Derby County	40	10	13	17	35	45	43
16	West Ham United	40	9	15	16	40	52	42
17	Charlton Athletic	40	9	15	16	38	52	42
18	Chelsea	40	9	15	16	50	68	42
19	Portsmouth	40	7	14	19	36	66	35
20	Watford	40	7	11	22	27	51	32
21	Oxford United	40	6	13	21	44	80	31

APPEARANCES

PLAYER	LGE	FAC	LC	TOT
McClair	40	3	5	48
Duxbury	39	3	5	47
Robson	36	2	5	43
Strachan	33 (3)	3	5	41 (3)
Anderson	30 (1)	3	4	37 (1)
Olsen	30 (7)	2 (1)	3 (1)	35 (9)
Whiteside	26 (1)	3	5	34 (1)
Gibson	26 (3)	2	5	33 (3)
Turner	24	3	3	30
Davenport	21 (13)	1 (1)	3 (1)	25 (15)
Bruce	21	3	–	24
McGrath	21 (1)	–	2	23 (1)
Moran	20 (1)	1	2	23 (1)
Blackmore	15 (7)	1 (1)	3 (1)	19 (9)
Moses	16 (1)	1	1 (1)	18 (2)
Walsh	16	–	2	18
Hogg	9 (1)	2	– (1)	11 (2)
O'Brien	6 (11)	– (2)	– (2)	6 (15)
Garton	5 (1)	–	2 (1)	7 (2)
Albiston	5 (6)	–	–	5 (6)
Graham	1	–	– (1)	1 (1)
Martin	– (1)	–	–	– (1)

GOALSCORERS

PLAYER	LGE	FAC	LC	TOT
McClair	24	2	5	31
Robson	11	–	–	11
Whiteside	7	1	2	10
Strachan	8	–	1	9
Davenport	5	–	1	6
Blackmore	3	–	–	3
Anderson	2	1	–	3
McGrath	2	–	1	3
Bruce	2	–	–	2
Gibson	2	–	–	2
O'Brien	2	–	–	2
Olsen	2	–	–	2
own goals	1	1	–	2

1988/89

FOOTBALL LEAGUE DIVISION ONE

DATE	OPPONENTS	SCORE	GOALSCORERS	ATTENDANCE
Aug 27	QUEENS PARK RANGERS	0-0		46,377
Sep 3	Liverpool	0-1		42,026
Sep 10	MIDDLESBROUGH	1-0	Robson	40,422
Sep 17	Luton Town	2-0	Davenport, Robson	11,010
Sep 24	WEST HAM UNITED	2-0	Davenport, Hughes	39,941
Oct 1	Tottenham Hotspur	2-2	Hughes, McClair	29,318
Oct 22	Wimbledon	1-1	Hughes	12,143
Oct 26	NORWICH CITY	1-2	Hughes	36,998
Oct 30	Everton	1-1	Hughes	27,005
Nov 5	ASTON VILLA	1-1	Bruce	44,804
Nov 12	Derby County	2-2	Hughes, McClair	24,080
Nov 19	SOUTHAMPTON	2-2	Hughes, Robson	37,277
Nov 23	SHEFFIELD WEDNESDAY	1-1	Hughes	30,849
Nov 27	Newcastle United	0-0		20,350
Dec 3	CHARLTON ATHLETIC	3-0	Hughes, McClair, Milne	31,173
Dec 10	Coventry City	0-1		19,936
Dec 17	Arsenal	1-2	Hughes	37,422
Dec 26	NOTTINGHAM FOREST	2-0	Hughes, Milne	39,582
Jan 1	LIVERPOOL	3-1	Beardsmore, Hughes, McClair	44,745
Jan 2	Middlesbrough	0-1		24,411
Jan 14	MILLWALL	3-0	Blackmore, Gill, Hughes	40,931
Jan 21	West Ham United	3-1	Martin, McClair, Strachan	29,822
Feb 5	TOTTENHAM HOTSPUR	1-0	McClair	41,243
Feb 11	Sheffield Wednesday	2-0	McClair 2	34,820
Feb 25	Norwich City	1-2	McGrath	23,155
Mar 12	Aston Villa	0-0		28,332
Mar 25	LUTON TOWN	2-0	Blackmore, Milne	36,335
Mar 27	Nottingham Forest	0-2		30,092
Apr 2	ARSENAL	1-1	og	37,977
Apr 8	Millwall	0-0		17,523
Apr 15	DERBY COUNTY	0-2		34,145
Apr 22	Charlton Athletic	0-1		12,055
Apr 29	COVENTRY CITY	0-1		29,799
May 2	WIMBLEDON	1-0	McClair	23,368
May 6	Southampton	1-2	Beardsmore	17,021
May 8	Queens Park Rangers	2-3	Blackmore, Bruce	10,017
May 10	EVERTON	1-2	Hughes	26,722
May 13	NEWCASTLE UNITED	2-0	McClair, Robson	30,379

FA CUP

DATE	OPPONENTS	SCORE	GOALSCORERS	ATTENDANCE
Jan 7	QUEENS PARK RGS. (Rd3)	0-0		36,222
Jan 11	Queens Park Rgs. (Rd3R)	2-2	Gill, Graham	22,236
Jan 23	QUEENS PARK RGS. (Rd3R2)	3-0	McClair 2, Robson	46,257
Jan 28	OXFORD UNITED (Rd4)	4-0	Bruce, Hughes, Robson, og	47,745
Feb 18	Bournemouth (Rd5)	1-1	Hughes	12,708
Feb 22	BOURNEMOUTH (Rd5R)	1-0	McClair	52,422
Mar 18	NOTTINGHAM FOREST (Rd6)	0-1		55,040

LEAGUE CUP

DATE	OPPONENTS	SCORE	GOALSCORERS	ATTENDANCE
Sep 28	Rotherham United (Rd2L1)	1-0	Davenport	12,588
Oct 12	ROTHERHAM UNITED (Rd2L2)	5-0	McClair 3, Bruce, Robson	20,597
Nov 2	Wimbledon (Rd3)	1-2	Robson	10,864

FINAL LEAGUE TABLE

		P	W	D	L	F	A	Pts
1	Arsenal	38	22	10	6	73	36	76
2	Liverpool	38	22	10	6	65	28	76
3	Nottingham Forest	38	17	13	8	64	43	64
4	Norwich City	38	17	11	10	48	45	62
5	Derby County	38	17	7	14	40	38	58
6	Tottenham Hotspur	38	15	12	11	60	46	57
7	Coventry City	38	14	13	11	47	42	55
8	Everton	38	14	12	12	50	45	54
9	Queens Park Rangers	38	14	11	13	43	37	53
10	Millwall	38	14	11	13	47	52	53
11	MANCHESTER UNITED	38	13	12	13	45	35	51
12	Wimbledon	38	14	9	15	50	46	51
13	Southampton	38	10	15	13	52	66	45
14	Charlton Athletic	38	10	12	16	44	58	42
15	Sheffield Wednesday	38	10	12	16	34	51	42
16	Luton Town	38	10	11	17	42	52	41
17	Aston Villa	38	9	13	16	45	56	40
18	Middlesbrough	38	9	12	17	44	61	39
19	West Ham United	38	10	8	20	37	62	38
20	Newcastle United	38	7	10	21	32	63	31

APPEARANCES

PLAYER	LGE	FAC	LC	TOT
Bruce	38	7	3	48
Hughes	38	7	3	48
Leighton	38	7	3	48
McClair	38	7	3	48
Robson	34	6	3	43
Donaghy	30	7		37
Blackmore	26 (2)	5 (1)	3	34 (3)
Strachan	21	5	2 (1)	28 (1)
Sharpe	19 (3)	5 (1)	2	26 (4)
Milne	19 (3)	7		26 (3)
Martin	20 (4)	4 (1)		24 (5)
McGrath	18 (2)	4 (1)	1	23 (3)
Beardsmore	17 (6)	3 (2)	1 (1)	21 (9)
Duxbury	16 (2)		3	19 (2)
Garton	13 (1)	–	2	15 (1)
Davenport	7 (1)	–	1 (1)	8 (2)
Olsen	6 (4)	–	1 (1)	7 (5)
Gill	4 (5)	2 (2)	–	6 (7)
Whiteside	6	–	–	6
Anderson	5 (1)	–	– (1)	5 (2)
Robins	1 (9)	1	– (1)	2(10)
Maiorana	2 (4)	–	–	2 (4)
O'Brien	1 (2)	–	1	2 (2)
Gibson	1 (1)	–	1	2 (1)
Wilson	– (4)	– (2)	–	– (6)
Brazil	– (1)	–	–	– (1)
Graham	–	– (1)	–	– (1)

GOALSCORERS

PLAYER	LGE	FAC	LC	TOT
Hughes	14	2	–	16
McClair	10	3	3	16
Robson	4	2	2	8
Bruce	2	1	1	4
Blackmore	3	–	–	3
Milne	3	–	–	3
Davenport	2	–	1	3
Beardsmore	2	–	–	2
Gill	1	1	–	2
Martin	1	–	–	1
McGrath	1	–	–	1
Strachan	1	–	–	1
Graham	–	1	–	1
own goals	1	1	–	2

1989/90

FOOTBALL LEAGUE DIVISION ONE

DATE	OPPONENTS	SCORE	GOALSCORERS	ATTENDANCE
Aug 19	ARSENAL	4-1	Bruce, Hughes, McClair, Webb	47,245
Aug 22	Crystal Palace	1-1	Robson	22,423
Aug 26	Derby County	0-2		22,175
Aug 30	NORWICH CITY	0-2		41,610
Sep 9	Everton	2-3	Beardsmore, McClair	37,916
Sep 16	MILLWALL	5-1	Hughes 3, Robson, Sharpe	42,746
Sep 23	Manchester City	1-5	Hughes	43,246
Oct 14	SHEFFIELD WEDNESDAY	0-0		41,492
Oct 21	Coventry City	4-1	Hughes 2, Bruce, Phelan	19,625
Oct 28	SOUTHAMPTON	2-1	McClair 2	37,122
Nov 4	Charlton Athletic	0-2		16,065
Nov 12	NOTTINGHAM FOREST	1-0	Pallister	34,182
Nov 18	Luton Town	3-1	Blackmore, Hughes, Wallace	11,141
Nov 25	CHELSEA	0-0		46,975
Dec 3	Arsenal	0-1		34,484
Dec 9	CRYSTAL PALACE	1-2	Beardsmore	33,514
Dec 16	TOTTENHAM HOTSPUR	0-1		36,230
Dec 23	Liverpool	0-0		37,426
Dec 26	Aston Villa	0-3		41,247
Dec 30	Wimbledon	2-2	Hughes, Robins	9,622
Jan 1	QUEENS PARK RANGERS	0-0		34,824
Jan 13	DERBY COUNTY	1-2	Pallister	38,985
Jan 21	Norwich City	0-2		17,370
Feb 3	MANCHESTER CITY	1-1	Blackmore	40,274
Feb 10	Millwall	2-1	Hughes, Wallace	15,491
Feb 24	Chelsea	0-1		29,979
Mar 3	LUTON TOWN	4-1	Hughes, McClair, Robins, Wallace	35,327
Mar 14	EVERTON	0-0		37,398
Mar 18	LIVERPOOL	1-2	og	46,629
Mar 21	Sheffield Wednesday	0-1		33,260
Mar 24	Southampton	2-0	Gibson, Robins	20,510
Mar 31	COVENTRY CITY	3-0	Hughes 2, Robins	39,172
Apr 14	Queens Park Rangers	2-1	Robins, Webb	18,997
Apr 17	ASTON VILLA	2-0	Robins 2	44,080
Apr 21	Tottenham Hotspur	1-2	Bruce	33,317
Apr 30	WIMBLEDON	0-0		29,281
May 2	Nottingham Forest	0-4		21,186
May 5	CHARLTON ATHLETIC	1-0	Pallister	35,389

FA CUP

DATE	OPPONENTS	SCORE	GOALSCORERS	ATTENDANCE
Jan 7	Nottingham Forest (Rd3)	1-0	Robins	23,072
Jan 28	Hereford United (Rd4)	1-0	Blackmore	13,777
Feb 18	Newcastle United (Rd5)	3-2	McClair, Robins, Wallace	31,748
Mar 11	Sheffield United (Rd6)	1-0	McClair	34,344
Apr 8	Oldham Athletic (SF) (at Maine Road)	3-3	Robson, Wallace, Webb	44,026
Apr 11	Oldham Athletic (SFR) (at Maine Road)	2-1	McClair, Robins	35,005
May 12	Crystal Palace (Final) (at Wembley)	3-3	Hughes 2, Robson	80,000
May 17	Crystal Palace (Final Replay) (at Wembley)	1-0	Martin	80,000

LEAGUE CUP

DATE	OPPONENTS	SCORE	GOALSCORERS	ATTENDANCE
Sep 20	Portsmouth (Rd2L1)	3-2	Ince 2, Wallace	18,072
Oct 3	PORTSMOUTH (Rd2L2)	0-0		26,698
Oct 25	TOTTENHAM HOTSPUR (Rd3)	0-3		45,759

FINAL LEAGUE TABLE

		P	W	D	L	F	A	Pts
1	Liverpool	38	23	10	5	78	37	79
2	Aston Villa	38	21	7	10	57	38	70
3	Tottenham Hotspur	38	19	6	13	59	47	63
4	Arsenal	38	18	8	12	54	38	62
5	Chelsea	38	16	12	10	58	50	60
6	Everton	38	17	8	13	57	46	59
7	Southampton	38	15	10	13	71	63	55
8	Wimbledon	38	13	16	9	47	40	55
9	Nottingham Forest	38	15	9	14	55	47	54
10	Norwich City	38	13	14	11	44	42	53
11	Queens Park Rangers	38	13	11	14	45	44	50
12	Coventry City	38	14	7	17	39	59	49
13	MANCHESTER UNITED	38	13	9	16	46	47	48
14	Manchester City	38	12	12	14	43	52	48
15	Crystal Palace	38	13	9	16	42	66	48
16	Derby County	38	13	7	18	43	40	46
17	Luton Town	38	10	13	15	43	57	43
18	Sheffield Wednesday	38	11	10	17	35	51	43
19	Charlton Athletic	38	7	9	22	31	57	30
20	Millwall	38	5	11	22	39	65	26

APPEARANCES

PLAYER	LGE	FAC	LC	TOT
McClair	37	8	3	48
Phelan	38	7	3	48
Hughes	36 (1)	8	3	47 (1)
Pallister	35	8	3	46
Leighton	35	7	3	45
Bruce	34	7	2	43
Martin	28 (4)	8	1	37 (4)
Ince	25 (1)	6 (1)	3	34 (2)
Wallace	23 (3)	6 (1)	2	31 (4)
Robson	20	4	3	27
Blackmore	19 (9)	2 (1)	–	21(10)
Anderson	14 (2)	4	1	19 (2)
Donaghy	13 (1)	1	3	17 (1)
Duxbury	12 (7)	2 (2)	1 (1)	15(10)
Sharpe	13 (5)	–	1 (1)	14 (6)
Webb	10 (1)	4	–	14 (1)
Robins	10 (7)	3 (3)	–	13(10)
Beardsmore	8(13)	1 (2)	1	10(15)
Gibson	5 (1)	1 (1)	–	6 (2)
Sealey	2	1	–	3
Bosnich	1	–	–	1
Maiorana	– (1)	–	– (1)	– (2)
Brazil	– (1)	–	–	– (1)
Graham	– (1)	–	–	– (1)
Milne	– (1)	–	–	– (1)

GOALSCORERS

PLAYER	LGE	FAC	LC	TOT
Hughes	13	2	–	15
Robins	7	3	–	10
McClair	5	3	–	8
Wallace	3	2	1	6
Robson	2	2	–	4
Bruce	3	–	–	3
Pallister	3	–	–	3
Blackmore	2	1	–	3
Webb	2	1	–	3
Beardsmore	2	–	–	2
Ince	–	–	2	2
Gibson	1	–	–	1
Phelan	1	–	–	1
Sharpe	1	–	–	1
Martin	–	1	–	1
own goal	1	–	–	1

1990/91

FOOTBALL LEAGUE DIVISION ONE

DATE	OPPONENTS	SCORE	GOALSCORERS	ATTENDANCE
Aug 25	COVENTRY CITY	2-0	Bruce, Webb	46,715
Aug 28	Leeds United	0-0		29,174
Sep 1	Sunderland	1-2	McClair	26,105
Sep 4	Luton Town	1-0	Robins	12,576
Sep 8	QUEENS PARK RANGERS	3-1	Robins 2, McClair	43,427
Sep 16	Liverpool	0-4		35,726
Sep 22	SOUTHAMPTON	3-2	Blackmore, Hughes, McClair	41,288
Sep 29	NOTTINGHAM FOREST	0-1		46,766
Oct 20	ARSENAL	0-1		47,232
Oct 27	Manchester City	3-3	McClair 2, Hughes	36,427
Nov 3	CRYSTAL PALACE	2-0	Wallace, Webb	45,724
Nov 10	Derby County	0-0		21,115
Nov 17	SHEFFIELD UNITED	2-0	Bruce, Hughes	45,903
Nov 25	CHELSEA	2-3	Hughes, Wallace	37,836
Dec 1	Everton	1-0	Sharpe	32,400
Dec 8	LEEDS UNITED	1-1	Webb	40,927
Dec 15	Coventry City	2-2	Hughes, Wallace	17,106
Dec 22	Wimbledon	3-1	Bruce 2, Hughes	9,644
Dec 26	NORWICH CITY	3-0	McClair 2, Hughes	39,801
Dec 29	ASTON VILLA	1-1	Bruce	47,485
Jan 1	Tottenham Hotspur	2-1	Bruce, McClair	29,399
Jan 12	SUNDERLAND	3-0	Hughes 2, McClair	45,934
Jan 19	Queens Park Rangers	1-1	Phelan	18,544
Feb 3	LIVERPOOL	1-1	Bruce	43,690
Feb 26	Sheffield United	1-2	Blackmore	27,570
Mar 2	EVERTON	0-2		45,656
Mar 10	Chelsea	2-3	Hughes, McClair	22,818
Mar 13	Southampton	1-1	Ince	15,701
Mar 16	Nottingham Forest	1-1	Blackmore	23,859
Mar 23	LUTON TOWN	4-1	Bruce 2, McClair, Robins	41,752
Mar 30	Norwich City	3-0	Bruce 2, Ince	18,282
Apr 2	WIMBLEDON	2-1	Bruce, McClair	36,660
Apr 6	Aston Villa	1-1	Sharpe	33,307
Apr 16	DERBY COUNTY	3-1	Blackmore, McClair, Robson	32,776
May 4	MANCHESTER CITY	1-0	Giggs	45,286
May 6	Arsenal	1-3	Bruce	40,229
May 11	Crystal Palace	0-3		25,301
May 20	TOTTENHAM HOTSPUR	1-1	Ince	46,791

FA CUP

DATE	OPPONENTS	SCORE	GOALSCORERS	ATTENDANCE
Jan 7	QUEENS PARK RGS. (Rd3)	2-1	Hughes, McClair	35,065
Jan 26	BOLTON WANDERERS (Rd4)	1-0	Hughes	43,293
Feb 18	Norwich City (Rd5)	1-2	McClair	23,058

LEAGUE CUP

DATE	OPPONENTS	SCORE	GOALSCORERS	ATTENDANCE
Sep 26	Halifax Town (Rd2L1)	3-1	Blackmore, McClair, Webb	6,841
Oct 10	HALIFAX TOWN (Rd2L2)	2-1	Anderson, Bruce	22,295
Oct 31	LIVERPOOL (Rd3)	3-1	Bruce, Hughes, Sharpe	42,033
Nov 28	Arsenal (Rd4)	6-2	Sharpe 3, Blackmore, Hughes, Wallace	40,844
Jan 16	Southampton (Rd5)	1-1	Hughes	21,011
Jan 23	SOUTHAMPTON (Rd5R)	3-2	Hughes 3	41,903
Feb 10	LEEDS UNITED (SFL1)	2-1	McClair, Sharpe	34,050
Feb 24	Leeds United (SFL2)	1-0	Sharpe	32,014
Apr 21	Sheffield Wednesday (Final) (at Wembley)	0-1		77,612

EUROPEAN CUP-WINNERS' CUP

DATE	OPPONENTS	SCORE	GOALSCORERS	ATTENDANCE
Sep 19	PECSI MUNKAS (Rd1L1)	2-0	Blackmore, Webb	28,411
Oct 3	Pecsi Munkas (Rd1L2)	1-0	McClair	17,000
Oct 23	WREXHAM (Rd2L1)	3-0	Bruce, McClair, Pallister	29,405
Nov 7	Wrexham (Rd2L2)	2-0	Bruce, Robins	13,327
Mar 6	MONTPELLIER (Rd3L1)	1-1	McClair	41,942
Mar 19	Montpellier (Rd3L2)	2-0	Blackmore, Bruce	18,000
Apr 10	Legia Warsaw (SFL1)	3-1	Bruce, Hughes, McClair	20,000
Apr 24	LEGIA WARSAW (SFL2)	1-1	Sharpe	44,269
May 15	Barcelona (Final) (at Feyenoord Stadium, Rotterdam)	2-1	Hughes 2	50,000

FINAL LEAGUE TABLE

		P	W	D	L	F	A	Pts
1	Arsenal **	38	24	13	1	74	18	83
2	Liverpool	38	23	7	8	77	40	76
3	Crystal Palace	38	20	9	9	50	41	69
4	Leeds United	38	19	7	12	65	47	64
5	Manchester City	38	17	11	10	64	53	62
6	MANCHESTER UNITED *	38	16	12	10	58	45	59
7	Wimbledon	38	14	14	10	53	46	56
8	Nottingham Forest	38	14	12	12	65	50	54
9	Everton	38	13	12	13	50	46	51
10	Tottenham Hotspur	38	11	16	11	51	50	49
11	Chelsea	38	13	10	15	58	69	49
12	Queens Park Rangers	38	12	10	16	44	53	46
13	Sheffield United	38	13	7	18	36	55	46
14	Southampton	38	12	9	17	58	69	45
15	Norwich City	38	13	6	19	41	64	45
16	Coventry City	38	11	11	16	42	49	44
17	Aston Villa	38	9	14	15	46	58	41
18	Luton Town	38	10	7	21	42	61	37
19	Sunderland	38	8	10	20	38	60	34
20	Derby County	38	5	9	24	37	75	24

* deducted 1 point for disciplinary reasons
** deducted 2 points for disciplinary reasons

APPEARANCES

PLAYER	LGE	FAC	LC	ECWC	TOT
Pallister	36	3	9	9	57
Blackmore	35	3	9	9	56
McClair	34 (2)	3	9	9	55 (2)
Sealey	31	3	8	8	50
Irwin	33 (1)	3	7 (1)	6	49 (2)
Bruce	31	3	7	8	49
Hughes	29 (2)	3	9	7 (1)	48 (3)
Phelan	30 (3)	1	7 (1)	8	46 (4)
Webb	31 (1)	2	7	6	46 (1)
Ince	31	2	6	7	46
Sharpe	20 (3)	3	7	6 (2)	36 (5)
Robson	15 (2)	3	5	4	27 (2)
Donaghy	17 (8)	–	3 (4)	2 (3)	22 (15)
Wallace	13 (6)	– (1)	1 (3)	2 (1)	16 (11)
Martin	7 (7)	1	2 (2)	3 (2)	13 (11)
Robins	7 (12)	– (1)	– (3)	2 (1)	9 (17)
Beardsmore	5 (7)	–	1	1 (1)	7 (8)
Walsh	5	–	–	1	6
Anderson	1	–	1	1	3
Ferguson	2 (3)	–	–	–	2 (3)
Bosnich	2	–	–	–	2
Giggs	1 (1)	–	–	–	1 (1)
Kanchelskis	1	–	–	–	1
Leighton	–	–	1	–	1
Whitworth	1	–	–	–	1
Wrattan	– (2)	–	–	–	– (2)

GOALSCORERS

PLAYER	LGE	FAC	LC	ECWC	TOT
McClair	13	2	2	4	21
Hughes	10	2	6	3	21
Bruce	13	–	2	4	19
Sharpe	2	–	6	1	9
Blackmore	4	–	2	2	8
Robins	4	–	–	1	5
Webb	3	–	1	1	5
Wallace	3	–	1	–	4
Ince	3	–	–	–	3
Giggs	1	–	–	–	1
Phelan	1	–	–	–	1
Robson	1	–	–	–	1
Anderson	–	–	1	–	1
Pallister	–	–	–	1	1

1991/92

FOOTBALL LEAGUE DIVISION ONE

DATE	OPPONENTS	SCORE	GOALSCORERS	ATTENDANCE
Aug 17	NOTTS COUNTY	2-0	Hughes, Robson	46,278
Aug 21	Aston Villa	1-0	Bruce	39,995
Aug 24	Everton	0-0		36,085
Aug 28	OLDHAM ATHLETIC	1-0	McClair	42,078
Aug 31	LEEDS UNITED	1-1	Robson	43,778
Sep 3	Wimbledon	2-1	Blackmore, Pallister	13,824
Sep 7	NORWICH CITY	3-0	Giggs, Irwin, McClair	44,946
Sep 14	Southampton	1-0	Hughes	19,264
Sep 21	LUTON TOWN	5-0	McClair 2, Bruce, Hughes, Ince	46,491
Sep 28	Tottenham Hotspur	2-1	Hughes, Robson	35,087
Oct 6	LIVERPOOL	0-0		44,997
Oct 19	ARSENAL	1-1	Bruce	46,594
Oct 26	Sheffield Wednesday	2-3	McClair 2	38,260
Nov 2	SHEFFIELD UNITED	2-0	Kanchelskis, og	42,942
Nov 16	Manchester City	0-0		38,180
Nov 23	WEST HAM UNITED	2-1	Giggs, Robson	47,185
Nov 30	Crystal Palace	3-1	Kanchelskis, McClair, Webb	29,017
Dec 7	COVENTRY CITY	4-0	Bruce, Hughes, McClair, Webb	42,549
Dec 15	Chelsea	3-1	Bruce, Irwin, McClair	23,120
Dec 26	Oldham Athletic	6-3	Irwin 2, McClair 2, Kanchelskis, Giggs	18,947
Dec 29	Leeds United	1-1	Webb	32,638
Jan 1	QUEENS PARK RANGERS	1-4	McClair	38,554
Jan 11	EVERTON	1-0	Kanchelskis	46,619
Jan 18	Notts County	1-1	Blackmore	21,055
Jan 22	ASTON VILLA	1-0	Hughes	45,022
Feb 1	Arsenal	1-1	McClair	41,703
Feb 8	SHEFFIELD WEDNESDAY	1-1	McClair	47,074
Feb 22	CRYSTAL PALACE	2-0	Hughes 2	46,347
Feb 26	CHELSEA	1-1	Hughes	44,872
Feb 29	Coventry City	0-0		23,967
Mar 14	Sheffield United	2-1	Blackmore, McClair	30,183
Mar 18	Nottingham Forest	0-1		28,062
Mar 21	WIMBLEDON	0-0		45,428
Mar 28	Queens Park Rangers	0-0		22,603
Mar 31	Norwich City	3-1	Ince 2, McClair	17,489
Apr 7	MANCHESTER CITY	1-1	Giggs	46,781
Apr 16	SOUTHAMPTON	1-0	Kanchelskis	43,972
Apr 18	Luton Town	1-1	Sharpe	13,410
Apr 20	NOTTINGHAM FOREST	1-2	McClair	47,576
Apr 22	West Ham United	0-1		24,197
Apr 26	Liverpool	0-2		38,669
May 2	TOTTENHAM HOTSPUR	3-1	Hughes 2, McClair	44,595

FA CUP

DATE	OPPONENTS	SCORE	GOALSCORERS	ATTENDANCE
Jan 15	Leeds United (Rd3)	1-0	Hughes	31,819
Jan 27	Southampton (Rd4)	0-0		19,506
Feb 5	SOUTHAMPTON (Rd4R) (United lost the tie on penalty kicks)	2-2	Kanchelskis, McClair	33,414

LEAGUE CUP

DATE	OPPONENTS	SCORE	GOALSCORERS	ATTENDANCE
Sep 25	CAMBRIDGE UNITED (Rd2L1)	3-0	Bruce, Giggs, McClair	30,934
Oct 9	Cambridge United (Rd2L2)	1-1	McClair	9,248
Oct 30	PORTSMOUTH (Rd3)	3-1	Robins 2, Robson	29,543
Dec 4	OLDHAM ATHLETIC (Rd4)	2-0	Kanchelskis, McClair	38,550
Jan 8	Leeds United (Rd5)	3-1	Blackmore, Giggs, Kanchelskis	28,886
Mar 4	Middlesbrough (SFL1)	0-0		25,572
Mar 11	MIDDLESBROUGH (SFL2)	2-1	Giggs, Sharpe	45,875
Apr 12	Nottingham Forest (Final) (at Wembley)	1-0	McClair	76,810

EUROPEAN CUP-WINNERS' CUP

DATE	OPPONENTS	SCORE	GOALSCORERS	ATTENDANCE
Sep 18	Athinaikos (Rd1L1)	0-0		5,400
Oct 2	ATHINAIKOS (Rd1L2)	2-0	Hughes, McClair	35,023
Oct 23	Athletico Madrid (Rd2L1)	0-3		40,000
Nov 6	ATHLETICO MADRID (Rd2L2)	1-1	Hughes	39,654

FINAL LEAGUE TABLE

		P	W	D	L	F	A	Pts
1	Leeds United	42	22	16	4	74	37	82
2	MANCHESTER UNITED	42	21	15	6	63	33	78
3	Sheffield Wednesday	42	21	12	9	62	49	75
4	Arsenal	42	19	15	8	81	46	72
5	Manchester City	42	20	10	12	61	48	70
6	Liverpool	42	16	16	10	47	40	64
7	Aston Villa	42	17	9	16	48	44	60
8	Nottingham Forest	42	16	11	15	60	58	59
9	Sheffield United	42	16	9	17	65	63	57
10	Crystal Palace	42	14	15	13	53	61	57
11	Queens Park Rangers	42	12	18	12	48	47	54
12	Everton	42	13	14	15	52	51	53
13	Wimbledon	42	13	14	15	53	53	53
14	Chelsea	42	13	14	15	50	60	53
15	Tottenham Hotspur	42	15	7	20	58	63	52
16	Southampton	42	14	10	18	39	55	52
17	Oldham Athletic	42	14	9	19	63	67	51
18	Norwich City	42	11	12	19	47	63	45
19	Coventry City	42	11	11	20	35	44	44
20	Luton Town	42	10	12	20	38	71	42
21	Notts County	42	10	10	22	40	62	40
22	West Ham United	42	9	11	22	37	59	38

APPEARANCES

PLAYER	LGE	FAC	LC	ECWC	TOT
McClair	41 (1)	3	8	4	56 (1)
Schmeichel	40	3	6	3	52
Pallister	37 (3)	3	8	3 (1)	51 (4)
Hughes	38 (1)	2 (1)	6	4	50 (2)
Irwin	37 (1)	3	7	2	49 (1)
Bruce	37	1	7	4	49
Ince	31 (2)	3	6 (1)	3	43 (3)
Giggs	32 (6)	2 (1)	6 (2)	1	41 (9)
Webb	29 (2)	3	6	3	41 (2)
Robson	26 (1)	2	5 (1)	3	36 (2)
Kanchelskis	28 (6)	2	4	1	35 (6)
Parker	24 (2)	3	6	2	35 (2)
Blackmore	19 (14)	1	4 (1)	1	25 (15)
Donaghy	16 (4)	2	3 (1)	–	21 (5)
Phelan	14 (4)	–	2 (1)	4	20 (5)
Sharpe	8 (6)	– (1)	1 (3)	–	9 (10)
Walsh	2	–	1	1	4
Robins	1 (1)	–	– (3)	2 (1)	3 (5)
Martin	– (1)	–	1	1 (2)	2 (3)
Ferguson	2 (2)	–	–	–	2 (2)
Beardsmore	–	–	–	1 (2)	1 (2)
Wallace	–	–	–	1 (1)	1 (1)
Wilkinson	–	–	1	–	1

GOALSCORERS

PLAYER	LGE	FAC	LC	ECWC	TOT
McClair	18	1	4	1	24
Hughes	11	1	–	2	14
Kanchelskis	5	1	2	–	8
Giggs	4	–	3	–	7
Bruce	5	–	1	–	6
Robson	4	–	1	–	5
Irwin	4	–	–	–	4
Blackmore	3	–	1	–	4
Ince	3	–	–	–	3
Webb	3	–	–	–	3
Sharpe	1	–	1	–	2
Robins	–	–	2	–	2
Pallister	1	–	–	–	1
own goal	1	–	–	–	1

1992/93

FA PREMIERSHIP

DATE	OPPONENTS	SCORE	GOALSCORERS	ATTENDANCE
Aug 15	Sheffield United	1-2	Hughes	28,070
Aug 19	EVERTON	0-3		31,901
Aug 22	IPSWICH TOWN	1-1	Irwin	31,704
Aug 24	Southampton	1-0	Dublin	15,623
Aug 29	Nottingham Forest	2-0	Giggs, Hughes	19,694
Sep 2	CRYSTAL PALACE	1-0	Hughes	29,736
Sep 6	LEEDS UNITED	2-0	Bruce, Kanchelskis	31,296
Sep 12	Everton	2-0	Bruce, McClair	30,002
Sep 19	Tottenham Hotspur	1-1	Giggs	33,296
Sep 26	QUEENS PARK RANGERS	0-0		33,287
Oct 3	Middlesbrough	1-1	Bruce	24,172
Oct 18	LIVERPOOL	2-2	Hughes 2	33,243
Oct 24	Blackburn Rovers	0-0		20,305
Oct 31	WIMBLEDON	0-1		32,622
Nov 7	Aston Villa	0-1		39,063
Nov 21	OLDHAM ATHLETIC	3-0	McClair 2, Hughes	33,497
Nov 28	Arsenal	1-0	Hughes	29,739
Dec 6	MANCHESTER CITY	2-1	Hughes, Ince	35,408
Dec 12	NORWICH CITY	1-0	Hughes	34,500
Dec 19	Chelsea	1-1	Cantona	34,464
Dec 26	Sheffield Wednesday	3-3	McClair 2, Cantona	37,708
Dec 28	COVENTRY CITY	5-0	Cantona, Giggs, Hughes, Irwin, Sharpe	36,025
Jan 9	TOTTENHAM HOTSPUR	4-1	Cantona, Irwin, McClair, Parker	35,648
Jan 18	Queens Park Rangers	3-1	Giggs, Ince, Kanchelskis	21,117
Jan 27	NOTTINGHAM FOREST	2-0	Hughes, Ince	36,085
Jan 30	Ipswich Town	1-2	McClair	22,068
Feb 6	SHEFFIELD UNITED	2-1	Cantona, McClair	36,156
Feb 8	Leeds United	0-0		34,166
Feb 20	SOUTHAMPTON	2-1	Giggs 2	36,257
Feb 27	MIDDLESBROUGH	3-0	Cantona, Giggs, Irwin	36,251
Mar 6	Liverpool	2-1	Hughes, McClair	44,374
Mar 9	Oldham Athletic	0-1		17,106
Mar 14	ASTON VILLA	1-1	Hughes	36,163
Mar 20	Manchester City	1-1	Cantona	37,136
Mar 24	ARSENAL	0-0		37,301
Apr 5	Norwich City	3-1	Cantona, Giggs, Kanchelskis	20,582
Apr 10	SHEFFIELD WEDNESDAY	2-1	Bruce 2	40,102
Apr 12	Coventry City	1-0	Irwin	24,249
Apr 17	CHELSEA	3-0	Cantona, Hughes, og	40,139
Apr 21	Crystal Palace	2-0	Hughes, Ince	30,115
May 3	BLACKBURN ROVERS	3-1	Giggs, Ince, Pallister	40,447
May 9	Wimbledon	2-1	Ince, Robson	30,115

FA CUP

DATE	OPPONENTS	SCORE	GOALSCORERS	ATTENDANCE
Jan 5	BURY (Rd3)	2-0	Gillespie, Phelan	30,668
Jan 23	BRIGHTON (Rd4)	1-0	Giggs	33,600
Feb 14	Sheffield United (Rd5)	1-2	Giggs	27,150

LEAGUE CUP

DATE	OPPONENTS	SCORE	GOALSCORERS	ATTENDANCE
Sep 23	Brighton (Rd2L1)	1-1	Wallace	16,649
Oct 7	BRIGHTON (Rd2L2)	1-0	Hughes	25,405
Oct 28	Aston Villa (Rd3)	0-1		35,964

UEFA CUP

DATE	OPPONENTS	SCORE	GOALSCORERS	ATTENDANCE
Sep 16	TORPEDO MOSCOW (Rd1L1)	0-0		19,998
Sep 29	Torpedo Moscow (Rd1L2)	0-0		11,357

(United lost the tie on penalty kicks)

FINAL LEAGUE TABLE

		P	W	D	L	F	A	Pts
1	MANCHESTER UNITED	42	24	12	6	67	31	84
2	Aston Villa	42	21	11	10	57	40	74
3	Norwich City	42	21	9	12	61	65	72
4	Blackburn Rovers	42	20	11	11	68	46	71
5	Queens Park Rangers	42	17	12	13	63	55	63
6	Liverpool	42	16	11	15	62	55	59
7	Sheffield Wednesday	42	15	14	13	55	51	59
8	Tottenham Hotspur	42	16	11	15	60	66	59
9	Manchester City	42	15	12	15	56	51	57
10	Arsenal	42	15	11	16	40	38	56
11	Chelsea	42	14	14	14	51	54	56
12	Wimbledon	42	14	12	16	56	55	54
13	Everton	42	15	8	19	53	55	53
14	Sheffield United	42	14	10	18	54	53	52
15	Coventry City	42	13	13	16	52	57	52
16	Ipswich Town	42	12	16	14	50	55	52
17	Leeds United	42	12	15	15	57	62	51
18	Southampton	42	13	11	18	54	61	50
19	Oldham Athletic	42	13	10	19	63	74	49
20	Crystal Palace	42	11	16	15	48	61	49
21	Middlesbrough	42	11	11	20	54	75	44
22	Nottingham Forest	42	10	10	22	41	62	40

APPEARANCES

PLAYER	PREM	FAC	LC	UC	TOT
Bruce	42	3	3	2	50
Pallister	42	3	3	2	50
McClair	41 (1)	3	3	2	49 (1)
Hughes	41	2	3	2	48
Irwin	40	3	3	2	48
Schmeichel	42	3	2	1	48
Ince	41	2	3	1	47
Giggs	40 (1)	2	2	1	45 (1)
Parker	31	3	2	- (1)	36 (1)
Sharpe	27	3	-	-	30
Cantona	21 (1)	1	-	-	22 (1)
Kanchelskis	14 (13)	1	2 (1)	1	18 (14)
Ferguson	15	-	1	-	16
Blackmore	12 (2)	- (1)	1	1	14 (3)
Phelan	5 (6)	2	-	1	8 (6)
Robson	5 (9)	- (1)	1	- (1)	6 (11)
Wallace	- (2)	1	1	2	4 (2)
Dublin	3 (4)	-	-	-	3 (4)
Webb	- (1)	-	1	2	3 (1)
Martin	-	-	1	1	2
Walsh	-	-	1	1	2
Gillespie	-	1 (1)	-	-	1 (1)
Beckham	-	-	- (1)	-	- (1)
Butt	- (1)	-	-	-	- (1)
Neville	-	-	-	- (1)	- (1)

GOALSCORERS

PLAYER	PREM	FAC	LC	UC	TOT
Hughes	15	-	1	-	16
Giggs	9	2	-	-	11
Cantona	9	-	-	-	9
McClair	9	-	-	-	9
Ince	6	-	-	-	6
Bruce	5	-	-	-	5
Irwin	5	-	-	-	5
Kanchelskis	3	-	-	-	3
Dublin	1	-	-	-	1
Pallister	1	-	-	-	1
Parker	1	-	-	-	1
Robson	1	-	-	-	1
Sharpe	1	-	-	-	1
Gillespie	-	1	-	-	1
Phelan	-	1	-	-	1
Wallace	-	-	1	-	1
own goal	1	-	-	-	1

1993/94

FA PREMIERSHIP

DATE	OPPONENTS	SCORE	GOALSCORERS	ATTENDANCE
Aug 15	Norwich City	2-0	Giggs, Robson	19,705
Aug 18	SHEFFIELD UNITED	3-0	Keane 2, Hughes	41,949
Aug 21	NEWCASTLE UNITED	1-1	Giggs	41,829
Aug 23	Aston Villa	2-1	Sharpe 2	39,624
Aug 28	Southampton	3-1	Cantona, Irwin, Sharpe	16,189
Sep 1	WEST HAM UNITED	3-0	Bruce, Cantona, Sharpe	44,613
Sep 11	Chelsea	0-1		37,064
Sep 19	ARSENAL	1-0	Cantona	44,009
Sep 25	SWINDON TOWN	4-2	Hughes 2, Cantona, Kanchelskis	44,583
Oct 2	Sheffield Wednesday	3-2	Hughes 2, Giggs	34,548
Oct 16	TOTTENHAM HOTSPUR	2-1	Keane, Sharpe	44,655
Oct 23	Everton	1-0	Sharpe	35,430
Oct 30	QUEENS PARK RANGERS	2-1	Cantona, Hughes	44,663
Nov 7	Manchester City	3-2	Cantona 2, Keane	35,155
Nov 20	WIMBLEDON	3-1	Hughes, Kanchelskis, Pallister	44,748
Nov 24	IPSWICH TOWN	0-0		43,300
Nov 27	Coventry City	1-0	Cantona	17,020
Dec 4	NORWICH CITY	2-2	Giggs, McClair	44,694
Dec 7	Sheffield United	3-0	Cantona, Hughes, Sharpe	26,746
Dec 11	Newcastle United	1-1	Ince	36,388
Dec 19	ASTON VILLA	3-1	Cantona 2, Ince	44,499
Dec 26	BLACKBURN ROVERS	1-1	Ince	44,511
Dec 29	Oldham Athletic	5-2	Giggs 2, Bruce, Cantona, Kanchelskis	16,708
Jan 1	LEEDS UNITED	0-0		44,724
Jan 4	Liverpool	3-3	Bruce, Giggs, Irwin	42,795
Jan 15	Tottenham Hotspur	1-0	Hughes	31,343
Jan 22	EVERTON	1-0	Giggs	44,750
Feb 5	Queens Park Rangers	3-2	Cantona, Giggs, Kanchelskis	21,267
Feb 26	West Ham United	2-2	Hughes, Ince	28,832
Mar 5	CHELSEA	0-1		44,745
Mar 16	SHEFFIELD WEDNESDAY	5-0	Cantona 2, Giggs, Hughes, Ince	43,669
Mar 19	Swindon Town	2-2	Ince, Keane	18,102
Mar 22	Arsenal	2-2	Sharpe 2	36,203
Mar 30	LIVERPOOL	1-0	Ince	44,751
Apr 2	Blackburn Rovers	0-2		20,886
Apr 4	OLDHAM ATHLETIC	3-2	Dublin, Giggs, Ince	44,686
Apr 16	Wimbledon	0-1		28,553
Apr 23	MANCHESTER CITY	2-0	Cantona 2	44,333
Apr 27	Leeds United	2-0	Giggs, Kanchelskis	41,125
May 1	Ipswich Town	2-1	Cantona, Giggs	22,559
May 4	SOUTHAMPTON	2-0	Hughes, Kanchelskis	44,705
May 8	COVENTRY CITY	0-0		44,717

FA CUP

DATE	OPPONENTS	SCORE	GOALSCORERS	ATTENDANCE
Jan 9	Sheffield United (Rd3)	1-0	Hughes	22,019
Jan 30	Norwich City (Rd4)	2-0	Cantona, Keane	21,060
Feb 20	Wimbledon (Rd5)	3-0	Cantona, Ince, Irwin	27,511
Mar 12	CHARLTON ATHLETIC (Rd6)	3-1	Kanchelskis 2, Hughes	44,347
Apr 10	Oldham Athletic (SF) (at Wembley)	1-1	Hughes	56,399
Apr 13	Oldham Athletic (SFR) (at Maine Road)	4-1	Giggs, Irwin, Kanchelskis, Robson	32,311

FA CUP

DATE	OPPONENTS	SCORE	GOALSCORERS	ATTENDANCE
May 14	Chelsea (Final) (at Wembley)	4-0	Cantona 2, Hughes, McClair	79,634

LEAGUE CUP

DATE	OPPONENTS	SCORE	GOALSCORERS	ATTENDANCE
Sep 22	Stoke City (Rd2L1)	1-2	Dublin	23,327
Oct 6	STOKE CITY (Rd2L2)	2-0	McClair, Sharpe	41,387
Oct 27	LEICESTER CITY (Rd3)	5-1	Bruce 2, Hughes, McClair, Sharpe	41,344
Nov 30	Everton (Rd4)	2-0	Giggs, Hughes	34,052
Jan 12	PORTSMOUTH (Rd5)	2-2	Cantona, Giggs	43,794
Jan 26	Portsmouth (Rd5R)	1-0	McClair	24,950
Feb 13	SHEFFIELD WEDNESDAY (SFL1)	1-0	Giggs	43,294
Mar 2	Sheffield Wednesday (SFL2)	4-1	Hughes 2, Kanchelskis, McClair	34,878
Mar 27	Aston Villa (Final) (at Wembley)	1-3	Hughes	77,231

EUROPEAN CUP

DATE	OPPONENTS	SCORE	GOALSCORERS	ATTENDANCE
Sep 15	Honved (Rd1L1)	3-2	Keane 2, Cantona	9,000
Sep 29	HONVED (Rd1L2)	2-1	Bruce 2	35,781
Oct 20	GALATASARAY (Rd2L1)	3-3	Cantona, Robson, og	39,346
Nov 3	Galatasaray (Rd2L2)	0-0		40,000

(United lost the tie on away goals rule)

FINAL LEAGUE TABLE

		P	W	D	L	F	A	Pts
1	MANCHESTER UNITED	42	27	11	4	80	38	92
2	Blackburn Rovers	42	25	9	8	63	36	84
3	Newcastle United	42	23	8	11	82	41	77
4	Arsenal	42	18	17	7	53	28	71
5	Leeds United	42	18	16	8	65	39	70
6	Wimbledon	42	18	11	13	56	53	65
7	Sheffield Wednesday	42	16	16	10	76	54	64
8	Liverpool	42	17	9	16	59	55	60
9	Queens Park Rangers	42	16	12	14	62	61	60
10	Aston Villa	42	15	12	15	46	50	57
11	Coventry City	42	14	14	14	43	45	56
12	Norwich City	42	12	17	13	65	61	53
13	West Ham United	42	13	13	16	47	58	52
14	Chelsea	42	13	12	17	49	53	51
15	Tottenham Hotspur	42	11	12	19	54	59	45
16	Manchester City	42	9	18	15	38	49	45
17	Everton	42	12	8	22	42	63	44
18	Southampton	42	12	7	23	49	66	43
19	Ipswich Town	42	9	16	17	35	58	43
20	Sheffield United	42	8	18	16	42	60	42
21	Oldham Athletic	42	9	13	20	42	68	40
22	Swindon Town	42	5	15	22	47	100	30

APPEARANCES

PLAYER	PREM	FAC	LC	EC	TOT
Bruce	41	7	8 (1)	4	60 (1)
Irwin	42	7	8 (1)	3	60 (1)
Pallister	41	7	9	3	60
Schmeichel	40	7	8	4	59
Parker	39 (1)	7	6	3	55 (1)
Ince	39	7	5	4	55
Hughes	36	7	8	2	53
Giggs	32 (6)	7	6 (2)	4	49 (8)
Keane	34 (3)	6	6 (1)	3	49 (4)
Cantona	34	5	5	4	48
Kanchelskis	28 (3)	6	9	-	43 (3)
Sharpe	26 (4)	1 (2)	2 (2)	4	33 (8)
McClair	12 (14)	1 (4)	6 (1)	-	19 (19)
Robson	10 (5)	1 (1)	5	4	20 (6)
Martin	1	-	3	1 (1)	5 (1)
Phelan	1 (1)	-	2	1 (3)	4 (4)
Dublin	1 (4)	1 (1)	1 (1)	- (1)	3 (7)
Ferguson	1 (2)	-	1 (1)	-	2 (3)
Walsh	2 (1)	-	-	-	2 (1)
Neville	1	-	-	- (1)	1 (1)
Sealey	-	- (1)	1	-	1 (1)
McKee	1	-	-	-	1
Butt	- (1)	- (1)	-	-	- (2)
Thornley	- (1)	-	-	-	- (1)

GOALSCORERS

PLAYER	PREM	FAC	LC	EC	TOT
Cantona	18	4	1	2	25
Hughes	12	4	5	-	21
Giggs	13	1	3	-	17
Sharpe	9	-	2	-	11
Kanchelskis	6	3	1	-	10
Ince	8	1	-	-	9
Keane	5	1	-	2	8
Bruce	3	-	2	2	7
McClair	1	1	4	-	6
Irwin	2	2	-	-	4
Robson	1	1	-	1	3
Dublin	1	-	1	-	2
Pallister	1	-	-	-	1
own goal	-	-	-	1	1

1994/95

FA PREMIERSHIP

DATE	OPPONENTS	SCORE	GOALSCORERS	ATTENDANCE
Aug 20	QUEENS PARK RANGERS	2-0	Hughes, McClair	43,214
Aug 22	Nottingham Forest	1-1	Kanchelskis	22,072
Aug 27	Tottenham Hotspur	1-0	Bruce	24,502
Aug 31	WIMBLEDON	3-0	Cantona, Giggs, McClair	43,440
Sep 11	Leeds United	1-2	Cantona	39,396
Sep 17	LIVERPOOL	2-0	Kanchelskis, McClair	43,740
Sep 24	Ipswich Town	2-3	Cantona, Scholes	22,559
Oct 1	EVERTON	2-0	Kanchelskis, Sharpe	43,803
Oct 8	Sheffield Wednesday	0-1		33,441
Oct 15	WEST HAM UNITED	1-0	Cantona	43,795
Oct 24	Blackburn Rovers	4-2	Kanchelskis 2, Cantona, Hughes	30,260
Oct 29	NEWCASTLE UNITED	2-0	Gillespie, Pallister	43,795
Nov 6	Aston Villa	2-1	Ince, Kanchelskis	32,136
Nov 10	MANCHESTER CITY	5-0	Kanchelskis 3, Cantona, Hughes	43,738
Nov 19	CRYSTAL PALACE	3-0	Cantona, Irwin, Kanchelskis	43,788
Nov 26	Arsenal	0-0		38,301
Dec 3	NORWICH CITY	1-0	Cantona	43,789
Dec 10	Queens Park Rangers	3-2	Scholes 2, Keane	18,948
Dec 17	NOTTINGHAM FOREST	1-2	Cantona	43,744
Dec 26	Chelsea	3-2	Cantona, Hughes, McClair	31,161
Dec 28	LEICESTER CITY	1-1	Kanchelskis	43,789
Dec 31	Southampton	2-2	Butt, Pallister	15,204
Jan 3	COVENTRY CITY	2-0	Cantona, Scholes	43,130
Jan 15	Newcastle United	1-1	Hughes	34,471
Jan 22	BLACKBURN ROVERS	1-0	Cantona	43,742
Jan 25	Crystal Palace	1-1	May	18,224
Feb 4	ASTON VILLA	1-0	Cole	43,795
Feb 11	Manchester City	3-0	Cole, Ince, Kanchelskis	26,368
Feb 22	Norwich City	2-0	Ince, Kanchelskis	21,824
Feb 25	Everton	0-1		40,011
Mar 4	IPSWICH TOWN	9-0	Cole 5, Hughes 2, Ince, Keane	43,804
Mar 7	Wimbledon	1-0	Bruce	18,224
Mar 15	TOTTENHAM HOTSPUR	0-0		43,802
Mar 19	Liverpool	0-2		38,906
Mar 22	ARSENAL	3-0	Hughes, Kanchelskis, Sharpe	43,623
Apr 2	LEEDS UNITED	0-0		43,712
Apr 15	Leicester City	4-0	Cole 2, Ince, Sharpe	21,281
Apr 17	CHELSEA	0-0		43,728
May 1	Coventry City	3-2	Cole 2, Scholes	21,885
May 7	SHEFFIELD WEDNESDAY	1-0	May	43,868
May 10	SOUTHAMPTON	2-1	Cole, Irwin	43,479
May 14	West Ham United	1-1	McClair	24,783

FA CUP

DATE	OPPONENTS	SCORE	GOALSCORERS	ATTENDANCE
Jan 9	Sheffield United (Rd3)	2-0	Cantona, Hughes	22,322
Jan 28	WREXHAM (Rd4)	5-2	Irwin 2, Giggs, McClair, og	43,222
Feb 19	LEEDS UNITED (Rd5)	3-1	Bruce, Hughes, McClair	42,744
Mar 12	QUEENS PARK RGS. (Rd6)	2-0	Irwin, Sharpe	42,830

FA CUP

DATE	OPPONENTS	SCORE	GOALSCORERS	ATTENDANCE
Apr 9	Crystal Palace (SF) (at Villa Park)	2-2	Irwin, Pallister	38,256
Apr 12	Crystal Palace (SFR) (at Villa Park)	2-0	Bruce, Pallister	17,987
May 20	Everton (Final) (at Wembley)	0-1		79,592

LEAGUE CUP

DATE	OPPONENTS	SCORE	GOALSCORERS	ATTENDANCE
Sep 21	Port Vale (Rd2L1)	2-1	Scholes 2	18,605
Oct 5	PORT VALE (Rd2L2)	2-0	May, McClair	31,615
Oct 26	Newcastle United (Rd3)	0-2		34,178

CHAMPIONS LEAGUE

DATE	OPPONENTS	SCORE	GOALSCORERS	ATTENDANCE
Sep 14	GOTHENBURG (P1)	4-2	Giggs 2, Kanchelskis, Sharpe	33,625
Sep 28	Galatasaray (P1)	0-0		28,605
Oct 19	BARCELONA (P1)	2-2	Hughes, Sharpe	40,064
Nov 2	Barcelona (P1)	0-4		114,273
Nov 23	Gothenburg (P1)	1-3	Hughes	36,350
Dec 7	GALATASARAY (P1)	4-0	Beckham, Davies, Keane, og	39,220

United failed to qualify from the group phase

FINAL LEAGUE TABLE

		P	W	D	L	F	A	Pts
1	Blackburn Rovers	42	27	8	7	80	39	89
2	MANCHESTER UNITED	42	26	10	6	77	28	88
3	Nottingham Forest	42	22	11	9	72	43	77
4	Liverpool	42	21	11	10	65	37	74
5	Leeds United	42	20	13	9	59	38	73
6	Newcastle United	42	20	12	10	67	47	72
7	Tottenham Hotspur	42	16	14	12	66	58	62
8	Queens Park Rangers	42	17	9	16	61	59	60
9	Wimbledon	42	15	11	16	48	65	56
10	Southampton	42	12	18	12	61	63	54
11	Chelsea	42	13	15	14	50	55	54
12	Arsenal	42	13	12	17	52	49	51
13	Sheffield Wednesday	42	13	12	17	49	57	51
14	West Ham United	42	13	11	18	44	48	50
15	Everton	42	11	17	14	44	51	50
16	Coventry City	42	12	14	16	44	62	50
17	Manchester City	42	12	13	17	53	64	49
18	Aston Villa	42	11	15	16	51	56	48
19	Crystal Palace	42	11	12	19	34	49	45
20	Norwich City	42	10	13	19	37	54	43
21	Leicester City	42	6	11	25	45	80	29
22	Ipswich Town	42	7	6	29	36	93	27

APPEARANCES

PLAYER	PREM	FAC	LC	CL	TOT
Pallister	42	7	2	6	57
Irwin	40	7	2	5	54
Ince	36	6	–	5	47
McClair	35 (5)	6 (1)	3	2	46 (6)
Bruce	35	5	1	5 (1)	46 (1)
Hughes	33 (1)	6	–	5	44 (1)
Schmeichel	32	7	–	3	42
Giggs	29	6 (1)	–	3	38 (1)
Sharpe	26 (2)	6 (1)	– (2)	3	35 (5)
Keane	23 (2)	6 (1)	1	4	34 (3)
Kanchelskis	25 (5)	2 (1)	–	5	32 (6)
Cantona	21	1	–	2	24
Neville G	16 (2)	4	2 (1)	1 (1)	23 (4)
Butt	11 (11)	3 (1)	3	5 (1)	22 (13)
May	15 (4)	1	2	4	22 (4)
Cole	17 (1)	–	–	–	17 (1)
Walsh	10	–	3	3	16
Scholes	6 (11)	1 (2)	3	– (2)	10 (15)
Davies	3 (2)	–	3	2	8 (2)
Beckham	2 (2)	1 (1)	3	1	7 (3)
Gillespie	3 (6)	–	3	–	6 (6)
Parker	1 (1)	–	–	2 (1)	3 (2)
Neville P	1 (1)	1	–	–	2 (1)
O'Kane	–	1	1 (1)	–	2 (1)
Casper	–	–	1	–	1
Tomlinson	–	–	– (2)	–	– (2)
Pilkington	– (1)	–	–	–	– (1)

GOALSCORERS

PLAYER	PREM	FAC	LC	CL	TOT
Kanchelskis	14	–	–	1	15
Cantona	12	1	–	–	13
Cole	12	–	–	–	12
Hughes	8	2	–	2	12
McClair	5	2	1	–	8
Scholes	5	–	2	–	7
Sharpe	3	1	–	2	6
Irwin	2	4	–	–	6
Ince	5	–	–	–	5
Bruce	2	2	–	–	4
Pallister	2	2	–	–	4
Giggs	1	1	–	2	4
Keane	2	–	–	1	3
May	2	–	1	–	3
Butt	1	–	–	–	1
Gillespie	1	–	–	–	1
Beckham	–	–	–	1	1
Davies	–	–	–	1	1
own goals	–	1	–	1	2

1995/96

FA PREMIERSHIP

DATE	OPPONENTS	SCORE	GOALSCORERS	ATTENDANCE
Aug 19	Aston Villa	1-3	Beckham	34,655
Aug 23	WEST HAM UNITED	2-1	Keane, Scholes	31,966
Aug 26	WIMBLEDON	3-1	Keane 2, Cole	32,226
Aug 28	Blackburn Rovers	2-1	Beckham, Sharpe	29,843
Sep 9	Everton	3-2	Sharpe 2, Giggs	39,496
Sep 16	BOLTON WANDERERS	3-0	Scholes 2, Giggs	32,812
Sep 23	Sheffield Wednesday	0-0		34,101
Oct 1	LIVERPOOL	2-2	Butt, Cantona	34,934
Oct 14	MANCHESTER CITY	1-0	Scholes	35,707
Oct 21	Chelsea	4-1	Scholes 2, Giggs, McClair	31,019
Oct 28	MIDDLESBROUGH	2-0	Cole, Pallister	36,580
Nov 4	Arsenal	0-1		38,317
Nov 18	SOUTHAMPTON	4-1	Giggs 2, Cole, Scholes	39,301
Nov 22	Coventry City	4-0	McClair 2, Beckham, Irwin	23,400
Nov 27	Nottingham Forest	1-1	Cantona	29,263
Dec 2	CHELSEA	1-1	Beckham	42,019
Dec 9	SHEFFIELD WEDNESDAY	2-2	Cantona 2	41,849
Dec 17	Liverpool	0-2		40,546
Dec 24	Leeds United	1-3	Cole	39,801
Dec 27	NEWCASTLE UNITED	2-0	Cole, Keane	42,024
Dec 30	QUEENS PARK RANGERS	2-1	Cole, Giggs	41,890
Jan 1	Tottenham Hotspur	1-4	Cole	32,852
Jan 13	ASTON VILLA	0-0		42,667
Jan 22	West Ham United	1-0	Cantona	24,197
Feb 3	Wimbledon	4-2	Cantona 2, Cole, og	25,380
Feb 10	BLACKBURN ROVERS	1-0	Sharpe	42,681
Feb 21	EVERTON	2-0	Keane, Giggs	42,459
Feb 25	Bolton Wanderers	6-0	Scholes 2, Beckham, Bruce, Butt, Cole	21,381
Mar 4	Newcastle United	1-0	Cantona	36,584
Mar 16	Queens Park Rangers	1-1	Cantona	18,817
Mar 20	ARSENAL	1-0	Cantona	50,028
Mar 24	TOTTENHAM HOTSPUR	1-0	Cantona	50,157
Apr 6	Manchester City	3-2	Cantona, Cole, Giggs	29,668
Apr 8	COVENTRY CITY	1-0	Cantona	50,332
Apr 13	Southampton	1-3	Giggs	15,262
Apr 17	LEEDS UNITED	1-0	Keane	48,382
Apr 28	NOTTINGHAM FOREST	5-0	Beckham 2, Cantona, Giggs, Scholes	53,926
May 5	Middlesbrough	3-0	Cole, Giggs, May	29,921

FA CUP

DATE	OPPONENTS	SCORE	GOALSCORERS	ATTENDANCE
Jan 6	SUNDERLAND (Rd3)	2-2	Butt, Cantona	41,563
Jan 16	Sunderland (Rd3R)	2-1	Cole, Scholes	21,378
Jan 27	Reading (Rd4)	3-0	Cantona, Giggs, Parker	14,780
Feb 18	MANCHESTER CITY (Rd5)	2-1	Cantona, Sharpe	42,692
Mar 11	SOUTHAMPTON (Rd6)	2-0	Cantona, Sharpe	45,446
Mar 31	Chelsea (SF) (at Villa Park)	2-1	Beckham, Cole	38,421
May 11	Liverpool (Final) (at Wembley)	1-0	Cantona	79,007

LEAGUE CUP

DATE	OPPONENTS	SCORE	GOALSCORERS	ATTENDANCE
Sep 20	YORK CITY (Rd2L1)	0-3		29,049
Oct 3	York City (Rd2L2)	3-1	Scholes 2, Cooke	9,386

UEFA CUP

DATE	OPPONENTS	SCORE	GOALSCORERS	ATTENDANCE
Sep 12	Rotor Volgograd (Rd1L1)	0-0		33,000
Sep 26	ROTOR VOLGOGRAD (Rd1L2)	2-2	Schmeichel, Scholes (United lost the tie on away goals rule)	29,724

FINAL LEAGUE TABLE

		P	W	D	L	F	A	Pts
1	MANCHESTER UNITED	38	25	7	6	73	35	82
2	Newcastle United	38	24	6	8	66	37	78
3	Liverpool	38	20	11	7	70	34	71
4	Aston Villa	38	18	9	11	52	35	63
5	Arsenal	38	17	12	9	49	32	63
6	Everton	38	17	10	11	64	44	61
7	Blackburn Rovers	38	18	7	13	61	47	61
8	Tottenham Hotspur	38	16	13	9	50	38	61
9	Nottingham Forest	38	15	13	10	50	54	58
10	West Ham United	38	14	9	15	43	52	51
11	Chelsea	38	12	14	12	46	44	50
12	Middlesbrough	38	11	10	17	35	50	43
13	Leeds United	38	12	7	19	40	57	43
14	Wimbledon	38	10	11	17	55	70	41
15	Sheffield Wednesday	38	10	10	18	48	61	40
16	Coventry City	38	8	14	16	42	60	38
17	Southampton	38	9	11	18	34	52	38
18	Manchester City	38	9	11	18	33	58	38
19	Queens Park Rangers	38	9	6	23	38	57	33
20	Bolton Wanderers	38	8	5	25	39	71	29

APPEARANCES

PLAYER	PREM	FAC	LC	UC	TOT
Schmeichel	36	6	1	2	45
Giggs	30 (3)	7	2	2	41 (3)
Cole	32 (2)	7	1	1	41 (2)
Butt	31 (1)	7	–	2	40 (1)
Irwin	31	6	1	1	39
Bruce	30	5	1 (1)	2	38 (1)
Keane	29	7	– (1)	2	38 (1)
Cantona	30	7	1	–	38
Neville G	30 (1)	5 (1)	1	1	37 (2)
Beckham	26 (7)	3	2	2	33 (7)
Sharpe	21 (10)	4 (2)	2	2	29 (12)
Neville P	21 (3)	6 (1)	1 (1)	1	29 (5)
Pallister	21	3	2	2	28
Scholes	16 (10)	– (2)	1	1 (1)	18 (13)
McClair	12 (10)	–	1	–	13 (10)
May	11 (5)	2	–	–	13 (5)
Parker	5 (1)	1 (1)	1	– (1)	7 (3)
Pilkington	2 (1)	1	1	–	4 (1)
Davies	1 (5)	–	1	– (1)	2 (6)
Cooke	1 (3)	–	1 (1)	– (1)	2 (5)
Prunier	2	–	–	–	2
O'Kane	– (1)	–	–	1	1 (1)
McGibbon	–	–	1	–	1
Thornley	– (1)	–	–	–	– (1)

GOALSCORERS

PLAYER	PREM	FAC	LC	UC	TOT
Cantona	14	5	–	–	19
Scholes	10	1	2	1	14
Cole	11	2	–	–	13
Giggs	11	1	–	–	12
Beckham	7	1	–	–	8
Keane	6	–	–	–	6
Sharpe	4	2	–	–	6
McClair	3	–	–	–	3
Butt	2	1	–	–	3
Bruce	1	–	–	–	1
Irwin	1	–	–	–	1
May	1	–	–	–	1
Pallister	1	–	–	–	1
Cooke	–	–	1	–	1
Parker	–	1	–	–	1
Schmeichel	–	–	–	1	1
own goal	1	–	–	–	1

1996/97

FA PREMIERSHIP

DATE	OPPONENTS	SCORE	GOALSCORERS	ATTENDANCE
Aug 17	Wimbledon	3-0	Beckham, Cantona, Irwin	25,786
Aug 21	EVERTON	2-2	Cruyff, og	54,943
Aug 25	BLACKBURN ROVERS	2-2	Cruyff, Solskjaer	54,178
Sep 4	Derby County	1-1	Beckham	18,026
Sep 7	Leeds United	4-0	Butt, Cantona, Poborsky, og	39,694
Sep 14	NOTTINGHAM FOREST	4-1	Cantona 2, Giggs, Solskjaer	54,984
Sep 21	Aston Villa	0-0		39,339
Sep 29	TOTTENHAM HOTSPUR	2-0	Solskjaer 2	54,943
Oct 12	LIVERPOOL	1-0	Beckham	55,128
Oct 20	Newcastle United	0-5		35,579
Oct 26	Southampton	3-6	Beckham, May, Scholes	15,253
Nov 2	CHELSEA	1-2	May	55,198
Nov 16	ARSENAL	1-0	og	55,210
Nov 23	Middlesbrough	2-2	Keane, May	30,063
Nov 30	LEICESTER CITY	3-1	Butt 2, Solskjaer	55,196
Dec 8	West Ham United	2-2	Beckham, Solskjaer	25,045
Dec 18	Sheffield Wednesday	1-1	Scholes	37,671
Dec 21	SUNDERLAND	5-0	Cantona 2, Solskjaer 2, Butt	55,081
Dec 26	Nottingham Forest	4-0	Butt, Beckham, Cole, Solskjaer	29,032
Dec 28	LEEDS UNITED	1-0	Cantona	55,256
Jan 1	ASTON VILLA	0-0		55,133
Jan 12	Tottenham Hotspur	2-1	Beckham, Solskjaer	33,026
Jan 18	Coventry City	2-0	Giggs, Solskjaer	23,085
Jan 29	WIMBLEDON	2-1	Cole, Giggs	55,314
Feb 1	SOUTHAMPTON	2-1	Cantona, Pallister	55,269
Feb 19	Arsenal	2-1	Cole, Solskjaer	38,172
Feb 22	Chelsea	1-1	Beckham	28,336
Mar 1	COVENTRY CITY	3-1	Poborsky, og 2	55,230
Mar 8	Sunderland	1-2	og	22,225
Mar 15	SHEFFIELD WEDNESDAY	2-0	Cole, Poborsky	55,267
Mar 22	Everton	2-0	Cantona, Solskjaer	40,079
Apr 5	DERBY COUNTY	2-3	Cantona, Solskjaer	55,243
Apr 12	Blackburn Rovers	3-2	Cantona, Cole, Scholes	30,476
Apr 19	Liverpool	3-1	Pallister 2, Cole	40,892
May 3	Leicester City	2-2	Solskjaer 2	21,068
May 5	MIDDLESBROUGH	3-3	Keane, Neville G, Solskjaer	54,489
May 8	NEWCASTLE UNITED	0-0		55,236
May 11	WEST HAM UNITED	2-0	Cruyff, Solskjaer	55,249

FA CUP

DATE	OPPONENTS	SCORE	GOALSCORERS	ATTENDANCE
Jan 5	TOTTENHAM HOTSPUR (Rd3)	2-0	Beckham, Scholes	52,445
Jan 25	WIMBLEDON (Rd4)	1-1	Scholes	53,342
Feb 4	Wimbledon (Rd4R)	0-1		25,601

LEAGUE CUP

DATE	OPPONENTS	SCORE	GOALSCORERS	ATTENDANCE
Oct 23	SWINDON TOWN (Rd3)	2-1	Poborsky, Scholes	49,305
Nov 27	Leicester City (Rd4)	0-2		20,428

CHAMPIONS LEAGUE

DATE	OPPONENTS	SCORE	GOALSCORERS	ATTENDANCE
Sep 11	Juventus (P1)	0-1		54,000
Sep 25	RAPID VIENNA (P1)	2-0	Beckham, Solskjaer	51,831
Oct 16	Fenerbahce (P1)	2-0	Beckham, Cantona	26,200
Oct 30	FENERBAHCE (P1)	0-1		53,297
Nov 20	JUVENTUS (P1)	0-1		53,529
Dec 4	Rapid Vienna (P1)	2-0	Cantona, Giggs	45,000
Mar 5	PORTO (QFL1)	4-0	Cantona, Cole, Giggs, May	53,425
Mar 19	Porto (QFL2)	0-0		40,000
Apr 9	Bor. Dortmund (SFL1)	0-1		48,500
Apr 23	BOR. DORTMUND (SFL2)	0-1		53,606

FINAL LEAGUE TABLE

		P	W	D	L	F	A	Pts
1	MANCHESTER UNITED	38	21	12	5	76	44	75
2	Newcastle United	38	19	11	8	73	40	68
3	Arsenal	38	19	11	8	62	32	68
4	Liverpool	38	19	11	8	62	37	68
5	Aston Villa	38	17	10	11	47	34	61
6	Chelsea	38	16	11	11	58	55	59
7	Sheffield Wednesday	38	14	15	9	50	51	57
8	Wimbledon	38	15	11	12	49	46	56
9	Leicester City	38	12	11	15	46	54	47
10	Tottenham Hotspur	38	13	7	18	44	51	46
11	Leeds United	38	11	13	14	28	38	46
12	Derby County	38	11	13	14	45	58	46
13	Blackburn Rovers	38	9	15	14	42	43	42
14	West Ham United	38	10	12	16	39	48	42
15	Everton	38	10	12	16	44	57	42
16	Southampton	38	10	11	17	50	56	41
17	Coventry City	38	9	14	15	38	54	41
18	Sunderland	38	10	10	18	35	53	40
19	Middlesbrough *	38	10	12	16	51	60	39
20	Nottingham Forest	38	6	16	16	31	59	34

* deducted 3 points for failure to fulfil fixture

APPEARANCES

PLAYER	PREM	FAC	LC	CL	TOT
Cantona	36	3	–	10	49
Schmeichel	36	3	–	9	48
Beckham	33 (3)	2	–	10	45 (3)
Neville G	30 (1)	3	1	10	44 (1)
Irwin	29 (2)	3	–	8	40 (2)
May	28 (1)	1	2	7 (1)	38 (2)
Johnsen	26 (5)	2	–	9	37 (5)
Pallister	27	1	–	8	36
Giggs	25 (1)	3	–	6 (1)	34 (2)
Solskjaer	25 (8)	– (3)	–	8 (2)	33 (13)
Butt	24 (2)	–	–	8 (1)	32 (3)
Keane	21	3	2	6	32
Poborsky	15 (7)	2	2	3 (3)	22 (10)
Scholes	16 (8)	2	2	– (4)	20 (12)
Neville P	15 (3)	–	1	2 (2)	18 (5)
Cruyff	11 (5)	–	1	3 (1)	15 (6)
Cole	10 (10)	2 (1)	–	2 (3)	14 (14)
McClair	4 (15)	1 (2)	2	– (3)	7 (20)
Clegg	3 (1)	1	1	–	5 (1)
van der Gouw	2	–	2	1	5
Casper	– (2)	1	2	– (1)	3 (3)
Thornley	1 (1)	–	2	–	3 (1)
O'Kane	1	–	1	–	2
Appleton	–	–	1 (1)	–	1 (1)
Davies	–	–	– (2)	–	– (2)
Cooke	–	–	– (1)	–	– (1)

GOALSCORERS

PLAYER	PREM	FAC	LC	CL	TOT
Solskjaer	18	–	–	1	19
Cantona	11	–	–	3	14
Beckham	8	1	–	2	11
Cole	6	–	–	1	7
Scholes	3	2	1	–	6
Butt	5	–	–	–	5
Giggs	3	–	–	2	5
May	3	–	–	1	4
Poborsky	3	–	1	–	4
Cruyff	3	–	–	–	3
Pallister	3	–	–	–	3
Keane	2	–	–	–	2
Irwin	1	–	–	–	1
Neville G	1	–	–	–	1
own goals	6	–	–	–	6

1997/98

FA PREMIERSHIP

DATE	OPPONENTS	SCORE	GOALSCORERS	ATTENDANCE
Aug 10	Tottenham Hotspur	2-0	Butt, og	26,359
Aug 13	SOUTHAMPTON	1-0	Beckham	55,008
Aug 23	Leicester City	0-0		21,221
Aug 27	Everton	2-0	Beckham, Sheringham	40,079
Aug 30	COVENTRY CITY	3-0	Cole, Keane, Poborsky	55,074
Sep 13	WEST HAM UNITED	2-1	Keane, Scholes	55,068
Sep 20	Bolton Wanderers	0-0		25,000
Sep 24	CHELSEA	2-2	Scholes, Solskjaer	55,163
Sep 27	Leeds United	0-1		39,952
Oct 4	CRYSTAL PALACE	2-0	Sheringham, og	55,143
Oct 18	Derby County	2-2	Cole, Sheringham	30,014
Oct 25	BARNSLEY	7-0	Cole 3, Giggs 2, Scholes, Poborsky	55,142
Nov 1	SHEFFIELD WEDNESDAY	6-1	Sheringham 2, Solskjaer 2, Cole, og	55,259
Nov 9	Arsenal	2-3	Sheringham 2	38,205
Nov 22	Wimbledon	5-2	Beckham 2, Butt, Cole, Scholes	26,309
Nov 30	BLACKBURN ROVERS	4-0	Solskjaer 2, og 2	55,175
Dec 6	Liverpool	3-1	Cole 2, Beckham	41,027
Dec 15	ASTON VILLA	1-0	Giggs	55,151
Dec 21	Newcastle United	1-0	Cole	36,767
Dec 26	EVERTON	2-0	Berg, Cole	55,167
Dec 28	Coventry City	2-3	Sheringham, Solskjaer	23,054
Jan 10	TOTTENHAM HOTSPUR	2-0	Giggs 2	55,281
Jan 19	Southampton	0-1		15,241
Jan 31	LEICESTER CITY	0-1		55,156
Feb 7	BOLTON WANDERERS	1-1	Cole	55,156
Feb 18	Aston Villa	2-0	Beckham, Giggs	39,372
Feb 21	DERBY COUNTY	2-0	Giggs, Irwin	55,170
Feb 28	Chelsea	1-0	Neville P	35,411
Mar 7	Sheffield Wednesday	0-2		39,427
Mar 11	West Ham United	1-1	Scholes	25,892
Mar 14	ARSENAL	0-1		55,174
Mar 28	WIMBLEDON	2-0	Johnsen, Scholes	55,306
Apr 6	Blackburn Rovers	3-1	Beckham, Cole, Scholes	30,547
Apr 10	LIVERPOOL	1-1	Johnsen	55,171
Apr 18	NEWCASTLE UNITED	1-1	Beckham	55,194
Apr 27	Crystal Palace	3-0	Butt, Cole, Scholes	26,180
May 4	LEEDS UNITED	3-0	Beckham, Giggs, Irwin	55,167
May 10	Barnsley	2-0	Cole, Sheringham	18,694

FA CUP

DATE	OPPONENTS	SCORE	GOALSCORERS	ATTENDANCE
Jan 4	Chelsea (Rd3)	5-3	Beckham 2, Cole 2, Sheringham	34,792
Jan 24	WALSALL (Rd4)	5-1	Cole 2, Solskjaer 2, Johnsen	54,669
Feb 15	BARNSLEY (Rd5)	1-1	Sheringham	54,700
Feb 25	Barnsley (Rd5R)	2-3	Cole, Sheringham	18,655

LEAGUE CUP

DATE	OPPONENTS	SCORE	GOALSCORERS	ATTENDANCE
Oct 14	Ipswich Town (Rd3)	0-2		22,173

CHAMPIONS LEAGUE

DATE	OPPONENTS	SCORE	GOALSCORERS	ATTENDANCE
Sep 17	Kosice (P1)	3-0	Berg, Cole, Irwin	9,950
Oct 1	JUVENTUS (P1)	3-2	Giggs, Scholes, Sheringham	53,428
Oct 22	FEYENOORD (P1)	2-1	Irwin, Scholes	53,188
Nov 5	Feyenoord (P1)	3-1	Cole 3	51,000
Nov 27	KOSICE (P1)	3-0	Cole, Sheringham, og	53,535
Dec 10	Juventus (P1)	0-1		47,786
Mar 4	Monaco (QFL1)	0-0		15,000
Mar 18	MONACO (QFL2) (United lost the tie on away goals rule)	1-1	Solskjaer	53,683

FINAL LEAGUE TABLE

		P	W	D	L	F	A	Pts
1	Arsenal	38	23	9	6	68	33	78
2	MANCHESTER UNITED	38	23	8	7	73	26	77
3	Liverpool	38	18	11	9	68	42	65
4	Chelsea	38	20	3	15	71	43	63
5	Leeds United	38	17	8	13	57	46	59
6	Blackburn Rovers	38	16	10	12	57	52	58
7	Aston Villa	38	17	6	15	49	48	57
8	West Ham United	38	16	8	14	56	57	56
9	Derby County	38	16	7	15	52	49	55
10	Leicester City	38	13	14	11	51	41	53
11	Coventry City	38	12	16	10	46	44	52
12	Southampton	38	14	6	18	50	55	48
13	Newcastle United	38	11	11	16	35	44	44
14	Tottenham Hotspur	38	11	11	16	44	56	44
15	Wimbledon	38	10	14	14	34	46	44
16	Sheffield Wednesday	38	12	8	18	52	67	44
17	Everton	38	9	13	16	41	56	40
18	Bolton Wanderers	38	9	13	16	41	61	40
19	Barnsley	38	10	5	23	37	82	35
20	Crystal Palace	38	8	9	21	37	71	33

APPEARANCES

PLAYER	PREM	FAC	LC	CL	TOT
Beckham	34 (3)	3 (1)	–	8	45 (4)
Neville G	34	2 (1)	–	8	44 (1)
Schmeichel	32	4	–	7	43
Pallister	33	3	–	6	42
Cole	31 (2)	3	1	6 (1)	41 (3)
Butt	31 (2)	1	–	7	39 (2)
Sheringham	28 (3)	2 (1)	–	7	37 (4)
Scholes	28 (3)	2	– (1)	6 (1)	36 (5)
Giggs	28 (1)	2	–	5	35 (1)
Neville P	24 (6)	3	1	5 (2)	33 (8)
Irwin	23 (2)	3 (1)	– (1)	6	32 (4)
Berg	23 (4)	2	–	5 (2)	30 (6)
Johnsen	18 (4)	3	1	5	27 (4)
Solskjaer	15 (7)	1 (1)	–	3 (3)	19 (11)
Keane	9	–	–	1	10
May	7 (2)	1	1	–	9 (2)
McClair	2 (11)	3	1	– (3)	6 (14)
Poborsky	3 (7)	–	1	2 (2)	6 (9)
van der Gouw	4 (1)	–	1	1	6 (1)
Curtis	3 (5)	–	1	–	4 (5)
Cruyff	3 (2)	– (1)	1	–	4 (3)
Thornley	– (5)	2	1	–	3 (5)
Clegg	1 (2)	2 (1)	–	– (1)	3 (4)
Nevland	– (1)	2 (1)	– (1)	–	2 (3)
Mulryne	1	– (1)	1	–	2 (1)
Pilkington	2	–	–	–	2
Brown	1 (1)	–	–	–	1 (1)
Higginbotham	– (1)	–	–	–	– (1)
Twiss	–	– (1)	–	–	– (1)
Wallwork	– (1)	–	–	–	– (1)

GOALSCORERS

PLAYER	PREM	FAC	LC	CL	TOT
Cole	15	5	–	5	25
Sheringham	9	3	–	2	14
Beckham	9	2	–	–	11
Scholes	8	–	–	2	10
Giggs	8	–	–	1	9
Solskjaer	6	2	–	1	9
Irwin	2	–	–	2	4
Butt	3	–	–	–	3
Johnsen	2	1	–	–	3
Keane	2	–	–	–	2
Poborsky	2	–	–	–	2
Berg	1	–	–	1	2
Neville P	1	–	–	–	1
own goals	5	–	–	1	6

1998/99

FA PREMIERSHIP

DATE	OPPONENTS	SCORE	GOALSCORERS	ATTENDANCE
Aug 15	LEICESTER CITY	2-2	Beckham, Sheringham	55,052
Aug 22	West Ham United	0-0		26,039
Sep 9	CHARLTON ATHLETIC	4-1	Solskjaer 2, Yorke 2	55,147
Sep 12	COVENTRY CITY	2-0	Johnsen, Yorke	55,198
Sep 20	Arsenal	0-3		38,142
Sep 24	LIVERPOOL	2-0	Irwin, Scholes	55,181
Oct 3	Southampton	3-0	Cole, Cruyff, Yorke	15,251
Oct 17	WIMBLEDON	5-1	Cole 2, Beckham, Giggs, Yorke	55,265
Oct 24	Derby County	1-1	Cruyff	30,867
Oct 31	Everton	4-1	Blomqvist, Cole, Yorke, og	40,079
Nov 8	NEWCASTLE UNITED	0-0		55,174
Nov 14	BLACKBURN ROVERS	3-2	Scholes 2, Yorke	55,198
Nov 21	Sheffield Wednesday	1-3	Cole	39,475
Nov 29	LEEDS UNITED	3-2	Butt, Keane, Solskjaer	55,172
Dec 5	Aston Villa	1-1	Scholes	39,241
Dec 12	Tottenham Hotspur	2-2	Solskjaer 2	36,079
Dec 16	CHELSEA	1-1	Cole	55,159
Dec 19	MIDDLESBROUGH	2-3	Butt, Scholes	55,152
Dec 26	NOTTINGHAM FOREST	3-0	Johnsen 2, Giggs	55,216
Dec 29	Chelsea	0-0		34,741
Jan 10	WEST HAM UNITED	4-1	Cole 2, Solskjaer, Yorke	55,180
Jan 16	Leicester City	6-2	Yorke 3, Cole 2, Stam	22,091
Jan 31	Charlton Athletic	1-0	Yorke	20,043
Feb 3	DERBY COUNTY	1-0	Yorke	55,174
Feb 6	Nottingham Forest	8-1	Solskjaer 4, Cole 2, Yorke 2	30,025
Feb 17	ARSENAL	1-1	Cole	55,171
Feb 20	Coventry City	1-0	Giggs	22,596
Feb 27	SOUTHAMPTON	2-1	Keane, Yorke	55,316
Mar 13	Newcastle United	2-1	Cole 2	36,776
Mar 21	EVERTON	3-1	Beckham, Neville G, Solskjaer	55,182
Apr 3	Wimbledon	1-1	Beckham	26,121
Apr 17	SHEFFIELD WEDNESDAY	3-0	Scholes, Sheringham, Solskjaer	55,270
Apr 25	Leeds United	1-1	Cole	40,255
May 1	ASTON VILLA	2-1	Beckham, og	55,189
May 5	Liverpool	2-2	Irwin, Yorke	44,702
May 9	Middlesbrough	1-0	Yorke	34,665
May 12	Blackburn Rovers	0-0		30,436
May 16	TOTTENHAM HOTSPUR	2-1	Beckham, Cole	55,189

FA CUP

DATE	OPPONENTS	SCORE	GOALSCORERS	ATTENDANCE
Jan 3	MIDDLESBROUGH (Rd3)	3-1	Cole, Giggs, Irwin	52,232
Jan 24	LIVERPOOL (Rd4)	2-1	Solskjaer, Yorke	54,591
Feb 14	FULHAM (Rd5)	1-0	Cole	54,798
Mar 7	CHELSEA (Rd6)	0-0		54,587
Mar 10	Chelsea (Rd6R)	2-0	Yorke 2	33,075
Apr 11	Arsenal (SF) (at Villa Park)	0-0		39,217
Apr 14	Arsenal (SFR) (at Villa Park)	2-1	Beckham, Giggs	30,223
May 22	Newcastle United (Final) (at Wembley)	2-0	Scholes, Sheringham	79,101

LEAGUE CUP

DATE	OPPONENTS	SCORE	GOALSCORERS	ATTENDANCE
Oct 28	BURY (Rd3)	2-0	Nevland, Solskjaer	52,495
Nov 11	NOTTINGHAM FOREST (Rd4)	2-1	Solskjaer 2	37,337
Dec 2	Tottenham Hotspur (Rd5)	1-3	Sheringham	35,702

CHAMPIONS LEAGUE

DATE	OPPONENTS	SCORE	GOALSCORERS	ATTENDANCE
Aug 12	LKS LODZ (QRdL1)	2-0	Cole, Giggs	50,906
Aug 26	LKS Lodz (QRdL2)	0-0		8,700
Sep 16	BARCELONA (P1)	3-3	Beckham, Giggs, Scholes	53,601
Sep 30	Bayern Munich (P1)	2-2	Scholes, Yorke	53,000
Oct 21	Brondby (P1)	6-2	Giggs 2, Cole, Keane, Solskjaer, Yorke	40,530
Nov 4	BRONDBY (P1)	5-0	Beckham, Cole, Neville P, Scholes, Yorke	53,250
Nov 25	Barcelona (P1)	3-3	Yorke 2, Cole	67,648
Dec 9	BAYERN MUNICH (P1)	1-1	Keane	54,434
Mar 3	INTERNAZIONALE (QFL1)	2-0	Yorke 2	54,430
Mar 17	Internazionale (QFL2)	1-1	Scholes	79,528
Apr 7	JUVENTUS (SFL1)	1-1	Giggs	54,487
Apr 21	Juventus (SFL2)	3-2	Cole, Keane, Yorke	64,500
May 26	Bayern Munich (Final) (at Nou Camp Stadium)	2-1	Sheringham, Solskjaer	90,000

FINAL LEAGUE TABLE

		P	W	D	L	F	A	Pts
1	MANCHESTER UNITED	38	22	13	3	80	37	79
2	Arsenal	38	22	12	4	59	17	78
3	Chelsea	38	20	15	3	57	30	75
4	Leeds United	38	18	13	7	62	34	67
5	West Ham United	38	16	9	13	46	53	57
6	Aston Villa	38	15	10	13	51	46	55
7	Liverpool	38	15	9	14	68	49	54
8	Derby County	38	13	13	12	40	45	52
9	Middlesbrough	38	12	15	11	48	54	51
10	Leicester City	38	12	13	13	40	46	49
11	Tottenham Hotspur	38	11	14	13	47	50	47
12	Sheffield Wednesday	38	13	7	18	41	42	46
13	Newcastle United	38	11	13	14	48	54	46
14	Everton	38	11	10	17	42	47	43
15	Coventry City	38	11	9	18	39	51	42
16	Wimbledon	38	10	12	16	40	63	42
17	Southampton	38	11	8	19	37	64	41
18	Charlton Athletic	38	8	12	18	41	56	36
19	Blackburn Rovers	38	7	14	17	38	52	35
20	Nottingham Forest	38	7	9	22	35	69	30

APPEARANCES

PLAYER	PREM	FAC	LC	CL	TOT
Schmeichel	34	8	–	13	55
Neville G	34	7	–	12	53
Beckham	33 (1)	7	– (1)	12	52 (2)
Keane	33 (2)	7	–	12	52 (2)
Stam	30	6 (1)	–	13	49 (1)
Yorke	32	5 (3)	–	11	48 (3)
Irwin	26 (3)	6	–	12	44 (3)
Cole	26 (6)	6 (1)	–	10	42 (7)
Scholes	24 (7)	3 (3)	– (1)	10 (2)	37 (13)
Giggs	20 (4)	5 (1)	1	9	35 (5)
Butt	22 (9)	5	2	4 (4)	33 (13)
Neville P	19 (9)	4 (3)	2	4 (2)	29 (14)
Blomqvist	20 (5)	3 (2)	– (1)	6 (1)	29 (9)
Johnsen	19 (3)	3 (2)	1	6 (2)	29 (7)
Berg	10 (6)	5	3	3 (1)	21 (7)
Solskjaer	9 (10)	4 (4)	3	1 (5)	17 (19)
Brown	11 (3)	2	– (1)	3 (1)	16 (5)
Sheringham	7 (10)	1 (3)	1	2 (2)	11 (15)
May	4 (2)	1	2	–	7 (2)
van der Gouw	4 (1)	–	3	–	7 (1)
Curtis	1 (3)	–	3	–	4 (3)
Greening	– (3)	– (1)	3	–	3 (4)
Clegg	–	–	3	–	3
Cruyff	– (5)	–	2	– (3)	2 (8)
Wilson	–	–	2	– (1)	2 (1)
Mulryne	–	–	2	–	2
Nevland	–	–	– (1)	–	– (1)
Notman	–	–	– (1)	–	– (1)
Wallwork	–	–	– (1)	–	– (1)

GOALSCORERS

PLAYER	PREM	FAC	LC	CL	TOT
Yorke	18	3	–	8	29
Cole	17	2	–	5	24
Solskjaer	12	1	3	2	18
Scholes	6	1	–	4	11
Giggs	3	2	–	5	10
Beckham	6	1	–	2	9
Keane	2	–	–	3	5
Sheringham	2	1	1	1	5
Johnsen	3	–	–	–	3
Irwin	2	1	–	–	3
Butt	2	–	–	–	2
Cruyff	2	–	–	–	2
Blomqvist	1	–	–	–	1
Neville G	1	–	–	–	1
Stam	1	–	–	–	1
Neville P	–	–	–	1	1
Nevland	–	–	1	–	1
own goals	2	–	–	–	2

1999/2000

FA PREMIERSHIP

DATE	OPPONENTS	SCORE	GOALSCORERS	ATTENDANCE
Aug 8	Everton	1-1	Yorke	39,141
Aug 11	SHEFFIELD WEDNESDAY	4-0	Cole, Scholes, Solskjaer, Yorke	54,941
Aug 14	LEEDS UNITED	2-0	Yorke 2	55,187
Aug 22	Arsenal	2-1	Keane 2	38,147
Aug 25	Coventry City	2-1	Scholes, Yorke	22,024
Aug 30	NEWCASTLE UNITED	5-1	Cole 4, Giggs	55,190
Sep 11	Liverpool	3-2	Cole, og 2	44,929
Sep 18	WIMBLEDON	1-1	Cruyff	55,189
Sep 25	SOUTHAMPTON	3-3	Yorke 2, Sheringham	55,249
Oct 3	Chelsea	0-5		34,909
Oct 16	WATFORD	4-1	Cole 2, Irwin, Yorke	55,188
Oct 23	Tottenham Hotspur	1-3	Giggs	36,072
Oct 30	ASTON VILLA	3-0	Cole, Keane, Scholes	55,211
Nov 6	LEICESTER CITY	2-0	Cole 2	55,191
Nov 20	Derby County	2-1	Butt, Cole	33,370
Dec 4	EVERTON	5-1	Solskjaer 4, Irwin	55,193
Dec 18	West Ham United	4-2	Giggs 2, Yorke 2	26,037
Dec 26	BRADFORD CITY	4-0	Cole, Keane, Fortune, Yorke	55,188
Dec 28	Sunderland	2-2	Butt, Keane	42,026
Jan 24	ARSENAL	1-1	Sheringham	58,293
Jan 29	MIDDLESBROUGH	1-0	Beckham	61,267
Feb 2	Sheffield Wednesday	1-0	Sheringham	39,640
Feb 5	COVENTRY CITY	3-2	Cole 2, Scholes	61,380
Feb 12	Newcastle United	0-3		36,470
Feb 20	Leeds United	1-0	Cole	40,160
Feb 26	Wimbledon	2-2	Cole, Cruyff	26,129
Mar 4	LIVERPOOL	1-1	Solskjaer	61,592
Mar 11	DERBY COUNTY	3-1	Yorke 3	61,619
Mar 18	Leicester City	2-0	Beckham, Yorke	22,170
Mar 25	Bradford City	4-0	Yorke 2, Beckham, Scholes	18,276
Apr 1	WEST HAM UNITED	7-1	Scholes 3, Beckham, Cole, Irwin, Solskjaer	61,611
Apr 10	Middlesbrough	4-3	Cole, Giggs, Fortune, Scholes	34,775
Apr 15	SUNDERLAND	4-0	Solskjaer 2, Berg, Butt	61,612
Apr 22	Southampton	3-1	Beckham, Solskjaer, og	15,245
Apr 24	CHELSEA	3-2	Yorke 2, Solskjaer	61,593
Apr 29	Watford	3-2	Cruyff, Giggs, Yorke	20,250
May 6	TOTTENHAM HOTSPUR	3-1	Beckham, Sheringham, Solskjaer	61,629
May 14	Aston Villa	1-0	Sheringham	39,217

FA CUP

DATE	OPPONENTS	SCORE	GOALSCORERS	ATTENDANCE

United did not compete in this season's competition

LEAGUE CUP

DATE	OPPONENTS	SCORE	GOALSCORERS	ATTENDANCE
Oct 13	Aston Villa (Rd3)	0-3		33,815

CHAMPIONS LEAGUE

DATE	OPPONENTS	SCORE	GOALSCORERS	ATTENDANCE
Sep 14	CROATIA ZAGREB (P1)	0-0		53,250
Sep 22	Sturm Graz (P1)	3-0	Cole, Keane, Yorke	16,480
Sep 29	OLYMPIQUE MARSEILLE (P1)	2-1	Cole, Scholes	53,993
Oct 19	Olympique Marseille (P1)	0-1		56,732
Oct 27	Croatia Zagreb (P1)	2-1	Beckham, Keane	27,500
Nov 2	STURM GRAZ (P1)	2-1	Keane, Solskjaer	53,745
Nov 23	Fiorentina (P2)	0-2		36,002
Dec 8	VALENCIA (P2)	3-0	Keane, Scholes, Solskjaer	54,606
Mar 1	GIRONDINS BORDEAUX (P2)	2-0	Giggs, Sheringham	59,786
Mar 7	Girondins Bordeaux (P2)	2-1	Keane, Solskjaer	30,130
Mar 15	FIORENTINA (P2)	3-1	Cole, Keane, Yorke	59,926
Mar 21	Valencia (P2)	0-0		40,419
Apr 4	Real Madrid (QFL1)	0-0		64,119
Apr 19	REAL MADRID (QFL2)	2-3	Beckham, Scholes	59,178

FINAL LEAGUE TABLE

		P	W	D	L	F	A	Pts
1	MANCHESTER UNITED	38	28	7	3	97	45	91
2	Arsenal	38	22	7	9	73	43	73
3	Leeds United	38	21	6	11	58	43	69
4	Liverpool	38	19	10	9	51	30	67
5	Chelsea	38	18	11	9	53	34	65
6	Aston Villa	38	15	13	10	46	35	58
7	Sunderland	38	16	10	12	57	56	58
8	Leicester City	38	16	7	15	55	55	55
9	West Ham United	38	15	10	13	52	53	55
10	Tottenham Hotspur	38	15	8	15	57	49	53
11	Newcastle United	38	14	10	14	63	54	52
12	Middlesbrough	38	14	10	14	46	52	52
13	Everton	38	12	14	12	59	49	50
14	Coventry City	38	12	8	18	47	54	44
15	Southampton	38	12	8	18	45	62	44
16	Derby County	38	9	11	18	44	57	38
17	Bradford City	38	9	9	20	38	68	36
18	Wimbledon	38	7	12	19	46	74	33
19	Sheffield Wednesday	38	8	7	23	38	70	31
20	Watford	38	6	6	26	35	77	24

APPEARANCES

PLAYER	PREM	FAC	LC	CL	TOT
Stam	33	–	–	13	46
Beckham	30 (1)	–	–	12	42 (1)
Giggs	30	–	–	11	41
Keane	28 (1)	–	–	12	40 (1)
Yorke	29 (3)	–	–	9 (2)	38 (5)
Scholes	27 (4)	–	–	11	38 (4)
Irwin	25	–	–	13	38
Cole	23 (5)	–	–	13	36 (5)
Silvestre	30 (1)	–	–	2 (2)	32 (3)
Neville P	25 (4)	–	–	6 (3)	31 (7)
Bosnich	23	–	1	7	31
Neville G	22	–	–	9	31
Berg	16 (6)	–	–	11 (1)	27 (7)
Butt	21 (11)	–	–	4 (2)	25 (13)
Solskjaer	15 (13)	–	1	4 (7)	20 (20)
Sheringham	15 (12)	–	–	3 (6)	18 (18)
van der Gouw	11 (3)	–	–	7	18 (3)
Fortune	4 (2)	–	–	1 (3)	5 (5)
Taibi	4	–	–	–	4
Cruyff	1 (7)	–	1	1 (3)	3 (10)
Greening	1 (3)	–	1	1 (1)	3 (4)
Wilson	1 (2)	–	–	2 (1)	3 (3)
Higginbotham	2 (1)	–	1	– (1)	3 (2)
Clegg	– (2)	–	1	1 (1)	2 (3)
Johnsen	2 (1)	–	–	–	2 (1)
Wallwork	– (5)	–	1	–	1 (5)
Curtis	– (1)	–	1	–	1 (1)
May	– (1)	–	–	1	1 (1)
Chadwick	–	–	1	–	1
O'Shea	–	–	1	–	1
Twiss	–	–	1	–	1
Culkin	– (1)	–	–	–	– (1)
Healy	–	–	– (1)	–	– (1)
Wellens	–	–	– (1)	–	– (1)

GOALSCORERS

PLAYER	PREM	FAC	LC	CL	TOT
Yorke	20	–	–	2	22
Cole	19	–	–	3	22
Solskjaer	12	–	–	3	15
Scholes	9	–	–	3	12
Keane	5	–	–	6	11
Beckham	6	–	–	2	8
Giggs	6	–	–	1	7
Sheringham	5	–	–	1	6
Butt	3	–	–	–	3
Cruyff	3	–	–	–	3
Irwin	3	–	–	–	3
Fortune	2	–	–	–	2
Berg	1	–	–	–	1
own goals	3	–	–	–	3

2000/01

FA PREMIERSHIP

DATE	OPPONENTS	SCORE	GOALSCORERS	ATTENDANCE
Aug 20	NEWCASTLE UNITED	2-0	Cole, Johnsen	67,477
Aug 22	Ipswich Town	1-1	Beckham	22,007
Aug 26	West Ham United	2-2	Beckham, Cole	25,998
Sep 5	BRADFORD CITY	6-0	Fortune 2, Sheringham 2, Beckham, Cole	67,447
Sep 9	SUNDERLAND	3-0	Scholes 2, Sheringham	67,503
Sep 16	Everton	3-1	Butt, Giggs, Solskjaer	38,541
Sep 23	CHELSEA	3-3	Beckham, Scholes, Sheringham	67,568
Oct 1	Arsenal	0-1		38,146
Oct 14	Leicester City	3-0	Sheringham 2, Solskjaer	22,132
Oct 21	LEEDS UNITED	3-0	Beckham, Yorke, og	67,523
Oct 28	SOUTHAMPTON	5-0	Sheringham 3, Cole 2	67,581
Nov 4	Coventry City	2-1	Beckham, Cole	21,079
Nov 11	MIDDLESBROUGH	2-1	Butt, Sheringham	67,576
Nov 18	Manchester City	1-0	Beckham	34,429
Nov 25	Derby County	3-0	Butt, Sheringham, Yorke	32,910
Dec 2	TOTTENHAM HOTSPUR	2-0	Scholes, Solskjaer	67,583
Dec 9	Charlton Athletic	3-3	Giggs, Keane, Solskjaer	20,043
Dec 17	LIVERPOOL	0-1		67,533
Dec 23	IPSWICH TOWN	2-0	Solskjaer 2	67,597
Dec 26	Aston Villa	1-0	Solskjaer	40,889
Dec 30	Newcastle United	1-1	Beckham	52,134
Jan 1	WEST HAM UNITED	3-1	Solskjaer, Yorke, og	67,603
Jan 13	Bradford City	3-0	Chadwick, Giggs, Sheringham	20,551
Jan 20	ASTON VILLA	2-0	Neville G, Sheringham	67,533
Jan 31	Sunderland	1-0	Cole	48,260
Feb 3	EVERTON	1-0	og	67,528
Feb 10	Chelsea	1-1	Cole	34,690
Feb 25	ARSENAL	6-1	Yorke 3, Keane, Sheringham, Solskjaer	67,535
Mar 3	Leeds United	1-1	Chadwick	40,055
Mar 17	LEICESTER CITY	2-0	Silvestre, Yorke	67,516
Mar 31	Liverpool	0-2		44,806
Apr 10	CHARLTON ATHLETIC	2-1	Cole, Solskjaer	67,505
Apr 14	COVENTRY CITY	4-2	Yorke 2, Giggs, Scholes	67,637
Apr 21	MANCHESTER CITY	1-1	Sheringham	67,535
Apr 28	Middlesbrough	2-0	Beckham, Neville P	34,417
May 5	DERBY COUNTY	0-1		67,526
May 13	Southampton	1-2	Giggs	15,526
May 19	Tottenham Hotspur	1-3	Scholes	36,072

FA CUP

DATE	OPPONENTS	SCORE	GOALSCORERS	ATTENDANCE
Jan 7	Fulham (Rd3)	2-1	Sheringham, Solskjaer	19,178
Jan 28	WEST HAM UNITED (Rd4)	0-1		67,029

LEAGUE CUP

DATE	OPPONENTS	SCORE	GOALSCORERS	ATTENDANCE
Oct 31	Watford (Rd3)	3-0	Solskjaer 2, Yorke	18,871
Nov 28	Sunderland (Rd4)	1-2	Yorke	47,543

CHAMPIONS LEAGUE

DATE	OPPONENTS	SCORE	GOALSCORERS	ATTENDANCE
Sep 13	ANDERLECHT (P1)	5-1	Cole 3, Irwin, Sheringham	62,749
Sep 19	Dynamo Kiev (P1)	0-0		65,000
Sep 26	PSV Eindhoven (P1)	1-3	Scholes	30,500
Oct 18	PSV EINDHOVEN (P1)	3-1	Scholes, Sheringham, Yorke	66,313
Oct 24	Anderlecht (P1)	1-2	Irwin	22,506
Nov 8	DYNAMO KIEV (P1)	1-0	Sheringham	66,776
Nov 21	PANATHINAIKOS (P2)	3-1	Scholes 2, Sheringham	65,024
Dec 6	Sturm Graz (P2)	2-0	Giggs, Scholes	16,500
Feb 14	Valencia (P2)	0-0		49,541
Feb 20	VALENCIA (P2)	1-1	Cole	66,715
Mar 7	Panathinaikos (P2)	1-1	Scholes	27,231
Mar 13	STURM GRAZ (P2)	3-0	Butt, Keane, Sheringham	66,404
Apr 3	BAYERN MUNICH (QFL1)	0-1		66,584
Apr 18	Bayern Munich (QFL2)	1-2	Giggs	60,000

FINAL LEAGUE TABLE

		P	W	D	L	F	A	Pts
1	MANCHESTER UNITED	38	24	8	6	79	31	80
2	Arsenal	38	20	10	8	63	38	70
3	Liverpool	38	20	9	9	71	39	69
4	Leeds United	38	20	8	10	64	43	68
5	Ipswich Town	38	20	6	12	57	42	66
6	Chelsea	38	17	10	11	68	45	61
7	Sunderland	38	15	12	11	46	41	57
8	Aston Villa	38	13	15	10	46	43	54
9	Charlton Athletic	38	14	10	14	50	57	52
10	Southampton	38	14	10	14	40	48	52
11	Newcastle United	38	14	9	15	44	50	51
12	Tottenham Hotspur	38	13	10	15	47	54	49
13	Leicester City	38	14	6	18	39	51	48
14	Middlesbrough	38	9	15	14	44	44	42
15	West Ham United	38	10	12	16	45	50	42
16	Everton	38	11	9	18	45	59	42
17	Derby County	38	10	12	16	37	59	42
18	Manchester City	38	8	10	20	41	65	34
19	Coventry City	38	8	10	20	36	63	34
20	Bradford City	38	5	11	22	30	70	26

APPEARANCES

PLAYER	PREM	FAC	LC	CL	TOT
Neville G	32	2	–	14	48
Barthez	30	1	–	12	43
Keane	28	2	–	13	43
Beckham	29 (2)	2	–	11 (1)	42 (3)
Silvestre	25 (5)	2	–	13 (1)	40 (6)
Scholes	28 (4)	–	–	12	40 (4)
Brown	25 (3)	1	1	9 (2)	36 (5)
Giggs	24 (7)	2	–	9 (2)	35 (9)
Butt	24 (4)	2	–	8 (3)	34 (7)
Sheringham	23 (6)	1 (1)	–	8 (3)	32 (10)
Neville P	24 (5)	1	2	4 (2)	31 (7)
Irwin	20 (1)	1	–	7	28 (1)
Solskjaer	19 (12)	1 (1)	2	3 (8)	25 (21)
Cole	15 (4)	1	–	10	26 (4)
Yorke	15 (7)	1 (1)	2	7 (4)	25 (12)
Stam	15	1	–	6	22
Johnsen	11	–	1	4	16
van der Gouw	5 (5)	1	2	2	10 (5)
Chadwick	6 (10)	– (1)	2	1 (2)	9 (13)
Fortune	6 (1)	–	2	– (1)	8 (2)
Wallwork	4 (8)	– (1)	2	– (1)	6 (10)
Greening	3 (4)	–	2	1 (1)	6 (5)
Stewart	3	–	– (2)	–	3 (2)
Clegg	–	–	2	–	2
Goram	2	–	–	–	2
O'Shea	–	–	2	–	2
May	1 (1)	–	–	–	1 (1)
Rachubka	1	–	– (1)	–	1 (1)
Healy	– (1)	–	– (1)	–	– (2)
Berg	– (1)	–	–	–	– (1)
Djordjic	– (1)	–	–	–	– (1)
Webber	–	–	– (1)	–	– (1)

GOALSCORERS

PLAYER	PREM	FAC	LC	CL	TOT
Sheringham	15	1	–	5	21
Solskjaer	10	1	2	–	13
Cole	9	–	–	4	13
Yorke	9	–	2	1	12
Scholes	6	–	–	6	12
Beckham	9	–	–	–	9
Giggs	5	–	–	2	7
Butt	3	–	–	1	4
Keane	2	–	–	1	3
Chadwick	2	–	–	–	2
Fortune	2	–	–	–	2
Irwin	–	–	–	2	2
Johnsen	1	–	–	–	1
Neville G	1	–	–	–	1
Neville P	1	–	–	–	1
Silvestre	1	–	–	–	1
own goals	3	–	–	–	3

2001/02

FA PREMIERSHIP

DATE	OPPONENTS	SCORE	GOALSCORERS	ATTENDANCE
Aug 19	FULHAM	3-2	van Nistelrooy 2, Beckham	67,534
Aug 22	Blackburn Rovers	2-2	Beckham, Giggs	29,836
Aug 26	Aston Villa	1-1	og	42,632
Sep 8	EVERTON	4-1	Beckham, Fortune, Giggs, Veron	67,534
Sep 15	Newcastle United	3-4	Giggs, van Nistelrooy, Veron	52,056
Sep 22	IPSWICH TOWN	4-0	Solskjaer 2, Cole, Johnsen	67,551
Sep 29	Tottenham Hotspur	5-3	Beckham, Blanc, Cole, van Nistelrooy, Veron	36,038
Oct 13	Sunderland	3-1	Cole, Giggs, og	48,305
Oct 20	BOLTON WANDERERS	1-2	Veron	67,559
Oct 27	LEEDS UNITED	1-1	Solskjaer	67,555
Nov 4	Liverpool	1-3	Beckham	44,361
Nov 17	LEICESTER CITY	2-0	van Nistelrooy, Yorke	67,651
Nov 25	Arsenal	1-3	Scholes	38,174
Dec 1	CHELSEA	0-3		67,544
Dec 8	WEST HAM UNITED	0-1		67,582
Dec 12	DERBY COUNTY	5-0	Solskjaer 2, Keane, Scholes, van Nistelrooy	67,577
Dec 15	Middlesbrough	1-0	van Nistelrooy	34,358
Dec 22	SOUTHAMPTON	6-1	van Nistelrooy 3, Keane, Neville P, Solskjaer	67,638
Dec 26	Everton	2-0	van Nistelrooy, Giggs	39,948
Dec 30	Fulham	3-2	Giggs 2, van Nistelrooy	21,159
Jan 2	NEWCASTLE UNITED	3-1	Scholes 2, van Nistelrooy	67,646
Jan 13	Southampton	3-1	Beckham, Solskjaer, van Nistelrooy	31,858
Jan 19	BLACKBURN ROVERS	2-1	Keane, van Nistelrooy	67,552
Jan 22	LIVERPOOL	0-1		67,599
Jan 29	Bolton Wanderers	4-0	Solskjaer 3, van Nistelrooy	27,350
Feb 2	SUNDERLAND	4-1	van Nistelrooy 2, Beckham, Neville P	67,587
Feb 10	Charlton Athletic	2-0	Solskjaer 2	26,475
Feb 23	ASTON VILLA	1-0	van Nistelrooy	67,592
Mar 3	Derby County	2-2	Scholes, Veron	33,041
Mar 6	TOTTENHAM HOTSPUR	4-0	Beckham 2, van Nistelrooy 2	67,599
Mar 16	West Ham United	5-3	Beckham 2, Butt, Scholes, Solskjaer	35,281
Mar 23	MIDDLESBROUGH	0-1		67,683
Mar 30	Leeds United	4-3	Solskjaer 2, Giggs, Scholes	40,058
Apr 6	Leicester City	1-0	Solskjaer	21,447
Apr 20	Chelsea	3-0	Scholes, Solskjaer, van Nistelrooy	41,725
Apr 27	Ipswich Town	1-0	van Nistelrooy	28,433
May 8	ARSENAL	0-1		67,580
May 11	CHARLTON ATHLETIC	0-0		67,571

FA CUP

DATE	OPPONENTS	SCORE	GOALSCORERS	ATTENDANCE
Jan 6	Aston Villa (Rd3)	3-2	van Nistelrooy 2, Solskjaer	38,444
Jan 26	Middlesbrough (Rd4)	0-2		17,624

LEAGUE CUP

DATE	OPPONENTS	SCORE	GOALSCORERS	ATTENDANCE
Nov 5	Arsenal (Rd3)	0-4		30,693

CHAMPIONS LEAGUE

DATE	OPPONENTS	SCORE	GOALSCORERS	ATTENDANCE
Sep 18	LILLE (P1)	1-0	Beckham	64,827
Sep 25	Deportivo La Coruna (P1)	1-2	Scholes	33,108
Oct 10	Olympiakos Piraeus (P1)	2-0	Beckham, Cole	73,537
Oct 17	DEPORTIVO LA CORUNA (P1)	2-3	van Nistelrooy 2	65,585
Oct 23	OLYMPIAKOS PIRAEUS (P1)	3-0	Giggs, Solskjaer, van Nistelrooy	66,769
Oct 31	Lille (P1)	1-1	Solskjaer	38,402
Nov 20	Bayern Munich (P2)	1-1	van Nistelrooy	59,000
Dec 5	BOAVISTA (P2)	3-0	van Nistelrooy 2, Blanc	66,274
Feb 20	Nantes Atlantique (P2)	1-1	van Nistelrooy	38,285
Feb 26	NANTES ATLANTIQUE (P2)	5-1	Solskjaer 2, Beckham, Silvestre, van Nistelrooy	66,492
Mar 13	BAYERN MUNICH (P2)	0-0		66,818
Mar 19	Boavista (P2)	3-0	Beckham, Blanc, Solskjaer	13,223
Apr 2	Deportivo La Coruna (QFL1)	2-0	Beckham, van Nistelrooy	32,351
Apr 10	DEPORTIVO LA CORUNA (QFL2)	3-2	Solskjaer 2, Giggs	65,875
Apr 24	BAYER LEVERKUSEN (SFL1)	2-2	van Nistelrooy, og	66,534
Apr 30	Bayer Leverkusen (SFL2)	1-1	Keane	22,500
	(United lost the tie on away goals rule)			

FINAL LEAGUE TABLE

		P	W	D	L	F	A	Pts
1	Arsenal	38	26	9	3	79	36	87
2	Liverpool	38	24	8	6	67	30	80
3	MANCHESTER UNITED	38	24	5	9	87	45	77
4	Newcastle United	38	21	8	9	74	52	71
5	Leeds United	38	18	12	8	53	37	66
6	Chelsea	38	17	13	8	66	38	64
7	West Ham United	38	15	8	15	48	57	53
8	Aston Villa	38	12	14	12	46	47	50
9	Tottenham Hotspur	38	14	8	16	49	53	50
10	Blackburn Rovers	38	12	10	16	55	51	46
11	Southampton	38	12	9	17	46	54	45
12	Middlesbrough	38	12	9	17	35	47	45
13	Fulham	38	10	14	14	36	44	44
14	Charlton Athletic	38	10	14	14	38	49	44
15	Everton	38	11	10	17	45	57	43
16	Bolton Wanderers	38	9	13	16	44	62	40
17	Sunderland	38	10	10	18	29	51	40
18	Ipswich Town	38	9	9	20	41	64	36
19	Derby County	38	8	6	24	33	63	30
20	Leicester City	38	5	13	20	30	64	28

APPEARANCES

PLAYER	PREM	FAC	LC	CL	TOT
Barthez	32	1	–	15	48
Neville G	31 (3)	2	–	14	47 (3)
Blanc	29	2	–	15	46
Scholes	30 (5)	2	–	13	45 (5)
Silvestre	31 (4)	2	–	10 (3)	43 (7)
van Nistelrooy	29 (3)	– (2)	–	14	43 (5)
Keane	28	2	–	11 (1)	41 (1)
Veron	24 (2)	1	–	13	38 (2)
Beckham	23 (5)	1	–	13	37 (5)
Giggs	18 (7)	– (1)	–	13	31 (8)
Solskjaer	23 (7)	2	–	5 (10)	30 (17)
Butt	20 (5)	2	–	8 (1)	30 (6)
Neville P	21 (7)	2	1	3 (4)	27 (11)
Brown	15 (2)	–	–	5 (2)	20 (4)
Irwin	10 (2)	–	–	8 (2)	18 (4)
Johnsen	9 (1)	–	–	8 (1)	17 (2)
Fortune	8 (6)	–	–	3 (2)	11 (8)
Carroll	6 (1)	1	1	1	9 (1)
Cole	7 (4)	–	–	1 (3)	8 (7)
Forlan	6 (7)	–	–	1 (4)	7 (11)
Chadwick	5 (3)	1 (1)	1	–	7 (4)
Yorke	4 (6)	– (1)	1	1 (2)	6 (9)
O'Shea	4 (5)	–	1	– (3)	5 (8)
Stewart	2 (1)	–	1	– (1)	3 (2)
May	2	–	–	1	3
Wallwork	– (1)	1	1	–	2 (1)
Davis	–	–	1	–	1
Djordjic	–	–	1	–	1
Roche	–	–	1	–	1
Stam	1	–	–	–	1
Webber	–	–	1	–	1
van der Gouw	– (1)	–	– (1)	–	– (2)
Clegg	–	–	– (1)	–	– (1)
Nardiello	–	–	– (1)	–	– (1)

GOALSCORERS

PLAYER	PREM	FAC	LC	CL	TOT
van Nistelrooy	23	2	–	10	35
Solskjaer	17	1	–	7	25
Beckham	11	–	–	5	16
Scholes	8	–	–	1	9
Giggs	7	–	–	2	9
Veron	5	–	–	–	5
Cole	4	–	–	1	5
Keane	3	–	–	1	4
Blanc	1	–	–	2	3
Neville P	2	–	–	–	2
Butt	1	–	–	–	1
Fortune	1	–	–	–	1
Johnsen	1	–	–	–	1
Yorke	1	–	–	–	1
Silvestre	–	–	–	1	1
own goals	2	–	–	1	3

2002/03

FA PREMIERSHIP

DATE	OPPONENTS	SCORE	GOALSCORERS	ATTENDANCE
Aug 17	WEST BROMWICH ALBION	1–0	Solskjaer	67,645
Aug 23	Chelsea	2–2	Beckham, Giggs	41,541
Aug 31	Sunderland	1–1	Giggs	47,586
Sep 3	MIDDLESBROUGH	1–0	van Nistelrooy	67,464
Sep 11	BOLTON WANDERERS	0–1		67,623
Sep 14	Leeds United	0–1		39,622
Sep 21	TOTTENHAM HOTSPUR	1–0	van Nistelrooy	67,611
Sep 28	Charlton Athletic	3–1	Giggs, Scholes, van Nistelrooy	26,630
Oct 7	EVERTON	3–0	Scholes 2, van Nistelrooy	67,629
Oct 19	Fulham	1–1	Solskjaer	18,103
Oct 26	ASTON VILLA	1–1	Forlan	67,619
Nov 2	SOUTHAMPTON	2–1	Forlan, Neville P	67,691
Nov 9	Manchester City	1–3	Solskjaer	34,649
Nov 17	West Ham United	1–1	van Nistelrooy	35,049
Nov 23	NEWCASTLE UNITED	5–3	van Nistelrooy 3, Scholes, Solskjaer	67,625
Dec 1	Liverpool	2–1	Forlan 2	44,250
Dec 7	ARSENAL	2–0	Scholes, Veron	67,650
Dec 14	WEST HAM UNITED	3–0	Solskjaer, Veron, og	67,555
Dec 21	Blackburn Rovers	0–1		30,475
Dec 26	Middlesbrough	1–3	Giggs	34,673
Dec 28	BIRMINGHAM CITY	2–0	Beckham, Forlan	67,640
Jan 1	SUNDERLAND	2–1	Beckham, Scholes	67,609
Jan 11	West Bromwich Albion	3–1	Scholes, Solskjaer, van Nistelrooy	27,129
Jan 18	CHELSEA	2–1	Forlan, Scholes	67,606
Feb 1	Southampton	2–0	Giggs, van Nistelrooy	32,085
Feb 4	Birmingham City	1–0	van Nistelrooy	29,475
Feb 9	MANCHESTER CITY	1–1	van Nistelrooy	67,646
Feb 22	Bolton Wanderers	1–1	Solskjaer	27,409
Mar 5	LEEDS UNITED	2–1	Silvestre, og	67,135
Mar 15	Aston Villa	1–0	Beckham	42,602
Mar 22	FULHAM	3–0	van Nistelrooy 3	67,706
Apr 5	LIVERPOOL	4–0	van Nistelrooy 2, Giggs, Solskjaer	67,639
Apr 12	Newcastle United	6–2	Scholes 3, Giggs, Solskjaer, van Nistelrooy	52,164
Apr 15	Arsenal	2–2	Giggs, van Nistelrooy	38,164
Apr 19	BLACKBURN ROVERS	3–1	Scholes 2, van Nistelrooy	67,626
Apr 27	Tottenham Hotspur	2–0	Scholes, van Nistelrooy	36,073
May 3	CHARLTON ATHLETIC	4–1	van Nistelrooy 3, Beckham	67,721
May 11	Everton	2–1	Beckham, van Nistelrooy	40,168

FA CUP

DATE	OPPONENTS	SCORE	GOALSCORERS	ATTENDANCE
Jan 4	PORTSMOUTH (Rd3)	4–1	van Nistelrooy 2, Beckham, Scholes	67,222
Jan 25	WEST HAM UNITED (Rd4)	6–0	Giggs 2, van Nistelrooy 2, Neville P, Solskjaer	67,181
Feb 15	ARSENAL (Rd5)	0–2		67,209

LEAGUE CUP

DATE	OPPONENTS	SCORE	GOALSCORERS	ATTENDANCE
Nov 5	LEICESTER CITY (Rd3)	2–0	Beckham, Richardson	47,848
Dec 4	Burnley (Rd4)	2–0	Forlan, Solskjaer	22,034
Dec 17	CHELSEA (Rd5)	1–0	Forlan	57,985
Jan 7	BLACKBURN ROVERS (SFL1)	1–1	Scholes	62,740
Jan 22	Blackburn Rovers (SFL2)	3–1	Scholes 2, van Nistelrooy	29,048
Mar 2	Liverpool (Final) (at Millennium Stadium)	0–2		74,500

CHAMPIONS LEAGUE

DATE	OPPONENTS	SCORE	GOALSCORERS	ATTENDANCE
Aug 14	Zalaegerszeg (QRdL1)	0–1		40,000
Aug 27	ZALAEGERSZEG (QRdL2)	5–0	van Nistelrooy 2, Beckham, Scholes, Solskjaer	66,814
Sep 18	MACCABI HAIFA (P1)	5–2	Giggs, Forlan, Solskjaer, van Nistelrooy, Veron	63,439
Sep 24	Bayer Leverkusen (P1)	2–1	van Nistelrooy 2	22,500
Oct 1	OLYMPIAKOS PIRAEUS (P1)	4–0	Giggs 2, Solskjaer, Veron	66,902
Oct 23	Olympiakos Piraeus (P1)	3–2	Blanc, Scholes, Veron	13,200
Oct 29	Maccabi Haifa (P1)	0–3		22,000
Nov 13	BAYER LEVERKUSEN (P1)	2–0	van Nistelrooy, Veron	66,185
Nov 26	Basel (P2)	3–1	van Nistelrooy 2, Solskjaer	29,501
Dec 11	DEPORTIVO LA CORUNA (P2)	2–0	van Nistelrooy 2	67,014
Feb 19	JUVENTUS (P2)	2–1	Brown, van Nistelrooy	66,703
Feb 25	Juventus (P2)	3–0	Giggs 2, van Nistelrooy	59,111
Mar 12	BASEL (P2)	1–1	Neville G	66,870
Mar 18	Deportivo La Coruna (P2)	0–2		25,000
Apr 8	Real Madrid (QFL1)	1–3	van Nistelrooy	75,000
Apr 23	REAL MADRID (QFL2)	4–3	Beckham 2, van Nistelrooy, og	66,708

FINAL LEAGUE TABLE

		P	W	D	L	F	A	Pts
1	MANCHESTER UNITED	38	25	8	5	74	34	83
2	Arsenal	38	23	9	6	85	42	78
3	Newcastle United	38	21	6	11	63	48	69
4	Chelsea	38	19	10	9	68	38	67
5	Liverpool	38	18	10	10	61	41	64
6	Blackburn Rovers	38	16	12	10	52	43	60
7	Everton	38	17	8	13	48	49	59
8	Southampton	38	13	13	12	43	46	52
9	Manchester City	38	15	6	17	47	54	51
10	Tottenham Hotspur	38	14	8	16	51	62	50
11	Middlesbrough	38	13	10	15	48	44	49
12	Charlton Athletic	38	14	7	17	45	56	49
13	Birmingham City	38	13	9	16	41	49	48
14	Fulham	38	13	9	16	41	50	48
15	Leeds United	38	14	5	19	58	57	47
16	Aston Villa	38	12	9	17	42	47	45
17	Bolton Wanderers	38	10	14	14	41	51	44
18	West Ham United	38	10	12	16	42	59	42
19	West Bromwich Albion	38	6	8	24	29	65	26
20	Sunderland	38	4	7	27	21	65	19

APPEARANCES

PLAYER	PREM	FAC	LC	CL	TOT
Silvestre	34	2	5	13	54
Giggs	32 (4)	3	4 (1)	13 (2)	52 (7)
van Nistelrooy	33 (1)	3	4	10 (1)	50 (2)
Scholes	31 (2)	2 (1)	4 (2)	9 (1)	46 (6)
Barthez	30	2	4	10	46
Beckham	27 (4)	3	5	10 (3)	45 (7)
Ferdinand	27 (1)	3	4	11	45 (1)
O'Shea	26 (6)	1	3	12 (4)	42 (10)
Solskjaer	29 (8)	1 (1)	1 (3)	9 (5)	40 (17)
Veron	21 (4)	1	4 (1)	11	37 (5)
Neville G	19 (7)	3	5	8 (2)	35 (9)
Neville P	19 (6)	2	4	10 (2)	35 (8)
Brown	22	1 (1)	5	6	34 (1)
Keane	19 (2)	3	2	6	30 (2)
Blanc	15 (4)	1	–	9	25 (4)
Butt	14 (4)	– (2)	– (1)	8	22 (7)
Forlan	7 (18)	– (2)	3 (2)	5 (8)	15 (30)
Carroll	8 (2)	1	2	3	14 (2)
Fortune	5 (4)	–	1	3 (3)	9 (7)
Richardson	– (2)	1	– (1)	2 (3)	3 (6)
Ricardo	– (1)	–	–	3 (1)	3 (2)
Pugh	– (1)	–	1	1 (2)	2 (3)
May	– (1)	–	2	– (1)	2 (2)
Fletcher	–	–	–	2	2
Chadwick	– (1)	–	1	– (3)	1 (4)
Stewart	– (1)	– (1)	1	– (1)	1 (3)
Nardiello	–	–	1	– (1)	1 (1)
Roche	– (1)	–	–	1	1 (1)
Lynch	–	–	–	1	1
Timm	–	–	–	– (1)	– (1)
Webber	–	–	–	– (1)	– (1)

GOALSCORERS

PLAYER	PREM	FAC	LC	CL	TOT
van Nistelrooy	25	4	1	14	44
Scholes	14	1	3	2	20
Solskjaer	9	1	1	4	15
Giggs	8	2	–	5	15
Beckham	6	1	1	3	11
Forlan	6	–	2	1	9
Veron	2	–	–	4	6
Neville P	1	1	–	–	2
Silvestre	1	–	–	–	1
Blanc	–	–	–	1	1
Brown	–	–	–	1	1
Neville G	–	–	–	1	1
Richardson	–	–	1	–	1
own goals	2	–	–	1	3

2003/04

FA PREMIERSHIP

DATE	OPPONENTS	SCORE	GOALSCORERS	ATTENDANCE
Aug 16	BOLTON WANDERERS	4–0	Giggs 2, Scholes, van Nistelrooy	67,647
Aug 23	Newcastle United	2–1	Scholes, van Nistelrooy	52,165
Aug 27	WOLVERHAMPTON W.	1–0	O'Shea	67,648
Aug 31	Southampton	0–1		32,066
Sep 13	Charlton Athletic	2–0	van Nistelrooy 2	26,078
Sep 21	ARSENAL	0–0		67,639
Sep 27	Leicester City	4–1	van Nistelrooy 3, Keane	32,044
Oct 4	BIRMINGHAM CITY	3–0	Giggs, Scholes, van Nistelrooy	67,633
Oct 18	Leeds United	1–0	Keane	40,153
Oct 25	FULHAM	1–3	Forlan	67,727
Nov 1	PORTSMOUTH	3–0	Forlan, Keane, Ronaldo	67,639
Nov 9	Liverpool	2–1	Giggs 2	44,159
Nov 22	BLACKBURN ROVERS	2–1	Kleberson, van Nistelrooy	67,748
Nov 30	Chelsea	0–1		41,932
Dec 6	ASTON VILLA	4–0	Forlan 2, van Nistelrooy 2	67,621
Dec 13	MANCHESTER CITY	3–1	Scholes 2, van Nistelrooy	67,643
Dec 21	Tottenham Hotspur	2–1	O'Shea, van Nistelrooy	35,910
Dec 26	EVERTON	3–2	Bellion, Butt, Kleberson	67,642
Dec 28	Middlesbrough	1–0	Fortune	34,738
Jan 7	Bolton Wanderers	2–1	Scholes, van Nistelrooy	27,668
Jan 11	NEWCASTLE UNITED	0–0		67,622
Jan 17	Wolverhampton W.	0–1		29,396
Jan 31	SOUTHAMPTON	3–2	Saha, Scholes, van Nistelrooy	67,758
Feb 7	Everton	4–3	Saha 2, van Nistelrooy 2	40,190
Feb 11	MIDDLESBROUGH	2–3	Giggs, van Nistelrooy	67,346
Feb 21	LEEDS UNITED	1–1	Scholes	67,744
Feb 28	Fulham	1–1	Saha	18,306
Mar 13	Manchester City	1–4	Scholes	47,284
Mar 20	TOTTENHAM HOTSPUR	3–0	Bellion, Giggs, Ronaldo	67,644
Mar 28	Arsenal	1–1	Saha	38,184
Apr 10	Birmingham City	2–1	Ronaldo, Saha	29,548
Apr 13	LEICESTER CITY	1–0	Neville G	67,749
Apr 17	Portsmouth	0–1		20,140
Apr 20	CHARLTON ATHLETIC	2–0	Neville G, Saha	67,477
Apr 24	LIVERPOOL	0–1		67,647
May 1	Blackburn Rovers	0–1		29,616
May 8	CHELSEA	1–1	van Nistelrooy	67,609
May 15	Aston Villa	2–0	Ronaldo, van Nistelrooy	42,573

FA CUP

DATE	OPPONENTS	SCORE	GOALSCORERS	ATTENDANCE
Jan 4	Aston Villa (Rd3)	2–1	Scholes 2	40,371
Jan 25	Northampton Town (Rd4)	3–0	Forlan, Silvestre, og	7,356
Feb 14	MANCHESTER CITY (Rd5)	4–2	van Nistelrooy 2, Ronaldo, Scholes	67,228
Mar 6	FULHAM (Rd6)	2–1	van Nistelrooy 2	67,614
Apr 3	Arsenal (SF) (at Villa Park)	1–0	Scholes	39,939
May 22	Millwall (Final) (at Millennium Stadium)	3–0	van Nistelrooy 2, Ronaldo	71,350

LEAGUE CUP

DATE	OPPONENTS	SCORE	GOALSCORERS	ATTENDANCE
Oct 28	Leeds United (Rd3)	3–2	Bellion, Djemba-Djemba, Forlan	37,546
Dec 3	West Bromwich Albion (Rd4)	0–2		25,282

CHAMPIONS LEAGUE

DATE	OPPONENTS	SCORE	GOALSCORERS	ATTENDANCE
Sep 16	PANATHINAIKOS (P1)	5–0	Butt, Djemba-Djemba, Fortune, Silvestre, Solskjaer	66,520
Oct 1	Stuttgart (P1)	1–2	van Nistelrooy	53,000
Oct 22	Glasgow Rangers (P1)	1–0	Neville P	48,730
Nov 4	GLASGOW RANGERS (P1)	3–0	van Nistelrooy 2, Forlan	66,707
Nov 26	Panathinaikos (P1)	1–0	Forlan	6,890
Dec 9	STUTTGART (P1)	2–0	Giggs, van Nistelrooy	67,141
Feb 25	Porto (Rd2L1)	1–2	Fortune	49,977
Mar 9	PORTO (Rd2L2)	1–1	Scholes	67,029

FINAL LEAGUE TABLE

		P	W	D	L	F	A	Pts
1	Arsenal	38	26	12	0	73	26	90
2	Chelsea	38	24	7	7	67	30	79
3	MANCHESTER UNITED	38	23	6	9	64	35	75
4	Liverpool	38	16	12	10	55	37	60
5	Newcastle United	38	13	17	8	52	40	56
6	Aston Villa	38	15	11	12	48	44	56
7	Charlton Athletic	38	14	11	13	51	51	53
8	Bolton Wanderers	38	14	11	13	48	56	53
9	Fulham	38	14	10	14	52	46	52
10	Birmingham City	38	12	14	12	43	48	50
11	Middlesbrough	38	13	9	16	44	52	48
12	Southampton	38	12	11	15	44	45	47
13	Portsmouth	38	12	9	17	47	54	45
14	Tottenham Hotspur	38	13	6	19	47	57	45
15	Blackburn Rovers	38	12	8	18	51	59	44
16	Manchester City	38	9	14	15	55	54	41
17	Everton	38	9	12	17	45	57	39
18	Leicester City	38	6	15	17	48	65	33
19	Leeds United	38	8	9	21	40	79	33
20	Wolverhampton Wanderers	38	7	12	19	38	77	33

APPEARANCES

PLAYER	PREM	FAC	LC	CL	TOT
O'Shea	32 (1)	6	2	6 (1)	46 (2)
Silvestre	33 (1)	5	–	6	44 (1)
Howard	32	4	–	7	43
Giggs	29 (4)	5	–	8	42 (4)
Neville G	30	4	1	7	42
van Nistelrooy	31 (1)	3 (1)	–	7	41 (2)
Neville P	29 (2)	2 (1)	1	7	39 (3)
Scholes	24 (4)	6	–	5	35 (4)
Keane	25 (3)	4 (1)	–	4	33 (4)
Fortune	18 (5)	3	1	6 (1)	28 (6)
Fletcher	17 (5)	4 (1)	2	3 (3)	26 (9)
Ferdinand	20	–	–	6	26
Ronaldo	15 (14)	5	1	3 (2)	24 (16)
Brown	15 (2)	5 (1)	–	2	22 (3)
Butt	12 (9)	3 (2)	2	4 (1)	21 (12)
Forlan	10 (14)	2	1	2 (2)	15 (16)
Kleberson	10 (2)	1	1	1 (1)	13 (3)
Djemba-Djemba	10 (5)	– (1)	1	1 (3)	12 (9)
Carroll	6	2 (1)	2	1	11 (1)
Saha	9 (3)	–	–	1 (1)	10 (4)
Solskjaer	7 (6)	1 (2)	–	1 (1)	9 (9)
Bellion	4 (10)	1 (1)	2	– (4)	7 (15)
Richardson	–	– (1)	2	–	2 (1)
Bardsley	–	– (1)	1	–	1 (1)
Pugh	–	– (1)	1	–	1 (1)
Tierney	–	–	1	–	1
Eagles	–	–	– (2)	–	– (2)
Johnson	–	–	– (1)	–	– (1)
Nardiello	–	–	– (1)	–	– (1)

GOALSCORERS

PLAYER	PREM	FAC	LC	CL	TOT
van Nistelrooy	20	6	–	4	30
Scholes	9	4	–	1	14
Giggs	7	–	–	1	8
Forlan	4	1	1	2	8
Saha	7	–	–	–	7
Ronaldo	4	2	–	–	6
Keane	3	–	–	–	3
Bellion	2	–	1	–	3
Fortune	1	–	–	2	3
Kleberson	2	–	–	–	2
Neville G	2	–	–	–	2
O'Shea	2	–	–	–	2
Butt	1	–	–	1	2
Djemba-Djemba	–	–	1	1	2
Silvestre	–	1	–	1	2
Neville P	–	–	–	1	1
Solskjaer	–	–	–	1	1
own goal	–	1	–	–	1

2004/05

FA PREMIERSHIP

DATE	OPPONENTS	SCORE	GOALSCORERS	ATTENDANCE
Aug 15	Chelsea	0-1		41,813
Aug 21	NORWICH CITY	2-1	Bellion, Smith	67,812
Aug 28	Blackburn Rovers	1-1	Smith	26,155
Aug 30	EVERTON	0-0		67,803
Sep 11	Bolton Wanderers	2-2	Bellion, Heinze	27,766
Sep 20	LIVERPOOL	2-1	Silvestre 2	67,857
Sep 25	Tottenham Hotspur	1-0	van Nistelrooy	36,103
Oct 3	MIDDLESBROUGH	1-1	Smith	67,988
Oct 16	Birmingham City	0-0		29,221
Oct 24	ARSENAL	2-0	Rooney, van Nistelrooy	67,862
Oct 30	Portsmouth	0-2		20,190
Nov 7	MANCHESTER CITY	0-0		67,863
Nov 14	Newcastle United	3-1	Rooney 2, van Nistelrooy	52,320
Nov 20	CHARLTON ATHLETIC	2-0	Giggs, Scholes	67,704
Nov 27	West Bromwich Albion	3-0	Scholes 2, van Nistelrooy	27,709
Dec 4	SOUTHAMPTON	3-0	Ronaldo, Rooney, Scholes	67,921
Dec 13	Fulham	1-1	Smith	21,940
Dec 18	CRYSTAL PALACE	5-2	Scholes 2, Smith, O'Shea, og	67,814
Dec 26	BOLTON WANDERERS	2-0	Giggs, Scholes	67,867
Dec 28	Aston Villa	1-0	Giggs	42,593
Jan 1	Middlesbrough	2-0	Fletcher, Giggs	34,199
Jan 4	TOTTENHAM HOTSPUR	0-0		67,962
Jan 15	Liverpool	1-0	Rooney	44,183
Jan 22	ASTON VILLA	3-1	Ronaldo, Saha, Scholes	67,859
Feb 1	Arsenal	4-2	Ronaldo 2, O'Shea, og	38,164
Feb 5	BIRMINGHAM CITY	2-0	Keane, Rooney	67,838
Feb 13	Manchester City	2-0	Rooney, og	47,111
Feb 26	PORTSMOUTH	2-1	Rooney 2	67,989
Mar 5	Crystal Palace	0-0		26,021
Mar 19	FULHAM	1-0	Ronaldo	67,959
Apr 2	BLACKBURN ROVERS	0-0		67,939
Apr 9	Norwich City	0-2		25,522
Apr 20	Everton	0-1		37,160
Apr 24	NEWCASTLE UNITED	2-1	Brown, Rooney	67,845
May 1	Charlton Athletic	4-0	Fletcher, Rooney, Scholes, Smith	26,789
May 7	WEST BROMWICH ALBION	1-1	Giggs	67,827
May 10	CHELSEA	1-3	van Nistelrooy	67,832
May 15	Southampton	2-1	Fletcher, van Nistelrooy	32,066

FA CUP

DATE	OPPONENTS	SCORE	GOALSCORERS	ATTENDANCE
Jan 8	EXETER CITY (Rd3)	0-0		67,551
Jan 19	Exeter City (Rd3R)	2-0	Ronaldo, Rooney	9,033
Jan 29	MIDDLESBROUGH (Rd4)	3-0	Rooney 2, O'Shea	67,251
Feb 19	Everton (Rd5)	2-0	Fortune, Ronaldo	38,664
Mar 12	Southampton (Rd6)	4-0	Scholes 2, Keane, Ronaldo	30,971
Apr 17	Newcastle United (SF) (at Millennium Stadium)	4-1	van Nistelrooy 2, Ronaldo, Scholes	69,280
May 21	Arsenal (Final) (at Millennium Stadium, United lost the tie on penalty kicks)	0-0		71,876

LEAGUE CUP

DATE	OPPONENTS	SCORE	GOALSCORERS	ATTENDANCE
Oct 26	Crewe Alexandra (Rd3)	3-0	Miller, Smith, og	10,103
Nov 10	CRYSTAL PALACE (Rd4)	2-0	Richardson, Saha	48,891
Dec 1	ARSENAL (Rd5)	1-0	Bellion	67,103
Jan 12	Chelsea (SFL1)	0-0		41,492
Jan 26	CHELSEA (SFL2)	1-2	Giggs	67,000

CHAMPIONS LEAGUE

DATE	OPPONENTS	SCORE	GOALSCORERS	ATTENDANCE
Aug 11	Dinamo Bucharest (QRdL1)	2-1	Giggs, og	58,000
Aug 25	DINAMO BUCHAREST (QRdL2)	3-0	Smith 2, Bellion	61,041
Sep 15	Olympique Lyon (P1)	2-2	van Nistelrooy 2	40,000
Sep 28	FENERBAHCE (P1)	6-2	Rooney 3, Bellion, Giggs, van Nistelrooy	67,128
Oct 19	Sparta Prague (P1)	0-0		20,654
Nov 3	SPARTA PRAGUE (P1)	4-1	van Nistelrooy 4	66,706
Nov 23	OLYMPIQUE LYON (P1)	2-1	Neville G, van Nistelrooy	66,398
Dec 8	Fenerbahce (P1)	0-3		35,000
Feb 23	AC MILAN (Rd2L1)	0-1		67,162
Mar 8	AC Milan (Rd2L2)	0-1		78,957

FINAL LEAGUE TABLE

		P	W	D	L	F	A	Pts
1	Chelsea	38	29	8	1	72	15	95
2	Arsenal	38	25	8	5	87	36	83
3	MANCHESTER UNITED	38	22	11	5	58	26	77
4	Everton	38	18	7	13	45	46	61
5	Liverpool	38	17	7	14	52	41	58
6	Bolton Wanderers	38	16	10	12	49	44	58
7	Middlesbrough	38	14	13	11	53	46	55
8	Manchester City	38	13	13	12	47	39	52
9	Tottenham Hotspur	38	14	10	14	47	41	52
10	Aston Villa	38	12	11	15	45	52	47
11	Charlton Athletic	38	12	10	16	42	58	46
12	Birmingham City	38	11	12	15	40	46	45
13	Fulham	38	12	8	18	52	60	44
14	Newcastle United	38	10	14	14	47	57	44
15	Blackburn Rovers	38	9	15	14	32	43	42
16	Portsmouth	38	10	9	19	43	59	39
17	West Bromwich Albion	38	6	16	16	36	61	34
18	Crystal Palace	38	7	12	19	41	62	33
19	Norwich City	38	7	12	19	42	77	33
20	Southampton	38	6	14	18	45	66	32

APPEARANCES

PLAYER	PREM	FAC	LC	CL	TOT
Silvestre	33 (2)	2 (2)	2	7 (1)	44 (5)
Scholes	29 (4)	5 (1)	1 (1)	7	42 (6)
Ferdinand	31	5	1	5	42
Ronaldo	25 (8)	6 (1)	2	7 (1)	40 (10)
Keane	28 (3)	4	1	6	39 (3)
Heinze	26	4	2	7	39
Rooney	24 (5)	6	1 (1)	6	37 (6)
Giggs	26 (6)	2 (2)	1	6	35 (8)
Carroll	26	3	-	5	34
Neville G	22	4	1	7	34
Brown	18 (3)	6	3	6 (1)	33 (4)
O'Shea	16 (7)	3 (1)	4	5	28 (8)
Smith	22 (9)	- (3)	1 (1)	3 (2)	26 (15)
Howard	12	4	5	5	26
Fletcher	18	1 (2)	3	3 (2)	25 (4)
van Nistelrooy	16 (1)	3	-	6 (1)	25 (2)
Fortune	12 (5)	5 (1)	4	3 (2)	24 (8)
Neville P	12 (7)	4 (1)	3	1 (5)	20 (13)
Djemba-Djemba	3 (2)	2	4	5	14 (2)
Saha	7 (7)	- (2)	4	- (2)	11 (11)
Kleberson	6 (2)	-	3	2 (1)	11 (3)
Miller	3 (5)	2 (2)	2	3 (2)	10 (9)
Bellion	1 (9)	1	3	2 (1)	7 (10)
Richardson	- (2)	1	3	1 (1)	5 (3)
Spector	2 (1)	1	- (1)	1 (1)	4 (3)
Eagles	-	1	1 (2)	1 (1)	3 (3)
Pique	-	1	- (1)	- (1)	1 (2)
Jones	-	1	- (1)	-	1 (1)
Forlan	- (1)	-	-	- (1)	- (2)
Rossi	-	-	- (2)	-	- (2)
Ebanks-Blake	-	-	- (1)	-	- (1)

GOALSCORERS

PLAYER	PREM	FAC	LC	CL	TOT
Rooney	11	3	-	3	17
van Nistelrooy	6	2	-	8	16
Scholes	9	3	-	-	12
Smith	6	-	1	2	9
Ronaldo	5	4	-	-	9
Giggs	5	-	1	2	8
Bellion	2	-	1	2	5
Fletcher	3	-	-	-	3
O'Shea	2	1	-	-	3
Silvestre	2	-	-	-	2
Keane	1	1	-	-	2
Saha	1	-	1	-	2
Brown	1	-	-	-	1
Heinze	1	-	-	-	1
Fortune	-	1	-	-	1
Miller	-	-	1	-	1
Neville G	-	-	-	1	1
Richardson	-	-	1	-	1
own goals	3	-	1	1	5

2005/06

FA PREMIERSHIP

DATE	OPPONENTS	SCORE	GOALSCORERS	ATTENDANCE
Aug 13	Everton	2-0	Rooney, van Nistelrooy	38,610
Aug 20	ASTON VILLA	1-0	van Nistelrooy	67,934
Aug 28	Newcastle United	2-0	Rooney, van Nistelrooy	52,327
Sep 10	MANCHESTER CITY	1-1	van Nistelrooy	67,839
Sep 18	Liverpool	0-0		44,917
Sep 24	BLACKBURN ROVERS	1-2	van Nistelrooy	67,765
Oct 1	Fulham	3-2	van Nistelrooy 2, Rooney	21,862
Oct 15	Sunderland	3-1	Rooney, Rossi, van Nistelrooy	39,085
Oct 22	TOTTENHAM HOTSPUR	1-1	Silvestre	67,856
Oct 29	Middlesbrough	1-4	Ronaldo	30,579
Nov 6	CHELSEA	1-0	Fletcher	67,864
Nov 19	Charlton Athletic	3-1	van Nistelrooy 2, Smith	26,730
Nov 27	West Ham United	2-1	O'Shea, Rooney	34,755
Dec 3	PORTSMOUTH	3-0	Rooney, Scholes, van Nistelrooy	67,684
Dec 11	EVERTON	1-1	Giggs	67,831
Dec 14	WIGAN ATHLETIC	4-0	Rooney 2, Ferdinand, van Nistelrooy	67,793
Dec 17	Aston Villa	2-0	Rooney, van Nistelrooy	37,128
Dec 26	WEST BROMWICH ALBION	3-0	Ferdinand, Scholes, van Nistelrooy	67,972
Dec 28	Birmingham City	2-2	Rooney, van Nistelrooy	28,459
Dec 31	BOLTON WANDERERS	4-1	Ronaldo 2, Saha, og	67,858
Jan 3	Arsenal	0-0		38,313
Jan 14	Manchester City	1-3	van Nistelrooy	47,192
Jan 22	LIVERPOOL	1-0	Ferdinand	67,874
Feb 1	Blackburn Rovers	3-4	van Nistelrooy 2, Saha	25,484
Feb 4	FULHAM	4-2	Ronaldo 2, Saha, og	67,884
Feb 11	Portsmouth	3-1	Ronaldo 2, van Nistelrooy	20,206
Mar 6	Wigan Athletic	2-1	Ronaldo, og	23,574
Mar 12	NEWCASTLE UNITED	2-0	Rooney 2	67,858
Mar 18	West Bromwich Albion	2-1	Saha 2	27,623
Mar 26	BIRMINGHAM CITY	3-0	Giggs 2, Rooney	69,070
Mar 29	WEST HAM UNITED	1-0	van Nistelrooy	69,522
Apr 1	Bolton Wanderers	2-1	Saha, van Nistelrooy	27,718
Apr 9	ARSENAL	2-0	Park, Rooney	70,908
Apr 14	SUNDERLAND	0-0		72,519
Apr 17	Tottenham Hotspur	2-1	Rooney 2	36,141
Apr 29	Chelsea	0-3		42,219
May 1	MIDDLESBROUGH	0-0		69,531
May 7	CHARLTON ATHLETIC	4-0	Richardson, Ronaldo, Saha, og	73,006

FA CUP

DATE	OPPONENTS	SCORE	GOALSCORERS	ATTENDANCE
Jan 8	Burton Albion (Rd3)	0-0		6,191
Jan 18	BURTON ALBION (Rd3R)	5-0	Rossi 2, Giggs, Richardson, Saha	53,564
Jan 29	Wolverhampton W. (Rd4)	3-0	Richardson 2, Saha	28,333
Feb 18	Liverpool (Rd5)	0-1		44,039

LEAGUE CUP

DATE	OPPONENTS	SCORE	GOALSCORERS	ATTENDANCE
Oct 26	BARNET (Rd3)	4-1	Ebanks-Blake, Miller, Richardson, Rossi	43,673
Nov 30	WEST BROMWICH ALBION (Rd4)	3-1	O'Shea, Ronaldo, Saha	48,924
Dec 20	Birmingham City (Rd5)	3-1	Saha 2, Park	20,454
Jan 11	Blackburn Rovers (SFL1)	1-1	Saha	24,348
Jan 25	BLACKBURN ROVERS (SFL2)	2-1	Saha, van Nistelrooy	61,636
Feb 26	Wigan Athletic (Final) (at Millennium Stadium)	4-0	Rooney 2, Ronaldo, Saha	66,866

CHAMPIONS LEAGUE

DATE	OPPONENTS	SCORE	GOALSCORERS	ATTENDANCE
Aug 9	DEBRECENI (QRdL1)	3-0	Ronaldo, Rooney, van Nistelrooy	51,701
Aug 24	Debreceni (QRdL2)	3-0	Heinze 2, Richardson	27,000
Sep 14	Villarreal (P1)	0-0		22,000
Sep 27	BENFICA (P1)	2-1	Giggs, van Nistelrooy	66,112
Oct 18	LILLE (P1)	0-0		60,626
Nov 2	Lille (P1)	0-1		65,000
Nov 22	VILLARREAL (P1)	0-0		67,471
Dec 7	Benfica (P1)	1-2	Scholes	61,000

United failed to qualify from the group phase

FINAL LEAGUE TABLE

		P	W	D	L	F	A	Pts
1	Chelsea	38	29	4	5	72	22	91
2	MANCHESTER UNITED	38	25	8	5	72	34	83
3	Liverpool	38	25	7	6	57	25	82
4	Arsenal	38	20	7	11	68	31	67
5	Tottenham Hotspur	38	18	11	9	53	38	65
6	Blackburn Rovers	38	19	6	13	51	42	63
7	Newcastle United	38	17	7	14	47	42	58
8	Bolton Wanderers	38	15	11	12	49	41	56
9	West Ham United	38	16	7	15	52	55	55
10	Wigan Athletic	38	15	6	17	45	52	51
11	Everton	38	14	8	16	34	49	50
12	Fulham	38	14	6	18	48	58	48
13	Charlton Athletic	38	13	8	17	41	55	47
14	Middlesbrough	38	12	9	17	48	58	45
15	Manchester City	38	13	4	21	43	48	43
16	Aston Villa	38	10	12	16	42	55	42
17	Portsmouth	38	10	8	20	37	62	38
18	Birmingham City	38	8	10	20	28	50	34
19	West Bromwich Albion	38	7	9	22	31	58	30
20	Sunderland	38	3	6	29	26	69	15

APPEARANCES

PLAYER	PREM	FAC	LC	CL	TOT
van der Sar	38	2	3	8	51
Ferdinand	37	1 (1)	4 (1)	8	50 (2)
O'Shea	34	2	3 (1)	7	46 (1)
Rooney	34 (2)	2 (1)	3 (1)	5	44 (4)
Silvestre	30 (3)	4	4 (1)	6	44 (4)
van Nistelrooy	28 (7)	2	1 (1)	8	39 (8)
Ronaldo	24 (9)	1 (1)	4	8	37 (10)
Fletcher	23 (4)	2 (1)	4	7	36 (5)
Neville	24 (1)	2 (1)	5	3 (1)	34 (3)
Giggs	22 (5)	1 (1)	3	4 (1)	30 (7)
Brown	17 (2)	4	5	3	29 (2)
Park	23 (10)	1 (1)	3	- (6)	27 (17)
Scholes	18 (2)	-	-	7	25 (2)
Smith	15 (6)	- (2)	1 (1)	7 (1)	23 (10)
Richardson	12 (10)	4	4 (1)	2 (3)	22 (14)
Saha	12 (7)	3 (1)	5	- (2)	20 (10)
Vidic	9 (2)	2	- (2)	-	11 (4)
Bardsley	3 (5)	2	1 (1)	2 (1)	8 (7)
Evra	7 (4)	- (1)	1 (1)	-	8 (6)
Rossi	1 (4)	2	3	- (2)	6 (6)
Howard	- (1)	2	3	-	5 (1)
Keane	4 (1)	-	-	1	5 (1)
Pique	1 (2)	2	1 (1)	-	4 (3)
Heinze	2 (2)	-	-	2	4 (2)
Solskjaer	- (3)	2	-	-	2 (3)
Jones	-	1	1 (2)	-	2 (2)
Miller	- (1)	-	1	- (1)	1 (2)
Ebanks-Blake	-	-	1	-	1
Eckersley	-	-	1	-	1
Martin	-	-	1	-	1
Gibson	-	-	- (1)	-	- (1)

GOALSCORERS

PLAYER	PREM	FAC	LC	CL	TOT
van Nistelrooy	21	-	1	2	24
Rooney	16	-	2	1	19
Saha	7	2	6	-	15
Ronaldo	9	-	2	1	12
Richardson	1	3	1	1	6
Giggs	3	1	-	1	5
Rossi	1	2	1	-	4
Ferdinand	3	-	-	-	3
Scholes	2	-	-	1	3
O'Shea	1	-	1	-	2
Park	1	-	1	-	2
Heinze	-	-	-	2	2
Fletcher	1	-	-	-	1
Silvestre	1	-	-	-	1
Smith	1	-	-	-	1
Ebanks-Blake	-	-	1	-	1
Miller	-	-	1	-	1
own goals	4	-	-	-	4

2006/07

FA PREMIERSHIP

DATE	OPPONENTS	SCORE	GOALSCORERS	ATTENDANCE
Aug 20	FULHAM	5-1	Rooney 2, Ronaldo, Saha, og	75,115
Aug 23	Charlton Athletic	3-0	Fletcher, Saha, Solskjaer	25,422
Aug 26	Watford	2-1	Giggs, Silvestre	19,453
Sep 9	TOTTENHAM HOTSPUR	1-0	Giggs	75,453
Sep 17	ARSENAL	0-1		75,595
Sep 23	Reading	1-1	Ronaldo	24,098
Oct 1	NEWCASTLE UNITED	2-0	Solskjaer 2	75,664
Oct 14	Wigan Athletic	3-1	Saha, Solskjaer, Vidic	20,631
Oct 22	LIVERPOOL	2-0	Ferdinand, Scholes	75,828
Oct 28	Bolton Wanderers	4-0	Rooney 3, Ronaldo	27,229
Nov 4	PORTSMOUTH	3-0	Ronaldo, Saha, Vidic	76,004
Nov 11	Blackburn Rovers	1-0	Saha	26,162
Nov 18	Sheffield United	2-1	Rooney 2	32,584
Nov 26	CHELSEA	1-1	Saha	75,948
Nov 29	EVERTON	3-0	Evra, O'Shea, Ronaldo	75,723
Dec 2	Middlesbrough	2-1	Fletcher, Saha	31,238
Dec 9	MANCHESTER CITY	3-1	Ronaldo, Rooney, Saha	75,858
Dec 17	West Ham United	0-1		34,966
Dec 23	Aston Villa	3-0	Ronaldo 2, Scholes	42,551
Dec 26	WIGAN ATHLETIC	3-1	Ronaldo 2, Solskjaer	76,018
Dec 30	READING	3-2	Ronaldo 2, Solskjaer	75,910
Jan 1	Newcastle United	2-2	Scholes 2	52,302
Jan 13	ASTON VILLA	3-1	Carrick, Park, Ronaldo	76,073
Jan 21	Arsenal	1-2	Rooney	60,128
Jan 31	WATFORD	4-0	Larsson, Ronaldo, Rooney, og	76,032
Feb 4	Tottenham Hotspur	4-0	Giggs, Ronaldo, Scholes, Vidic	36,146
Feb 10	CHARLTON ATHLETIC	2-0	Fletcher, Park	75,883
Feb 24	Fulham	2-1	Giggs, Ronaldo	24,459
Mar 3	Liverpool	1-0	O'Shea	44,403
Mar 17	BOLTON WANDERERS	4-1	Park 2, Rooney 2	76,058
Mar 31	BLACKBURN ROVERS	4-1	Carrick, Park, Scholes, Solskjaer	76,098
Apr 7	Portsmouth	1-2	O'Shea	20,223
Apr 17	SHEFFIELD UNITED	2-0	Carrick, Rooney	75,540
Apr 21	MIDDLESBROUGH	1-1	Richardson	75,967
Apr 28	Everton	4-2	Eagles, O'Shea, Rooney, og	39,682
May 5	Manchester City	1-0	Ronaldo	47,244
May 9	Chelsea	0-0		41,794
May 13	WEST HAM UNITED	0-1		75,927

FA CUP

DATE	OPPONENTS	SCORE	GOALSCORERS	ATTENDANCE
Jan 7	ASTON VILLA (Rd3)	2-1	Larsson, Solskjaer	74,924
Jan 27	PORTSMOUTH (Rd4)	2-1	Rooney 2	71,137
Feb 17	READING (Rd5)	1-1	Carrick	70,608
Feb 27	Reading (Rd5R)	3-2	Heinze, Saha, Solskjaer	23,821
Mar 10	Middlesbrough (Rd6)	2-2	Ronaldo, Rooney	33,308
Mar 19	MIDDLESBROUGH (Rd6R)	1-0	Ronaldo	71,325
Apr 14	Watford (SF) (at Villa Park)	4-1	Rooney 2, Richardson, Ronaldo	37,425
May 19	Chelsea (Final) (at Wembley)	0-1		89,826

LEAGUE CUP

DATE	OPPONENTS	SCORE	GOALSCORERS	ATTENDANCE
Oct 25	Crewe Alexandra (Rd3)	2-1	Lee, Solskjaer	10,046
Nov 7	Southend United (Rd4)	0-1		11,532

CHAMPIONS LEAGUE

DATE	OPPONENTS	SCORE	GOALSCORERS	ATTENDANCE
Sep 13	GLASGOW CELTIC (P1)	3-2	Saha 2, Solskjaer	74,031
Sep 26	Benfica (P1)	1-0	Saha	61,000
Oct 17	COPENHAGEN (P1)	3-0	O'Shea, Richardson, Scholes	72,020
Nov 1	Copenhagen (P1)	0-1		40,000
Nov 21	Glasgow Celtic (P1)	0-1		60,632
Dec 6	BENFICA (P1)	3-1	Giggs, Saha, Vidic	74,955
Feb 20	Lille Metropole (Rd2L1)	1-0	Giggs	41,000
Mar 7	LILLE METROPOLE (Rd2L2)	1-0	Larsson	75,182
Apr 4	AS Roma (QFL1)	1-2	Rooney	77,000
Apr 10	AS ROMA (QFL2)	7-1	Carrick 2, Ronaldo 2, Evra, Rooney, Smith	74,476
Apr 24	AC MILAN (SFL1)	3-2	Rooney 2, Ronaldo	73,820
May 2	AC Milan (SFL2)	0-3		78,500

FINAL LEAGUE TABLE

		P	W	D	L	F	A	Pts
1	MANCHESTER UNITED	38	28	5	5	83	27	89
2	Chelsea	38	24	11	3	64	24	83
3	Liverpool	38	20	8	10	57	27	68
4	Arsenal	38	19	11	8	63	35	68
5	Tottenham Hotspur	38	17	9	12	57	54	60
6	Everton	38	15	13	10	52	36	58
7	Bolton Wanderers	38	16	8	14	47	52	56
8	Reading	38	16	7	15	52	47	55
9	Portsmouth	38	14	12	12	45	42	54
10	Blackburn Rovers	38	15	7	16	52	54	52
11	Aston Villa	38	11	17	10	43	41	50
12	Middlesbrough	38	12	10	16	44	49	46
13	Newcastle United	38	11	10	17	38	47	43
14	Manchester City	38	11	9	18	29	44	42
15	West Ham United	38	12	5	21	35	59	41
16	Fulham	38	8	15	15	38	60	39
17	Wigan Athletic	38	10	8	20	37	59	38
18	Sheffield United	38	10	8	20	32	55	38
19	Charlton Athletic	38	8	10	20	34	60	34
20	Watford	38	5	13	20	29	59	28

APPEARANCES

PLAYER	PREM	FAC	LC	CL	TOT
Rooney	33 (2)	5 (2)	1	12	51 (4)
Ronaldo	31 (3)	6 (1)	1	11	49 (4)
Carrick	29 (4)	7	–	12	48 (4)
Ferdinand	33	7	–	8 (1)	48 (1)
van der Sar	32	3	–	12	47
Scholes	29 (1)	3 (1)	–	10 (1)	42 (3)
Giggs	25 (5)	6	–	8	39 (5)
Vidic	25	5	–	8	38
Neville	24	3	–	6	33
Heinze	17 (5)	6	2	7 (1)	32 (6)
Brown	17 (5)	6	2	7	32 (5)
Evra	22 (2)	3 (1)	– (1)	4 (3)	29 (7)
O'Shea	16 (16)	2 (3)	1	8 (3)	27 (22)
Fletcher	16 (8)	3 (3)	1	6 (3)	26 (14)
Saha	18 (6)	2	–	5 (3)	25 (9)
Solskjaer	9 (10)	3 (3)	1	2 (4)	15 (17)
Silvestre	6 (8)	2	2	3	13 (8)
Richardson	8 (7)	2 (1)	2	– (4)	12 (12)
Kuszczak	6	5	2	–	13
Park	8 (6)	4 (1)	–	– (1)	12 (8)
Smith	6 (3)	2 (1)	2	1 (3)	11 (7)
Larsson	5 (2)	3 (1)	–	2	10 (3)
Jones D	–	–	2	–	2
Lee	1	–	– (2)	–	1 (2)
Eagles	1 (1)	–	–	–	1 (1)
Dong	1	–	–	–	1
Gray	–	–	1	–	1
Jones R	–	–	1	–	1
Marsh	–	–	1	–	1
Shawcross	–	–	– (2)	–	– (2)
Barnes	–	–	– (1)	–	– (1)

GOALSCORERS

PLAYER	PREM	FAC	LC	CL	TOT
Ronaldo	17	3	–	3	23
Rooney	14	5	–	4	23
Saha	8	1	–	4	13
Solskjaer	7	2	1	1	11
Scholes	6	–	–	1	7
Giggs	4	–	–	2	6
Carrick	3	1	–	2	6
Park	5	–	–	–	5
O'Shea	4	–	–	1	5
Vidic	3	–	–	1	4
Fletcher	3	–	–	–	3
Larsson	1	1	–	1	3
Richardson	1	1	–	1	3
Evra	1	–	–	1	2
Eagles	1	–	–	–	1
Ferdinand	1	–	–	–	1
Silvestre	1	–	–	–	1
Heinze	–	1	–	–	1
Lee	–	–	1	–	1
Smith	–	–	–	1	1
own goals	3	–	–	–	3

2007/08

FA PREMIER LEAGUE

DATE	OPPONENTS	SCORE	GOALSCORERS	ATTENDANCE
Aug 12	READING	0-0		75,655
Aug 15	Portsmouth	1-1	Scholes	20,510
Aug 19	Manchester City	0-1		44,955
Aug 26	TOTTENHAM HOTSPUR	1-0	Nani	75,696
Sep 1	SUNDERLAND	1-0	Saha	75,648
Sep 15	Everton	1-0	Vidic	39,364
Sep 23	CHELSEA	2-0	Saha, Tevez	75,663
Sep 29	Birmingham City	1-0	Ronaldo	26,526
Oct 6	WIGAN ATHLETIC	4-0	Ronaldo 2, Rooney, Tevez	75,300
Oct 20	Aston Villa	4-1	Rooney 2, Ferdinand, Giggs	42,640
Oct 27	MIDDLESBROUGH	4-1	Tevez 2, Nani, Rooney	75,720
Nov 3	Arsenal	2-2	Ronaldo, og	60,161
Nov 11	BLACKBURN ROVERS	2-0	Ronaldo 2	75,710
Nov 24	Bolton Wanderers	0-1		25,028
Dec 3	FULHAM	2-0	Ronaldo 2	75,055
Dec 8	DERBY COUNTY	4-1	Tevez 2, Giggs, Ronaldo	75,725
Dec 16	Liverpool	1-0	Tevez	44,459
Dec 23	EVERTON	2-1	Ronaldo 2	75,749
Dec 26	Sunderland	4-0	Saha 2, Ronaldo, Rooney	47,360
Dec 29	West Ham United	1-2	Ronaldo	34,966
Jan 1	BIRMINGHAM CITY	1-0	Tevez	75,459
Jan 12	NEWCASTLE UNITED	6-0	Ronaldo 3, Tevez 2, Ferdinand	75,965
Jan 19	Reading	2-0	Ronaldo, Rooney	24,135
Jan 30	PORTSMOUTH	2-0	Ronaldo 2	75,415
Feb 2	Tottenham Hotspur	1-1	Tevez	36,075
Feb 10	MANCHESTER CITY	1-2	Carrick	75,970
Feb 23	Newcastle United	5-1	Ronaldo 2, Rooney 2, Saha	52,291
Mar 1	Fulham	3-0	Hargreaves, Park, og	25,314
Mar 15	Derby County	1-0	Ronaldo	33,072
Mar 19	BOLTON WANDERERS	2-0	Ronaldo 2	75,476
Mar 23	LIVERPOOL	3-0	Brown, Nani, Ronaldo	76,000
Mar 29	ASTON VILLA	4-0	Rooney 2, Ronaldo, Tezev	75,932
Apr 6	Middlesbrough	2-2	Ronaldo, Rooney	33,952
Apr 13	ARSENAL	2-1	Hargreaves, Ronaldo	75,967
Apr 19	Blackburn Rovers	1-1	Tevez	30,316
Apr 26	Chelsea	1-2	Rooney	41,828
May 3	WEST HAM UNITED	4-1	Ronaldo 2, Carrick, Tevez	76,013
May 11	Wigan Athletic	2-0	Giggs, Ronaldo	25,133

FA CUP

DATE	OPPONENTS	SCORE	GOALSCORERS	ATTENDANCE
Jan 5	Aston Villa (Rd3)	2-0	Ronaldo, Rooney	33,630
Jan 27	TOTTENHAM HOTSPUR (Rd4)	3-1	Ronaldo 2, Tevez	75,369
Feb 16	ARSENAL (Rd5)	4-0	Fletcher 2, Nani, Rooney	75,550
Mar 8	PORTSMOUTH (Rd6)	0-1		75,463

LEAGUE CUP

DATE	OPPONENTS	SCORE	GOALSCORERS	ATTENDANCE
Sep 26	Coventry City (Rd3)	0-2		74,055

CHAMPIONS LEAGUE

DATE	OPPONENTS	SCORE	GOALSCORERS	ATTENDANCE
Sep 19	Sporting Lisbon (P1)	1-0	Ronaldo	39,514
Oct 2	AS ROMA (P1)	1-0	Rooney	73,652
Oct 23	Dynamo Kiev (P1)	4-2	Ronaldo 2, Ferdinand, Rooney	43,000
Nov 7	DYNAKO KIEV (P1)	4-0	Pique, Ronaldo, Rooney, Tevez	75,017
Nov 27	SPORTING LISBON (P1)	2-1	Ronaldo, Tevez	75,162
Dec 12	AS Roma (P1)	1-1	Pique	29,490
Feb 20	Olympique Lyonnais (Rd2L1)	1-1	Tevez	39,230
Mar 4	OLYMPIQUE LYONNAIS (Rd2L2)	1-0	Ronaldo	75,520
Apr 1	AS Roma (QFL1)	2-0	Ronaldo, Rooney	60,931
Apr 9	AS ROMA (QFL2)	1-0	Tevez	74,423
Apr 23	Barcelona (SFL1)	0-0		95,949
Apr 29	BARCELONA (SFL2)	1-0	Scholes	75,061
May 21	Chelsea (Final)	1-1	Ronaldo	67,310

(at Luzhniki Stadium, United won the tie 6-5 on penalty kicks)

FINAL LEAGUE TABLE

		P	W	D	L	F	A	Pts
1	MANCHESTER UNITED	38	27	6	5	80	22	87
2	Chelsea	38	25	10	3	65	26	85
3	Arsenal	38	24	11	3	74	31	83
4	Liverpool	38	21	13	4	67	28	76
5	Everton	38	19	8	11	55	33	65
6	Aston Villa	38	16	12	10	71	51	60
7	Blackburn Rovers	38	15	13	10	50	48	58
8	Portsmouth	38	16	9	13	48	40	57
9	Manchester City	38	15	10	13	45	53	55
10	West Ham United	38	13	10	15	42	50	49
11	Tottenham Hotspur	38	11	13	14	66	61	46
12	Newcastle United	38	11	10	17	45	65	43
13	Middlesbrough	38	10	12	16	43	53	42
14	Wigan Athletic	38	10	10	18	34	51	40
15	Sunderland	38	11	6	21	36	59	39
16	Bolton Wanderers	38	9	10	19	36	54	37
17	Fulham	38	8	12	18	38	60	36
18	Reading	38	10	6	22	41	66	36
19	Birmingham City	38	8	11	19	46	62	35
20	Derby County	38	1	8	29	20	89	11

APPEARANCES

PLAYER	PREM	FAC	LC	CL	TOT
Ferdinand	35	4	–	11	50
Brown	34 (2)	4	– (1)	9 (1)	47 (4)
Evra	33	4	–	10	47
Ronaldo	31 (3)	3	–	11	45 (3)
Vidic	32	3	–	9	44
van der Sar	29	4	–	10	43
Tevez	31 (3)	2	–	6 (6)	39 (9)
Carrick	24 (7)	3 (1)	– (1)	11 (1)	38 (10)
Rooney	25 (2)	3 (1)	–	10 (1)	38 (4)
Giggs	26 (5)	2	–	4 (5)	32 (10)
Scholes	22 (2)	1 (2)	–	7	30 (4)
Nani	16 (10)	2	1	7 (4)	26 (14)
Anderson	16 (8)	2 (2)	1	6 (3)	25 (13)
Hargreaves	16 (7)	2 (1)	–	5 (3)	23 (11)
O'Shea	10 (18)	1 (1)	1	4 (2)	16 (21)
Park	8 (4)	2	–	4	14 (4)
Kuszczak	8 (1)	– (1)	1	3 (2)	12 (4)
Fletcher	5 (11)	1	–	5 (1)	11 (12)
Saha	6 (11)	1 (1)	–	3 (2)	10 (14)
Pique	5 (4)	–	1	3	9 (4)
Simpson	1 (2)	– (1)	1	2 (1)	4 (4)
Silvestre	3	–	–	1 (1)	4 (1)
Eagles	1 (3)	–	1	1	3 (3)
Evans	–	–	1	1 (1)	2 (1)
Dong	–	–	1	– (1)	1 (1)
Bardsley	–	–	1	–	1
Foster	1	–	–	–	1
Martin	–	–	1	–	1
Campbell	– (1)	–	– (1)	–	– (2)
Neville	–	–	–	– (1)	– (1)

GOALSCORERS

PLAYER	PREM	FAC	LC	CL	TOT
Ronaldo	31	3	–	8	42
Tevez	14	1	–	4	19
Rooney	12	2	–	4	18
Saha	5	–	–	–	5
Nani	3	1	–	–	4
Giggs	3	–	–	–	3
Ferdinand	2	–	–	1	3
Carrick	2	–	–	–	2
Hargreaves	2	–	–	–	2
Scholes	1	–	–	1	2
Fletcher	–	2	–	–	2
Pique	–	–	–	2	2
Brown	1	–	–	–	1
Park	1	–	–	–	1
Vidic	1	–	–	–	1
own goals	2	–	–	–	2

2008/09

FA PREMIER LEAGUE

DATE	OPPONENTS	SCORE	GOALSCORERS	ATTENDANCE
Aug 17	NEWCASTLE UNITED	1-1	Fletcher	75,512
Aug 25	Portsmouth	1-0	Fletcher	20,540
Sep 13	Liverpool	1-2	Tevez	44,192
Sep 21	Chelsea	1-1	Park	41,760
Sep 27	BOLTON WANDERERS	2-0	Ronaldo, Rooney	75,484
Oct 4	Blackburn Rovers	2-0	Brown, Rooney	27,321
Oct 18	WEST BROMWICH ALBION	4-0	Berbatov, Nani, Ronaldo, Rooney	75,451
Oct 25	Everton	1-1	Fletcher	36,069
Oct 29	WEST HAM UNITED	2-0	Ronaldo 2	75,397
Nov 1	HULL CITY	4-3	Ronaldo 2, Carrick, Vidic	75,398
Nov 8	Arsenal	1-2	Rafael	60,106
Nov 15	STOKE CITY	5-0	Ronaldo 2, Berbatov, Carrick, Welbeck	75,369
Nov 22	Aston Villa	0-0		42,585
Nov 30	Manchester City	1-0	Rooney	47,320
Dec 6	SUNDERLAND	1-0	Vidic	75,400
Dec 13	Tottenham Hotspur	0-0		35,882
Dec 26	Stoke City	1-0	Tevez	27,500
Dec 29	MIDDLESBROUGH	1-0	Berbatov	75,294
Jan 11	CHELSEA	3-0	Berbatov, Rooney, Vidic	75,455
Jan 14	WIGAN ATHLETIC	1-0	Rooney	73,917
Jan 17	Bolton Wanderers	1-0	Berbatov	26,021
Jan 27	West Bromwich Albion	5-0	Ronaldo 2, Berbatov, Tevez, Vidic	26,105
Jan 31	EVERTON	1-0	Ronaldo	75,399
Feb 8	West Ham United	1-0	Giggs	34,958
Feb 18	FULHAM	3-0	Berbatov, Rooney, Scholes	75,437
Feb 21	BLACKBURN ROVERS	2-1	Ronaldo, Rooney	75,000
Mar 4	Newcastle United	2-1	Berbatov, Rooney	51,636
Mar 14	LIVERPOOL	1-4	Ronaldo	75,569
Mar 21	Fulham	0-2		25,652
Apr 5	ASTON VILLA	3-2	Ronaldo 2, Macheda	75,409
Apr 11	Sunderland	2-1	Macheda, Scholes	45,408
Apr 22	PORTSMOUTH	2-0	Carrick, Rooney	74,895
Apr 25	TOTTENHAM HOTSPUR	5-2	Ronaldo 2, Rooney 2, Berbatov	75,458
May 2	Middlesbrough	2-0	Giggs, Park	33,767
May 10	MANCHESTER CITY	2-0	Ronaldo, Tevez	75,464
May 13	Wigan Athletic	2-1	Carrick, Tevez	21,286
May 16	ARSENAL	0-0		75,468
May 24	Hull City	1-0	Gibson	24,945

FA CUP

DATE	OPPONENTS	SCORE	GOALSCORERS	ATTENDANCE
Jan 4	Southampton (Rd3)	3-0	Gibson, Nani, Welbeck	31,901
Jan 24	TOTTENHAM HOTSPUR (Rd4)	2-1	Berbatov, Scholes	75,014
Feb 15	Derby County (Rd5)	4-1	Gibson, Nani, Ronaldo, Welbeck	32,103
Mar 7	Fulham (Rd6)	4-0	Tevez 2, Park, Rooney	24,662
Apr 19	Everton (SF)	0-0		88,141
	(at Wembley Stadium, United lost the tie 2-4 on penalty kicks)			

LEAGUE CUP

DATE	OPPONENTS	SCORE	GOALSCORERS	ATTENDANCE
Sep 23	MIDDLESBROUGH (Rd3)	3-1	Giggs, Nani, Ronaldo	53,729
Nov 11	QUEENS PARK RANGERS (Rd4)	1-0	Tevez	62,539
Dec 3	BLACKBURN ROVERS (Rd5)	5-3	Tevez 4, Nani	53,997
Jan 7	Derby County (SFL1)	0-1		30,194
Jan 20	DERBY COUNTY (SFL2)	4-2	Nani, O'Shea, Ronaldo, Tevez	73,374
Mar 1	Tottenham Hotspur (Final)	0-0		88,217
	(at Wembley Stadium, United won the tie 4-1 on penalty kicks)			

CHAMPIONS LEAGUE

DATE	OPPONENTS	SCORE	GOALSCORERS	ATTENDANCE
Sep 17	VILLARREAL (P1)	0-0		74,944
Sep 30	Aalborg (P1)	3-0	Berbatov 2, Rooney	10,346
Oct 21	GLASGOW CELTIC (P1)	3-0	Berbatov 2, Rooney	74,655
Nov 5	Glasgow Celtic (P1)	1-1	Giggs	58,903
Nov 25	Villarreal (P1)	0-0		22,529
Dec 10	AALBORG (P1)	2-2	Rooney, Tevez	74,382
Feb 24	Internazionale (Rd2L1)	0-0		80,018
Mar 11	INTERNAZIONALE (Rd2L2)	2-0	Ronaldo, Vidic	74,769
Apr 7	PORTO (QFL1)	2-2	Rooney, Tevez	74,517
Apr 15	Porto (QFL2)	1-0	Ronaldo	50,000
Apr 29	ARSENAL (SFL1)	1-0	O'Shea	74,733
May 5	Arsenal (SFL2)	3-1	Ronaldo 2, Park	59,867
May 27	Barcelona (Final)	0-2		62,467
	(at Olympic Stadium, Rome)			

FINAL LEAGUE TABLE

		P	W	D	L	F	A	Pts
1	MANCHESTER UNITED	38	28	6	4	68	24	90
2	Liverpool	38	25	11	2	77	27	86
3	Chelsea	38	25	8	5	68	24	83
4	Arsenal	38	20	12	6	68	37	72
5	Everton	38	17	12	9	55	37	63
6	Aston Villa	38	17	11	10	54	48	62
7	Fulham	38	14	11	13	39	34	53
8	Tottenham Hotspur	38	14	9	15	45	45	51
9	West Ham United	38	14	9	15	42	45	51
10	Manchester City	38	15	5	18	58	50	50
11	Wigan Athletic	38	12	9	17	34	45	45
12	Stoke City	38	12	9	17	38	55	45
13	Bolton Wanderers	38	11	8	19	41	53	41
14	Portsmouth	38	10	11	17	38	57	41
15	Blackburn Rovers	38	10	11	17	40	60	41
16	Sunderland	38	9	9	20	34	54	36
17	Hull City	38	8	11	19	39	64	35
18	Newcastle United	38	7	13	18	40	59	34
19	Middlesbrough	38	7	11	20	28	57	32
20	West Bromwich Albion	38	8	8	22	36	67	32

APPEARANCES

PLAYER	PREM	FAC	LC	CL	TOT
Vidic	33 (1)	4	2 (2)	9	48 (3)
Ronaldo	31 (2)	2	2 (2)	11 (1)	46 (5)
van der Sar	33	2	–	10	45
O'Shea	20 (10)	3 (1)	6	12	41 (11)
Evra	28	2 (1)	1 (1)	10 (1)	41 (3)
Ferdinand	24	3	1	11	39
Rooney	25 (5)	1 (1)	– (1)	11 (2)	37 (9)
Berbatov	29 (2)	2 (1)	–	5 (4)	36 (7)
Carrick	24 (4)	3	– (1)	9	36 (5)
Fletcher	25 (1)	2 (1)	– (1)	8	35 (3)
Tevez	18 (11)	3	5 (1)	4 (5)	30 (17)
Park	21 (4)	3	1	5 (4)	30 (8)
Evans	16 (1)	2 (1)	5	6 (1)	29 (3)
Giggs	15 (13)	2	3 (1)	6 (5)	26 (19)
Anderson	11 (6)	3	5 (1)	7 (2)	26 (9)
Nani	7 (6)	2	6	6 (1)	21 (7)
Rafael	12 (4)	2	5	2 (2)	21 (6)
Neville	13 (3)	2	3	3 (1)	21 (4)
Scholes	14 (7)	1 (1)	2 (1)	3 (3)	20 (12)
Gibson	1 (2)	2 (1)	5 (1)	1 (1)	9 (5)
Foster	2	3	3	1	9
Welbeck	1 (2)	3 (2)	4 (1)	–	8 (5)
Brown	6 (2)	–	1	– (2)	7 (4)
Kuszczak	3 (1)	–	2	2	7 (1)
Possebon	– (3)	– (2)	3	–	3 (5)
Macheda	2 (2)	1	–	–	3 (2)
Hargreaves	1 (1)	–	–	1	2 (1)
Fabio	–	2	–	–	2
Amos	–	–	1	–	1
Campbell	1	–	–	–	1
De Laet	1	–	–	–	1
Martin, Lee	1	–	–	–	1
Eckersley	– (2)	– (2)	–	–	– (4)
Manucho	– (1)	–	– (2)	–	– (3)
Tosic	– (2)	– (1)	–	–	– (3)
Chester	–	–	– (1)	–	– (1)

GOALSCORERS

PLAYER	PREM	FAC	LC	CL	TOT
Ronaldo	18	1	2	4	25
Rooney	12	1	–	4	17
Tevez	5	2	6	2	15
Berbatov	9	1	–	4	14
Nani	1	2	3	–	6
Vidic	4	–	–	1	5
Carrick	4	–	–	–	4
Giggs	2	–	1	1	4
Park	2	1	–	1	4
Fletcher	3	–	–	–	3
Scholes	2	1	–	–	3
Gibson	1	2	–	–	3
Welbeck	1	2	–	–	3
Macheda	2	–	–	–	2
O'Shea	–	–	1	1	2
Brown	1	–	–	–	1
Rafael	1	–	–	–	1

2009/10

FA PREMIER LEAGUE

DATE	OPPONENTS	SCORE	GOALSCORERS	ATTENDANCE
Aug 16	BIRMINGHAM CITY	1-0	Rooney	75,062
Aug 19	Burnley	0-1		20,872
Aug 22	Wigan Athletic	5-0	Rooney 2, Berbatov, Nani, Owen	18,164
Aug 29	ARSENAL	2-1	Rooney, og	75,095
Sep 12	Tottenham Hotspur	3-1	Anderson, Giggs, Rooney	35,785
Sep 20	MANCHESTER CITY	4-3	Fletcher 2, Owen, Rooney	75,066
Sep 26	Stoke City	2-0	Berbatov, O'Shea	27,500
Oct 03	SUNDERLAND	2-2	Berbatov, og	75,114
Oct 17	BOLTON WANDERERS	2-1	Valencia, og	75,103
Oct 25	Liverpool	0-2		44,188
Oct 31	BLACKBURN ROVERS	2-0	Berbatov, Rooney	74,658
Nov 8	Chelsea	0-1		41,836
Nov 21	EVERTON	3-0	Carrick, Fletcher, Valencia	75,169
Nov 28	Portsmouth	4-1	Rooney 3, Giggs	20,482
Dec 5	West Ham United	4-0	Gibson, Rooney, Scholes, Valencia	34,980
Dec 12	ASTON VILLA	0-1		75,130
Dec 15	WOLVERHAMPTON W.	3-0	Rooney, Valencia, Vidic	73,709
Dec 19	Fulham	0-3		25,700
Dec 27	Hull City	3-1	Berbatov, Rooney, og	24,627
Dec 30	WIGAN ATHLETIC	5-0	Berbatov, Carrick, Rafael, Rooney, Valencia	74,560
Jan 9	Birmingham City	1-1	og	28,907
Jan 16	BURNLEY	3-0	Berbatov, Diouf, Rooney	75,120
Jan 23	HULL CITY	4-0	Rooney 4	73,933
Jan 31	Arsenal	3-1	Park, Rooney, og	60,091
Feb 6	PORTSMOUTH	5-0	Berbatov, Carrick, Rooney, og 2	74,684
Feb 10	Aston Villa	1-1	og	42,788
Feb 20	Everton	1-3	Berbatov	39,448
Feb 23	WEST HAM UNITED	3-0	Rooney 2, Owen	73,797
Mar 6	Wolverhampton Wanderers	1-0	Scholes	28,883
Mar 14	FULHAM	3-0	Rooney 2, Berbatov	75,207
Mar 21	LIVERPOOL	2-1	Park, Rooney	75,216
Mar 27	Bolton Wanderers	4-0	Berbatov 2, Gibson, og	25,370
Apr 3	CHELSEA	1-2	Macheda	75,217
Apr 11	Blackburn Rovers	0-0		29,912
Apr 17	Manchester City	1-0	Scholes	47,019
Apr 24	TOTTENHAM HOTSPUR	3-1	Giggs 2, Nani	75,268
May 2	Sunderland	1-0	Nani	47,641
May 9	STOKE CITY	4-0	Fletcher, Giggs, Park, og	75,316

FA CUP

DATE	OPPONENTS	SCORE	GOALSCORERS	ATTENDANCE
Jan 3	LEEDS UNITED (Rd3)	0-1		74,526

LEAGUE CUP

DATE	OPPONENTS	SCORE	GOALSCORERS	ATTENDANCE
Sep 23	WOLVERHAMPTON W. (Rd3)	1-0	Welbeck	51,116
Oct 27	Barnsley (Rd4)	2-0	Owen, Welbeck	20,019
Dec 1	TOTTENHAM HOTSPUR (Rd5)	2-0	Gibson 2	57,212
Jan 19	Manchester City (SFL1)	1-2	Giggs	46,067
Jan 27	MANCHESTER CITY (SFL2)	3-1	Carrick, Rooney, Scholes	74,576
Feb 28	Aston Villa (Final)	2-1	Owen, Rooney	88,596
	(at Wembley Stadium)			

CHAMPIONS LEAGUE

DATE	OPPONENTS	SCORE	GOALSCORERS	ATTENDANCE
Sep 15	Besiktas (P1)	1-0	Scholes	32,000
Sep 30	WOLFSBURG (P1)	2-1	Carrick, Giggs	74,037
Oct 21	CSKA Moscow (P1)	1-0	Valencia	51,250
Nov 3	CSKA MOSCOW (P1)	3-3	Owen, Scholes, og	73,718
Nov 25	BESIKTAS (P1)	0-1		74,242
Dec 08	Wolfsburg (P1)	3-1	Owen 3	29,000
Feb 16	AC Milan (Rd2L1)	3-2	Rooney 2, Scholes	80,000
Mar 10	AC MILAN (Rd2L2)	4-0	Rooney 2, Fletcher, Park	74,595
Mar 30	Bayern Munich (QFL1)	1-2	Rooney	66,000
Apr 7	BAYERN MUNICH (QFL2)	3-2	Nani 2, Gibson	74,482
	(United lost the tie on away goals rule)			

FINAL LEAGUE TABLE

		P	W	D	L	F	A	Pts
1	Chelsea	38	27	5	6	103	32	86
2	MANCHESTER UNITED	38	27	4	7	86	28	85
3	Arsenal	38	23	6	9	83	41	75
4	Tottenham Hotspur	38	21	7	10	67	41	70
5	Manchester City	38	18	13	7	73	45	67
6	Aston Villa	38	17	13	8	52	39	64
7	Liverpool	38	18	9	11	61	35	63
8	Everton	38	16	13	9	60	49	61
9	Birmingham City	38	13	11	14	38	47	50
10	Blackburn Rovers	38	13	11	14	41	55	50
11	Stoke City	38	11	14	13	34	48	47
12	Fulham	38	12	10	16	39	46	46
13	Sunderland	38	11	11	16	48	56	44
14	Bolton Wanderers	38	10	9	19	42	67	39
15	Wolverhampton Wanderers	38	9	11	18	32	56	38
16	Wigan Athletic	38	9	9	20	37	79	36
17	West Ham United	38	8	11	19	47	66	35
18	Burnley	38	8	6	24	42	82	30
19	Hull City	38	6	12	20	34	75	30
20	Portsmouth *	38	7	7	24	34	66	19

* deducted 9 points for going into administration

APPEARANCES

PLAYER	PREM	FAC	LC	CL	TOT
Evra	37 (1)	–	3	7 (2)	47 (3)
Rooney	32	1	2 (1)	6 (1)	41 (2)
Fletcher	29 (1)	–	3	6 (1)	38 (2)
Valencia	29 (5)	– (1)	2 (2)	6 (3)	37 (11)
Carrick	22 (8)	–	4 (1)	6 (2)	32 (11)
Vidic	24	–	2	7	33
Scholes	24 (4)	–	1 (1)	7	32 (5)
Nani	19 (4)	–	2	8	29 (4)
Berbatov	24 (9)	1	2	1 (5)	28 (14)
van der Sar	21	–	2	6	29
Evans	18	1	5	3	27
Brown	18 (1)	1	4 (1)	2 (2)	25 (4)
Neville	15 (2)	1	3 (1)	6	25 (3)
Giggs	20 (5)	– (1)	2	1 (2)	23 (8)
Anderson	10 (4)	1	3	5	19 (4)
Ferdinand	12 (1)	–	1	6	19 (1)
Park	10 (7)	–	2	5 (1)	17 (8)
Rafael	8	–	4	3 (1)	15 (1)
O'Shea	12 (3)	–	–	2 (1)	14 (4)
Kuszczak	8	1	3	2	14
Gibson	6 (9)	1	2 (1)	3 (1)	12 (11)
Owen	5 (14)	– (1)	3 (1)	3 (3)	11 (19)
Foster	9	–	1	2	12
Welbeck	1 (4)	1	3	2	7 (4)
Fabio	1 (4)	1	2	2	6 (4)
Obertan	1 (6)	1	2	1 (2)	5 (8)
Macheda	1 (4)	–	2 (1)	2	5 (5)
De Laet	2	–	1 (2)	–	3 (2)
Diouf	– (5)	–	– (1)	–	– (6)
Tosic	–	–	– (2)	–	– (2)
Hargreaves	– (1)	–	–	–	– (1)
King	–	–	– (1)	–	– (1)

GOALSCORERS

PLAYER	PREM	FAC	LC	CL	TOT
Rooney	26	–	2	5	33
Berbatov	12	–	–	–	12
Owen	3	–	2	4	9
Giggs	5	–	1	1	7
Valencia	5	–	–	2	7
Scholes	3	–	1	3	7
Nani	4	–	–	2	6
Fletcher	4	–	–	1	5
Carrick	3	–	1	1	5
Gibson	2	–	2	1	5
Park	3	–	–	1	4
Welbeck	–	–	2	–	2
Anderson	1	–	–	–	1
Diouf	1	–	–	–	1
Macheda	1	–	–	–	1
O'Shea	1	–	–	–	1
Rafael	1	–	–	–	1
Vidic	1	–	–	–	1
own goals	10	–	–	–	10

2010/11

FA PREMIER LEAGUE

DATE	OPPONENTS	SCORE	GOALSCORERS	ATTENDANCE
Aug 16	NEWCASTLE UNITED	3-0	Berbatov, Fletcher, Giggs	75,221
Aug 22	Fulham	2-2	Scholes, og	25,643
Aug 28	WEST HAM UNITED	3-0	Berbatov, Nani, Rooney	75,061
Sep 11	Everton	3-3	Berbatov, Fletcher, Vidic	36,556
Sep 19	LIVERPOOL	3-2	Berbatov 3	75,213
Sep 26	Bolton Wanderers	2-2	Nani, Owen	23,926
Oct 2	Sunderland	0-0		41,709
Oct 16	WEST BROMWICH ALBION	2-2	Hernandez, Nani	75,272
Oct 24	Stoke City	2-1	Hernandez 2	27,372
Oct 30	TOTTENHAM HOTSPUR	2-0	Nani, Vidic	75,223
Nov 6	WOLVERHAMPTON W.	2-1	Park 2	75,285
Nov 10	Manchester City	0-0		47,679
Nov 13	Aston Villa	2-2	Macheda, Vidic	40,073
Nov 20	WIGAN ATHLETIC	2-0	Evra, Hernandez	74,181
Nov 27	BLACKBURN ROVERS	7-1	Berbatov 5, Nani, Park	74,850
Dec 13	ARSENAL	1-0	Park	75,227
Dec 26	SUNDERLAND	2-0	Berbatov, og	75,269
Dec 28	Birmingham City	1-1	Berbatov	28,242
Jan 1	West Bromwich Albion	2-1	Hernandez, Rooney	25,499
Jan 4	STOKE CITY	2-1	Hernandez, Nani	73,401
Jan 16	Tottenham Hotspur	0-0		35,828
Jan 22	BIRMINGHAM CITY	5-0	Berbatov 3, Giggs, Nani	75,326
Jan 25	Blackpool	3-2	Berbatov 2, Hernandez	15,574
Feb 1	ASTON VILLA	3-1	Rooney 2, Vidic	75,256
Feb 5	Wolverhampton W.	1-2	Nani	28,811
Feb 12	MANCHESTER CITY	2-1	Nani, Rooney	75,322
Feb 26	Wigan Athletic	4-0	Hernandez 2, Fabio, Rooney	18,140
Mar 1	Chelsea	1-2	Rooney	41,825
Mar 6	Liverpool	1-3	Hernandez	44,753
Mar 19	BOLTON WANDERERS	1-0	Berbatov	75,486
Apr 2	West Ham United	4-2	Rooney 3, Hernandez	34,546
Apr 9	FULHAM	2-0	Berbatov, Valencia	75,339
Apr 19	Newcastle United	0-0		49,025
Apr 23	EVERTON	1-0	Hernandez	75,300
May 1	Arsenal	0-1		60,107
May 8	CHELSEA	2-1	Hernandez, Vidic	75,445
May 14	Blackburn Rovers	1-1	Rooney	29,867
May 22	BLACKPOOL	4-2	Anderson, Owen, Park, og	75,400

FA CUP

DATE	OPPONENTS	SCORE	GOALSCORERS	ATTENDANCE
Jan 9	LIVERPOOL (Rd3)	1-0	Giggs	74,727
Jan 29	Southampton (Rd4)	2-1	Hernandez, Owen	28,792
Feb 19	CRAWLEY TOWN (Rd5)	1-0	Brown	74,778
Mar 12	ARSENAL (Rd6)	2-0	Fabio, Rooney	74,693
Apr 16	Manchester City (SF) (at Wembley Stadium)	0-1		86,549

LEAGUE CUP

DATE	OPPONENTS	SCORE	GOALSCORERS	ATTENDANCE
Sep 22	Scunthorpe United (Rd3)	5-2	Owen 2, Gibson, Park, Smalling	9,077
Oct 26	WOLVERHAMPTON W. (Rd4)	3-2	Bebe, Hernandez, Park	46,083
Nov 30	West Ham United (Rd5)	0-4		33,551

CHAMPIONS LEAGUE

DATE	OPPONENTS	SCORE	GOALSCORERS	ATTENDANCE
Sep 14	GLASGOW RANGERS (P1)	0-0		74,408
Sep 29	Valencia (P1)	1-0	Hernandez	52,689
Oct 20	BURSASPOR (P1)	1-0	Nani	72,610
Nov 2	Bursaspor (P1)	3-0	Bebe, Fletcher, Obertan	19,050
Nov 24	Glasgow Rangers (P1)	1-0	Rooney	49,764
Dec 7	VALENCIA (P1)	1-1	Anderson	74,513
Feb 23	Olympique Marseille (R2L1)	0-0		58,000
Mar 15	OLYMPIQUE MARSEILLE (R2L2)	2-1	Hernandez 2	73,996
Apr 6	Chelsea (QFL1)	1-0	Rooney	37,915
Apr 12	CHELSEA (QFL2)	2-1	Hernandez, Park	74,672
Apr 26	Schalke 04 (SFL1)	2-0	Giggs, Rooney	54,142
May 4	SCHALKE 04 (SFL2)	4-1	Anderson 2, Gibson, Valencia	74,637
May 28	Barcelona (Final) (at Wembley Stadium)	1-3	Rooney	87,695

FINAL LEAGUE TABLE

		P	W	D	L	F	A	Pts
1	MANCHESTER UNITED	38	23	11	4	78	37	80
2	Chelsea	38	21	8	9	69	33	71
3	Manchester City	38	21	8	9	60	33	71
4	Arsenal	38	19	11	8	72	43	68
5	Tottenham Hotspur	38	16	14	8	55	46	62
6	Liverpool	38	17	7	14	59	44	58
7	Everton	38	13	15	10	51	45	54
8	Fulham	38	11	16	11	49	43	49
9	Aston Villa	38	12	12	14	48	59	48
10	Sunderland	38	12	11	15	45	56	47
11	West Bromwich Albion	38	12	11	15	56	71	47
12	Newcastle United	38	11	13	14	56	57	46
13	Stoke City	38	13	7	18	46	48	46
14	Bolton Wanderers	38	12	10	16	52	56	46
15	Blackburn Rovers	38	11	10	17	46	59	43
16	Wigan Athletic	38	9	15	14	40	61	42
17	Wolverhampton Wanderers	38	11	7	20	46	66	40
18	Birmingham City	38	8	15	15	37	58	39
19	Blackpool	38	10	9	19	55	78	39
20	West Ham United	38	7	12	19	43	70	33

APPEARANCES

PLAYER	PREM	FAC	LC	CL	TOT
Evra	34 (1)	3	–	9 (1)	46 (2)
Vidic	35	2	–	9	46
van der Sar	33	2	–	10	45
Nani	31 (2)	2 (1)	–	9 (3)	42 (6)
Carrick	23 (5)	3	1	11	38 (5)
Rooney	25 (3)	1 (1)	–	9	35 (4)
Berbatov	24 (8)	2	–	6 (1)	32 (9)
Fletcher	24 (2)	1 (1)	1	5 (2)	31 (5)
Ferdinand	19	2	1	7	29
O'Shea	18 (2)	4	1	5 (1)	28 (3)
Hernandez	15 (12)	4 (1)	2 (1)	6 (3)	27 (17)
Giggs	19 (6)	1 (2)	1	6 (2)	27 (10)
Rafael	15 (1)	3	1 (1)	6 (1)	25 (3)
Park	13 (2)	1	2	8 (1)	24 (3)
Smalling	11 (5)	2 (2)	3	7 (2)	23 (9)
Scholes	16 (6)	2 (1)	–	4 (3)	22 (10)
Anderson	14 (4)	2 (2)	2	4 (2)	22 (8)
Evans	11 (2)	2	2	2 (1)	17 (3)
Fabio	5 (6)	3 (1)	2	5 (2)	15 (9)
Gibson	6 (6)	3	2	3	14 (6)
Valencia	8 (2)	1 (1)	–	5 (2)	14 (5)
Brown	4 (3)	2 (1)	2 (1)	2	10 (5)
Kuszczak	5	1	2	2	10
Obertan	3 (4)	2	2 (1)	1 (2)	8 (7)
Macheda	2 (5)	–	2 (1)	1 (1)	5 (7)
Owen	1 (10)	1 (1)	1	– (2)	3 (13)
Bebe	– (2)	1	2 (1)	– (1)	3 (4)
Neville	3	–	– (1)	–	3 (1)
Amos	–	–	1	1	2
Lindegaard	–	2	–	–	2
Hargreaves	1	–	–	–	1
Morrison	–	–	– (1)	–	– (1)

GOALSCORERS

PLAYER	PREM	FAC	LC	CL	TOT
Berbatov	20	–	–	–	20
Hernandez	13	1	1	4	19
Rooney	11	1	–	4	16
Nani	9	–	–	1	10
Park	5	–	2	1	8
Vidic	5	–	–	–	5
Owen	2	1	2	–	5
Giggs	2	1	–	1	4
Anderson	1	–	–	3	4
Fletcher	2	–	–	1	3
Fabio	1	1	–	–	2
Valencia	1	–	–	1	2
Bebe	–	–	1	1	2
Gibson	–	–	1	1	2
Evra	1	–	–	–	1
Macheda	1	–	–	–	1
Scholes	1	–	–	–	1
Brown	–	1	–	–	1
Obertan	–	–	–	1	1
Smalling	–	–	1	–	1
own goals	3	–	–	–	3

2011/12

FA PREMIER LEAGUE

DATE	OPPONENTS	SCORE	GOALSCORERS	ATTENDANCE
Aug 14	West Bromwich Albion	2-1	Rooney, og	25,360
Aug 22	TOTTENHAM HOTSPUR	3-0	Anderson, Rooney, Welbeck	75,498
Aug 28	ARSENAL	8-2	Rooney 3, Young 2, Nani, Park, Welbeck	75,448
Sep 10	Bolton Wanderers	5-0	Rooney 3, Hernandez 2	25,944
Sep 18	CHELSEA	3-1	Nani, Rooney, Smalling	75,455
Sep 24	Stoke City	1-1	Nani	27,582
Oct 1	NORWICH CITY	2-0	Anderson, Welbeck	75,514
Oct 15	Liverpool	1-1	Hernandez	45,065
Oct 23	MANCHESTER CITY	1-6	Fletcher	75,487
Oct 29	Everton	1-0	Hernandez	35,494
Nov 5	SUNDERLAND	1-0	og	75,570
Nov 19	Swansea City	1-0	Hernandez	20,295
Nov 26	NEWCASTLE UNITED	1-1	Hernandez	75,594
Dec 3	Aston Villa	1-0	Jones	40,053
Dec 10	WOLVERHAMPTON W.	4-1	Nani 2, Rooney 2	75,627
Dec 18	Queens Park Rangers	2-0	Carrick, Rooney	18,033
Dec 21	Fulham	5-0	Berbatov, Giggs, Nani, Rooney, Welbeck	25,700
Dec 26	WIGAN ATHLETIC	5-0	Berbatov 3, Park, Valencia	75,183
Dec 31	BLACKBURN ROVERS	2-3	Berbatov 2	75,146
Jan 4	Newcastle United	0-3		52,299
Jan 14	BOLTON WANDERERS	3-0	Carrick, Scholes, Welbeck	75,444
Jan 22	Arsenal	2-1	Valencia, Welbeck	60,093
Jan 31	STOKE CITY	2-0	Berbatov, Hernandez	74,719
Feb 5	Chelsea	3-3	Rooney 2, Hernandez	41,668
Feb 11	LIVERPOOL	2-1	Rooney 2	74,844
Feb 26	Norwich City	2-1	Giggs, Scholes	26,811
Mar 4	Tottenham Hotspur	3-1	Young 2, Rooney	36,034
Mar 11	WEST BROMWICH ALBION	2-0	Rooney 2	75,598
Mar 18	Wolverhampton W.	5-0	Hernandez 2, Evans, Valencia, Welbeck	27,494
Mar 26	FULHAM	1-0	Rooney	75,570
Apr 2	Blackburn Rovers	2-0	Valencia, Young	26,532
Apr 8	QUEENS PARK RANGERS	2-0	Rooney, Scholes	75,505
Apr 11	Wigan Athletic	0-1		18,115
Apr 15	ASTON VILLA	4-0	Rooney 2, Nani, Welbeck	75,138
Apr 22	EVERTON	4-4	Rooney 2, Nani, Welbeck	75,522
Apr 30	Manchester City	0-1		47,259
May 6	SWANSEA CITY	2-0	Scholes, Young	75,496
May 13	Sunderland	1-0	Rooney	46,452

FA CUP

DATE	OPPONENTS	SCORE	GOALSCORERS	ATTENDANCE
Jan 9	Manchester City (Rd3)	3-2	Rooney 2, Welbeck	46,808
Jan 29	Liverpool (Rd4)	1-2	Park	43,952

LEAGUE CUP

DATE	OPPONENTS	SCORE	GOALSCORERS	ATTENDANCE
Sep 20	Leeds United (Rd3)	3-0	Owen 2, Giggs	31,031
Oct 25	Aldershot (Rd4)	3-0	Berbatov, Owen, Valencia	7,044
Nov 30	CRYSTAL PALACE (QF)	1-2	Macheda	52,624

CHAMPIONS LEAGUE

DATE	OPPONENTS	SCORE	GOALSCORERS	ATTENDANCE
Sep 14	Benfica (P1)	1-1	Giggs	59,671
Sep 27	BASEL (P1)	3-3	Welbeck 2, Young	73,115
Oct 18	Otelul Galati (P1)	2-0	Rooney 2	49,500
Nov 2	OTELUL GALATI (P1)	2-0	Valencia, og	74,847
Nov 22	BENFICA (P1)	2-2	Berbatov, Fletcher	74,853
Dec 7	Basel (P1)	1-2	Jones	36,894

EUROPA LEAGUE

DATE	OPPONENTS	SCORE	GOALSCORERS	ATTENDANCE
Feb 16	Ajax (R32L1)	2-0	Hernandez, Young	51,000
Feb 23	AJAX (R32L2)	1-2	Hernandez	67,328
Mar 8	ATHLETIC BILBAO (R16L1)	2-3	Rooney 2	59,265
Mar 15	Athletic Bilbao (R16L2)	1-2	Rooney	40,000

FINAL LEAGUE TABLE

		P	W	D	L	F	A	Pts
1	Manchester City	38	28	5	5	93	29	89
2	MANCHESTER UNITED	38	28	5	5	89	33	89
3	Arsenal	38	21	7	10	74	49	70
4	Tottenham Hotspur	38	20	9	9	66	41	69
5	Newcastle United	38	19	8	11	56	51	65
6	Chelsea	38	18	10	10	65	46	64
7	Everton	38	15	11	12	50	40	56
8	Liverpool	38	14	10	14	47	40	52
9	Fulham	38	14	10	14	48	51	52
10	West Bromwich Albion	38	13	8	17	45	52	47
11	Swansea City	38	12	11	15	44	51	47
12	Norwich City	38	12	11	15	52	66	47
13	Sunderland	38	11	12	15	45	46	45
14	Stoke City	38	11	12	15	36	53	45
15	Wigan Athletic	38	11	10	17	42	62	43
16	Aston Villa	38	7	17	14	37	53	38
17	Queens Park Rangers	38	10	7	21	43	66	37
18	Bolton Wanderers	38	10	6	22	46	77	36
19	Blackburn Rovers	38	8	7	23	48	78	31
20	Wolverhampton Wanderers	38	5	10	23	40	82	25

APPEARANCES

PLAYER	PREM	FAC	LC	CL/EL	TOT
Evra	37	2	–	7	46
Rooney	32 (2)	1	–	7	40 (2)
De Gea	29	1	–	8	38
Carrick	27 (3)	2	1	6 (1)	36 (4)
Ferdinand	29 (1)	1	–	6	36 (1)
Evans	28 (1)	1	1	5 (3)	35 (4)
Jones	25 (4)	1	1	7 (2)	34 (6)
Valencia	22 (5)	2	3	5 (1)	32 (6)
Nani	24 (5)	1	–	6 (3)	31 (8)
Welbeck	23 (7)	2	– (1)	1 (4)	26 (12)
Young	19 (6)	–	–	7	26 (6)
Hernandez	18 (10)	– (1)	–	4 (3)	22 (14)
Giggs	14 (11)	2	1	5	22 (11)
Smalling	14 (5)	2	1	5 (2)	22 (7)
Park	10 (7)	1	3	5 (2)	19 (9)
Scholes	14 (3)	1 (1)	–	– (2)	15 (6)
Rafael	10 (2)	1	1	3	15 (2)
Fabio	2 (3)	–	3	7	12 (3)
Berbatov	5 (7)	– (1)	3	3 (1)	11 (9)
Anderson	8 (2)	– (1)	–	3 (1)	11 (4)
Lindegaard	8	1	–	2	11
Cleverley	5 (5)	–	1	3	9 (5)
Fletcher	7 (1)	–	–	2	9 (1)
Vidic	6	–	1	2	9
Amos	1	–	3	–	4
Owen	– (1)	–	2	1	3 (1)
Diouf	–	–	3	–	3
Fryers	– (2)	–	2 (1)	– (1)	2 (4)
Macheda	– (3)	–	2	– (1)	2 (4)
Gibson	1	–	1	–	2
Pogba	– (3)	–	– (3)	– (1)	– (7)
Morrison	–	–	– (2)	–	– (2)
Cole	–	–	– (1)	–	– (1)
Keane M	–	–	– (1)	–	– (1)
Keane W	– (1)	–	–	–	– (1)

GOALSCORERS

PLAYER	PREM	FAC	LC	CL/EL	TOT
Rooney	27	2	–	5	34
Hernandez	10	–	–	2	12
Welbeck	9	1	–	2	12
Berbatov	7	–	1	1	9
Nani	8	–	–	–	8
Young	6	–	–	2	8
Valencia	4	–	1	1	6
Scholes	4	–	–	–	4
Giggs	2	–	1	1	4
Park	2	1	–	–	3
Owen	–	–	3	–	3
Anderson	2	–	–	–	2
Carrick	2	–	–	–	2
Fletcher	1	–	–	1	2
Jones	1	–	–	1	2
Evans	1	–	–	–	1
Smalling	1	–	–	–	1
Macheda	–	–	1	–	1
own goals	2	–	–	1	3

OTHER COMPETITIVE MATCHES

CHARITY SHIELD / COMMUNITY SHIELD

DATE	OPPONENTS	SCORE	GOALSCORERS	ATTENDANCE	VENUE
Apr 27 1908	Queens Park Rangers	1-1	Meredith	6,000	Stamford Bridge
Apr 29 1908	Queens Park Rangers	4-0	Turnbull J 3, Wall	6,000	Stamford Bridge
Sep 25 1911	Swindon Town	8-4	Halse 6, Turnbull A, Wall	10,000	Stamford Bridge
Oct 6 1948	Arsenal	3-4	Burke, Rowley, og	31,000	Highbury
Sep 24 1952	NEWCASTLE UNITED	4-2	Rowley 2, Byrne, Downie	11,381	Old Trafford
Oct 24 1956	Manchester City	1-0	Viollet	30,495	Maine Road
Oct 22 1957	ASTON VILLA	4-0	Taylor 3, Berry	27,923	Old Trafford
Aug 17 1963	Everton	0-4		54,840	Goodison Park
Aug 14 1965	LIVERPOOL (Trophy shared)	2-2	Best, Herd	48,502	Old Trafford
Aug 12 1967	TOTTENHAM HOTSPUR (Trophy shared)	3-3	Charlton 2, Law	54,106	Old Trafford
Aug 13 1977	Liverpool (Trophy shared)	0-0		82,000	Wembley
Aug 20 1983	Liverpool	2-0	Robson 2	92,000	Wembley
Aug 10 1985	Everton	0-2		82,000	Wembley
Aug 18 1990	Liverpool (Trophy shared)	1-1	Blackmore	66,558	Wembley
Aug 7 1993	Arsenal (United won 5-4 on penalty kicks)	1-1	Hughes	66,519	Wembley
Aug 14 1994	Blackburn Rovers	2-0	Cantona, Ince	60,402	Wembley
Aug 11 1996	Newcastle United	4-0	Beckham, Butt, Cantona, Keane	73,214	Wembley
Aug 3 1997	Chelsea (United won 4-2 on penalty kicks)	1-1	Johnsen	73,636	Wembley
Aug 9 1998	Arsenal	0-3		67,342	Wembley
Aug 1 1999	Arsenal	1-2	Yorke	70,185	Wembley
Aug 13 2000	Chelsea	0-2		65,148	Wembley
Aug 12 2001	Liverpool	1-2	van Nistelrooy	70,227	Millennium Stadium
Aug 10 2003	Arsenal (United won 4-3 on penalty kicks)	1-1	Silvestre	59,293	Millennium Stadium
Aug 8 2004	Arsenal	1-3	Smith	63,317	Millennium Stadium
Aug 5 2007	Chelsea (United won 3-0 on penalty kicks)	1-1	Giggs	80,731	Wembley
Aug 10 2008	Portsmouth (United won 3-1 on penalty kicks)	0-0		84,808	Wembley
Aug 9 2009	Chelsea (United lost 1-4 on penalty kicks)	2-2	Nani, Rooney	85,896	Wembley
Aug 8 2010	Chelsea	3-1	Berbatov, Hernandez, Valencia	84,623	Wembley
Aug 9 2011	Manchester City	3-2	Nani 2, Smalling	77,169	Wembley

The matches listed here are classed as competitive matches for the purposes of the appearances and goalscoring records in this volume.

EUROPE/SOUTH AMERICA INTER-CONTINENTAL CUP

DATE	OPPONENTS	SCORE	GOALSCORERS	ATTENDANCE	VENUE
Sep 25 1968	Estudiantes de la Plata	0-1		55,000	Boca Juniors Stadium
Oct 16 1968	ESTUDIANTES DE LA PLATA (United lost 1-2 on aggregate)	1-1	Morgan	63,500	Old Trafford
Nov 30 1999	Palmeiras	1-0	Keane	53,372	Olympic Stadium, Tokyo

CLUB WORLD CUP

DATE	OPPONENTS	SCORE	GOALSCORERS	ATTENDANCE	VENUE
Dec 18 2008	Gamba Osaka	5-3	Rooney 2, Fletcher, Ronaldo, Vidic	67,618	Yokohama Stadium
Dec 21 2008	Liga de Quito	1-0	Rooney	62,619	Yokohama Stadium

CLUB WORLD CHAMPIONSHIP

DATE	OPPONENTS	SCORE	GOALSCORERS	ATTENDANCE	VENUE
Jan 6 2000	Rayos del Necaxa	1-1	Yorke	50,000	Maracana Stadium
Jan 8 2000	Vasca da Gama	1-3	Butt	73,000	Maracana Stadium
Jan 11 2000	South Melbourne (United failed to qualify from the group phase)	2-0	Fortune 2	25,000	Maracana Stadium

EUROPEAN SUPER CUP

DATE	OPPONENTS	SCORE	GOALSCORERS	ATTENDANCE	VENUE
Nov 19 1991	RED STAR BELGRADE	1-0	McClair	22,110	Old Trafford
Aug 27 1999	Lazio	0-1		14,461	Stade Louis II, Monaco
Aug 29 2008	Zenit St. Petersburg	1-2	Vidic	18,500	Stade Louis II, Monaco

TEST MATCHES

DATE	OPPONENTS	SCORE	GOALSCORERS	ATTENDANCE	VENUE
Apr 22 1893	Birmingham City	1-1	Farman	4,000	Victoria Ground
Apr 27 1893	Birmingham City (United retained their Division One status)	5-2	Farman 3, Cassidy, Coupar	6,000	Bramall Lane
Apr 28 1894	Liverpool (United were relegated to Division Two)	0-2		3,000	Ewood Park
Apr 27 1895	Stoke City (United remained in Division Two)	0-3		10,000	Cobridge Stadium
Apr 19 1897	Burnley	0-2		10,000	Turf Moor
Apr 21 1897	BURNLEY	2-0	Boyd, Jenkyns	7,000	Bank Street
Apr 24 1897	SUNDERLAND	1-1	Boyd	18,000	Bank Street
Apr 26 1897	Sunderland (United remained in Division Two)	0-2		6,000	Newcastle Road

APPEARANCES

PLAYER	CS	ICC	ESC	CWC	TM	TOT
Albiston, Arthur	3	-	-	-	-	3
Anderson	1	-	1	2	-	4
Anderson, John	1	-	-	-	-	1
Aston, John (Jnr)	2	-	-	-	-	2
Aston, John (Snr)	2	-	-	-	-	2
Bailey, Gary	2	-	-	-	-	2
Bannister, Jimmy	2	-	-	-	-	2
Barrett, Frank	-	-	-	-	4	4
Barthez, Fabien	2	-	-	-	-	2
Beckham, David	5 (1)	1	1	1 (1)	-	8 (2)
Bell, Alex	3	-	-	-	-	3
Bellion, David	1	-	-	-	-	1
Berbatov, Dimitar	1 (2)	-	-	-	-	1 (2)
Berg, Henning	1 (1)	-	1	1	-	3 (1)
Berry, Johnny	3	-	-	-	-	3
Best, George	2	2	-	-	-	4
Blackmore, Clayton	1	-	1	-	-	2
Blanchflower, Jackie	1	-	-	-	-	1
Bosnich, Mark	1	1	-	2	-	4
Boyd, Henry	-	-	-	-	3	3
Brennan, Shay	2	1	-	-	-	3
Brown, Wes	1 (1)	-	- (1)	-	-	1 (2)
Bruce, Steve	3	-	1	-	-	4
Bryant, William	-	-	-	-	4	4
Buchan, Martin	1	-	-	-	-	1
Burgess, Herbert	2	-	-	-	-	2
Burke, Ronnie	1	-	-	-	-	1
Burns, Francis	-	1	-	-	-	1
Butt, Nicky	6	1	-	2	-	9
Byrne, Roger	3	-	-	-	-	3
Campbell, Fraizer	- (1)	-	-	-	-	- (1)
Cantona, Eric	3	-	-	-	-	3
Cantwell, Noel	2	-	-	-	-	2
Carey, Johnny	2	-	-	-	-	2
Carrick, Michael	4 (1)	-	-	1	-	5 (1)
Cartwright, Walter	-	-	-	-	2	2
Cassidy, Joe	-	-	-	-	7	7
Charlton, Bobby	3	2	-	-	-	5
Chilton, Allenby	2	-	-	-	-	2
Clarkin, John	-	-	-	-	2	2
Clements, John	-	-	-	-	2	2
Cleverley, Tom	- (1)	-	-	-	-	- (1)
Cole, Andrew	3 (1)	-	1	2	-	6 (1)
Colman, Eddie	1	-	-	-	-	1
Coppell, Steve	1	-	-	-	-	1
Coupar, Jimmy	-	-	-	-	2	2
Crerand, Pat	3	2	-	-	-	5
Crompton, Jack	1	-	-	-	-	1
Cruyff, Jordi	1 (3)	-	- (1)	1 (1)	-	2 (5)
Curtis, John	-	-	- (1)	-	-	- (1)
Davidson, Will	-	-	-	-	1	1
Davies, John	-	-	-	-	2	2
De Gea, David	1	-	-	-	-	1
Delaney, Jimmy	1	-	-	-	-	1
Djemba-Djemba, Eric	1 (1)	-	-	-	-	1 (1)
Donaghy, Mal	1	-	-	-	-	1
Donaldson, Bob	-	-	-	-	8	8
Doughty, Roger	-	-	-	-	3	3
Douglas, William	-	-	-	-	1	1
Dow, John	-	-	-	-	1	1
Downie, John	1	-	-	-	-	1
Draycott, Billy	-	-	-	-	4	4
Duckworth, Dick	3	-	-	-	-	3
Dunne, Pat	1	-	-	-	-	1
Dunne, Tony	3	2	-	-	-	5
Duxbury, Mike	2	-	-	-	-	2
Eagles, Chris	- (1)	-	-	-	-	- (1)
Edmonds, Hugh	1	-	-	-	-	1
Edwards, Duncan	2	-	-	-	-	2
Erentz, Fred	-	-	-	-	7	7
Evans, Johnny	2 (1)	-	-	- (2)	-	2 (3)
Evra, Patrice	4	-	1	2	-	7
Fabio da Silva	1 (1)	-	-	-	-	1 (1)
Fall, Joe	-	-	-	-	1	1
Farman, Alf	-	-	-	-	3	3
Ferdinand, Rio	5	-	1	2	-	8
Fitzsimmons, Tommy	-	-	-	-	2	2
Fletcher, Darren	2 (3)	-	1	- (2)	-	3 (5)
Forlan, Diego	- (2)	-	-	-	-	- (2)
Fortune, Quinton	2 (1)	-	-	1 (1)	-	3 (2)
Foster, Ben	1	-	-	-	-	1
Foulkes, Bill	4	2	-	-	-	6
Gaskell, David	1 (1)	-	-	-	-	1 (1)
Gibson, Don	1	-	-	-	-	1
Gidman, John	1 (1)	-	-	-	-	1 (1)
Giggs, Ryan	11 (2)	1	- (1)	3	-	15 (3)
Giles, Johnny	1	-	-	-	-	1
Gillespie, Matthew	-	-	-	-	4	4
Goodwin, Fred	1	-	-	-	-	1
Graham, Arthur	1	-	-	-	-	1
Greenhoff, Brian	1	-	-	-	-	1
Greenhoff, Jimmy	1	-	-	-	-	1
Greening, Jonathan	-	-	- (1)	1	-	1 (1)
Halse, Harold	1	-	-	-	-	1
Hamill, Mickey	1	-	-	-	-	1
Herd, David	2	-	-	-	-	2
Hernandez, Javier	- (1)	-	-	-	-	- (1)
Higginbotham, Danny	-	-	-	1	-	1
Hill, Gordon	1	-	-	-	-	1
Hofton, Leslie	1	-	-	-	-	1
Hogg, Graeme	1	-	-	-	-	1
Hood, Billy	-	-	-	-	2	2
Howard, Tim	2	-	-	-	-	2
Hughes, Mark	4	-	1	-	-	5
Ince, Paul	3	-	1	-	-	4
Irwin, Denis	8	1	1	2	-	12
Jenkyns, Caesar	-	-	-	-	4	4
Johnsen, Ronny	3	-	-	-	-	3
Jones, Phil	- (1)	-	-	-	-	- (1)
Jones, Mark	1	-	-	-	-	1
Kanchelskis, Andrei	2	-	1	-	-	3
Keane, Roy	8	1	1	2	-	12
Kidd, Brian	1	1	-	-	-	2
Law, Denis	3	2	-	-	-	5
Macari, Lou	1	-	-	-	-	1
Martin, Lee	-	-	1	-	-	1
May, David	2 (1)	-	-	-	-	2 (1)
McCartney, John	-	-	-	-	1	1
McClair, Brian	2	-	1	-	-	3
McCreery, David	- (1)	-	-	-	-	- (1)
McGrath, Paul	1	-	-	-	-	1
McIlroy, Sammy	1	-	-	-	-	1
McNaught, James	-	-	-	-	5	5
McNulty, Thomas	1	-	-	-	-	1
McQueen, Gordon	1	-	-	-	-	1
Meredith, Billy	3	-	-	-	-	3
Mitchell, Andrew	-	-	-	-	3	3
Mitten, Charlie	1	-	-	-	-	1
Moger, Harry	2	-	-	-	-	2
Moran, Kevin	1	-	-	-	-	1
Morgan, Willie	-	2	-	-	-	2
Morris, Johnny	1	-	-	-	-	1
Moses, Remi	- (1)	-	-	-	-	- (1)
Muhren, Arnold	1	-	-	-	-	1
Nani	3 (2)	-	1	1	-	5 (2)
Neville, Gary	5 (1)	1	2	3 (1)	-	11 (2)
Neville, Phil	4 (2)	-	1	2 (1)	-	7 (3)
Nicholl, Jimmy	1	-	-	-	-	1
Olsen, Jesper	1	-	-	-	-	1
O'Shea, John	5 (1)	-	- (1)	-	-	5 (2)
Owen, Michael	1 (1)	-	-	-	-	1 (1)
Pallister, Gary	5	-	1	-	-	6
Park, Ji-Sung	2	-	- (1)	1	-	3 (1)
Parker, Paul	1	-	-	-	-	1
Pearson, Stan	1	-	-	-	-	1
Pearson, Stuart	1	-	-	-	-	1
Peden, Jack	-	-	-	-	1	1
Pegg, David	2	-	-	-	-	2
Perrins, George	-	-	-	-	4	4
Peters, James	-	-	-	-	1	1
Phelan, Mike	1	-	-	-	-	1
Picken, Jack	1	-	-	-	-	1
Poborsky, Karel	- (1)	-	-	-	-	- (1)
Quixall, Albert	1	-	-	-	-	1
Rachubka, Paul	-	-	-	- (1)	-	- (1)
Rafael da Silva	- (1)	-	-	1	-	1 (1)
Richardson, Kieran	- (1)	-	-	-	-	- (1)
Roberts, Charlie	3	-	-	-	-	3
Robins, Mark	- (1)	-	-	-	-	- (1)
Robson, Bryan	2 (1)	-	-	-	-	2 (1)
Ronaldo, Cristiano	1	-	-	2	-	3
Rooney, Wayne	4	-	1	1 (1)	-	6 (1)
Rowley, Jack	2	-	-	-	-	2
Sadler, David	-	2	-	-	-	2
Sartori, Carlo	- (1)	-	-	-	-	- (1)
Schmeichel, Peter	5	-	1	-	-	6
Scholes, Paul	10 (1)	1	2	1	-	14 (1)
Sealey, Les	1	-	-	-	-	1
Setters, Maurice	1	-	-	-	-	1
Sharpe, Lee	1	-	-		-	1
Sheringham, Teddy	2 (2)	- (1)	1	- (2)	-	3 (5)
Silvestre, Mikael	5	1	-	2	-	8
Smalling, Chris	1 (1)	-	-	-	-	1 (1)
Smith, Alan	1	-	-	-	-	1
Smith, Dick	-	-	-	-	1	1
Solskjaer, Ole	2 (2)	1	1	2 (1)	-	6 (3)
Spector, Jonathan	- (1)	-	-	-	-	- (1)
Stacey, George	3	-	-	-	-	3
Stam, Jaap	3 (1)	1	1	2	-	7 (1)
Stapleton, Frank	2	-	-	-	-	2
Stepney, Alex	2	2	-	-	-	4
Stewart, Willie	-	-	-	-	2	2
Stiles, Nobby	2	1	-	-	-	3
Stone, Herbert	-	-	-	-	1	1
Taylor, Tommy	2	-	-	-	-	2
Tevez, Carlos	1	-	1	2	-	4
Turnbull, Jimmy	2	-	-	-	-	2
Turnbull, Sandy	2	-	-	-	-	2
Valencia, Antonio	1 (1)	-	-	-	-	1 (1)
van der Sar, Edwin	3	-	1	2	-	6
van der Gouw, Raimond	-	-	1	1	-	2
van Nistelrooy, Ruud	2	-	-	-	-	2
Vidic, Nemanja	4	-	1	2	-	7
Viollet, Dennis	2	-	-	-	-	2
Wall, George	3	-	-	-	-	3
Wallace, Danny	1	-	-	-	-	1
Wallwork, Ronnie	-	-	-	1	-	1
Warner, Jack	1	-	-	-	-	1
Webb, Neil	-	-	1	-	-	1
Welbeck, Danny	1	-	-	-	-	1
Whelan, William	2	-	-	-	-	2

PLAYER	CS	ICC	ESC	CWC	TOT
Whiteside, Norman	2	-	-	-	2
Wilkins, Ray	1	-	-	-	1
Wilson, Mark	-	-	-	1	1
Wood, Ray	3	-	-	-	3
Young, Ashley	1	-	-	-	1
Yorke, Dwight	1 (2)	- (1)	-	2	3(3)

GOALSCORERS

PLAYER	CS	ICC	ESC	CWC	TM	TOT
Beckham, David	1	-	-	-	-	1
Berbatov, Dimitar	1	-	-	-	-	1
Berry, Johnny	1	-	-	-	-	1
Best, George	1	-	-	-	-	1
Blackmore, Clayton	1	-	-	-	-	1
Boyd, Henry	-	-	-	-	2	2
Burke, Ronnie	1	-	-	-	-	1
Butt, Nicky	1	-	-	1	-	2
Byrne, Roger	1	-	-	-	-	1
Cantona, Eric	2	-	-	-	-	2
Cassidy, Joe	-	-	-	-	1	1
Charlton, Bobby	2	-	-	-	-	2
Coupar, Jimmy	-	-	-	-	1	1
Downie, John	1	-	-	-	-	1
Farman, Alf	-	-	-	-	4	4
Fletcher, Darren	-	-	-	1	-	1
Fortune, Quinton	-	-	-	2	-	2
Giggs, Ryan	1	-	-	-	-	1
Halse, Harold	6	-	-	-	-	6
Herd, David	1	-	-	-	-	1
Hernandez, Javier	1	-	-	-	-	1
Hughes, Mark	1	-	-	-	-	1
Ince, Paul	1	-	-	-	-	1
Jenkyns, Caesar	-	-	-	-	1	1
Johnsen, Ronny	1	-	-	-	-	1
Keane, Roy	1	1	-	-	-	2
Law, Denis	1	-	-	-	-	1
McClair, Brian	-	-	1	-	-	1
Meredith, Billy	1	-	-	-	-	1
Morgan, Willie	-	1	-	-	-	1
Nani	3	-	-	-	-	3
Robson, Bryan	2	-	-	-	-	2
Ronaldo, Cristiano	-	-	-	1	-	1
Rooney, Wayne	1	-	-	3	-	4
Rowley, Jack	3	-	-	-	-	3
Silvestre, Mikael	1	-	-	-	-	1
Smalling, Chris	1	-	-	-	-	1
Smith, Alan	1	-	-	-	-	1
Taylor, Tommy	3	-	-	-	-	3
Turnbull, Jimmy	3	-	-	-	-	3
Turnbull, Sandy	1	-	-	-	-	1
Valencia, Antonio	1	-	-	-	-	1
van Nistelrooy, Ruud	1	-	-	-	-	1
Vidic, Nemanja	-	-	1	1	-	2
Viollet, Dennis	1	-	-	-	-	1
Wall, George	2	-	-	-	-	2
Yorke, Dwight	1	-	-	1	-	2
own goal	1	-	-	-	-	1

THE TOP 10 APPEARANCE MAKERS

OVERALL COMPETITION	APPS	SUBS	TOTAL
1 Giggs, Ryan	769	(140)	909
2 Charlton, Bobby	756	(2)	758
3 Scholes, Paul	567	(130)	697
4 Foulkes, Bill	685	(3)	688
5 Neville, Gary	566	(36)	602
6 Stepney, Alex	539		539
7 Dunne, Tony	534	(1)	535
8 Irwin, Denis	511	(18)	529
9 Spence, Joe	510		510
10 Albiston, Arthur	467	(18)	485

ALL LEAGUE MATCHES	APPS	SUBS	TOTAL
1 Giggs, Ryan	537	(101)	638
2 Charlton, Bobby	604	(2)	606
3 Foulkes, Bill	563	(3)	566
4 Scholes, Paul	396	(87)	483
5 Spence, Joe	481		481
6 Stepney, Alex	433		433
7 Silcock, Jack	423		423
8 Dunne, Tony	414		414
9 Neville, Gary	380	(20)	400
10 Rowley, Jack	380		380

FA PREMIER LEAGUE	APPS	SUBS	TOTAL
1 Giggs, Ryan	504	(94)	598
2 Scholes, Paul	396	(87)	483
3 Neville, Gary	380	(20)	400
4 Keane, Roy	309	(17)	326
5 Irwin, Denis	286	(10)	296
6 Ferdinand, Rio	267	(3)	270
7 Butt, Nicky	210	(60)	270
8 Beckham, David	237	(28)	265
9 Neville, Phil	210	(53)	263
10 O'Shea, John	188	(68)	256

LEAGUE DIVISION ONE	APPS	SUBS	TOTAL
1 Charlton, Bobby	604	(2)	606
2 Foulkes, Bill	563	(3)	566
3 Dunne, Tony	414	–	414
4 Stepney, Alex	393	–	393
5 Albiston, Arthur	362	(15)	377
6 Best, George	361	–	361
7 Rowley, Jack	355	–	355
8 Chilton, Allenby	352	–	352
9 Buchan, Martin	335	–	335
10 Robson, Bryan	311	(5)	316

LEAGUE DIVISION TWO	APPS	SUBS	TOTAL
1 Erentz, Fred	229	–	229
2 Cartwright, Walter	228	–	228
3 Stafford, Harry	183	–	183
4 Spence, Joe	169	–	169
5 Griffiths, Billy	157	–	157
6 Silcock, Jack	152	–	152
7 Cassidy, Joe	148	–	148
8 Schofield, Alf	147	–	147
9 Morgan, Billy	143	–	143
10 Manley, Tom	134	–	134

FA CUP	APPS	SUBS	TOTAL
1 Charlton, Bobby	78		78
2 Giggs, Ryan	60	(10)	70
3 Foulkes, Bill	61		61
4 Dunne, Tony	54	(1)	55
5 Neville, Gary	44	(3)	47
6 Best, George	46		46
7 Hughes, Mark	45	(1)	46
=8 Keane, Roy	44	(2)	46
Law, Denis	44	(2)	46
10 Scholes, Paul	31	(15)	46

LEAGUE CUP	APPS	SUBS	TOTAL
1 Robson, Bryan	50	(1)	51
2 McClair, Brian	44	(1)	45
3 Albiston, Arthur	38	(2)	40
4 Hughes, Mark	37	(1)	38
5 Giggs, Ryan	32	(6)	38
6 Pallister, Gary	36		36
7 Stepney, Alex	35		35
=8 Bruce, Steve	32	(2)	34
Duxbury, Mike	32	(2)	34
10 Irwin, Denis	28	(3)	31

ALL EUROPEAN MATCHES	APPS	SUBS	TOTAL
1 Giggs, Ryan	125	(20)	145
2 Scholes, Paul	112	(20)	132
3 Neville, Gary	109	(8)	117
4 Beckham, David	79	(4)	83
5 Keane, Roy	81	(1)	82
6 Solskjaer, Ole Gunnar	36	(45)	81
7 Ferdinand, Rio	79	(1)	80
8 O'Shea, John	61	(15)	76
9 Irwin, Denis	73	(2)	75
10 Butt, Nicky	58	(13)	71

EUROPEAN CUP / CL	APPS	SUBS	TOTAL
1 Giggs, Ryan	119	(20)	139
2 Scholes, Paul	111	(17)	128
3 Neville, Gary	108	(7)	115
4 Beckham, David	77	(4)	81
5 Solskjaer, Ole Gunnar	36	(45)	81
6 Keane, Roy	79	(1)	80
7 Ferdinand, Rio	77	(1)	78
8 O'Shea, John	61	(15)	76
9 Silvestre, Mikael	61	(8)	69
10 Butt, Nicky	56	(13)	69

THE TOP 10 GOALSCORERS

OVERALL COMPETITION	GOALS	APPS	STRIKE RATE
1 Charlton, Bobby	249	758	32.8
2 Law, Denis	237	404	58.7
3 Rowley, Jack	211	424	49.8
4 Rooney, Wayne	181	365	49.6
=5 Best, George	179	470	38.1
Viollet, Dennis	179	293	61.1
7 Spence, Joe	168	510	32.9
=8 Giggs, Ryan	163	909	17.9
Hughes, Mark	163	467	34.9
10 Scholes, Paul	154	697	22.1

ALL LEAGUE MATCHES	GOALS	APPS	STRIKE RATE
1 Charlton, Bobby	199	606	32.8
2 Rowley, Jack	182	380	47.9
3 Law, Denis	171	309	55.3
4 Viollet, Dennis	159	259	61.4
5 Spence, Joe	158	481	32.9
6 Best, George	137	361	37.9
7 Rooney, Wayne	129	251	51.4
8 Pearson, Stan	127	312	40.7
9 Hughes, Mark	120	345	34.8
10 Herd, David	114	202	56.4

FA PREMIER LEAGUE	GOALS	APPS	STRIKE RATE
1 Rooney, Wayne	129	251	51.4
2 Giggs, Ryan	107	598	17.9
3 Scholes, Paul	106	483	21.9
4 van Nistelrooy, Ruud	95	150	63.3
5 Cole, Andrew	93	195	47.7
6 Solskjaer, Ole Gunnar	91	235	38.7
7 Ronaldo, Cristiano	84	196	42.9
8 Cantona, Eric	64	143	44.8
9 Beckham, David	62	265	23.4
10 Berbatov, Dimitar	48	108	44.4

LEAGUE DIVISION ONE	GOALS	APPS	STRIKE RATE
1 Charlton, Bobby	199	606	32.8
2 Rowley, Jack	173	355	48.7
3 Law, Denis	171	309	55.3
4 Viollet, Dennis	159	259	61.4
5 Best, George	137	361	38.0
6 Pearson, Stan	125	301	41.5
7 Herd, David	114	202	56.4
8 Taylor, Tommy	112	166	67.5
9 Spence, Joe	106	312	34.0
10 Turnbull, Sandy	90	220	40.9

LEAGUE DIVISION TWO	GOALS	APPS	STRIKE RATE
1 Cassidy, Joe	90	148	60.8
2 Spence, Joe	52	169	30.8
3 Peddie, Jack	46	96	47.9
4 Lochhead, Arthur	40	111	36.0
=5 Bamford, Tommy	39	69	56.5
Mutch, George	39	84	46.4
7 Smith, Dick	35	93	37.6
8 Donaldson, Bob	33	81	40.7
=9 Boyd, Henry	32	52	61.5
Manley, Tom	32	134	23.9

FA CUP	GOALS	APPS	STRIKE RATE
1 Law, Denis	34	46	73.9
2 Rowley, Jack	26	42	61.9
=3 Best, George	21	46	45.7
Pearson, Stan	21	30	70.0
5 Charlton, Bobby	19	78	24.4
6 Hughes, Mark	17	46	37.0
7 Herd, David	15	35	42.9
=8 McClair, Brian	14	45	31.1
Rooney, Wayne	14	26	53.8
van Nistelrooy, Ruud	14	14	100.0

LEAGUE CUP	GOALS	APPS	STRIKE RATE
1 McClair, Brian	19	45	42.2
2 Hughes, Mark	16	38	42.1
=3 Giggs, Ryan	10	38	26.3
Macari, Lou	10	27	37.0
=5 Best, George	9	25	36.0
Coppell, Steve	9	25	36.0
Scholes, Paul	9	21	42.9
Sharpe, Lee	9	23	39.1
Whiteside, Norman	9	29	31.0
=10 Charlton, Bobby	7	24	29.2
Kidd, Brian	7	20	35.0
Owen, Michael	7	7	100.0
Saha, Louis	7	9	77.8
Solskjaer, Ole Gunnar	7	11	63.6

ALL EUROPEAN MATCHES	GOALS	APPS	STRIKE RATE
1 van Nistelrooy, Ruud	38	47	80.9
2 Rooney, Wayne	30	70	42.9
3 Giggs, Ryan	29	145	20.0
4 Law, Denis	28	33	84.8
5 Scholes, Paul	26	132	19.7
6 Charlton, Bobby	22	45	48.9
7 Solskjaer, Ole Gunnar	20	81	24.7
8 Cole, Andrew	19	50	38.0
9 Ronaldo, Cristiano	16	55	29.1
10 Beckham, David	15	83	18.1

EUROPEAN CUP / CL	GOALS	APPS	STRIKE RATE
1 van Nistelrooy, Ruud	38	47	80.9
2 Giggs, Ryan	29	139	20.9
3 Rooney, Wayne	27	67	40.3
4 Scholes, Paul	25	128	19.5
5 Solskjaer, Ole Gunnar	20	81	24.7
6 Cole, Andrew	19	49	38.8
7 Ronaldo, Cristiano	16	55	29.1
8 Beckham, David	15	81	18.5
=9 Keane, Roy	14	80	17.5
Law, Denis	14	18	77.8

The 'Strike Rate' referred to in the above tables is calculated as goals scored per 100 games played

PLAYER ROLL CALL

PLAYER	PREMIER LGE		DIVISION ONE		DIVISION TWO		FA CUP		LEAGUE CUP		EC / CL		ECWC		UEFA CUP		OTHER GAMES		TOTALS		DEBUT
	APPS	GLS	APPS	GLS	APPS	GLS	APPS	GLS	APPS	GLS	APPS	GLS	APPS	GLS	APPS	GLS	APPS	GLS	APPS	GLS	
A																					
AINSWORTH, Alf	–	–	–	–	2	–	–	–	–	–	–	–	–	–	–	–	–	–	2	–	3 Mar 1934
AITKEN, John	–	–	–	–	2	1	–	–	–	–	–	–	–	–	–	–	–	–	2	1	7 Sep 1895
ALBINSON, George	–	–	–	–	–	–	1	–	–	–	–	–	–	–	–	–	–	–	1	–	12 Jan 1921
ALBISTON, Arthur	–	–	362 (15)	6	2	–	36	–	38 (2)	1	–	–	12	–	14 (1)	–	3	–	467 (18)	7	9 Oct 1974
ALLAN, Jack	–	–	3	–	32	21	1	1	–	–	–	–	–	–	–	–	–	–	36	22	3 Sep 1904
ALLEN, Reg	–	–	75	–	–	–	5	–	–	–	–	–	–	–	–	–	–	–	80	–	19 Aug 1950
ALLMAN, Arthur	–	–	12	–	–	–	–	–	–	–	–	–	–	–	–	–	–	–	12	–	13 Feb 1915
AMBLER, Alfred	–	–	–	–	10	1	–	–	–	–	–	–	–	–	–	–	–	–	10	1	2 Sep 1899
AMOS, Ben	1	–	–	–	–	–	–	–	5	–	1	–	–	–	–	–	–	–	7	–	23 Sep 2008
ANDERSON	59 (24)	4	–	–	–	–	8 (5)	–	11 (1)	–	25 (7)	3	–	–	– (1)	–	4	–	107 (38)	7	1 Sep 2007
ANDERSON, George	–	–	80	37	–	–	6	2	–	–	–	–	–	–	–	–	–	–	86	39	9 Sep 1911
ANDERSON, John	–	–	33	1	–	–	6	1	–	–	–	–	–	–	–	–	1	–	40	2	20 Dec 1947
ANDERSON, Trevor	–	–	13 (6)	2	–	–	–	–	–	–	–	–	–	–	–	–	–	–	13 (6)	2	31 Mar 1973
ANDERSON, Viv	–	–	50 (4)	2	–	–	7	1	6 (1)	1	–	–	1	–	–	–	–	–	64 (5)	4	15 Aug 1987
ANDERSON, Willie	–	–	7 (2)	–	–	–	2	–	–	–	1	–	–	–	–	–	–	–	10 (2)	–	28 Dec 1963
APPLETON, Michael	–	–	–	–	–	–	–	–	1 (1)	–	–	–	–	–	–	–	–	–	1 (1)	–	23 Oct 1996
ARKESDEN, Tommy	–	–	–	–	70	28	9	5	–	–	–	–	–	–	–	–	–	–	79	33	14 Feb 1903
ASTLEY, Joe	–	–	2	–	–	–	–	–	–	–	–	–	–	–	–	–	–	–	2	–	17 Mar 1926
ASTON, John (Jnr)	–	–	139 (16)	25	–	–	5 (2)	1	12 (3)	–	8	1	–	–	–	–	2	–	166 (21)	27	12 Apr 1965
ASTON, John (Snr)	–	–	253	29	–	–	29	1	–	–	–	–	–	–	–	–	2	–	284	30	18 Sep 1946
B																					
BAILEY, Gary	–	–	294	–	–	–	31	–	28	–	–	–	8	–	12	–	2	–	375	–	18 Nov 1978
BAIN, David	–	–	–	–	22	9	1	–	–	–	–	–	–	–	–	–	–	–	23	9	14 Oct 1922
BAIN, James	–	–	–	–	2	1	–	–	–	–	–	–	–	–	–	–	–	–	2	1	16 Sep 1899
BAIN, Jimmy	–	–	3	–	1	–	–	–	–	–	–	–	–	–	–	–	–	–	4	–	7 Feb 1925
BAINBRIDGE, Bill	–	–	–	–	–	–	1	1	–	–	–	–	–	–	–	–	–	–	1	1	9 Jan 1946
BAIRD, Harry	–	–	14	3	35	12	4	3	–	–	–	–	–	–	–	–	–	–	53	18	23 Jan 1937
BALDWIN, Tommy	–	–	–	–	2	–	–	–	–	–	–	–	–	–	–	–	–	–	2	–	18 Jan 1975
BALL, Billy	–	–	–	–	4	–	–	–	–	–	–	–	–	–	–	–	–	–	4	–	8 Nov 1902
BALL, Jack	–	–	23	11	24	6	3	1	–	–	–	–	–	–	–	–	–	–	50	18	11 Sep 1929
BALL, John	–	–	22	–	–	–	1	–	–	–	–	–	–	–	–	–	–	–	23	–	10 Apr 1948
BAMFORD, Tommy	–	–	29	14	69	39	11	4	–	–	–	–	–	–	–	–	–	–	109	57	20 Oct 1934
BANKS, Jack	–	–	–	–	40	–	4	1	–	–	–	–	–	–	–	–	–	–	44	1	7 Sep 1901
BANNISTER, Jimmy	–	–	57	7	–	–	4	1	–	–	–	–	–	–	–	–	2	–	63	8	1 Jan 1907
BARBER, Jack	–	–	–	–	3	1	1	1	–	–	–	–	–	–	–	–	–	–	4	2	6 Jan 1923
BARDSLEY, Phil	3 (5)	–	–	–	–	–	2 (1)	–	3 (1)	–	2 (1)	–	–	–	–	–	–	–	10 (8)	–	3 Dec 2003
BARLOW, Cyril	–	–	29	–	–	–	1	–	–	–	–	–	–	–	–	–	–	–	30	–	7 Feb 1920
BARNES, Michael	–	–	–	–	–	–	–	–	– (1)	–	–	–	–	–	–	–	–	–	– (1)	–	25 Oct 2006
BARNES, Peter	–	–	19 (1)	2	–	–	–	–	5	2	–	–	–	–	–	–	–	–	24 (1)	4	31 Aug 1985
BARRETT, Frank	–	–	–	–	118	–	14	–	–	–	–	–	–	–	–	–	4	–	136	–	26 Sep 1896
BARSON, Frank	–	–	60	4	80	–	12	–	–	–	–	–	–	–	–	–	–	–	152	4	9 Sep 1922
BARTHEZ, Fabien	92	–	–	–	–	–	4	–	4	–	37	–	–	–	–	–	2	–	139	–	13 Aug 2000
BEADSWORTH, Arthur	–	–	–	–	9	1	3	1	–	–	–	–	–	–	–	–	–	–	12	2	25 Oct 1902
BEALE, Robert	–	–	105	–	–	–	7	–	–	–	–	–	–	–	–	–	–	–	112	–	2 Sep 1912
BEARDSLEY, Peter	–	–	–	–	–	–	–	–	1	–	–	–	–	–	–	–	–	–	1	–	6 Oct 1982
BEARDSMORE, Russell	–	–	30 (26)	4	–	–	4 (4)	–	3 (1)	–	–	–	2 (3)	–	–	–	–	–	39 (34)	4	24 Sep 1988
BEBE, Tiago	– (2)	–	–	–	–	–	1	–	2 (1)	1	– (1)	1	–	–	–	–	–	–	3 (4)	2	22 Sep 2010
BECKETT, R	–	–	–	–	–	–	1	–	–	–	–	–	–	–	–	–	–	–	1	–	30 Oct 1886
BECKHAM, David	237 (28)	62	–	–	–	–	22 (2)	6	10 (2)	1	77 (4)	15	–	–	2	–	8 (2)	1	356 (38)	85	23 Sep 1992
BEDDOW, John	–	–	3	–	30	12	1	3	–	–	–	–	–	–	–	–	–	–	34	15	25 Feb 1905
BEHAN, Billy	–	–	–	–	1	–	–	–	–	–	–	–	–	–	–	–	–	–	1	–	3 Mar 1934
BELL, Alex	–	–	202	5	76	5	28	–	–	–	–	–	–	–	–	–	3	–	309	10	24 Jan 1903
BELLION, David	5 (19)	4	–	–	–	–	2 (1)	–	5	2	2 (5)	2	–	–	–	–	1	–	15 (25)	8	27 Aug 2003
BENNION, Ray	–	–	193	2	93	–	15	1	–	–	–	–	–	–	–	–	–	–	301	3	27 Aug 1921
BENT, Geoff	–	–	12	–	–	–	–	–	–	–	–	–	–	–	–	–	–	–	12	–	11 Dec 1954
BERBATOV, Dimitar	82 (26)	48	–	–	–	–	5 (2)	1	5	1	14 (11)	5	–	–	1	–	1 (2)	1	108 (41)	56	13 Sep 2008
BERG, Henning	49 (17)	2	–	–	–	–	7	–	3	–	19 (4)	1	–	–	–	–	3 (1)	–	81 (22)	3	13 Aug 1997
BERRY, Bill	–	–	13	1	–	–	1	–	–	–	–	–	–	–	–	–	–	–	14	1	17 Nov 1906
BERRY, Johnny	–	–	247	37	–	–	15	4	–	–	11	3	–	–	–	–	3	1	276	45	1 Sep 1951
BEST, George	–	–	361	137	–	–	46	21	25	9	21	9	2	–	11	2	4	1	470	179	14 Sep 1963
BIELBY, Paul	–	–	2 (2)	–	–	–	–	–	–	–	–	–	–	–	–	–	–	–	2 (2)	–	13 Mar 1974
BIRCH, Brian	–	–	11	4	–	–	4	1	–	–	–	–	–	–	–	–	–	–	15	5	27 Aug 1949
BIRCHENOUGH, Herbert	–	–	–	–	25	–	5	–	–	–	–	–	–	–	–	–	–	–	30	–	25 Oct 1902
BIRKETT, Cliff	–	–	9	2	–	–	4	–	–	–	–	–	–	–	–	–	–	–	13	2	2 Dec 1950
BIRTLES, Gary	–	–	57 (1)	11	–	–	4	1	2	–	–	–	–	–	–	–	–	–	63 (1)	12	22 Oct 1980
BISSETT, George	–	–	40	10	–	–	2	–	–	–	–	–	–	–	–	–	–	–	42	10	15 Nov 1919
BLACK, Dick	–	–	–	–	8	3	–	–	–	–	–	–	–	–	–	–	–	–	8	3	23 Apr 1932
BLACKMORE, Clayton	12 (2)	–	138 (34)	19	–	–	15 (6)	1	23 (2)	3	–	–	10	2	1	–	2	1	201 (44)	26	16 May 1984
BLACKMORE, Peter	–	–	–	–	1	–	1	–	–	–	–	–	–	–	–	–	–	–	2	–	21 Oct 1899
BLACKSTOCK, Tommy	–	–	3	–	31	–	4	–	–	–	–	–	–	–	–	–	–	–	38	–	3 Oct 1903
BLANC, Laurent	44 (4)	1	–	–	–	–	3	–	–	–	24	3	–	–	–	–	–	–	71 (4)	4	8 Sep 2001
BLANCHFLOWER, Jackie	–	–	105	26	–	–	6	1	–	–	5	–	–	–	–	–	1	–	117	27	24 Nov 1951
BLEW, Horace	–	–	–	–	1	–	–	–	–	–	–	–	–	–	–	–	–	–	1	–	13 Apr 1906
BLOMQVIST, Jesper	20 (5)	1	–	–	–	–	3 (2)	–	– (1)	–	6 (1)	–	–	–	–	–	–	–	29 (9)	1	9 Sep 1998
BLOTT, Sam	–	–	19	2	–	–	–	–	–	–	–	–	–	–	–	–	–	–	19	2	1 Sep 1909
BOGAN, Tommy	–	–	29	7	–	–	4	–	–	–	–	–	–	–	–	–	–	–	33	7	8 Oct 1949
BOND, Ernie	–	–	20	4	–	–	1	–	–	–	–	–	–	–	–	–	–	–	21	4	18 Aug 1951
BONTHRON, Bob	–	–	28	–	91	3	15	–	–	–	–	–	–	–	–	–	–	–	134	3	5 Sep 1903
BOOTH, William	–	–	–	–	2	–	–	–	–	–	–	–	–	–	–	–	–	–	2	–	26 Dec 1900
BOSNICH, Mark	23	–	3	–	–	–	–	–	1	–	7	–	–	–	–	–	4	–	38	–	30 Apr 1990
BOYD, Billy	–	–	–	–	6	4	–	–	–	–	–	–	–	–	–	–	–	–	6	4	9 Feb 1935
BOYD, Henry	–	–	–	–	52	32	7	1	–	–	–	–	–	–	–	–	3	2	62	35	20 Jan 1897
BOYLE, Tommy	–	–	16	6	–	–	1	–	–	–	–	–	–	–	–	–	–	–	17	6	30 Mar 1929
BRADBURY, Len	–	–	2	1	–	–	–	–	–	–	–	–	–	–	–	–	–	–	2	1	28 Jan 1939
BRADLEY, Warren	–	–	63	20	–	–	4	1	–	–	–	–	–	–	–	–	–	–	67	21	15 Nov 1958
BRATT, Harold	–	–	–	–	–	–	–	–	1	–	–	–	–	–	–	–	–	–	1	–	2 Nov 1960
BRAZIL, Alan	–	–	18 (13)	8	–	–	– (1)	–	4 (3)	3	–	–	–	–	2	1	–	–	24 (17)	12	25 Aug 1984
BRAZIL, Derek	–	–	– (2)	–	–	–	–	–	–	–	–	–	–	–	–	–	–	–	– (2)	–	10 May 1989
BREEDON, Jack	–	–	23	–	12	–	–	–	–	–	–	–	–	–	–	–	–	–	35	–	31 Aug 1935
BREEN, Tommy	–	–	32	–	33	–	6	–	–	–	–	–	–	–	–	–	–	–	71	–	28 Nov 1936
BRENNAN, Shay	–	–	291 (1)	3	–	–	36	3	4	–	11	–	2	–	11	–	3	–	358 (1)	6	19 Feb 1958
BRETT, Frank	–	–	10	–	–	–	–	–	–	–	–	–	–	–	–	–	–	–	10	–	27 Aug 1921
BRIGGS, Ronnie	–	–	9	–	–	–	2	–	–	–	–	–	–	–	–	–	–	–	11	–	21 Jan 1961
BROOKS, William	–	–	–	–	3	3	–	–	–	–	–	–	–	–	–	–	–	–	3	3	22 Oct 1898
BROOME, Albert	–	–	–	–	1	–	–	–	–	–	–	–	–	–	–	–	–	–	1	–	28 Apr 1923
BROOMFIELD, Herbert	–	–	9	–	–	–	–	–	–	–	–	–	–	–	–	–	–	–	9	–	21 Mar 1908
BROWN, James (1932-34)	–	–	–	–	40	17	1	–	–	–	–	–	–	–	–	–	–	–	41	17	3 Sep 1892
BROWN, James (1935-39)	–	–	34	–	68	1	8	–	–	–	–	–	–	–	–	–	–	–	110	1	17 Sep 1932
BROWN, James (1892-93)	–	–	7	–	–	–	–	–	–	–	–	–	–	–	–	–	–	–	7	–	31 Aug 1935
BROWN, Robert	–	–	4	–	–	–	–	–	–	–	–	–	–	–	–	–	–	–	4	–	31 Jan 1948
BROWN, Wes	203 (29)	3	–	–	–	–	32 (3)	1	23 (4)	–	54 (11)	1	–	–	–	–	1 (2)	–	313 (49)	5	4 May 1998
BROWN, William	–	–	–	–	7	2	–	–	–	–	–	–	–	–	–	–	–	–	7	2	1 Sep 1896
BRUCE, Steve	148	11	161	25	–	–	41	3	32 (2)	6	9 (1)	2	12	4	4	–	4	–	411 (3)	51	19 Dec 1987
BRYANT, Billy	–	–	64	16	84	26	9	–	–	–	–	–	–	–	–	–	–	–	157	42	3 Nov 1934
BRYANT, William	–	–	–	–	109	27	14	6	–	–	–	–	–	–	–	–	4	–	127	33	1 Sep 1896
BUCHAN, George	–	–	– (3)	–	–	–	–	–	– (1)	–	–	–	–	–	–	–	–	–	– (4)	–	15 Sep 1973

PLAYER ROLL CALL

PLAYER	PREMIERSHIP		DIVISION ONE		DIVISION TWO		FA CUP		LEAGUE CUP		EC / CL		ECWC		UEFA CUP		OTHER GAMES		TOTALS		DEBUT
	APPS	GLS	APPS	GLS	APPS	GLS	APPS	GLS	APPS	GLS	APPS	GLS	APPS	GLS	APPS	GLS	APPS	GLS	APPS	GLS	
BUCHAN, Martin	–	–	335	4	41	–	39	–	30	–	–	–	4	–	6	–	1	–	456	4	4 Mar 1972
BUCKLE, Ted	–	–	20	6	–	–	4	1	–	–	–	–	–	–	–	–	–	–	24	7	4 Jan 1947
BUCKLEY, Frank	–	–	3	–	–	–	–	–	–	–	–	–	–	–	–	–	–	–	3	–	29 Sep 1906
BULLOCK, Jimmy	–	–	10	3	–	–	–	–	–	–	–	–	–	–	–	–	–	–	10	3	20 Sep 1930
BUNCE, William	–	–	–	–	2	–	–	–	–	–	–	–	–	–	–	–	–	–	2	–	4 Oct 1902
BURGESS, Herbert	–	–	49	–	–	–	3	–	–	–	–	–	–	–	–	–	2	–	54	–	1 Jan 1907
BURKE, Ronnie	–	–	28	16	–	–	6	6	–	–	–	–	–	–	–	–	1	1	35	23	26 Oct 1946
BURKE, Tom	–	–	–	–	–	–	1	–	–	–	–	–	–	–	–	–	–	–	1	–	30 Oct 1886
BURNS, Francis	–	–	111 (10)	6	–	–	11 (1)	–	10 (1)	–	10 (1)	1	–	–	–	–	1	–	143 (13)	7	2 Sep 1967
BUTT, Nicky	210 (60)	21	–	–	–	–	23 (6)	1	7 (1)	–	56 (13)	2	–	–	2	–	9	2	307 (80)	26	21 Nov 1992
BYRNE, David	–	–	–	–	4	3	–	–	–	–	–	–	–	–	–	–	–	–	4	3	21 Oct 1933
BYRNE, Roger	–	–	245	17	–	–	18	2	–	–	14	–	–	–	–	–	3	1	280	20	24 Nov 1951

C

CAIRNS, James	–	–	–	–	1	–	–	–	–	–	–	–	–	–	–	–	–	–	1	–	15 Apr 1895
CAIRNS, Jim	–	–	–	–	1	–	–	–	–	–	–	–	–	–	–	–	–	–	1	–	8 Oct 1898
CAMPBELL, Fraizer	1 (1)	–	–	–	–	–	–	–	– (1)	–	–	–	–	–	–	–	– (1)	–	1 (3)	–	19 Aug 2007
CAMPBELL, William	–	–	5	1	–	–	–	–	–	–	–	–	–	–	–	–	–	–	5	1	25 Nov 1893
CANTONA, Eric	142 (1)	64	–	–	–	–	17	10	6	1	16	5	–	–	–	–	3	2	184 (1)	82	6 Dec 1992
CANTWELL, Noel	–	–	123	6	–	–	14	2	–	–	3	–	4	–	–	–	2	–	146	8	26 Nov 1960
CAPE, Jack	–	–	4	1	55	17	1	–	–	–	–	–	–	–	–	–	–	–	60	18	27 Jan 1934
CAPPER, Freddy	–	–	1	–	–	–	–	–	–	–	–	–	–	–	–	–	–	–	1	–	23 Mar 1912
CAREY, Johnny	–	–	288	13	16	3	38	1	–	–	–	–	–	–	–	–	2	–	344	17	25 Sep 1937
CARMAN, James	–	–	–	–	3	1	–	–	–	–	–	–	–	–	–	–	–	–	3	1	25 Dec 1897
CAROLAN, Joseph	–	–	66	–	–	–	4	–	1	–	–	–	–	–	–	–	–	–	71	–	22 Nov 1958
CARRICK, Michael	149 (31)	14	–	–	–	–	18 (1)	1	6 (3)	1	53 (3)	3	–	–	2 (1)	–	5 (1)	–	233 (40)	19	23 Aug 2006
CARROLL, Roy	46 (3)	–	–	–	–	–	7 (1)	–	5	–	10	–	–	–	–	–	–	–	68 (4)	–	26 Aug 2001
CARSON, Adam	–	–	13	3	–	–	–	–	–	–	–	–	–	–	–	–	–	–	13	3	3 Sep 1892
CARTMAN, Bert	–	–	–	–	3	–	–	–	–	–	–	–	–	–	–	–	–	–	3	–	16 Dec 1922
CARTWRIGHT, Walter	–	–	–	–	228	8	27	–	–	–	–	–	–	–	–	–	2	–	257	8	7 Sep 1895
CASHMORE, Arthur	–	–	3	–	–	–	–	–	–	–	–	–	–	–	–	–	–	–	3	–	13 Sep 1913
CASPER, Chris	– (2)	–	–	–	–	–	1	–	3	–	– (1)	–	–	–	–	–	–	–	4 (3)	–	5 Oct 1994
CASSIDY, Joe	–	–	4	–	148	90	15	9	–	–	–	–	–	–	–	–	7	1	174	100	31 Mar 1893
CASSIDY, Laurie	–	–	4	–	–	–	–	–	–	–	–	–	–	–	–	–	–	–	4	–	10 Apr 1948
CHADWICK, Luke	11 (14)	2	–	–	–	–	1 (2)	–	5	–	1 (5)	–	–	–	–	–	–	–	18 (21)	2	13 Oct 1999
CHALMERS, Stewart	–	–	–	–	34	1	1	–	–	–	–	–	–	–	–	–	–	–	35	1	1 Oct 1932
CHAPMAN, Billy	–	–	26	–	–	–	–	–	–	–	–	–	–	–	–	–	–	–	26	–	18 Sep 1926
CHARLTON, Bobby	–	–	604 (2)	199	–	–	78	19	24	7	28	10	6	4	11	8	5	2	756 (2)	249	6 Oct 1956
CHESTER, James	–	–	–	–	–	–	–	–	– (1)	–	–	–	–	–	–	–	–	–	– (1)	–	20 Jan 2009
CHESTER, Reg	–	–	–	–	13	1	–	–	–	–	–	–	–	–	–	–	–	–	13	1	31 Aug 1935
CHESTERS, Arthur	–	–	7	–	2	–	–	–	–	–	–	–	–	–	–	–	–	–	9	–	28 Dec 1929
CHILTON, Allenby	–	–	352	3	–	–	37	–	–	–	–	–	–	–	–	–	2	–	391	3	5 Jan 1946
CHISNALL, Phil	–	–	35	8	–	–	8	1	–	–	–	–	4	1	–	–	–	–	47	10	2 Dec 1961
CHORLTON, Tom	–	–	4	–	–	–	–	–	–	–	–	–	–	–	–	–	–	–	4	–	11 Oct 1913
CHRISTIE, David	–	–	2	–	–	–	–	–	–	–	–	–	–	–	–	–	–	–	2	–	7 Sep 1908
CHRISTIE, John	–	–	–	–	1	–	–	–	–	–	–	–	–	–	–	–	–	–	1	–	28 Feb 1903
CLARK, Joe	–	–	–	–	9	–	–	–	–	–	–	–	–	–	–	–	–	–	9	–	30 Sep 1899
CLARK, Jonathan	–	–	– (1)	–	–	–	–	–	–	–	–	–	–	–	–	–	–	–	– (1)	–	10 Nov 1976
CLARKIN, John	–	–	12	5	55	18	5	–	–	–	–	–	–	–	–	–	2	–	74	23	13 Jan 1894
CLAYTON, Gordon	–	–	2	–	–	–	–	–	–	–	–	–	–	–	–	–	–	–	2	–	16 Mar 1957
CLEAVER, Harry	–	–	–	–	1	–	–	–	–	–	–	–	–	–	–	–	–	–	1	–	4 Apr 1903
CLEGG, Michael	4 (5)	–	–	–	–	–	3 (1)	–	7 (1)	–	1 (2)	–	–	–	–	–	–	–	15 (9)	–	23 Nov 1996
CLEMENTS, John	–	–	36	–	–	–	4	–	–	–	–	–	–	–	–	–	2	–	42	–	3 Oct 1891
CLEMPSON, Frank	–	–	15	2	–	–	–	–	–	–	–	–	–	–	–	–	–	–	15	2	18 Feb 1950
CLEVERLEY, Tom	5 (5)	–	–	–	–	–	–	–	1	–	–	–	–	–	3	–	– (1)	–	9 (6)	–	7 Aug 2011
COCKBURN, Henry	–	–	243	4	–	–	32	–	–	–	–	–	–	–	–	–	–	–	275	4	5 Jan 1946
COLE, Andrew	161 (34)	93	–	–	–	–	19 (2)	9	2	–	42 (7)	19	–	–	1	–	6 (1)	–	231 (44)	121	22 Jan 1995
COLE, Larnell	–	–	–	–	–	–	–	–	– (1)	–	–	–	–	–	–	–	–	–	– (1)	–	20 Sep 2011
COLLINSON, Cliff	–	–	7	–	–	–	–	–	–	–	–	–	–	–	–	–	–	–	7	–	2 Nov 1946
COLLINSON, Jimmy	–	–	–	–	62	16	9	1	–	–	–	–	–	–	–	–	–	–	71	17	16 Nov 1895
COLMAN, Eddie	–	–	85	1	–	–	9	–	–	–	13	1	–	–	–	–	1	–	108	2	12 Nov 1955
COLVILLE, James	–	–	9	1	–	–	1	–	–	–	–	–	–	–	–	–	–	–	10	1	12 Nov 1892
CONNACHAN, James	–	–	–	–	4	–	–	–	–	–	–	–	–	–	–	–	–	–	4	–	5 Nov 1898
CONNAUGHTON, John	–	–	3	–	–	–	–	–	–	–	–	–	–	–	–	–	–	–	3	–	4 Apr 1972
CONNELL, Tom	–	–	2	–	–	–	–	–	–	–	–	–	–	–	–	–	–	–	2	–	22 Dec 1978
CONNELLY, John	–	–	79 (1)	22	–	–	13	2	1	–	8	6	–	–	11	5	–	–	112 (1)	35	22 Aug 1964
CONNOR, Ted	–	–	15	2	–	–	–	–	–	–	–	–	–	–	–	–	–	–	15	2	27 Dec 1909
COOKE, Terry	1 (3)	–	–	–	–	–	–	–	1 (2)	1	–	–	–	–	– (1)	–	–	–	2 (6)	1	16 Sep 1995
COOKSON, Sam	–	–	12	–	–	–	1	–	–	–	–	–	–	–	–	–	–	–	13	–	26 Dec 1914
COPE, Ronnie	–	–	93	2	–	–	10	–	1	–	2	–	–	–	–	–	–	–	106	2	29 Sep 1956
COPPELL, Steve	–	–	311 (1)	53	9 (1)	1	36	4	25	9	–	–	4	3	7 (1)	–	1	–	393 (3)	70	1 Mar 1975
COUPAR, Jimmy	–	–	21	5	11	4	–	–	–	–	–	–	–	–	–	–	2	1	34	10	3 Sep 1892
COYNE, Peter	–	–	1 (1)	1	–	–	–	–	–	–	–	–	–	–	–	–	–	–	1 (1)	1	21 Feb 1976
CRAIG, T	–	–	–	–	–	–	2	1	–	–	–	–	–	–	–	–	–	–	2	1	18 Jan 1889
CRAVEN, Charlie	–	–	11	2	–	–	–	–	–	–	–	–	–	–	–	–	–	–	11	2	27 Aug 1938
CRERAND, Pat	–	–	304	10	–	–	43	4	4	–	24	1	6	–	11	–	5	–	397	15	23 Feb 1963
CROMPTON, Jack	–	–	191	–	–	–	20	–	–	–	–	–	–	–	–	–	1	–	212	–	5 Jan 1946
CROOKS, Garth	–	–	6 (1)	2	–	–	–	–	–	–	–	–	–	–	–	–	–	–	6 (1)	2	19 Nov 1983
CROWTHER, Stan	–	–	13	–	–	–	5	–	–	–	2	–	–	–	–	–	–	–	20	–	
CRUYFF, Jordi	15 (19)	8	–	–	–	–	– (1)	–	5	–	4 (7)	–	–	–	–	–	2 (5)	–	26 (32)	8	11 Aug 1996
CULKIN, Nick	– (1)	–	–	–	–	–	–	–	–	–	–	–	–	–	–	–	–	–	– (1)	–	22 Aug 1999
CUNNINGHAM, John	–	–	–	–	15	2	2	–	–	–	–	–	–	–	–	–	–	–	17	2	5 Nov 1898
CUNNINGHAM, Laurie	–	–	3 (2)	1	–	–	–	–	–	–	–	–	–	–	–	–	–	–	3 (2)	1	19 Apr 1983
CURRY, Joe	–	–	13	–	–	–	1	–	–	–	–	–	–	–	–	–	–	–	14	–	21 Nov 1908
CURTIS, John	4 (9)	–	–	–	–	–	–	–	5	–	–	–	–	–	–	–	– (1)	–	9 (10)	–	14 Oct 1997

D

DALE, Billy	–	–	60	–	4	–	4	–	–	–	–	–	–	–	–	–	–	–	68	–	25 Aug 1928
DALE, Herbert	–	–	–	–	–	–	1	–	–	–	–	–	–	–	–	–	–	–	1	–	25 Oct 1890
DALE, Joe	–	–	2	–	–	–	–	–	–	–	–	–	–	–	–	–	–	–	2	–	27 Sep 1947
DALTON, Ted	–	–	1	–	–	–	–	–	–	–	–	–	–	–	–	–	–	–	1	–	25 Mar 1908
DALY, Gerry	–	–	71 (3)	12	36 (1)	11	9 (1)	5	17	4	–	–	–	–	4	–	–	–	137 (5)	32	25 Aug 1973
DAVENPORT, Peter	–	–	73 (19)	22	–	–	2 (2)	–	8 (2)	4	–	–	–	–	–	–	–	–	83 (23)	26	15 Mar 1986
DAVIDSON, Will	–	–	28	1	12	1	3	–	–	–	–	–	–	–	–	–	1	–	44	2	2 Sep 1893
DAVIES, Alan	–	–	6 (1)	–	–	–	2	–	–	–	–	–	– (1)	1	–	–	–	–	8 (2)	1	1 May 1982
DAVIES, Joe	–	–	–	–	–	–	2	–	–	–	–	–	–	–	–	–	–	–	2	–	30 Oct 1886
DAVIES, John	–	–	7	–	–	–	1	–	–	–	–	–	–	–	–	–	2	–	10	–	14 Jan 1893
DAVIES, L	–	–	–	–	–	–	1	–	–	–	–	–	–	–	–	–	–	–	1	–	30 Oct 1886
DAVIES, Ron	–	–	–	–	– (8)	–	– (2)	–	–	–	–	–	–	–	–	–	–	–	– (10)	–	30 Nov 1974
DAVIES, Simon	4 (7)	–	–	–	–	–	–	–	4 (2)	–	2	1	–	–	– (1)	–	–	–	10 (10)	1	21 Sep 1994
DAVIES, Wyn	–	–	15 (1)	4	–	–	1	–	–	–	–	–	–	–	–	–	–	–	16 (1)	4	23 Sep 1972
DAVIS, Jimmy	–	–	–	–	–	–	–	–	1	–	–	–	–	–	–	–	–	–	1	–	5 Nov 2001
DAWSON, Alex	–	–	80	45	–	–	10	8	3	1	–	–	–	–	–	–	–	–	93	54	22 Apr 1957
DEAN, Harold	–	–	–	–	2	–	–	–	–	–	–	–	–	–	–	–	–	–	2	–	26 Sep 1931
DE GEA, David	29	–	–	–	–	–	1	–	–	–	4	–	–	–	4	–	1	–	39	–	7 Aug 2011
DE LAET, Ritchie	3	–	–	–	–	–	–	–	1 (2)	–	–	–	–	–	–	–	–	–	4 (2)	–	24 May 2009
DELANEY, Jimmy	–	–	164	25	–	–	19	3	–	–	–	–	–	–	–	–	1	–	184	28	31 Aug 1946

PLAYER ROLL CALL

PLAYER	PREMIER LGE		DIVISION ONE		DIVISION TWO		FA CUP		LEAGUE CUP		EC / CL		ECWC		UEFA CUP		OTHER GAMES		TOTALS		DEBUT
	APPS	GLS	APPS	GLS	APPS	GLS	APPS	GLS	APPS	GLS	APPS	GLS	APPS	GLS	APPS	GLS	APPS	GLS	APPS	GLS	
DEMPSEY, Mark	–	–	1	–	–	–	–	–	–	–	–	–	– (1)	–	–	–	–	–	1 (1)	–	2 Nov 1983
DENMAN, J	–	–	–	–	–	–	1	–	–	–	–	–	–	–	–	–	–	–	1	–	5 Dec 1891
DENNIS, Billy	–	–	–	–	3	–	–	–	–	–	–	–	–	–	–	–	–	–	3	–	13 Oct 1923
DEWAR, Neil	–	–	–	–	36	14	–	–	–	–	–	–	–	–	–	–	–	–	36	14	11 Feb 1933
DIOUF, Mame	– (5)	1	–	–	–	–	–	–	3 (1)	–	–	–	–	–	–	–	–	–	3 (6)	1	9 Jan 2010
DJEMBA-DJEMBA, Eric	13 (7)	–	–	–	–	–	2 (1)	–	5	1	6 (3)	1	–	–	–	–	1 (1)	–	27 (12)	2	10 Aug 2003
DJORDJIC, Bojan	– (1)	–	–	–	–	–	–	–	1	–	–	–	–	–	–	–	–	–	1 (1)	–	19 May 2001
DOHERTY, John	–	–	25	7	–	–	1	–	–	–	–	–	–	–	–	–	–	–	26	7	6 Dec 1952
DONAGHY, Bernard	–	–	–	–	3	–	–	–	–	–	–	–	–	–	–	–	–	–	3	–	4 Nov 1905
DONAGHY, Mal	–	–	76 (13)	–	–	–	10	–	9 (5)	–	–	–	2 (3)	–	–	–	1	–	98 (21)	–	30 Oct 1988
DONALD, Ian	–	–	4	–	–	–	–	–	2	–	–	–	–	–	–	–	–	–	6	–	7 Oct 1970
DONALDSON, Bob	–	–	50	23	81	33	16	10	–	–	–	–	–	–	–	–	8	–	155	66	3 Sep 1892
DONG, Fangzhuo	1	–	–	–	–	–	–	–	1	–	– (1)	–	–	–	–	–	–	–	2 (1)	–	9 May 2007
DONNELLY, not known	–	–	–	–	–	–	1	–	–	–	–	–	–	–	–	–	–	–	1	–	15 Mar 1909
DONNELLY, Tony	–	–	34	–	–	–	3	–	–	–	–	–	–	–	–	–	–	–	37	–	25 Oct 1890
DOUGAN, Tommy	–	–	4	–	–	–	–	–	–	–	–	–	–	–	–	–	–	–	4	–	29 Mar 1939
DOUGHTY, Jack	–	–	–	–	–	–	3	3	–	–	–	–	–	–	–	–	–	–	3	3	30 Oct 1886
DOUGHTY, Roger	–	–	–	–	–	–	5	1	–	–	–	–	–	–	–	–	3	–	8	1	18 Jan 1889
DOUGLAS, William	–	–	7	–	48	–	1	–	–	–	–	–	–	–	–	–	1	–	57	–	3 Feb 1894
DOW, John	–	–	2	–	46	6	1	–	–	–	–	–	–	–	–	–	1	–	50	6	24 Mar 1894
DOWNIE, Alex	–	–	55	2	117	10	19	2	–	–	–	–	–	–	–	–	–	–	191	14	22 Nov 1902
DOWNIE, John	–	–	110	35	–	–	5	1	–	–	–	–	–	–	–	–	1	1	116	37	5 Mar 1949
DRAYCOTT, Billy	–	–	–	–	81	6	10	–	–	–	–	–	–	–	–	–	4	–	95	6	1 Sep 1896
DUBLIN, Dion	4 (8)	2	–	–	–	–	1 (1)	–	1 (1)	1	– (1)	–	–	–	–	–	–	–	6 (11)	3	15 Aug 1992
DUCKWORTH, Dick	–	–	206	4	19	7	26	–	–	–	–	–	–	–	–	–	3	–	254	11	19 Dec 1903
DUNN, William	–	–	–	–	10	–	2	–	–	–	–	–	–	–	–	–	–	–	12	–	4 Sep 1897
DUNNE, Pat	–	–	45	–	–	–	7	–	1	–	2	–	–	–	11	–	1	–	67	–	8 Sep 1964
DUNNE, Tony	–	–	414	2	–	–	54 (1)	–	21	–	23	–	6	–	11	–	5	–	534 (1)	2	15 Oct 1960
DUXBURY, Mike	–	–	274 (25)	6	–	–	20 (5)	1	32 (2)	–	–	–	8	–	9 (1)	–	2	–	345 (33)	7	23 Aug 1980
DYER, Jimmy	–	–	–	–	1	–	–	–	–	–	–	–	–	–	–	–	–	–	1	–	14 Oct 1905

E

EAGLES, Chris	2 (4)	1	–	–	–	–	1	–	2 (4)	–	2 (1)	–	–	–	–	–	– (1)	–	7 (10)	1	28 Oct 2003
EARP, John	–	–	–	–	–	–	1	–	–	–	–	–	–	–	–	–	–	–	1	–	30 Oct 1886
EBANKS-BLAKE, Sylvan	–	–	–	–	–	–	–	–	1 (1)	1	–	–	–	–	–	–	–	–	1 (1)	1	26 Oct 2004
ECKERSLEY, Adam	–	–	–	–	–	–	–	–	1	–	–	–	–	–	–	–	–	–	1	–	26 Oct 2005
ECKERSLEY, Richard	– (2)	–	–	–	–	–	– (2)	–	–	–	–	–	–	–	–	–	–	–	– (4)	–	24 Jan 2009
EDGE, Alf	–	–	–	–	–	–	3	3	–	–	–	–	–	–	–	–	–	–	3	3	3 Oct 1891
EDMONDS, Hugh	–	–	43	–	–	–	7	–	–	–	–	–	–	–	–	–	1	–	51	–	11 Feb 1911
EDWARDS, Duncan	–	–	151	20	–	–	12	1	–	–	12	–	–	–	–	–	2	–	177	21	4 Apr 1953
EDWARDS, Paul	–	–	52 (2)	–	–	–	10	–	4	1	–	–	–	–	–	–	–	–	66 (2)	1	19 Aug 1969
ELLIS, David	–	–	–	–	11	–	–	–	–	–	–	–	–	–	–	–	–	–	11	–	25 Aug 1923
ERENTZ, Fred	–	–	51	2	229	7	23	–	–	–	–	–	–	–	–	–	7	–	310	9	3 Sep 1892
ERENTZ, Harry	–	–	–	–	6	–	3	–	–	–	–	–	–	–	–	–	–	–	9	–	8 Jan 1898
EVANS, George	–	–	–	–	–	–	1	1	–	–	–	–	–	–	–	–	–	–	1	1	4 Oct 1890
EVANS, Jonny	73 (4)	1	–	–	–	–	6 (1)	–	14	–	14 (5)	–	–	–	3 (1)	–	2 (3)	–	112 (14)	1	26 Sep 2007
EVANS, Sidney	–	–	–	–	6	2	–	–	–	–	–	–	–	–	–	–	–	–	6	2	12 Apr 1924
EVRA, Patrice	198 (8)	2	–	–	–	–	14 (3)	–	5 (3)	–	45 (7)	1	–	–	2	–	7	–	271 (21)	3	14 Jan 2006

F

FABIO, da Silva	8 (13)	1	–	–	–	–	6 (1)	1	7	–	12 (2)	–	–	–	2	–	1 (1)	–	36 (17)	2	24 Jan 2009
FALL, Joe	–	–	23	–	–	–	3	–	–	–	–	–	–	–	–	–	1	–	27	–	2 Sep 1893
FARMAN, Alf	–	–	46	18	5	–	7	6	–	–	–	–	–	–	–	–	3	4	61	28	18 Jan 1889
FEEHAN, John	–	–	12	–	–	–	2	–	–	–	–	–	–	–	–	–	–	–	14	–	5 Nov 1949
FELTON, G	–	–	–	–	–	–	1	–	–	–	–	–	–	–	–	–	–	–	1	–	25 Oct 1890
FERDINAND, Rio	267 (3)	6	–	–	–	–	26 (1)	–	12 (1)	–	77 (1)	1	–	–	2	–	8	–	392 (6)	7	27 Aug 2002
FERGUSON, Danny	–	–	4	–	–	–	–	–	–	–	–	–	–	–	–	–	–	–	4	–	7 Apr 1928
FERGUSON, Darren	16 (2)	–	4 (5)	–	–	–	–	–	2 (1)	–	–	–	–	–	–	–	–	–	22 (8)	–	26 Feb 1991
FERGUSON, John	–	–	–	–	8	1	–	–	–	–	–	–	–	–	–	–	–	–	8	1	29 Aug 1931
FERRIER, Ron	–	–	6	1	12	3	1	–	–	–	–	–	–	–	–	–	–	–	19	4	4 Sep 1935
FIELDING, Bill	–	–	6	–	–	–	1	–	–	–	–	–	–	–	–	–	–	–	7	–	25 Jan 1947
FISHER, James	–	–	–	–	42	2	4	1	–	–	–	–	–	–	–	–	–	–	46	3	20 Oct 1900
FITCHETT, John	–	–	–	–	16	1	2	–	–	–	–	–	–	–	–	–	–	–	18	1	21 Mar 1903
FITTON, Arthur	–	–	–	–	12	2	–	–	–	–	–	–	–	–	–	–	–	–	12	2	26 Mar 1932
FITZPATRICK, John	–	–	111 (6)	8	–	–	11	1	12	1	7	–	–	–	–	–	–	–	141 (6)	10	24 Feb 1965
FITZSIMMONS, David	–	–	–	–	28	–	3	–	–	–	–	–	–	–	–	–	–	–	31	–	7 Sep 1895
FITZSIMMONS, Tommy	–	–	27	6	–	–	1	–	–	–	–	–	–	–	–	–	2	–	30	6	19 Nov 1892
FLETCHER, Darren	164 (33)	17	–	–	–	–	14 (9)	2	14 (1)	–	47 (12)	3	–	–	–	–	3 (5)	1	242 (60)	23	12 Mar 2003
FLETCHER, Peter	–	–	2 (5)	–	–	–	–	–	–	–	–	–	–	–	–	–	–	–	2 (5)	–	14 Apr 1973
FOGGON, Alan	–	–	– (3)	–	–	–	–	–	–	–	–	–	–	–	–	–	–	–	– (3)	–	21 Aug 1976
FOLEY, G	–	–	–	–	7	1	–	–	–	–	–	–	–	–	–	–	–	–	7	1	17 Mar 1900
FORD, Joe	–	–	5	–	–	–	–	–	–	–	–	–	–	–	–	–	–	–	5	–	31 Mar 1909
FORLAN, Diego	23 (40)	10	–	–	–	–	2 (2)	1	4 (2)	3	8 (15)	3	–	–	–	–	– (2)	–	37 (61)	17	29 Jan 2002
FORSTER, Tommy	–	–	35	–	–	–	1	–	–	–	–	–	–	–	–	–	–	–	36	–	8 Nov 1919
FORSYTH, Alex	–	–	60 (2)	3	39	1	10	1	7	–	–	–	– (1)	–	–	–	–	–	116 (3)	5	6 Jan 1973
FORTUNE, Quinton	53 (23)	6	–	–	–	–	8 (1)	1	8	–	16 (12)	2	–	–	–	–	3 (2)	2	88 (38)	11	30 Aug 1999
FOSTER, Ben	12	–	–	–	–	–	3	–	4	–	3	–	–	–	–	–	1	–	23	–	15 Mar 2008
FOULKES, Bill	–	–	563 (3)	7	–	–	61	–	3	–	35	2	6	–	11	–	6	–	685 (3)	9	13 Dec 1952
FRAME, Tommy	–	–	–	–	51	4	1	–	–	–	–	–	–	–	–	–	–	–	52	4	1 Oct 1932
FRYERS, Ezekiel	– (2)	–	–	–	–	–	–	–	2 (1)	–	– (1)	–	–	–	–	–	–	–	2 (4)	–	20 Sep 2011

G

GALLIMORE, Stanley	–	–	28	5	44	14	4	1	–	–	–	–	–	–	–	–	–	–	76	20	11 Oct 1930
GARDNER, Dick	–	–	4	–	12	1	2	–	–	–	–	–	–	–	–	–	–	–	18	1	28 Dec 1935
GARTON, Billy	–	–	39 (2)	–	–	–	3	–	5 (1)	–	–	–	–	–	– (1)	–	–	–	47 (4)	–	26 Sep 1984
GARVEY, James	–	–	–	–	6	–	–	–	–	–	–	–	–	–	–	–	–	–	6	–	1 Sep 1900
GASKELL, David	–	–	96	–	–	–	16	–	1	–	1	–	4	–	–	–	1 (1)	–	119 (1)	–	24 Oct 1956
GAUDIE, Ralph	–	–	–	–	7	–	1	–	–	–	–	–	–	–	–	–	–	–	8	–	5 Sep 1903
GIBSON, Colin	–	–	74 (5)	9	–	–	8 (1)	–	7	–	–	–	–	–	–	–	–	–	89 (6)	9	30 Nov 1985
GIBSON, Darron	14 (17)	3	–	–	–	–	6 (1)	2	10 (3)	3	7 (2)	2	–	–	–	–	–	–	37 (23)	10	26 Oct 2005
GIBSON, Don	–	–	108	–	–	–	6	–	–	–	–	–	–	–	–	–	1	–	115	–	26 Aug 1950
GIBSON, Richard	–	–	11	–	–	–	1	–	–	–	–	–	–	–	–	–	–	–	12	–	27 Aug 1921
GIBSON, Terry	–	–	14 (9)	1	–	–	1 (1)	–	– (2)	–	–	–	–	–	–	–	–	–	15 (12)	1	2 Feb 1986
GIDMAN, John	–	–	94 (1)	4	–	–	9	–	5	–	–	–	1 (1)	–	6 (1)	–	1 (1)	–	116 (4)	4	29 Aug 1981
GIGGS, Ryan	504 (94)	107	33 (7)	5	–	–	60 (10)	11	32 (6)	10	119 (20)	29	1	–	5	–	15 (3)	1	769 (140)	163	2 Mar 1991
GILES, Johnny	–	–	99	10	–	–	13	2	2	1	–	–	–	–	–	–	1	–	115	13	12 Sep 1959
GILL, Tony	–	–	5 (5)	1	–	–	2 (2)	1	–	–	–	–	–	–	–	–	–	–	7 (7)	2	3 Jan 1987
GILLESPIE, Keith	3 (6)	1	–	–	–	–	1 (1)	1	3	–	–	–	–	–	–	–	–	–	7 (7)	2	5 Jan 1993
GILLESPIE, Matthew	–	–	–	–	74	17	11	4	–	–	–	–	–	–	–	–	4	–	89	21	28 Nov 1896
GIPPS, Tommy	–	–	23	–	–	–	–	–	–	–	–	–	–	–	–	–	–	–	23	–	25 Dec 1912
GIVENS, Don	–	–	4 (4)	1	–	–	–	–	1	–	–	–	–	–	–	–	–	–	5 (4)	1	9 Aug 1969
GLADWIN, George	–	–	20	1	7	–	1	–	–	–	–	–	–	–	–	–	–	–	28	1	27 Feb 1937
GODSMARK, Gilbert	–	–	–	–	9	4	–	–	–	–	–	–	–	–	–	–	–	–	9	4	3 Feb 1900
GOLDTHORPE, Ernie	–	–	–	–	27	15	3	1	–	–	–	–	–	–	–	–	–	–	30	16	11 Nov 1922

PLAYER ROLL CALL

PLAYER	PREMIER LGE APPS	PREMIER LGE GLS	DIVISION ONE APPS	DIVISION ONE GLS	DIVISION TWO APPS	DIVISION TWO GLS	FA CUP APPS	FA CUP GLS	LEAGUE CUP APPS	LEAGUE CUP GLS	EC / CL APPS	EC / CL GLS	ECWC APPS	ECWC GLS	UEFA CUP APPS	UEFA CUP GLS	OTHER GAMES APPS	OTHER GAMES GLS	TOTALS APPS	TOTALS GLS	DEBUT
GOODWIN, Billy	–	–	7	1	–	–	–	–	–	–	–	–	–	–	–	–	–	–	7	1	28 Aug 1920
GOODWIN, Fred	–	–	95	7	–	–	8	1	–	–	3	–	–	–	–	–	1	–	107	8	20 Nov 1954
GORAM, Andy	2	–	–	–	–	–	–	–	–	–	–	–	–	–	–	–	–	–	2	–	14 Apr 2001
GOTHERIDGE, James	–	–	–	–	–	–	1	–	–	–	–	–	–	–	–	–	–	–	1	–	30 Oct 1886
GOURLAY, John	–	–	–	–	1	–	–	–	–	–	–	–	–	–	–	–	–	–	1	–	18 Feb 1899
GOWLING, Alan	–	–	64 (7)	18	–	–	6 (2)	2	7 (1)	1	–	–	–	–	–	–	–	–	77 (10)	21	30 Mar 1968
GRAHAM, Arthur	–	–	33 (4)	5	–	–	1	–	6	1	–	–	6 (1)	1	–	–	1	–	47 (5)	7	20 Aug 1983
GRAHAM, Deiniol	–	–	1 (1)	–	–	–	– (1)	1	– (1)	–	–	–	–	–	–	–	–	–	1 (3)	1	7 Oct 1987
GRAHAM, George	–	–	41 (1)	2	– (1)	–	2	–	1	–	–	–	–	–	–	–	–	–	44 (2)	2	6 Jan 1973
GRAHAM, John	–	–	4	–	–	–	–	–	–	–	–	–	–	–	–	–	–	–	4	–	11 Nov 1893
GRASSAM, Billy	–	–	–	–	29	13	8	1	–	–	–	–	–	–	–	–	–	–	37	14	3 Oct 1903
GRAY, David	–	–	–	–	–	–	–	–	1	–	–	–	–	–	–	–	–	–	1	–	25 Oct 2006
GREAVES, Ian	–	–	67	–	–	–	6	–	–	–	2	–	–	–	–	–	–	–	75	–	2 Oct 1954
GREEN, Eddie	–	–	–	–	9	4	–	–	–	–	–	–	–	–	–	–	–	–	9	4	26 Aug 1933
GREENHOFF, Brian	–	–	179 (1)	9	39 (2)	4	24	2	19	2	–	–	2	–	4	–	1	–	268 (3)	17	8 Sep 1973
GREENHOFF, Jimmy	–	–	94 (3)	26	–	–	18 (1)	9	4	1	–	–	1	–	1	–	1	–	119 (4)	36	20 Nov 1976
GREENING, Jonathan	4 (10)	–	–	–	–	–	– (1)	–	6	–	2 (2)	–	–	–	–	–	1 (1)	–	13 (14)	–	28 Oct 1998
GREENWOOD, Wilson	–	–	–	–	3	–	–	–	–	–	–	–	–	–	–	–	–	–	3	–	20 Oct 1900
GREGG, Harry	–	–	210	–	–	–	24	–	2	–	9	–	2	–	–	–	–	–	247	–	21 Dec 1957
GRIFFITHS, Billy	–	–	–	–	157	27	18	3	–	–	–	–	–	–	–	–	–	–	175	30	1 Apr 1899
GRIFFITHS, Clive	–	–	7	–	–	–	–	–	–	–	–	–	–	–	–	–	–	–	7	–	27 Oct 1973
GRIFFITHS, Jack	–	–	56	–	109	1	8	–	–	–	–	–	–	–	–	–	–	–	173	1	17 Mar 1934
GRIMES, Ashley	–	–	62 (28)	10	–	–	5	1	6	–	–	–	– (2)	–	4	–	–	–	77 (30)	11	20 Aug 1977
GRIMSHAW, Tony	–	–	– (1)	–	–	–	–	–	– (1)	–	–	–	–	–	–	–	–	–	– (2)	–	10 Sep 1975
GRIMWOOD, John	–	–	99	5	97	3	9	–	–	–	–	–	–	–	–	–	–	–	205	8	11 Oct 1919
GRUNDY, John	–	–	–	–	11	3	–	–	–	–	–	–	–	–	–	–	–	–	11	3	28 Apr 1900
GYVES, William	–	–	–	–	–	–	1	–	–	–	–	–	–	–	–	–	–	–	1	–	25 Oct 1890

H

PLAYER	PREMIER LGE APPS	PREMIER LGE GLS	DIVISION ONE APPS	DIVISION ONE GLS	DIVISION TWO APPS	DIVISION TWO GLS	FA CUP APPS	FA CUP GLS	LEAGUE CUP APPS	LEAGUE CUP GLS	EC / CL APPS	EC / CL GLS	ECWC APPS	ECWC GLS	UEFA CUP APPS	UEFA CUP GLS	OTHER GAMES APPS	OTHER GAMES GLS	TOTALS APPS	TOTALS GLS	DEBUT
HACKING, Jack	–	–	–	–	32	–	2	–	–	–	–	–	–	–	–	–	–	–	34	–	17 Mar 1934
HALL, Jack (1933–1936)	–	–	–	–	67	–	6	–	–	–	–	–	–	–	–	–	–	–	73	–	30 Sep 1933
HALL, Jack (1926)	–	–	3	–	–	–	–	–	–	–	–	–	–	–	–	–	–	–	3	–	6 Feb 1926
HALL, Proctor	–	–	–	–	8	2	–	–	–	–	–	–	–	–	–	–	–	–	8	2	26 Mar 1904
HALSE, Harold	–	–	109	41	–	–	15	9	–	–	–	–	–	–	–	–	1	6	125	56	28 Mar 1908
HALTON, Reg	–	–	4	1	–	–	–	–	–	–	–	–	–	–	–	–	–	–	4	1	12 Dec 1936
HAMILL, Mickey	–	–	57	2	–	–	2	–	–	–	–	–	–	–	–	–	1	–	60	2	16 Sep 1911
HANLON, Jimmy	–	–	63	20	–	–	6	2	–	–	–	–	–	–	–	–	–	–	69	22	26 Nov 1938
HANNAFORD, Charlie	–	–	11	–	–	–	1	–	–	–	–	–	–	–	–	–	–	–	12	–	28 Dec 1925
HANSON, Jimmy	–	–	135	44	3	3	9	5	–	–	–	–	–	–	–	–	–	–	147	52	15 Nov 1924
HARDMAN, Harold	–	–	4	–	–	–	–	–	–	–	–	–	–	–	–	–	–	–	4	–	19 Sep 1908
HARGREAVES, Owen	18 (9)	2	–	–	–	–	2 (1)	–	–	–	6 (3)	–	–	–	–	–	–	–	26 (13)	2	19 Aug 2007
HARRIS, Frank	–	–	46	2	–	–	3	–	–	–	–	–	–	–	–	–	–	–	49	2	14 Feb 1920
HARRIS, Tom	–	–	4	1	–	–	–	–	–	–	–	–	–	–	–	–	–	–	4	1	30 Oct 1926
HARRISON, Charlie	–	–	–	–	–	–	1	–	–	–	–	–	–	–	–	–	–	–	1	–	18 Jan 1889
HARRISON, William	–	–	44	5	–	–	2	–	–	–	–	–	–	–	–	–	–	–	46	5	23 Oct 1920
HARROP, Bobby	–	–	10	–	–	–	1	–	–	–	–	–	–	–	–	–	–	–	11	–	5 Mar 1958
HARTWELL, William	–	–	–	–	3	–	1	–	–	–	–	–	–	–	–	–	–	–	4	–	30 Apr 1904
HASLAM, George	–	–	17	–	8	–	2	–	–	–	–	–	–	–	–	–	–	–	27	–	25 Feb 1922
HAWKSWORTH, Tony	–	–	1	–	–	–	–	–	–	–	–	–	–	–	–	–	–	–	1	–	27 Oct 1956
HAWORTH, Ronald	–	–	2	–	–	–	–	–	–	–	–	–	–	–	–	–	–	–	2	–	28 Aug 1926
HAY, Tom	–	–	–	–	–	–	1	–	–	–	–	–	–	–	–	–	–	–	1	–	18 Jan 1890
HAYDOCK, Frank	–	–	6	–	–	–	–	–	–	–	–	–	–	–	–	–	–	–	6	–	20 Aug 1960
HAYES, Vince	–	–	53	–	62	2	13	–	–	–	–	–	–	–	–	–	–	–	128	2	25 Feb 1901
HAYWOOD, Joe	–	–	26	–	–	–	–	–	–	–	–	–	–	–	–	–	–	–	26	–	22 Nov 1913
HEALY, David	– (1)	–	–	–	–	–	–	–	– (2)	–	–	–	–	–	–	–	–	–	– (3)	–	13 Oct 1999
HEATHCOTE, Joe	–	–	–	–	7	–	1	–	–	–	–	–	–	–	–	–	–	–	8	–	16 Dec 1899
HEINZE, Gabriel	45 (7)	1	–	–	–	–	10	1	4	–	16 (1)	2	–	–	–	–	–	–	75 (8)	4	11 Sep 2004
HENDERSON, William	–	–	10	2	24	15	2	–	–	–	–	–	–	–	–	–	–	–	36	17	26 Nov 1921
HENDRY, James	–	–	2	1	–	–	–	–	–	–	–	–	–	–	–	–	–	–	2	1	15 Oct 1892
HENRYS, Arthur	–	–	3	–	–	–	3	–	–	–	–	–	–	–	–	–	–	–	6	–	3 Oct 1891
HERD, David	–	–	201 (1)	114	–	–	35	15	1	1	8	5	6	3	11	6	2	1	264 (1)	145	19 Aug 1961
HERNANDEZ, Javier	33 (22)	23	–	–	–	–	4 (2)	1	2 (1)	1	7 (6)	4	–	–	3	2	– (1)	1	49 (32)	32	8 Aug 2010
HERON, Tommy	–	–	3	–	–	–	–	–	–	–	–	–	–	–	–	–	–	–	3	–	5 Apr 1958
HEYWOOD, Herbert	–	–	–	–	4	2	–	–	–	–	–	–	–	–	–	–	–	–	4	2	6 May 1933
HIGGINBOTHAM, Danny	2 (2)	–	–	–	–	–	–	–	1	–	– (1)	–	–	–	–	–	1	–	4 (3)	–	10 May 1998
HIGGINS, Alexander	–	–	–	–	10	–	–	–	–	–	–	–	–	–	–	–	–	–	10	–	12 Oct 1901
HIGGINS, Mark	–	–	6	–	–	–	2	–	–	–	–	–	–	–	–	–	–	–	8	–	9 Jan 1986
HIGSON, James	–	–	–	–	5	1	–	–	–	–	–	–	–	–	–	–	–	–	5	1	1 Mar 1902
HILDITCH, Clarence	–	–	207	6	94	1	21	–	–	–	–	–	–	–	–	–	–	–	322	7	30 Aug 1919
HILL, Gordon	–	–	100 (1)	39	–	–	17	6	7	4	–	–	4	1	4	1	1	–	133 (1)	51	15 Nov 1975
HILLAM, Charlie	–	–	–	–	8	–	–	–	–	–	–	–	–	–	–	–	–	–	8	–	26 Aug 1933
HINE, Ernie	–	–	–	–	51	12	2	–	–	–	–	–	–	–	–	–	–	–	53	12	11 Feb 1933
HODGE, James	–	–	79	2	–	–	7	–	–	–	–	–	–	–	–	–	–	–	86	2	17 Apr 1911
HODGE, John	–	–	30	–	–	–	–	–	–	–	–	–	–	–	–	–	–	–	30	–	27 Dec 1913
HODGES, Frank	–	–	20	4	–	–	–	–	–	–	–	–	–	–	–	–	–	–	20	4	18 Oct 1919
HOFTON, Leslie	–	–	17	–	–	–	1	–	–	–	–	–	–	–	–	–	1	–	19	–	18 Feb 1911
HOGG, Graeme	–	–	82 (1)	1	–	–	8	–	7 (1)	–	–	–	4	–	6	–	1	–	108 (2)	1	7 Jan 1984
HOLDEN, Dick	–	–	78	–	28	–	11	–	–	–	–	–	–	–	–	–	–	–	117	–	24 Apr 1905
HOLT, Edward	–	–	–	–	1	1	–	–	–	–	–	–	–	–	–	–	–	–	1	1	28 Apr 1900
HOLTON, Jim	–	–	49	5	14	–	2	–	4	–	–	–	–	–	–	–	–	–	69	5	20 Jan 1973
HOMER, Tom	–	–	25	14	–	–	–	–	–	–	–	–	–	–	–	–	–	–	25	14	30 Oct 1909
HOOD, Billy	–	–	33	6	–	–	3	–	–	–	–	–	–	–	–	–	2	–	38	6	1 Oct 1892
HOOPER, Arthur	–	–	7	1	–	–	–	–	–	–	–	–	–	–	–	–	–	–	7	1	22 Jan 1910
HOPKIN, Fred	–	–	70	8	–	–	4	–	–	–	–	–	–	–	–	–	–	–	74	8	30 Aug 1919
HOPKINS, James	–	–	–	–	1	–	–	–	–	–	–	–	–	–	–	–	–	–	1	–	18 Mar 1899
HOPKINSON, Samuel	–	–	17	4	34	6	2	2	–	–	–	–	–	–	–	–	–	–	53	12	17 Jan 1931
HOUSTON, Stewart	–	–	164 (1)	7	40	6	22	1	16	2	–	–	2 (1)	–	4	–	–	–	248 (2)	16	1 Jan 1974
HOWARD, Tim	44 (1)	–	–	–	–	–	10	–	8	–	12	–	–	–	–	–	2	–	76 (1)	–	10 Aug 2003
HOWARTH, John	–	–	4	–	–	–	–	–	–	–	–	–	–	–	–	–	–	–	4	–	2 Jan 1922
HOWELLS, E	–	–	–	–	–	–	1	–	–	–	–	–	–	–	–	–	–	–	1	–	30 Oct 1886
HUDSON, Edward	–	–	11	–	–	–	–	–	–	–	–	–	–	–	–	–	–	–	11	–	24 Jan 1914
HUGHES, Mark	110 (1)	35	226 (8)	85	–	–	45 (1)	17	37 (1)	16	7	2	13 (3)	5	10	2	5	1	453 (14)	163	26 Oct 1983
HULME, Aaron	–	–	4	–	–	–	–	–	–	–	–	–	–	–	–	–	–	–	4	–	25 Apr 1908
HUNTER, George	–	–	22	2	–	–	1	–	–	–	–	–	–	–	–	–	–	–	23	2	14 Mar 1914
HUNTER, Reg	–	–	1	–	–	–	–	–	–	–	–	–	–	–	–	–	–	–	1	–	27 Dec 1958
HUNTER, William	–	–	3	2	–	–	–	–	–	–	–	–	–	–	–	–	–	–	3	2	29 Mar 1913
HURST, Daniel	–	–	–	–	16	4	5	–	–	–	–	–	–	–	–	–	–	–	21	4	6 Sep 1902

I

PLAYER	PREMIER LGE APPS	PREMIER LGE GLS	DIVISION ONE APPS	DIVISION ONE GLS	DIVISION TWO APPS	DIVISION TWO GLS	FA CUP APPS	FA CUP GLS	LEAGUE CUP APPS	LEAGUE CUP GLS	EC / CL APPS	EC / CL GLS	ECWC APPS	ECWC GLS	UEFA CUP APPS	UEFA CUP GLS	OTHER GAMES APPS	OTHER GAMES GLS	TOTALS APPS	TOTALS GLS	DEBUT
IDDON, Richard	–	–	2	–	–	–	–	–	–	–	–	–	–	–	–	–	–	–	2	–	29 Aug 1925
INCE, Paul	116	19	87 (3)	6	–	–	26 (1)	1	23 (1)	2	9	–	10	–	1	–	4	1	276 (5)	29	16 Sep 1989
INGLIS, Bill	–	–	14	1	–	–	–	–	–	–	–	–	–	–	–	–	–	–	14	1	20 Mar 1926
IRWIN, Denis	286 (10)	18	70 (2)	4	–	–	42 (1)	7	28 (3)	–	62 (2)	4	8	–	3	–	12	–	511 (18)	33	18 Aug 1990

PLAYER ROLL CALL

PLAYER	PREMIER LGE		DIVISION ONE		DIVISION TWO		FA CUP		LEAGUE CUP		EC / CL		ECWC		UEFA CUP		OTHER GAMES		TOTALS		DEBUT
	APPS	GLS	APPS	GLS	APPS	GLS	APPS	GLS	APPS	GLS	APPS	GLS	APPS	GLS	APPS	GLS	APPS	GLS	APPS	GLS	
J																					
JACKSON, Tommy	-	-	18 (1)	-	-	-	-	-	4	-	-	-	-	-	-	-	-	-	22 (1)	-	16 Aug 1975
JACKSON, William	-	-	-	-	61	12	3	2	-	-	-	-	-	-	-	-	-	-	64	14	2 Sep 1899
JAMES, Steve	-	-	116	4	13	-	12	-	17 (1)	-	-	-	2	-	-	-	-	-	160 (1)	4	12 Oct 1968
JENKYNS, Caesar	-	-	-	-	35	5	8	-	-	-	-	-	-	-	-	-	4	1	47	6	1 Sep 1896
JOHN, Roy	-	-	15	-	-	-	-	-	-	-	-	-	-	-	-	-	-	-	15	-	29 Aug 1936
JOHNSEN, Ronny	85 (14)	7	-	-	-	-	8 (2)	1	3	-	32 (3)	-	-	-	-	-	3	1	131 (19)	9	17 Aug 1996
JOHNSON, Eddie	-	-	-	-	-	-	-	-	- (1)	-	-	-	-	-	-	-	-	-	- (1)	-	28 Oct 2003
JOHNSON, Samuel	-	-	-	-	1	-	-	-	-	-	-	-	-	-	-	-	-	-	1	-	20 Mar 1901
JOHNSTON, Billy	-	-	43	13	28	11	6	3	-	-	-	-	-	-	-	-	-	-	77	27	15 Oct 1927
JONES, David (1937)	-	-	-	-	1	-	-	-	-	-	-	-	-	-	-	-	-	-	1	-	11 Dec 1937
JONES, David (2004)	-	-	-	-	-	-	1	-	2 (1)	-	-	-	-	-	-	-	-	-	3 (1)	-	1 Dec 2004
JONES, Mark	-	-	103	1	-	-	7	-	-	-	10	-	-	-	-	-	1	-	121	1	7 Oct 1950
JONES, Owen	-	-	-	-	2	-	-	-	-	-	-	-	-	-	-	-	-	-	2	-	3 Sep 1898
JONES, Peter	-	-	1	-	-	-	-	-	-	-	-	-	-	-	-	-	-	-	1	-	19 Oct 1957
JONES, Phil	25 (4)	1	-	-	-	-	1	-	1	-	4 (2)	1	-	-	3	-	- (1)	-	34 (7)	2	7 Aug 2011
JONES, Richard	-	-	-	-	-	-	1	-	2 (2)	-	-	-	-	-	-	-	-	-	3 (2)	-	26 Oct 2005
JONES, Tom	-	-	86	-	103	-	11	-	-	-	-	-	-	-	-	-	-	-	200	-	8 Nov 1924
JONES, Tommy	-	-	-	-	20	4	-	-	-	-	-	-	-	-	-	-	-	-	22	4	25 Aug 1934
JORDAN, Joe	-	-	109	37	-	-	11 (1)	2	4	2	-	-	-	-	-	-	1	-	125 (1)	41	28 Jan 1978
JOVANOVIC, Nikki	-	-	20 (1)	4	-	-	1	-	2	-	-	-	-	-	2	-	-	-	25 (1)	4	2 Feb 1980
K																					
KANCHELSKIS, Andrei	67 (21)	23	29 (6)	5	-	-	11 (1)	4	15 (1)	3	5	1	1	-	1	-	3	-	132 (29)	36	11 May 1991
KEANE, Michael	-	-	-	-	-	-	-	-	- (1)	-	-	-	-	-	-	-	-	-	- (1)	-	25 Oct 2011
KEANE, Roy	309 (17)	33	-	-	-	-	44 (2)	2	12 (2)	-	79 (1)	14	2	-	12	2	-	-	458 (22)	51	7 Aug 1993
KEANE, Will	- (1)	-	-	-	-	-	-	-	-	-	-	-	-	-	-	-	-	-	- (1)	-	31 Dec 2011
KELLY, Jimmy	-	-	- (1)	-	-	-	-	-	-	-	-	-	-	-	-	-	-	-	- (1)	-	20 Dec 1975
KENNEDY, Fred	-	-	-	-	17	4	1	-	-	-	-	-	-	-	-	-	-	-	18	4	6 Oct 1923
KENNEDY, Patrick	-	-	1	-	-	-	-	-	-	-	-	-	-	-	-	-	-	-	1	-	2 Oct 1954
KENNEDY, William	-	-	-	-	30	11	3	1	-	-	-	-	-	-	-	-	-	-	33	12	7 Sep 1895
KERR, Hugh	-	-	-	-	2	-	-	-	-	-	-	-	-	-	-	-	-	-	2	-	9 Mar 1904
KIDD, Brian	-	-	195 (8)	52	-	-	24 (1)	8	20	7	16	3	-	-	-	-	2	-	257 (9)	70	12 Aug 1967
KING, Joshua	-	-	-	-	-	-	-	-	- (1)	-	-	-	-	-	-	-	-	-	- (1)	-	23 Sep 2009
KINLOCH, Joe	-	-	1	-	-	-	-	-	-	-	-	-	-	-	-	-	-	-	1	-	29 Oct 1892
KINSEY, Albert	-	-	-	-	-	-	1	1	-	-	-	-	-	-	-	-	-	-	1	1	9 Jan 1965
KLEBERSON, Jose	16 (4)	2	-	-	-	-	1	-	4	-	3 (2)	-	-	-	-	-	-	-	24 (6)	2	27 Aug 2003
KNOWLES, Frank	-	-	46	1	-	-	1	-	-	-	-	-	-	-	-	-	-	-	47	1	30 Mar 1912
KOPEL, Frank	-	-	8 (2)	-	-	-	1	-	-	-	1	-	-	-	-	-	-	-	10 (2)	-	9 Sep 1967
KUSZCZAK, Tomasz	30 (2)	-	-	-	-	-	7 (1)	-	10	-	9 (2)	-	-	-	-	-	-	-	56 (5)	-	17 Sep 2006
L																					
LANCASTER, Joe	-	-	2	-	-	-	2	-	-	-	-	-	-	-	-	-	-	-	4	-	14 Jan 1950
LANG, Tommy	-	-	8	-	4	1	1	-	-	-	-	-	-	-	-	-	-	-	13	1	11 Apr 1936
LANGFORD, Len	-	-	-	-	15	-	-	-	-	-	-	-	-	-	-	-	-	-	15	-	22 Sep 1934
LAPPIN, Harry	-	-	-	-	27	4	-	-	-	-	-	-	-	-	-	-	-	-	27	4	27 Apr 1901
LARSSON, Henrik	5 (2)	1	-	-	-	-	3 (1)	1	-	-	2	1	-	-	-	-	-	-	10 (3)	3	7 Jan 2007
LAW, Denis	-	-	305 (4)	171	-	-	44 (2)	34	11	3	18	14	5	6	10	8	5	1	398 (6)	237	18 Aug 1962
LAWSON, Reg	-	-	-	-	3	-	-	-	-	-	-	-	-	-	-	-	-	-	3	-	1 Sep 1900
LAWTON, Nobby	-	-	36	6	-	-	7	-	1	-	-	-	-	-	-	-	-	-	44	6	9 Apr 1960
LEE, Edwin	-	-	-	-	11	5	-	-	-	-	-	-	-	-	-	-	-	-	11	5	25 Mar 1899
LEE, Kieran	1	-	-	-	-	-	-	-	- (2)	1	-	-	-	-	-	-	-	-	1 (2)	1	25 Oct 2006
LEIGH, Tom	-	-	-	-	43	15	3	-	-	-	-	-	-	-	-	-	-	-	46	15	17 Mar 1900
LEIGHTON, Jim	-	-	73	-	-	-	14	-	7	-	-	-	-	-	-	-	-	-	94	-	27 Aug 1988
LEONARD, Harry	-	-	10	5	-	-	-	-	-	-	-	-	-	-	-	-	-	-	10	5	11 Sep 1920
LEWIS, Eddie	-	-	20	9	-	-	4	2	-	-	-	-	-	-	-	-	-	-	24	11	29 Nov 1952
LIEVESLEY, Leslie	-	-	-	-	2	-	-	-	-	-	-	-	-	-	-	-	-	-	2	-	25 Mar 1932
LIEVESLEY, Wilfred	-	-	-	-	2	-	1	-	-	-	-	-	-	-	-	-	-	-	3	-	20 Jan 1923
LINDEGAARD, Anders	8	-	-	-	-	-	3	-	-	-	2	-	-	-	-	-	-	-	13	-	29 Jan 2011
LINKSON, Oscar	-	-	55	-	-	-	4	-	-	-	-	-	-	-	-	-	-	-	59	-	24 Oct 1908
LIVINGSTONE, George	-	-	43	4	-	-	3	-	-	-	-	-	-	-	-	-	-	-	46	4	23 Jan 1909
LOCHHEAD, Arthur	-	-	36	10	111	40	6	-	-	-	-	-	-	-	-	-	-	-	153	50	27 Aug 1921
LONGAIR, William	-	-	-	-	1	-	-	-	-	-	-	-	-	-	-	-	-	-	1	-	20 Apr 1895
LONGTON, not known	-	-	-	-	-	-	1	-	-	-	-	-	-	-	-	-	-	-	1	-	30 Oct 1886
LOWRIE, Tommy	-	-	13	-	-	-	1	-	-	-	-	-	-	-	-	-	-	-	14	-	7 Apr 1948
LYDON, George	-	-	1	-	2	-	-	-	-	-	-	-	-	-	-	-	-	-	3	-	25 Dec 1930
LYNCH, Mark	-	-	-	-	-	-	-	-	1	-	-	-	-	-	-	-	-	-	1	-	18 Mar 2003
LYNER, David	-	-	-	-	3	-	-	-	-	-	-	-	-	-	-	-	-	-	3	-	23 Sep 1922
LYNN, Sammy	-	-	13	-	-	-	-	-	-	-	-	-	-	-	-	-	-	-	13	-	3 Jan 1948
LYONS, George	-	-	-	-	4	-	1	-	-	-	-	-	-	-	-	-	-	-	5	-	23 Apr 1904
M																					
MACARI, Lou	-	-	275 (16)	67	36 (2)	11	31 (3)	8	22 (5)	10	-	-	4	-	5 (1)	1	1	-	374 (27)	97	20 Jan 1973
MACDONALD, Ken	-	-	9	2	-	-	-	-	-	-	-	-	-	-	-	-	-	-	9	2	3 Mar 1923
MACDOUGALL, Ted	-	-	18	5	-	-	-	-	-	-	-	-	-	-	-	-	-	-	18	5	7 Oct 1972
MACHEDA, Federico	5 (14)	4	-	-	-	-	1	-	6 (2)	1	3 (2)	-	-	-	-	-	-	-	15 (18)	5	5 Apr 2009
MACKIE, Charlie	-	-	-	-	5	3	2	1	-	-	-	-	-	-	-	-	-	-	7	4	3 Sep 1904
MAIORANA, Jules	-	-	2 (5)	-	-	-	-	-	- (1)	-	-	-	-	-	-	-	-	-	2 (6)	-	14 Jan 1989
MANLEY, Tom	-	-	54	8	134	32	7	1	-	-	-	-	-	-	-	-	-	-	195	41	5 Dec 1931
MANN, Frank	-	-	113	2	67	3	17	-	-	-	-	-	-	-	-	-	-	-	197	5	17 Mar 1923
MANN, Herbert	-	-	-	-	13	2	-	-	-	-	-	-	-	-	-	-	-	-	13	2	29 Aug 1931
MANNS, Tom	-	-	-	-	2	-	-	-	-	-	-	-	-	-	-	-	-	-	2	-	3 Feb 1934
MANUCHO	- (1)	-	-	-	-	-	-	-	- (2)	-	-	-	-	-	-	-	-	-	- (3)	-	23 Sep 2008
MARSH, Philip	-	-	-	-	-	-	-	-	1	-	-	-	-	-	-	-	-	-	1	-	25 Oct 2006
MARSHALL, Arthur	-	-	-	-	-	-	6	-	-	-	-	-	-	-	-	-	-	-	6	-	9 Mar 1903
MARTIN, Lee (1990s)	1	-	55 (17)	1	-	-	13 (1)	1	8 (2)	-	1 (1)	-	4 (4)	-	1	-	1	-	84 (25)	2	9 May 1988
MARTIN, Lee (2000s)	1	-	-	-	-	-	-	-	2	-	-	-	-	-	-	-	-	-	3	-	26 Oct 2005
MARTIN, Mick	-	-	26 (6)	2	7 (1)	-	2	-	1	-	-	-	-	-	-	-	-	-	36 (7)	2	24 Jan 1973
MATHIESON, William	-	-	10	2	-	-	-	-	-	-	-	-	-	-	-	-	-	-	10	2	3 Sep 1892
MAY, David	68 (17)	6	-	-	-	-	6	-	9	1	13 (2)	1	-	-	-	-	2 (1)	-	98 (20)	8	14 Aug 1994
McBAIN, Neil	-	-	21	-	21	2	1	-	-	-	-	-	-	-	-	-	-	-	43	2	26 Nov 1921
McCALLIOG, Jim	-	-	11	4	20	3	1	-	5 (1)	-	-	-	-	-	-	-	-	-	37 (1)	7	16 Mar 1974
McCARTHY, Pat	-	-	1	-	-	-	-	-	-	-	-	-	-	-	-	-	-	-	1	-	20 Jan 1912
McCARTNEY, John	-	-	-	-	18	1	1	-	-	-	-	-	-	-	-	-	-	-	20	1	8 Sep 1894
McCARTNEY, William	-	-	-	-	13	-	-	-	-	-	-	-	-	-	-	-	-	-	13	-	5 Sep 1903
McCLAIR, Brian	106 (56)	18	190 (3)	70	-	-	38 (7)	14	44 (1)	19	2 (6)	-	13	5	2	-	3	1	398 (73)	127	15 Aug 1987
McCLELLAND, Jimmy	-	-	5	1	-	-	-	-	-	-	-	-	-	-	-	-	-	-	5	1	2 Sep 1936
McCRAE, James	-	-	9	-	-	-	4	-	-	-	-	-	-	-	-	-	-	-	13	-	16 Jan 1926
McCREERY, David	-	-	48 (37)	7	- (2)	-	1 (6)	-	4 (4)	1	-	-	3	-	1 (3)	-	- (1)	-	57 (53)	8	15 Oct 1974
McDONALD, Willie	-	-	-	-	27	4	-	-	-	-	-	-	-	-	-	-	-	-	27	4	23 Apr 1932
McFARLANE, Bob	-	-	-	-	-	-	3	-	-	-	-	-	-	-	-	-	-	-	3	-	3 Oct 1891
McFARLANE, Noel	-	-	1	-	-	-	-	-	-	-	-	-	-	-	-	-	-	-	1	-	13 Feb 1954

PLAYER ROLL CALL

PLAYER	PREMIER LGE		DIVISION ONE		DIVISION TWO		FA CUP		LEAGUE CUP		EC / CL		ECWC		UEFA CUP		OTHER GAMES		TOTALS		DEBUT
	APPS	GLS	APPS	GLS	APPS	GLS	APPS	GLS	APPS	GLS	APPS	GLS	APPS	GLS	APPS	GLS	APPS	GLS	APPS	GLS	
McFETTERIDGE, David	–	–	–	–	1	–	–	–	–	–	–	–	–	–	–	–	–	–	1	–	13 Apr 1895
McGARVEY, Scott	–	–	13 (12)	3	–	–	–	–	–	–	–	–	–	–	–	–	–	–	13 (12)	3	13 Sep 1980
McGIBBON, Pat	–	–	–	–	–	–	–	–	1	–	–	–	–	–	–	–	–	–	1	–	20 Sep 1995
McGILLIVRAY, Charlie	–	–	–	–	8	–	1	–	–	–	–	–	–	–	–	–	–	–	9	–	26 Aug 1933
McGILLIVRAY, John	–	–	3	–	–	–	1	–	–	–	–	–	–	–	–	–	–	–	4	–	11 Jan 1908
McGLEN, Billy	–	–	110	2	–	–	12	–	–	–	–	–	–	–	–	–	–	–	122	2	31 Aug 1946
McGRATH, Chris	–	–	12 (16)	1	–	–	–	–	– (2)	–	–	–	3 (1)	–	–	–	–	–	15 (19)	1	23 Oct 1976
McGRATH, Paul	–	–	159 (4)	12	–	–	15 (3)	2	13	2	–	–	2	–	2	–	1	–	192 (7)	16	10 Nov 1982
McGUINNESS, Wilf	–	–	81	2	–	–	2	–	–	–	2	–	–	–	–	–	–	–	85	2	8 Oct 1955
McILROY, Sammy	–	–	279 (21)	50	41 (1)	7	35 (3)	6	25 (3)	6	–	–	4	–	6	2	1	–	391 (28)	71	6 Nov 1971
McILVENNY, Eddie	–	–	2	–	–	–	–	–	–	–	–	–	–	–	–	–	–	–	2	–	19 Aug 1950
McKAY, Bill	–	–	49	5	120	10	13	–	–	–	–	–	–	–	–	–	–	–	182	15	17 Mar 1934
McKEE, Colin	1	–	–	–	–	–	–	–	–	–	–	–	–	–	–	–	–	–	1	–	8 May 1994
McLACHLAN, George	–	–	65	4	45	–	6	–	–	–	–	–	–	–	–	–	–	–	116	4	21 Dec 1929
McLENAHAN, Hugh	–	–	45	8	67	3	4	1	–	–	–	–	–	–	–	–	–	–	116	12	4 Feb 1928
McMILLAN, Sammy	–	–	15	6	–	–	–	–	–	–	–	–	–	–	–	–	–	–	15	6	4 Nov 1961
McMILLEN, Walter	–	–	–	–	27	2	2	–	–	–	–	–	–	–	–	–	–	–	29	2	16 Sep 1933
McNAUGHT, James	–	–	26	1	114	11	17	–	–	–	–	–	–	–	–	–	5	–	162	12	2 Sep 1893
McNULTY, Thomas	–	–	57	–	–	–	2	–	–	–	–	–	–	–	–	–	1	–	60	–	15 Apr 1950
McPHERSON, Frank	–	–	87	37	72	8	16	7	–	–	–	–	–	–	–	–	–	–	175	52	25 Aug 1923
McQUEEN, Gordon	–	–	184	20	–	–	21	2	16	4	–	–	4	–	3	–	1	–	229	26	25 Feb 1978
McSHANE, Harry	–	–	56	8	–	–	1	–	–	–	–	–	–	–	–	–	–	–	57	8	13 Sep 1950
MEEHAN, Tommy	–	–	51	6	–	–	2	–	–	–	–	–	–	–	–	–	–	–	53	6	1 Sep 1919
MELLOR, Jack	–	–	37	–	79	–	6	–	–	–	–	–	–	–	–	–	–	–	122	–	15 Sep 1930
MENZIES, Alex	–	–	23	4	–	–	2	–	–	–	–	–	–	–	–	–	–	–	25	4	17 Nov 1906
MEREDITH, Billy	–	–	303	35	–	–	29	–	–	–	–	–	–	–	–	–	3	1	335	36	1 Jan 1907
MEW, Jack	–	–	133	–	53	–	13	–	–	–	–	–	–	–	–	–	–	–	199	–	26 Oct 1912
MILARVIE, Bob	–	–	–	–	–	–	1	–	–	–	–	–	–	–	–	–	–	–	1	–	4 Oct 1890
MILLAR, George	–	–	–	–	6	5	1	–	–	–	–	–	–	–	–	–	–	–	7	5	22 Dec 1894
MILLER, James	–	–	–	–	4	1	–	–	–	–	–	–	–	–	–	–	–	–	4	1	15 Mar 1924
MILLER, Liam	3 (6)	–	–	–	–	–	2 (2)	–	3	2	3 (3)	–	–	–	–	–	–	–	11 (11)	2	11 Aug 2004
MILLER, Tom	–	–	25	7	–	–	2	1	–	–	–	–	–	–	–	–	–	–	27	8	25 Sep 1920
MILNE, Ralph	–	–	19 (4)	3	–	–	7	–	–	–	–	–	–	–	–	–	–	–	26 (4)	3	19 Nov 1988
MITCHELL, Andrew (1890s)	–	–	54	–	–	–	4	–	–	–	–	–	–	–	–	–	3	–	61	–	10 Sep 1892
MITCHELL, Andrew (1930s)	–	–	–	–	1	–	–	–	–	–	–	–	–	–	–	–	–	–	1	–	18 Mar 1933
MITCHELL, John	–	–	–	–	–	–	3	–	–	–	–	–	–	–	–	–	–	–	3	–	30 Oct 1886
MITTEN, Charlie	–	–	142	50	–	–	19	11	–	–	–	–	–	–	–	–	1	–	162	61	31 Aug 1946
MOGER, Harry	–	–	170	–	72	–	22	–	–	–	–	–	–	–	–	–	2	–	266	–	10 Oct 1903
MOIR, Ian	–	–	45	5	–	–	–	–	–	–	–	–	–	–	–	–	–	–	45	5	1 Oct 1960
MONTGOMERY, Archie	–	–	–	–	3	–	–	–	–	–	–	–	–	–	–	–	–	–	3	–	16 Sep 1905
MONTGOMERY, James	–	–	27	1	–	–	–	–	–	–	–	–	–	–	–	–	–	–	27	1	13 Mar 1915
MOODY, John	–	–	–	–	50	–	1	–	–	–	–	–	–	–	–	–	–	–	51	–	26 Mar 1932
MOORE, Charlie	–	–	215	–	94	–	19	–	–	–	–	–	–	–	–	–	–	–	328	–	30 Aug 1919
MOORE, Graham	–	–	18	4	–	–	1	1	–	–	–	–	–	–	–	–	–	–	19	5	9 Nov 1963
MORAN, Kevin	–	–	228 (3)	21	–	–	18	1	24 (1)	2	–	–	8	–	5 (1)	–	1	–	284 (5)	24	30 Apr 1979
MORGAN, Billy	–	–	–	–	143	6	9	1	–	–	–	–	–	–	–	–	–	–	152	7	2 Mar 1897
MORGAN, Hugh	–	–	–	–	20	4	3	–	–	–	–	–	–	–	–	–	–	–	23	4	15 Dec 1900
MORGAN, Willie	–	–	204	22	32 (2)	3	27	4	24 (1)	3	4	1	–	–	–	–	2	1	293 (3)	34	28 Aug 1968
MORGANS, Kenny	–	–	17	–	–	–	2	–	–	–	4	–	–	–	–	–	–	–	23	–	21 Dec 1957
MORRIS, Johnny	–	–	83	32	–	–	9	3	–	–	–	–	–	–	–	–	1	–	93	35	26 Oct 1946
MORRISON, Ravel	–	–	–	–	–	–	–	–	– (3)	–	–	–	–	–	–	–	–	–	– (3)	–	26 Oct 2010
MORRISON, Tommy	–	–	–	–	29	7	7	1	–	–	–	–	–	–	–	–	–	–	36	8	25 Dec 1902
MORTON, Ben	–	–	–	–	1	–	–	–	–	–	–	–	–	–	–	–	–	–	1	–	16 Nov 1935
MOSES, Remi	–	–	143 (7)	7	–	–	11	1	22 (2)	4	–	–	5 (1)	–	7	–	– (1)	–	188 (11)	12	19 Sep 1981
MUHREN, Arnold	–	–	65 (5)	13	–	–	8	1	11	1	–	–	5	–	3	3	1	–	93 (5)	18	28 Aug 1982
MULRYNE, Philip	1	–	–	–	–	–	– (1)	–	3	–	–	–	–	–	–	–	–	–	4 (1)	–	14 Oct 1997
MURRAY, Robert	–	–	–	–	4	–	–	–	–	–	–	–	–	–	–	–	–	–	4	–	28 Aug 1937
MUTCH, George	–	–	28	7	84	39	8	3	–	–	–	–	–	–	–	–	–	–	120	49	25 Aug 1934
MYERSCOUGH, Joe	–	–	20	5	13	3	1	–	–	–	–	–	–	–	–	–	–	–	34	8	4 Sep 1920

N

PLAYER	PREMIER LGE		DIVISION ONE		DIVISION TWO		FA CUP		LEAGUE CUP		EC / CL		ECWC		UEFA CUP		OTHER GAMES		TOTALS		DEBUT
NANI	97 (27)	25	–	–	–	–	7 (1)	3	9	3	34 (10)	3	–	–	2 (1)	–	5 (2)	3	154 (41)	37	5 Aug 2007
NARDIELLO, Daniel	–	–	–	–	–	–	–	–	1 (2)	–	– (1)	–	–	–	–	–	–	–	1 (3)	–	5 Nov 2001
NEVILLE, Gary	380 (20)	5	–	–	–	–	44 (3)	–	22 (3)	–	108 (7)	2	–	–	1 (1)	–	11 (2)	–	566 (36)	7	16 Sep 1992
NEVILLE, Phil	210 (53)	5	–	–	–	–	25 (6)	1	16 (1)	–	42 (22)	2	–	–	1	–	7 (3)	–	301 (85)	8	28 Jan 1995
NEVIN, George	–	–	–	–	4	–	1	–	–	–	–	–	–	–	–	–	–	–	5	–	6 Jan 1934
NEVLAND, Erik	– (1)	–	–	–	–	–	2 (1)	–	– (2)	1	–	–	–	–	–	–	–	–	2 (4)	1	14 Oct 1997
NEWTON, Percy	–	–	–	–	2	–	–	–	–	–	–	–	–	–	–	–	–	–	2	–	3 Feb 1934
NICHOLL, Jimmy	–	–	188 (8)	3	– (1)	–	22 (4)	1	14	1	–	–	4	1	6	–	1	–	235 (13)	6	5 Apr 1975
NICHOLSON, Jimmy	–	–	58	5	–	–	7	1	3	–	–	–	–	–	–	–	–	–	68	6	24 Aug 1960
NICOL, George	–	–	6	2	–	–	1	–	–	–	–	–	–	–	–	–	–	–	7	2	11 Feb 1928
NOBLE, Bobby	–	–	31	–	–	–	2	–	–	–	–	–	–	–	–	–	–	–	33	–	9 Apr 1966
NORTON, Joe	–	–	37	3	–	–	–	–	–	–	–	–	–	–	–	–	–	–	37	3	24 Jan 1914
NOTMAN, Alex	–	–	–	–	–	–	–	–	– (1)	–	–	–	–	–	–	–	–	–	– (1)	–	2 Dec 1998
NUTTALL, Tom	–	–	16	4	–	–	–	–	–	–	–	–	–	–	–	–	–	–	16	4	23 Mar 1912

O

PLAYER	PREMIER LGE		DIVISION ONE		DIVISION TWO		FA CUP		LEAGUE CUP		EC / CL		ECWC		UEFA CUP		OTHER GAMES		TOTALS		DEBUT
OBERTAN, Gabriel	4 (10)	–	–	–	–	–	3	–	4 (1)	–	2 (4)	1	–	–	–	–	–	–	13 (15)	1	27 Oct 2009
O'BRIEN, George	–	–	–	–	1	–	–	–	–	–	–	–	–	–	–	–	–	–	1	–	7 Apr 1902
O'BRIEN, Liam	–	–	16 (15)	2	–	–	– (2)	–	1 (2)	–	–	–	–	–	–	–	–	–	17 (19)	2	20 Dec 1986
O'CONNELL, Pat	–	–	34	2	–	–	1	–	–	–	–	–	–	–	–	–	–	–	35	2	2 Sep 1914
O'KANE, John	1 (1)	–	–	–	–	–	1	–	2 (1)	–	–	–	–	–	1	–	–	–	5 (2)	–	21 Sep 1994
OLIVE, Les	–	–	2	–	–	–	–	–	–	–	–	–	–	–	–	–	–	–	2	–	11 Apr 1953
OLSEN, Jesper	–	–	119 (20)	21	–	–	13 (3)	2	10 (3)	1	–	–	–	–	6 (1)	–	1	–	149 (27)	24	25 Aug 1984
O'NEIL, Tommy	–	–	54	–	–	–	7	–	7	–	–	–	–	–	–	–	–	–	68	–	5 May 1971
O'SHAUGHNESSY, T	–	–	–	–	–	–	1	–	–	–	–	–	–	–	–	–	–	–	1	–	25 Oct 1890
O'SHEA, John	188 (68)	10	–	–	–	–	22 (6)	1	25 (1)	2	61 (15)	2	–	–	–	–	5 (2)	–	301 (92)	15	13 Oct 1999
OWEN, Bill	–	–	–	–	1	–	–	–	–	–	–	–	–	–	–	–	–	–	1	–	15 Oct 1898
OWEN, George	–	–	–	–	–	–	1	–	–	–	–	–	–	–	–	–	–	–	1	–	18 Jan 1889
OWEN, Jack	–	–	–	–	–	–	6	–	–	–	–	–	–	–	–	–	–	–	6	–	18 Jan 1889
OWEN, Michael	6 (25)	5	–	–	–	–	1 (2)	1	6 (1)	7	4 (5)	4	–	–	–	–	1 (1)	–	18 (34)	17	9 Aug 2009
OWEN, W	–	–	–	–	17	1	–	–	–	–	–	–	–	–	–	–	–	–	17	1	22 Sep 1934

P

PLAYER	PREMIER LGE		DIVISION ONE		DIVISION TWO		FA CUP		LEAGUE CUP		EC / CL		ECWC		UEFA CUP		OTHER GAMES		TOTALS		DEBUT
PAGE, Louis	–	–	–	–	12	–	–	–	–	–	–	–	–	–	–	–	–	–	12	–	25 Mar 1932
PALLISTER, Gary	206	8	108 (3)	4	–	–	38	2	36	–	23	–	12 (1)	1	4	–	6	–	433 (4)	15	30 Aug 1989
PAPE, Albert	–	–	2	–	16	5	–	–	–	–	–	–	–	–	–	–	–	–	18	5	7 Feb 1925
PARK, Ji-Sung	93 (41)	19	–	–	–	–	12 (2)	2	11	3	24 (15)	3	–	–	3	–	3 (1)	–	146 (59)	27	9 Aug 2005
PARKER, Paul	76 (3)	1	24 (2)	–	–	–	14 (1)	1	15	–	5 (1)	–	2	–	– (2)	–	1	–	137 (9)	2	17 Aug 1991
PARKER, Samuel	–	–	11	–	–	–	1	–	–	–	–	–	–	–	–	–	–	–	12	–	13 Jan 1894
PARKER, Thomas	–	–	9	–	8	–	–	–	–	–	–	–	–	–	–	–	–	–	17	–	11 Oct 1930
PARKINSON, Robert	–	–	–	–	15	7	–	–	–	–	–	–	–	–	–	–	–	–	15	7	11 Nov 1899
PARTRIDGE, Teddy	–	–	112	16	36	–	12	2	–	–	–	–	–	–	–	–	–	–	160	18	9 Oct 1920
PATERSON, Steve	–	–	3 (3)	–	–	–	–	–	2	–	–	–	–	–	– (2)	–	–	–	5 (5)	–	29 Sep 1976

PLAYER ROLL CALL

PLAYER	PREMIER LGE		DIVISION ONE		DIVISION TWO		FA CUP		LEAGUE CUP		EC / CL		ECWC		UEFA CUP		OTHER GAMES		TOTALS		DEBUT
	APPS	GLS	APPS	GLS	APPS	GLS	APPS	GLS	APPS	GLS	APPS	GLS	APPS	GLS	APPS	GLS	APPS	GLS	APPS	GLS	
PAYNE, Ernest	–	–	2	1	–	–	–	–	–	–	–	–	–	–	–	–	–	–	2	1	27 Feb 1909
PEARS, Steve	–	–	4	–	–	–	1	–	–	–	–	–	–	–	–	–	–	–	5	–	12 Jan 1985
PEARSON, Mark	–	–	68	12	–	–	7	1	3	1	2	–	–	–	–	–	–	–	80	14	19 Feb 1958
PEARSON, Stan	–	–	301	125	11	2	30	21	–	–	–	–	–	–	–	–	1	–	343	148	13 Nov 1937
PEARSON, Stuart	–	–	108	38	30 (1)	17	22	5	12	5	–	–	3	1	3	–	1	–	179 (1)	66	17 Aug 1974
PEDDIE, Jack	–	–	16	6	96	46	9	6	–	–	–	–	–	–	–	–	–	–	121	58	6 Sep 1902
PEDEN, Jack	–	–	28	7	–	–	3	1	–	–	–	–	–	–	–	–	1	–	32	8	2 Sep 1893
PEGG, David	–	–	127	24	–	–	9	–	–	–	12	4	–	–	–	–	2	–	150	28	6 Dec 1952
PEGG, Dick	–	–	–	–	41	13	10	7	–	–	–	–	–	–	–	–	–	–	51	20	6 Sep 1902
PEGG, Ken	–	–	2	–	–	–	–	–	–	–	–	–	–	–	–	–	–	–	2	–	15 Nov 1947
PEPPER, Frank	–	–	–	–	7	–	1	–	–	–	–	–	–	–	–	–	–	–	8	–	10 Dec 1898
PERRINS, George	–	–	55	–	37	–	6	–	–	–	–	–	–	–	–	–	4	–	102	–	3 Sep 1892
PETERS, James	–	–	–	–	46	13	4	1	–	–	–	–	–	–	–	–	1	–	51	14	8 Sep 1894
PHELAN, Mike	6 (7)	–	82 (7)	2	–	–	10	1	14 (2)	–	1 (3)	–	12	–	1	–	1	–	127 (19)	3	19 Aug 1989
PICKEN, Jack	–	–	80	19	33	20	8	7	–	–	–	–	–	–	–	–	1	–	122	46	2 Sep 1905
PILKINGTON, Kevin	4 (2)	–	–	–	–	–	1	–	1	–	–	–	–	–	–	–	–	–	6 (2)	–	19 Nov 1994
PINNER, Mike	–	–	4	–	–	–	–	–	–	–	–	–	–	–	–	–	–	–	4	–	4 Feb 1961
PIQUE, Gerard	6 (6)	–	–	–	–	–	3	–	2 (2)	–	3 (1)	2	–	–	–	–	–	–	14 (9)	2	26 Oct 2004
POBORSKY, Karel	18 (14)	5	–	–	–	–	2	–	3	1	5 (5)	–	–	–	–	–	– (1)	–	28 (20)	6	11 Aug 1996
POGBA, Paul	– (3)	–	–	–	–	–	–	–	– (3)	–	–	–	–	–	– (1)	–	–	–	– (7)	–	20 Sep 2011
PORTER, Billy	–	–	2	–	59	–	4	–	–	–	–	–	–	–	–	–	–	–	65	–	19 Jan 1935
POSSEBON, Rodrigo	– (3)	–	–	–	–	–	– (2)	–	3	–	–	–	–	–	–	–	–	–	3 (5)	–	17 Aug 2008
POTTS, Arthur	–	–	27	5	–	–	2	–	–	–	–	–	–	–	–	–	–	–	29	5	26 Dec 1913
POWELL, Jack	–	–	–	–	–	–	4	–	–	–	–	–	–	–	–	–	–	–	4	–	30 Oct 1886
PRENTICE, John	–	–	1	–	–	–	–	–	–	–	–	–	–	–	–	–	–	–	1	–	2 Apr 1920
PRESTON, Stephen	–	–	–	–	33	14	1	–	–	–	–	–	–	–	–	–	–	–	34	14	7 Sep 1901
PRINCE, Albert	–	–	1	–	–	–	–	–	–	–	–	–	–	–	–	–	–	–	1	–	27 Feb 1915
PRINCE, D	–	–	2	–	–	–	–	–	–	–	–	–	–	–	–	–	–	–	2	–	4 Nov 1893
PRUNIER, William	2	–	–	–	–	–	–	–	–	–	–	–	–	–	–	–	–	–	2	–	30 Dec 1995
PUGH, Danny	– (1)	–	–	–	–	–	– (1)	–	2	–	1 (2)	–	–	–	–	–	–	–	3 (4)	–	18 Sep 2002
PUGH, James	–	–	1	–	1	–	–	–	–	–	–	–	–	–	–	–	–	–	2	–	29 Apr 1922

Q

PLAYER	PREMIER LGE APPS	PREMIER LGE GLS	DIVISION ONE APPS	DIVISION ONE GLS	DIVISION TWO APPS	DIVISION TWO GLS	FA CUP APPS	FA CUP GLS	LEAGUE CUP APPS	LEAGUE CUP GLS	EC / CL APPS	EC / CL GLS	ECWC APPS	ECWC GLS	UEFA CUP APPS	UEFA CUP GLS	OTHER GAMES APPS	OTHER GAMES GLS	TOTALS APPS	TOTALS GLS	DEBUT
QUINN, Jack	–	–	2	–	–	–	–	–	–	–	–	–	–	–	–	–	–	–	2	–	3 Apr 1909
QUIXALL, Albert	–	–	165	50	–	–	14	4	1	2	–	–	3	–	–	–	1	–	184	56	20 Sep 1958

R

PLAYER	PREMIER LGE APPS	PREMIER LGE GLS	DIVISION ONE APPS	DIVISION ONE GLS	DIVISION TWO APPS	DIVISION TWO GLS	FA CUP APPS	FA CUP GLS	LEAGUE CUP APPS	LEAGUE CUP GLS	EC / CL APPS	EC / CL GLS	ECWC APPS	ECWC GLS	UEFA CUP APPS	UEFA CUP GLS	OTHER GAMES APPS	OTHER GAMES GLS	TOTALS APPS	TOTALS GLS	DEBUT
RACHUBKA, Paul	1	–	–	–	–	–	–	–	– (1)	–	–	–	–	–	–	–	– (1)	–	1 (2)	–	11 Jan 2000
RADCLIFFE, George	–	–	–	–	1	–	–	–	–	–	–	–	–	–	–	–	–	–	1	–	12 Apr 1899
RADFORD, Charlie	–	–	27	–	64	1	5	–	–	–	–	–	–	–	–	–	–	–	96	1	7 May 1921
RAFAEL, da Silva	45 (7)	2	–	–	–	–	6	–	11 (1)	–	11 (4)	–	–	–	3	–	1 (1)	–	77 (13)	2	17 Aug 2008
RAMSAY, Robert	–	–	–	–	–	–	1	–	–	–	–	–	–	–	–	–	–	–	1	–	4 Oct 1890
RAMSDEN, Charlie	–	–	14	3	–	–	2	–	–	–	–	–	–	–	–	–	–	–	16	3	24 Sep 1927
RATTIGAN, not known	–	–	–	–	–	–	1	–	–	–	–	–	–	–	–	–	–	–	1	–	25 Oct 1890
RAWLINGS, Bill	–	–	35	19	–	–	1	–	–	–	–	–	–	–	–	–	–	–	36	19	14 Mar 1928
READ, Bert	–	–	–	–	35	–	7	–	–	–	–	–	–	–	–	–	–	–	42	–	6 Sep 1902
REDMAN, Billy	–	–	36	–	–	–	2	–	–	–	–	–	–	–	–	–	–	–	38	–	7 Oct 1950
REDWOOD, Hubert	–	–	56	1	30	2	7	1	–	–	–	–	–	–	–	–	–	–	93	4	21 Sep 1935
REID, Tom	–	–	60	36	36	27	5	4	–	–	–	–	–	–	–	–	–	–	101	67	2 Feb 1929
RENNOX, Charlie	–	–	56	24	4	–	8	1	–	–	–	–	–	–	–	–	–	–	68	25	14 Mar 1925
RICARDO, Felipe	– (1)	–	–	–	–	–	–	–	–	–	3 (1)	–	–	–	–	–	–	–	3 (2)	–	18 Sep 2002
RICHARDS, Billy	–	–	–	–	9	1	–	–	–	–	–	–	–	–	–	–	–	–	9	1	21 Dec 1901
RICHARDS, Charlie	–	–	–	–	8	1	3	1	–	–	–	–	–	–	–	–	–	–	11	2	6 Sep 1902
RICHARDSON, Kieran	20 (21)	2	–	–	–	–	8 (2)	4	11 (2)	3	5 (11)	2	–	–	–	–	– (1)	–	44 (37)	11	18 Sep 2002
RICHARDSON, Lance	–	–	38	–	–	–	4	–	–	–	–	–	–	–	–	–	–	–	42	–	1 May 1926
RIDDING, Bill	–	–	–	–	42	14	2	–	–	–	–	–	–	–	–	–	–	–	44	14	25 Dec 1931
RIDGWAY, Joe	–	–	–	–	14	–	3	–	–	–	–	–	–	–	–	–	–	–	17	–	11 Jan 1896
RIMMER, Jimmy	–	–	34	–	–	–	3	–	6	–	2 (1)	–	–	–	–	–	–	–	45 (1)	–	15 Apr 1968
RITCHIE, Andy	–	–	26 (7)	13	–	–	3 (1)	–	3 (2)	–	–	–	–	–	–	–	–	–	32 (10)	13	26 Dec 1977
ROACH, John	–	–	–	–	–	–	2	–	–	–	–	–	–	–	–	–	–	–	2	–	5 Jan 1946
ROBBIE, David	–	–	–	–	1	–	–	–	–	–	–	–	–	–	–	–	–	–	1	–	28 Sep 1935
ROBERTS, Charlie	–	–	207	13	64	9	28	1	–	–	–	–	–	–	–	–	3	–	302	23	23 Apr 1904
ROBERTS, Robert	–	–	2	–	–	–	–	–	–	–	–	–	–	–	–	–	–	–	2	–	27 Dec 1913
ROBERTS, W.A	–	–	–	–	9	2	1	–	–	–	–	–	–	–	–	–	–	–	10	2	18 Feb 1899
ROBERTSON, Alex	–	–	–	–	28	10	6	–	–	–	–	–	–	–	–	–	–	–	34	10	5 Sep 1903
ROBERTSON, Sandy	–	–	–	–	33	1	2	–	–	–	–	–	–	–	–	–	–	–	35	1	5 Sep 1903
ROBERTSON, Thomas	–	–	–	–	3	–	–	–	–	–	–	–	–	–	–	–	–	–	3	–	5 Sep 1903
ROBERTSON, William	–	–	–	–	47	1	3	–	–	–	–	–	–	–	–	–	–	–	50	1	17 Mar 1934
ROBINS, Mark	–	–	19 (29)	11	–	–	4 (4)	3	– (7)	2	–	–	4 (2)	1	–	–	– (1)	–	27 (43)	17	12 Oct 1988
ROBINSON, James	–	–	21	3	–	–	–	–	–	–	–	–	–	–	–	–	–	–	21	3	3 Jan 1920
ROBINSON, Matt	–	–	–	–	10	–	–	–	–	–	–	–	–	–	–	–	–	–	10	–	26 Sep 1931
ROBSON, Bryan	15 (14)	2	311 (5)	72	–	–	33 (2)	10	50 (1)	5	4	1	13	4	9 (1)	3	2 (1)	2	437 (24)	99	7 Oct 1981
ROCHE, Lee	– (1)	–	–	–	–	–	–	–	1	–	1	–	–	–	–	–	–	–	2 (1)	–	5 Nov 2001
ROCHE, Paddy	–	–	44	–	2	–	4	–	3	–	–	–	–	–	–	–	–	–	53	–	8 Feb 1975
ROGERS, Martyn	–	–	1	–	–	–	–	–	–	–	–	–	–	–	–	–	–	–	1	–	22 Oct 1977
RONALDO, Cristiano	157 (39)	84	–	–	–	–	23 (3)	13	10 (2)	4	51 (4)	16	–	–	–	–	3	1	244 (48)	118	16 Aug 2003
ROONEY, Wayne	230 (21)	129	–	–	–	–	20 (6)	14	7 (4)	4	63 (4)	27	–	–	3	3	6 (1)	4	329 (36)	181	28 Sep 2004
ROSSI, Giuseppe	1 (4)	1	–	–	–	–	2	2	3 (2)	1	– (2)	–	–	–	–	–	–	–	6 (8)	4	10 Nov 2004
ROTHWELL, Charles	–	–	1	–	1	1	1	2	–	–	–	–	–	–	–	–	–	–	3	3	2 Dec 1893
ROTHWELL, Herbert	–	–	–	–	22	–	6	–	–	–	–	–	–	–	–	–	–	–	28	–	25 Oct 1902
ROUGHTON, George	–	–	47	–	39	–	6	–	–	–	–	–	–	–	–	–	–	–	92	–	12 Sep 1936
ROUND, Elijah	–	–	2	–	–	–	–	–	–	–	–	–	–	–	–	–	–	–	2	–	9 Oct 1909
ROWE, Jocelyn	–	–	1	–	–	–	–	–	–	–	–	–	–	–	–	–	–	–	1	–	5 Mar 1914
ROWLEY, Harry	–	–	111	28	62	27	7	–	–	–	–	–	–	–	–	–	–	–	180	55	27 Oct 1928
ROWLEY, Jack	–	–	355	173	25	9	42	26	–	–	–	–	–	–	–	–	2	3	424	211	23 Oct 1937
ROYALS, Ezra	–	–	7	–	–	–	–	–	–	–	–	–	–	–	–	–	–	–	7	–	23 Mar 1912
RYAN, Jimmy	–	–	21 (3)	4	–	–	1	–	–	–	2	–	–	–	–	–	–	–	24 (3)	4	4 May 1966

S

PLAYER	PREMIER LGE APPS	PREMIER LGE GLS	DIVISION ONE APPS	DIVISION ONE GLS	DIVISION TWO APPS	DIVISION TWO GLS	FA CUP APPS	FA CUP GLS	LEAGUE CUP APPS	LEAGUE CUP GLS	EC / CL APPS	EC / CL GLS	ECWC APPS	ECWC GLS	UEFA CUP APPS	UEFA CUP GLS	OTHER GAMES APPS	OTHER GAMES GLS	TOTALS APPS	TOTALS GLS	DEBUT
SADLER, David	–	–	266 (6)	22	–	–	22 (1)	1	22	1	14	3	2	–	–	–	2	–	328 (7)	27	24 Aug 1963
SAGAR, Charles	–	–	10	4	20	16	3	4	–	–	–	–	–	–	–	–	–	–	33	24	2 Sep 1905
SAHA, Louis	52 (34)	28	–	–	–	–	6 (4)	3	9	7	9 (10)	4	–	–	–	–	–	–	76 (48)	42	31 Jan 2004
SAPSFORD, George	–	–	52	16	–	–	1	1	–	–	–	–	–	–	–	–	–	–	53	17	26 Apr 1920
SARTORI, Carlo	–	–	26 (13)	4	–	–	9	1	3 (2)	–	2	1	–	–	–	–	– (1)	–	40 (16)	6	9 Oct 1968
SARVIS, William	–	–	–	–	1	–	–	–	–	–	–	–	–	–	–	–	–	–	1	–	23 Sep 1922
SAUNDERS, James	–	–	–	–	12	–	1	–	–	–	–	–	–	–	–	–	–	–	13	–	26 Dec 1901
SAVAGE, Ted	–	–	–	–	4	–	1	–	–	–	–	–	–	–	–	–	–	–	5	–	1 Jan 1938
SAWYER, F	–	–	–	–	6	–	–	–	–	–	–	–	–	–	–	–	–	–	6	–	14 Oct 1899
SCANLON, Albert	–	–	115	34	–	–	6	1	3	–	3	–	–	–	–	–	–	–	127	35	20 Nov 1954
SCHMEICHEL, Peter	252	–	40	–	–	–	41	–	17	–	36	–	3	–	3	1	6	–	398	1	17 Aug 1991
SCHOFIELD, Alf	–	–	10	2	147	28	22	5	–	–	–	–	–	–	–	–	–	–	179	35	1 Sep 1900
SCHOFIELD, George	–	–	1	–	–	–	–	–	–	–	–	–	–	–	–	–	–	–	1	–	4 Sep 1920
SCHOFIELD, Joseph	–	–	–	–	2	–	–	–	–	–	–	–	–	–	–	–	–	–	2	–	26 Mar 1904
SCHOFIELD, Percy	–	–	1	–	–	–	–	–	–	–	–	–	–	–	–	–	–	–	1	–	1 Oct 1921

PLAYER ROLL CALL

PLAYER	PREMIER LGE		DIVISION ONE		DIVISION TWO		FA CUP		LEAGUE CUP		EC / CL		ECWC		UEFA CUP		OTHER GAMES		TOTALS		DEBUT
	APPS	GLS	APPS	GLS	APPS	GLS	APPS	GLS	APPS	GLS	APPS	GLS	APPS	GLS	APPS	GLS	APPS	GLS	APPS	GLS	
SCHOLES, Paul	396 (87)	106	–	–	–	–	31 (15)	13	14 (7)	9	111 (17)	25	–	–	1 (3)	1	14 (1)	–	567 (130)	154	21 Sep 1994
SCOTT, Jack	–	–	3	–	–	–	–	–	–	–	–	–	–	–	–	–	–	–	3	–	4 Oct 1952
SCOTT, John	–	–	23	–	–	–	1	–	–	–	–	–	–	–	–	–	–	–	24	–	27 Aug 1921
SEALEY, Les	–	–	33	–	–	–	4 (1)	–	9	–	–	–	8	–	–	–	1	–	55 (1)	–	14 Apr 1990
SETTERS, Maurice	–	–	159	12	–	–	25	1	2	–	–	–	6	1	1	–	1	–	194	14	16 Jan 1960
SHARPE, Lee	100 (16)	17	60 (17)	4	–	–	22 (7)	3	15 (8)	9	7	2	6 (2)	1	2	–	1	–	213 (50)	36	24 Sep 1988
SHARPE, William	–	–	–	–	–	–	2	–	–	–	–	–	–	–	–	–	–	–	2	–	4 Oct 1890
SHAWCROSS, Ryan	–	–	–	–	–	–	–	–	– (2)	–	–	–	–	–	–	–	–	–	– (2)	–	25 Oct 2006
SHELDON, John	–	–	26	1	–	–	–	–	–	–	–	–	–	–	–	–	–	–	26	1	27 Dec 1910
SHERINGHAM, Teddy	73 (31)	31	–	–	–	–	4 (5)	5	1	1	20 (11)	9	–	–	–	–	3 (5)	–	101 (52)	46	3 Aug 1997
SIDEBOTTOM, Arnold	–	–	4	–	12	–	2	–	2	–	–	–	–	–	–	–	–	–	20	–	23 Apr 1973
SILCOCK, Jack	–	–	271	2	152	–	26	–	–	–	–	–	–	–	–	–	–	–	449	2	30 Aug 1919
SILVESTRE, Mikael	225 (24)	6	–	–	–	–	19 (2)	1	13 (1)	–	61 (8)	2	–	–	–	–	8	1	326 (35)	10	11 Sep 1999
SIMPSON, Danny	1 (2)	–	–	–	–	–	– (1)	–	1	–	2 (1)	–	–	–	–	–	–	–	4 (4)	–	26 Sep 2007
SIVEBAEK, Johnny	–	–	29 (2)	1	–	–	2	–	1	–	–	–	–	–	–	–	–	–	32 (2)	1	9 Feb 1986
SLATER, J.F	–	–	–	–	–	–	4	–	–	–	–	–	–	–	–	–	–	–	4	–	4 Oct 1890
SLOAN, Tom	–	–	4 (7)	–	–	–	–	–	– (1)	–	–	–	–	–	–	–	–	–	4 (8)	–	18 Nov 1978
SMALLING, Chris	25 (10)	1	–	–	–	–	4 (2)	–	4	1	10 (3)	–	–	–	2 (1)	–	1 (1)	1	46 (17)	3	28 Aug 2010
SMITH, Alan	43 (18)	7	–	–	–	–	2 (6)	–	4 (2)	1	11 (6)	3	–	–	–	–	1	1	61 (32)	12	8 Aug 2004
SMITH, Albert	–	–	5	1	–	–	–	–	–	–	–	–	–	–	–	–	–	–	5	1	22 Jan 1927
SMITH, Dick	–	–	–	–	93	35	7	2	–	–	–	–	–	–	–	–	1	–	101	37	8 Sep 1894
SMITH, Jack	–	–	19	6	17	8	5	1	–	–	–	–	–	–	–	–	–	–	41	15	2 Feb 1938
SMITH, Lorenzo	–	–	–	–	8	1	2	–	–	–	–	–	–	–	–	–	–	–	10	1	22 Nov 1902
SMITH, Tom	–	–	40	3	43	9	7	4	–	–	–	–	–	–	–	–	–	–	90	16	19 Jan 1924
SMITH, William	–	–	–	–	16	–	1	–	–	–	–	–	–	–	–	–	–	–	17	–	14 Sep 1901
SNEDDON, J	–	–	–	–	–	–	3	1	–	–	–	–	–	–	–	–	–	–	3	1	3 Oct 1891
SOLSKJAER, Ole Gunnar	151 (84)	91	–	–	–	–	15 (15)	8	8 (3)	7	36 (45)	20	–	–	–	–	6 (3)	–	216 (150)	126	25 Aug 1996
SPECTOR, Jonathan	2 (1)	–	–	–	–	–	1	–	– (1)	–	1 (1)	–	–	–	–	–	– (1)	–	4 (4)	–	8 Aug 2004
SPENCE, Joe	–	–	312	106	169	52	29	10	–	–	–	–	–	–	–	–	–	–	510	168	30 Aug 1919
SPENCER, Charlie	–	–	46	–	–	–	2	–	–	–	–	–	–	–	–	–	–	–	48	–	15 Sep 1928
SPRATT, Walter	–	–	13	–	–	–	–	–	–	–	–	–	–	–	–	–	–	–	13	–	6 Feb 1915
STACEY, George	–	–	241	9	–	–	26	–	–	–	–	–	–	–	–	–	3	–	270	9	12 Oct 1907
STAFFORD, Harry	–	–	–	–	183	–	17	1	–	–	–	–	–	–	–	–	–	–	200	1	3 Apr 1896
STAM, Jaap	79	1	–	–	–	–	7 (1)	–	–	–	32	–	–	–	–	–	7 (1)	–	125 (2)	1	9 Aug 1998
STAPLETON, Frank	–	–	204 (19)	60	–	–	21	7	26 (1)	6	–	–	8	4	6 (1)	1	2	–	267 (21)	78	29 Aug 1981
STEPHENSON, R	–	–	–	–	1	1	–	–	–	–	–	–	–	–	–	–	–	–	1	1	11 Jan 1896
STEPNEY, Alex	–	–	393	2	40	–	44	–	35	–	15	–	4	–	4	–	4	–	539	2	17 Sep 1966
STEWARD, Alfred	–	–	204	–	105	–	17	–	–	–	–	–	–	–	–	–	–	–	326	–	23 Oct 1920
STEWART, Michael	5 (2)	–	–	–	–	–	– (1)	–	2 (2)	–	– (2)	–	–	–	–	–	–	–	7 (7)	–	31 Oct 2000
STEWART, William	–	–	–	–	46	7	3	–	–	–	–	–	–	–	–	–	–	–	49	7	19 Nov 1932
STEWART, Willie	–	–	54	4	22	1	9	–	–	–	–	–	–	–	–	–	2	–	87	5	4 Oct 1890
STILES, Nobby	–	–	311	17	–	–	38	–	7	–	23	2	2	–	11	–	3	–	395	19	1 Oct 1960
STONE, Herbert	–	–	2	–	4	–	–	–	–	–	–	–	–	–	–	–	1	–	7	–	26 Mar 1894
STOREY-MOORE, Ian	–	–	39	11	–	–	–	–	4	1	–	–	–	–	–	–	–	–	43	12	11 Mar 1972
STRACHAN, Gordon	–	–	155 (5)	33	–	–	22	2	12 (1)	1	–	–	–	–	6	2	–	–	195 (6)	38	25 Aug 1984
STREET, Ernest	–	–	–	–	1	–	2	–	–	–	–	–	–	–	–	–	–	–	3	–	7 Feb 1903
SUTCLIFFE, John	–	–	–	–	21	–	7	–	–	–	–	–	–	–	–	–	–	–	28	–	5 Sep 1903
SWEENEY, Eric	–	–	27	6	–	–	5	1	–	–	–	–	–	–	–	–	–	–	32	7	13 Feb 1926

T

PLAYER	PREMIER LGE		DIVISION ONE		DIVISION TWO		FA CUP		LEAGUE CUP		EC / CL		ECWC		UEFA CUP		OTHER GAMES		TOTALS		DEBUT
	APPS	GLS	APPS	GLS	APPS	GLS	APPS	GLS	APPS	GLS	APPS	GLS	APPS	GLS	APPS	GLS	APPS	GLS	APPS	GLS	
TAIBI, Massimo	4	–	–	–	–	–	–	–	–	–	–	–	–	–	–	–	–	–	4	–	11 Sep 1999
TAPKEN, Norman	–	–	14	–	–	–	2	–	–	–	–	–	–	–	–	–	–	–	16	–	26 Dec 1938
TAYLOR, Chris	–	–	27	6	1	–	2	1	–	–	–	–	–	–	–	–	–	–	30	7	17 Jan 1925
TAYLOR, Ernie	–	–	22	2	–	–	6	1	–	–	2	1	–	–	–	–	–	–	30	4	19 Feb 1958
TAYLOR, Tommy	–	–	166	112	–	–	9	5	–	–	14	11	–	–	–	–	2	3	191	131	7 Mar 1953
TAYLOR, Walter	–	–	1	–	–	–	–	–	–	–	–	–	–	–	–	–	–	–	1	–	2 Jan 1922
TEVEZ, Carlos	49 (14)	19	–	–	–	–	5	3	5 (1)	6	10 (11)	6	–	–	–	–	4	–	73 (26)	34	15 Aug 2007
THOMAS, Harry	–	–	101	12	27	–	7	1	–	–	–	–	–	–	–	–	–	–	135	13	22 Apr 1922
THOMAS, Mickey	–	–	90	11	–	–	13	2	5	2	–	–	–	–	2	–	–	–	110	15	25 Nov 1978
THOMPSON, John	–	–	2	1	1	–	–	–	–	–	–	–	–	–	–	–	–	–	3	1	21 Nov 1936
THOMPSON, William	–	–	3	–	–	–	–	–	–	–	–	–	–	–	–	–	–	–	3	–	21 Oct 1893
THOMSON, Arthur	–	–	3	1	–	–	2	–	–	–	–	–	–	–	–	–	–	–	5	1	26 Jan 1929
THOMSON, Ernest	–	–	4	–	–	–	–	–	–	–	–	–	–	–	–	–	–	–	4	–	14 Sep 1907
THOMSON, James	–	–	6	1	–	–	–	–	–	–	–	–	–	–	–	–	–	–	6	1	13 Dec 1913
THORNLEY, Ben	1 (8)	–	–	–	–	–	2	–	3	–	–	–	–	–	–	–	–	–	6 (8)	–	26 Feb 1994
TIERNEY, Paul	–	–	–	–	–	–	–	–	1	–	–	–	–	–	–	–	–	–	1	–	3 Dec 2003
TIMM, Mads	–	–	–	–	–	–	–	–	–	–	– (1)	–	–	–	–	–	–	–	– (1)	–	29 Oct 2002
TOMLINSON, Graeme	–	–	–	–	–	–	–	–	– (2)	–	–	–	–	–	–	–	–	–	– (2)	–	5 Oct 1994
TOMS, Billy	–	–	13	3	–	–	1	1	–	–	–	–	–	–	–	–	–	–	14	4	4 Oct 1919
TOPPING, Henry	–	–	–	–	12	1	–	–	–	–	–	–	–	–	–	–	–	–	12	1	5 Apr 1933
TOSIC, Zoran	– (2)	–	–	–	–	–	– (1)	–	– (2)	–	–	–	–	–	–	–	–	–	– (5)	–	24 Jan 2009
TRANTER, Wilf	–	–	1	–	–	–	–	–	–	–	–	–	–	–	–	–	–	–	1	–	7 Mar 1964
TRAVERS, George	–	–	21	4	–	–	–	–	–	–	–	–	–	–	–	–	–	–	21	4	7 Feb 1914
TURNBULL, Jimmy	–	–	67	36	–	–	9	6	–	–	–	–	–	–	–	–	2	3	78	45	28 Sep 1907
TURNBULL, Sandy	–	–	220	90	–	–	25	10	–	–	–	–	–	–	–	–	2	1	247	101	1 Jan 1907
TURNER, Chris	–	–	64	–	–	–	8	–	7	–	–	–	–	–	–	–	–	–	79	–	14 Dec 1985
TURNER, John	–	–	–	–	3	–	1	–	–	–	–	–	–	–	–	–	–	–	4	–	22 Oct 1898
TURNER, not known	–	–	–	–	–	–	1	–	–	–	–	–	–	–	–	–	–	–	1	–	25 Oct 1890
TURNER, Robert	–	–	–	–	2	–	–	–	–	–	–	–	–	–	–	–	–	–	2	–	08 Oct 1898
TWISS, Michael	–	–	–	–	–	–	– (1)	–	1	–	–	–	–	–	–	–	–	–	1 (1)	–	25 Feb 1998
TYLER, Sidney	–	–	–	–	1	–	–	–	–	–	–	–	–	–	–	–	–	–	1	–	10 Nov 1923

U

PLAYER	PREMIER LGE		DIVISION ONE		DIVISION TWO		FA CUP		LEAGUE CUP		EC / CL		ECWC		UEFA CUP		OTHER GAMES		TOTALS		DEBUT
	APPS	GLS	APPS	GLS	APPS	GLS	APPS	GLS	APPS	GLS	APPS	GLS	APPS	GLS	APPS	GLS	APPS	GLS	APPS	GLS	
URE, Ian	–	–	47	1	–	–	8	–	10	–	–	–	–	–	–	–	–	–	65	1	23 Aug 1969

V

PLAYER	PREMIER LGE		DIVISION ONE		DIVISION TWO		FA CUP		LEAGUE CUP		EC / CL		ECWC		UEFA CUP		OTHER GAMES		TOTALS		DEBUT
	APPS	GLS	APPS	GLS	APPS	GLS	APPS	GLS	APPS	GLS	APPS	GLS	APPS	GLS	APPS	GLS	APPS	GLS	APPS	GLS	
VALENCIA, Antonio	59 (12)	10	–	–	–	–	3 (2)	–	5 (2)	1	16 (5)	4	–	–	– (1)	–	1 (1)	1	84 (23)	16	9 Aug 2009
VALENTINE, Bob	–	–	–	–	10	–	–	–	–	–	–	–	–	–	–	–	–	–	10	–	25 Mar 1905
VAN DER GOUW, Raimond	26 (11)	–	–	–	–	–	1	–	8 (1)	–	11	–	–	–	–	–	2	–	48 (12)	–	3 Feb 1896
VAN DER SAR, Edwin	186	–	–	–	–	–	13	–	5	–	56	–	–	–	–	–	6	–	266	–	21 Sep 1996
VAN NISTELROOY, Ruud	137 (13)	95	–	–	–	–	11 (3)	14	5 (1)	2	45 (2)	38	–	–	–	–	2	1	200 (19)	150	9 Aug 2005
VANCE, James	–	–	–	–	11	1	–	–	–	–	–	–	–	–	–	–	–	–	11	1	12 Aug 2001
VERON, Juan-Sebastian	45 (6)	7	–	–	–	–	2	–	4 (1)	–	24	4	–	–	–	–	–	–	75 (7)	11	19 Aug 2001
VIDIC, Nemanja	164 (3)	14	–	–	–	–	16	–	5 (4)	–	44	2	–	–	–	–	7	2	236 (7)	18	25 Jan 2006
VINCENT, Ernest	–	–	–	–	64	1	1	–	–	–	–	–	–	–	–	–	–	–	65	1	6 Feb 1932
VIOLLET, Dennis	–	–	259	159	–	–	18	5	2	1	12	13	–	–	–	–	2	1	293	179	11 Apr 1953
VOSE, George	–	–	65	–	130	1	14	–	–	–	–	–	–	–	–	–	–	–	209	1	26 Aug 1933

PLAYER ROLL CALL

PLAYER	PREMIER LGE		DIVISION ONE		DIVISION TWO		FA CUP		LEAGUE CUP		EC / CL		ECWC		UEFA CUP		OTHER GAMES		TOTALS		DEBUT
	APPS	GLS	APPS	GLS	APPS	GLS	APPS	GLS	APPS	GLS	APPS	GLS	APPS	GLS	APPS	GLS	APPS	GLS	APPS	GLS	

W

PLAYER	APPS	GLS	APPS	GLS	APPS	GLS	APPS	GLS	APPS	GLS	APPS	GLS	APPS	GLS	APPS	GLS	APPS	GLS	APPS	GLS	DEBUT
WALDRON, Colin	–	–	3	–	–	–	–	–	1	–	–	–	–	–	–	–	–	–	4	–	4 Oct 1976
WALKER, Dennis	–	–	1	–	–	–	–	–	–	–	–	–	–	–	–	–	–	–	1	–	20 May 1963
WALKER, Robert	–	–	–	–	2	–	–	–	–	–	–	–	–	–	–	–	–	–	2	–	14 Jan 1899
WALL, George	–	–	281	86	6	3	29	9	–	–	–	–	–	–	–	–	3	2	319	100	7 Apr 1906
WALLACE, Danny	– (2)	–	36 (9)	6	–	–	7 (2)	2	4 (3)	3	–	–	3 (2)	–	2	–	1	–	53 (18)	11	20 Sep 1989
WALLWORK, Ronnie	4 (15)	–	–	–	–	–	1 (1)	–	4 (1)	–	– (1)	–	–	–	–	–	1	–	10 (18)	–	25 Oct 1997
WALSH, Gary	12 (1)	–	37	–	–	–	–	–	7	–	3	–	2	–	1	–	–	–	62 (1)	–	13 Dec 1986
WALTON, Joe	–	–	21	–	–	–	2	–	–	–	–	–	–	–	–	–	–	–	23	–	26 Jan 1946
WALTON, John	–	–	2	–	–	–	–	–	–	–	–	–	–	–	–	–	–	–	2	–	29 Sep 1951
WARBURTON, Arthur	–	–	20	6	15	4	4	–	–	–	–	–	–	–	–	–	–	–	39	10	8 Mar 1930
WARNER, Jack	–	–	102	1	–	–	13	1	–	–	–	–	–	–	1	–	–	–	116	2	5 Nov 1938
WARNER, Jimmy	–	–	22	–	–	–	–	–	–	–	–	–	–	–	–	–	–	–	22	–	3 Sep 1892
WASSALL, Jackie	–	–	34	5	11	1	2	–	–	–	–	–	–	–	–	–	–	–	47	6	9 Nov 1935
WATSON, Willie	–	–	11	–	–	–	–	–	3	–	–	–	–	–	–	–	–	–	14	–	26 Sep 1970
WEALANDS, Jeffrey	–	–	7	–	–	–	–	–	1	–	–	–	–	–	–	–	–	–	8	–	2 Apr 1983
WEBB, Neil	– (1)	–	70 (4)	8	–	–	9	1	14	1	–	–	9	1	2	–	1	–	105 (5)	11	19 Aug 1989
WEBBER, Danny	–	–	–	–	–	–	–	–	1 (1)	–	– (1)	–	–	–	–	–	–	–	1 (2)	–	28 Nov 2000
WEBSTER, Colin	–	–	65	26	–	–	9	4	–	–	–	–	–	–	–	–	–	–	79	31	28 Nov 1953
WEDGE, Frank	–	–	–	–	2	2	–	–	–	–	–	–	–	–	–	–	–	–	2	2	20 Nov 1897
WELBECK, Danny	25 (13)	10	–	–	–	–	6 (2)	3	7 (2)	2	3 (1)	2	–	–	– (3)	–	1	–	42 (21)	17	23 Sep 2008
WELLENS, Richard	–	–	–	–	–	–	–	–	– (1)	–	–	–	–	–	–	–	–	–	– (1)	–	13 Oct 1999
WEST, Enoch	–	–	166	72	–	–	15	8	–	–	–	–	–	–	–	–	–	–	181	80	1 Sep 1910
WETHERELL, Joe	–	–	–	–	2	–	–	–	–	–	–	–	–	–	–	–	–	–	2	–	21 Sep 1896
WHALLEY, Arthur	–	–	97	6	–	–	9	–	–	–	–	–	–	–	–	–	–	–	106	6	27 Dec 1909
WHALLEY, Bert	–	–	24	–	8	–	6	–	–	–	–	–	–	–	–	–	–	–	38	–	30 Nov 1935
WHELAN, Anthony	–	–	– (1)	–	–	–	–	–	–	–	–	–	–	–	–	–	–	–	– (1)	–	29 Nov 1980
WHELAN, William	–	–	79	43	–	–	6	4	–	–	11	5	–	–	2	–	–	–	98	52	26 Mar 1955
WHITEFOOT, Jeff	–	–	93	–	–	–	2	–	–	–	–	–	–	–	–	–	–	–	95	–	15 Apr 1950
WHITEHOUSE, Jimmy	–	–	–	–	59	–	5	–	–	–	–	–	–	–	–	–	–	–	64	–	15 Sep 1900
WHITEHURST, Walter	–	–	1	–	–	–	–	–	–	–	–	–	–	–	–	–	–	–	1	–	14 Sep 1955
WHITESIDE, Kerr	–	–	1	–	–	–	–	–	–	–	–	–	–	–	–	–	–	–	1	–	18 Jan 1908
WHITESIDE, Norman	–	–	193 (13)	47	–	–	24	10	26 (3)	9	–	–	5 (1)	1	6 (1)	–	2	–	256 (18)	67	24 Apr 1982
WHITNEY, John	–	–	–	–	3	–	–	–	–	–	–	–	–	–	–	–	–	–	3	–	29 Feb 1896
WHITTAKER, Walter	–	–	–	–	3	–	–	–	–	–	–	–	–	–	–	–	–	–	3	–	14 Mar 1896
WHITTLE, John	–	–	–	–	1	–	–	–	–	–	–	–	–	–	–	–	–	–	1	–	16 Jan 1932
WHITWORTH, Neil	–	–	1	–	–	–	–	–	–	–	–	–	–	–	–	–	–	–	1	–	13 Mar 1991
WILCOX, Tom	–	–	2	–	–	–	–	–	–	–	–	–	–	–	–	–	–	–	2	–	24 Oct 1908
WILKINS, Ray	–	–	158 (2)	7	–	–	10	1	14 (1)	1	6	1	2	–	1	–	–	–	191 (3)	10	18 Aug 1979
WILKINSON, Harry	–	–	–	–	8	–	1	–	–	–	–	–	–	–	–	–	–	–	9	–	26 Dec 1903
WILKINSON, Ian	–	–	–	–	–	–	–	–	1	–	–	–	–	–	–	–	–	–	1	–	9 Oct 1991
WILLIAMS, Bill	–	–	–	–	4	–	–	–	–	–	–	–	–	–	–	–	–	–	4	–	7 Sep 1901
WILLIAMS, Frank	–	–	3	–	–	–	–	–	–	–	–	–	–	–	–	–	–	–	3	–	13 Sep 1930
WILLIAMS, Fred	–	–	–	–	8	–	2	4	–	–	–	–	–	–	–	–	–	–	10	4	6 Sep 1902
WILLIAMS, Harry (1904–6)	–	–	1	–	32	7	4	1	–	–	–	–	–	–	–	–	–	–	37	8	10 Sep 1904
WILLIAMS, Harry (1922–3)	–	–	–	–	5	2	–	–	–	–	–	–	–	–	–	–	–	–	5	2	28 Aug 1922
WILLIAMS, Joe	–	–	3	1	–	–	–	–	–	–	–	–	–	–	–	–	–	–	3	1	25 Mar 1907
WILLIAMS, Rees	–	–	31	2	–	–	4	–	–	–	–	–	–	–	–	–	–	–	35	2	8 Oct 1927
WILLIAMSON, John	–	–	2	–	–	–	–	–	–	–	–	–	–	–	–	–	–	–	2	–	17 Apr 1920
WILSON, David	–	–	– (4)	–	–	–	– (2)	–	–	–	–	–	–	–	–	–	–	–	– (6)	–	23 Nov 1988
WILSON, Edgar	–	–	–	–	–	–	1	–	–	–	–	–	–	–	–	–	–	–	1	–	18 Jan 1889
WILSON, Jack	–	–	121	3	9	–	10	–	–	–	–	–	–	–	–	–	–	–	140	3	4 Sep 1926
WILSON, Mark	1 (2)	–	–	–	–	–	–	–	2	–	2 (2)	–	–	–	–	–	1	–	6 (4)	–	21 Oct 1998
WILSON, Tommy	–	–	1	–	–	–	–	–	–	–	–	–	–	–	–	–	–	–	1	–	15 Feb 1908
WINTERBOTTOM, Walter	–	–	21	–	4	–	2	–	–	–	–	–	–	–	–	–	–	–	27	–	28 Nov 1936
WOMBWELL, Dick	–	–	14	–	33	3	4	–	–	–	–	–	–	–	–	–	–	–	51	3	18 Mar 1905
WOOD, John	–	–	–	–	15	1	1	–	–	–	–	–	–	–	–	–	–	–	16	1	26 Aug 1922
WOOD, Nicky	–	–	2 (1)	–	–	–	–	–	– (1)	–	–	–	–	–	–	–	–	–	2 (2)	–	26 Dec 1985
WOOD, Ray	–	–	178	–	–	–	15	–	–	–	12	–	–	–	–	–	3	–	208	–	3 Dec 1949
WOODCOCK, Wilf	–	–	58	20	–	–	3	1	–	–	–	–	–	–	–	–	–	–	61	21	1 Nov 1913
WORRALL, Harry	–	–	6	–	–	–	–	–	–	–	–	–	–	–	–	–	–	–	6	–	30 Nov 1946
WRATTEN, Paul	–	–	– (2)	–	–	–	–	–	–	–	–	–	–	–	–	–	–	–	– (2)	–	2 Apr 1991
WRIGGLESWORTH, Billy	–	–	23	6	4	1	7	2	–	–	–	–	–	–	–	–	–	–	34	9	23 Jan 1937

Y

PLAYER	APPS	GLS	APPS	GLS	APPS	GLS	APPS	GLS	APPS	GLS	APPS	GLS	APPS	GLS	APPS	GLS	APPS	GLS	APPS	GLS	DEBUT
YATES, William	–	–	3	–	–	–	–	–	–	–	–	–	–	–	–	–	–	–	3	–	15 Sep 1906
YORKE, Dwight	80 (16)	48	–	–	–	–	6 (5)	3	3	2	28 (8)	11	–	–	–	–	3 (3)	2	120 (32)	66	22 Aug 1998
YOUNG, Arthur	–	–	2	–	–	–	–	–	–	–	–	–	–	–	–	–	–	–	2	–	27 Oct 1906
YOUNG, Ashley	19 (6)	6	–	–	–	–	–	–	–	–	3	1	–	–	4	1	1	–	27 (6)	8	7 Aug 2011
YOUNG, Tony	–	–	62 (6)	1	7 (8)	–	5	–	5 (4)	–	–	–	–	–	–	–	–	–	79 (18)	1	29 Aug 1970

Above *Although primarily signed as a provider, Sir Alex Ferguson praised winger Ashley Young's contribution of eight goals in his debut season, which included this fine curling effort against Swansea at Old Trafford. 'There's definitely a goal in that lad,' said Sir Alex. 'He's a good finisher.'*

Opposite *Sir Alex Ferguson acknowledges the applause of supporters in the stands at Ewood Park after United clinched their record-breaking 19th title on 14 May 2011.*

INDEX

Italic page numbers indicate illustrations

A

Albiston, Arthur 151, 156–7, 160–1, 164–5, 169, 175, 184
Anderson 262, *270*
Arsenal 51, 53, 68, 159–60, 164–6, 222, 245, 268, 272, 291
Aston, John (Jnr) 108, 113, *113*, 118–19, 129, *129*
Aston, John (Snr) 54, 55, 57–60, *61*, 64
Aston Villa 18, 19, 20, 27, 53, 78–9
Atkinson, Ron 163–4, *163*, 170, 175–7, 179–80, 195

B

Bailey, Gary 159, 161, *161*, 181
Bamlett, Herbert 22, 36, 38, 39
Barcelona *154*, 167–70, *169*, 188–92, *192*, 193, 264, 273, 288, 290
Barson, Frank 32, 37, *37*
Bayern Munich 202, 225, 226–9, 234, 278
Beckham, David *219*, 242–3, *243*
  1995/96 208, 214
  1996/97 211
  1998/99 218, 221, 222, 227
  1999/2000 *231*, 232, 233
  leaving 240
  return visit 278, *278*
Bell, Alex 47
Benfica 107, 111, 115–16, 118–21
Bennion, Ray 47, *47*
Bent, Geoff 81, *82*, 83
Berbatov, Dimitar 265, 268, *268*, 281, *282*
Berry, Johnny 67, *67*, 71, 78, 82
Best, George 102–3, *103*, 128–9, *128*
  1963/64 101, *101*
  1964/65 104–5
  1965/66 107, *107*
  1966/67 108, 109

  1967/68 113, 114, *114*, 115, 120–1, *120*
  1968/69 123–4
  1969/70 132, 133
  1970/71 134
  1972/73 138
  death 250
  leaving 140
Birtles, Garry 162, *163*, 164
Blackburn Rovers 13, 22, 27
Blackpool 15, 53, 54–7, 71
Bolton Wanderers 18, 20, 84, *85*, 265
Brennan, Shay 84, 105, *126*, 127
Brighton 22, 166–7, *167*, 168
Bristol City 15, 18, 22, 23
Bruce, Steve 181, *181*, 183–5, 186–7, 188–9, 193, 198
Buchan, Martin 135, 142, 152, *152*, 161
Busby Babes 66–85, 95
Busby, Sir Matt *48*, 49–50, *49*, 62–3, 67, 287
  1947/48 55
  1950/51 60
  1952/53 69–70
  1957/58 84
  1960/61 87–9
  1961/62 89
  1963/64 100
  1965/66 107
  1966/67 *86*, 108, 109
  1967/68 111, 114, 116–17, 118, 120, 121
  funeral 206
  as general manager 123, 124–5, 133–4, 138–9, 147
  Munich crash 80–1
  Murphy 95
Byrne, Roger 67, 68–9, 70, 71, 72, 78, 81, 83

C

Cantona, Eric 216–17, *217*
  1992/93 198–9, *199*
  1993/94 203, 204–6, 205
  1994/95 206–8, *207*
  1995/96 210–11, *212–13*, 214
  1996/97 211
  retirement 215

Carey, Johnny 44, *44*, 51, 55, *55*, 64, 68, 70
Carrick, Michael 253, *253*, 260
Champions League
  1996/97 215
  1997/98 215–18
  1998/99 218, 223–9
  1999/2000 232–3
  2000/01 234
  2001/02 234–5, 239
  2002/03 240
  2003/04 240
  2004/05 245
  2005/06 250
  2006/07 255, 258–9
  2007/08 264, 266–7
  2008/09 271, *271*, 273
  2009/10 278
  2010/11 287–8, 290
  2011/12 293
Charlton, Bobby *85*, 92–3, *125*, 129, 295
  1958/59 84
  1960/61 87–9
  1964/65 105
  1965/66 107
  1966/67 108, 109
  1967/68 116, 118, *119*, 121
  1969/70 131
  debut 1953 72
  last match 139, *139*
  50th anniversary of arrival at Old Trafford 254
Chelsea 18, 68, 96, 204–5, 244–5, 250, 253–5, 259–60, 262–4, 275, 278, 281, 286, 288
Chilton, Allenby 51, 54, 65, 69
Cleverley, Tom 291
Cole, Andy 206, *208*, 221, *221*, 222, 225, 234
Colman, Eddie 81, 82
Connelly, John 105, 106, 107, 108
Coppell, Steve 143–4, *143*, 146, 152, 160, 161, 187
Crerand, Pat 127, *127*
  1962/63 89
  1964/65 105

1965/66 107
1966/67 108, 109, *109*
1967/68 115
  leaving 134
Crickmer, Walter 39, 44, 50
Crompton, Jack 51, 54, 55, 60, 64, 81, *95*
Crystal Palace 187, 189, 206–7

D

Davies, John Henry 15, 18, 20, 27, 36
De Gea, David 290, *290*
Delaney, Jimmy 50, 51, 53, 65
Division One
  1892/93 13–14
  1893/94 14
  1906/07 18
  1907/08 19–20
  1908/09 20–2
  1909/10 27
  1910/11 27
  1911/12 27
  1914/15 27
  1920/21 31
  1925/26 32
  1926/27 36
  1928/29 38
  1930/31 38–9
  1936/37 44
  1938/39 44
  1946/47 50
  1947/48 51–3
  1949/50 57–60
  1950/51 60
  1951/52 67–9
  1952/53 69–70
  1953/54 70
  1954/55 70–1
  1955/56 71–2
  1956/57 72–3, 79
  1958/59 84
  1959/60 87
  1960/61 87–9
  1961/62 89
  1962/63 89, 96
  1963/64 96–7, 100–1
  1964/65 101–5
  1966/67 108–9

1965/66 107
1966/67 108, 109, *109*
1967/68 115
  leaving 134
  1967/68 117, 123
  1968/69 123–4
  1969/70 131
  1970/71 133–4
  1971/72 135, 138
  1972/73 138–9
  1973/74 139–41
  1975/76 143–4
  1976/77 145
  1977/78 156–7
  1978/79 158
  1979/80 161–2
  1980/81 162–3
  1981/82 164
  1982/83 164
  1983/84 167
  1984/85 170
  1985/86 175
  1986/87 176–7, 179–81
  1987/88 181–3
  1988/89 184–5
  1989/90 185–6
  1990/91 187
  1991/92 192, 196
Division Two
  1894/95 14
  1902/03 16
  1903/04 16, 18
  1905/06 18
  1924/25 32
  1931/32 39
  1932/33 39
  1933/34 39
  1935/36 39–42
  1937/38 44
  1974/75 141–3
Docherty, Tommy 138–40, 141–9, *148*, 156
Duncan, Scott 39–42, *40–1*, 44
Dunne, Tony 87, 105, 109, *126*, 127, 131

E

Edwards, Duncan 69–70, 72–3, 78, 80, 81, 82–3
Estudiantes 123–4, *123*
European Cup
  1956/57 73–8
  1965/66 105–7
  1967/68 111–17, 118–21

1968/69 124
1993/94 204–6
European Cup-Winners' Cup
  1963/64 97–100, *97*
  1977/78 *156*, 157
  1983/84 154, *167–70*
  1990/91 187–92,
    190–2, 193
Everton 171, 174, 208, 259, 271
Evra, Patrice *282*, 293,

F

FA Charity Shield/
Community Shield 20, *22*,
  27, *290*
FA Cup
  1905/06 18
  1906/07 *19*
  1907/08 20
  1908/09 22, 23–6
  1911/12 27
  1925/26 32–4, *34*
  1947/48 53–7, *54–5*
  1948/49 57
  1950/51 60
  1952/53 69
  1956/57 78–9
  1957/58 81, *81–4*
  1961/62 89
  1962/63 96, 98–9, *98*
  1963/64 97
  1969/70 131–3
  1975/76 *130*, 144–5
  1976/77 145–6, *146*,
    148–9, *148–9*
  1978/79 158–60, *158*, *160*
  1982/83 164–7, *167*, 1
    68, *168*
  1984/85 170–5, *172–3*
  1986/87 180
  1989/90 186–7, 189, *189*
  1993/94 204, 205
  1994/95 208
  1995/96 210–11, *212–13*, 214
  1998/99 218, 222–3, *223*
  1999/2000 231
  2003/04 240, 244, 246–7
  2004/05 245
  2005/06 250
  2006/07 261
  2008/09 271
  2009/10 279
  2010/11 287

FA Premier League
  1992/93 197–9
  1993/94 203–4
  1994/95 206–8
  1995/96 208–10
  1996/97 211, 215
  1998/99 218–22
  1999/2000 231–2
  2000/01 233–4
  2001/02 234, 239
  2002/03 239–40
  2003/04 240
  2004/05 244
  2005/06 250
  2006/07 252, 253–5, 261,
    259–61, *261*
  2008/09 265, 268, *269*
  2009/10 275, 279
  2010/11 281–3, 286, *287*
  2011/12 290, 294
  creation 196–7
Fairs Cup 105
Ferdinand, Rio 239, 240,
  240, 262
Ferguson, Sir Alex 200–1, *201*
  1986/87 177, *177*,
    179–81, *179*, *363*
  1987/88 181–4
  1988/89 184–5
  1989/90 185–7
  1990/91 187–92
  1991/92 192, 196
  1992/93 198, *199*
  1993/94 203–4
  1995/96 208
  1996/97 211
  1998/99 225, 226–7, 228
  2001/02 234–5
  2002/03 239
  2003/04 244
  2006/07 253–5, 258,
    259–61
  2007/08 262, 264, 267,
    268–9
  2008/09 269, *269*, 273
  2009/10 278
  2010/11 286, 290
  2011/12 295
  Beckham 242
  Busby 206
  Cantona 216
  Record 19th title 286–7
FIFA Club World Cup 269, *270*

First World War 28, 31
Football Alliance 13
Football League *see* **Division**
  One; Division Two
Foster, Ben 270
Foulkes, Bill 69, *69*, 128
  1958/59 84
  1964/65 104, 105
  1966/67 108
  1967/68 115
  leaving 131
  Munich 81, 83

G

Galatasaray 204–6
Gamba Osaka 269
Gibson, Darron 278, *279*
Giggs, Ryan 192, 198, 222, *223*,
  224, 226, 227, 271, *271*, 274
Glazer family 245, 250
Greenhoff, Brian 140, 142,
  144–5, 151, *151*, 159
Greenhoff, Jimmy 152
  1976/77 145, 146,
    146, 148–9
  1978/79 158, 159, *159*
  leaving 164
Gregg, Harry 81, 84, 109

H

Hargreaves, Owen 262
Herd, David *90–1*, 99, *104*,
  105, 106, 107, *107*, 109
Hernandez, Javier
  'Chicharito' 286, *286*
Hilditch, Clarrie 36, *36*, 47
Hill, Gordon 143–4, *144*, 145,
  153, 157
hooliganism 142–3, 157, 161
Hughes, Mark 170, 194, *194*
  1984/85 171, *171*, 174
  1985/86 175–6, *175*
  1988/89 184
  1989/90 185, 187, *188*
  1990/91 193, *193*
  1992/93 198
  1993/94 204, 205
  leaving 208

I

Ince, Paul 185, 198, 208

J

Jones, Mark 69, 81, 83
Jones, Phil 290, *290*
Jordan, Joe 157, 159, 160,
  161, 164
Juventus 145, 170, 224–5

K

Kanchelskis, Andrei 192,
  203, 208, 233
Keane, Roy 203, 222, 224,
  248–9, *249*
  1998/99 221–2, 224
  1999/2000 232, 233
  2003/04 244, *244*
  leaving 250
Kidd, Brian 129
  1967/68 111, *111*, 113, 116, 121
  1969/70 131–2
  as coach 211
  sold 1973 140

L

Lancashire Cup (1941) 45
Lancashire and Yorkshire
  Railway (L&YR) 11–13
Larsson, Henrik 255, *255*, 258
Law, Denis 37, *88*, 100
  1962/63 89, 96, 99
  1963/64 97, *97*, 100–1
  1964/65 104–5
  1965/66 106, *106*, 107
  1966/67 108–9
  1967/68 116
  1968/69 124
  1969/70 131
  move to Manchester City
    141, *141*
League Cup
  1985/86 177
  1990/91 187
  1991/92 196, *197*
  1993/94 203
  2005/06 250, *251*
  2008/09 270
  2009/10 279
  2010/11 287
Leeds United 18, 101–4, 133,
  146, 192, 196
Leicester City 32, 96, 98–9, *98*
Lille 255
Liverpool
  1893/94 14

1914/15 27–8
1926/27 36
1946/47 51
1947/48 53
1976/77 146, 148–9
1978/79 158–9, *159*
1984/85 170–1
1987/88 183–4
1995/96 210–11, 214
2008/09 268–9
2010/11 287
2011/12 293, *294*
match-fixing scandal
  1915 28

M

Macari, Lou 153, *153*, 170
  1973/74 140, *141*
  1975/76 144
  1976/77 145, 149
  1979/80 161
McClair, Brian 180, *182*,
  196, *197*
  1990/91 188
  1993/94 204, 205
  1994/95 208
  1995/96 214
  1996/97 215
  1997/98 218
McCreery, David 153, *153*
McGrath, Paul 170, 171, 175,
  184, 185
McGuinness, Wilf 84, 124–5,
  124, 131, 133, 139
McIlroy, Sammy 142, 145, 151,
  151, 160, *160*
McQueen, Gordon 157, *157*,
  158, 160, 161, 175
Manchester City
  1891/92 13
  1905/06 18–19
  1925/26 *34*
  1947/48 51–3
  1954/55 70–1
  1955/56 72
  1962/63 89
  1967/68 117, 123
  1973/74 140–1
  1986/87 180
  2007/08 263, *263*
  2011/12 291, 294
  Second World War 45
Manchester Cup 13

Mangnall, Ernest 16, 18–20, 23, 27, 29, 29, 31
Martin, Mick 140, 140
match-fixing scandal 1915 27–8
Maxwell, Robert 170
Meredith, Billy 19, 20, 21, 27, 31, 35
Milan, AC 259, 278
Millwall 39, 244, 247
Mitten, Charlie 51, 53, 58–9, 60, 65
Montpellier 187–8, 190–1
Moran, Kevin 171, 174, 184
Morris, Johnny 51, 53, 55–7, 56, 60, 65
Munich air crash 79–81, 89
50th anniversary 263
Murphy, Jimmy 50, 69–70, 80–1, 81, 84, 94–5, 94, 139

N
Nani 262
Neville, Gary 208, 222, 222, 228, 244, 258–9, 269, 282, 284, 285
Newcastle United 22, 27, 210, 211, 215, 222
Newton Heath L&YR FC 11–16
Nicholl, Jimmy 150, 150, 161
North American tour (1952) 69
Northampton Town 132, 133
Nottingham Forest 13, 186–7

O
O'Farrell, Frank 134–5, 135, 138
O'Shea, John 258, 258, 272
Old Trafford 27–8, 31, 44, 50, 57, 101, 260
Owen, Michael 275, 279, 280

P
Pallister, Gary 178, 185, 185, 198
Park, Ji-sung 250, 272, 273
Pearson, Stan 51, 53, 55, 65, 68, 69, 281
Pearson, Stuart 141–2, 142, 143, 145, 148, 153, 156, 157
Pegg, David 69, 81, 82
Powell, Jack 11–12
Pozzo, Vittorio 16–17

Q
Queens Park Rangers 20, 22
Quito, LDU 269, 270
Quixall, Albert 84, 89, 96

R
Reading 255
Real Madrid 76–8, 77, 111, 114–15, 233, 240
Roberts, Charlie 16–18, 17, 20, 23, 27, 28, 47
Robson, Bryan 195, 195
1981/82 164
1982/83 166, 166, 168
1983/84 154, 169, 169
1984/85 171
1985/86 175, 175

1987/88 181
1989/90 187
1990/91 190–1, 193
1993/94 205
Rocca, Louis 16, 44
Roma, AS 258–9, 258
Ronaldo, Christiano 240, 241, 250, 253, 255, 258–61, 259, 262, 263, 266–7, 272, 273, 276, 277
leaving 275
Rooney, Wayne 245, 245, 253, 254, 254, 258–60, 264, 269, 270, 278, 280, 281, 283, 283
Rowley, Jack 51, 53, 54–5, 54, 57, 65, 68–9

S
Sadler, David 109, 115, 129, 140
St Etienne 156, 157
St John, Ian 100, 100
Sarajevo 112–13
Schalke 04 288
Schmeichel, Peter 234, 236–7, 236
1991/92 192
1992/93 198
1993/94 203
1998/99 222, 229
Scholes, Paul 208, 209, 221, 222, 224, 233, 244, 254, 264, 292–3, 292–3
Second World War 44–5, 51
Sexton, Dave 155–7, 155, 160–3
Sheffield United 19, 51, 143

Sheringham, Teddy 202, 222, 224, 227, 234
Silcock, John (Jack) 32, 46, 46
Smalling, Chris 289, 291
Smith, Alan 258, 258
Solskjaer, Ole Gunnar 202, 221, 222, 227–8, 228, 239
Southampton 39, 145, 146
Spence, Joe 32, 32, 36, 46
Sporting Lisbon 97, 100
Stapleton, Frank 164, 167, 169, 171, 181, 265
Stepney, Alex 112, 126, 126, 150
1966/67 109
1967/68 112–13, 114, 115, 118, 119–21
1973/74 140
1974/75 142
leaving 157
Steward, Alf 32, 33, 46–7
Stiles, Norbert (Nobby) 87, 104, 105, 108, 128, 128
1965/66 107
1966/67 109
1967/68 120
1968/69 123, 123
leaving 134
Strachan, Gordon 170, 171, 184, 196
Sunderland 27, 32, 36

T
Taylor, Tommy 69, 71, 72–6, 77, 78, 81, 83
Tevez, Carlos 262, 264, 265, 266, 275, 279

Thomas, Mickey 157, 158, 159, 161
Turnbull, Sandy 19, 23, 26, 27, 28

U
UEFA Cup, 1976/77 145

V
Valencia, Antonio 275, 275, 295
Van der Sar, Edwin 258, 260, 266–7, 290
Van Nistelrooy, Ruud 235, 238, 244, 253, 256, 257
Vidic, Nemanja 260, 262, 282
Viollet, Dennis 69, 69, 71, 72, 73–6, 82, 84, 87, 87

W
Walthamstow Avenue 68, 69
Welbeck, Danny 291, 291
Whelan, Liam 72–3, 74–5, 80, 81, 82, 83
Whiteside, Norman 164, 166, 166, 167, 168, 171, 174, 175
Wilkins, Ray 160–1, 161, 162
Willem II 97, 97
Wood, Ray 71, 78, 78, 82
World Club Championship 123–4, 123

Y
Yorke, Dwight 220, 221, 222, 224–5, 225, 234
Young, Ashley 290, 362

PICTURE CREDITS

The publishers would like to thank the following for providing photographs and for permission to reproduce copyright material. While every effort has been made to trace and acknowledge the copyright holders, we would like to apologise should there have been any errors or omissions.

All pictures supplied by Empics, except: Action Images pages 219, 220, 221, 224 (top), 233, 235; Cliff Butler page 13; Colorsport pages 44, 46, 48, 49, 56, 63, 82 (inset), 112, 128, 143 (right), 144, 147, 190–191, 192, 193, 212–213; Getty Images pages 17, 28, 34, 38, 43, 52, 58–59, 70, 71, 74–75, 87, 93, 106, 110, 115, 118, 121, 138, 154, 169; *Illustrated London News* pages 18, 22 (bottom); *Manchester Evening News* pages 15, 21, 24–25, 32, 35, 36, 37, 45, 67, 81 (right), 107, 123, 150 (top); Manchester United/John Peters pages 202, 203, 204, 222, 223, 229, 230, 232, 234, 236, 239, 240, 243, 244, 245, 249, 250–251, 252, 253, 254, 255, 256, 258, 259, 260, 261, 262, 263, 264, 265, 266, 267, 268, 269, 270, 271, 272, 273, 274, 275, 277, 278, 279, 280, 281, 282, 283, 284, 286, 287, 289, 290, 291, 292–3, 294, 295, 362, 363, 364–5; Roger Mellor page 10; Popperfoto page 23.